"This rich multidimensional study will be the state-of-the-art introduction to the Old Testament for some time to come. In addition to a book-by-book introduction, this valuable resource by these two accomplished scholars includes much useful information concerning ancient Near Eastern history, geography, and cultural context and concerning alternative theological interpretations, canon, and studies of personalities. This information-packed book is made even more attractive by insightful artwork and witty links to contemporary life. The authors note that one does not 'read' a library but 'study' it. That is what they do with the library of the Old Testament: they study it. And they invite the reader to study it with them as they guide, instruct, and persuade."

—**Walter Brueggemann**, Columbia Theological Seminary (emeritus)

"In *Introducing the Old Testament*, Jacobson and Chan offer an excellent resource for studying and teaching the Old Testament. Drawing on their years of experience as educators, the authors have clearly thought about diverse audiences when writing this book. The book's organization is clear and easy to follow, focusing especially on historical, literary, and theological themes in the Old Testament. In addition to its insightful scholarship, *Introducing the Old Testament* includes many maps, images, artistic pieces, and online resources that assist and enhance biblical study. Overall, Jacobson and Chan provide a wealth of knowledge in this critical, creative, and visually stimulating volume."

—**Jaime L. Waters**, Boston College School of Theology and Ministry

"This is a textbook written by top-notch scholars who are also extraordinary teachers. Their love of Old Testament study and their commitment to student learning shine through in every chapter. With an affable voice, good humor, and rigorous scholarship, the book offers hospitality to all students, whether they come to the Old Testament classroom with enthusiasm, reluctance, or indifference. Jacobson and Chan approach their subject with joy and humility rather than dogmatism, always keeping the biblical text and its world at the center of their analysis. I can't wait to use this book in my seminary courses!"

—**Cameron Howard**, Luther Seminary

"In this impressive volume, Jacobson and Chan have sought to present readers with something that is 'beautiful, well organized, and easy to use.' They (and Baker Academic) have succeeded admirably on all of these fronts and yet still more: here is an engagement of the Old Testament that pays equal attention to its theological, literary, and historical depths, that is accompanied by numerous readerly helps, and that is handsomely illustrated and spiritedly written to boot. I predict this introduction, unlike so many others presently on the market, will have a very long shelf life, with enduring usefulness in a wide range of classroom settings."

—**Brent A. Strawn**, Duke University

INTRODUCING
THE OLD
TESTAMENT

INTRODUCING THE OLD TESTAMENT

A Historical, Literary, and Theological Survey

Rolf A. Jacobson
and
Michael J. Chan

Baker Academic
a division of Baker Publishing Group
Grand Rapids, Michigan

Published by Baker Academic
a division of Baker Publishing Group
Grand Rapids, Michigan
www.bakeracademic.com

Printed in the United States of America

Library of Congress Cataloging-in-Publication Data
Names: Jacobson, Rolf A., author. | Chan, Michael J., author.
Title: Introducing the Old Testament : a historical, literary, and theological survey / Rolf A. Jacobson and Michael J. Chan.
Description: Grand Rapids, Michigan : Baker Academic, a division of Baker Publishing Group, [2023] | Includes bibliographical references and index.
Identifiers: LCCN 2022026501 | ISBN 9780801049255 (cloth) | ISBN 9781493438051 (ebook) | ISBN 9781493438068 (pdf)
Subjects: LCSH: Bible. Old Testament—Introductions.
Classification: LCC BS1140.3 .J335 2023 | DDC 221.6/6—dc23/eng/20220803
LC record available at https://lccn.loc.gov/2022026501

Baker Publishing Group publications use paper produced from sustainable forestry practices and post-consumer waste whenever possible.

23   24   25   26   27   28   29   7   6   5   4   3   2   1

For our wives, Amy and Katherine

And for Jim Kinney

Contents

Maps

Preface

Welcome to the Old Testament! If you are reading these words, you are most likely a teacher or a student in a course on the Old Testament. The Old Testament is an astounding book—really, an astounding library. It contains thirty-nine books in the Protestant Christian way of approaching it. These books contain stories, laws, poems, songs, prophecies of many types, proverbs, genealogies, liturgies, and much more. Much of the Old Testament is beautiful, but some is troubling and even a little terrifying. One doesn't *read* a library— one *studies* a library. Welcome to the study of this wonderful, ancient library.

The Old Testament (in Judaism, it is called the "Tanak," a term we'll explain below) is among the most influential books in world history, because it is central to the religious lives of both Jews and Christians. The main figure or character in the book is the Lord, the God of Israel. The main human figures in the book are ancient Israelites—descendants of two Mesopotamian migrants, Abraham and Sarah. You may or may not be a person of faith; you may not be sure if you are a person of faith. This book does not assume either that you are or that you are not. But we have written the book so that believers, nonbelievers, doubters, inquirers, those who are curious, and those who simply have to take a required course are all welcome.

This book is the companion volume to Mark Allan Powell's *Introducing the New Testament*. In the preface to that book, Powell wrote, "My intent in writing this book is to help you have an interesting, enjoyable, and intellectually rewarding experience."[1] Mark's book is all of those things, and more! It is also beautiful, well organized, and easy to use. We have followed Mark's pattern and hope you will experience this book as all of those things too.

A Brief Orientation to the Book

Here is a brief overview of this book. A few chapters deal with general topics— such as "The Old Testament World," "The Old Testament Writings," and introductory chapters on the Pentateuch, historical books, prophetic literature, and other writings. But most chapters deal with one or two books of the Old Testament. These chapters share a common organization:

- Background (the author, composition and development, genre, and outline of the book)
- Literary Interpretation (a summary of the book's content and analysis of major literary themes)
- Theological Interpretation (major theological themes of the book and major theological issues with interpreting the book)
- Historical Interpretation (what the book says about history and what interpreters can learn about history by studying the book carefully—we often talk about the history in the book and the history behind the book)
- For Further Reading (if you want to learn more about a book or want to write a term paper about something in the book, these books might help)

Following the example set by Powell, there are a few things that are distinctive about this particular Old Testament introduction, things that might set it apart from other textbooks that you have used (and from some other Old Testament introductions).

The Chapters Can Be Read in Almost Any Order

After a few introductory chapters, we have organized the book according to the order of books in the Protestant Old Testament canon. But many professors will want to introduce the chapters in a different order, and they will have good reasons for doing so. One good reason for doing this is that the books were not written in the order of the canon. Nor does the story in the Old Testament go book by book. From Genesis through Ezra-Nehemiah, the story does go mostly in order. But the prophetic books are not in historical order.

- Some professors may want to start with the oldest materials and then create their own order.
- Some professors might want to proceed in canonical order, but then sprinkle chapters on most of the prophetic books in as you read through 1–2 Kings, Ezra, and Nehemiah (because the prophetic books generally are placed within that time span of the story).
- Some professors might use the book in two different courses, so they may only want to assign some chapters of this book for each course.

- Some professors might want to read Genesis through Ezra-Nehemiah in canonical order, but then read the chapters on the Prophets in a reconstructed historical order. Here is one possible reconstruction: Amos, Hosea, Isaiah 1–39, Micah, Jeremiah, Nahum, Habakkuk, Zephaniah, Ezekiel, Daniel (?), Isaiah 40–66, Joel, Zephaniah, Haggai, Zechariah, Malachi, Daniel (?).
- Some professors might want to follow the order of the Jewish canon, which presents the order a bit differently than Protestant Christian Bibles.

If the professor seems to be skipping around, there are good reasons for it!

The Book Presents Different Sides of Many Important Debates, Often without Resolving Them

The book is somewhat unique in its approach. Many Old Testament introductions will be written from one dominant approach to some central debate about the Old Testament. We have not written that kind of a textbook. Many introductions will also present various disputed topics and then argue for one solution to those topics. For the most part we have steered clear of that, but on some occasions we do say what we think about a given debate. Here's an example: You may have noticed above that we distinguished between Isaiah 1–39 and Isaiah 40–66 and separated them in the historical order of prophets. We agree with those scholars who think the two halves of the book date to different times. But many people we respect do not share our view. No worries. When we talk about scholarly debates, because of limitations of space, we generally do not list the names of scholars on the various sides of issues. We assume that your professor will offer you some guidance with regard to evaluating the different ideas and will also help you find additional secondary literature on any particular question you might have. We agree with what Powell wrote in the preface to *Introducing the New Testament*: "The goal of this book is engagement, not indoctrination. However, if we should ever meet, I will be happy to tell you what I think you should believe about all sorts of things!"[2] And we will also be willing to tell you how we have changed our minds about all sorts of issues over the years! In fact, researching and writing this book sparked us to change our minds regarding many issues.

The Book Draws on the Rich Resources of Christian and Jewish Art

You probably have already noticed this book's extensive use of artwork—assuming you were not so intrigued by this preface that you took to reading it before looking at anything else. This book contains the usual maps and a few historical photos that characterize conventional Old Testament introductions. But, following Powell's lead, it also offers about 150 reproductions of artwork from many lands and many centuries. Why? With Powell, we believe the following.

- First, we simply want this book to be beautiful. Genesis says that God put the first man in the garden, where God made to grow all sorts of trees "that are beautiful to see and good to eat" (2:9 AT [authors' translation]). Life should include some beauty, and so should learning. By the way, there is also a great deal of beautiful music and literature inspired by the Old Testament. We can't put it in this textbook, but don't miss the wonder!
- Second, the artwork also illustrates good, bad, and quirky things about the history of the interpretation of the Old Testament. Study the art and read the captions, where we have teased out how the art is interpreting parts of the Old Testament. The art continues and adds to the learning.
- Third, the art comes predominantly from parts of the world where the Old Testament has been more influential for the longest time. So, yes, there is a great deal of European fine art from the Christian tradition in the book. But we have tried to represent something of the global impact of the Old Testament by including Jewish art and art from Christianity around the world. Different cultures and ethnicities see and hear different things in the Bible. Let the art be a guide to how different cultures receive the witness of the Old Testament.
- The individual works often depict either important themes of a book or controversial aspects of a book and how it has been interpreted. They have not been chosen haphazardly! Ask questions about what the fine art is doing. And here's a hint: ask your professor about the art (it might be a way of making class more interesting).

The Book Has a Companion Website That Features Numerous Additional Resources

The website (www.IntroducingOT.com) accompanying this book is filled with materials that you may find useful in this course and beyond. If you like, you can print and reproduce many of these materials for use in teaching the Old Testament to others, should you find yourself in a position to do that. The website includes things like chapter objectives, pedagogical suggestions, discussion prompts, quizzes, a test bank, PowerPoint slides, flash cards for glossary terms, self-quizzes, chapter summaries, and study questions.

About Writing This Book and Acknowledging Awesome People

As we wrote this book, one of us was the primary author of a given chapter. The other then reviewed, made suggestions, and offered edits. We have decided not to indicate which chapters or parts of chapters were written by each of us. Because of this—believe it or not—neither of us agrees with everything in the book! Coauthoring a book is like being married: you have to know when to compromise and say, "I understand where you are coming from. Let's move forward with your perspective." Speaking of marriage, we are pleased to dedicate this book to our wives, Amy Dewald and Katherine Chan. Each is a gift from the divine. We also are pleased to dedicate this book to our excellent (always) and patient (to a point) editor, Jim Kinney. He, too, is a gift from the divine.

We wish to thank the board and administration of Luther Seminary (St. Paul, MN) for the callings and support that afforded us the chance to write this book. We have both been professors at Luther Seminary during the years in which it took shape. We thank Luther for everything from the lights in our offices, to a sabbatical during which Rolf began this project, to the tremendous support the administration and board offer for research and writing. As we finish this project, Michael has accepted a new appointment at Concordia College (Moorhead, MN), where he will continue to serve the church, among college students. We will miss serving together but are grateful for the years we have shared at Luther Seminary. We also want to thank our current and former Old Testament colleagues, who on many occasions shared wisdom that has made it into this book. They also helped us think through many and various interpretive matters. They are Diane Jacobson, Mark Throntveit, Dick Nysse, Fred Gaiser, Kathryn Schifferdecker, Cameron Howard, and Mark Hillmer. We also acknowledge two colleagues who are now deceased: Terry Fretheim and Jim Limburg. Karl Jacobson, Rolf's brother and also an Old Testament scholar, also deserves our gratitude for many conversations with both of us. Finally, we thank the students of Luther Seminary for the passion they bring to learning. Their questions, curiosity, and commitment to the text have made us better students of the Old Testament. We also want to thank Mark Allan Powell for blessing our efforts to write a companion volume to his text and for assisting with the selection of some of the images. The glossary also contains many of Mark's definitions in order to provide consistency for students.

Along with Jim Kinney at Baker Academic, we are also grateful for the critical assistance of Brandy Scritchfield and James Korsmo. We produced a manuscript; they turned it into a book that feels like a work of art and is masterfully made.

Part 1

THE
OLD TESTAMENT

Context and Scope

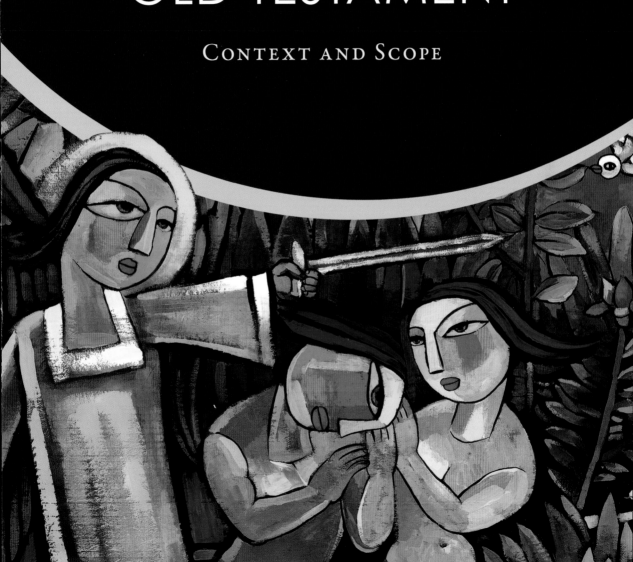

The Old Testament World

Few books, if any, have had a greater impact on the world than the book Christians call "the Old Testament." The Old Testament has shaped how people think about what it is to be a human being. It has shaped how people think about the universe. It has impacted how people conceive of the earth and its many creatures and features. It has influenced the basic elements of human society—including things such as marriage, family, childhood, and old age. It has played a role in the evolution of ethics, the development of laws, and the rise of the arts. It has shaped how people think about both the past and the future. And, perhaps most of all, the Old Testament has influenced how people think about God and about spiritual matters.

In light of the Old Testament's great influence in shaping our world, it is surprising how little most people know about the world that shaped the Old Testament. All the books of the Old Testament were written by people who lived in an actual world—what we are calling in this chapter "the Old Testament world." This may seem like an obvious statement, but many readers of the Old Testament often fail to appreciate this fact. Perhaps the reason for this is that many readers approach the Old Testament in search of "timeless truths"—and the concept of timeless truths tends to obscure the time-bounded character of the text. In order to understand the Old Testament properly—indeed, to understand why and how the Old Testament's witness remains valid and applicable in the modern world—knowing and understanding the contours of the Old Testament world is essential.

Why does such knowledge matter? In two words: understanding and misunderstanding. Knowledge of the Old Testament world can help one understand the meaning of various passages. And perhaps even more importantly, knowledge of the Old Testament world can help a reader avoid misunderstanding various passages.

testament A written account of a covenant. It is in this sense that parts of the Bible are called the Old Testament and the New Testament.

Time Periods

ancestors Sometimes referred to as the patriarchs or matriarchs; generally includes Abraham/Sarah, Isaac/Rebekah, Jacob/Rachel/Leah.

Period of the Ancestors: Prior to 1500 BCE

The oldest traditions in the Old Testament date to a time that is often called the period of the ancestors or the period of the patriarchs and matriarchs. This time period can be considered prehistory because its events and people are very difficult to date historically. Most likely these stories date from a time before 1500 BCE. During this era, Israel's story began. And the story began as a family story—the stories of Abraham and Sarah, Isaac and Rebekah, Jacob and his wives and consorts, and Joseph and his brothers.

BCE An abbreviation for "before the common era"; in academic studies, BCE is typically used for dates in place of BC ("before Christ").

Slavery in Egypt and the Exodus: Ca. 1500–1240 BCE

The book of Genesis ends by recounting how Jacob and his family end up in Egypt. The book of Exodus starts by describing how the Israelites had grown numerous and were enslaved by the Egyptians. Exodus then tells the foundational story of Israel's identity: the exodus from Egypt. This story describes Israel's rescue by God from Egyptian slavery, Israel's new covenantal relationship with God, the gift of the law, and Israel's journey through the wilderness.

Israel (1) The entire people descended from Abraham and Sarah; (2) the Northern Kingdom centered in Samaria; (3) a symbolic name given to Jacob, the patriarch.

Egypt An ancient imperial power in northeast Africa, organized around the Nile River.

Emergence of Israel and Settlement in the Land: Ca. 1200–1000 BCE

Following the exodus and Israel's journey through the wilderness, the nation of Israel comes of age in the "promised land" of Canaan. There is debate about the nature of Israel's emergence in the land. Was it a giant military conquest?

Exodus The second book of the Pentateuch. It describes the liberation of the Israelites from the oppressive rule of Pharaoh and the subsequent giving of the law at Sinai.

the law The law of Moses or any regulations the Jewish people understood as delineating faithfulness to God in terms of the covenant he had made with Israel; often used synonymously with Torah.

Box 1.1

Basic Old Testament Chronology

Prior to 1500	Period of the ancestors
Ca. 1500–1240	Slavery in Egypt, exodus, and journey to Canaan
Ca. 1200–1000	Emergence of Israel and settlement in the land
Ca. 1025–928	United monarchy (Saul, David, and Solomon)
Ca. 922–586	Divided monarchy
Ca. 922–722/721	Israel (the Northern Kingdom) exists until Assyria conquers it
Ca. 922–586	Judah (the Southern Kingdom) exists until Babylon conquers it
586–537	Exile
539–333	Persian period (the return and the diaspora) Return (many exiled Judeans return to Judah) Diaspora (many exiled Judeans choose to live as a dispersed people in locations throughout the ancient Near East)
332–63	Hellenistic period

Note: All dates are BCE.

Was it a political revolution? Was it a peaceful immigration into previously unsettled areas? Was it a combination of all three? Scholars disagree on this, but all agree that at the end of the second millennium BCE, a people called Israel emerged in Canaan. Sometimes this era is called "the tribal league" because during these years Israel was not a centralized nation ruled by a king but rather a loose affiliation of twelve tribes that were led by various leaders called "judges" (charismatic leaders). During these early years, Israel's existence was constantly threatened by rival people who lived nearby—such as the Arameans, Moabites, Canaanites, Philistines, Midianites, and Ammonites. According to books like Judges and 1 Samuel, Israel did not have a human king because God was considered the nation's king.

judges The translation of a Hebrew term more properly translated "deliverers" or "saviors."

United Monarchy: Ca. 1025–922 BCE

The system of charismatic judges leading the people eventually failed. When this failure occurred, the people demanded a human king. For about a century, the twelve tribes of Israel were united under a single king. Three men ruled successively over the unified nation: Saul, David, and Solomon. King David made Jerusalem the capital of the united Israel, and his son Solomon built a temple in Jerusalem to centralize the worship of Israel's God. According to the biblical text, during David's rule the nation of Israel briefly achieved the status of a powerful empire. But by the end of the reign of David's son Solomon, the nation was fragmenting due to both internal and external pressures.

Canaanite A term used to describe the inhabitants of the Holy Land prior to Israel's emergence there.

Divided Monarchy: Ca. 922–586 BCE

Following Solomon's reign, the twelve tribes split into two kingdoms—a northern kingdom called Israel and a southern kingdom called Judah. During this period, the relationship between the two nations was sometimes friendly. At other times, the nations were in rivalry with each other, and sometimes they were even at war with each other. Even though both nations worshiped Yahweh, "the God of Abraham, Isaac, and Jacob," they had rival religious structures and some differing theological teachings.

Judah The Southern Kingdom centered in Jerusalem.

Northern Kingdom: Ca. 922–722/721 BCE

The Northern Kingdom (which the Bible often refers to as Israel, Ephraim, Jacob, or Joseph) was composed of the ten Israelite tribes that lived in the northern part of the land. This nation was formed when ten tribes rebelled against the Davidic kings who ruled from Jerusalem. Israel was more populous and prosperous than Judah, the Southern Kingdom, but it was plagued by internal political instability (its kings were often overthrown from within by

Northern Kingdom The ten tribes that broke away from Judah after Solomon's reign. It had alternative cultic sites at Dan and Bethel.

political rivals) and by external military threats (Israel was more vulnerable militarily than the mountain-bound Southern Kingdom). The capital of Israel was eventually located in the city of Samaria, and its religious centers included Bethel and Dan (where the first king, Jeroboam, erected golden calves in the worship sanctuaries), as well as numerous "high places" and other sites, such as Gilgal and Shechem, where sacrifices were performed and offerings were received. The Northern Kingdom was eventually conquered by the Assyrian Empire. After several failed attempts to rebel against Assyria, Samaria was destroyed in 722/721 BCE; its leading citizens were forcibly exiled; and foreign people were resettled into the land. (The descendants of the Northern Kingdom were later called Samaritans.)

Southern Kingdom: Ca. 922–586 BCE

Two tribes—Judah and Benjamin—composed the Southern Kingdom, which took the name of Judah (the more powerful of its two tribes). Although the nation of Judah was neither as wealthy nor as powerful as its northern neighbor, it enjoyed several other important advantages. These advantages mainly centered on the city of Jerusalem, a well-fortified city and the political and religious center of the country. Judah experienced political stability because it had the Davidic monarchy—all of its kings hailed from the line of King David. The country also had a stable religious life, centering on the temple in Jerusalem, where offerings were received and sacrifices were performed. The Southern Kingdom was able to survive the Assyrian threat that brought about Israel's demise, lasting for approximately 150 more years, although in its final years it was a vassal nation of the Babylonian Empire. After Judah rebelled several times, the Babylonians sacked Jerusalem—razing the temple, tearing down the city's walls, and forcing the prominent citizens into exile in Babylon (many other leading citizens fled to places such as Egypt and Damascus).

Exile: 586–537 BCE

After Babylon subdued Jerusalem, a period of exile followed. In a series of deportations (in 597, 586, and 582), many prominent citizens of Jerusalem and Judah were taken to live as exiles in the land of Babylon. During this period, other Judeans also fled to Egypt and elsewhere.

Persian Period: 539–333 BCE

In 539 BCE, Cyrus the Great of Persia conquered Babylon. Soon thereafter, Cyrus gave the Judean exiles in Babylon permission to return home, resettle in Jerusalem, and rebuild the temple.

Fig. 1.1. This nineteenth-century painting is titled *The Captivity of the Tribes of Israel*. Viewers might ask, "Which one?" since the people of Israel were enslaved, conquered, exiled, or otherwise subdued by many of the world's great empires. Sadly, the "captivity" to which the artist refers is a pogrom of Jews that occurred in France in the fifteenth century, reminding us that the suffering of the Jewish people has continued for millennia after the writing of what Christians call "the Old Testament."

The return. Following Cyrus's edict that the Judeans could return to the promised land, many who were living in exile did so and joined in the resettling and restoration of the land. But Judah was not reestablished as an independent nation with a king. Rather, the Persian province of Yehud was created. In 515 BCE, a new temple built on the foundations of Solomon's temple was dedicated. This temple lasted until the Romans destroyed an expanded version of it in 70 CE. The period of time from 515 BCE to 70 CE is known as the Second Temple

Cyrus the Great Persian emperor who conquered the ancient Near East and permitted exiled Jews to return to their land and rebuild their temple.

Persia A large area east of Mesopotamia and north of the Persian Gulf; the center of the Persian Empire, which ruled large portions of the ancient Near East from 539 to 332 BCE.

CE An abbreviation for "common era"; in academic studies, CE is typically used for dates in place of AD (*anno Domini*, "in the year of the Lord").

Second Temple period The era in Jewish history between the dedication of the second Jerusalem temple in 515 BCE and its destruction in 70 CE.

synagogue A congregation of Jews who gather for worship, prayer, and Bible study, or the place where they gather for these purposes.

diaspora Jews living in exile outside the Holy Land; also called the dispersion.

Torah The law of Moses, as contained in the Pentateuch; or, frequently, a synonym for the Pentateuch (referring, then, to the first five books of the Hebrew Bible).

ancient Near East Geographical area that runs east-west from Egypt to Mesopotamia and north-south from Turkey to the Arabian Peninsula.

Hellenistic Affected by Hellenism, that is, the influence of Greek and Roman culture, customs, philosophy, and modes of thought. For example, Jewish people were said to be "hellenized" when they adopted Greco-Roman customs or came to believe propositions derived from Greek philosophy.

Seleucids The Syrian dynastic family that ruled Palestine during the years 198–167 BCE.

period. This was one of the most transformational and productive periods in Jewish history.

The diaspora. Although many exiles returned to live again in or near Jerusalem, many did not. Those who continued to live at a distance from the land formed Jewish communities in the midst of foreign lands and began to gather and worship in local synagogues. Thus began what is known as the diaspora—marking a major change in the identity of the people of Israel. Prior to the exile, the people thought of themselves as a holy nation, living in a holy land, centered on a holy temple and the chosen family of Davidic kings. The exile and diaspora initiated a lengthy and complex process of change that fundamentally transformed Jewish identity. The emphasis on Torah observance among many modern Jewish communities testifies to these seismic shifts.

Hellenistic Period: 332–63 BCE

Persian rule of the ancient Near East lasted until the rise of the Greeks, led by the youthful Alexander the Great. Palestine fell under Alexander's rule in 332 BCE. The period of time that followed is known broadly as the Hellenistic period—referring to the time when Greek culture and language heavily influenced many contemporary Jews. Greek became the international language. After Alexander's death in 323, his generals and officials fought for control of his empire. Two of these generals succeeded in gaining control of large territories—Ptolemy in Egypt and Seleucus in Asia Minor. Judea, which was located near the border of these two territories, owed allegiance first to the Ptolemaic Empire (320–198 BCE) and then later to the Seleucid Empire (198–167 BCE).

In the middle of the second century BCE, Jewish fighters rebelled against the Seleucid overlord, Antiochus IV Epiphanes (175–164 BCE), achieving independence for a time. They were responding to his harsh religious and political repression. Their recapture and rededication of the temple initiated a period of native Jewish rule over Judea known as the Hasmonean period (165–37 BCE), named after the ruling dynasty. During this period, the latest books of the Old Testament were most likely written and other books that had evolved over the centuries probably reached their final form.

Ages of Empires

In large part, the Old Testament recounts the story of the people of Israel. It narrates Israel's understanding of itself as having begun when God called an aged couple—Abraham and Sarah—to be the founders of a chosen people. The story unfolds as this chosen family survives early threats, grows to be a substantial people, eventually becomes an independent nation, declines under many different pressures, and survives as a holy people of a holy book.

Throughout the long story of the Old Testament, this chosen people, Israel, was beset by powers and principalities greater than itself. Over the centuries, Israel was often besieged by the great empires that rose and fell around it—Egypt, Assyria, Babylon, Persia, Greece, the Ptolemies, the Seleucids, and Rome. Familiarity with these great (and near-great) empires and the imperial pressures they imposed on Israel provides useful context for understanding various texts from the Old Testament. Here, only a brief sketch of the major empires is given. In later chapters, additional context will be provided.

Egyptian Empire(s)

The land of Egypt was host to many great rulers and dynasties. Throughout Israel's long history, Egypt exercised profound influence—both benign and malignant—on the chosen people. This can be seen in the mixed array of stories about Egypt in the Pentateuch. On the one hand, Egypt was a safe harbor during famine under the capable administration of Joseph in Genesis. On the other hand, Egypt was Israel's oppressor in the book of Exodus. Later on in Israel's history, kings occasionally looked to Egypt for protection and no doubt benefited economically from trade relations.

Over the centuries, Egyptian power and influence over the Levant—the land along the eastern Mediterranean Sea—waxed and waned. Historians

Antiochus IV Epiphanes A second-century-BCE king of the Seleucid Empire (based in Syria) who was responsible for religiously persecuting Jews living in Judea. These events influenced the latter chapters of the book of Daniel.

Hasmonean The family name of the Jewish rebels who led a successful revolt against the Syrians in 167 BCE.

principalities Powerful spiritual beings that exercise their influence in a dimension not perceptible to human senses.

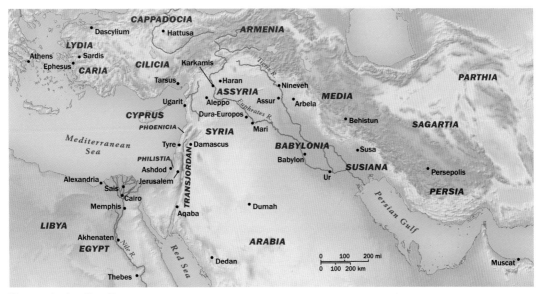

Map 1.1. Ancient Near East

distinguish between various epochs of Egyptian empire, such as the Old Kingdom (2686–2218 BCE), the Middle Kingdom (2055–1650 BCE), the New Kingdom (1550–1069 BCE), and the Late Period (664–332 BCE). Between each of these eras were transitory interregnums during which Egyptian power was low or internal divisions were being sorted out.

In terms of ancient Israel, the New Kingdom (1550–1069 BCE) had a great impact. During this period, Egyptian power reached its zenith—with Egyptian hegemony reaching as far south as Ethiopia and as far north as Syria. The events recounted in the book of Exodus likely occurred during this era. Especially important here is to note that during the thirteenth and twelfth centuries BCE—precisely when Israel was emerging as a people in the Holy Land—Egypt lost control of that area. Toward the end of the New Kingdom, internal disorders and divisions grew rampant. The golden age of Israel's kingdom (from Saul's reign in ca. 1020 BCE through the fall of the Southern Kingdom in 586 BCE) coincided with a time in which Egypt's power was greatly diminished. In the Late Period, a resurgent Egypt reappeared and played a role in the final years of the Southern Kingdom.

Regional Powers in Israel's Neighborhood

Israel's history was not only shaped by the great riverine civilizations of Egypt and Mesopotamia. Smaller kingdoms in Israel's geographical neighborhood also had significant influence (Aram, Ammon, Edom, Moab, Philistia, etc.). These regional powers played a variety of roles depending on the circumstances. Sometimes they were allies; sometimes they were adversaries; and sometimes they were trade partners. The full range of state relations existed among Israel and its neighbors.

The Philistines are but one example. In the twelfth century BCE, this seafaring people settled in five cities (Gaza, Ashdod, Ashkelon, Gath, and Ekron) along the coast of the Mediterranean. During the Israelite periods of the judges and early monarchy, the Philistines and Israelites were often at loggerheads. This was so much the case that, in a good portion of the Old Testament, the Philistines appear as iconic adversaries of Israel.

Significant amounts of cultural and religious intermingling happened among these regional powers. From the ninth through sixth centuries BCE (especially during the time of the Northern Kingdom of Israel), powers to Israel's north and east—Aram, Sidon, and Tyre to the north; Ammon, Moab, and Edom to the east—vexed Israel and Judah. Their religious and cultural practices were imitated by some within Israel and Judah, including royalty, which caused some division within Israel and Judah. The Edomites seem to have played an especially destructive role in the siege and sack of Jerusalem in 586 BCE. Testimony to the Judahites' bitterness regarding these events is found in several biblical books, including the entire book of Obadiah.

Neo-Assyrian Empire (934–609 BCE)

According to Genesis, the story of Israel started when Abraham and Sarah uprooted their household from Mesopotamia—the fertile land between and around the Tigris and Euphrates Rivers—and transplanted it to Palestine. The story of the kingdoms of Israel and Judah climaxed when two Mesopotamian empires—Assyria and Babylon, respectively—subdued those kingdoms. As was the case with Egypt, both the Babylonian and Assyrian Empires consisted of multiple empires over many epochs. It is specifically the Neo-Assyrian and Neo-Babylonian Empires that played important roles in the world of the Old Testament.

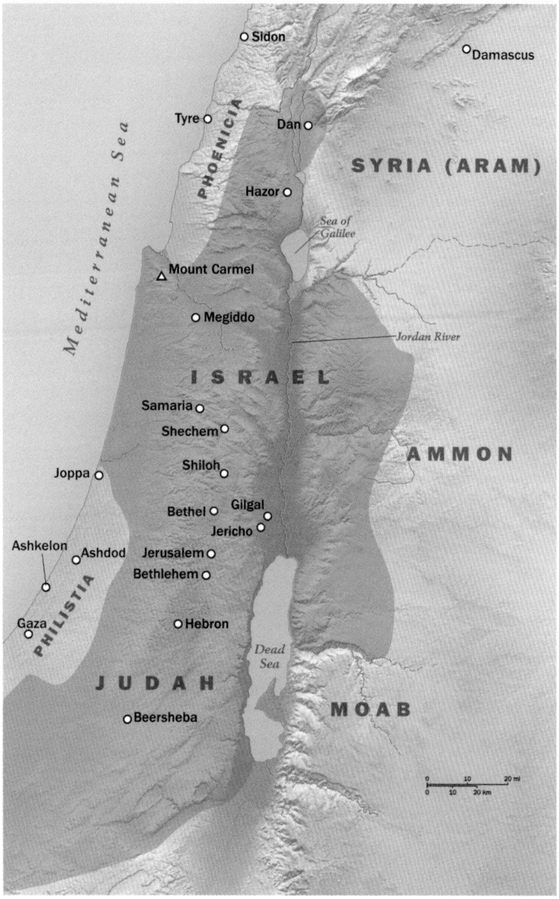

The Neo-Assyrian Empire rose from the ashes of past empires beginning in 934 BCE under kings such as Assur-dan II and Tukulti-ninurta II. The empire reached its zenith during the expansionist reign of Tiglath-pileser III (745–727 BCE). Over the next three centuries, many countries and kings bent their knees to various Neo-Assyrian kings. The Northern Kingdom of Israel was no exception. The Assyrian king Shalmaneser III brought Israel under heel as a vassal nation in 841 BCE. Following several attempted rebellions, Israel was defeated, its capital city of Samaria destroyed in 722/721, and its citizens deported, while a more docile foreign population was resettled in the land of Israel. The Assyrians also threatened the Southern Kingdom of Judah but did not utterly destroy it. Neo-Assyrian rule over the ancient Near East endured for the next century, until finally giving way in 609 BCE to a new empire.

Neo-Babylonian Empire (627–539 BCE)

As with the Egyptian and Assyrian Empires, the Babylonian Empire had several incarnations over the centuries. The one that most directly affected the

Map 1.2. Israel and its neighbors from the tenth through the seventh centuries

Neo-Assyrian Empire An empire based in northern Mesopotamia that ruled much of the ancient Near East from the middle of the eighth century BCE until approximately 609 BCE.

Neo-Babylonian Empire An empire based in southern Mesopotamia that ruled much of the ancient Near East from 612 to 539 BCE.

people of ancient Israel was the Neo-Babylonian Empire, a relatively short-lived empire that nonetheless played a major role in the fate and fortunes of the kingdom of Judah. Babylon first forced Judah to submit in 597 BCE, but when it continued to rebel, Babylon eventually sacked Jerusalem and forced several waves of Jews into exile.

Persian (or Achaemenid) Empire (550–333 BCE)

Yehud A term for the province of Judah during the Persian period.

The Achaemenid king, Cyrus the Great, was responsible for overthrowing the Babylonian Empire. In a move that was both self-serving and generous, Cyrus granted the exiled captives permission to return to their homelands. The Persian religion was Zoroastrianism, but the empire tolerated and even encouraged local populations to keep their own gods, temples, and religious traditions. When Persia conquered Babylon, many captive peoples, including the exiled Judeans, were allowed to return home and reestablish their religious institutions. With respect to local government, Persia granted considerable local autonomy, but the landed was divided into provinces of the Persian Empire with appointed governors. Judah became the province Yehud, no longer an independent nation or vassal kingdom with its own dynastic kings.

priests In Second Temple Judaism, people authorized to oversee the sacrificial system in the Jerusalem temple; closely associated with the Sadducees.

prophet Someone claiming to bear a message from a divine source.

Box 1.2

War in the Ancient Near East

The famous story of King David's adulterous relationship with Bathsheba in 2 Samuel 11 begins, "In the spring of the year, the time when kings go out to battle . . ." War was a regular feature of life in the Old Testament. The annual rhythm that included times for planting, tending, and harvesting of crops also tragically included "a time for war," as the poet writes in Ecclesiastes 3. In the Old Testament world, the main purpose of war was to subjugate foreign territories for economic exploitation. A conquered nation was required to send the conquering empire annual tribute in the forms of silver and gold, male and female slaves, and crops and livestock.

Over the centuries that encompass the Old Testament, the technologies and tactics of war developed. Early innovation included the use of horses and chariots in war and the development of body armor and weapons (first made of bronze and then of iron). Later, cities were fortified with walls and gates for purposes of defense. This fortification led invading armies to develop tactics and weapons for siege warfare. These included battering rams to attack city gates, great siege ramps to gain the rams access to the city gates, and engines of war to overcome city walls. Besieging armies would also excavate beneath city walls in order, quite literally, to undermine their foundations. Kings were expected to lead their nations' armies, while priests and prophets were expected to provide ritual and prayer support in times of war. The role that religion played in war and conquest differed from nation to nation.

Greek Empire and Empires of the Ptolemies and Seleucids (334–167 BCE)

With the appearance of Alexander the Great on the battlefields of the ancient Near East, a sea change took place in the region. The international language shifted to Greek, and the influences of Greek culture spread. But a unified Greek Empire under Alexander was short lived. In the wake of his premature death, the empire split into smaller entities (including the Ptolemaic and Seleucid kingdoms), each of which waxed and waned over several centuries. The influences of Greek culture and empire on Second Temple Judaism were sometimes experienced as threats. Judah was at times ruled by the empire of the Ptolemies, based in Egypt, and at other times by the empire of the Seleucids, based in Syria. In these alternating periods of domination, taxation and required tributes were heavy, but especially during a particular era of Seleucid domination of Judah, the explicit oppression of Jewish religious life became intense, ultimately resulting in the desecration of the temple.

Second Temple Judaism A general term for the diverse culture, practices, and beliefs of Jewish people during the Second Temple period (515 BCE–70 CE).

Geography of the Old Testament World

Many readers of the Old Testament do not have an appreciation of the role of "place" in the texts of the Old Testament. Nor do many readers have a strong sense of the geography of either the land of Canaan or its broader region—known as the ancient Near East. The emphasis on the Bible as "the word" by some religions may have contributed to this lack of appreciation and lack of knowledge. But because the story of the Old Testament takes place in and around specific places, basic knowledge of Old Testament geography is essential.

Palestine (Canaan, the Promised Land)

The story of the people of Israel began when God said to Abram, "Leave your land . . . for the land that I will show you" (Gen. 12:1 CEB). From that point

---

Box 1.3

Empires of the Old Testament World

Empire	Era	Homeland	Language	Key Leaders	Key Gods
Egyptian	1550–1069	Egypt	Egyptian	Akhenaten, Ramesses III	Horus, Re
Neo-Assyrian	934–609	Mesopotamia	Akkadian	Tiglath-pileser III, Sargon	Assur, Ishtar
Neo-Babylonian	627–539	Mesopotamia	Akkadian	Nebuchadnezzar	Marduk, Sîn
Persian	550–333	Iran	Aramaic	Cyrus, Artaxerxes	Ahura Mazda
Greek	334–167	Macedonia	Greek	Alexander, Seleucus	Zeus, Mars

Note: All dates are BCE.

onward, the so-called "promised land" looms as a major feature of the story. What was this land—later described as "a land flowing with milk and honey" (Exod. 3:17)—really like?

The "land of Israel" refers to a slender strip of land that runs north to south along the eastern edge of the Mediterranean Sea. Israel is relatively small—a little smaller than New Jersey. The Mediterranean Sea marked the western border—although the southern part of the coastal area was occupied by the cities of the Philistines. On the east, the border was the desert that makes up the northwest section of the Arabian Peninsula. In biblical times, the region of Bashan and the nations of Ammon, Moab, and Edom were arranged along this eastern border. To the south was a wilderness/desert area known as the Negev; to the north were the nations of Phoenicia and Aram (Syria).

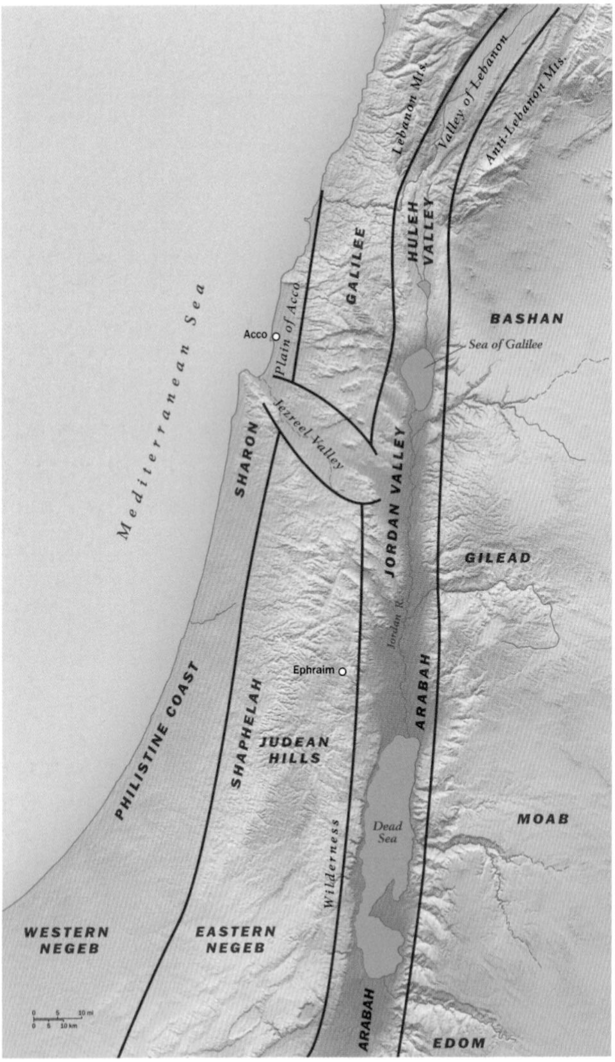

Within the land, the Jordan River flows from the Sea of Galilee (also called the Sea of Kinneret) in the north to the Dead Sea in the south. A low, mountainous spine runs north and south just west of the Jordan River. In these mountains, herds of goats and sheep were tended, and crops were grown on human-made terraces. The southern highlands formed the center of the Southern Kingdom of Judah, where Jerusalem was located. To the west of this central range are plains, valleys, and lowlands. The key cities of Bethel, Shechem, and Samaria were located in this region.

The northern end of the land is also mountainous, with Mount Carmel to the northwest protruding into the Mediterranean Sea and the high point of Mount Hermon (7,326 ft.) farther to the north, as if to look down on the rest of the land. The

Map 1.3. Geographical map of ancient Israel

major break in the north-south mountain range is the Valley of Jezreel, which runs east and west from Mount Carmel in the west to the Jordan Valley in the east. This valley was prime agricultural land, serving as the breadbasket of ancient Israel.

The area east of the Jordan River is called the Transjordan. Israelites lived in this area, but as was the case with all border areas, neighboring countries contested with Israel for dominion over the territory (cf. 1 Kings 22).

The climate of Israel is arid and warm—with lengthy, dry summer months and a comparatively short rainy season. In the rainy season, otherwise dry creek beds known as wadis temporarily run with water. Droughts and dry years were common. In the absence of rain, natural springs and human-made wells were highly prized and could provide the point of conflict.

Israel was at a crossroads in the ancient world. Two important international roads were part of the land's terrain. These two highways facilitated international trade (and war) and were sources of taxes for the kingdoms through which they ran. The Way of the Sea ran north and south along the edge of the Mediterranean Sea—especially connecting Egypt to Israel, Lebanon, and Asia Minor. The King's Highway also ran north and south, but along the east side of the Jordan River—especially connecting the Arabian Peninsula to Mesopotamia. Multiple smaller east-west roads connected the two major north-south roads, creating an international crossroads in Palestine.

Within the land, there was a national boundary between Israel and Judah. There were also tribal boundaries—between Ephraim and Dan, for instance. Various places in the land had holy sites—Shechem, Bethel, Dan, Gilgal, and most importantly, Jerusalem.

Most of the population lived in villages, with a minority living in larger towns. The villages were often located near springs for water or on hilltops for defense.

Ancient Near East—Cradle of Civilizations

The larger known world during the time of the Old Testament is referred to as the ancient Near East (ANE). Broadly speaking, this area included the lands surrounding the eastern Mediterranean Sea as well as Mesopotamia, Egypt, Iran, and modern-day Turkey.

Considered as a whole and over a long period of history, this region proved a fertile ground for the growth of cultures, languages (including the development of writing), arts, and sciences. Great civilizations and religions emerged in the ANE. In addition to the Egyptian, Assyrian, Babylonian, Persian, and Greek civilizations already mentioned, great civilizations such as the Hittites, Sumerians, and various Mediterranean kingdoms were born in the region. The

Jordan River A major river system in Israel running north-south and connecting the Sea of Galilee and the Dead Sea.

Transjordan The geographic region of Israel east of the Jordan River.

Sumerians are often credited with being the first civilization to develop writing. Writing in the ANE began as a kind of pictographic orthography that developed into a syllabic form of writing—a form of writing in which characters represent two- or three-phoneme clusters. The invention of the alphabet—a form of writing in which an individual character represents a single phoneme—most likely occurred along the northeast coast of the Mediterranean.

Israel, located at a key crossroads of the ANE, both reaped the rewards of its location and paid the penalty for it. The greatest downside was probably the constant threat of war and imperial domination. Israel was often either a pawn in the game of empires or caught in the crossfire between empires. But there were other downsides. Being located at the crossroads exposed Israel to epidemics and to adverse social conventions, such as slavery and the promulgation of social classes and economic inequalities.

But Israel's location provided numerous advantages as well, such as access to international trade. Israel had access to foreign markets for its most tradable commodities—especially olive oil and wine, neither of which grew in Egypt or Mesopotamia. Israel was also exposed to many salutary cultural influences, including the development of legal codes; technological developments such as pottery, the cultivation of agriculture, the milling of grain, and the forging of bronze and iron; and cultural evolutions in philosophy, astronomy, math, and architecture.

polytheism The belief that there are multiple gods.

henotheism A belief in multiple gods but with the added belief that one god rules over the others.

monolatry The worship of a single god without denying the existence of others.

monotheism The belief that there is only one God.

Judaism A general term for the religious systems and beliefs of the Jewish people. In Jesus's day, there were varieties of Judaism, though all shared certain fundamental ideas and practices.

Box 1.4

Polytheism, Henotheism, Monolatry, Monotheism

For most peoples of the ancient Near East, the world was full of deities. It was not until much later in Israel's life that belief in a single deity actually won out. Scholars use several technical terms to describe the various ways people conceptualize the divine world. *Polytheism* is a belief in many gods. *Henotheism* is also polytheistic, but it claims that one deity rules all others. *Monolatry*, similarly, affirms the existence of multiple gods, but its adherents choose to worship only one among them. *Monotheism* is belief in a single God. Judaism, Christianity, and Islam lay claim to this belief system.

Belief in multiple deities was the default in the ANE. Whether talking about the official Egyptian pantheon or popular religion in Phoenicia, belief in multiple gods shaped the everyday lives of people in the ANE, including Israel. Israelite religion developed in this environment. In its early stages, ancient Israel's religion is probably best described as henotheistic: they believed in multiple gods but placed the Lord at the top of the divine hierarchy. This belief is reflected in Deuteronomy 32:8–9 and Psalm 82:1–4. Judaism eventually became a monotheistic religion, but only after a very long time.

Religious Landscape of the Ancient Near East

The ancient Near East was a religiously diverse part of the world. Religious beliefs were evident in all aspects of life, from birth to the afterlife. Quite unlike people in modern, secular Western nations such as America, ancient Near Easterners viewed the world as "enchanted"—that is, it was filled with gods, goddesses, demons, and semidivine beings who blessed, afflicted, and otherwise impeded everyday life in a variety of ways. This rich belief in an enchanted cosmos left its mark in the archaeological record in the form of ritual texts, mythologies, graves, divine images, sculpture, architecture, and more. Not surprisingly, the people of this region developed a rich array of practices and professions that allowed them to negotiate this complex, largely unseen world.

> **demon** An evil (or "unclean") spirit capable of possessing people and incapacitating them with some form of illness or disability.

Daily Life in Ancient Israel

Kinship-Based Social System

Every society develops norms and customs that help organize the complicated set of daily human interactions. Biblical Israel was a kinship society, meaning that extended family networks formed the warp and woof of the societal tapestry. The structure of Israel's kinship relations is evident in the following passage, in which the leader Joshua was tasked by God with sorting through the people of Israel: "So Joshua rose early in the morning, and brought *Israel* near *tribe* by *tribe*, and the *tribe* of Judah was taken. He brought near the *clans* of Judah, and the *clan* of the Zerahites was taken; and he brought near the *clan* of the Zerahites, *family* by *family*, and Zabdi was taken. And he brought near his *household* one by one, and Achan son of Carmi son of Zabdi son of Zerah, of the *tribe* of Judah, was taken" (Josh. 7:16–18; emphasis added).

Notice that there are four layers of social relationships to which an individual belonged. The highest level of kinship was the "people" (i.e., Israel), and the lowest level was the "household":

People (Israel)
|
Tribe (Judah)
|
Clan (Zerah)
|
Household (Zabdi, grandfather of Achan)
|
Individual (Achan)

Every person in Israel would have known the people, tribe, clan, and household to which they belonged. The "household" was literally that—a three-generation family living together in one house. In such a house, the father and mother of the house lived with all of their sons and the sons' wives and children, all of their unmarried daughters, and all of their unmarried grandchildren.

This web of kinship provided the relational networks in which ancient Israelites found their personal identity, their sense of purpose and belonging, and also their economic role. An ancient Israelite's purpose was to work together with all blood relatives to contribute to the well-being of the household, clan, tribe, and ultimately, people. If a person became ill or handicapped, indebted or endangered, a relative was expected to step up and care for them.

The Hebrew language had a special term—go'el, often translated as "redeemer" or "kinsman-redeemer"—for the family member who fulfilled obligations to a relative in need. The identity of this "redeemer" would depend on what a person's need was (relief from debt, disability, injury, starvation, homelessness, childlessness, slavery, death, etc.) and who was available to meet their need. Hebrew also had a special term for those people who did not belong to a household or clan or tribe. A "family-less person" was called a ger, usually translated as "sojourner" or "resident alien." In the ancient world, nobody wanted to be a "sojourner," because sojourners had no family to help them if they were hurt, injured, starving, homeless, disabled, childless, enslaved, and so on.

In a kinship-based society, the social value of hospitality cannot be emphasized enough. Hospitality was not a voluntary action that a person extended to friends and colleagues. It was a society-wide obligation that every household was duty bound to extend to strangers, foreigners, travelers, and sojourners. Because the societal weave was based on familial relationships, the societal welfare demanded that households offer temporary shelter and food to anyone who was brought by life circumstance into a household's territory at the end of a day. The stories of Abraham and Sarah preparing a lavish feast for three travelers (Gen. 18:1–15) and of Jesus sending seventy followers into the land of Samaria (Luke 11:1–11), as well as many other passages, illustrate the importance of the value of hospitality.

Daily Food and Drink

When Jesus's disciples asked him for instruction in how to pray, one of the petitions that he commended to them was, "Give us each day our daily bread" (Luke 11:3 NIV). As this prayer indicates, bread—along with wine, grains, and olive oil—was a staple of the Israelite diet. In fact, bread (Hebrew: lehem) was so important to the ancient Israelite that the word for "food" is the same as the word for "bread." Bread was food. The two basic breads in ancient Israel were an unleavened type of pan bread baked on a hot, flat surface (either stone

Fig. 1.2. Along with olives and figs, grapes were an essential part of the Mediterranean diet during the biblical period. Grapes could be eaten or used to make wine. This picture shows Joshua and Caleb bringing grapes to the Israelites who are about to enter the "promised land" as a testimony of the fertility they will encounter there.

or metal) and a risen bread baked in a clay oven built into the ground. It is estimated that 50–75 percent of daily caloric intake for many Israelites came from bread alone. Grapes and olives grew in abundance in Israel, and these two crops could be preserved for future consumption or trade—grapes could be preserved as wine and olives as olive oil. Together, bread, wine, and olive oil—the "Mediterranean triad"—were the staples of the ancient diet.

But this did not mean that bread was the only thing ancient Israelites ate. Fruits, vegetables, beans, and dairy products (from cattle, sheep, and goats) were also important to the ancient diet. But these other foods were available on seasonal bases.

It is sometimes said that ancient Israelites rarely, if ever, consumed meat. It is more accurate to say that for most Israelites, access to meat and fish was not a daily luxury. Animals were primarily kept and tended not to produce meat but for the other contributions they made to society—sheep and goats for the production of wool and dairy products, oxen and donkeys as the engines of agriculture, and poultry (a later development) for eggs and feathers. Only secondarily were animals tended for their meat. And as can be expected, there was an unequal distribution of meat and fish—the prosperous and the powerful enjoyed meat more often than poor people.

anoint To use oil to symbolize the selection of a royal figure.

In this vein, the Old Testament recalls that before the prophet Samuel anointed Saul as Israel's first king, he warned the people of the greedy, exploitative ways of kings. As part of this warning, he cautioned that the king "will take the best of your fields and vineyards and olive orchards and give them to his courtiers. He will take one-tenth of your grain and of your vineyards and give it to his officers and his courtiers. He will take . . . the best of your cattle and donkeys. . . . He will take one-tenth of your flocks" (1 Sam. 8:14–17). In light of this warning, the description of King Solomon's lavish ways implies a strong critique of the inequitable distribution of food: "Solomon's provision for one day was thirty cors of choice flour, and sixty cors of meal, ten fat oxen, and twenty pasture-fed cattle, one hundred sheep, besides deer, gazelles, roebocks, and fatted fowl" (1 Kings 4:22–23). Similarly, the prophet Amos castigated the wealthy for their conspicuous consumption:

> Woe to those who lie on beds of ivory . . .
> and eat lambs from the flock
> and calves from the midst of the stall, . . .

Box 1.5

Is There a Biblical Diet?

Some readers of the Old Testament assume that the biblical diet was healthier than other diets and therefore that descriptions of food in the Bible hold a sort of divinely revealed key to a healthy life. It is true that some modern studies have shown that the "Mediterranean diet," centered on grain, wine, and olive oil, is healthier than diets that are high in saturated fats and refined sugars. But this does not mean that the ancient Israelites were healthier than people today. Research suggests that the diet of many or most ancient Israelites was severely lacking in key nutrients. One scholar concludes, "Our current state of knowledge suggests that the population of Iron Age Israel generally suffered from an inadequate diet, poor health, and low life expectancy."*

Iron Age The period of human culture from 1200 BCE to 586 BCE; the period in which Israel developed from a loose confederation of tribes into a kingdom.

The Old Testament also includes long lists of "clean" and "unclean foods" (see Lev. 11 and Deut. 14). The meaning and purpose of these food laws will be discussed in later chapters, but it should simply be noted here that the Israelites' daily diet was impacted by these laws.

* Nathan McDonald, *What Did the Ancient Israelites Eat? Diet in Biblical Times* (Grand Rapids: Eerdmans, 2008), 87.

who drink wine in bowls,
        and anoint themselves with the finest oils. (Amos 6:4–6 ESV)

Work and Professions

A variety of work and professions were available to ancient Israelites. As the above discussion of food implies, for those living in rural areas and villages, most of life was devoted to agricultural work.

For men, this most likely meant directly tending crops and herds—planting, tending, harvesting, and processing grain; pruning, harvesting, and crushing grapes and olives; and herding, grooming, slaughtering, and butchering the flocks. Herding the flocks seems to have been especially assigned to younger men and boys.

For women, this most likely meant the crucial responsibilities of running the household economy. This included preparing the daily meals for the extended household—processing, preserving, and preparing food. It also involved processing agricultural by-products to produce clothing, including spinning and weaving yarn and crafting clothing. Israelite clothing was made from linen (produced from flax), wool (produced from sheep and goat hair), and leather (produced from animal skins). The importance of clothing and the amount of labor needed to produce clothing for the household must not be underestimated. Many people only had one set of garments and one cloak, as the statute in Deuteronomy 24:12–13 indicates: "If [a person leaves a garment in pledge for

---

Box 1.6

The Gezer Calendar

The rhythm of the entire Israelite year revolved around agriculture, as an ancient Hebrew document called the Gezer Calendar attests. The year began in the fall, with the harvest:

Two months of ingathering [Sept.–Oct.]
Two months of sowing [Nov.–Dec.]
Two months of late planting [Jan.–Feb.]
One month of cutting flax [March]
One month of harvesting barley [April]
One month of harvesting and measuring grain
    [May]
Two months of pruning [June–July]
A month of summer fruit [Aug.]*

* Translation based on F. W. Dobbs-Allsopp, J. J. M. Roberts, C. L. Seow, Richard E Whitaker, *Hebrew Inscriptions: Texts from the Biblical Period of the Monarchy with Concordance* (New Haven: Yale University Press, 2005), 157.

Fig. 1.3. Gezer Calendar

a borrowed item], you shall not sleep in the garment given you as the pledge. You shall give the pledge back by sunset, so that your neighbor may sleep in the cloak and bless you." The crucial role that women played in leading the household economy is illustrated by the list of the accomplishments of a "valorous wife" in Proverbs 31.

In the larger towns, more trades and professions were available. Israel had potters, weavers, tanners, carpenters, masons, smiths, traders, bakers, courtiers, fishers, and soldiers/guards, among others.

Israel also had religious professionals. There was a unique tribe—the Levites—to whom the profession of priest was given. An Israelite priest filled many roles, including butcher (as in most early religions), healer (in charge of ritual purity and cleanliness), worship specialist (Levites served as singers, musicians, scribes, and chroniclers), religious educator, diviner of the future, tutor of the young, and treasurer. The profession of priest will be discussed more in later chapters, as will the role of another religious professional—the prophet.

scribes Professionals skilled in teaching, copying, and interpreting texts; in Second Temple Judaism, closely associated with the Pharisees.

Conclusion

The world of the Old Testament is a complicated and foreign place for most modern readers. The purpose of this chapter has been to provide new readers of the Old Testament with a basic knowledge of some prominent features of that world. The treatment here does not claim to be exhaustive. As we delve more deeply into the individual books and literary genres of the Old Testament, we will explore more contours of this ancient world.

genre A type or form of literature (e.g., poetry, letter, narrative).

FOR FURTHER READING: **The Old Testament World**

Borowski, Oded. *Daily Life in Biblical Times*. Archaeology and Biblical Studies 5. Leiden: Brill, 2003.

Frank, Harry Thomas, and Roger S. Boraas. *Hammond Atlas of the Bible Lands*. Union, NJ: Hammond, 2002.

Greer, Jonathan S., John W. Hilber, and John H. Walton. *Behind the Scenes of the Old Testament: Cultural, Social, and Historical Contexts*. Grand Rapids: Baker Academic, 2018.

King, Philip J., and Lawrence E. Stager. *Life in Biblical Israel*. Library of Ancient Israel. Louisville: Westminster John Knox, 2001.

MacDonald, Nathan. *What Did the Ancient Israelites Eat? Diet in Biblical Times*. Grand Rapids: Eerdmans, 2008.

Miller, J. Maxwell, and John H. Hayes. *A History of Ancient Israel and Judah*. 2nd ed. Louisville: Westminster John Knox, 2006.

Van De Mieroop, Marc. *A History of the Ancient Near East, ca. 3000–323 BC*. 3rd ed. Blackwell History of the Ancient World. Chichester, UK: Wiley & Sons, 2016.

בן שלש עשרה למצות

The Old Testament Writings

Scripture The sacred writings of the Bible, believed to be inspired by God and viewed as authoritative for faith and practice.

Tanak (TNK) An acronym for the Jewish Bible: Torah (Pentateuch), Nevi'im (Prophets), Ketuvim (Writings).

Aramaic A Semitic language similar to Hebrew and used primarily in the Old Testament books of Daniel and Ezra-Nehemiah. It was also the native tongue for Jesus and many other Jews living in Palestine during the New Testament period.

Toward the end of the Gospel of Luke, one of the most prominent books of the Christian New Testament, the author records that Jesus said to his disciples, "'Everything written about me in the Law from Moses, the Prophets, and the Psalms must be fulfilled.' Then he opened their minds to understand the scriptures" (Luke 24:44b–45 CEB). These words of Jesus show two very important things about the collection of texts that Christians call the "Old Testament." The first is that, already in the time of Jesus, Jews (recall that Jesus was a Jew) organized their sacred texts into three sections—the Law, the Prophets, and the Psalms (more on this below). The second thing Jesus's words show is that in the New Testament, "scriptures" refers not to the New Testament or to what later became the whole of the Christian Bible. Rather, in the New Testament, "scriptures" refers to texts now collected under the label of "Old Testament." The first generation of Christians regarded what we now call the Old Testament as Scripture (cf. 2 Peter 3:2, 16).

The book that Christians know as the Old Testament was first of all the book that Second Temple Jews knew as "the scriptures." It is a book that more

---

Box 2.1

Different Names for the Old Testament

Several terms are used to describe the collection of texts that Christians typically call the "Old Testament." Jews often refer to it as the "Tanak," an acronym for Torah (Pentateuch), Nevi'im (Prophets), and Ketuvim (Writings). While the books of the Jewish Tanak are identical to the books found in most Protestant Bibles, the Tanak orders the books differently, and that is reflected in its three major divisions. In academic circles, it is common to refer to the Old Testament as the "Hebrew Bible," despite the fact that it also includes several chapters written in Aramaic. Still others refer to the Old Testament as the "First Testament," in hopes of overcoming the often-negative connotations of the word *old*.

than one religion regards as holy Scripture. The book is venerated by Jews and Christians but also by Samaritans and, to a lesser degree, by Muslims. For this reason, it is right to say that few books, if any, have had a greater impact in human history than the book Christians call the Old Testament.

Overview

The book that we call the Old Testament is really a small library: there are many books in the Old Testament. And these books are not all of the same type, nor were they all written by the same person, during the same era, or even in the same fashion. The Old Testament writings are diverse in several key ways. They have different literary genres—some are narrative, some are poetry, some are laws, and so on. They have different topics. Some are about history, some are about wisdom, some are about prophecy, and so on. Some are collections of pieces written by many different hands, while some reflect the work of one individual. Some books were composed earlier (before the Babylonian exile), while some took shape later (after the exile). And so on.

Old Testament Canons

When we set out to provide an overview of the Old Testament writings, we immediately run into a problem. Different religious traditions count the books differently and put the books in different orders. Some religious traditions also include a handful of additional books in the Old Testament.

How did it happen that various traditions came to have their Old Testaments differ in these ways? There is a relatively simple historical answer.

Box 2.2

What Is a Canon?

A wit once wrote, "Not to be confused with a large weapon (this canon only has one *n*), the canon is the list of books comprising the authoritative, written Word of God . . . which sinners often use as a large weapon to bash each other."* The word *canon* means an "official list." An Old Testament canon, therefore, refers to a list of books that are accepted as being part of the Old Testament. Differing traditions have differing lists—differing canons. But it is not just churches that have canons. For example, there are various Shakespearean canons. Most everyone accepts *Hamlet* and *King Lear* as plays officially penned by Shakespeare—they are in nearly every Shakespearean canon. But plays such as *Pericles, Prince of Tyre* or *Arden of Faversham* are disputed—they appear on some lists but not others.

* Rolf A. Jacobson, ed., *Crazy Talk: A Not-So-Stuffy Dictionary of Theological Terms*, rev. ed. (Minneapolis: Fortress, 2017), 40.

Throughout the Old Testament period, the Israelites spoke Hebrew, and their Scriptures were—quite naturally—written in Hebrew. But at the end of the Old Testament time period, with the rise of the Greek Empire and the diaspora of Second Temple Jews across the ancient world, the daily language of most Jews became Greek. When this happened, the Jewish Scriptures were gradually translated from Hebrew into Greek. Then some new books were written . . . in Greek. The collection of translated books and new Greek books is known as the Septuagint, or sometimes the Old Greek version. Thus, the situation arose in antiquity in which there were two sets of Jewish Scriptures: a set in Hebrew and a slightly longer set in Greek.

After the life of Jesus of Nazareth and the destruction of the second temple in 70 CE, Second Temple Judaism eventually evolved into rabbinic Judaism, on the one hand, and Christianity, on the other hand. Rabbinic Judaism chose as its Scriptures only those Old Testament books that existed in Hebrew. Early Christianity chose as its Scriptures the Old Testament books that existed in Greek. The Roman Catholic and Orthodox Churches accept this Greek canon as the canon of the Old Testament. When the Protestant Reformation broke away from Roman Catholicism, the Protestant churches, following the lead of Martin Luther, adopted the Jewish canonical list and so excluded from their canon the extra books.

Fig. 2.1. This nineteenth-century painting portrays Hebrew scribes (in the words of the artist) "compiling and editing the canon of Scripture from ancient documents and records." Such compiling and editing did occur, but of course the process involved a large number of people over a long period of time.

Septuagint A Greek translation of the Old Testament produced during the last three centuries BCE. The Septuagint (abbreviated LXX) includes fifteen extra books that Protestants call the Apocrypha (eleven of these are classed as deutero-canonical writings by Roman Catholics).

The Jewish Three-Part Canon (the TaNaK) and the Christian Five-Part Canon

At the beginning of this chapter, the words of Jesus and the Gospel writer Luke were cited: "'Everything written about me in the Law from Moses, the Prophets, and the Psalms must be fulfilled.' Then he opened their minds to understand the scriptures" (Luke 24:44–45 CEB). As was noted, the essential Jewish three-part

Box 2.3

Old Testament Canons

What follows is a chart that shows four different tables of contents for the Old Testament.

Before examining the chart, it may be helpful to imagine each "book" as a scroll. For many centuries, the Old Testament writings were written and preserved as scrolls. It was not until after the time of Jesus of Nazareth that some of his followers began to collect the Scriptures as a large book, with individual pages sewn together with a binding (this type of book is called a codex). When each book was a scroll, the order in which the scrolls were collected was more fluid. Even which books were regarded as Scripture was more fluid. But once a set of books began to be sewn together and bound in a single volume, then the issues of canon and order became more fixed.

Jewish	Protestant	Catholic	Orthodox
Torah	**Law/Pentateuch**	**Law/Pentateuch**	**Law/Pentateuch**
Genesis	Genesis	Genesis	Genesis
Exodus	Exodus	Exodus	Exodus
Leviticus	Leviticus	Leviticus	Leviticus
Numbers	Numbers	Numbers	Numbers
Deuteronomy	Deuteronomy	Deuteronomy	Deuteronomy
Prophets	**Historical Books**	**Historical Books**	**Historical Books**
Former Prophets	Joshua	Joshua	Joshua
Joshua	Judges	Judges	Judges
Judges	Ruth	Ruth	Ruth
Samuel	1–2 Samuel	1–2 Samuel	1–2 Samuel*
Kings	1–2 Kings	1–2 Kings	1–2 Kings*
Latter Prophets	1–2 Chronicles	1–2 Chronicles	1–2 Chronicles†
Isaiah	Ezra	Ezra	1 Esdras
Jeremiah	Nehemiah	Nehemiah	2 Esdras (Ezra and Nehemiah)
Ezekiel	Esther	Tobit	Tobit
Scroll of the Twelve		Judith	Judith
Hosea		Esther (and additions)	Esther (and additions)
Joel		1–2 Maccabees	1–3 Maccabees‡
Amos			
Obadiah			
Jonah			
Micah			
Nahum			
Habakkuk			
Zephaniah			
Haggai			
Zechariah			
Malachi			

Protestant Reformation A religious movement of the sixteenth century that sought to reform the Roman Catholic Church and that led to the establishment of Protestant churches.

organization of the Jewish Scriptures is apparent here: (1) the Law of Moses, (2) the Prophets, and (3) the Psalms. The "Law of Moses" refers to the five books of the Pentateuch (in Hebrew called the Torah). "The Prophets" refers to the totality of both the Former Prophets and the Latter Prophets. And "the Psalms" refers to the Writings—because the book of Psalms is the first book of the Writings.

Jewish	Protestant	Catholic	Orthodox
Writings	**Poetry**	**Poetry**	**Poetry**
Psalms	Job	Job	Psalms (and Ps 151)
Job	Psalms	Psalms	Job
Proverbs	Proverbs	Proverbs	Odes (and the Prayer of
Ruth	Ecclesiastes	Ecclesiastes	Manasseh)
Song of Songs	Song of Songs	Song of Songs	Proverbs
Ecclesiastes		Wisdom of Solomon	Ecclesiastes
Lamentations		Ecclesiasticus (Sirach)	Song of Songs
Esther			Wisdom of Solomon
Daniel			Ecclesiasticus (Sirach)
Ezra-Nehemiah			
Chronicles			
	Major Prophets	**Major Prophets**	**Major Prophets**
	Isaiah	Isaiah	Isaiah
	Jeremiah	Jeremiah	Jeremiah
	Lamentations	Lamentations	Baruch
	Ezekiel	Baruch and Letter of	Lamentations
	Daniel	Jeremiah	Epistle of Jeremiah
		Ezekiel	Ezekiel
		Daniel	Daniel
	Minor Prophets	**Minor Prophets**	**Minor Prophets****
	Hosea	Hosea	Hosea
	Joel	Joel	Joel
	Amos	Amos	Amos
	Obadiah	Obadiah	Obadiah
	Jonah	Jonah	Jonah
	Micah	Micah	Micah
	Nahum	Nahum	Nahum
	Habakkuk	Habakkuk	Habakkuk
	Zephaniah	Zephaniah	Zephaniah
	Haggai	Haggai	Haggai
	Zechariah	Zechariah	Zechariah
	Malachi	Malachi	Malachi

* Orthodox Churches call these books 1, 2, 3, and 4 Kingdoms.
† Orthodox Churches call these books 1–2 Paralipomenon.
‡ 4 Maccabees appears in an appendix.
** In the Orthodox canon, the Minor Prophets precede the Major Prophets.

As noted earlier, this three-part organization of the canon led to an acronym, by which Jews refer to the totality of their Scriptures, based on the first letter of the Hebrew words for the Law (*Torah*), the Prophets (*Nevi'im*), and the Writings (*Ketuvim*): TaNaK, or more commonly, the Tanak.

This different way of organizing the books of the Old Testament is about more than trivia. First, speaking very generally, the Jewish organization of the canon most likely preserves something of the historical order in which the sections of the Old Testament were finalized: the Pentateuch was the first part of the canon to be completed, with the Prophets next, and the Writings completed last.

Second, the three-part organization grants the first part, the Pentateuch, relatively more authority than the other parts of the canon. This is reflected in

Fig. 2.2. How did the writings of the Old Testament come together for us? This fanciful woodcut from the fifteenth century presents a simpler answer than the one described in this textbook: God opened a window in heaven and dictated the Bible word for word to some attentive Israelite (in European dress).

Sadducees One of the major Jewish groups during the Second Temple period; the Sadducees were closely associated with the temple in Jerusalem and were concerned with maintaining the sacrificial system; most priests appear to have been Sadducees.

Sabbath A day of the week set aside for worship and for rest from normal endeavors; for Jews, the Sabbath is the last day of the week (Saturday); for most Christians, it is the first (Sunday).

the facts that the Pentateuch was the first collection to be translated into Greek and that the Samaritans, a religious group related to the Jews, only recognize the Pentateuch (their own version of it) as Scripture. Similarly, in Jesus's day, the Jewish group known as the Sadducees only accepted the Pentateuch as Scripture. Even today, the authority of the Torah is affirmed in synagogal worship, where the entire Torah is read in Sabbath worship over the course of each year. No other part of the Tanak is mandated to be read in full every year.

Third, the genre with which a reader labels a piece of literature can greatly affect the meaning derived from a passage. For example, the Christian canon labels the book of Daniel as prophecy—with significant ramifications for the interpretation of Daniel. The Jewish canon considers Daniel one of the Writings—with equally significant interpretive ramifications.

Fourth, the order in which a set of literature is read can impact its interpretation. As noted in the chart above, the order in which the books appear is different in the Protestant Old Testament and the Jewish Tanak. The Tanak culminates with the closing chapter of 2 Chronicles, which describes the return of the tribes to Jerusalem. The Christian Old Testament culminates with the closing verses of Malachi, which announce that the day of the Lord is coming. It warns the audience to heed "the teaching of my servant Moses" (meaning the laws of the Pentateuch) and promises that "I will send you the prophet Elijah before the great and terrible day of the LORD comes. He will turn the hearts of parents to their children and the hearts of children to their parents, so that I will not come and strike the land with a curse." The differing expectations that arise from these two different conclusions to the Old Testament are significant. Jews will say as part of some religious observances, "Next year in Jerusalem." Many Christians, on the other hand, sing the song of Zechariah (Luke 1:68–79), the father of John the Baptist, who sings at his son's birth:

> And you, my child, will be called a prophet of the Most High;
> for you will go on before the Lord to prepare the way for him. (v. 76 NIV)

Here one can clearly see how the order of books in different traditions shapes a slightly different story. Order matters!

And yet it probably is not quite right even to say that there is a "Christian order of books" and a "Jewish order of books." The two oldest and best Hebrew manuscripts from the Jewish tradition have a differing order for the Writings. These manuscripts, known as the Leningrad Codex and the Aleppo Codex, order the Writings in the following way: Chronicles, Psalms, Job, Proverbs, Ruth, Song of Songs, Ecclesiastes, Lamentations, Esther, Daniel, Ezra-Nehemiah. It would probably be most correct to say that there were many different ways of ordering the books of the Old Testament—one of those ways survived in Christianity, and another survived in Judaism.

faith A strong belief in God or religious doctrines; often an orientation of complete trust and confidence in God that transforms one's life and being.

The Christian five-part organization of the Old Testament places greater emphasis on gathering books of similar genre together in common sections. Thus, the books of Ruth, Esther, 1–2 Chronicles, Ezra, and Nehemiah are taken from the Writings section and placed with the books of Joshua, Judges, 1–2 Samuel, and 1–2 Kings. Read together, these twelve books bear witness to a story that begins at creation (1 Chron. 1:1) and ends with the return from exile (2 Chron. 36:22–23).

Nuremberg Bible / The Stapleton Collection / Bridgeman Images

Fig. 2.3. In the Middle Ages, the Bible was preserved, disseminated, and illustrated in monasteries and other places. Sometimes these manuscripts were produced for use in a monastery; other times wealthy patrons commissioned them for their own purposes.

Box 2.4

How Did We Get the Bible We Have Today?

How did an ancient, once-disparate library of ancient Israelite texts become what we know today as the Old Testament? This is a complicated question, in large part because each individual book has its own unique compositional history. A number of important milestones can be sketched. In its earliest stages, the Old Testament books were written in Hebrew and Aramaic, but mostly in Hebrew. In the third century BCE, when many of the Old Testament books were approaching their final form, a group of Jewish scholars in Alexandria translated the Pentateuch from Hebrew into Greek. Other Old Testament books would follow, ultimately resulting in the Septuagint (abbreviated LXX). Many are surprised to learn that the Septuagint was actually the book of the early Christians and even continues to be used by churches within the Orthodox tradition today. By contrast, most Protestant Christians today use translations that rely largely upon Hebrew manuscripts. In the fourth and fifth centuries CE, Jerome broke with tradition by returning to the Hebrew and Aramaic sources in his Latin translation of the Old Testament. This work became known as the Vulgate, and it remains the official translation of the Roman Catholic Church. The upshot is that even in today's religious environment, Christians do not necessarily use the same Bible. Some are more reliant on the Greek and some on the Hebrew.

A few observations about these four differing Old Testament canons are in order:

- The Jewish and Protestant canons contain the same books, but the books are categorized, numbered, and ordered differently.
- The Roman Catholic Church and the various Orthodox Churches include all the books that are in the Jewish and Protestant canons, plus a few more books/chapters. These additional materials are sometimes called apocryphal or deuterocanonical, but it is more respectful to call them disputed.
- All the books in the Jewish/Protestant canon are written in the Hebrew language (several chapters in Ezra and Daniel are written in Aramaic, a language closely related to Hebrew). All the additional books/chapters in the Catholic and Orthodox canons are in Greek; some of them originated in Hebrew, but the Hebrew copies were not preserved. So an easy way to understand why Jews and Protestants do not accept the disputed (apocryphal/deuterocanonical) materials is that they were not preserved in Hebrew.
- All the additions that the Roman Catholic Church accepts are also accepted by the Orthodox Churches. In addition, various Orthodox Churches accept a few more: the Eastern Orthodox Church accepts Psalm 151; the Syrian Orthodox Church accepts 2 Baruch; the Ethiopian Orthodox Church accepts 4 Baruch, 1 Enoch, Jubilees, and 1, 2, 3 Meqabyan.
- One significant difference between major Christian groups is that Protestant translations of the Old Testament regard the Hebrew text as authoritative and translate from the Hebrew. Orthodox churches regard the Greek text as authoritative and translate from the Greek text known as the Septuagint. Roman Catholic Bible translations used to be based on the ancient Latin translation known as the Vulgate, but recent Roman Catholic translations have been based on the Hebrew and Greek texts.

Overall, the amount of text in the disputed canonical books is small when compared with the text in the books that are accepted by all traditions. The main story of the Old Testament and the major ethical and theological teachings are available in the books that are commonly accepted.

The poetic books are also gathered by genre. This section does not offer a common message or bear a common witness. Rather, it forms a collection of spiritual poetry for use in the life of faith.

The prophetic books are split into two sections: the Major Prophets and the Minor Prophets. These terms are misleading, because one might wrongly assume the "major" prophets are more important than the "minor" prophets. The title only means to communicate the relative length of the books. The books of Isaiah, Jeremiah (with Lamentations), Ezekiel, and Daniel are books that each take a whole scroll. The twelve other prophetic books are included in one scroll—called the Scroll of the Twelve or the Book of the Twelve. This scroll of so-called Minor Prophets has had a major impact on church and synagogue. Among them, the ongoing relevance of the books of Amos, Hosea, Joel, Micah, Jonah, Habakkuk, and Malachi is especially important.

For the most part, prophetic books contain collections of the messages of the prophet for whom the book is named. For example, the book of Amos is a collection of the messages of Amos. It is most likely the case that the prophets themselves did not write down their messages, but rather that followers of each prophet recorded and preserved a selection of their messages.

The Organization of the Protestant Bible

Pentateuch (also called the Law or the Torah). The first five books of the Old Testament—**Genesis, Exodus, Leviticus, Numbers, and Deuteronomy**—are called the Pentateuch (based on the Greek words *penta* and *teuchos*, "five books"). These books are about origins—origins of the universe, origins of the people of Israel, and origins of the laws that God gave to Israel. In terms of the story of Israel, these books take us from the time of Abraham and Sarah (ca. 1800–1500 BCE) to the death of Moses (ca. 1240 BCE).

Historical Books. The books of **Joshua, Judges, Ruth, 1–2 Samuel, 1–2 Kings, 1–2 Chronicles, Ezra, Nehemiah, and Esther** describe the long arc of Israel's story from the death of Moses (ca. 1240 BCE) to the return from exile. These books journey through the periods of the judges, the kings, the exile, to the time when the exiled people return to the land and rebuild Jerusalem's walls and the temple (ca. 450 BCE.) The disputed books of 1–2 Maccabees continue the story of the people of Israel down through the Hellenistic period (including the persecution of the Jews under the Seleucids and the revolt by the Maccabees). In the Jewish canon, the books of Joshua, Judges, Samuel, and Kings are called the Former Prophets because prophetic figures feature prominently in them. The books of Ruth, Ezra-Nehemiah, and Esther are in the Writings section of the Jewish canon.

Poetry. The books of **Job, Psalms, Proverbs, Ecclesiastes, and the Song of Songs (or the Song of Solomon)** are the poetic books. Job, Proverbs, and

compositional history A description of how a text came to be in its present form.

manuscript In biblical studies, an ancient handwritten document containing a book or portion of the Bible.

Vulgate A Latin translation of the Bible produced by Jerome in the fourth century CE; it was virtually the only Bible used in Western Christianity for over a thousand years.

Apocrypha Books of the Old Testament with varying degrees of scriptural status and authority among Protestant, Roman Catholic, and Orthodox Christians; many of these books were included in the Septuagint but not the Hebrew Bible.

deuterocanonical writings A term used primarily by Roman Catholics for eleven of the fifteen books that Protestants call the Apocrypha; the books are regarded as a "secondary canon," part of Scripture but distinct from both Old and New Testament writings.

persecution A program or campaign to exterminate, drive away, or subjugate people based on their membership in a religious, ethnic, or social group.

Maccabees Literally, "hammers"; the nickname given to Jewish rebels who led a successful revolt against the Syrians in 167 BCE.

wisdom literature / wisdom tradition Biblical and other ancient materials that focus on common-sense observations about life; examples include the books of Proverbs, Job, and Ecclesiastes.

vision A revelatory, visual medium typically experienced by prophets and apocalyptic visionaries.

Ecclesiastes are considered wisdom literature, a genre that features wise sayings and proverbs, as well as poetic investigations of some of life's most difficult questions, such as why the innocent suffer. The book of Psalms contains spiritual poetry and worship songs that express joy and sorrow, trust and doubt, thanksgiving and pain, wisdom and questioning. The Song of Songs is a love poem. In the Jewish canon, all of these books are in the Writings section.

Major Prophets. The Christian canon distinguishes between the Major and the Minor Prophets, based on the relative lengths of the books. The Major Prophets include Isaiah, Jeremiah (with Lamentations), Ezekiel, and Daniel. The books of Isaiah, Jeremiah, and Ezekiel contain prophetic messages from each of these prophets, along with some narrative descriptions of the prophets' actions. Some interpreters believe that the scroll of Isaiah contains messages from more than one prophet (more will be said on this in a later chapter). The book of Lamentations, which contains five songs of lament over the destruction of Jerusalem, is included among the Major Prophets because tradition holds that Jeremiah composed these poems. Daniel does not contain the messages of the prophet by that name but rather narrative depictions of Daniel's life, along with apocalyptic visions. The five books are organized chronologically: Isaiah came before Jeremiah, who came before Ezekiel, who came before Daniel.

Minor Prophets. The Minor Prophets are **Hosea, Joel, Amos, Obadiah, Jonah, Micah, Nahum, Habakkuk, Zephaniah, Haggai, Zechariah, and Malachi.** Except for the book of Jonah, which contains a narrative about that prophet, these books are collections of the prophetic messages of the respective prophets. As with the Major Prophets, the sequence of the twelve books is organized roughly by chronology. This is only a rule of thumb—note, for example, that Amos lived before Hosea—but it can be a helpful guide for locating the books within the overarching story of the Old Testament.

Development of the Old Testament Canon

In terms of what is possible to know with certainty about the development of the Old Testament canon, we are about to dive into deep waters. The question is this: As a group, how did the Old Testament writings develop? There is significant disagreement among scholars about how to answer this question. Most of the questions we pose about the Bible's composition are simply unanswerable given the data at hand. That said, we dive into the deep end.

What We Know

We can say with great certainty that the writings of the Old Testament developed over a very long period of time. How long of a period? At least a millennium. The oldest chapters in the Old Testament date to the twelfth century BCE, and perhaps earlier. The most recent chapters in the Old Testament date to the second century BCE. The process of sorting out which documents would be accepted into the collection that Christians now call the Old Testament went on a bit longer—at least as late as 90 CE. The process was lengthy, to say the least.

We also know that the process was highly complex. This is true of the development of specific books as well as the canon as a whole. The book of Psalms, for instance, seems to have developed over a very long time period. It is a collection of collections, including psalms of David, of Ascent, of Asaph, and of the Korahites. The process by which the whole book finally came into shape may well have taken over a thousand years. It is impossible to make anything more than educated guesses about the details of that development.

We also know that the development of the Old Testament canon involved selection. There were other ancient writings that did not make it into the canon. Some of these documents still exist. These include mostly late documents, such as 1–2 Enoch, 4–6 Maccabees, the Odes of Solomon, and the Testament of the Twelve Patriarchs. Also included are some documents from the Dead Sea Scrolls, which were found beginning in 1946 after being hidden away for centuries in desert caves. In addition to fragmentary copies of every biblical book except Esther, archaeologists discovered noncanonical books that the Dead Sea community clearly regarded as sacred, such as the Damascus Document, the War Scroll, and the Community Rule.

Some of the documents that were not included in the canon have been lost. Numbers 21:14 refers to a document called the "Book of the Wars of the Lord." Similarly, 1 and 2 Kings often refer to both the "Book of the Annals of

Dead Sea Scrolls A collection of Jewish documents copied and preserved between 250 BCE and 70 CE.

Qumran A site in Palestine near the Dead Sea where it is believed the Essenes had their monastic community; many of the Dead Sea Scrolls were found in close proximity to this settlement.

Box 2.5

The Dead Sea Scrolls

The Dead Sea Scrolls (DSS) are the most important archaeological find of the twentieth century, at least when it comes to the study of the Bible. The term *DSS* refers to hundreds of Hebrew, Greek, and Aramaic texts that have been discovered in proximity to the Dead Sea since 1946, most famously at the site called Khirbet Qumran. These scrolls date from roughly 250 BCE to 70 CE and contain both biblical and extrabiblical texts. Most scholars assume that the community at Khirbet Qumran was a sectarian group of Jews that had a role in both preserving and even creating some of the DSS. The scrolls are especially important for helping students of the Bible understand the compositional history of biblical texts. For example, there is a well-preserved copy of Isaiah, often called the Great Isaiah Scroll (IQIsaᵃ) that largely demonstrates the stability of the Isaiah tradition to the present day. This kind of stability is true for Isaiah but not necessarily true for all biblical texts. When modern scholars translate the Bible from Hebrew into English, they largely rely on a medieval manuscript from 1008 CE, over a thousand years after the texts themselves were written.

John Millar Watt / © Look and Learn / Bridgeman Images

Fig. 2.4. The Dead Sea Scrolls are a group of ancient Jewish texts. They include many of the oldest surviving manuscripts of the Old Testament. This painting depicts a boy discovering the first scroll.

the Kings of Israel" (e.g., 1 Kings 14:19; 15:31; 2 Kings 1:18) and the "Book of the Annals of the Kings of Judah" (e.g., 1 Kings 14:29; 15:7; 2 Kings 8:23). The authors of 1 and 2 Kings apparently drew on these books as resources. Similarly, the books of Chronicles refer to the "Annals of King David" (1 Chron. 27:24), the "Annals of Jehu son of Hanani" (2 Chron. 20:34), and the "Annals of the Kings of Israel" (2 Chron. 33:18), while "the annals of your ancestors" and the "Book of the Annals" are mentioned in Ezra 4:15 and Nehemiah 12:23, respectively. All of these books are lost and presumed destroyed.

Jeremiah 36 tells the intriguing story of King Jehoiakim of Judah burning what may have been an early version of the book of Jeremiah: "Jeremiah called Baruch son of Neriah, and Baruch wrote on a scroll at Jeremiah's dictation all the words of the LORD that [the LORD] had spoken to [Jeremiah]" (36:4). These messages, apparently, were critical of the king, because as the columns of the scroll were read to him, he "would cut it up with a scribe's knife and throw it into the fire" (36:23 NJPS). Jeremiah dictated another scroll, but one wonders if the second scroll was perfectly identical to the first. Were any messages left out?

This story offers a window into how at least some of the prophetic books were composed. A prophet, who may not have been literate, dictated the prophetic messages to a scribe. The scribe collected and preserved the messages. But we know that there were prophets in Israel and Judah whose messages were not preserved. Was there once a collection of prophetic messages from well-known prophets such as Elijah (1 Kings 17–19) or Micaiah (1 Kings 22) or the prophetess Huldah (2 Kings 22:14–20)? Jeremiah 26 describes "another man prophesying in the name of the LORD, Uriah son of Shemaiah from Kiriath-jearim. He prophesied against this city and against the land in words exactly like those of Jeremiah" (v. 20). The prophet fled for his life to Egypt, but the king sent men who "brought him to King Jehoiakim, who struck him down with the sword and dumped his dead body into the burial place of the common people" (v. 23 ESV).

Were the words of the prophet Uriah, or other unknown prophets, ever written down? Whether or not they were, it is clear that the development of the Old Testament canon was a complex process that included selection and editing.

A Plausible Reconstruction

Although the process of canonical development was long and complex, it is still possible to suggest a plausible reconstruction of how it happened, relying primarily on the text of the Old Testament itself.

Phase 1: Oral transmission of many traditions. Almost all reconstructions of the canonical process emphasize a first stage that is usually described as the oral tradition. In this stage, there is little or no access to writing. Cultures pass on wisdom about important events, people, ideas, and traditions through oral transmission. In the case of the Old Testament, the oral tradition dates to the early period of Israel's history. But even in later times—because literacy was limited to a small percentage of the population—important traditions existed first only orally.

oral tradition Material passed on by word of mouth; early Christians relied on oral tradition as well as written sources when writing the Gospels.

Phase 2: Limited written traditions. Many who study the Old Testament believe that it preserves several very early documents. These were incorporated into larger, more coherent narratives. Scholars often rely on comparative historical linguistics to make judgments about which passages are very old. Hebrew, like most languages, developed and changed over a long period of time. Just as English speakers can distinguish between Old English (or perhaps we should say "ye olde English") and modern English, students of Biblical Hebrew can recognize passages that are older. Biblical scholars refer to this older form of Hebrew as Archaic Biblical Hebrew (as opposed to Standard/Classical Biblical Hebrew or Late Biblical Hebrew). As with all things scholarly, there are differences of opinion about which passages are to be considered early. The following represent some of the more agreed-upon examples:

- The testament of Jacob. Genesis 49:1–27 consists of a lengthy song in which the patriarch Jacob blesses his twelve sons prior to his death. At least a portion of the poem is believed to be quite ancient.
- The Songs of Moses and Miriam. Exodus 15:2–18 and 15:20–21 are called, respectively, the Song of Moses and the Song of Miriam. The songs

celebrate God's deliverance of Israel from Pharaoh's chariots around 1280 BCE. The passages are most likely very old.

- An early creedal fragment. Exodus 34:6–7 contains a short poem that many believe to be very early. The fragment emphasizes the Lord's name (Yahweh) and his constitutive character: "merciful and gracious, slow to anger, and abounding in steadfast love and faithfulness."
- Moses's farewell blessing. Deuteronomy 33:2–29, Moses's farewell song of blessing, is considered one of the older poems in the Old Testament.
- The Song of Deborah. Judges 5 contains a long, ancient song in the voices of the judges Deborah and Barak. The song likely dates to the twelfth century BCE.
- Psalm 68. A long, very difficult-to-interpret song is preserved as the sixty-eighth psalm. The poem is believed to be as early as the tenth century BCE.
- The Song of the Bow. In 2 Samuel 1:19–27, the narrative recounts a song of mourning King David sang over the death of his friend Jonathan. Some scholars believe this song is from the time of David.

Other passages are believed to be quite ancient, but this list gives a sense of where some of the older passages preserved in Scripture can be found and also of the sort of narrative context into which these fragments were later integrated.

Phase 3: Development and collection of larger textual units. As the oral tradition was passed on and new generations added their own traditions, larger textual units developed. It is most likely that individual books were developed first—such as Genesis or Deuteronomy—and then at a later time, books were gathered into larger groups—such as the Pentateuch, Hexateuch, or the Prophets. The Pentateuch probably developed first, followed by the Prophets and then the Writings.

It is also likely that, even after these larger groups were gathered, individual books continued to evolve. For instance, a version of the book of Psalms was probably gathered fairly early and considered the first or lead scroll in the Writings collection. Some collection of the Psalms of David likely made up most of this early Psalter, but the book continued to grow, as collections such as the Songs of Ascent or the Psalms of Asaph were added. (More on this in the chapter on the Psalms.)

If we take the biblical text itself as the guide, it is possible to draw some cautious conclusions about how and when the growth of individual books and collections may have happened. Several specific biblical passages are most important: 2 Kings 22:3–13; 2 Kings 25:27–30; Ezra 7:1–10; and Nehemiah 8:1–8.

- The book of the law (ca. 622 BCE; 2 Kings 22:3–13). Second Kings 22 gives an account of the discovery of "the book of the law" in the temple. King Josiah of Judah (640–609 BCE) is described as a reform-minded king. This reform was necessary, according to 2 Kings, because during the reigns of Josiah's grandfather and father, worship of Yahweh was corrupted. Josiah's reform included repairing the temple in Jerusalem. As repairs got underway, it was reported to Josiah that "the book of the law [was found] in the house of the LORD" (2 Kings 22:8). Many scholars believe that this "book of the law" was a form of the book of Deuteronomy (more will be said about this in the chapter dealing with Deuteronomy). If so, one can conclude that the book of Deuteronomy was largely developed sometime before 622 BCE.

- The Deuteronomistic History (ca. 585–540 BCE; 2 Kings 25:27–30). Just a few chapters later, the narrator of 2 Kings brings the book to a close with

Fig. 2.5. The scribe Ezra (see the book of Ezra) is portrayed as writing the book of the law of Moses from memory in 458 BCE. Ezra was a key figure following the Babylonian exile in establishing the Jewish people as a religious people with a holy book rather than a holy nation with a holy king.

the following description: "In the thirty-seventh year of the exile of King Jehoiachin of Judah, on the twenty-seventh day of the twelfth month, King Evil-merodach of Babylon, in the year he became king, took note of King Jehoiachin of Judah and released him from prison. He spoke kindly to him, and gave him a throne above those of other kings who were with him in Babylon. His prison garments were removed, and [Jehoiachin] received regular rations by his favor for the rest of his life. A regular allotment of food was given him at the instance of the king—an allotment for each day—all the days of his life" (NJPS). Biblical scholars believe that these words, which describe how the exiled Judean monarch Jehoiachin was released from prison in exile, were written sometime between 586 and 540 BCE. The sequence of books from Deuteronomy through 2 Kings (excluding Ruth, which was composed separately) forms

Deuteronomistic History / Deuteronomic History An academic term for the narrative unit from Deuteronomy through Kings.

a lengthy, sustained narrative about the story of the people of Israel in the land of Canaan—from the time when Israel first emerged as a distinct people in the land until the last king of Judah was exiled. Scholars call this block of books the Deuteronomistic History. If scholars are correct about the compositional history of this collection, it means that by 540 BCE a major part of the Old Testament writings—Deuteronomy through 2 Kings (except for Ruth)—was finished.

- The book of the law of Moses (ca. 440 BCE; Ezra 7:1–10; Neh. 8:1–8). At the end of the exile, with the blessing of King Cyrus of Persia, some of the Judean exiles returned to the land of Israel and began the great task of restoring Jerusalem. Among them were Nehemiah, the appointed governor, and Ezra, who is described as "a scribe skilled in the law of Moses" (Ezra 7:6). Nehemiah 8 offers an account of how "all the people gathered together into the square" and how Ezra read and explained "the book of the law of Moses" (8:1). Many scholars believe that the book Ezra read from that day was the complete Pentateuch. (Some scholars think there is reason to believe that the Persian king also blessed the completion and dissemination of the Pentateuch.) If this is correct, we can conclude that by about 440 BCE, most of the books from Genesis through 2 Kings were basically complete and had been collected together.

Phase 4: Further development and collection. Over many following centuries, other books were written or developed. For some, such as the book of the prophet Haggai, this process was very brief. The book of Haggai describes the ministry of the prophet by the same name, who proclaimed messages from God for just a few months in the year 520 BCE. It is likely that the small book came together relatively quickly and simply. The book of Psalms, however, as has already been mentioned, most likely had an extremely lengthy and complicated developmental process. New books were written, some of which were accepted as authoritative (such as Ruth, Esther, and Daniel), while others were not. Some books continued to develop, the Hebrew Scriptures were translated into Greek, and so on.

A watershed moment for the development of the Old Testament writings occurred in 70 CE. In response to a rebellion by certain Jews in Judea, the Romans destroyed the second temple. During the years just prior to this destruction, rival groups of Jews made competing claims about their Jewish identity. These groups included the Sadducees, Pharisees, Essenes, and Zealots. Many scholars believe that after the temple's destruction the future of Judaism evolved largely out of the Pharisees—a lay-led movement of law-observant pietists. Pharisaic Judaism eventually evolved into rabbinic Judaism—a Judaism that was text centered rather than temple centered, whose worship was marked

Pharisees One of the major Jewish groups active during the Second Temple period. The Pharisees were largely associated with synagogues and placed high value on faithfulness to Torah; most rabbis and many scribes were Pharisees.

Essenes Ascetic, separatist Jews who lived in private communities; they probably are to be identified with the group that lived at Qumran and preserved a library of manuscripts now known as the Dead Sea Scrolls.

by spiritualized worship in dispersed synagogues rather than a sacrifice-oriented worship in a central temple, and which was led by educated rabbis rather than hereditary priests.

rabbis Jewish teachers, many of whom had disciples or followers; closely associated with the Pharisees.

As part of the normalization of Second Temple Judaism into rabbinic Judaism, an authoritative list of scriptural books was developed. Some scholars believe that at a rabbinic meeting in the Judean coastal town of Jamnia (Yabneh) in approximately 90 CE, the book of Ecclesiastes and probably the Song of Songs were accepted as authoritative. At the same time, early Christianity was deciding which biblical books (and what sequence of books) the followers of Jesus would accept. Most likely, the individual books of what Christians call the Old Testament were essentially completed, but it was probably not until the fourth or fifth centuries that both rabbinic Judaism and early Christianity definitively named their official canons.

Phase 5: Stabilization and vocalization of the consonantal text. A final stage of the development of the Old Testament literature needs to be described—the stage in which the text was stabilized.

Biblical Hebrew used one of the earliest alphabetic writing systems—meaning that individual written symbols represented individual phonemes (rather than writing systems in which individual symbols represented words or complete syllables). For many centuries, written Hebrew was a consonantal writing system—symbols represented only consonantal sounds, not vowel sounds. The largest collection of ancient biblical texts, the Dead Sea Scrolls, is purely consonantal.

As the consonantal text of the Old Testament was copied over the centuries, some developments and changes occurred to the text. Sometimes textual developments were accidental—for instance, a scribal copyist might make a small mistake. Other changes to the text were intentional—for example, a scribe might correct what he thought was a mistake or insert a clarifying remark.

This gradual evolution of the text came to a rather sudden halt around the time the second temple was destroyed and Judaism became a text-centered rather than temple-centered religion. In order to stop further evolution of the text, a careful system of cross-checking was developed, whereby the consonantal text could be—for the most part—consistently copied. This is referred to as the stabilizing of the text.

Eventually, a system of symbols representing vowel phonemes was also developed (actually, several systems were developed, but one prevailed). It is not known exactly when the vowel system was invented or by whom—the best guess is that this occurred around 600 CE. These symbols also took time to evolve and stabilize. It was not until as late as 1000 CE that texts including both consonants and vowels were stabilized. The task of adding vowel marks to an existing consonantal text is called "pointing." This work of stabilizing the fully pointed text was performed by a group of Jewish scribes called the

Masoretes. The textual tradition that these scribes produced is referred to as the Masoretic Text. All modern versions of the Hebrew Scriptures are based on the work of the Masoretes and the Masoretic Text.

Quoting Chapter and Verse

Many readers may have heard a statement such as "He can quote *The Baseball Almanac* chapter and verse" or "She can cite the US Constitution book, chapter, and verse." These refer to someone who is very knowledgeable about a given field. The source of the phrase, of course, is the Bible—which has been divided into books, chapters, and verses.

But the biblical writers did not themselves write the chapter and verse numbers, which were added many years after the various biblical books were written. The chapter numbers were invented first. The system that is found in most Bibles today was devised by Archbishop Stephen Langton in about 1200 CE. He inserted chapter numbers into a Latin translation of the Bible, and these numbers eventually made it into almost all versions of the Bible. The current system of verse numbers in the Old Testament was devised by Joseph Athias in 1661. The basic rule of thumb is that there is one sentence per verse. So, the verse numbers are someone's interpretation of where sentences start and end.

But the origins of the chapter-and-verse system lie with Jewish scribes who divided the Old Testament writings into sentences and paragraphs. Long before Langton and Athias started their numbering, Jewish rabbis were sectioning the text. The sections they created were not numbered and do not correspond to the present chapter and verse numbers. In Hebrew, the larger sections are called *parashiyyot* (basically meaning "paragraphs"). These paragraphs come in two sizes—larger and smaller. A larger section is called a *parashah*

Box 2.6

Who Were the Masoretes?

The Masoretes were Jewish scribes dedicated to preserving the text of the Hebrew Bible. They developed a careful system of copying the consonantal Hebrew text; developed symbols for vowels, accents, and cantillation marks; and created a system of notations called the *masorah* (from which the group's name was derived). It is not known who first developed the vowels, accents, cantillation marks, or marginal notes. Two famous groups of Masoretes were the ben Asher and ben Naphtali families. All existing Hebrew masoretic manuscripts are from the ben Asher tradition. No Hebrew manuscripts from the ben Naphtali family have survived, although alternative readings from the ben Naphtali tradition have been preserved in the form of notations. The two oldest and best masoretic texts are known as the Leningrad Codex, which is a complete manuscript, and the Aleppo Codex, which is missing most of the Pentateuch and much of the Writings. The most famous Masorete was Aaron ben Asher, who was said to have pointed (added vowels to) the Aleppo Codex himself.

petuhah ("open paragraph"), and a smaller section is called a *parashah setumah* ("closed paragraph"). The Jewish tradition also divides the text at the level of the individual verse (*pasuq*). At the end of each sentence an accent mark called a *silluq* indicates the end of a sentence. Again, these "verses" are not numbered, and they do not correspond exactly to the present system of numbering. When it comes to some books, such as the Psalms, the verse numbers in modern Jewish Bibles differ slightly from those found in Christian Bibles.

A great bit of wisdom from the Jewish tradition in the Talmud is this: "One who reads in the Torah may not read less than three verses" (Mishnah Megillah 4:4 AT). This shows that the rabbis whose learning went into the Talmud in the centuries after Jesus were thinking of the Bible in terms of verses. It also offers a wise warning—do not pull one verse out of context, because you are likely to misinterpret it.

Fig. 2.6. The Aleppo Codex is the oldest complete Hebrew manuscript of the Old Testament. It was written ca. 920 CE in the city of Tiberias. The great Jewish figure Maimonides examined it and testified to its authority and accuracy. It had been housed in a synagogue in Aleppo, Syria, but it disappeared for a time after anti-Jewish riots in 1947. Much of the manuscript was preserved and is now housed in Jerusalem, although most of the Pentateuch is now missing.

Aside from being handy trivia, there is also an important intellectual point about the Old Testament here—the chapter and verse numbers are not actually part of the Bible. They were only added to make it easy to find a passage or to refer to a specific text. The chapter and verse numbers are not authoritative.

Talmud A collection of sixty-three books that contain Jewish civil and canonical law based on interpretations of Scripture.

Interpretation of the Historical World "behind" and "in" the Text

Throughout this book, we will be making a distinction between the "historical world in the text" and the "historical world behind the text." The distinction is fairly straightforward.

Mishnah A collection of rabbinic discussions about the interpretation of the law of Moses; the Mishnah forms one major part of the Jewish Talmud.

The Historical World behind the Text

Every text is historical in the sense that it has a history. Every text is written at a certain moment in history in a particular historical context. The author of a text has a history. The historical context shapes how a text was originally interpreted and what it originally meant. Certain social customs and norms from a given historical context may have influenced the author(s) of a text. And so on. All of these things (and more) are included in what we are calling "the historical world behind the text."

The more that interpreters can know about the authors of a text or about the historical context in which a text was written—the social conditions and norms, the historical events and how they were understood, the economic and technological systems, the religious practices and beliefs—the better their understandings of the text will be.

However, the texts usually assume that their readers and interpreters already know and are familiar with the historical and social locations. The authors of these texts did not know that they would be read and interpreted thousands of years later. They had no way of knowing how the world would change and which elements of their social location would no longer be assumed or understood in the future. Therefore, interpreting and "reconstructing" the world behind the text is often a matter of deduction (and sometimes of guesswork). And as should come as no surprise, modern interpreters often reconstruct the world behind the text in very different ways. There are often sharp and significant disagreements between scholars about the world behind the text. For example, when it comes to reconstructing the social location from which the book of Deuteronomy was produced, some scholars believe the book originated in prophetic communities, others believe it originated in priestly communities, and still others believe that it grew out of wisdom or scribal circles.[1] Where a reader imagines a text originated may at times significantly impact the way that reader interprets its meaning.

social location A person's social identity in terms of factors such as age, gender, race, nationality, social class, and marital status.

The Historical World in the Text

Every text has a historical world behind it. In addition, some texts have a historical world in the text. Texts that make historical claims about the past or that tell stories about the past are said to have a "historical world in the text." Such texts can be evaluated and interpreted based on the ways in which they portray the historical past. For example, some texts in the Old Testament recount the story of the Babylonian conquest of Jerusalem in 586 BCE. These texts include 2 Kings 24–25, 2 Chronicles 36, Jeremiah 25–39, and some other texts. These texts can be interpreted to help readers understand the history in the text.

This type of interpretation can be fraught with significant ideological and theological tensions. Some readers who come from traditions that emphasize the authority (or even inerrancy) of the Bible have been taught that they must believe every word of the Bible. When it comes to the historical world in the Bible, this means that some readers are uncomfortable with this type of historical interpretation. Some other readers who come from backgrounds that are highly suspicious of religion, and the Bible in particular, are eager to dismiss any historical claims of biblical texts. In this textbook, the goal is to present the most salient issues about the historical world presented in the text and invite readers into the conversation about this world.

FOR FURTHER READING: The Old Testament Writings

Collins, John J., Craig Evans, and Lee Martin McDonald. *Ancient Jewish and Christian Scriptures: New Developments in Canon Controversy*. Louisville: Westminster John Knox, 2020.

Evans, Craig A., and Emanuel Tov. *Exploring the Origins of the Bible: Canon Formation in Historical, Literary, and Theological Perspective*. Acadia Studies in Bible and Theology. Grand Rapids: Baker Academic, 2008.

Kugel, James. *The Bible as It Was*. Cambridge, MA: Harvard University Press, 1999.

Law, Timothy Michael. *When God Spoke Greek: The Septuagint and the Making of the Christian Bible*. Oxford: Oxford University Press, 2013.

McDonald, Lee Martin. *The Formation of the Biblical Canon*. Vol. 1, *The Old Testament: Its Authority and Canonicity*. Edinburgh: Bloomsbury T&T Clark, 2021.

Wegner, Paul D. *The Journey from Texts to Translations*. Grand Rapids: Baker, 1999.

Part 2

FROM CREATION TO INHERITANCE

The Pentateuch

Overview

The first five books of the Bible—Genesis, Exodus, Leviticus, Numbers, and Deuteronomy—are most commonly called the Pentateuch. This name is derived from the Greek name *pentateuchos* ("five books"). In Judaism, these books can be referred to as the *Chumash*, a form of the Hebrew word for "five," but they are most often called the Torah—meaning "instruction." Torah is an appropriate name due to the large amount of ethical-legal material found in Exodus, Leviticus, Numbers, and Deuteronomy. When the Old Testament was translated in antiquity into Greek, the term *nomos* ("law") was used to render the Hebrew *torah*, with the unhappy result that in many Christian traditions the Pentateuch is often referred to as the Law. This term is unfortunate, both because it too often carries highly negative connotations and because it overlooks the fact that the narrative of Genesis 1–Exodus 20 has been more influential than the laws of the other sections. These pentateuchal books are also often called the Books of Moses, both because Moses is the central human character in Exodus–Deuteronomy and because traditionally Moses was held to be their author.

The Pentateuch was most likely the earliest subsection of the Old Testament to come together—both the Prophets and the Writings came together later. It was also the first section of the Old Testament to be translated into Greek (the Septuagint). The Pentateuch also can claim a broader sphere of influence than the Prophets and the Writings. In the first century, during the time of Jesus, the group of Jews called the Sadducees only acknowledged the Pentateuch—not the Prophets or Writings—as authoritative Scripture. This is still the case today with the relatively small religious group known as the Samaritans, who only acknowledge their version of the Pentateuch, called the Samaritan Pentateuch, as Scripture. The Pentateuch also has a greater role in the religious life of modern Judaism, where the entire Torah is covered in Sabbath worship over a one-year period of time.

Within various Christian traditions, the Pentateuch has had a tremendous impact. Many of the most well-known stories and passages of the Bible come from the Pentateuch, including the following:

- creation in seven days
- Adam, Eve, the serpent, and the forbidden fruit
- the flood
- Sarah laughing at God and giving birth in old age
- Jacob and the ladder from heaven and wrestling with God
- the plagues and the exodus
- the Ten Commandments
- the golden calf
- the great commandments to love God and your neighbor as yourself
- the *Shema*, a confessional statement about the singularity of God

Shema The central affirmation of Jewish faith. Based on Deuteronomy 6:4–9; 11:13–21; Numbers 15:37–41, it was recited daily. *Shema* is the Hebrew word for "Hear!"

But the influence of the Pentateuch goes far beyond a few popular stories. The Pentateuch's influence reaches into the smallest corners of daily life. It has affected everything from the way society organizes the calendar (the powerful rhythm of the seven-day week, with some days to work and some to rest and worship, is a result of the Pentateuch), to common names that many children are given (Adam, Noah, Sarah, Isaac, Rebekah, Jacob, Leah, Rachel, Joseph, and Benjamin still rank among the most popular names), to how people think about the law (the pattern of legal principles and precedents is established in the Pentateuch). And, most significantly, the Pentateuch has deeply impacted how human beings conceive of God, the universe, and ourselves as created "in the image of God."

Authorship and Composition

As is the case with most Old Testament books, the pentateuchal books are anonymous. Nowhere in any of the five books is an author named. Perhaps the best approach then would be to read and interpret them as anonymous volumes.

Fig. 3.1. This scene shows the Israelites crossing the Red Sea with Miriam singing and dancing: "Then the prophet Miriam, Aaron's sister, took a tambourine in her hand; and all the women went out after her with tambourines and with dancing. And Miriam sang to them: 'Sing to Yahweh, for he has triumphed gloriously; horse and rider he has cast into the sea'" (Exod. 15:20–21, modified).

But everyone enjoys a good mystery—or even better, a good conspiracy theory. Telling people that a piece of literature is anonymous is the best way to get them to wonder who the author is.

The Tradition of Mosaic Authorship

For thousands of years, tradition has ascribed authorship of the Pentateuch to Moses. This is for at least two reasons. First, Moses is the main human character from Exodus, which begins with the account of his birth, through Deuteronomy, which ends with the account of his death. Second, beginning in Exodus 20, God reveals the law through Moses, who delivers it to the people. For this reason, the many legal and ethical passages of the Pentateuch are called the Mosaic law.

The tradition of attributing the Pentateuch to Moses began very early. Already in the Old Testament, at least by the time of the exile (ca. 540 BCE) and most likely before the exile (ca. 620 BCE), this tradition existed (Josh. 1:1–9; 2 Kings 14:6; 23:25). The New Testament writers and early authors of the Talmud assume it, as do later Christian leaders such as Augustine, Aquinas, Luther, and Calvin.

The Documentary Hypothesis

Beginning in the Enlightenment, thinkers such as Thomas Hobbes (1588–1679) and Baruch Spinoza (1632–77) began to question the tradition that Moses authored the Pentateuch. They pointed out that Moses could not have written the account of his own death (Deut. 34), that some pentateuchal laws seem to contradict each other (compare Exod. 21:1–11 with Deut. 15:1–18), that some stories are inexplicably told twice (such as two stories in which Abraham's wife Sarah is temporarily taken into the harem of another man; Gen. 12:10–20 and 20:1–18), and that anachronisms occur in the Pentateuch (such as the phrase "at that time the Canaanites were in the land" in Gen. 12:6, implying that Genesis was written at a later date when Israel occupied the land).

anachronism
Something that appears in a text from a different time (e.g., an automobile appearing in a medieval text).

Jean Astruc (1684–1766) drew attention to the fact that Genesis uses two different names for God—Yahweh (the proper name of God, usually translated as "the LORD") and Elohim (the common noun simply meaning "God" or "gods"). Isolating the passages that call God "Yahweh" from those that refer simply to "God," Astruc hypothesized that the Pentateuch was a joint composition woven together from two separate source documents. By working backward from the text, Astruc believed he could reconstruct the two different sources. The source that used the name Yahweh came to be called "J" (because the German spelling of "Yahweh" is "Jahweh"), and the source that referred to God as Elohim became "E." This view came to be known as the Documentary Hypothesis. With two sources initially distinguished, other consistent differences were noticed. For example, the place names in J are consistently in Judah, the Southern Kingdom, while those in E tend to be in the northern territories. J uses rich anthropomorphic language, while E is more pedantic.

Hermann Hupfeld (1796–1866) argued that E was really two documents that both referred to the deity as Elohim. For one he retained the name E, and the other he coined "P," because it focused on "priestly" concerns.

Documentary Hypothesis A theory that explains the composition of the Pentateuch by proposing that its final form is compiled from at least four different sources, commonly referred to as the J, E, D, and P sources.

Wilhelm DeWette (1780–1849) argued that the central sections of the book of Deuteronomy (chaps. 12–26) had once been a separate source. He connected this hypothetical "D" with the scroll that was found in the temple by the priest Hilkiah during the reign of King Josiah (ca. 622 BCE).

Thus, the four sources of the Documentary Hypothesis were named J (the Yahwist), E (the Elohist), D (the Deuteronomic source), and P (the Priestly source).

The two scholars most closely associated with the Documentary Hypothesis are Karl Heinrich Graf (1815–69) and Julius Wellhausen (1844–1918). Graf argued that the order of the sources, from oldest to youngest, was J–E–D–P. Wellhausen refined the hypothesis by writing a lengthy and careful argument in which he theorized social and historical locations for each document.

Work continued on the hypothesis for much of the twentieth century. Scholars who accept the Documentary Hypothesis disagree on details, such as when a given document was written, where and who wrote it, and even whether a given element was actually a document or was just a new layer of revisions. At the high point of its popularity, the hypothesis looked something like this:

J—the Yahwist, written ca. 950 BCE in Judah, the eventual Southern Kingdom

E—the Elohist, written ca. 850 BCE in Israel, the Northern Kingdom

[J and E were combined in the eighth century.]

D—the Deuteronomic source, written ca. 750 BCE in the Northern Kingdom, Israel[1]

P—the Priestly source, written ca. 550–500 BCE in exile in Babylon

[All four sources were combined during or after the exile.]

The four sources were combined over time in the following sequence:

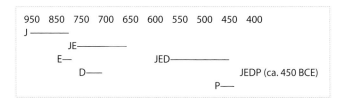

Currently, there is no consensus view on how the Pentateuch was developed. Some scholars (especially Europeans) see the Pentateuch as part of larger compositional units such as the Hexateuch (Genesis–Joshua) or the Enneateuch (Genesis–Kings). Whatever the case may be, the precise nature of the Pentateuch's compositional history will likely remain a mystery.

One of the most important aspects of the Documentary Hypothesis is that a literary document reflects the social time period in which it was written. Therefore, to understand a document, one must read it against the background of the time, place, and ideology in which it was composed. The point of the Documentary Hypothesis is that a reader should interpret the J sections of the Pentateuch against the social background of Jerusalem around 950 BCE—the time when Solomon was reigning over a large empire and building the temple. But the P sections should be interpreted against the background of priestly concerns and the exile or postexile, when Israel was no longer an independent nation with its own king but a province of the Persian Empire led by priests such as Ezra.

The Documentary Hypothesis was not just about reconstructing the history behind the Pentateuch but about locating the sources of the Pentateuch in history in order that they might be better understood and interpreted more accurately. Scholars interested in identifying and studying these aspects of a text are called source critics.

Not all biblical interpreters accept the Documentary Hypothesis. Interpreters within conservative traditions—both Jewish and Christian—continue to advocate for Moses as the author of the Pentateuch. One argument they advance is that throughout the Pentateuch Moses is described as the human who receives the laws from God. A second argument they make is that the ancients were not concerned with small discrepancies, repetitions, and contradictions, so for a modern interpreter to conclude on the basis of these that there was more than one source behind the Pentateuch is a fallacious application of anachronistic standards.

The strongest argument for the Documentary Hypothesis is that hypothesizing separate sources is the best way to explain the different names for God, the repetitions that occur in the Pentateuch, and discrepancies between passages. Furthermore, once separate passages are identified on the basis of terms for God, deeper sets of differences between the sources emerge, such as geographic

---

Box 3.1

Repeated Stories in Genesis

doublet In literature, a pair or duplication of references.

Students of the Bible notice that Genesis contains "doublets." These are stories that seem to replicate literary structure, motifs, and themes from other stories. For example, there are two creation accounts (1:1–2:4a; 2:4b–2:25), with distinct emphases and in some cases mutually exclusive claims. There are two accounts in which Abraham pretends that Sarah, his wife, is his sister (12:10–20; 20:1–18). Yahweh's covenant with Abraham is another example. Variations occur in both Genesis 15 and 17, with markedly different literary and theological emphases. Genesis 37 contains two different descriptions of Joseph being sold into slavery. In the case of 37:25–27, he is sold to the Ishmaelites, but in vv. 23–24, 28, and 36, he is snatched up by Midianites after having been throw into a pit by his brothers.

covenant In the Bible, an agreement or pact between God and human beings that establishes the terms of their ongoing relationship.

These doublets have played an important role in scholarly reconstructions of the Pentateuch's compositional history. In some cases, the doublets may indicate that two independent stories have been woven together into a single story (e.g., Gen. 37). The doublets may even indicate that two stories rely on a third source. In other instances, the compositional history is less apparent and may be better explained as a literary feature of the text.

references (J refers to places mostly in Judah; E refers mostly to places in Israel) and differing names for common geographic locations. For example, J and P call the mountain where the law was given "Sinai," and D calls it "Horeb."

Recent Developments and the Decline of the Consensus

As noted above, many interpreters in conservative traditions have never accepted the Documentary Hypothesis and still hold to Mosaic authorship. But beginning in the 1970s, scholars from more liberal traditions who had previously accepted the hypothesis began to question it. Scholars such as Thomas Thompson, John van Seters, Norman Whybray, Rolf Rendtdorff, Hans Heinrich Schmidt, and Erhard Blum have criticized various elements of the hypothesis. In its place, two other schools of thought have been proposed: (1) refining, redating, and reordering and (2) ongoing revision.

Refining, redating, and reordering. One approach to the Documentary Hypothesis tends to keep many of its assumptions and conclusions in place while challenging other aspects of it. For example, it has been argued that the J source never existed. Other source critics have argued that the P material was not a separate source but an editorial layer. Or it has been debated whether there is really anything at all of the E source. Or it has been argued that the P source includes not just priestly material but also an "H" source composed of "holiness" material (and, of course, it is debated as to which of these is older).

Box 3.2

Reading Literature against a Social Location

The idea of reading a piece of literature against the background of its social location is relevant for interpreting other kinds of literature besides biblical literature. Consider these three famous North American biographies of Abraham Lincoln:

- Carl Sandberg, *Abraham Lincoln: The Prairie Years and The War Years* (1939)
- Benjamin Thomas, *Abraham Lincoln: A Biography* (1952)
- David Herbert Donald, *Lincoln* (1996)

Note that each biography was published in a different era of American history. A person can read each biography in order to learn about Lincoln and his times. But if one reads all three, one would learn not only about Lincoln and his times but also about Sandberg and his times, Thomas and his times, and Donald and his times. Sandberg's biography is romantic and effusive. Thomas cuts through the romantic view of Lincoln and focuses on trying to understand the president's personality and character. Donald strives for accuracy and produces a respectful yet critical biography. In short, biographical texts tell us something not only about their subject matter but also about their author.

Ongoing revision. A second approach sees the whole process as much messier than the Documentary Hypothesis allowed—that the JEDP model is simply too neat. These scholars argue that many redundancies and discrepancies in the Pentateuch are not evidence of two or three sources but of many different editorial changes over a long period of time. Some imagine a fluid but stable process of editorial updating, while others see a messier process in which disparate fragments were brought together. These scholars tend to date the formation of the Pentateuch much later than Wellhausen and his admirers do, some as late as 166–150 BCE.

The criticism of the Documentary Hypothesis from more liberal schools of thought has not silenced those who support the theory. The hypothesis still has many supporters. But it is unlikely that the field of biblical studies will ever again see one widely supported hypothesis about the authorship and sources of the Pentateuch. Rather, there will likely be many competing views.

Literary and Canonical Approaches

At roughly the same time that scholars were beginning to challenge the Documentary Hypothesis and the work of source critics, a separate set of biblical

---

Box 3.3

J and P in the Flood Story

Genesis 6–9 is the account of Noah, his ark, and the great flood. Scholars who accept the Documentary Hypothesis point out that the name for God changes and also that the number of animals changes in the account. They conclude that two, once-separate sources are behind this now unified text. In what follows, the hypothetical J source is underlined, and the P source is italicized.

> 6:19 *"And of every living thing, of all flesh, you shall bring two of every kind into the ark, to keep them alive with you; they shall be male and female.* 20 *Of the birds according to their kinds, and of the animals according to their kinds, of every creeping thing of the ground according to its kind, two of every kind shall come in to you, to keep them alive.* 21 *Also take with you every kind of food that is eaten, and store it up; and it shall serve as food for you and for them."* 22 *Noah did this; he did all that God commanded him.*
> 7:1 Then the LORD said to Noah, "Go into the ark, you and all your household, for I have seen that you alone are righteous before me in this generation. 2 Take with you seven pairs of all clean animals, the male and its mate; and a pair of the animals that are not clean, the male and its mate; 3 and seven pairs of the birds of the air also, male and female, to keep their kind alive on the face of all the earth. 4 For in seven days I will send rain on the earth for forty days and forty nights; and every living thing that I have made I will blot out from the face of the ground." 5 And Noah did all that the LORD had commanded him. 6 *Noah was six hundred years old when the flood of waters came on the earth.* 7 *And Noah with his sons and his wife and his sons' wives went into the ark to escape the waters of the flood.* 8 *Of clean animals, and of animals that are not clean, and of birds, and of everything that creeps on the ground,* 9 *two and two, male and female, went into the ark with Noah, as God had commanded Noah.* 10 *And after seven days the waters of the flood came on the earth.* (Gen. 6:19–7:10)

Fig. 3.2. The story of God's covenant with Abraham is repeated in several different ways in Genesis. The most famous may be in Genesis 15, where Abraham laments to God that he remains childless. God responds, "Look toward heaven and count the stars, if you are able to count them. . . . So shall your offspring be" (Gen. 15:5 NJPS).

scholars began to advocate for a complete paradigm shift for approaching biblical interpretation. These scholars argued for a shift away from interpretive approaches that dissected a text to approaches that looked at the text in its final form.

Recall from the above description of the Documentary Hypothesis about reading texts in their social location. The interpretive point of the hypothesis was that by isolating the source of a given text, a reader can read that text against the background of its social location. So a text from P, for example, could be read against the social location of a group of priestly exiles in Babylon, who were struggling to maintain their identity and make sense of their faith in Yahweh after the destruction of their nation, city, and temple.

This approach was all well and good as long as readers were confident that the particular passage they were trying to understand had been correctly matched with the right source, and that the social location of that source—including its who, where, when, and why—had been correctly reconstructed. In other words, this reading strategy was based on one's ability to reconstruct what was happening "behind the text."

But what happens when one does not have confidence in the ability of scholars to reconstruct the historical and social contexts? What context is left? The literary context! "Literary" and "canonical" approaches to interpreting the Pentateuch start with the fact that the only *sure context* in which a passage from Genesis, for example, can be located is Genesis itself.

Take this example of Genesis 12:1–3: "Now the LORD said to Abram, 'Go from your country and your kindred and your father's house to the land that I will show you. I will make of you a great nation, and I will bless you, and make your name great, so that you will be a blessing. I will bless those who bless you, and the one who curses you I will curse; and in you all the families of the earth shall be blessed.'" "Behind-the-text" scholars would have noted that the name of God here is "the LORD"—and so identified this text with the J source. Assuming that the J source was from the time of Solomon, when the kingdom was great and thriving, they might interpret the passage in light of that particular social location. In order to engage the meaning of the text, a source critic asked a set of questions: Who wrote this? Why and when? What were society's conditions? What were the great questions of the time? Who was the audience to whom these words were addressed? A literary critic, by contrast, inquires into the plot, characters, narrative sequence, and narrative setting of a book. Regarding Genesis 12, the literary interpreter might ask: What has happened before in Genesis? What do we know of the character Abram? What do we know of the character God? Reading ahead, are future events foreshadowed in this passage? How does this passage advance the plot of Genesis?

Canonical approaches to Old Testament interpretation, while not identical to literary approaches, share with most literary approaches a focus on the final form of the text. Rather than trying to understand the traditions and communities behind the text of the Pentateuch, they focus on the texts as they now exist in their final, canonical form. The argument is that the text as we have it is what is authoritative for communities of faith—not what happened to create the text. In the case of the Pentateuch, reconstructed and hypothetical J, E, D, and P documents are not authoritative, but rather the whole of the Pentateuch in its current literary form.

It should be noted, however, that literary-canonical approaches do not simply discard history as a category irrelevant to biblical interpretation. Scholars do not simply read the Pentateuch as if it were a modern novel. History is still important, if for no other reason than the fact that the Pentateuch is an ancient document, which was written in an ancient language. The very act of translating the Pentateuch from Biblical Hebrew into any modern language requires historical awareness. The explanation of ancient practices—such as polygamy, the expectation of offering hospitality to strangers, or offering animal sacrifice—is an act of historical translation.

Types of Literature in the Pentateuch

The Old Testament is not so much a book as it is a library. And not all of the books in this small library share the same literary genre. In fact, many of the books of the Old Testament are themselves collections of literature that contain more than one genre of literature. In this way, the books of the Pentateuch may have more in common with a newspaper (whether a physical copy or online) than a modern novel or biography. A modern novel or biography usually sustains one genre for the entire book. But a newspaper bundles many types of literature in each edition—there are news accounts, opinion essays, advertisements, stock reports, comic strips, horoscopes, advice columns, travel and fashion features, recipes, and so on. In a similar way, rolled up in each of the scrolls of the Pentateuch is a variety of literary genres.

Theological Narratives

Much of the Pentateuch is given over to a form of literature that can be called theological narrative. This term attempts to capture the style, content, and intention of the pentateuchal stories. The style of these theological narratives is storytelling, and they employ an anonymous narrator—someone is telling the stories, but that voice is not identified. This anonymous narrator is sometimes referred to as the "implied narrator." The audience is left to trust the authority of the narrator, assuming that when the narrator of the stories says something, its accuracy can be trusted. Some readers imagine the voice as that of Moses—but any two readers might imagine Moses very differently. Some readers imagine simply an anonymous voice. The point is that the implied narrator of the story is different than the historical author.

Another feature of theological narratives is that they have an audience. Beginning readers will most likely assume that the stories are being directed at "us"—the modern audience. And while it is true that religious traditions that venerate the Old Testament do consider these stories as directed at themselves in some way, it is also true that readers who engage the Pentateuch critically learn to imagine an ancient "implied audience." To put this another way, anyone who engages the Pentateuch in any depth will soon realize that it was composed and collected for a different audience than "us." The Pentateuch was composed for an ancient, Israelite audience. Embedded in its stories are many hints that help the reader construct an imagined audience for the Pentateuch. For example, Genesis 12:6 says, "Abram passed through the land to the place at Shechem, to the oak of Moreh. At that time the Canaanites were in the land." A first-time reader of Genesis will know very little about the land that the narrator is describing—about what Shechem is, why the oak of Moreh is mentioned, and who the Canaanites were and why it is important. But even a first-time reader will realize that this story was originally composed for an implied audience who knew these things as well as their significance.

These narratives are human narratives, with human characters. Abraham and Sarah, Jacob and Rachel, Moses and Miriam are characters in these theological stories. To call them characters does not mean that they were not historical figures. Nor does the term malign the historical accuracy of these stories. There are some scholars who doubt the historical accuracy of the pentateuchal narratives, but even those who accept their historical accuracy will recognize that in the theological narratives of the Pentateuch, Abraham and Sarah and the others are characters. (This is also true of any family stories someone might tell about their grandpa or grandma. When someone tells a story about grandma, it does not mean grandma does not exist or never existed; but for the length of that story, "grandma" is a character in the story.)

One of the most important things about the characters in Old Testament narratives is that, for the most part, the narrator tells what the characters did and what they said. We are rarely told why they did or said something, and we are almost never told what they felt or thought. In Genesis 12, for example, we read that "the LORD said to Abram, 'Go from your country and your kindred and your father's house to the land that I will show you. . . .' So Abram went." The narrative does not say why God commanded this. Or how Abram felt. Or what his wife Sarah thought of the idea. This does not mean that the reader cannot (or must not) wonder about such things. It just means that usually the narrator does not give this sort of information. In this sense, the narratives of the Pentateuch are spare. They say a great deal but use very few words to say it.

In terms of intention, the Pentateuch's narratives are theological. That is, these narratives were composed, collected, and preserved over the centuries by a faith community that believed the stories communicate messages that are essential and true about who God is, about who "we" are, about God's good creation, and about how God is at work in his creation. All the stories of the Pentateuch are theological in that their overriding concern is with God.

In addition to the leading human characters, such as Abraham, Sarah, and Moses, the leading character of the entire Pentateuch is Israel's God, whose name is Yahweh.

To emphasize that the narratives of the Pentateuch are theological does not cast aspersions on their historical nature. Rather, calling these stories theological narratives places the emphasis where it belongs. Only in the last few centuries (since the Enlightenment) has the genre of "historical narrative" arisen, in which the purported goal is simply to be as objectively accurate about history as possible. (We say "purported" because nobody really ever tells a story just to be accurate.) The stories of the Pentateuch are self-consciously theological. Their subject is God, and their intention is to say something true about that God.

Legal Material

A tremendous amount of the Pentateuch is devoted to transmitting Israel's legal and ethical tradition. Many people who are new readers of the Bible—and especially of the Old Testament—primarily expect that they will encounter legal prohibitions and commandments when they open its pages for the first time. Although there is less legal material than many people expect, the Old Testament does pass on the heart of ancient Israel's legal and ethical wisdom.

But here is an interesting thing about Israel's legal tradition. Israel considered the laws they received from God to be a good and wonderful gift! Israel did not chafe under the law or consider it a burden. Nor did Israel think that following the laws was a means to earn salvation by "works righteousness" (more on that in a later chapter). Rather, the laws revealed to Israel were seen as a sign of God's favor: "Observe them carefully, for this will show your wisdom and understanding to the nations, who will hear about all these decrees and say, 'Surely this great nation is a wise and understanding people.' What other

---

Box 3.4

Legal Collections in the Pentateuch

The Pentateuch has several collections of ancient Israel's legal traditions, including these:

- the Covenant Code (Exod. 20:23–23:33)
- the Holiness Code (Lev. 17–26)
- laws about Levitical and refuge cities, murder and inheritance (Num. 35–36)
- the Deuteronomic Code (Deut. 12–26)

Israel was not the only ancient Near Eastern society with law codes. There is evidence that legal wisdom was shared between societies. The most famous ancient Near Eastern law code is the Code of Hammurabi (ca. 1770 BCE).

nation is so great as to have their gods near them the way the LORD our God is near us whenever we pray to him? And what other nation is so great as to have such righteous decrees and laws as this body of laws I am setting before you today?" (Deut. 4:6–8 NIV).

As noted above in the discussion of the Pentateuch as theological narrative, readers will immediately recognize that much of the law was composed for an animal-powered agrarian society in the ancient world, a foreign way of life for most modern readers. There are laws about oxen and donkeys, reaping and gleaning fields, lending at interest and letting the soil rest every seven years, and kings and priests. Modern readers may understandably question whether there is any continuing relevance in these legal traditions. On the other hand, the Pentateuch also contains laws that seem relevant for all times and places: "You shall love your neighbor as yourself" (Lev. 19:18b); "You shall not murder" (Exod. 20:13); "You shall not commit adultery" (Exod. 20:14); "You shall not steal" (Exod. 20:15). The legal texts of the Pentateuch address many of the issues that have been points of human interaction throughout the ages: financial matters (including trade, fair weights and measures, and especially property issues); family matters (including household laws, marriage, and inheritance); public safety (including murder, accidental death, and damage to another person's property); and the most basic of all material goods: food.

For readers who have grown up in a society that respects law and has a tradition of respecting human rights, it may be hard to imagine life without law and order. But much of the ancient world was precisely that kind of world. Israel's ethical and legal traditions were seen as a miraculous divine gift. The chapters in this book that deal specifically with Exodus, Leviticus, and Deuteronomy will delve more deeply into the Pentateuch's legal traditions. For now, it is enough to say that the reader of the Pentateuch will encounter collections of legal material.

Ritual and Religious Material

Less common than legal material is the related genre of ritual and religious material. The Pentateuch includes directions for Israel's worship spaces, for worship services that served a variety of ancient needs, and for maintaining ritual purity. Among the Pentateuch's collections of ritual and religious materials are laws concerning the following:

- the tabernacle, ark of the covenant, and priesthood (Exod. 25–30; Lev. 8–10)
- offerings and sacrifices (Lev. 1–7; 27)

purity codes Regulations derived from the Torah that specified what was clean or unclean or holy or profane for the Jewish people, enabling them to live in the presence of a holy God and in a way that was distinct from their neighbors.

tabernacle The portable tent-shrine that housed the ark of the covenant and was used as the central place of worship for the Israelites prior to the construction of the temple in Jerusalem.

- ritual purity (Lev. 11–16)
- the purity of the people (Num. 5–10)
- other ritual requirements (Num. 15; 17–19; 28–30)

Texts concerning ritual and religious matters will be addressed more extensively in the chapters on Leviticus and Numbers.

Songs and Poetry

Although none of the five pentateuchal books are considered poetic, sections of poetry are interspersed throughout the Pentateuch. In particular, the following poetic sections are worth noting:

- the testament of Jacob (Gen. 49:1–27)
- the Song of the Sea, also known as the Songs of Moses and Miriam (Exod. 15:1–18, 21)
- a creedal fragment (Exod. 34:6–7)
- the Aaronic Blessing (Num. 6:24–26)
- Balaam's prophetic speeches (Num. 23:7–10, 18b–24; 24:3–9, 15–24)
- the Song of Moses (Deut. 32:1–43)
- Moses's farewell blessing (Deut. 33:2–29)

There are many other short, important poetic fragments and passages in the Pentateuch (such as Num. 21:14, 17–18, 27–30). The above simply represent some of the most important and well known. The purpose of these poetic interludes in the longer narrative of the Pentateuch varies. They often represent older poems that have been preserved and incorporated into a later prose book (see chap. 2). They often serve the narrative plot as the final words of an important figure (the testament of Jacob; Moses's two farewell poems). They can preserve a very important element from Israel's worship (the creedal fragment in Exod. 34; the Aaronic Blessing). Or they can interrupt the narrative to accentuate the importance of an event (the Song of the Sea; Balaam's speeches). Readers who grow interested in any of these poems may want to skip to chapter 18, where the rhythms and functions of biblical poetry are introduced.

© 2014, Baker Publishing Group. Courtesy of Musée du Louvre; Autorisation de photographer et de filmer. Louvre, Paris, France.

Fig. 3.3. The Code of Hammurabi is a collection of case law that was collected and disseminated under the reign of the Babylonian king Hammurabi (1792–1750 BCE). It is the longest and most well-preserved legal code from the ancient Near East, and it contains some laws similar to biblical case law, some of which will be discussed below.

Genealogies

Another common—but often skipped—genre in the Pentateuch is genealogy. A genealogy is a chronological listing of how two or more generations are related to each other: so-and-so gave birth to so-and-so, who gave birth to so-and-so. Utilizing the more archaic language of the King James Version of the Bible, people used to refer to these as the "begats": "Adam lived an hundred and thirty years, and begat a son in his own likeness, and after his image; and called his name Seth. . . . And Seth lived an hundred and five years, and begat Enos. . . . And Enos lived ninety years and begat Cainan" (Gen. 5:3, 6, 9 KJV).

There are genealogies throughout the Bible. The books of 1–2 Chronicles, Ezra, and Nehemiah make pronounced use of genealogies in the Old Testament, and the Gospels of Matthew and Luke feature genealogies that connect the story of Jesus to the story of the Old Testament. In the Pentateuch, there are genealogies throughout. Scholars who accept the Documentary Hypothesis identify genealogies especially with the J and P sources of the Pentateuch. In Genesis particularly, one finds genealogies in chapters 4, 5, 11, 25, and 30.

In the Pentateuch, the genealogies function in three important ways. First, and perhaps most importantly, they underscore the theological point that God is active in history and that history is moving into the future with purpose. Life is not simply one thing after another until we die. There is divine direction in creation. The genealogies demonstrate this by serving as narrative glue between the various time epochs in the Pentateuch. Embedded in the genealogies is a particular theological view of history: there is order; there is purpose.

Box 3.5

Understanding a Literary Plot

Most broadly understood, a literary plot can be described as a sequence of events that are related to each other and move toward a resolution. Along this vein, the philosopher Aristotle said that a plot must have a beginning, a middle, and an end.

A simpler definition is that a plot is the story of a given *problem* that occurred and the *actions and events* that bring the problem to a *resolution*. The problem usually emerges after the characters and setting have been introduced—Hamlet is the prince of Denmark; Frodo is a hobbit with a special ring who lives in the Shire; Harry is a boy with a weird scar who lives with his aunt's family.

Once the characters have been introduced, the problem typically appears. Hamlet's uncle killed his father. What will Hamlet do? Frodo's ring belongs to the dark lord and must be destroyed. How will this be accomplished? Harry's scar is the remnant of an attack on him by the dark lord (See a pattern?), who is not quite done with Harry yet. Will Harry or the dark lord prevail?

Second, and almost as important, the genealogies imply that all human life is connected. In a human family in which difference often leads to bloodshed, the genealogies point to the interrelatedness of humankind. In the kinship-based ancient world (see chap. 1), the genealogies show how Israel had a familial connection with the nations that surrounded it. With this claim of distant familial connectedness came a complementary ethical claim. Relatives, no matter how distantly related, are family who owe each other hospitality and refuge.

Third, the genealogies of the Pentateuch were sources of identity. Much more than in the modern era, identity in ancient Israel was tribe and clan based. If people did not know their genealogies in the ancient world, they did not know who they were. This is apparent in the genealogy of the priestly tribe of Levi as laid out in Exodus 6:16–27. In ancient Israel, being a priest was a familial, hereditary calling.

The Plot

The Pentateuch is a body of literature that has a plot. This is the case regardless of an interpreter's view on how the Pentateuch came together. Every reader can discern a plot unfolding over the course of its pages, though not every interpreter will describe that plot in the same, or even similar, terms. Describing a plot is a subjective, rather than objective, activity.

One important way to understand the plot of the Pentateuch is to see it as the interweaving development of three themes: (1) the Creator's continuing commitment to a good but broken creation; (2) the Lord's choice of the family of Abraham and Sarah (originally called Abram and Sarai) to be a blessing to people in a broken creation; and (3) Israel learning to live as God's own people in a hostile world.

The Creator's Commitment

In the Old Testament, the setting of the story is creation. The benevolent Creator fashions an orderly creation with humanity, the crown of creation, made in the Creator's image. Then comes the problem: brokenness enters creation when forbidden fruit is eaten (more on this in chap. 4). The rest of the plot is a complicated answer to a simple question: What is the benevolent Creator going to do with a broken creation—a creation in which the human creatures have rebelled because they want to be like God (Gen. 3:5), in which human creatures murder each other (4:8), in which human "wickedness" and "evil" (6:5) are great? Perhaps the central message of the story of Noah and the great flood (Gen. 6–9) is that rather than destroying the broken creation and starting over, the Creator chooses a different way to respond to sin.

sin Any act, thought, word, or state of being contrary to the will of God.

The Lord's Choice of Abraham and Sarah

Faced with a creation that is broken, in which the families of the earth are broken and scattered, the Lord chooses Abraham and Sarah to be a means of blessing to the broken creation. "Leave your land, your family, and your father's household for the land that I will show you. I will make of you a great nation and will bless you. I will make your name respected, and you will be a blessing. I will bless those who bless you, those who curse you I will curse; all the families of the earth will be blessed because of you" (Gen. 12:1–3 CEB). God promises Abraham and Sarah three things: a land, many descendants, and the blessing. One way to frame the rest of the plot of the Pentateuch is as the history of God's endangered promises. Throughout the books, one or more of these three promises is always at risk. But God finds ways to stay faithful to the promises.

God's People Learn to Live in a Hostile World

But the plot of the Pentateuch should not only be seen in terms of the action of God. Although the chosen people—descendants of Abraham and Sarah—are recipients of continual divine action, they are not *merely* recipients. They have the will and the inclination to act on their own behalf. At times, this will and inclination prove rather poor—they often are their own worst enemy. They prove capable of great wickedness and folly. At other times, members of the chosen people prove that they are capable of surprising wisdom, mercy, and loyalty.

After recounting God's choice of Abraham and Sarah and his threefold promise to them, Genesis traces the story through the next three generations of the family. The promises are constantly threatened by the normal woes of the broken creation: childlessness, war, famine, human evil, parents playing favorites with children, brothers betraying each other, family not acting as family to each other, and on and on. At times, the family is split up and divided against itself; at other times, a family member seems to learn grace. At the end of the book of Genesis, the family is together, but they are not in the promised land; they are living instead in the land of Egypt.

The rest of the pentateuchal plot traces the long and tortured journey by which Israel regains its place in the promised land. Led by Moses as it journeys toward home, Israel must overcome slavery; hunger and lack of water in the wilderness; its own disobedience, rebellion, and hard-heartedness; and opposition from foreign kings and people. Along the way, Israel tries to learn to trust God, follow his laws, and reorder itself according to his will. The book of Deuteronomy ends with Israel on the banks of the river Jordan, looking over to the promised land, about to enter. And then Israel learns it has one more hurdle to overcome. Moses, who led the people out of Egypt and through the wilderness for forty years, will not be going into the land with them. They must deal with the future under the guidance of an unproven leader—Joshua.

FOR FURTHER READING: **The Pentateuch**

Alter, Robert. *The Five Books of Moses: A Translation with Commentary.* New York: Norton, 2004.

Baden, Joel S., and Jeffrey Stackert, eds. *The Oxford Handbook of the Pentateuch.* Oxford: Oxford University Press, 2021.

Fretheim, Terence E. *The Pentateuch.* Interpreting Biblical Texts. Nashville: Abingdon, 1996.

Goldstein, Elyse, ed. *The Women's Torah Commentary: New Insights from Women Rabbis on the 54 Torah Portions.* Woodstock, VT: Jewish Lights, 2000.

Mann, Thomas W. *The Book of the Torah.* 2nd ed. Eugene, OR: Cascade Books, 2013.

Schnittjer, Gary Edward. *The Torah Story: An Apprenticeship on the Pentateuch.* Grand Rapids: Zondervan, 2006.

Ska, Jean-Louis. *Introduction to Reading the Pentateuch.* Winona Lake, IN: Eisenbrauns, 2006.

Sweeney, Marvin A. *The Pentateuch.* Core Biblical Studies. Nashville: Abingdon, 2017.

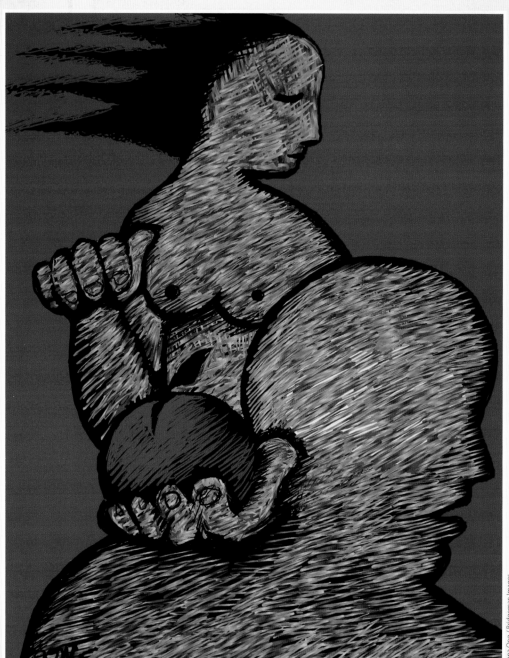

Genesis

The title "Genesis," derived from the Greek word for "to be born," means "beginning." The book of Genesis famously begins with the words "In the beginning." The Jewish name for the book (*Bereshit*) comes from these first words, meaning "in [the] beginning."

It is not surprising, then, that Genesis is about beginnings. It is about the beginning of the universe as God's creation. It is about the beginning of life on earth. It is about the beginning of sin and brokenness. It is about the beginning of civilization. It is about the beginning of diversity and variety. And it is about the beginning of the people Israel, whom God chose to be a people "blessed to be a blessing" (see Gen. 12:1–3).

Background

Composition and Development

Like most of the books of the Old Testament, the book of Genesis is anonymous. Nowhere in its pages is any author identified.

According to historic tradition, Moses is the author of Genesis. For reasons discussed in chapter 3, "The Pentateuch," many modern critics no longer consider Moses the author of Genesis. The most widely accepted scholarly view is that the book of Genesis is the product of a lengthy and complicated history. Although many theories attempt to reconstruct this historical development, it is not possible to do so with anything close to 100 percent certainty. For a more detailed introduction to theories regarding the development and composition of Genesis, see that earlier discussion.

What can be said with a fair degree of certainty is that the book was copied, preserved, and disseminated by faithful, Second Temple scribes in the years following the Babylonian exile. The scribes who preserved the book did so because they believed it communicated truths about the origins of creation, the people of Israel, and God's enduring commitment to be in relationship with both creation and Israel.

Genre

The book of Genesis is a mixed composition of several types of literature. These include theological narratives (the bulk of the book), genealogies, songs, and poetry (especially Gen. 49).

The genealogies in particular need additional comment. The editorial placement of genealogies by the book's editors/authors is a clue to how the ancients may have understood the book as a whole. As discussed in the previous chapter, pentateuchal genealogies function in at least three important ways: they show God at work in history, they point to the connectedness of all life, and they were sources of identity for ancient Israel.

But genealogies in Genesis also function to move the plot of the story forward in significant ways. The editors placed genealogies at the intersection of major stories, linking together the various "generations" of the Genesis narrative. These genealogies are usually introduced by the formula "These are the generations/descendants of . . ." or something similar (see Gen. 5:1).

Genesis 1:1–2:4a—Creation by the word, including the twice-given command "Be fruitful and multiply" (1:22 and 1:28)

Genesis 2:4a: "These are the generations of the heavens and the earth when they were created."

Genesis 2:4b–4:26—The creation of Adam and Eve, the beginnings of brokenness, and the beginnings of civilization

Genesis 5: "This is the list of the descendants of Adam" (5:1).

Genesis 6–9—The great flood and the preservation of creation

Genesis 10: "These are the descendants of Noah's sons" (10:1).

Genesis 11:1–9—The tower of Babel

Genesis 11:10–32: "These are the descendants of Shem" (11:10).

Genesis 12:1–25:11—The story of Abraham, Sarah, and Hagar

Genesis 25:12–28: "These are the descendants of Ishmael, Abraham's son. . . . These are the descendants of Isaac, Abraham's son" (25:12, 19).

Genesis 25:29–35:29—The story of Isaac and Rebekah

Genesis 36: "These are the descendants of Esau" (36:1).

Genesis 37:1–46:7—The story of Joseph and his family

Genesis 46:8–27: "Now these are the names of the Israelites, Jacob and his offspring, who came to Egypt" (46:8).

Genesis 46:28–50:26—Jacob and Joseph die in Egypt

The significance of the genealogies in the story of Genesis becomes even clearer in light of the command that God gives twice in Genesis 1: "Be fruitful and multiply." God first gives this command to the creatures that live in the water and in the sky (1:22) and then to the human beings and, by extension, to other creatures that live on the land (1:26). The genealogies are signs of the creatures faithfully fulfilling God's initial command. As it is fulfilled, life thrives on earth. Far from being insignificant "filler," the genealogies show creation teeming—practically bursting at the seams—in faithfulness to God.

The genealogies also show that human beings and other creatures participate in God's ongoing act of creation. They indicate that all life on earth is interconnected. From the first "generation" of the heavens and earth to the first "generation" of humans—and on through the ages—all creatures are extended family. They are connected to each other. And in the view of the authors of Genesis, significantly, all creatures are connected to their Creator.

Literary Interpretation

Reading about literature in a secondary textbook is never a substitute for reading the primary literature itself. This is true whether one is reading Jane Austen, William Shakespeare, or the Bible. But because having an initial grasp of the overall story can be helpful when approaching a book, a brief summary of the Genesis story in its larger units is offered here.

The beginnings of life, brokenness, and God's commitment to creation (Gen. 1–11). As noted earlier, the opening chapters of Genesis are about origins: the beginnings of the world, its brokenness, and God's response. Genesis 1–2 offers complementary pictures of creation (Gen. 1:1–2:4a and 2:4b–3:24). Genesis 1 focuses on the big picture of a transcendent God from a cosmic point of view.

Looking down from space, as it were, Genesis 1 shows a creation in which everything fits and is in balance: light and darkness; heaven and earth; air, water, and land; creatures to fill the air, the water, and the land; and humanity, created in God's image, to care for and have dominion over the earth. Genesis 2 focuses on the smaller picture of an immanent God. Digging fingers in the clay like a potter, God molds man and woman, places them in a garden, gives them work to do ("serve and guard" the earth), and issues one rule to follow for their own safekeeping (do not eat the forbidden fruit). Genesis 3 tells how man and woman rebel against God and God's order. They want to "be like God, knowing good and evil" (3:5). But knowing good from evil does not mean one has the ability to do good and refrain from evil. The first murder follows, when one brother kills another (4:1–16).

Fig. 4.1. The flood-and-ark story is a favorite among visual artists. They often depict the wonders of nature and creation while avoiding or obscuring the terror of the story, the Lord's decision, "I will blot out from the earth the human beings that I have created" (Gen. 6:7a).

Genesis 6–9 tells the story of the great flood. God regards the creation and, seeing that "the earth was filled with violence" (6:11), he briefly considers starting over. Like a potter whose vessel doesn't come out right, God considers destroying what he has made and remolding it from the beginning. But because God loves creation—and especially a man named Noah and his family—he sends a flood but preserves creation. Here is the main promise of the flood story: God's response to a violent creation will not be violence and destruction. God promises not to destroy creation by flood; he will find another way to address the beloved but rebellious-and-violent creation. After the flood, creation remains broken. Noah's first act after the flood is to get drunk, which leads to one of his sons taking advantage of him. Genesis 11 tells how human rebellion against God continues, as humanity (foolishly and frankly humorously) seeks to "make a name" for themselves by building a great tower. God confuses people's language and scatters them across the face of the earth. The earth is now a place of rebellion (against God) and confusion (humans do not understand each other). Thus ends the first major section of Genesis.

The beginnings of the people Israel: Abraham and Sarah (Gen. 12:1–25:18). Perhaps the greatest surprise in the plot of Genesis comes in 12:1–3. God's response to the brokenness and rebellion—and the new situation in which the families of the earth are estranged and scattered—is to call Abraham and

The Names "Abraham" and "Sarah"

Two of the main characters in Genesis are Abraham and Sarah, whose names mean "father of many" and "princess," respectively. But when these characters are introduced at the end of Genesis 11, they are called "Abram" and "Sarai." In Genesis 15, God declares, "No longer shall your name be Abram, but your name shall be Abraham, for I have made you the ancestor of a multitude of nations" (17:5). A few verses later, "God said to Abraham, 'As for Sarai your wife, you shall not call her Sarai, but Sarah shall be her name. . . . I will give you a son by her. I will bless her, and she shall give rise to nations; kings of people shall come from her'" (17:15–16).

The giving of new names to characters is a common and important motif in the Bible. Divinely ordained name changes move the story line ahead. In this case, the new names are not that much different—scholars believe that *Abram* and *Sarai* are really just different linguistic forms of *Abraham* and *Sarah*—but note that in the story, the name change reaffirms God's central promise to Abraham and, even more importantly, God's promise to Sarah. God's promise is not just to Abraham but also to Sarah. God values her not simply because she is Abraham's wife. God values her as herself, as Sarah. God has a promise specifically for Sarah.

Later in Genesis, God appears to Jacob and wrestles with him all night. After this "long night of the soul," Jacob demands a blessing. God replies, "You shall no longer be called Jacob, but Israel, for you have striven with God and with humans, and have prevailed" (32:28).

Fig. 4.2. The story of Sodom and Gomorrah serves to illustrate that even after the flood, human beings are incapable of avoiding evil. Indeed, at times those in power and even entire societies seem bent on doing evil. The sin of the cities is not primarily sexual in nature but rather a generalized inclination toward evil rather than good. Lot and his family are delivered from the destruction of the city, but in a strange detail Lot's wife looks back at the destruction and is turned into a pillar of salt.

Sarah. God scattered people because they had sought to "make a name" for themselves. Now he chooses Abraham and Sarah, promising them "a great name" and that they will be the parents of a great nation that will fulfill a priestly function—being the means through which "all the families of the earth shall be blessed" (12:3). Although the focus in this discussion is on Genesis, a reader could step back and, taking in the entire sweep of the Old Testament, consider the promise of this "priestly calling" the underpinning of the plot of the Old Testament.

Through the cycle of stories related to Abraham and Sarah, God's threefold promise of land, descendants, and a blessing is endangered—sometimes by Abraham, sometimes by Sarah, sometimes by nature, sometimes by other humans, and sometimes even by God. Right away in Genesis 12:10–20, a famine hits, driving Abraham and Sarah away from the promised land to Egypt. In Egypt, Abraham—not yet the great man of faith that he will later be recognized as—presents Sarah as his sister rather than his wife, and Sarah is taken into Pharaoh's harem. In spite of Abraham's faithlessness, God rescues them and returns them to the land. But new problems arise when their possessions grow so abundant that the land cannot support all of the family's livestock and helpers, and strife arises between the various herders. Here, God's abundant blessings create a danger for the threefold promise. The crisis is solved when Abraham's nephew Lot takes his share of the holdings and moves on.

As the years go by, Abraham and Sarah remain childless. In Genesis 15, God renews his promises to Abraham, this time making the commitment more profound by entering into a covenant with Abraham: "On that day the LORD made a covenant with Abram" (15:18). In spite of the renewed promise and covenant, Abraham and Sarah remained childless. Genesis 16 narrates the story of Sarah's decision to give her slave girl Hagar to Abraham in order to provide an heir for him. Hagar likely had little choice in this arrangement; the narrative does not even bother to record whether she consents. Hagar gives birth to a son, Ishmael. In Genesis 17, God again renews the promises, again in the form of a covenant. Abraham laughs and then pleads, "O that Ishmael might live in your sight" (17:18). God responds by emphasizing Sarah's membership in the covenant and the promise to her: "I will bless her, and she shall give rise to nations. . . . Your wife Sarah shall bear you a son. . . . I will establish my covenant with him" (17:16–19). In Genesis 18, when God again repeats the promise that Sarah shall have a son, she also laughs at the promise.

In a digression that emphasizes the brokenness of creation, the story of Sodom and Gomorrah is related. The horrific story relates the attempted rape of guests and Lot's willingness to put his daughters at risk. The city and Lot's wife are destroyed. Abraham's mournful lament resonates to this day: "Shall not the Judge of all the earth do what is just?" (18:25).

Box 4.3

Ellen Davis on Genesis 22

Genesis 22 is a much-debated story. Some say that the story amounts to divine child abuse. Others fault Abraham because he did not argue with God, as he did when God announced he would punish Sodom and Gomorrah. Ellen Davis offers a different perspective:

> As we read this story on Good Friday, it is at last clear why Abraham can afford to trust God with his only and beloved son. In every circumstance and beyond all reason, God can be trusted with the child, for God's heart is wholly the heart of a parent. Today with faith's eye we see our God standing, just as Abraham does, an anguished parent yearning over his "adorable, true, and only Son" bound on the wood. So, in the strange idiom of Christian faith, we know God as the One whose heart has been torn wide open by the conflict between love for his Son and love for the world—and, stranger than strange, God's heart, once ripped open, has the capacity to love all the more.*

* Ellen F. Davis, "Vulnerability, the Condition of Covenant," in *The Art of Reading Scripture*, ed. Ellen F. Davis and Richard B. Hays (Grand Rapids: Eerdmans, 2003), 288.

Sarah finally does give birth to a son, who is named Isaac, "he laughs," a play on Abraham and Sarah's laughter at God's promise. In a chilling act after the birth of her own son, Sarah drives Hagar and her son, Ishmael, into the wilderness. There, facing death, Hagar is met by God, who faithfully preserves her and her son.

The beginnings of the people Israel—Jacob, Leah, and Rachel (Gen. 25:19–36:43). If the main plot question in Abraham and Sarah's part of the story is, How will God keep the divine promises when they have no child? the plot question in the next section is, Which son shall inherit the blessing? Isaac and Rebekah have twin sons: Isaac favors the older twin, Esau, whereas Rebekah favors Jacob, the younger son. By law the older child would be heir to the blessing. With the help of his mother, Jacob steals the blessing from Esau (Gen. 27). As a result, Jacob must flee from his family and the promised land. Forced into exile by his own crimes, Jacob meets God at a place he called Bethel ("House of God"), where God renews the covenantal promises (Gen. 28).

Jacob takes shelter with his mother's brother Laban. There, the cheater becomes cheated. Jacob desires to marry Laban's younger daughter, Rachel. After Jacob works for seven years, Laban tricks him into marrying his older daughter, Leah. Outraged by this trickery, Jacob confronts Laban, who finally agrees to give him Rachel in marriage after a week, but only in exchange for seven more years of work. Sleeping with his two wives and their two servants—Bilhah and Zilpah—Jacob fathers twelve sons and one daughter, Dinah. After playing a trick on Laban, Jacob sets out to return to the land that God had promised his people. On the way back, God again encounters Jacob, renewing the covenantal promise yet again and changing Jacob's name to Israel, meaning "he strives with God."

Box 4.4

Plot, Characters, and Truth

When interpreters apply literary concepts such as plot, characters, and audience to a story, it does not mean that the story did not happen historically or that the characters were not genuine historical people. By studying biblical texts as literature, we acknowledge and appreciate that ancient Israel's scribes were not merely stenographers. In many cases, they were literary artists with highly refined skills in storytelling, persuasion, and subtlety. Ancient scribes crafted these texts so that they would be heard, digested, and believed by the communities in which they lived. If we are to interpret the Old Testament fruitfully, then ancient Israel's literature needs to be appreciated not only as testimonies to the past but also as works of artistry. The fact that Israel's Scriptures are art does not mean that they are not true. The category of truth far transcends mere historical fact. When reading the stories in Genesis, the real question is, How is this story telling me the truth?

Genesis 34 recounts a story of Jacob's daughter, Dinah. There is some controversy about the story. The traditional interpretation is that Dinah is raped and abducted by a non-Israelite named Shechem. Dinah's brothers rescue her, slay Shechem and the males of the city, and plunder all the loot. Jacob reacts angrily against his sons, who respond, "Should our sister be treated like a whore?" (34:31). Jacob returns to Bethel and settles there (Gen. 35).

The beginnings of the people Israel—Joseph and his brothers (Gen. 37–50). The last fourteen chapters of Genesis are the story of Joseph and his brothers. Like his father and mother before him, Jacob plays favorites among his children. He loves Joseph more than the others and favors him with a special coat. The Lord also seems to favor Joseph, who is given dreams and the gift of interpreting dreams. The ten older boys do not like their favored little brother much. One day, they waylay him, and on the advice of Judah, one of the brothers, they sell him to some slavers, who take him to Egypt where he is sold to an official named Potiphar. The brothers smear animal blood on Joseph's coat and give it to Jacob as evidence of Joseph's death. And there you have the recurring themes of the Joseph story: favoritism, jealousy, God's presence with Joseph, injustice and faithlessness, false evidence, and dreams.

Genesis 38 is a brief interlude in Joseph's story, and it describes an event in which Joseph's older brother Judah proves faithless but then repents. Judah refuses to provide for his daughter-in-law, Tamar, following the death of her husband. Left with no recourse, Tamar disguises herself as a temple prostitute (38:21) and has sex with Judah. When it is reported to Judah that Tamar is pregnant, he sentences her to die. When Tamar presents evidence to Judah that he is the father of her child, Judah repents and declares, "She is more righteous than I" (38:26 NIV). It appears Judah is changing.

Meanwhile, Joseph's story with its established themes continues in Egypt. In Potiphar's household, God is with Joseph, who prospers and rises to be

---

Box 4.5

Role Models?

Readers who have been raised in homes or communities where the Bible is revered often assume that characters in the Bible—whether in the Old Testament or in the New—are to be understood as role models, figures to be emulated. This is not the case, however. The Bible presents men and women as they truly are—complex, morally ambiguous, and sometimes conflicted. In many cases, characters partake in troubling actions—and their behavior is neither celebrated nor condemned. The story of the rape of Dinah and her brothers' revenge is such a case. The brothers rescue Dinah. So far so good. But they kill all the men of Shechem and plunder the city's wealth. Troubling. Then Jacob rebukes them and appears only to think about himself: "You have brought trouble on me by making me odious to the inhabitants of the land" (34:30). Also troubling. The narrative does not clarify whether Jacob or his sons are in the right, or if all the parties (except Dinah) are in the wrong.

Fig. 4.3. In the story of "Jacob's ladder," God appears to Jacob following his flight from Esau's wrath. God reiterates the covenantal promises that had first been made to Abraham and Sarah.

head of Potiphar's household, save for Potiphar himself. After a failed attempt to seduce Joseph, Potiphar's wife presents her husband with false evidence that Joseph tried to rape her, and he is sent to prison. God is with Joseph in prison. He prospers, is favored by the chief jailer, and rises to be in charge of all prisoners. When two prisoners have dreams, Joseph interprets them. The one prisoner is set free but faithlessly forgets Joseph in prison. When Pharaoh has dreams, the former prisoner brings Joseph to the king's attention, and he interprets Pharaoh's dreams—saying there will be seven years of abundance

Box 4.6

The Plots of Genesis

In a narrative work, the plot is the major story line (or story lines) that move the narrative forward. In a very simple sense, "plot" can be described as a situation that must be resolved and the steps characters take to resolve it. Because Genesis is a narrative book, it is helpful to apply the concept of plot to it. This can help the reader make sense of the meaning of the book. And as is the case with most good stories, more than one plot is often at work in a story. When analyzing the plot of a story, it is often helpful to phrase the plot in the form of a question that the story is trying to answer. We can call these "plot questions."

Genesis has two major plots: one grand plot that has to do with all of creation and a second that has to do with the origins of the people of Israel. In terms of the first, the situation that must be resolved is that the Creator crafts a creation, but it is broken. The plot question is, What will the Creator do with a creation that is broken, violent, and in rebellion?

The second major plot is introduced in Genesis 12 when God promises Abraham a land, descendants who will become a great nation, and a blessing. But as soon as Abraham arrives in the "promised land" with Sarah and their entire household, problems arise. The audience already knows that Sarah was "barren; she had no children" (11:30 NET). This situation poses a problem for the Lord's promise of descendants who will be a great nation. Then a second problem arises: "Now there was a famine in the land. So Abram went down to Egypt" (12:10). The plot question is, How is God going to keep the threefold promise that was made to Abraham and Sarah?

In addition to these greater plotlines, the story of Genesis has many smaller stories and story lines. When interpreting one of the individual stories in Genesis, it is often helpful to ask two different levels of questions. First, on a more macro level, how does this particular story fit into the overall plot and story of Genesis? How does this story help either to resolve or to further complicate the major situation to be resolved in the plot? Second, on a more micro level, what is the situation to be resolved within the smaller story?

As an example of this, consider a smaller story within the larger story line of Abraham and Sarah. One of the most important issues in their story is that Sarah is childless. Within the larger story line of Genesis, this is a problem: How can God's promise of a great nation of descendants be kept if the mother of Israel is barren? This is problem enough. But in Genesis 16, Sarah suggests to Abraham that he have a child with her slave girl, Hagar. The child born of this coupling is Ishmael. Ishmael's birth introduces new complications into the story. Will Ishmael be Abraham's heir? If so, what about Sarah? Will she then be left out? If not, what will happen to Hagar and Ishmael? Will God have a place for them?

followed by seven years of famine. Joseph prospers and rises to be head of all Egypt, save for Pharaoh himself. The famine hits in the promised land, and Jacob sends his ten older sons—he now favors the twelfth son, Benjamin, who stays behind—to Egypt to buy grain. Joseph tests the brothers in various ways, including by planting false evidence on them.

In the end, Joseph reveals himself to his brothers. The brothers rightly fear retribution, but Joseph welcomes the entire family. He utters the famous words "Even though you intended to do me harm, God intended it for good" (50:20 AT).

Genesis ends with the family reunited. But God's threefold promise is still endangered, because Abraham's descendants are in Egypt, not in the promised land. Joseph underscores this unresolved situation in his final words: "I am about to die. But God will surely come to your aid and take you up out of this land to the land he promised on oath to Abraham, Isaac and Jacob" (50:24 NIV).

Theological Interpretation

God the Creator and Sustainer of Life

What portrait of God does Genesis paint? The first picture of God that the reader encounters is God as the Creator and sustainer of life. The act of God's creation is both a onetime event and an ongoing process. With respect to creation being a onetime event, Genesis bears witness that creation came into being solely as the act of God. In Genesis 1, God speaks, and everything comes into existence. God speaks, and there is light. God speaks again, and a space for life is formed—"an expanse in the midst of the water. . . . God called the expanse Sky" (vv. 6, 8 NJPS). God speaks again, and the seas and dry land emerge (vv. 9–10). God speaks again, and the sun, moon, and stars come into being (vv. 14–19).

Aside from the actions in which God directly creates various things in Genesis 1, it is interesting to note that creation is also an indirect and ongoing process. God uses things that are already created to continue the creative process. God speaks, and "the earth brought forth vegetation" (v. 12). God says, "Let the waters bring forth swarms of living creatures" (v. 20). God says, "Let the earth bring forth living creatures of every kind" (v. 24). And God commands the living creatures, including human beings, to "be fruitful and multiply" (vv. 22, 28) in order that the creative process might continue.

It is also worth noting that creation is understood as the act of bringing order out of chaos. In creating, God transforms the chaotic and inhospitable "formless void" (v. 2) into a hospitable, life-sustaining environment. Note some of the verbs that describe God's actions: God *separates* light from the darkness (v. 4), waters from waters (v. 7), and day from night (v. 14). God *gathers* together the waters of the earth so that dry land can emerge (v. 10). God also imposes order on chaos by creating a hierarchy as part of creation. God sets the sun and the moon in the sky to "rule" over the day and the night (v. 18). God *creates* humanity—both male and female—in his image and gives them the responsibility of having "dominion" (vv. 26, 28) over "every living thing that moves upon the earth" and to "subdue" the earth. These two terms do not mean humans may do whatever they like to earth but rather that they are to continue God's creative act of creating hospitable space in which life can flourish.

The Enuma Elish

Israel's neighbors had stories that were both similar to and different from Israel's stories. One of the most famous is the Enuma Elish, which originated in Mesopotamia (the land around the Tigris and Euphrates Rivers in parts of present-day Syria, Iraq, and Iran). The story recounts creation as a conflict among gods. The story famously begins:

> When on high the heaven had not been named,
> Firm ground below had not been called by name,
> Naught but primordial Apsu, their begetter,
> (And) Mummu-Tiamat, she who bore them all,
> Their waters comingling in a single body;
> No reed hut had been matted, no marsh land had appeared,
> When no gods whatsoever had been brought into being . . .*

The story relates how the two originating gods, Apsu and Tiamat (representing fresh water and salt water), give life to other gods. A conflict then arises, which results in the death of both Apsu and Tiamat. Marduk slays Tiamat:

> Then joined issue Tiamat and Marduk, wisest of gods;
> They strove in single combat, locked in battle. . . .
> He released the arrow, it tore her belly,
> It cut through her insides, splitting the heart.
> Having thus subdued her, he extinguished her life.
> He cast down her body to stand upon it. . . .
> He split like a shellfish into two parts:
> Half of her he set up and ceiled it as sky.†

Having made the sky from her remains, he then fashions places in the sky for the gods Anu, Enlil, and Ea. Marduk creates night and day, the moon, clouds and rain. Marduk sacrifices the god Kingu, and out of his blood they created humankind.

* "The Creation Epic," trans. E. A. Speiser, in *Ancient Near Eastern Texts Relating to the Old Testament*, ed. James Pritchard, 2nd ed. (Princeton: Princeton University Press, 1955), 60–61.
† "The Creation Epic," 69.

Zunkir, CC BY-SA 4.0 / Wikimedia Commons

Fig. 4.4. Israel's neighbors in the ancient Near East had creation myths that were in some ways similar to Israel's creation texts (Gen. 1–3; Job 38–41; Ps. 104). Israel's neighbors' stories almost always include violence between the gods.

God's indirect activity of establishing agents tasked with acting on God's behalf to bring order to the world includes natural law, such as the sun and the moon ruling over the day and night. One also thinks here of laws such as the law of gravity, which is necessary to sustain life. It also includes moral law, such as granting humanity the responsibility to exercise caretaking of the earth. It is tragic, as the rest of the book of Genesis bears witness, that humanity in its brokenness so often fails at this God-given responsibility.

The first chapters of Genesis are narratives that communicate basic beliefs about life and the universe. Israel's neighbors had their own narratives about creation. In some of these non-Israelite stories, creation results from deities fighting one another (theomachy). In the Enuma Elish, a creation story from Mesopotamia, the god Marduk slays Tiamat, the goddess of the sea, and forms heaven and earth from her corpse. Creation is an act that requires violence and death—indeed, creation is the act of multiple gods in combat with each other. The very stuff of creation, moreover, is itself divine. In Genesis, creation is the act of the one God whose creative acts include blessing (1:22, 28), rather than violence.

As has already been mentioned in this chapter, God's commitment to his creation persists in spite of the brokenness and violence that come to characterize it. One profound meaning of the flood story (Gen. 6–9) is that the Creator will not destroy the creation on account of its evil and violence. God remains committed to his creation, and he promises, "Never again will I curse the ground because of humans, even though every inclination of the human heart is evil from childhood. And never again will I destroy all living creatures, as I have done" (8:21 NIV).

The Relational God

The portrait of God that emerges in Genesis is the picture of a relational God who interacts with his beloved creation. In Genesis 1, God creates various things and pronounces them all "good." A careful analysis of the chapter, however, suggests that "goodness" in Genesis is a relational term. Things are not good in and of themselves. Rather, they are good when they are in relational balance with each other:

- darkness and light
- the heavens and the earth
- sea, air, and dry land
- bodies to fill the heavens
- living things to fill the sea, the air, and the dry land
- humanity created in God's image to have responsible dominion over all
- a day of rest to balance the days of labor

This relational picture of goodness is approached from another angle in Genesis 2 when God sees the newly created solitary man and remarks, "It is not good that the man should be alone" (2:18).

The Covenant God

A primary way in which the God of Genesis chooses to be in relationship with creation is through the forging and keeping of covenants. A covenant is

Michelangelo Caravaggio

Fig. 4.5. Genesis 22 relates the terrifying text in which God tests Abraham by commanding him to sacrifice his son Isaac. But God provides a ram to be sacrificed in Isaac's place. Abraham passes God's test, but in Genesis the two never speak to each other again. Sarah dies and is buried. A proper wife, Rebekah, is found for Isaac (Gen. 24), thus making possible the continuation of the family and the blessing. Abraham remarries and has more children, who play no role in the biblical story, but their existence rather strongly suggests that Genesis 22–25 is at least as much about Sarah and God's covenant with her as it is about Abraham.

a particular type of relationship—a formal and solemn agreement in which partners radically commit to each other for the long haul. Although the Old Testament portrays covenants between human partners, covenant primarily describes both God's commitment and his faithfulness to that commitment.

In Genesis, there are two primary covenants—the covenants with and through Noah and then with and through Abraham and Sarah. Most importantly, these covenants emphasize God's agency in choosing to enter the covenant and his fidelity in keeping the covenantal promises. It is helpful to think of a covenant as having at least four parts: (1) the choice; (2) the partners; (3) the sign; and (4) the promise(s).

Covenant with Noah. God's covenant with and through Noah is a one-sided affair that God initiates. Once the waters of the flood subside, God unilaterally chooses to initiate the covenant: "I establish my covenant with you, that never again shall all flesh be cut off by the waters of the flood. . . . I have set my bow in the cloud, and it shall be a sign of the covenant between me and the earth. . . . I will see it and remember the everlasting covenant between God and every living creature of all flesh that is on the earth" (Gen. 9:11, 13, 16 ESV).

Several important aspects should be noted here. First, the covenant is an act of divine freedom; it was "my covenant," an act solely of God's will—God's choice. Second, the covenant is between God and "every living creature of all flesh." God's commitment here is not only to humanity; God's gracious eyes are on the larger horizon of all the earth. Third and fourth, the sign of the covenant is the rainbow, and the promise is that God will never again send a flood to destroy all life. Note that the promise is phrased in the negative, outlining what God will not do: "I will never . . . never again . . . never again . . . never again" (8:21; 9:11, 15). Having freely initiated the covenant, God freely limits himself by committing to that which he will *not* do. This freedom-limiting promise of God is emphasized by the fact that he places the rainbow in the sky not to remind humans of the divine promise but as a self-reminder: "I will see it and remember the everlasting covenant." Although the promise is couched in negative language ("I will never"), it actually constitutes the positive commitment of God to endure in relationship with all the earth—in spite of the earth's brokenness and violence.

Covenant with Abraham and Sarah. The second major covenant in Genesis is with Abraham and Sarah. As detailed earlier in this chapter, God initiates a relationship with Abraham by making a threefold promise: to give Abraham descendants who will be a great nation, a promised land for them to live in, and a blessing through which "all the families of the earth shall be blessed" (12:3). The initial promise is later reaffirmed twice in covenant-making ceremonies. In Genesis 15, Abraham laments that because he has not yet produced a child, a slave, Eliezer of Damascus, would be his heir. God reaffirms the promise—"Look toward heaven and count the stars. . . . So shall your descendants be" (15:5). Abraham believes the promise, and "on that day the LORD made a covenant with [him]" (15:18). As detailed earlier, God renews the covenant some years later, following the birth of Ishmael to Hagar, and explicitly includes Sarah and her son in the covenant: "Your wife Sarah shall bear you a son, and you shall name him Isaac. I will establish my covenant with him as an everlasting covenant" (17:19).

circumcision A surgical procedure to remove the foreskin of a penis; in the Jewish tradition, the rite is a sign of the covenant God made with Israel.

Again, the covenantal relationship is initiated by God, who elects Abraham and Sarah and their offspring as the partners in the covenant. The sign of the covenant is the circumcision of male children. The covenantal promises of Genesis 12 are repeated as the promises of the covenant: descendants who will be a great nation, a promised land, and a blessing through which all the families of the earth shall be blessed.

The Blessing God

More must be said about the matter of blessing. Throughout Genesis, God is not portrayed as a disinterested and detached creator but as a God whose commitment to creation includes the intent to bless the creation. Blessing is a concept that implies granting favorable gifts, experiences, and capacities to the creation. The first blessing that God grants is the ability for creation to be continuous, to participate as "created cocreators" with God in the ongoing creation. "God blessed them, and God said to them, 'Be fruitful and multiply, and fill the earth and subdue it'" (1:28; see also 1:22 and 9:1). Thus, God's blessings are first an act through which he sustains creation and allows other beings to participate in creation.

God's blessings are also acts of reconciliation and redemption. According to Genesis 12–17, his election of Abraham, Sarah, and their offspring as the chosen people has a reconciling function. The family of Abraham and Sarah is chosen not merely for its own welfare but so that through it "all the families of the earth shall be blessed" (12:3). God's election of Israel therefore is about God's ongoing desire to be reconciled with the families of earth. Throughout Genesis, the ancestors experience blessings in many forms—from the fertility of their flocks to the appearance of water in their wells—as do others with whom they come into friendly contact. As the plot of Genesis unfolds, the blessing passes from Abraham and Sarah to Isaac, from Isaac and Rebekah to Jacob, and from Jacob to "the twelve tribes of Israel, . . . blessing each one of them with a suitable blessing" (49:28). As the blessing is passed down, so is the mission of the blessing. For example, after blessing Jacob, God appears to him and announces, "Your offspring shall be like the dust of the earth . . . ; and all the families of the earth shall be blessed in you and in your offspring" (28:14; see also 26:4).

In Genesis, God's blessings are also his redemptive gifts. Each of the female ancestors of Israel is described at one point as barren—Sarah, Rebekah, and Rachel. In the ancient world, the tragic reality was that being childless meant shame for a woman and also the possibility of having no one to care for her in old age. The granting of children to these barren women is understood in Genesis as an act of divine redemption and blessing: "I will bless [Sarah], and moreover I will give you a son by her" (17:16). Similarly, Genesis says that when Joseph languished as a slave in Potiphar's household or in prison, the Lord was with Joseph and "the LORD blessed the Egyptian's house for Joseph's sake; the blessing of the LORD was on all that he had" (39:5).

God's Faithfulness to His Promises

One more important theological theme should be emphasized—the God of Genesis makes and keeps promises. This notion is embedded deeply in themes that have already been developed. The making and keeping of promises is integral to the covenants. The plot of Genesis as the continual "endangering" of the threefold promises (land, descendants, blessing) has entirely to do with God's improbable means of keeping promises. The passing of the blessing to

redemption A theological term derived from commerce (where it means "purchase" or "buy back"); associated with the concept that human salvation was costly to God, requiring the death of Jesus.

election In theology, the notion or doctrine that people may be chosen by God for salvation or some predetermined destiny.

fertility A condition that results in abundance in agriculture, sustenance, and descendants.

shame A negative status, implying disgrace and unworthiness.

each generation and the unfolding of that blessing in the lives of both Israel's ancestors and those who come into friendly contact with them—this too is entirely about promises. But it is worth noting separately that the God of Genesis not only speaks creation into being with the word; he also primarily works through the making and keeping of promises.

Another way of naming this theme is to describe the faithfulness (or fidelity) of God. God is faithful and remains committed to his beloved creation. God is also faithful to Israel, in spite of its failings. God is faithful to the promises made to Abraham and Sarah.

Historical Interpretation

As noted in chapter 2, "The Old Testament Writings," we are distinguishing between two ways of approaching the Old Testament with historical questions. On the one hand, a reader can wonder about the historical world "behind the text." This approach inquires into the type of world and community that produced the book of Genesis and first read the book. On the other hand, a reader can inquire about the historical world "in the text." This second approach inquires into the world and history that the book itself describes. Both historical approaches have fruitful uses and both have their limitations. In this and subsequent chapters, we will consider the historical world both "behind the text" and "in the text."

In addition, historical approaches to Genesis are often interested in trying to reconstruct the history of the book of Genesis itself: Who wrote it? When, where, and in what stages did it develop? Questions about the historical development of Genesis are addressed in chapter 3, "The Pentateuch."

The Historical World behind the Text

What world and community produced the book of Genesis? What can we confidently or reasonably know about this world? When a reader inquires into the world behind Genesis, the text of Genesis is the place to start. More specifically, a reader can be alert to places in the text that seem to show the awareness of a gap between the events and epoch the story is narrating and the period when the story was being written or edited.

Taken at face value, the events narrated in Genesis occurred between 2000 and 1500 BCE. But there are several verses that seem aware of a historical gap between this period and the time when the text was written or edited:

- Genesis 12:6 says, "Abram passed through the land to the place at Shechem, to the oak of Moreh. At that time the Canaanites were in the land." This last sentence seems to indicate the book was written or edited at a time

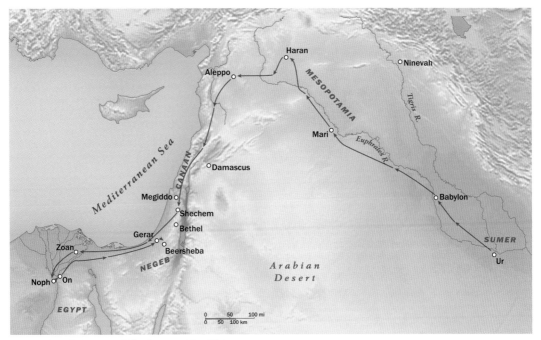

Map 4.1. Possible route of Abraham and Sarah's journeys

after the Canaanites were no longer in the land—that is, 1000 BCE at the earliest.

- Genesis 36:31 says, "These are the kings who reigned in the land of Edom, before any king reigned over the Israelites." This seems to indicate the book was written or edited after the institution of kingship was introduced in Israel—that is, sometime after 1020 BCE.
- Genesis 21:34 says, "Abraham lived as an immigrant in the Philistines' land for a long time" (CEB). The "Philistines' land" refers to an area on the southwest coast of the land of Israel around the cities of Gaza, Ashdod, Ashkelon, Ekron, and Gath. The Philistines did not migrate to this area until after 1175 BCE. So most likely the text in its final form dates from after this period.

Based on passages such as these, scholars conclude that the book of Genesis did not reach its final, edited form until a time long after the events it narrates. There are two important conclusions to draw from this observation.

First, even in the ancient world, there was a historical distance between the events, social practices and norms, and cultural contexts that are described in Genesis. This reminds the reader that Genesis requires cross-cultural interpretation. An informed reader needs to appreciate the challenges this poses. For example, the modern reader brings preconceived ideas about what a "person" is, or what a "family" is, or what it means or does not mean for a woman to be "barren." The conceptions that the reader brings may or may not equate with the ideas that the community that produced Genesis had. A careful reader attempts to be aware of the distance between one's own ideas and the text's ideas.

Second, the distance between the historical world in the text and the historical world behind the text as Genesis reached its final form suggests that, at the very least, the book of Genesis preserves some very old traditions. Some of these are discussed below.

The Historical World in the Text

Genesis portrays Israel's ancestors as engaging in many practices that later were not practiced—and some of which were explicitly prohibited by biblical law. For instance, the male ancestors are portrayed as having multiple wives. But in postexilic, Second Temple Judaism, the norm was to be married to one wife. Furthermore, Jacob marries two sisters, Leah and Rachel (see Gen. 29). But later biblical law prohibits this practice: "You shall not take a woman as a rival to her sister" (Lev. 18:18). Similarly, the second of the Ten Commandments prohibits making or worshiping idols or other graven images. But Jacob's wife Rachel steals "her father's household gods" (that is, his graven-image idols; see Gen. 31:19, 30–35).

There are other examples of this sort of thing. That the book of Genesis describes the ancestors engaging in practices that are contrary to Israel's laws and in behaviors that may have been embarrassing to Israel suggests that the traditions in Genesis were ancient even when the book reached its final form. For the most part, it is impossible to date just how old the traditions in Genesis are. It may be reasonable to guess that the traditions date from the second millennium BCE.

But one more caveat needs to be noted. In terms of understanding the meaning of the Genesis narratives, it is at best limiting and at worst completely misleading to ask only historical questions such as, Is this exactly the way it happened? Sometimes historical questions may not be the best questions.

As an example, consider how Genesis describes the ages of various people. Early in Genesis, people are described as living incredibly long lives. Adam is said to be 930 years old when he dies (5:5). Methuselah, the longest lived of the ancients, lives to age 969 (5:23). As the book of Genesis develops, people generally live shorter and shorter lives. God decrees that the measure of human lives shall be 120 years (6:3), but for a few more chapters characters still live to be far older than that. Abraham is said to be about 100 years old when Isaac is born, with Sarah nearly as old—well past childbearing years. Are these dates to be taken at face value? Were Abraham and Sarah literally that old? Perhaps there are other meanings in the reported ages. Perhaps the mostly consistent decline in the reported age of characters is a signal that the narrative is moving away from the more mythic stories of creation toward that which is more historical.

Perhaps the point is not precisely that Abraham and Sarah were literally 100 and 90 when Isaac was born but that the birth of Isaac was miraculous—occurring when it should have been physically impossible.

A final question about "the historical world in the text." To what degree can readers consider Abraham, Sarah, Hagar, Ishmael, Isaac, Rebekah, Jacob, Rachel, Leah, and the rest as genuinely historical people? As the plot of Genesis moves from the prehistorical accounts of the beginnings of creation and life, the narrative clearly communicates that the story is moving into history. Some interpreters regard the ancestral figures and the stories about them as completely genuine, and they argue that persons of faith must believe every detail of the stories. Other interpreters regard the ancestral figures as completely legendary with no historical validity—similar to the Greek story of Hercules, the German saga of Siegfried and Kriemhild, or the tale of Atlantis.

Still other interpreters choose a middle road between the two extremes. They regard the ancestors as historical figures, around whom layers of tradition and stories have grown. There was a time when modern skeptics believed that the city of Troy (with the story of the Trojan horse) never existed. Other skeptics regarded the Norwegian tales of the explorer Leif Erikson's voyages to what is now North America as purely legendary. But archaeology has provided evidence both of Troy and of Scandinavian settlements in North America. In a similar way, some interpreters believe that it is likely that Abraham, Sarah, Hagar, and the rest once walked the earth.

archaeology The study of human history and prehistory through the excavation of sites and analysis of artifacts, material culture, and other physical remains.

FOR FURTHER READING: Genesis

Brueggemann, Walter. *Genesis.* Interpretation: A Bible Commentary for Teaching and Preaching. Atlanta: John Knox, 1986.

Fretheim, Terence E. *Abraham: Trials of Family and Faith.* Studies on Personalities of the Old Testament. Columbia: University of South Carolina Press, 2007.

Galambush, Julie. *Reading Genesis: A Literary and Theological Commentary.* Macon, GA: Smyth & Helwys, 2018.

Kvam, Kristen E., Linda S. Schearing, and Valarie H. Ziegler, eds. *Eve and Adam: Jewish, Christian, and Muslim Readings on Genesis and Gender.* Bloomington: Indiana University Press, 1999.

Sarna, Nahum M. *Genesis: The Traditional Hebrew Text with the New JPS Translation.* JPS Torah Commentary. Philadelphia: Jewish Publication Society of America, 2001.

Trible, Phyllis. *God and the Rhetoric of Sexuality.* Overtures to Biblical Theology. Philadelphia: Fortress, 1978.

Wenham, Gordon J. *Genesis 1–15.* Word Biblical Commentary 1. Waco: Word, 1987.

———. *Genesis 16–50.* Word Biblical Commentary 2. Waco: Word, 1994.

Exodus

The title "Exodus," which is related to the English word *exit*, means "going out." As Exodus begins, the people of Israel are held captive as slaves in Egypt. The book narrates how the Lord sets the people free from captivity and then makes them his own people by forging a new covenant with them at a wilderness mountain called Sinai. Exodus emphasizes God's liberating act whereby he claimed the people as his own. The Hebrew name for the book is *Shemot*, "names," and derives from the first words of the book: "These are the names of the sons of Israel who came to Egypt." This title emphasizes that the book of Exodus continues the story that began in the book of Genesis. It also points to the particular identity of the people whom God frees and claims in Exodus—this is not some generic people, just any people. This is a particular people, the tribes and family of Israel: Reuben, Simeon, Levi, Judah, Issachar, Zebulon, Benjamin, Dan, Naphtali, Gad, Asher, and Joseph—the sons of Jacob. Before Exodus was ever our story, it was their story.

The story that Exodus tells is the most important story in the Old Testament. It is the story of Israel's rescue from captivity by God's hand, and it is the story of the covenant God makes with Israel. The reason it is the most important story is because the exodus story is the foundational story that defines who God is and who Israel is. Forever after the exodus, the Lord is the one "who brought you out of the land of Egypt, out of the house of slavery" (Exod. 20:2). Corresponding to this, Israel is the people whom God brought out of Egypt: "You are a people holy to the Lord your God; the Lord your God has chosen you out of all the peoples on earth to be his people, his treasured possession. . . . The Lord has brought you out with a mighty hand, and redeemed you from the house of slavery, from the hand of Pharaoh king of Egypt" (Deut. 7:6, 8b).

When the prophets need to remind Israel who they are or who God is, they invoke the exodus because it is Israel's foundational story. This is true when a prophet wants to admonish Israel with a word of judgment:

> O my people, what have I done to you?
> > In what way have I wearied you? Answer me!
> For I brought you up from the land of Egypt,
> > and redeemed you from the house of slavery. (Mic. 6:3–4a)

This is also true when a prophet wants to proclaim a message of hope and deliverance:

> When Israel was a child, I loved him,
> > and out of Egypt I called my son. . . .
> Yet it was I who taught Ephraim to walk;
> > I took them up in my arms,
> > but they did not know that I healed them.
> I led them with bands of human kindness,
> > with cords of love. . . .
> My heart winces within me;
> > my compassion grows warm and tender. (Hosea 11:1, 3–4, 8c CEB)

Because the book of Exodus tells Israel's foundational story, it is also one of the most overtly theological books in the Old Testament, and even in the whole Bible. That is, its stories, laws, poems, and descriptions make explicitly theological claims—claims about who the God of Israel is, who Israel is in relationship to God, what a right relationship with God looks like, how God's people regard and treat their neighbors, where God's presence is to be found, and what that presence is like.

Background

Composition and Development

Like many biblical books, the book of Exodus is anonymous, though Moses is said to write at least portions of it (see Exod. 34:27–28; 38:21). According to ancient tradition, Moses was the author of the book, a fitting tradition because he is the main human character in Exodus. Chapter 1 narrates his birth, and for the rest of the book he is the dominant human figure.

Many scholars today do not consider Moses the author of Exodus. Among the many reasons for this conclusion is that the narrative is told in third person about Moses: "Moses went down from the mountain to the people. He consecrated the people" (19:14). If Moses were both the author and the main character, one would expect a first-person narrative: "I went down from the mountain to the people. I consecrated the people." For other reasons scholars do not regard Moses as the author of Exodus, see chapter 3, "The Pentateuch."

The most widely accepted scholarly view is that the book of Exodus we have today, like other books of the Pentateuch, is the end product of a lengthy and complicated history. The book certainly contains many ancient traditions, but it very likely reached its final form sometime shortly after the people returned from the Babylonian exile (ca. 539 BCE). The book was then preserved, copied, and disseminated by scribes who did so because the book's narratives and laws communicated the very identity of the people, God's "treasured possession out of all the peoples" (Exod. 19:5).

Genre

The book of Exodus is composed of several types of literature: narratives about the people's escape from Egypt and years wandering in the desert, laws that form Israel's basic identity, cultic descriptions that detail Israel's most sacred worship spaces and objects, and a few poems that express the heart of Israel's ancient faith.

Literary Interpretation

The exodus: God rescues the people from Egypt (Exod. 1:1–15:21). The story of Exodus takes off with one of the most famous and haunting lines in the Bible: "Now a new king arose over Egypt, who did not know Joseph" (1:8). The narrative never supplies the name of this new pharaoh. Based on some internal clues in Exodus, the most likely guess is Pharaoh Ramesses II (ca. 1290–1224 BCE). The narrative mostly refers to the king by using the anonymous title "Pharaoh." This may be intentional, a sort of ancient equivalent of "the Man"—referring to an authority only by title communicates the coldness of the relationship between the one in power and those under his power. Referring to Pharaoh by name is not necessary. As the great Old Testament scholar Walter Brueggemann has often quipped to us, "You meet one Pharaoh, you've met them all."

Pharaoh's two dominant traits are ignorance and fear. He is ignorant of history in that "he did not know Joseph." That is, he does not know of all the blessings that accrued to Egypt through the gifts of Joseph—who is now long dead. He does not know that Israel was extended a hospitable welcome by a past pharaoh (see Gen. 45:16–20; 47:1–6). He is also ruled by fear that the Israelites have grown too numerous: "Look, the Israelite people are more numerous and more powerful than we" (Exod. 1:9). Therefore, Pharaoh's regime begins a systematic oppression and genocide of the Israelites—ruthlessly imposing labor demands on the Israelites and ordering that all newborn boys be killed.

Pharaoh's oppression of the Israelites poses the major plot question of the first fifteen chapters: Who will be the lord of the Israelites—the Lord or Pharaoh? God's response to Pharaoh is to raise up a leader from among the Israelites—Moses, who fled Egypt because of a crime. Called by God, Moses returns to Egypt where he acts as God's agent in the struggle between the Lord and Pharaoh to see who will be lord of the Israelite people. After ten plagues, the Lord prevails, and Pharaoh lets the people go. But then Pharaoh changes his mind and makes one final attempt to retain Israel as slaves, which ends in disaster for Egypt and deliverance for Israel.

The undermining of Pharaoh's regime begins at the bottom of the social order, as Shiphrah and Puah—two enslaved, Hebrew midwives who "feared God" (1:17)—defy Pharaoh's order to murder the newborn boys. Among the newborns is Moses, whose mother places him in a basket and sets it afloat on

Fig. 5.1. At the beginning of Exodus, almost all of the action centers around women who resist Pharaoh's command to kill the Israelite slave boys upon birth.

the river when she can no longer hide him. Pharaoh's own daughter finds the baby and takes him into her household, and Moses's sister arranges for his own mother to be his wet nurse. "After Moses had grown up" (2:11), he killed an Egyptian who was beating a Hebrew slave. As a result, he flees Egypt.

Then comes another of the most famous lines from the Bible: "The Israelites were groaning under the bondage and cried out. . . . God heard their moaning, and God remembered His covenant with Abraham and Isaac and Jacob"

Box 5.2

The Name of God

In Exodus 3, God reveals the divine name to Moses. "God said to Moses, 'I AM WHO I AM.' He said further, 'Thus you shall say to the Israelites, "I AM has sent me to you."' God also said to Moses, 'Thus you shall say to the Israelites, "The LORD . . . has sent me to you": This is my name forever'" (vv. 13–15).

Most scholars believe that the name of God was originally pronounced something like *Yahweh* (*yah-wuh*). But because the second commandment warns against misusing God's name, relatively late during the Old Testament period the people stopped saying the name out loud and instead substituted the Hebrew word for "lord"—*adonai* (*ah-doe-nigh*)—for the name. To this day, many faithful Jews will not pronounce the divine name and will instead say "The Lord," or "The Name," or "*Ha-Shem*" (Hebrew for "The Name") in place of the divine name. Out of respect for Jews and Judaism, many Christians also decline to say the divine name. Most English translations of the Bible print "the LORD" (in small capital letters) wherever the Hebrew text has the divine name.

No ancient Israelite ever called God "Jehovah" (or Jahovah/Yahowah). In order to remind themselves never to say the divine name out loud, ancient Hebrew scribes printed the vowels to the Hebrew word <u>adonai</u> under the four consonants of the divine name—*yhwh*. Early translators of the Bible misunderstood this convention and mistakenly invented a new word made of the vowels of one word and the consonants of another. The term "Jehovah/Yahowah" results from taking the consonants from *Yahweh* (*Jhvh* in German) and vowels from *adonai* to create:

Yhwh + a o a = Yahowah (or Jehovah)

This was a mistake that began to appear in the thirteenth century CE. Jehovah was never God's name.

Even though the divine name is no longer pronounced by some observant Jews and many Christians who respect Jewish tradition, other Jews and Christians do use the name "Yahweh." Whether pronounced or not, the name remains important for both rabbinic Judaism and Christianity. As two scholars recently wrote, "The name Yahweh . . . is the center of the Old Testament." The gift of the name allows people to say both what God is and what God is not. "The proper name of this God names God's distinctive character and the presence invoked by those who place their lives under his name."*

In this book, we use "Yahweh" and "the Lord" (no small caps) interchangeably.

* Reinhard Feldmeier and Hermann Spieckermann, *God of the Living: A Biblical Theology*, trans. Mark E. Biddle (Waco: Baylor University Press, 2011), 23, 25.

(2:23–24 NJPS). The Lord, who is faithful to his divine promises, remembers the promises he gave to the ancestors.

God then calls Moses. Speaking out of a bush that burns yet is not consumed, God says, "The cry of the Israelites has now come to me. . . . So come, I will send you to Pharaoh to bring my people, the Israelites, out of Egypt" (3:9–10). Moses resists God's call, but God is persistent. God reveals his divine name—Yahweh—to Moses and equips Moses with abilities to perform miraculous signs. Moses still defers, claiming that he is not much of a public speaker. God provides his brother, Aaron, to speak for him, and in the end, Moses relents to God's will and accepts the call.

Exodus 4–15 narrates the conflict between Pharaoh and the Lord to determine whose people Israel will be—will Israel serve the enslaving Pharaoh, or will Israel serve the liberating Lord? The contest includes several famous

Box 5.3

The Ten Plagues

The ten plagues that God unleashes against Egypt are among the most memorable motifs in the story. They include the following:

Water to blood	7:14–25
Frogs	8:1–15
Gnats	8:16–19
Flies	8:20–32
Livestock diseased	9:1–7
Boils	9:8–12
Hail	9:13–25
Locusts	10:1–20
Darkness	10:21–29
Death of firstborn sons	11:1–12:32

Readers often miss two points. First, the plagues lift up creation's involvement in Israel's liberation and Egypt's judgment. God does not act alone in these instances but acts in partnership with creational forces that operate as his agents. Second, ancient Jewish interpreters recognized that the plagues are organized according to an intentional and literarily significant structure. The first nine plagues fall into three cycles (1–3, 4–6, 7–9). The first, fourth, and seventh plagues begin with God commanding Moses to stand before Pharaoh in the morning (7:15; 8:20; 9:13). Each cycle, moreover, contains a purpose clause at the beginning indicating why the plagues were sent: "By this you shall know that I am the LORD" (7:17); "that you may know that I the LORD am in this land" (8:22); "so that you may know that there is no one like me in all the earth" (9:14). These purpose clauses answer Pharaoh's jeering question in Exodus 5:2: "Who is the LORD, that I should heed him and let Israel go? I do not know the LORD, and I will not let Israel go."

elements, including the sending of ten plagues, the "hardening of Pharaoh's heart," the first Passover, and the rescue of the people at the Red Sea. Returning to Egypt, Moses confronts Pharaoh, "Thus says the Lord, the God of Israel, 'Let my people go'" (5:1). Pharaoh refuses—"I do not know the Lord, and I will not let Israel go" (5:2)—and increases the suffering of Israel. In order to compel Pharaoh to relent, the Lord sends ten plagues against Egypt. Throughout the plagues, the narrative reports both that Pharaoh "hardened his heart" and that the Lord "hardened Pharaoh's heart."

Cosimo Roselli

Fig. 5.2. The story of the people worshiping the golden calf is often interpreted as the worship of a false god. In the story, however, Aaron forges the calf and then declares a "festival to the Lord" (32:5), suggesting that the calf was a false image not of a foreign god but of Yahweh, who was understood to be invisibly enthroned on the calf.

The last plague, the death of all firstborn sons, is also the first Passover. Every Israelite household slaughters a lamb and places the blood of the lamb on the doorposts so that the house would not be visited by death. Pharaoh at last lets Israel go but then changes his mind and sends his army after them. In a miraculous delivery, the Egyptians drown while the Israelites pass through the sea and escape into the desert.

The journey to Mount Sinai (Exod. 15:22–18:27). Immediately after their escape into the desert, the newly freed people turn on both Moses and God, complaining that they will starve or die of thirst. God provides both food and water.

The covenant at Mount Sinai (Exod. 19:1–24:18). Exodus 19–20 describes a new covenant. At Mount Sinai, God reestablishes a covenantal relationship with the people. He promises as part of this covenant—often called the Sinaitic or Mosaic covenant—that the people will be "my treasured possession" (19:5). The covenant includes a mission: "You shall be for me a priestly kingdom and a holy nation" (19:6). This covenant includes moral requirements: the Lord gives the Ten Commandments as relational requirements that come with Israel's election as God's people. And like earlier covenants, the covenant includes a sign. Here, the sign is the keeping of the Sabbath (31:16–17).

Israel's worship and the presence of God (Exod. 25:1–40:38). The bulk of the book's remaining chapters is dedicated to the giving of more laws and descriptions of Israel's sacred spaces, personnel (priests), and objects (Exod. 24–31, 34–40).

One dramatic event is narrated in Exodus 32—the story of Aaron and the forging of a golden calf. While Moses is on the mountain receiving divine instruction, the people lose confidence that he will return. They demand that

Moses's brother, Aaron, make a god that they can see. In response to the people's request, Aaron makes a golden calf and declares a "festival to the LORD" (32:5). The Lord is initially of a mind to abandon Israel, who so quickly violated the covenant. But Moses intercedes on the people's behalf, reminding the Lord of the divine promises to Abraham, Isaac, and Jacob. "And the LORD changed his mind about the disaster that he planned to bring on his people" (32:14). The Lord renews the covenant and sends the people from Sinai.

Before leaving Sinai, the people construct the tabernacle (a tent that served as a moving temple), the ark of the covenant (the wooden box in which the tablets of the Ten Commandments were kept), and other key sacred items.

Decalogue A synonym for the Ten Commandments.

The book closes with a description of the "glory of the LORD" descending and filling the tabernacle. Thus, the story that started with God hearing

---

Box 5.4

The Ten Commandments

The Ten Commandments are the most famous legal-ethical code in history. Although many different religious traditions honor the Ten Commandments, various traditions have numbered the commandments differently. The Hebrew text of Exodus 20 does not number the individual commandments. But based on Exodus 34:28, it is clear that the tradition of "ten commandments" is ancient: "[Moses] wrote on the tablets the words of the covenant, the ten commandments." In Jewish tradition, the Decalogue is called the "Ten Words"— note that the first word is not a commandment but a statement about Yahweh and his relationship to Israel. There are at least three major ways of numbering the commandments:

Jewish	Catholic, Lutheran, Orthodox	Reformed, Anglican, Other Protestants
1. I am the Lord your God.		
2. Have no other gods (and make no graven images).	1. Have no other gods (and make no graven images).	1. Have no other gods.
		2. Make no graven images.
3. Do not misuse God's name.	2. Do not misuse God's name.	3. Do not misuse God's name.
4. Keep the Sabbath.	3. Keep the Sabbath.	4. Keep the Sabbath.
5. Honor father and mother.	4. Honor father and mother.	5. Honor father and mother.
6. Do not murder.	5. Do not murder.	6. Do not murder.
7. Do not commit adultery.	6. Do not commit adultery.	7. Do not commit adultery.
8. Do not steal.	7. Do not steal.	8. Do not steal.
9. Do not bear false witness against a neighbor.	8. Do not bear false witness against a neighbor.	9. Do not bear false witness against a neighbor.
10. Do not covet your neighbor's spouse or house.	9. Do not covet your neighbor's spouse.	10. Do not covet your neighbor's spouse or house.
	10. Do not covet your neighbor's house.	

Box 5.5

The Plots of Exodus

The book of Exodus has three major plotlines.

A continuation of Genesis. The opening lines of the book of Exodus indicate that the narrative continues the story that begins in Genesis: "These are the names of the sons of Israel who came to Egypt with Jacob, each with his household." As we recounted in chapter 4, "Genesis," the plot of Genesis revolves around God's promises to Abraham: descendants who will be a great nation, a promised land, and a blessing through which all the families of the earth shall be blessed (Gen. 12:1–3). The plot advances as the promises are endangered in many and various ways and as God finds unexpected and gracious ways to keep the promises. But the book closes with the twelve sons of Jacob and their households dwelling in Egypt rather than in the promised land. A famine had chased them out of the land. The reason they found hospitable welcome in Egypt was because Joseph, one of Jacob's sons, had used his God-given gifts to serve Pharaoh. As Pharaoh was blessed on account of Joseph, Joseph had risen until he was "ruler over all the land of Egypt" (45:26).

Exodus's opening lines also note that Abraham and Sarah's descendants are well on the way to becoming a great nation, as the people have grown from the original couple: "The total number of people born to Jacob was seventy" (Exod. 1:5). After the death of Joseph and his entire generation, an unspecified time passes (according to Exod. 12:40, the duration of the sojourn in Egypt was 430 years). During these years, the Israelites were busy: "The Israelites were fruitful and prolific; they multiplied and grew exceedingly strong, so that the land was filled with them" (1:7). This report echoes God's imperative in the creation story that humankind is to "be fruitful and multiply, and fill the earth" (Gen. 1:28). Ominously, the Israelites' faithfulness to the divine command leads, in part, to Pharaoh's attention: "Behold, the people of Israel are too many and too mighty for us" (1:9 ESV). The note that "the land was filled with them" reminds the reader, however, that they are in the wrong land: they are in Egypt rather than God's promised land.

Who is lord of Israel—Pharaoh or God? The first fifteen chapters of Exodus are devoted to a contest between Pharaoh and God to determine who will be lord of Israel. As noted earlier, this conflict is prefigured in Pharaoh's question, "Who is the LORD, that I should heed him and let Israel go?" (5:2). The subsequent plagues are a response to Pharaoh's questions and a demonstration that Yahweh is the true sovereign over Israel.

Can Israel belong to God? Another plot element begins in Exodus 16, after the people are freed from Egypt. This layer of plot can be defined by the following questions: Can Israel belong to God? Does Israel have what it takes to trust God's guidance and follow God into a new future? Does Israel have what it takes to be in relationship with God? Can Israel be faithful to the God who set them free? What will God do in response to Israel?

Exodus also has smaller stories and plotlines that either contribute to the larger plots or act as excurses within the broader narrative. The smaller stories are worth reading and understanding in their own right. But it is also often the case that it is fruitful to inquire how the smaller stories contribute to the overall plotlines. As an example, Exodus 18 tells the relatively long story of how the responsibilities of leadership exhaust Moses. His father-in-law, Jethro, advises him to delegate authority to various "middle-manager" figures, who can then share the burdens of leadership. The story has meaning on its own, but within the broader sweep of Exodus and the Old Testament, the story is a subtle reminder that finite, flesh-and-blood human beings—whether they are ill-intentioned like Pharaoh or well-intentioned like Moses—cannot alone be the leaders of the people; they need help. They are not able to bear up under the burdens of leadership. This plotline will return again in later books, when Israel demands (and is given) human kings.

Fig. 5.3. Charles Wilbert White portrays Harriet Tubman as "Black Moses," highlighting her role in helping to secure the freedom of enslaved African Americans in an exodus-like deliverance.

the groans of the people in Egypt ends with God living among God's chosen people.

Theological Interpretation

God the Deliverer and Israel the Delivered

The dominant theological theme of the book of Exodus is deliverance. The God we meet in Exodus is the one who delivers. The exodus act shows who God is—one who delivers the oppressed, frees the enslaved, and cares for the lost. The act also stamps Israel with an indelible identity: they are God's redeemed, delivered, freed people.

As mentioned at the beginning of this chapter, the exodus act forever reveals who God is. The God of the Old Testament is the God "who brought you up out of the land of Egypt, out of the house of slavery" (20:2). The only way to know the God of Israel is to know this story. The exodus story does not merely tell what God did once upon a time; it reveals who God is for all time. As the Old Testament interpreter Terence Fretheim has written, the God of Exodus "is the champion of the poor and those pushed to the margins of life; God is the one who liberates them from the pharaohs of this world. As God acted then, so God can be expected to act again."[1] As the text of Exodus itself says, "God heard their groaning. . . . God looked upon the Israelites, and God took notice of them" (2:24).

For this reason, oppressed communities throughout history, throughout the world have found hope in this story. The word *found* is not even quite right. The story has given hope; it has injected hope and life into hopeless, mostly dead, and marginalized communities.

The political dimension of the exodus story must not be ignored. In the United States, many churches have tacitly agreed to leave political questions on the sideline. "No politics in the pulpit," the motto goes. In these contexts, the story of the exodus is often spiritualized. "God, who delivered Israel" becomes "God, who delivers us from sin." While the mantra of no politics in the pulpit and the accompanying spiritualization of the exodus story have served the church well in many cases, the exodus story challenges those interpretations. God desires that people be free. Not only spiritually free, but politically and physically free.

Readers of Exodus are often troubled by the divine violence they find in the story. God destroys people and property to free his people from Egypt. But this violence is related to the matter of God's politics. The freedom that God desires for people is a flesh-and-blood, political freedom. At odds with God's intent are the pharaohs of this world, who hold flesh-and-blood people in physical, iron-fetters-and-chains bondage. When these two contradictory forces collide, there will be conflict. And at times, when the pharaohs harden their hearts and cling tightly to their slaves, God's liberating actions require violence to free those in bondage.

The purpose of divine violence in Exodus is freedom, and its duration is temporary. God does not conquer Egypt for the purpose of empire building but to free Israel from the emperor's grasp. Once this freedom is achieved, violence ceases.

Even so, many readers legitimately struggle with God unleashing such violence in Exodus. After all, when God is pictured as the source of destruction, is it not easy for God's people to claim his endorsement for their own violence? On the other hand, the divine violence in the exodus story signals that God is not at peace with the oppressive structures of the world. The world as it is does not reflect God's will, and God is prepared to act in order that slaves might be freed and the oppressed might know mercy.

Women Participating in God's Work

In the two opening chapters of Exodus, God is seemingly absent in the story of his people—though the text hints at his presence. The first hint comes in the first chapter with the statement that the Israelites had multiplied, become numerous, and filled the land—an allusion to the divine command in Genesis 1 to be fruitful, multiply, and fill the earth and also to the promise of descendants made to Abraham and Sarah. Although God's hand appears to be absent when Pharaoh oppresses his people, hints of his presence are found in the actions of several women.

First, there are Shiphrah and Puah—two enslaved Hebrew midwives. They "fear God" and therefore engage in a dangerous act of civil disobedience, refusing to kill the newborn boys. It is hard for the modern, Western mind to wrap itself around how revolutionary and countercultural this story would have been in the ancient world. In the social hierarchy of the time, it would have been almost impossible to imagine any more marginalized, powerless persons than Shiphrah and Puah. They are female, enslaved, from a marginalized ethnic group, and barren. Yet as a sign of their worthiness and participation in God's work, the narrative supplies their names, while Pharaoh's personal name is omitted.

Other women are integral to God's work in Exodus. Moses's mother, his sister (later identified as Miriam), and Pharaoh's daughter each have a part in the unlikely story of Moses's birth, his rescue from the river, and his survival into adulthood. Miriam plays a role later in the rescue of the people at the Red Sea (Exod. 15). She is identified there as a prophet—a sign that women could be public religious leaders in ancient Israel. Her song, "Sing to the Lord, for he has triumphed gloriously; horse and rider he has thrown into the sea" (15:21), comes in the narrative after the longer song of Moses (15:1–18), but many historical critics believe that her song is the earlier of the two. She offers the call to praise—"Sing to the Lord!"—and Moses lifts his voice in response—"I will sing to the Lord."

The role of women in Exodus is representative of a broader biblical theme of God working through the powerless and the least likely. In Exodus, this includes the women already mentioned, as well as Moses—the fugitive guilty of murder. Moses resists God's call both because he is afraid and because he does not possess the oratory gifts of a leader: "O my Lord, I have never been eloquent . . . ; but I am slow of speech and slow of tongue" (4:10). Perhaps we are to understand Moses as having a speech impediment. So God provides his brother, Aaron. In the same way that a prophet speaks for God, Aaron is to speak for Moses, an unlikely agent called by God.

Israel's Self-Critique: A "Stiff-Necked" People

In Exodus 32:9, God calls his newly freed people "stiff-necked." Not exactly a compliment. One powerful, recurring theme in Exodus is the unflattering ways in which Israel's own story reflects on Israel. To put it bluntly, in Exodus, God's people come off as an ungrateful, faithless, frightened, weak-willed lot. And that is the point.

When the fugitive Moses returns with the surprising news that God has commissioned him to lead the people out of Egypt, the Israelites are on board: "The people believed; and when they heard that the LORD had given heed to the Israelites and that he had seen their misery, they bowed down and worshiped" (4:31).

But when the going gets tough, their "belief" does not last long. Moses demands that Pharaoh let the people go, and the king responds by multiplying their sorrows. He commands his task masters, "You shall no longer give the people straw to make bricks, as before; let them go and gather straw. . . . But you shall require of them the same quantity of bricks" (5:7–8). What did the people expect—that Pharaoh would just let his slaves go? The people respond by blaming Moses and Aaron: "You have made us stink in the sight of Pharaoh" (5:21 ESV). And Moses himself implores God, "Why did you ever send me?" (5:22).

After the tenth plague, the death of the firstborn sons, Pharaoh lets the people go. But as they near the border of Egypt, Pharaoh changes his mind and leads his army in pursuit to recapture the Israelites. With Pharaoh's chariots bearing down on them, the Israelites again show little faith: "Was it because there are

Fig. 5.4. The deliverance of the people from slavery and Pharaoh's domination is the good-news moment of the Old Testament. The story signals who the Lord is: "I am the LORD your God, who brought you out of the land of Egypt, out of the house of slavery" (Exod. 20:2). The deliverance at the sea is a favorite scene for artists of all kinds.

no graves in Egypt that you have taken us away to die in the wilderness? . . . For it would have been better for us to serve the Egyptians than to die in the wilderness" (14:11–12).

In spite of the people's fear and lack of faith, God shows up and rescues them from Pharaoh's thundering chariots. But as soon as they are on the other side of the sea, the complaints resume. First, they complain about the lack of water: "What shall we drink?" (15:24). And God gives water. Next, it's the lack of food: "If only we had died by the hand of the LORD in the land of Egypt, when we sat by the fleshpots and ate our fill of bread; for you have brought us out into this wilderness to kill this whole assembly with hunger" (16:3). And God provides food. Then the people renew the water complaint: "Why did you bring us out of Egypt, to kill us and our children and livestock with thirst?" (17:3).

After arriving at Mount Sinai, the people enter into a covenant relationship with God and promise, "Everything that the LORD has spoken we will do" (19:8). Then God gives the Ten Commandments, which begin, "You shall have no other gods before me. You shall not make for yourself an idol" (20:3–4). But that is exactly what the people do. As Moses lingers on the mountaintop receiving instruction from the Lord, the people grow afraid and demand a god that they can see—an idolatrous depiction of Yahweh: "Come, make a god for

Box 5.6

National Founding Stories

Most nations airbrush their founding stories, conveniently leaving out the unflattering episodes and polishing up the flattering stories until they reflect a nearly perfect image. In the USA, we downplay the truth about founding fathers. Of the first ten presidents, eight owned slaves (only John Adams and his son John Quincy Adams did not). And we make up stories to portray these presidents as better than they were, such as the ahistorical account of George Washington cutting down the cherry tree and then saying, "I cannot tell a lie."

But Israel seeks to tell a different type of story—a true story about God and God's creation. This means, first and foremost, Israel must be relentless in telling the truth about itself. If Israel were to gloss over the unflattering parts of its own story, who would believe it? We might paraphrase the story as follows: "We are God's chosen people. But God didn't choose us and remain faithful to us because of any redeeming qualities in us. God chose us and rescued us in order that we might be his 'priestly kingdom' and a 'holy nation,' a means of blessing all the families of the world. What did we do in response? We complained, feared, rebelled, and would gladly have returned to slavery. But God was faithful and would not let us go. In spite of our stubborn resistance to his choice of us, God remained faithful. But to this very day, we remain God's stiff-necked people."

us, who shall go before us" (32:1, modified).[2] It is this particular action that provokes God to call Israel "stiff-necked" (v. 9). But even this was forgiven: "And the LORD changed his mind about the disaster he planned to bring on his people" (v. 14).

This extended theme of Israel's stubborn, stiff-necked rebellion against God is remarkable. What other nation tells their founding story with such honesty?

The Gracious Gift of the Law

Many people who live in so-called developed countries take the law for granted. Sometimes we take it so much for granted that we start to think of the law as a set of unnecessary burdens.

But imagine what it would be like to live in a culture with little or no law. In such a society, the strong could take what they wanted from the weak—their land, property, even their children. A grocer might sell spoiled food, or a farmer might sell diseased livestock—and nobody could do anything about it. There would be no traffic laws to facilitate safe travel. And so on.

Beginning in the book of Exodus, God bestows an enormous blessing on the people: divine law. The Israelite people came into being during a time in which some law codes were known, the most famous of which is the Code of Hammurabi. Israel's law codes have some similarities with these other law codes, yet they also have one major difference: the Ten Commandments—a concise list of universal prohibitions and duties. There seems to be nothing quite like the Ten Commandments among the laws of Israel's neighbors.

Some biblical scholars have found it helpful to differentiate between absolute law (also called *apodictic* or *universal law*), on the one hand, and conditional law (also called *casuistic* or *case law*), on the other hand.

Scholars use the term *absolute law* to refer to laws that are universal (or at least close to universal). These laws are universal/absolute because they are to be kept at all times and in all places. The Ten Commandments are absolute law. You shall not kill (ever). You shall not commit adultery (ever). You shall not steal (ever). Other absolute laws include "You shall love the LORD your God with all your heart, and with all your soul, and with all your might" (Deut. 6:5) and "Love your neighbor as yourself" (Lev. 19:18). In the Bible, the terms *command*, *word*, or *law* (Hebrew: *torah*) are used for the absolute law. The absolute law functions like the US Constitution: it names Israel's highest values, principles, and rights.

Scholars use the terms *conditional* and *casuistic* to refer to laws that only apply in certain circumstances. These laws often include "if" or "when" clauses: "When you see the donkey of one who hates you lying under its burden and you would hold back from setting it free, you must help to set it free" (Exod. 23:5).

Box 5.7

Ancient Near Eastern Law Codes

Israel's laws must be understood in the context of other ancient law codes, such as the Code of Hammurabi (ca. 1750 BCE), the Code of Ur-Nammu (ca. 2050 BCE), the Laws of Eshnunna (ca. 1930 BCE), the laws of Lipit-Ishtar (ca. 1870 BCE), and the Hittite laws (ca. 1650 BCE). These codes most likely developed as summaries of judicial decisions made by rulers and other judges.

These codes are both similar and dissimilar to Israel's law codes. Unlike Israelite law, they lack anything like the Ten Commandments—a brief, clear set of universal prohibitions and duties. But like Israelite law, the codes contain many examples of specific judicial decisions pertaining to common legal problems. Most of the laws in the Code of Hammurabi begin, "If a man . . ." Here are two famous laws from the Code of Hammurabi that are very similar to biblical laws:

- "If a man destroy the eye of another man, they shall destroy his eye. If one break a man's bone, they shall break his bone. If one destroy the eye of a freeman or break the bone of a freeman he shall pay one mana of silver. If one destroy the eye of a man's slave or break a bone of a man's slave he shall pay one-half his price" (law no. 196). Compare Exodus 21:23–24: "If any harm follows [a fight], then you shall give life for life, eye for eye, tooth for tooth, hand for hand, foot for foot, burn for burn, wound for wound, stripe for stripe."

- "If an ox, while going along the street, gore a man and cause his death, no claims of any kind can be made. If a man's ox be addicted to goring and have manifested to him his failing, that it is addicted to goring, and, nevertheless, he have neither blunted his horns, nor fastened up his ox; then if his ox gore a free man and cause his death, he shall give 30 shekels of silver. If it be a man's slave, he shall give 20 shekels of silver" (law no. 250). Compare Exodus 21:28–30: "When an ox gores a man or a woman to death, the ox shall be stoned, and its flesh shall not be eaten, but the owner of the ox shall not be liable. But if the ox has been accustomed to gore in the past, and its owner has been warned but has not kept it in, and it kills a man or a woman, the ox shall be stoned, and its owner also shall be put to death. If a ransom is imposed on him, then he shall give for the redemption of his life whatever is imposed on him" (ESV).*

In comparison, Deuteronomy reads, "For what other great nation has a god so near to it as the LORD our God is whenever we call to him? And what other great nation has statutes and ordinances as just as this entire law that I am setting before you today?" (Deut. 4:7–8).

* Translations of the Code of Hammurabi are from Martha T. Roth, *Law Collections from Mesopotamia and Asia Minor*, Writings from the Ancient World (Atlanta: Society of Biblical Literature, 1995).

These laws are conditional because they are for specific times, places, people, and circumstances. In terms of times, there are laws that apply to the annual religious festivals (see Exod. 23:14–19), to the maximum term that a person can be held in slavery (Deut. 15:12–18), to the "year of jubilee," when all property that had been sold is returned to permanent owners (Lev. 25:8–55), and so on. In terms of places, there are laws concerning legitimate and illegitimate places of worship (Deut. 12:1–27); "cities of refuge," where people could seek asylum (Deut. 19:1–13); property boundaries and disposition of fields (Exod. 21:28–36; Lev. 19:9–10; Deut. 19:14); and the like. In terms of people, there are laws concerning priests (Lev. 21:1–24), slaves (Deut. 15:12–18), judges (Deut. 17:8–13), kings (Deut. 17:14–20), captives (Deut. 21:10–14), the poor (Deut. 24:10–15, 17–18), and so on. In terms of circumstances, there are laws concerning harvest (Deut. 24:19–22), offerings (Lev. 22), war (Deut. 20), sex and marriage (Deut. 22:13–30; 24:1–5), and so on. In the Bible, the many conditional laws are referred to as *decrees*, *statutes*, *precepts*, *judgments*, and *ordinances*.

As Psalm 119 (a very long ode praising God's law) bears witness, Israel considered God's law a gracious gift:

> I treasure your word in my heart. . . .
> I delight in the ways of your decrees
>   as much as in all riches. (Ps. 119:11, 14)

Israel believed that through the law, God was acting to create a more just society and to set apart Israel as a "holy nation" that mirrored God's holiness.

The Creator God

The Old Testament scholar Terence Fretheim has argued persuasively that "a theology of creation" is a major theme in Exodus. Noting that the theme of creation is overlooked in many studies of Exodus, Fretheim argues that the book is actually "shaped in a decisive way by a creation theology."[3]

It is the Creator God who hears Israel's cries and moves to rescue the people from slavery. Moreover, the people themselves attract Pharaoh's fearful gaze precisely because they are faithful to the creative imperative to be fruitful, multiply, and fill the earth. It is also creation theology that "provides the *cosmic purpose* behind God's redemptive activity on Israel's behalf."[4] Because Israel has a divinely bestowed role to play in God's redemptive purposes for creation, he moves to save Israel: "But this is why I have let you live: to show you my power, and to make my name resound through all the earth" (9:16). Exodus 9:29 says, "The earth is the LORD's," and the exodus story is part of the longer story of God working to redeem the rebellious creation.

The creation theme is also evident in that elements of God's creation are integral to the conflict between God and Pharaoh. Pharaoh attempts to subjugate part of God's creation (Israel), and his means of pursuing this ungodly goal is anticreational: the murder of newborn children. Because God has a creational purpose for Israel and because God is Creator of all, he harnesses elements of the good creation—water, frogs, gnats, flies, livestock, boils, hail, darkness, locusts, and the firstborn—to contest Pharaoh's false claim to lordship over Israel. The miraculous delivery at the sea and the provision of food and water in the wilderness continue the creative theme. The description in chapters 25–31 of the tabernacle as God's proscribed means of being present in creation is contrasted with Aaron's forging of the golden calf in chapter 32. The use of gold to image the Creator is doomed to fail because the Creator cannot be contained in a created image.

The book ends with a description of the descent of the divine glory in fire and clouds, placing a literary exclamation point on the theme of creation: "For the cloud of the LORD was on the tabernacle by day, and fire was in the cloud by night" (40:38). Again, Fretheim notes, "Redemption is for the purpose of creation, a new life within the larger creation, a return to the world as God intended it to be."[5]

The Lord: A God of Covenant and Fidelity

As noted above, in the book of Exodus God reveals the divine name—Yahweh, "the LORD"—to the people. Along with the divine name, the narrative of Exodus also reveals God's character. God's actions speak more clearly about who he is than any creed—through the acts of hearing their cries and rescuing Israel from the house of slavery in Egypt, of guiding and providing for them in the wilderness, of entering into covenant with them at Mount Sinai and giving them the law, and of continually being faithful in forgiving them and ignoring their stiff-necked rebellion. These actions—hearing and rescuing, guiding and providing, covenanting and giving law, forgiving and sustaining—communicate who the Lord is.

Yet Exodus 34 does contain an ancient, creed-like fragment. In the narrative, it is unclear whether Moses or the Lord is speaking, but a majority of interpreters view God as the speaker. The fragment is thus God's self-revelation: it provides his personal disclosure of the divine character:

> The LORD passed before him, and proclaimed,
>> "The LORD, the LORD,
>> a God merciful and gracious,
>> slow to anger,
>> and abounding in steadfast love and faithfulness,

creed A confessional statement summarizing key articles of faith.

revelation In theology, the disclosure (usually by God) of things that could not be known otherwise.

keeping steadfast love for the thousandth generation,
forgiving iniquity and transgression and sin,
yet by no means clearing the guilty,
but visiting the iniquity of the parents
upon the children
and the children's children,
to the third and the fourth generation." (Exod. 34:6–7)

The key theological terms that describe God's character are *merciful*, *gracious*, *steadfast love*, and *faithfulness*. Together, these terms define the character of the covenanting God whose name is the Lord as being made up of love and fidelity. To put it another way, the God who enters into a permanent covenantal relationship with Israel at Sinai is a God who is loving, forgiving, patient, and merciful. Punishment for violating the covenant will come, but God is slow to anger. When those punishments are given, they may last three or four generations, but God's loving fidelity will endure to "the thousandth generation."

The gift of the divine name—Yahweh, "the Lord"—and the creedal self-disclosure of the Lord's character go together. And together, these divinely disclosed gifts—name and character—allow the people of God to experience spirituality as a relationship with a personal God rather than as a vague, numinous presence or a set of relationships with multiple gods, some of whom war with each other. As Feldmeier and Spieckermann have written, the gift of the name provides the condition for a relationship with God. It designates God first as an "other" who is separate from creation but who is available and near within creation. The name "demarcates the boundary between God and human . . . [yet] makes the boundary passable in order to grant God's presence to those who request it."[6] And again, "The proper name of God names God's distinctive character and the presence invoked by those who place their lives under his name."[7]

Historical Interpretation

The Historical World behind the Text

What world and community produced the book of Exodus? What can we confidently or reasonably know about this world? Many of the answers to these questions will be the same as those given regarding the book of Genesis. But one additional point is worth noting: there is clearly a distance between the events narrated and the time when the narrative was written down. Some have concluded that although many of the traditions in Exodus are surely very old, the book in its final form was likely written down shortly before or after

540 BCE—when the Judean exiles who had been deported to Babylon began to make their way back to the promised land. If this conclusion is accurate, then the ancient story of the exodus may have served the exiles in a fashion very similar to its original purpose. The exiles would have had an easy time relating to the story of God's rescue of the chosen people from foreign soil to their restoration to the land. The pain of being held captive in a foreign land would have existentially connected with the exiles. All of the fear, lack of faith, complaining, and stiff-necked resistance to God's rescue would have made sense. And the promise of the redeeming God's faithfulness to Israel may have sparked hope in the hearts of at least some of the returnees.

The Historical World in the Text

As is the case with the book of Genesis, it seems clear that the book of Exodus preserves some very old traditions. The oldest of these traditions may have been the revelation of the divine name, the Ten Commandments and the book of the covenant legal code in Exodus 21–23, the creed-like fragment in Exodus 34, and the tradition of a people escaping from Egypt and fleeing to the land of Palestine.

The major question that many historical approaches put to the book of Exodus concerns the historicity of the exodus itself. Was there a pharaoh who enslaved the descendants of Jacob? Were Moses, Aaron, and Miriam historical figures, or are they better understood as mythic figures? Did a group of Israelites escape from Egypt, wander in the wilderness, and eventually come into the land? If so, what date can be assigned to the exodus?

Again, it should be maintained that historical questions such as these may not always be the most important or even the most interesting questions. Many books and studies have been dedicated to these questions, so only a few comments will be made here.

First, the traditional reading of the exodus story that imagines the entire people of Israel enslaved in Egypt and then the entire people of Israel crossing the Sea and wandering together in the wilderness needs to be held lightly. The entire "people" who understood themselves as ancient "Israelites" probably emerged from several earlier groups. Some probably escaped Egyptian tyranny. Others, like the women Rahab (Josh. 2), Tamar (Gen. 38), and Ruth, probably were Canaanites or Moabites who married into Israel or joined for other reasons. Others were probably wandering nomads who gave up the nomadic life and settled with Israel. Still others may have been people who dwelt in Canaanite cities and left to settle in more rural areas where ancient Israel was emerging in the land. And so on. That is to say that not all of the ancient Israelites descended exclusively from the people who escaped from Egypt. But

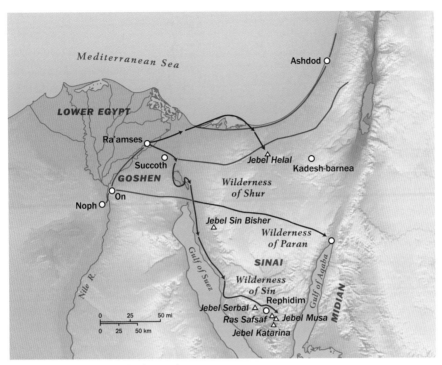

Map 5.1. Proposed routes for the exodus

when these foreigners joined Israel, the exodus story became their story—even if their "ancestors" were not technically present for the actual event. Because the exodus story is the paradigmatic story of who God is and who Israel is, the story became everyone's story.

A similar phenomenon can be seen in United States history. Not every American is descended from the early colonists who settled in northeastern North America following the journey of the *Mayflower* in 1620 or from early American leaders who signed the Declaration of Independence. Some Americans—American Indians—trace their presence in North America back thousands of years. Others trace their roots through Spanish settlers who settled in Florida, Central America, and California. Others trace their roots through enslaved Africans who were transported on slave ships. Others trace their roots through Asian immigrants who came from the Far East and traveled eastward across the Pacific. And so on. But national stories such as those of the landing at Plymouth Rock or the Fourth of July still capture the imaginations of many Americans. These founding narratives still shape the nation even though not everyone is descended from ancestors who were part of those stories. In a similar way, the exodus came to be the defining story of ancient

Israel, even though it is likely that only some ancient Israelites could trace their roots back to Egypt.

Second, many who inquire into the historical story in the text of Exodus seek to answer questions such as, Where was Mount Sinai? What route did the Israelites take to Sinai and then from Sinai to the land? What was the manna that the Israelites ate in the wilderness? And so on. As one could expect, there are multiple proposals in response to each question. As an example, see the map here, which identifies three proposed routes that the Israelites may have taken through the wilderness.

Third, a major question concerns when to date the exodus (if one accepts that it was a historical event). The two pharaohs of the exodus—the one who oppressed Israel and the one who refused to let them go—are not named. There are a couple of important points of reference that some historians use to try to date the event. First, a rough date can be hazarded based on the report that the Israelite slaves worked on the supply cities of Pithom and Rameses (Exod. 1:11). Because of archaeological dating of these cities, many historians date the events of Exodus to the fourteenth through thirteenth centuries BCE—although it is important to note that no archaeological evidence of the Israelites in Egypt has ever been unearthed.

A second point of reference historians use to date the exodus is the important archaeological artifact known as the Merneptah Stele. A stele is an inscribed stone monument. The stele in question describes the military victories of Pharaoh Merneptah, who reigned from 1213 to 1203 BCE. Most of the stele describes Merneptah's victories over the Libyans, but toward the end the narrative turns to the land of Canaan. The stele records the pharaoh's boast that "Israel is laid waste and his seed is no more."[8] This reference seems to place Israel in the land of Canaan by the year 1200 BCE, which means that the exodus must have occurred earlier.

Based on these two data, many scholars posit a date of around 1300–1220 BCE for the exodus.

FOR FURTHER READING: **Exodus**

Brenner, Athalya, ed. *A Feminist Companion to Exodus to Deuteronomy*. Feminist Companion to the Bible 6. Sheffield: Sheffield Academic Press, 1994.

Croatto, J. Severino. *Exodus: A Hermeneutics of Freedom*. Translated by Salvator Attanasio. 1981. Reprint, Eugene, OR: Wipf & Stock, 2021.

Dozeman, Thomas B., ed. *Methods for Exodus*. Methods in Biblical Interpretation. Cambridge: Cambridge University Press, 2010.

Durham, John I. *Exodus*. Word Biblical Commentary 3. Waco: Word, 1987.

Fretheim, Terence E. *Exodus*. Interpretation: A Bible Commentary for Teaching and Preaching. Louisville: John Knox, 1991.

Sarna, Nahum M. *Exodus: The Traditional Hebrew Text with the New JPS Translation*. JPS Torah Commentary. Philadelphia: Jewish Publication Society of America, 2004.

Leviticus

Here is a fun fact about the book of Leviticus: when Rob Bell founded Mars Hill Bible Church—which became one of the fastest growing and largest congregations in America—he preached through the book of Leviticus for the first year.[1] Readers who are even a little familiar with the book of Leviticus might be surprised . . . no, shocked . . . by this curious fact because much of what Leviticus is about—such things as (in Bell's words) "menstrual blood," "hold the pork," and "avoid road kill"—may seem absurdly irrelevant to life in the postmodern age. But it was not long until eight to eleven thousand people were worshiping weekly at Mars Hill in Grand Rapids, Michigan.

Here are more facts about Leviticus: The book contains one of the most well-loved laws in the Old Testament and also one of the most controversial laws. The well-loved law is one of the two laws that Jesus later said were the most important: "Love your neighbor as yourself" (Lev. 19:18). Both Judaism and Christianity adhere strongly to this law, as well as to certain other laws. The highly controversial law prohibits male homosexual activity: "You shall not lie with a male as with a woman" (Lev. 18:22). Within both Judaism and Christianity, there is intense debate over the status of this statute, as well as many other laws in Leviticus. As this indicates, a major issue for interpreters of Leviticus regards the degree (if any) to which these ancient laws are applicable to contemporary faith communities. More will be said on this later in the chapter.

The common English name for the book, Leviticus, comes from the book's title in ancient Greek translation—*leuitikos*—meaning, "concerning the Levites (Levitical priests)." This title may be slightly misleading because many of the regulations in Leviticus apply to the entire people, not just the Levites. But the title is very important, because it highlights the role of the Levitical priests as the means through which the identity and character of the people

The Levites

The Levites were Israel's priestly tribe. According to the Genesis narrative, Jacob (whose name was changed by God to "Israel") had twelve sons. Each of these sons became the ancestral father of one of the tribes of Israel. Eleven of these tribes were normal tribes—with each inhabiting a designated territory within Israel and with members serving as farmers, vinedressers, shepherds, warriors, and so on. But the tribe of Levi was a priestly tribe. It did not have a designated territory, although there were cities set aside for the Levites (Num. 35:1–8). The Levites did not own property or receive an inheritance of land, but were scattered among the other tribes, serving as priests in the cities, towns, and villages of Israel.

According to Exodus, the deliverer Moses came from the tribe of Levi (Exod. 2:1), and his brother, Aaron, became Israel's first high priest (29:1–9).

of Israel were both forged and maintained. Even though not all the laws of Leviticus concern only the Levites, the book does accentuate the reality that the stewardship of Israel's identity as a separate, holy people was entrusted in large part to its priests.

The Jewish name for the book of Leviticus—*Wayyiqra'*—is taken from the first word of the book in Hebrew: "and [the Lord] proclaimed." This title is an important signal about the meaning of Leviticus: the book is cast narratively as a lengthy set of ritual and legal requirements that the Lord dictated to Moses as soon as "the glory of the Lord" had descended into the midst of the "tent of meeting" in the midst of the people (Exod. 40:34).

Background

Composition and Development

Like most of the books of the Old Testament, the book of Leviticus is anonymous. Nowhere in its text is any author identified. But as the first words of the book imply—"the Lord proclaimed to Moses" (AT)—the book is cast as a series of statues that the Lord dictated to Moses. It is not surprising, then, that according to many traditions, Moses is considered the author of Leviticus. For reasons that are discussed in chapter 3, many modern critics no longer hold to this idea. As with the other books of the Pentateuch, the most widely accepted scholarly view is that the current book of Leviticus is the end product of a lengthy and complicated history.

It is clear that the book of Leviticus was copied, preserved, and disseminated by faithful Second Temple scribes in the years following the Babylonian exile. After the exile, major changes occurred in the identity and makeup of the chosen people. The Judeans ceased to be part of a geographical kingdom—living as an autonomous nation in one geographic area, ruled by a king. Instead, they became a widely dispersed people, held together primarily by religious customs and laws and led by priests. The book of Leviticus played a large role in forming this new identity. The importance of this point can hardly be overemphasized.

The book of Leviticus contains two major sections—chapters 1–16 and 17–27. Chapters 1–16 are often called the Priestly Code. Many scholars identify these chapters with the P (Priestly) source of the Pentateuch (see chap. 3 above). Chapters 17–27 are often called the Holiness Code ("H"), because of the oft-repeated statement in those chapters that the Israelites are to be holy as the Lord is holy: "You shall be holy, for I the LORD your God am holy" (19:2; see also 20:7–8, 26; 21:8, 23; 22:9, 16, 33).

Genre

The book of Leviticus is mainly composed of a variety of laws. These laws regulated Israel's worship life, the ethical conduct of all Israelites, and the community's purity. There are only two brief narrative passages in Leviticus. When all is said and done, Leviticus functions as a kind of priestly handbook, educating those designated for this important role.

Literary Interpretation

The book of Leviticus continues the story of Genesis and Exodus, but unlike Exodus, which begins several hundred years after the concluding events of Genesis, Leviticus is an immediate continuation of the events that conclude the book of Exodus. From a narrative perspective, basically no time at all elapses between Exodus and Leviticus. The last event that happens in Exodus is that "the glory of the LORD" descends and fills the tent of meeting. Because God's glory is now in the tent, Moses cannot enter. And yet God still has things to say to Moses (apparently, God did not say everything there was to say during the forty days that he instructed Moses on the mountaintop). So God starts speaking from within the tent while Moses, outside the tent, listens. The speech that God delivers is the entire book of Leviticus. Reading the last verses of Exodus and the first verses of Leviticus together illustrates this point:

> And the cloud covered the tent of meeting, and the glory of the Lord filled the tabernacle. Now Moses was unable to go into the tent of meeting because the cloud was in it, and the glory of the Lord filled the tabernacle. (Whenever the cloud was lifted up from the tabernacle, the children of Israel would set out on each stage

of their journey; but if the cloud was not lifted up, they would not set out until the day that it was lifted up. For the cloud of the Lord was on the tabernacle by day, and fire was in the cloud by night, before the eyes of all the house of Israel at each stage of their journey.) And he proclaimed to Moses, and the Lord spoke to him from the tent of meeting, saying, "Speak to the children of Israel and say to them . . ." (Exod. 40:34–Lev. 1:2a AT)

Thus, the book of Leviticus is cast as the first words that the Lord speaks to the people once he has taken up residence in their midst. As such, the book begins to flesh out a picture of what a people who are literally gathered around the word of the Lord will look like.

That Leviticus is to be read as a continuation of the story that began in Genesis and Exodus is made even more clear by the way the book immediately begins to detail ritual prescriptions, without offering any context for the rituals. In Leviticus 1–3, a series of ritual prescriptions is given for differing types of offerings—but the situations that would call for these various offerings are not explained. It is assumed that the audience already knows what situations would call for various offerings and who "the sons of Aaron" are:

- Leviticus 1 prescribes various "burnt offering" rituals (see vv. 3, 10, 14).
- Leviticus 2 prescribes various "grain offering" rituals (see vv. 1, 4, 11, 14).
- Leviticus 3 prescribes various "well-being" sacrifices (see vv. 1, 6, 12).
- Leviticus 4 prescribes various rituals for when different people "sin unintentionally" (see vv. 1, 3, 13, 22, 27, 32).

Dura-Europos synagogue

Fig. 6.1. The tabernacle and its priests (Jewish, third century CE)

It is worth noting that what qualifies as "sin" is not defined. Presumably, the reader of the narrative needs to refer back to Exodus—and especially to Exodus 20–23, the Ten Commandments and the book of the covenant—in order to understand what sin is.

Stories within Leviticus—Individual Laws as Brief Narratives

While scholars might have to struggle to find a plot in the book of Leviticus, the laws of Leviticus are often brief narratives in themselves. For example, consider the following regulation from Leviticus 4:22–26:

> When a ruler sins, doing unintentionally any one of all the things that by commandments of the LORD his God ought not to be done and incurs guilt, once the sin that he has committed is made known to him, he shall bring as his offering a male goat without blemish. He shall lay his hand on the head of the goat; it shall be slaughtered at the spot where the burnt offering is slaughtered before the LORD; it is a sin offering. The priest shall take some of the blood of the sin offering with his finger and put it on the horns of the altar of burnt offering, and pour out the rest of its blood at the base of the altar of burnt offering. All its fat he shall turn into smoke on the altar, like the fat of the sacrifice of well-being. Thus the priest shall make atonement on his behalf for his sin, and he shall be forgiven.

Notice that this law is a brief story. The regulation, like many laws in Leviticus, presents a hypothetical legal situation: "If x happens, a person shall do y." It describes "one thing" that might happen (in this case, the unintentional sin of the ruler), and then prescribes what "other thing" is to happen next (in this case, the gift of a goat to atone for the ruler's unintentional sin).

As readers approach these storylike laws in Leviticus, they are invited to imagine themselves or other people as the person in the story. Or, better yet, readers are invited to apply the brief narrative-like laws to their own stories. Thus, modern readers might ask themselves, What should I do when I unintentionally do something that might make me unclean or guilty? What does my religious community teach about what should be done in such a circumstance? In this way, the brief narrative-like laws can shape the stories of modern readers.

A Time for Instruction in Holiness

The most striking feature of the narrative of Leviticus is also one of the easier features to overlook—namely, that Leviticus encompasses an extended period of divine instruction during which Israel's journey from Egypt to the land is halted. In fact, the reception of the Levitical law at Sinai is the very center of the Pentateuch and its longest section. Think about it this way: Israel is standing

atonement In the context of Levitical law, atonement is most prominently associated with the Day of Atonement, a day of purification and confession when the people are cleansed before Yahweh.

at Sinai receiving the law from Exodus 19:2 to Numbers 10:11, at which point they depart from the mountain.

As noted above, the book of Exodus concludes with the description that "whenever the cloud was lifted up from the tabernacle, the children of Israel would set out on each stage of their journey." A reader might naturally expect the next book to pick up the story and detail the next stages of the journey toward the land. But the journey does not commence until the book of Numbers. For the entirety of Leviticus, the journey stops as Israel receives divine instruction through Moses. The narrative's long delay in the journey emphasizes how important Israel considered the gift of the law. As we will explore next, the law was divine instruction for Israel concerning what it meant for Israel to belong to God.

Theological Interpretation

Leviticus is highly technical, detailed literature that was originally intended for priestly use on behalf of the people. But theological riches are buried in the details.

The Holy God and a People Made Holy by God

The two most enduring theological themes in the book of Leviticus are holiness and divine law—and these two themes are related. The relationship between them can be seen in the way the narrative introduces and concludes the important set of laws in Leviticus 19. These laws are introduced: "The LORD said to Moses, 'Speak to the entire assembly of Israel and say to them: "Be holy because I, the LORD your God, am holy"'" (19:1–2 NIV). The chapter concludes: "I am the LORD your God, who brought you out of Egypt. Keep all my decrees and all my laws and follow them. I am the LORD" (19:36b–37 NIV).

Because the Lord is holy, the people in whose midst the Lord chose to dwell must be holy also. That is, the human community that the Lord gathers around the divine presence must take on the character of the Lord. The Lord is holy, so the people must be holy. And how does the Lord transfer the divine attribute of holiness to the people? By dwelling in their midst and giving the law. In order to withstand the holiness of God, the people must be holy.

At this point, we must be very careful. Leviticus does not say that by keeping the law people become holy or that by keeping the law people can become more and more holy. Rather, the keeping of the law is itself holiness. By keeping the law, the human community shares in God's holiness. The distinction made here is nuanced but vital. An example from the realm of music may help. When people sing or play music, they participate in the music—they do

Box 6.3

Common Offerings in Leviticus

Type of Offering	Description and Relevant Texts
Sin offering	For unintentional violations of Yahweh's law (4:1–35)
Guilt offering	A type of sin offering that required reparations and a 1/5 penalty (5:14–26)
Burnt offering	A dedicatory offering that took place on the north side of the altar (1:3–16)
Grain offering	A dedicatory offering made of choice flour, oil, and frankincense (2:1–16)
Well-being offering	A voluntarily offering expressing gladness and gratitude, with specific regulations related to how the meat should be consumed (3:1–17; 7:11–36)

not become the music. People can never *be music* itself. But as they sing, they experience music. In the thought-world of Leviticus, God's holy nature is like that. God alone is holy. People themselves can never *be holy* in the way God is. But by practicing God's holy law, the people experience and participate in God's holiness.

Atonement

Even though Leviticus understands the keeping of the law as the practice through which people experience and share in God's holiness, it also knows and teaches that human beings cannot keep the law with perfection. In fact,

William Holman Hunt

Fig. 6.2. This depicts the Jewish ritual of the Day of Atonement described in Leviticus 16 and 22. The red wool around the base of the goat's horns represents the sins of the people.

Box 6.4

Atonement

It has become something of a cliché to begin discussions of atonement by pointing out that the term derives from the combination of the words *at + one* in Middle English. But as the linguistic background of the term shows, "atonement" refers to the reconciliation between God and humans that is necessary because of the disruptive power of human sins.

The word is especially important in Leviticus, where rituals are described in which the Levitical priest can offer a sacrificial offering in atonement for a person's (or persons') sins. The act of atonement is about the guilt or debt of the human sinner. The sacrifice of an atoning offering does not change God; rather, it removes the guilt or pays off the penalty incurred by the person who has sinned. Sin disturbs a person's relationship with God. It is this ruptured relationship that must be tended—not God's anger per se. Thus, the atoning offering mends the damaged relationship.

Leviticus knows that humans cannot keep the divine law with anything even approaching perfection. The arrangement of the laws in the book signals this. The first three chapters describe a set of ritual offerings through which humans can rightly worship God and approach the divine presence. And then Leviticus 4 introduces the category of "unintentional sins"—sins that can be committed by various individuals (the priest, the ruler, or "anyone," v. 27) and also by the community ("the whole congregation," v. 13). It then prescribes sin-offering rituals by which the priests can "atone" for the unintentional sins of the people.

The important biblical concept of atonement is first introduced in Leviticus. The concepts of sin and atonement go hand in hand.

Leviticus 16 details the ritual for an annual, communal Day of Atonement (Hebrew: *yom kippur*). This is the most important day on the ritual calendar. The purpose of the annual Day of Atonement is laid out clearly in verse 30 (AT): "For on this day atonement will be made on your behalf, to cleanse you from all of your sins. In Yahweh's presence you must be clean." As part of the ritual, the high priest sacrifices a goat. The priest confesses the people's sins while laying hands on a second goat, thereby symbolically transferring the people's sins to the goat. The goat is then released into the wilderness, symbolically carrying the people's sins away. Finally, the high priest enters the holy of holies (the most sacred part of the tabernacle—later temple—complex) and purifies the tent of meeting and the altar, thereby making expiation for the priests and the entire people (16:33–34). These purgation exercises ensure that God's holy presence can remain among his people.

expiation A ritual that cleanses or removes defilement.

Theological and Social Dimensions of Sin

Theological dimension. In Leviticus, as is generally the case in the Old Testament, a sin is any action that violates the will of God: "If any ordinary person sins unintentionally by breaking one of the Lord's commands, doing something that shouldn't be done . . ." (4:27 CEB). In Leviticus, a sin may consist of doing something that God forbids (a "sin of commission") or of failing to do something that God commands, such as failing to testify in a public dispute when one knows something relevant to the dispute (a "sin of omission"; see 5:1). As mentioned above, a person's sins can be either known or unknown, intentional or unintentional.

As understood in Leviticus, sins disturb or rupture the relationship between an individual and God (or between the people and God). Most often, Leviticus uses the metaphors of guilt and debt to describe the nature of the disturbance or rupture that sin causes in the divine-human relationship. In response to the debt caused by the sin, the system of rituals presents various offerings or gifts that the priest may present on behalf of a person in order to atone for the sin: "Thus the priest shall make atonement on your behalf for the sin that you have committed, and you shall be forgiven" (4:35). Leviticus also uses the metaphor of violation—that is, of violating a rule or acting unfaithfully—to describe the consequences of a sin (see 5:14–16). In this case, the offering is described as a fine or penalty that a person must pay to expunge guilt.

Social dimension. In addition to recognizing that sin ruptures the relationship between God and people, Leviticus also recognizes that sins often have significant social dimensions. That is, Leviticus recognizes that through sin, we humans often harm each other and rupture our relationships with one another. Thus, as part of the atonement ritual overseen by the priests, repayment of a debt with interest is required. For example, Leviticus 6:1–7 describes that when one person deprives another of property by some illicit means, the total value of the property must be repaid, plus another 20 percent. Thus, atonement in Leviticus has both theological and ethical dimensions. People cannot mend their relationship with God unless they are also prepared to mend their relationship with a wronged neighbor.

Another perspective on the social dimension of human sin can be seen in the various sin offerings in Leviticus 4. Greater responsibility and accountability are put on the leaders of the community—specifically, on the priest and the ruler. A priest's sin can bring "guilt on the people" (v. 3), whereas sins of "the ordinary people" bring guilt only on themselves (v. 27). For this reason, the required offering for the sin of a priest is a bull (v. 4), while the sin offering for an ordinary person is a female goat (v. 28). The sin offering for a ruler is a male goat, which perhaps signifies a more costly atoning gift because the communal cost of a ruler's sin might be greater than that of an ordinary citizen.

Ritual Purity

According to Leviticus 10:10, the priests were called by God to "distinguish between the holy and common, and between the clean and the unclean." These categories are central to understanding Leviticus, but they are not primarily about hygiene—at least not as we think about hygiene. Terms like *clean* and *unclean*, *holy* and *profane*, or *common*, have to do with the ritual status of persons, objects, or materials.

When a thing or an entity is holy, it is set apart from that which is common or profane. The term *profane* might seem negative to English speakers since it sounds like *profanity*. But *profane* in the Old Testament simply describes something that is ritually common and thereby unsuitable to be in contact with the holy. For example, many of the purity laws in Leviticus are intended to preserve the holy status of the tabernacle/temple. For ancient Israel, the presence of the holy God was potentially dangerous (Lev. 10:1–20). As a result, laws that clearly define what is clean and unclean (i.e., suitable or unsuitable to be in contact with the holy) were intended to protect people from harm and the temple from contamination.

Some sources of impurity are avoidable, and some are not. For instance, eating unclean food or having sexual relations with a menstruating woman are largely avoidable. Giving birth and having intercourse, however, are natural parts of human life. In fact, in both cases one must do these things in order to obey Yahweh's command to "be fruitful and multiply" (Gen. 1:28). Moving in and out of ritual states of cleanness and uncleanness was simply part of daily human existence. Moving from a state of uncleanness to cleanness was generally a matter of following prescribed steps that might include washing or even simply waiting for a predetermined time to elapse.

The food laws are an especially noteworthy part of this larger system of ritual purity. Foods that are unclean include pork, shellfish, the flesh of scavenger animals, the fat of all animals, and the flesh of animals with its blood still in it. The meaning of these dietary laws is debated. One theory is that the dietary laws prescribe a diet that is mostly vegetarian—a recognition that human consumption of other animals as food is morally problematic. Another theory is that the food laws functioned as ancient precursors to modern food-safety laws—an early recognition that foods such as pork, shellfish, and raw meat are more likely to carry disease or bacteria that causes illness.

No matter what the original purpose of the food laws was, these laws serve two other important functions. First, the laws are important social identity markers—those who keep them are set apart as different from the rest of humanity. Being intentionally and publicly different from other human beings helps preserve a community's identity. Second, the food laws are signs of lives devoted to God—those who keep the laws devote themselves to God, down to every bite of food they eat.

The purposes of other cleanliness laws are similarly debated. These laws especially focus on various bodily emissions that make a person ritually unclean and the rituals through which a person would rejoin the community. The main concern was to prevent the impurity of individual people from contaminating the community.

Fig. 6.3. This modern Jewish painting illustrates the Levitical law requiring the "unclean" person to remain outside the camp. Here, the isolation from the community is emphasized by the barrenness of the landscape.

Social Laws

The most important—and most heavily debated—laws in Leviticus are those found in chapters 18–19. Leviticus 18 contains laws dealing with sexuality, whereas Leviticus 19 contains an eclectic set of moral statutes.

As mentioned in the introduction to this chapter, the sexual laws in Leviticus 18 are among the most controversial laws in the entire Bible. These laws indicate a profound awareness that human sexual activity has the power to shape human community in both positive and negative ways. There is a special awareness that people from surrounding cultures participated in sexual practices that Israel found objectionable: "You shall not do as they do in the land of Egypt . . . [or] in the land of Canaan" (18:3). The chapter forbids incest (sex with one's father, mother, stepmother, sister, granddaughter, aunt, uncle, and so on; vv. 6–18), sex with a woman during her menstrual period (v. 19), adultery (v. 20), male homosexual activity (v. 22), and sex with animals (v. 23). Leviticus 19 also prohibits prostitution and the sexual abuse of slaves.

Leviticus views human sexuality quite differently than modern, Western people do. In the Western world, sexuality is viewed through the lens of individualism. Every person is free to act in their own interests, as long as it does not violate the freedom of anyone else. In ancient Israel, sexuality was viewed through the lens of the community's survival. Each person owed their life and actions to the community—especially to one's "house." This obligation included one's sexual actions. Sexual activity was to be directed toward procreation and the survival of the community. People were not to engage in sexual practices such as incest or adultery, which might cause strife in the community. The length and intensity of the laws against incest are noteworthy (18:6–18). The household and family are the basic building blocks of society, and Leviticus takes great pains to stipulate that the household must be a place free of the sort of sexual violence and exploitation that goes along with incest. In the middle of the chapter, child sacrifice is also prohibited (v. 21). Israel's God was understood as unequivocally devoted to life.

Leviticus 19 contains an eclectic mix of social laws, including prohibitions against slander, worshiping idols, theft, fraud, bullying the handicapped, hatred, and the use of dishonest weights and measures. The chapter also prescribes actions a person must practice, including respect of the elderly, provision of food for the poor, love of one's neighbors and of displaced persons, just actions in legal disputes, and granting everyone rest on the Sabbath.

Israel understood its God as committed to fostering the conditions in which all life can thrive. These laws were seen as God's gracious intrusions into the chaos of the human community in order to create a more trustworthy and just world.

The Sabbatical Year and the Year of Jubilee

For modern people who have grown up in a capitalist, free-market economy, Leviticus 25 makes for strange reading. The reason for this is that the assumptions of the ancient economy were very different than those that govern economic systems today.

Leviticus 25:1–7 describes the Sabbatical Year—how every seven years the land is to be given rest; the fields are not planted, and vineyards are not pruned. This law is part of a larger set of laws for the Sabbatical Year that include the Year of Jubilee described in verses 8–55. Every fifty years (seven years times seven years), all land that has been sold in the past forty-nine years is to revert to the family to whom it originally belonged: "You shall return, every one of you, to your property and every one of you to your family" (v. 10). The reason for this is that the land belongs to the Lord: "The land must not be permanently sold because the land is mine. You are just immigrants and foreign guests of mine" (v. 23 CEB). Additionally, slaves are to be freed and all debts forgiven.

Some skeptical modern readers wonder if the ancient Israelites really kept these laws. This skepticism is largely the result of the vast difference in the economic assumptions between the ancient and the modern worlds. But there is good reason to suppose that the Sabbatical and Jubilee laws were kept—at least partially. Israel's neighbors had similar laws about property reverting to original owners and debts being canceled. As Moshe Weinfeld has shown, Israel's Sabbatical and Jubilee laws were, "functionally speaking, identical with the

Mesopotamian *misharum* and *duraru(m)*" laws.[2] Israel's economy was based on assumptions very different than our own and relied on the Sabbatical and Jubilee years to remain viable.

Historical Interpretation

Leviticus is difficult literature to read. This is understandable, since, historically, it was written for a highly specialized class of individuals—the priests—whose job it was to "distinguish between the holy and the common, and between the unclean and the clean" and "to teach the people of Israel all the statutes that the LORD has spoken to them through Moses" (Lev. 10:10–11). Throughout Israel's history, Leviticus helped priests fulfill their responsibilities to one another and to God. Those priests and the cultic apparatus they oversaw no longer exist. And yet Leviticus remains an important source of Jewish law, theology, and philosophy.

FOR FURTHER READING: **Leviticus**

Balentine, Samuel E. *Leviticus*. Interpretation: A Bible Commentary for Teaching and Preaching. Louisville: Westminster John Knox, 2003.

Hayes, Christine. *What's Divine about Divine Law? Early Perspectives*. Princeton: Princeton University Press, 2017.

Levine, Baruch A. *Leviticus: The Traditional Hebrew Text with the New JPS Translation*. JPS Torah Commentary. Philadelphia: Jewish Publication Society of America, 2003.

Milgrom, Jacob. *Leviticus: A Book of Ritual and Ethics*. Continental Commentaries. Minneapolis: Fortress, 2004.

Nelson, Richard D. *Raising Up a Faithful Priest: Community and Priesthood in Biblical Theology*. Louisville: Westminster John Knox, 1993.

Weinfeld, Moshe. *Social Justice in Ancient Israel and in the Ancient Near East*. Minneapolis: Fortress, 1995.

7

Numbers

The book of Numbers takes its name from a population census that is reported in the first chapter of the book. According to Numbers 1:2, this census was taken at God's command: "Take a census of all the congregation of the people of Israel, by clans, by fathers' houses, according to the number of names" (ESV).

But the fourth book of the Old Testament is not about math or counting or even about a census. Rather, the book of Numbers is about the journey of God's people through the wilderness to the edge of the promised land. The Hebrew name of the book, "In the Wilderness" (*Bemidbar*), better captures this book's content.

The book could also be titled "Exodus: The Sequel," because it continues the story of the exodus generation and features many of the same characters—Moses, Miriam, Aaron, Caleb, and Joshua. The book of Exodus ends with the divine presence descending upon the newly constructed tabernacle and ark of the covenant. Leviticus provides a sort of interlude in which the Lord dictates sets of laws and rituals through Moses. The book of Numbers then resumes the story of the exodus, with the people poised to resume their journey toward the promised land.

While the book of Numbers deals with many concerns, two major themes rise to the top. First, Numbers is about the life of faith as a journey in which God's people have no place or land of their own. On this journey, God's people have left one place, the land of chains and slavery in which they do not belong, but they have not yet reached the next place, the promised land in which they will find true belonging and place. More on this theme below.

Second, Numbers is about the transition from one generation of people to the next. At the start of the book, the chosen people are made up of the exodus generation—the men and women who walked through the sea on dry land and with whom God made a covenant at Sinai. By the end of the book, the chosen people are the sons and daughters of the exodus generation, which has almost completely died off. The contrast between these generations is a key theme of Numbers.

Background

Composition and Development

As is the case with the other books of the Pentateuch, the book of Numbers is an anonymous book. And like the other four books of the Pentateuch, historic tradition holds that Moses was the book's author. For a longer discussion of the tradition of Mosaic authorship and for a summary of modern criticism of that tradition, see chapter 3, "The Pentateuch."

There are very strong reasons for concluding that the book was compiled from earlier sources and traditions by an anonymous editor (or editors). In the ancient world, a long document was almost never the product of a single person who was its "author." Rather, books such as Numbers often had complex histories of editing and amending. It seems likely that the book of Numbers contains narratives and legal material that are quite ancient, dating to very early in Israel's history.

On the one hand, the book as a whole is framed largely by a perspective at home in Israel's priestly circles. Note the extended description of the census, organization, duties, and ritual importance of the priestly tribe of Levi in chapters 3–5. Note also the description of the offerings and vessels for the sanctuary in chapters 7–8 and 10:1–10 and the importance of the Passover celebration in 9:1–14. This material suggests that priestly scribes may have been among the editors who compiled earlier material into the final form of this book. If this is correct, the most likely date for this to have happened was during the Babylonian exile—after the time when kings and prophets led the chosen people and when Israel's priests assumed the mantle of leadership.

Box 7.1

Outline

1. The old generation: the exodus and wilderness (1–25)
   a. The first census (1–4)
   b. Ritual requirements and departure from Sinai (5–10)
   c. Journey of unfaithfulness (11–25)
2. The new generation: entrance to the land (26–36)
   a. The second census (26–27)
   b. A ritual calendar and vows (28–30)
   c. Journey of opportunity and hope (31–36)

Box 7.2

The Plots of Numbers

The story of Numbers has two significant plotlines—a plotline about moving from Mount Sinai to the Jordan River and a plotline about one generation of God's people giving way to the next. These two plotlines are interwoven.

The "travel" plotline explores the question, How will this band of escaped slaves survive in the wilderness and reach the promised land? Readers might also ask plot questions such as the following: Who will lead the people? What obstacles will they face? What route will they take around these obstacles? How will they hold up in harsh conditions? Will they make it to the promised land?

The "generational" plotline explores the issue of the transition from the exodus generation—those God brought out of Egypt and with whom he established the covenant at Mount Sinai—to a new "entrance generation" poised to enter the promised land. Dennis Olson has concluded that "the transition from the old generation of the wilderness to the new generation of hope and promise on the edge of the promised land forms the primary structure and theme for the book of Numbers."* The main question of the book is, Who from among the people will reach the promised land?

According to Olson, the first major portion of the book (chaps. 1–25) "recounts the eventual death of the old generation of God's people. . . . [This death] is brought on by the people's relentless rebellion against God." The second major portion of the book (chaps. 26–36) recounts the emergence of a new generation: "New life and hope, not rebellion and death, characterize this new generation's story."†

Numbers also contains smaller stories and other types of literature. One important set of texts concerns the role of the priestly tribe of Levi within the organization of the people. Related to this concern is a set of ritual texts that are to govern the worship life of the people once they enter the land. Another important story line concerns the place of women within the people. Related to this are two narrative passages about the five daughters of Zelophehad, who died in the wilderness without any sons. The daughters begged Moses that they be allowed to be their father's heirs, which they were allowed to do.

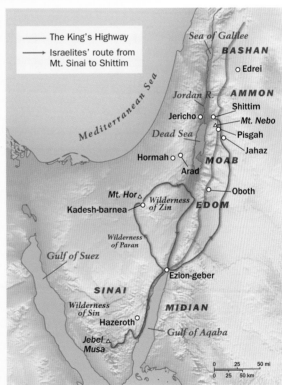

Map 7.1. Route of the Israelites from Mount Sinai to the Jordan River

* Dennis T. Olson, *Numbers*, Interpretation: A Bible Commentary for Teaching and Preaching (Louisville: John Knox, 1996), 4.
† Olson, *Numbers*, 4–5.

On the other hand, the book also includes nonpriestly narratives, laws, itineraries, and censuses—some of which are clearly much older than the exile. Some of these include creedal and liturgical fragments (such as 6:24–26; 10:35–36; 14:18), the troubling description of the ritual regarding a woman suspected of adultery (5:11–31), and the prophetic oracles of the prophet Balaam (23:7–10, 18–24; 24:3–9, 15–24). Some of this material was quite ancient even at the time of the exile. In addition, sections of narrative in chapters 11–14 and 20–24 likely predate the final, priestly work.

Genre

As noted above, Numbers is composed of an impressive variety of literary types: narratives, censuses, laws, itineraries, liturgical directions, and creedal fragments. But in its final form, it is the narrative that holds all these genres together and weaves them into a coherent book. More specifically, it is the dual narrative movements of the exodus generation giving way to the next generation and of the people journeying from Sinai to the Jordan that hold the book together.

Literary Interpretation

An extraordinarily large part of the pentateuchal narrative takes place at Mount Sinai. The people arrive at Sinai in Exodus 19. They spend the rest of Exodus, all of Leviticus, and the first nine chapters of Numbers cooling their heels at Sinai.

The old generation: The first census (Num. 1–4). The book of Numbers begins on an ominous note, recounting a census taken of all men "from twenty years old and upward, everyone in Israel able to go to war" (1:3). This beginning signals that Israel's path into the land will not be easy, a fact that plays out in the rest of the book, where the people encounter resistance, battle, and even a foreign king's attempt to get God to curse Israel.

Chapter 2 consists of a highly stylized description of Israel's order of march, with the twelve rank-and-file tribes marching in cohorts—three to a side—centered on the Levites, who bear the ark of the covenant and the tabernacle. Chapters 3–4 are devoted to the responsibilities of the Levites, according to their ancestral houses: Gershon, Kohath, and Merari.

The old generation: Ritual requirements and departure from Sinai (Num. 5–10). Significant space in these next chapters is given to legal and ritual regulations. It should be noted that while modern people distinguish intellectually between "legal" and "ritual" categories, the ancient Israelites did not. There was no separation of worship life, legal life, and citizenship or government. The important ritual texts in the first part of Numbers include requirements concerning the redemption of firstborn males (3:40–51), dealing with unclean persons (5:1–4), confession of sin and restitution for injury (5:5–10), a painful ritual for an accused woman (5:11–31), the priestly benediction (6:22–27), offerings for Israel's leaders (7:1–89), the seven lamps of the tabernacle (8:1–4), and the consecration of the Levites (8:5–26).

The complete set of the census lists and ritual requirements builds up to the story of the people keeping the second Passover at Sinai (9:1–14). All the people, including the ritually unclean, keep the Passover. At this point in Numbers, the narrative has painted the portrait of a people who are highly organized. They are literally centered on God both in their encampment and as they are marching. They are centered on God in their legal life and in their worship life. For leadership, the people are given the very presence of God's glory appearing over the tent of meeting with the appearance of a cloud by day and fire by night.

Finally, with great pageantry and the sound of two silver trumpets, the people set off from Sinai (10:11–13). This section of Numbers closes with two battle cries, ominously echoing the note of battle with which the book began:

> When the Ark was to set out, Moses would say:
>> Advance, O Lord!
>> May Your enemies be scattered,
>> And may Your foes flee before You!
> And when it halted, he would say:
>> Return, O Lord,
>> You who are Israel's myriads of thousands! (10:35–36 NJPS)

Box 7.3

Ordeal for Suspected Adultery

Numbers 5:11–31 describes one of the most disturbing rituals in the Hebrew Bible. The ritual is initiated by a jealous husband who suspects that his wife may have committed adultery (a corollary option is not provided for jealous wives). He brings her to a priest, who is to facilitate a ritual that is intended to determine the guilt or innocence of the woman. After taking a vow, the woman drinks a ritual concoction. If her belly distends and her thigh sags, then she is guilty of the crime (the language of the thigh that sags is ambiguous but likely refers to a distended uterus). If not, then she is innocent. Either way, the text claims, the husband is clear of all guilt (v. 31), suffering nothing for falsely accusing his wife. The ritual needs to be understood as an attempt to conjure divinatory evidence in a situation in which evidence is typically impossible to find. In an enchanted world like that of the Old Testament—that is, people believed the world was filled with gods, goddesses, demons, and semidivine beings who blessed and afflicted creation—such a ritual would have seemed reasonable. The fact that the ritual seems to presume the woman's guilt and does nothing to dissuade false accusation was, unfortunately, also reasonable within a patriarchal society that had a vested interest in controlling women's bodies.

The old generation: Journey of unfaithfulness (Num. 11–25). The people leave Mount Sinai and set out for Mount Hor, and soon they are complaining about the hardships of their journey. Similar to the way Exodus recounts that as soon as the people had passed out of Egypt, they complained that God had only delivered them in order to let them die by thirst and hunger (Exod. 15:22–17:7), Numbers reports that the people complained that they lacked meat; they "remember[ed] the fish . . . , the cucumbers, the melons, the leeks, the onions, and the garlic" (Num. 11:5). The Lord responds by providing the people with quail to eat. When the people arrive at Hazeroth, Moses's own brother and sister, Aaron and Miriam, join in the complaining against Moses (Num. 12).

Numbers 13–14 recounts a seminal event in the people's journey to the promised land. At the Lord's direction, Moses sends spies into the promised land. They return with good news and bad news. The good news is that the land "flows with milk and honey" (13:27; meaning it is rich and fertile). The bad news is that the land is strongly fortified with walled cities stoutly defended by oversized occupants (the spies "seemed like grasshoppers" to them [13:33]). One of the spies, Caleb, urges the people to trust God and proceed into the promised land, but the people rebel—once again complaining against Moses and Aaron: "Would that we had died in the land of Egypt!" (14:2). As in the story of the golden calf in Exodus 32, Moses stands between the rebellious people and God, asking him to forgive their sin. God does forgive, but with one caveat: "Not one of those who saw my glory and the signs I performed in Egypt and in the wilderness but who disobeyed me and tested me ten times—not one of them will ever see the land I promised on oath to their ancestors" (14:22–23 NIV). The people then attempt to reverse course, invading the land, but the Lord is not with them and the invasion fails.

Box 7.4

Land of Milk and Honey

The phrase "land of milk and honey" is used throughout the Pentateuch to describe the land given by Yahweh to Abraham, Sarah, and their descendants (see, e.g., Exod. 3:8, 17; 33:3; Num. 13:27; 14:8; 16:13–14; Deut. 6:3). The phrase is a shorthand way of describing the land's fertility, abundance, and suitability for human life. Tellingly, the words *honey* and *milk* are also used in tandem to describe the woman in the Song of Songs—a book overflowing with the imagery of fertility.

Fertility may seem a strange topic to the modern ear, especially given the highly scientific nature of agriculture in the modern Western world. But for the ancient Israelites, fertility was a divine gift, one that could not be taken for granted. Fertility was literally a matter of life and death. For ancient Israel, Yahweh was also a fertility God who ensured that the land was abundant and that future generations were born.

Fig. 7.1. One proposed explanation for why Moses is not allowed to enter the promised land is that his action of striking the rock symbolizes his own power rather than God's.

Anticipating the people's arrival in the promised land ("When you come into the land you are to inhabit . . ."), God gives another set of ritual laws in Numbers 15. The people respond with another rebellion! Several Levite priests—Korah, Dathan, and Abiram—attempt to replace Moses as the chief intercessor before God and the leader of the people (chap. 16). This rebellion results in the deaths not only of the three rebels but also of 250 other men. This causes the "whole people" to rebel against Moses and Aaron, which sparks the outbreak of a plague. Aaron steps in front of the spreading plague, halting its progress. Seemingly in reward for this act of faithfulness, the Lord appoints Aaron and his descendants to serve as the high priests of the people (chaps. 17–18). Additional priestly regulations and laws follow (chap. 19).

Finally, the people arrive at the wilderness of Zin (chap. 20). There, Moses's sister, Miriam, herself a prophet, dies. Guess what happens next? The people again rebel against God! The occasion this time is a lack of water: "If only we too had died when our brothers perished in the Lord's presence! Why have you brought the Lord's assembly into this desert to kill us and our animals here?" (20:3–4 CEB). The Lord instructs Moses to take his staff and to "command the rock before their eyes to yield its water." Moses takes his staff, but instead of commanding the rock, "he struck the rock twice with his staff." Water gushes forth abundantly. But, apparently because Moses struck the rock

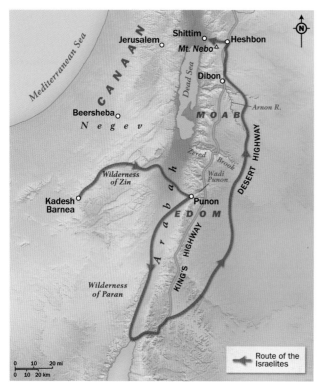

Map 7.2. The route from the Wilderness of Zin around Edom and other countries

rather than speaking to it, the Lord is displeased with Moses and Aaron and tells them that they will not be allowed to enter the promised land.

The people seek to pass through the kingdom of Edom along a road called the King's Highway but are refused passage. Moses's brother, Aaron, the first high priest, dies and is buried at a place called Mount Hor (scholars are unsure of its precise location). His son Eleazar becomes high priest in his place.

As the people depart Mount Hor, they again complain against the Lord: "Why have you brought us up out of Egypt to die in the wilderness? For there is no food and no water, and we detest this miserable food" (21:5). The Lord sends venomous snakes to plague the people, who then repent and beg Moses for help. Moses fashions a bronze serpent to be placed on a pole, which protects all who look on it from the serpents.

On the way to the land, Israel again requests peaceful passage through various territories. This time when they are refused passage, the Lord provides a series of military victories for them: over the king of Arad, over King Sihon of the Amorites, over King Og of Bashan.

This series of military victories leads King Balak of Moab to fear the Israelites. In one of the more entertaining narratives in the Pentateuch, Balak summons the prophet Balaam to curse the Israelites. Balaam warns the king that a prophet does not choose his own word; rather, "whatever [God] shows me I will tell you" (23:3). Instead of cursing the Israelites, the prophet blesses them according to the Lord's will. Balak is not satisfied. Thinking that getting a prophecy is a matter of how much one pays, or how much one sacrifices to God, or where one prays, or how many times one prays, Balak induces Balaam to prophesy four different times in an effort to have him curse Israel. Each time, the message gets worse for Balak and more favorable for Israel.

Ironically, even as the Lord is blessing Israel through the non-Israelite prophet Balaam, the Israelites are again forsaking the Lord by worshiping the false god Baal of Peor. The Lord sends a plague to punish them, but Aaron's grandson

baal/Baal A Hebrew word meaning "master" or "lord" and also used for a Canaanite deity encountered in the Old Testament.

Phinehas slays two people responsible for the sin, and thus "the plague was stopped" (25:8). For this faithful act, Phinehas is granted God's "covenant of peace," "a covenant of perpetual priesthood" (25:12–13). The plague nevertheless kills twenty-four thousand people—the remainder of the exodus generation who had so consistently complained against and rebelled against the Lord and finally chose a god other than the Lord. As Dennis Olson comments, "The story of Israel's worship of an alien god in Numbers 25 brings to an end the life of the first generation of Israelites who came out of Egypt. . . . They have left the stage to make room for a new generation who will again stand on the edge of the promised land. The advent of this new generation of hope is marked by the second census list of Israel's twelve tribes in Numbers 26."[1]

The new generation: The second census (Num. 26–27). The passage of the unfaithful wilderness generation marks an important time for the people of Israel. The new generation has the opportunity to respond differently to God. As noted above, a second census hints at the hope associated with this fresh start.

Fig. 7.2. Moses and the plague of serpents

A member of the tribe of Manasseh, Zelophehad, dies in the wilderness but has only daughters to survive him—no son to inherit either his name or his property. His daughters—Mahlah, Noah, Hoglah, Milcah, and Tirzah—request of the Israelite leaders that they be allowed to perpetuate their father's name and inherit his property. The Lord responds, "The daughters of Zelophehad are right in what they are saying; you shall indeed let them possess an inheritance among their father's brothers and pass the inheritance of their father on to them. You shall also say to the Israelites, 'If a man dies, and has no son, then you shall pass his inheritance on to his daughter'" (27:7–8). The Lord's positive regard for these women, their rights, and the future rights of all Israelite women shows that the new "generation of hope" bears hope not just for Israel's men but also for their women—hope not yet of equal footing, but at least of less unequal footing with regard to the law.

The new generation: A ritual calendar and vows (Num. 28–30). Joshua is appointed Moses's eventual successor (Num. 27:12–23), which gives the Lord an opportunity to issue more laws (chaps. 28–30). Noteworthy among these is the establishment of a religious calendar for the Israelites to follow in the promised land.

The new generation: Journey of opportunity and hope (Num. 31–36). The Lord then grants Israel victory over the Midianites and over the territory known as the Transjordan—the land that belonged to the Israelites on the east side of the Jordan River. In a final section, Numbers reviews the stages of the journey from Egypt to the Jordan River. The book then describes the disposition of the promised land and closes with another discourse on the daughters of Zelophehad (36:1–12).

Theological Interpretation

From One Generation to the Next

As noted earlier in this chapter, one of the most important themes in Numbers is the transition from the old, rebellious exodus generation to the new promised-land generation of hope. As also noted, Dennis Olson has argued that the transition from the unfaithful exodus generation to the faithful entrance generation is the primary narrative theme of the book.

Within this overall literary arc, a supporting narrative theme concerns the death of certain Israelite leaders and the passing of the torch of leadership. During the wilderness wandering, both Aaron and Miriam die. The narrative also includes the word from God that Moses will not reach the promised land. As the book nears its end, the reader wonders what will become of Moses's leadership. Aaron is confirmed in Numbers as Israel's first high priest. His staff of leadership is successfully passed on to his son Eleazar, who walks in his father's footsteps. The narrative also includes the promise that Eleazar's son Phinehas had earned for Aaron's lineage the "covenant of perpetual priesthood" (25:13). Moses's mantle of leadership, on the other hand, passed not to his son Gershom but to another Israelite: Joshua son of Nun. At this point in the people's history, leadership of the priesthood was hereditary, but leadership of the people was not. If Miriam married or had children, it is not reported. Sadly, the biblical text is less interested in Miriam—almost certainly because she was a woman. But as noted above, Mahlah, Noah, Hoglah, Milcah, and Tirzah, the daughters of Zelophehad, step forward to demand and receive their father's inheritance.

This narrative theme of one generation passing the torch of leadership and the mantle of faith on to the next raises the important theological issue of how faith and character are—or are not—passed on. The main theme of the book seems to be that an unfaithful, rebellious generation can give way to a

Fig. 7.3. The story of the daughters of Zelophehad highlights a positive regard for the welfare of women in ancient Israel, especially since these stories are connected with the "generation of hope" as the people prepare to enter the land.

faithful, obedient generation. Often when older people complain about the next generations, it seems that they are worried about the infidelity of their heirs. The narrative of Numbers promises that the faithful can follow the unfaithful, just as readily as the other way around. Sometimes the children are more faithful than their parents!

According to Numbers, the passing of the torch of leadership is also a complex, unpredictable matter. Children do not always walk in the ways of their parents. Each son or daughter makes their own choices in the new circumstances in which they find themselves. Even great leaders such as Moses, Aaron, and Miriam are flawed. Moses has his moment of weakness, and for that he is not allowed into the promised land. Aaron and Miriam speak against Moses because of his marriage to a Cushite woman, and they rebel against his authority (chap. 12).

Law and Promise

Numbers indicates that God works through law and promise. On the one hand, God holds people—especially leaders—accountable to divine law. Each of Israel's leaders is held accountable when they transgress God's law. God works through the law to uphold life. God's life-giving purposes are also witnessed by the myriad ritual and moral laws that pepper the narrative of Numbers. Yet God's law develops and changes to serve life, as indicated by the account of Mahlah, Noah, Hoglah, Milcah, and Tirzah—Zelophehad's daughters. But law is not enough. God also works through promise—God binds himself to the line of Aaron in a perpetual "covenant of peace" for the sake of Aaron's grandson Phinehas.

The Theology of the Journey

The Jewish name for Numbers is "In the Wilderness." The second major narrative theme of the book of Numbers is the theme of journeying through the wilderness. On the one hand, the book purports to narrate a geographical journey from Mount Sinai, to Mount Hor, to the plains of Moab and the verge of the Jordan. On the other hand, this physical journey has significant spiritual and moral dimensions. It is a *hard journey*. It is a *journey from slavery toward freedom*. It is a journey in which the people experience both *scarcity and abundance*. It is a journey that is charted precisely *through the "wild-ness"*—a place that is outside of human society. And it is a *journey with God*, a time when God guides the people physically by way of fire and cloud, a time when Israel and God get to know each other.

A hard journey. Numbers insists that the journey from Sinai to the Jordan was a hard journey. Along the way, the people faced hostile nations (Amalekites, Edomites, Amorites, Moabites, Bashanites, Midianites, and so on). They faced scarcity of water and food. They faced venomous serpents, quarrels between their own leaders, and rebellions. The relatively extreme extent to which Numbers goes to relate these many difficulties is a reminder that Israel viewed the life of faith as far from a rosy path; life with God is not easy. And yet life with God beats the alternative. The destination is worth the hardships of the journey.

From slavery toward freedom. The book of Numbers begins with Israel still at Mount Sinai, where its covenant relationship with God was consummated. It ends with Israel on the verge of the Jordan, looking across toward the promised land. This journey—the stages of which are reviewed in Numbers 33—continues Israel's longer journey from bondage in a foreign land to freedom, nationhood, and residence in a land of their own. As Israel makes this journey, the hardships it encounters often make it long for Egypt—where, in spite of the whips and chains, they at least had water, vegetables, and a variety of meat. How often the people cry out, "Would that we had died in Egypt!" But with divine assurance and prophetic-priestly leadership, the people march on toward freedom and a land of their own.

Scarcity and abundance. The theme of scarcity and abundance is critical to Numbers. Time and again, the book recounts how the people complained when they experienced scarcity. The people were on a journey from being "no people" in a land of bondage to being God's people in an abundant land that "flows with milk and honey" (13:27). Despite this promise, the scarcity of water, fruit, vegetables, and meat—and even the monotony of eating manna—led the people to complain and rebel. God's response to this complaint? Abundance. The abundant provision of water, manna, and quail. The narrative not only emphasizes humanity's characteristic lack of faith; it also simultaneously emphasizes that abundance is a characteristic of both the Creator and the good creation. Humans are prone to fearing they never have enough. The Creator, through the creation, provides abundantly.

Through the wild-ness. As many interpreters of Numbers have pointed out, the wilderness setting that dominates the book is itself important. The journey is through the wilderness—or "wild area"—the area that is outside human society. Many interpreters who come from interpreting communities "outside" the mainstream—such as feminist, womanist, and African American communities—have found this metaphor a powerful symbol for both their struggle and their hope. For Katharine Sakenfeld, the wilderness symbolizes that "those engaged in feminist biblical study . . . find themselves in an environment where there is far less certainty or ordinary source of sustenance." It also "symbolizes a context of living in continuing hope for 'land,' a hope not just for space but for place within the scholarly community," and finally it symbolizes "a place of dissension and dispute along the journey, even as it did for Israel of old."[2] The wilderness serves as an important metaphor for those who struggle still with God, with God's people, with the Bible, or with life itself. As Karl Jacobson writes, "In the midst of the 'wildernesses' of our time—the wildernesses of loss, of mistrust, of human-on-human crime, of religious pluralism, of searching for genuine, life-changing faith in an increasingly complicated and wild world—the story of Israel 'in the wilderness' is potentially meaningful."[3]

A journey with God. A related theme is that Israel's journey through the hardships, scarcity, and wild-ness of the wilderness is a journey with God—a

feminist criticism
An academic approach that analyzes texts from a feminist perspective.

womanist criticism
An academic approach that focuses on the lived experiences of African American women, with a focus on experiences of oppression and the longing for liberation.

Box 7.5

"Poor Wayfaring Stranger"

The metaphor of journeying through life's wilderness on the way to the Jordan and the promised land was also a metaphor for the African American experience of enduring and escaping slavery. As the spiritual "Poor Wayfaring Stranger" has it,

> I know dark clouds will gather round me,
> I know my way is rough and steep.
> The beauteous fields lie just before me,
> Where God's redeemed their vigils keep.
> I'm only going over Jordan,
> I'm only going over home.

journey in which Israel and God are just getting to know each other. Two of Israel's later prophets, Amos and Hosea, seem to have looked back on the wilderness period with a certain fondness. Hosea said,

> I will now allure her [Israel],
>> and bring her into the wilderness,
>> and speak tenderly to her.
> From there I will give her her vineyards. . . .
> She shall respond as in the days of her youth,
>> as at the time when she came out of the land of Egypt. (Hosea 2:14–15; see also Amos 5:25)

Holy Blessing, People, Leaders, and Worship

Not to be missed in the book of Numbers is all the material about the priestly tribe of Levi and the worship life of the people. There is an intense focus on the priestly leadership of the Levites. The census of the Levites—and the special Levitical subgroups of the Kohathites, Gershonites, and Merarites—takes an extraordinary amount of space (chaps. 3–4). In addition, there is a description of the holy order of the Nazirites (6:1–21). Numbers contains important ritual texts, such as the redemption of the firstborn (3:40–51), confession of sin and reconciliation (5:5–10), offerings (15:1–21; 28:1–29:40), and the ceremony of the red heifer (19:1–22). The book includes descriptions of worship materials such as the silver trumpets (10:1–10) and significant accounts of the people worshiping, including the account of their Passover observance as they depart Sinai (9:1–14).

In addition to these positive emphases on the worship life of the people, the transition from the old wilderness generation of rebellion to the new promised-land generation of hope takes place as the old generation forsakes the Lord to worship the alien god Baal of Peor (chap. 25). This occurs immediately after the Lord blesses the people through the non-Israelite prophet Balaam. The point of all this seems to be that it is the Lord's intention to bless Israel continuously with unmerited grace. This divine blessing flows to the people through the priestly tribe of Levi—remember that Moses was a Levite—via the liturgies and rituals that God established. The holy people of the Lord must be a worshiping people, for in worship the relationship with the Lord is maintained and the Lord's unmerited grace is poured out in blessing, forgiveness, and favor. Yet when the people sin, the priestly leaders play the role of stepping between the Lord and the people to intercede for them, as did Moses (14:13–20), or to atone for their sin, as did Phinehas (25:6–13). This theme of the pouring out of divine blessing and favor is best captured in the most famous passage from Numbers, the so-called priestly blessing:

The LORD spoke to Moses, saying: Speak to Aaron and his sons, saying, Thus you shall bless the Israelites: You shall say to them,

> The LORD bless you and keep you;
> The LORD make his face to shine upon you, and be gracious to you;
> The LORD lift up his countenance upon you, and give you peace.

So shall they put my name on the Israelites, and I will bless them. (6:22–27)

Historical Interpretation

As was noted in chapter 2 and has been discussed in earlier chapters, there are two major ways a reader can approach Numbers from a historical perspective. A reader might inquire into the world "behind the text"—that is, the historical situation that occasioned Numbers to be written. Or a reader might inquire into the world "in the text"—that is, the historicity of the events Numbers narrates.

The Historical World behind the Text

What world and community produced the book of Numbers? Taken at face value, Numbers recounts events that occurred between the time Israel departed from Egypt and the time they entered the promised land. It is most likely that the book of Numbers did not reach its final form until many years after the events it narrates. It also seems likely, from a close examination of the text of Numbers, that the book in its final form is a composite work—having been sewn carefully together from a variety of older sources—such as the "Book of the Wars of the LORD," mentioned in Numbers 21:14. It also seems evident that some of these older narratives, laws, rituals, and census lists that the collectors of Numbers included were already quite ancient at the time Numbers was compiled. Candidates for the most ancient of these preexisting sources include the fragment from the "Book of the Wars of the LORD" (21:14–18), the priestly benediction (6:22–27), the ancient creed-like fragment (14:18), and the ancient battle cry (10:35–36).

But when was the final form of the book compiled? It is almost certain that earlier versions existed, but it seems likely that Numbers reached its final form during the time of the exile, between 597 and 539 BCE. During this time, when the people were again captive and forced to live outside the promised land, the ancient narrative of their people journeying toward the homeland would have been particularly inspiring and hopeful.

Finally, the theme of a failed generation of rebellion giving way to a new generation of obedience and hope fits the time of the exile too. The Judean exiles blamed the destruction of Jerusalem in 586 BCE and the exile in Babylon on the failed leadership of the generations who had lived in the decades leading up to the exile. The message of hope for a new, obedient generation returning to the promised land would have resonated strongly with the exiles.

The Historical World in the Text

Very often, when modern readers engage an ancient historical text, the first—and often only—question they ask is, Did the events it recounts happen exactly the way the text says they happened? While that question is valid, in the case of Numbers it does not get one very far. The book of Numbers is not attempting to describe history for the sake of history. Rather, it is trying to tell its story in order to move the people of God to make changes in their lives. Numbers wants to move the people to obedience and faith. Its strategy for creating this movement is embedding ritual and legal texts in a highly stylized, overarching narrative.

For example, the book of Numbers narrates a carefully crafted marching order for the people of God (2:1–34). The people were to camp and march

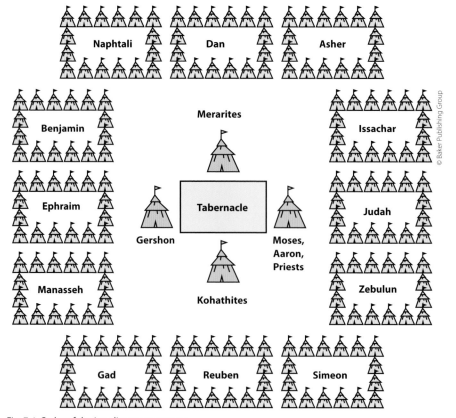

Fig. 7.4. Order of the Israelite encampment

with the tabernacle—containing the ark of the covenant—in the middle of their formation, surrounded immediately by Moses, Aaron, and the Levites. The tribes of Judah, Issachar, and Zebulun were to camp on the east; Reuben, Simeon, and Gad on the south; Ephraim, Manasseh, and Benjamin on the west; and Dan, Asher, and Naphtali on the north. Over the tabernacle, the presence of the Lord burned as a fire by night and hovered as a cloud by day. If the cloud stayed in one place for a day, or two, or a month, the Israelites would stay encamped there. When it moved, the Israelites would follow.

The point of this stylized order of march is more spiritual than historical. The idea is that the Lord had placed the divine presence at the very center of the people's communal existence. And the spiritual go-between that mediated between the Lord and the people was the tribe of Levi—and in particular, the tribe's leaders.

This is not to say that the book of Numbers does not in all likelihood contain very ancient historical material. Rather, it is to say that the point is not to preserve historical information, but to convey the spiritual message of the book. That message could be summed up any number of ways, but here we will let Numbers 35:34 have the last word: "I the LORD dwell among the Israelites."

FOR FURTHER READING: **Numbers**

Leveen, Adriane. *Memory and Tradition in the Book of Numbers*. New York: Cambridge University Press, 2008.

Milgrom, Jacob. *Numbers: The Traditional Hebrew Text with the New JPS Translation*. JPS Torah Commentary. Philadelphia: Jewish Publication Society of America, 2003.

Olson, Dennis T. *Numbers*. Interpretation: A Bible Commentary for Teaching and Preaching. Louisville: John Knox, 1996.

Sakenfeld, Katharine Doob. "Numbers." In *Women's Bible Commentary*, 3rd ed., edited by Carol A. Newsom, Sharon H. Ringe, and Jacqueline E. Lapsley, 79–87. Louisville: Westminster John Knox, 2012.

Deuteronomy

The title "Deuteronomy"—which in Greek means "second law" (*deutero* + *nomos*)—is given to this book because Deuteronomy is, to some extent, a repetition of the laws given earlier in the Pentateuch. This is especially the case because the Ten Commandments, the heart of Israel's law, are given first in Exodus 20 and then again in Deuteronomy 5.

The Hebrew name for the book—'*elleh haddebarim*, "These are the words," or less formally, *Sefer Debarim*, "Book of words"—is also significant because the book contains almost no actions or narratives, only the words of Moses: "These are the words that Moses spoke to all Israel beyond the Jordan—in the wilderness" (1:1a). The only new activity that takes place in Deuteronomy is Moses's death and burial, reported in 34:5–8.

The book of Deuteronomy contains the last words of Moses—his farewell speech, if you will. Readers may remember that in the book of Numbers, God announced to Moses that it would not be his role to lead the people into the promised land. But God gave Moses a consolation prize: a long goodbye speech to the people of Israel. The book of Deuteronomy is that speech.

But two other introductory emphases in the first few verses of Deuteronomy are noteworthy: the continuing journey of the Israelites and God's faithfulness to his promise. First, even though there is no real narrative action in the book of Deuteronomy, the first chapter continues the story of the Israelites' journey: "The LORD our God spoke to us at Horeb [another name for Mount Sinai], saying, 'You have stayed long enough at this mountain. Resume your journey'" (1:6–7a). This note is a reminder that Deuteronomy is simply a way station on Israel's journey from slavery in Egypt to freedom in the promised land—an important pause, but still just a stop along the way.

The second emphasis is in the Lord's words, "See, I have set the land before you; go in and take possession of the land that I swore to your ancestors, to Abraham, to Isaac, and to Jacob, to give to them and to their descendants after them" (1:8). Deuteronomy is a continuation of the promise given to Abraham: "Leave your land, your family, and your father's household for the land that I will show you. I will make of you a great nation and will bless you. I will make your name respected, and you will be a blessing. I will bless those who bless you, those who curse you I will curse; all the families of the earth will be blessed because of you" (Gen. 12:1–3 CEB). The central, driving force of the narrative is the faithfulness of God to his promises.

As a book, Deuteronomy is both an ending and a beginning. It is the fifth and final book in the Pentateuch, furnishing the last chapter in the story of Israel's founding narrative. It marks the last chapter in the long and remarkable story of Moses, Israel's most important founding figure. But Deuteronomy is also the first book in a set of books that historians call the Deuteronomistic History—which recounts the story of Israel from its entry into the promised land all the way to the destruction of Jerusalem and the exile. (For more on the Deuteronomistic History, see chap. 9.)

Background

Composition and Development

As with the other four books of the Pentateuch, the book of Deuteronomy is an anonymous book, though tradition holds that Moses was its author. As is also the case with the other books of the Pentateuch, Deuteronomy was likely not written at one time but developed over time—a process that cannot be fully recovered.

One compelling idea about the development of the book of Deuteronomy, however, is so important that it needs to be described. This view holds that the central part of Deuteronomy (4:44–28:68) was an independent scroll at one time.

Second Kings 2 describes how the reforming King Josiah of Jerusalem opened up the royal treasury in order to refurbish the Jerusalem temple in 622 BCE. No expense was to be spared. Then the king received an urgent message from

---

> ### Box 8.1
>
> ### *Deuteronomy as Ending and Beginning*
>
> | Pentateuch | Deuteronomistic History |
> |------------|-------------------------|
> | Genesis | Deuteronomy |
> | Exodus | Joshua |
> | Leviticus | Judges* |
> | Numbers | 1–2 Samuel |
> | Deuteronomy | 1–2 Kings |
>
> * The book of Ruth is not considered part of the Deuteronomistic History. It was written separately from these books. In the Jewish ordering of the Hebrew Bible, Ruth is part of the Writings (see chap. 2).

Fig. 8.1. This colorful scene from the French Liebig cards series shows King Josiah reading the book of the law that was discovered in the temple (ca. 620 BCE). Second Kings 22:10 says that the scribe Shaphan read the scroll to the king. (It is likely that most kings at the time were illiterate.)

the high priest, Hilkiah: "I have found the book of the law in the house of the LORD" (2 Kings 22:8). Second Kings 23 then describes a series of reforms that Josiah enacted.

What was this "book of the law" (literally, "the scroll of Torah"; Hebrew: *sefer hattorah*) that was found in the temple? Because the reforms described in 2 Kings 23 closely mirror the regulations found in the central part of Deuteronomy, many scholars believe that the "book of the law" found in the temple was, indeed, Deuteronomy 4:44–28:68 (or at least an early version of those chapters).

If this was the case, as seems likely to many scholars, it is also likely that Deuteronomy 1:1–4:43 and 29:1–34:12 were added to this core, either during the time of King Josiah (died 609 BCE) or during the Babylonian exile (586–539 BCE).

For ease of reference here, the central core of the book of Deuteronomy will be referred to as the Deuteronomic Book of Torah. But where did this book come from? Recall that in 922 BCE, following the death of King Solomon, the united kingdom of Israel split into two kingdoms. The kingdom to the north was called Israel, and the southern was Judah. In 722/721 BCE, the Northern

What Does Torah Mean?

The traditional translation of the Hebrew term *torah* as "law" is misleading. A better translation is "instruction," based on the fact that the word *torah* is related to the Hebrew verb *yarah*, meaning "instruct." But even "instruction" or "teaching" do not quite get at the richness of the Hebrew word—which eventually came to refer to all of the narratives, laws, rituals, blessings, and other literature in the first five books of the Bible. As Clinton McCann has written, the term "is anything but an invitation to pedantry, legalism, or self-righteousness. On the contrary, it is an invitation to be *open to God's instruction* and to the reality of *God's reign in the world*."* Deuteronomy, then, is divine instruction that opens up one's imagination to the reality of God's reign in the world. For Deuteronomy, torah is something that is to be remembered, pondered, and studied by all, and most especially by kings (17:14–20).

* J. Clinton McCann Jr., *A Theological Introduction to the Book of Psalms: The Psalms as Torah* (Nashville: Abingdon, 1993), 27.

Kingdom fell to the Assyrian Empire, and many of its citizens were exiled. But we also know that many of its citizens fled south and joined themselves to the Southern Kingdom, Judah. Because the Deuteronomic Book of Torah reflects many traditions of the Northern Kingdom, scholars believe that it was brought south to Jerusalem by refugees from the north. If this is correct, it seems likely that this core book contained ancient traditions about Moses that the Northern Kingdom had preserved.

Genre

united kingdom
The kingdom of Israel ruled by Saul, David, and Solomon. It divided into Northern and Southern Kingdoms after Solomon's death.

The book of Deuteronomy is composed of speeches by Moses, presented in rhetorically moving ways. Speeches in the Old Testament are often given at significant points in a narrative and contain important theological insights. This is certainly true for the book of Deuteronomy, which comes at the pivotal moment when Israel is posed to enter into Canaan. Prominent scholar Patrick D. Miller explores the theological range of the words of Torah that come to us in Deuteronomy. On the one hand, "the book has some of the prophetic spirit. . . . This is discernible in several of its emphases: its zeal for obedience to the covenant law; its focus on the issue of apostasy; its insistent claim that the Lord is Israel's only God; its concern for social justice." The book also shows concern for the daily walk of faith: "Deuteronomy is law that is taught and preached, not simply promulgated." The book also conveys "the deep concern . . . for passing on the formative story and its implications for life."[1]

Deuteronomy is preached law, intending to fortify, remind, and exhort. Miller continues: "These speeches are proper preaching in any age—the proclamation of the redemptive grace of God as a basis for exhortation to obedience. Deuteronomy, through the mouth of Moses, reminds the people of God's grace in the past. On that basis it calls them to a thankful, obedient response, instructing them in the way and character of obedience."[2] Given its rhetorical power, it is no surprise that Deuteronomy has proven to be so memorable and impactful.

Literary Interpretation

Similar to Leviticus, Deuteronomy does not contain a narrative of action and movement. Rather, it consists of the four sermons of Moses. These four sermons do, however, look backward to the wilderness journey and anticipate the entrance into the land. Each sermon is introduced by a similar narrative formula, yet each introduction stresses the unique character of that particular sermon: words, instruction, covenant, and blessing.

First sermon: Words (story) (Deut. 1:1–4:43). The first of Moses's four sermons is introduced simply as "words" (Hebrew: *debarim*). In Hebrew, the word *dabar* can mean a word, matter, thing, promise, command, story, sermon, and so on. Here, the term is defined by the content of Moses's first speech, which is found in 1:6–4:40. Moses tells Israel's story, from the time of the departure from Mount Sinai ("Resume your journey, and go," 1:6) until their arrival at the Transjordan, across from the promised land ("So we remained in the valley opposite Beth-peor," 3:29).

Box 8.4

The Plot of Deuteronomy

Speeches play an important role in the Old Testament, especially when they are embedded within narratives. Deuteronomy exemplifies this literary principle. The core of the book is a lengthy speech from Moses, given just as Israel is poised to enter into Canaan—a land promised generations ago to their ancestors, Abraham and Sarah. Keep in mind, however, that the generation of Israelites Moses is addressing in Deuteronomy is not the same generation that departed from Egypt. Apart from a small remnant, the generation addressed in Deuteronomy only knew the events surrounding the exodus through secondhand reporting. The original generation died in the wilderness after refusing to trust in Yahweh's ability to give them victory over their opponents in the land of Canaan (Num. 14:20–38).

How can a people accustomed to wandering take up a new identity as landed folk? How does one recapture the glory and majesty of the exodus and the Sinai revelation in the eyes of a people who did not experience it directly? How does one prepare a people for a new leader? These are questions that the plot of Deuteronomy attempts to address. It does so by reciting Israel's history and recounting the Sinai law in a way that is memorable and moving. Offering one last gift before his death, Moses reminds Israel of its obligations to Yahweh, to one another, and to those outside the community.

At least two aspects of this story are vital for understanding Deuteronomy. The first is that the story Moses tells reveals that Israel's history with God is the history of God's constant, unrelenting love and goodness. Moses sums this up in his prayer for permission to cross over and enter the promised land: "O Lord God, you have only begun to show your servant your greatness and your mighty hand. For what god is there in heaven or on earth who can do such works and mighty acts as yours?" (3:24 ESV). With insight that anticipates the ancient Christian maxim "it is not possible not to sin" (Latin: *Non posse non peccare*), Moses foresees that there will come a day when Israel will not be faithful to the Lord. The Lord will punish Israel, Moses promises, but also remain gracious and faithful: "In your distress, when all these things have happened to you in time to come, you will return to the Lord your God and heed him. Because *the Lord your God is a merciful God, he will neither abandon you nor destroy you; he will not forget the covenant with your ancestors that he swore to them*" (4:30–31; emphasis added).

A second crucial aspect of the story that Moses tells in the first sermon is that Israel's history and relationship with the Lord is completely unique—totally unparalleled and absolutely unequaled by any nation or god. The reason for this, in the worldview of Deuteronomy, is that there is no other god like the Lord who deserves their love and loyalty. As Moses says,

> For what other great nation has a god so near to it as the Lord our God is whenever we call to him? And what other great nation has statutes and ordinances as just as this entire law that I am setting before you today? (Deut. 4:7–8)

> For ask now about former ages, long before your own, ever since the day that God created human beings on the earth; ask from one end of heaven to the other: has anything so great as this ever happened or has its like ever been heard of? Has any people ever heard the voice of a god speaking out of a fire, as you have heard, and lived? Or has any god ever attempted to go and take a nation for himself from the midst of another nation, by trials, by signs and wonders, by war, by a mighty hand and an outstretched arm, and by terrifying displays of power, as the Lord your God did for you in Egypt before your very eyes? To you it was shown so that you would acknowledge that the Lord is God; there is no other besides him. From heaven he made you hear his voice to discipline you. On earth he showed you his great fire, while you heard his words coming out of the fire. And because he loved your ancestors, he chose their descendants after them. He brought you out of Egypt with his own presence, by his great power, driving out before you nations greater and mightier than yourselves, to bring you in, giving you their land for a possession, as it is still today. So acknowledge today and take to heart that the Lord is God in heaven above and on the earth beneath; there is no other. (Deut. 4:32–39)

signs and wonders
Spectacular acts (miracles) performed by people who access either divine or demonic supernatural power.

Fig. 8.2. God tells Moses that he cannot enter the promised land. But in the final chapter of Deuteronomy, which recounts Moses's farewell speech, Moses climbs Mount Nebo and is given a view of the land.

According to Moses's first sermon, Israel's history tells the story of God's unearned but freely given grace and love. The story Moses tells also emphasizes God's nearness to Israel. This is evident both in the gift of the law and in the history of God's gracious responses to Israel's cries for deliverance: "The Lord has taken you and brought you out of the iron-smelter, out of Egypt, to become a people of his very own possession, as you are now" (4:20).

Second sermon: Instruction (Deut. 4:44–28:68). The second sermon of Moses in Deuteronomy is introduced as the "instruction" (Hebrew: *torah*) that Moses set before the people of Israel. As noted earlier in this chapter, this lengthy sermon forms the main part of Deuteronomy. As was also mentioned, the word *torah* does not mean "law" as it has been traditionally mistranslated, but rather "instruction," or perhaps simply "scripture."

"Scripture" is an appropriate subtitle for this section of Deuteronomy because the introductory verses to the second sermon define God's covenant with Israel not as simply an action of the past but as an ongoing promise from God: "Moses preached to all Israel, and said to them: 'Hear, O Israel, the statutes and ordinances that I am addressing to you today; you shall learn them and observe them diligently. The Lord our God made a covenant with us at Horeb. Not only with our fathers and mothers did the Lord make this covenant, but with us—we, these ones, here, today, all of us, the living!'" (5:1–3 AT).

Note the last line: "Not only with our fathers and mothers did the Lord make this covenant, but with us—we, these ones, here, today, all of us, the living!" Recall that the book of Numbers described how the entire generation that had been present at Sinai died during the wilderness years and that it was their children who entered the promised land. The people left standing to hear Moses's four sermons were the children and grandchildren of the exodus generation. So at the merely historical level, Moses's claim that "the Lord our God made a covenant with us" and "not only with our fathers and mothers" is not accurate. But the point of Deuteronomy is that at the deeper, theological level, the covenant initiated at Horeb (Sinai) did not end with the death of the wilderness generation but is valid forever. The point is that the Bible does not merely relate what happened to some ancient Israelites; rather, it relates who God is still today.

The remainder of this second sermon includes some of the most important legal and theological material in the entire Old Testament, including the Ten Commandments (5:6–21), the great Shema (6:4–9), the law of the king (17:14–20), and the ancient liturgy of firstfruits (26:1–15). More will be said about each of these important texts below in the section called "Theological Interpretation."

Third sermon: Covenant (Deut. 29:1–32:52). The third sermon in Deuteronomy takes up the theme of the covenant. This sermon consists of a renewal of the covenant first established at Mount Horeb (Sinai). As Dennis Olson has seen, the nature of this renewal is that the commandments of the law are turned into promises: "Sole trust in imperatives, threats, and laws cannot ultimately save the community from the encroaching powers, both internal and external, that bring the community's eventual destruction and death (28:15–68)."[3]

The covenant initiated at Horeb included the legal prescription that all male members of the covenant have their foreskins circumcised. The third sermon of Deuteronomy twice employs a distinctive phrase that rarely occurs elsewhere in the Old Testament, namely that God will circumcise the peoples' hearts. Noting first that Deuteronomy 6:5 and 10:16 command the people to "love the LORD your God with all your heart, and with all your soul, and with all your might" and to "circumcise, then, the foreskin of your heart," Olson writes: "In the new covenant section in 30:6, the same phrase is used as a clear echo of chapter 10. The command is dramatically transformed, however. . . . The *command* has become a *promise*: 'Moreover, the LORD your God *will circumcise* your heart and the heart of your descendants, so that you *will love* the LORD your God will all your heart and with all your soul, in order that you may live.' Commanded *human* action has now become a promised *divine* gift."[4]

This renewal of the covenant occurs in part as a response to the impending crisis of Moses's death. The third sermon also, therefore, describes how Joshua was again designated as Moses's successor and includes a long farewell song from Moses (chap. 32).

Fourth sermon: Blessing (Deut. 33:1–34:12). The fourth and final sermon in Deuteronomy consists of Moses's farewell blessing. In this sermon, the dying priest-prophet blesses each of the tribes of Israel in succession, from

firstfruits An agricultural term for crops collected at the beginning of the harvest season; Jesus is called the "firstfruits of the resurrection" because his resurrection is thought to precede and anticipate the general resurrection of all.

Reuben (33:6) through Asher (33:24). By ending with a blessing, the book of Deuteronomy reminds its readers that, from the time of Abraham, God has been committed to building an entire people, beginning with a barren couple. Yahweh's people-building project has reached a turning point, and it is time for them to have a more permanent home. Ronald Clements notes that the laws of Deuteronomy include a list of curses for those who violate the covenant and its requirements (see chaps. 28–30). "But curse cannot be the ultimate fate of Israel as a nation, and the grounds for believing this are set out here in the context of the hymnic celebration of God's power. So this final formulaic blessing with which Moses parts from the tribes and their representatives is a final pointer to trust in the power of God as the only source and assurance of ultimate success. It is, in the most literal sense, a poem that bids, 'Fare well!'"[5]

Theological Interpretation

Instruction (Torah) in the Service of Life

One of the most important passages in Deuteronomy occurs toward the end of the book. Most of the legal material—the commandments and laws—in the book occurs in chapters 5–26. Having covered those commandments, Deuteronomy then urges Israel to obey the law and in so doing to "choose life":

> Now what I am commanding you today is not too difficult for you or beyond your reach. . . . No, the word is very near you; it is in your mouth and in your heart so you may obey it.
>
> See, I set before you today life and prosperity, death and destruction. For I command you today to love the LORD your God, to walk in obedience to him, and to keep his commands, decrees and laws; then you will live. . . . I have set before you life and death, blessings and curses. Now choose life, so that you and your children may live. (30:11, 14–16a, 19b NIV)

According to Deuteronomy, the miracle that God works through the law is life itself. God uses the law to create an environment within creation where life can thrive and blessings can multiply. Just as the laws of nature make life itself possible, the laws that God gave to Israel through Moses make human life livable.

The themes of blessing and prosperity fit here also. Deuteronomy teaches that through the law God works to create blessing and prosperity. But this cause-and-effect relationship between keeping the law and experiencing its rewards needs to be commented on. Keeping the law itself is what creates blessing, according to Deuteronomy. If everyone in a society or community keeps the law, the community will prosper because the law itself is life. So choose life! Life is the choice that Deuteronomy urges.

One God: The Ten Commandments and the Great Shema

The most famous passages in Deuteronomy are, without a doubt, the Ten Commandments and the great Shema. Because the Ten Commandments are also given in Exodus 20, see chapter 5, "Exodus," for discussion on them.

Here the focus will be on a passage that has been critically important in Judaism, Deuteronomy 6:4–9. These verses form the first paragraph of a prayer known in Judaism as the Shema, which observant Jews recite twice daily, in the morning and in the evening (Deut. 11:13–21 and Num. 15:37–41 make up the rest of the Shema). The prayer takes its name from the Hebrew word for "hear," which is the first word in the passage.

> Hear, O Israel: The LORD is our God, the LORD alone. You shall love the LORD your God with all your heart, and with all your soul, and with all your might. Keep these words that I am commanding you today in your heart. Recite them to your children and talk about them when you are at home and when you are away, when you lie down and when you rise. Bind them as a sign on your hand, fix them as an emblem on your forehead, and write them on the doorposts of your house and on your gates. (6:4–9)

Judaism is not a creedal religion—meaning that it does not have official creeds (from the Latin *credo*, meaning "I believe") that are recited publicly as statements of beliefs. But the great Shema functions something like a creed in Judaism.

One phrase in verse 4 is especially important: "The LORD is our God, the LORD alone." The first half of this sentence declares the central tenet of Israel's faith: Israel belongs to the Lord. The meaning of the second half of the sentence is debated. It can be translated two different ways, each with a slightly different emphasis:

- "The LORD is our God, the LORD is one" (NASB). This translation, which is the traditional rendering of the verse, emphasizes the oneness of God—there is only one God.
- "The LORD is our God, the LORD alone." This translation, which most scholars believe is closer to the original meaning of the sentence, emphasizes the exclusive nature of Israel's loyalty to God—Israel will worship and serve only the Lord.

The Shema is the positive expression of the first commandment, which negatively commands Israel's loyalty to God: "You shall have no other gods before

The Great Shema in Phylacteries

As Deuteronomy 6:4–9 indicates, the Shema was to be fixed to the body and on the doorposts of houses and gates (see also Exod. 13:1–16; Deut. 11:13–21). Within Judaism, this takes the form of tefillin, black boxes containing Bible verses and strapped to the left hand and the forehead during morning services. These are also called phylacteries, a term that seems to have its roots in Matthew 23:5, where Jesus uses the word in a critique of the Pharisees.

Franz Obermüller / The Stapleton Collection / Bridgeman Images

Fig. 8.3. Phylacteries are two leather boxes, containing Torah passages, which are worn on the left hand, in accordance with Deuteronomy 6:8: "Bind them as a sign on your hand."

me." The Shema states it positively: "You shall love the LORD your God with all your heart, and with all your soul, and with all your might" (6:5). Many centuries after Moses, Jesus was asked which is the greatest commandment. Agreeing with the rabbis of his day, Jesus responded by quoting Deuteronomy 6:5 (see Matt. 22:36–37).

Miller has argued persuasively that "one proper way of understanding Deuteronomy is as an explication of the Great Commandment, as that is also embodied and explicated in the Shema and the Ten Commandments." The rest of the book interprets and applies the Shema: "Focusing on the Great Commandment and the Decalogue identifies a center around which other things revolve. It enables a reduction of the whole to its most important point, spelling it out in specifics and implications."[6]

God's people are to love God, as the Shema sets forth. And God's people are to love their neighbor, as the Decalogue spells out. All of the laws and instructions of the book of Deuteronomy are to be interpreted in light of these two emphases.

phylactery A small case containing Scripture texts and worn on the forehead or left arm by pious Jews in obedience to the law (see Exod. 13:9, 16; Deut. 6:8; 11:18).

A Theology of Memory and Rescue: "Remember That You Were a Slave"

Deuteronomy also gives voice to a theology of memory. The book urges Israel to remember both the suffering of its past and also its gracious salvation at the hand of the Lord. One place early in the book of Deuteronomy where this emphasis can be detected is in the commandment to keep the Sabbath. As noted already, the Ten Commandments appear twice (Exod. 20 and Deut. 5), with the only significant difference between the two versions occurring in the motive clause of the Sabbath commandment (italicized below):

Remember the sabbath day, and keep it holy. Six days you shall labor and do all your work. But the seventh day is a sabbath to the LORD your God; you shall not do any work—you, your son or your daughter, your male or female slave, your livestock, or the alien resident in your towns. *For in six days the LORD made heaven and earth, the sea, and all that is in them, but rested the seventh day; therefore the LORD blessed the sabbath day and consecrated it.* (Exod. 20:8–11)

Observe the sabbath day and keep it holy, as the LORD your God commanded you. Six days you shall labor and do all your work. But the seventh day is a sabbath to the LORD your God; you shall not do any work—you, or your son or your daughter, or your male or female slave, or your ox or your donkey, or any of your livestock, or the resident alien in your towns, so that your male and female slave may rest as well as you. *Remember that you were a slave in the land of Egypt, and the LORD your God brought you out from there with a mighty hand and an outstretched arm; therefore the LORD your God commanded you to keep the sabbath day.* (Deut. 5:12–15)

Exodus evidences a theology of imitation and sanctity. The reasons to keep the Sabbath are to imitate God and because God has consecrated the day as holy. Deuteronomy prefers a theology of memory and rescue. The reason to keep the Sabbath is for the sake of remembering Israel's own suffering and the gracious rescue by God.

This theology pervades the book of Deuteronomy. Israel is to remember its own oppression and suffering and therefore show mercy to those who are oppressed or experience suffering. This theme can be seen in the law that slavery—a universal reality in the ancient world—was not to be a permanent status in Israel.

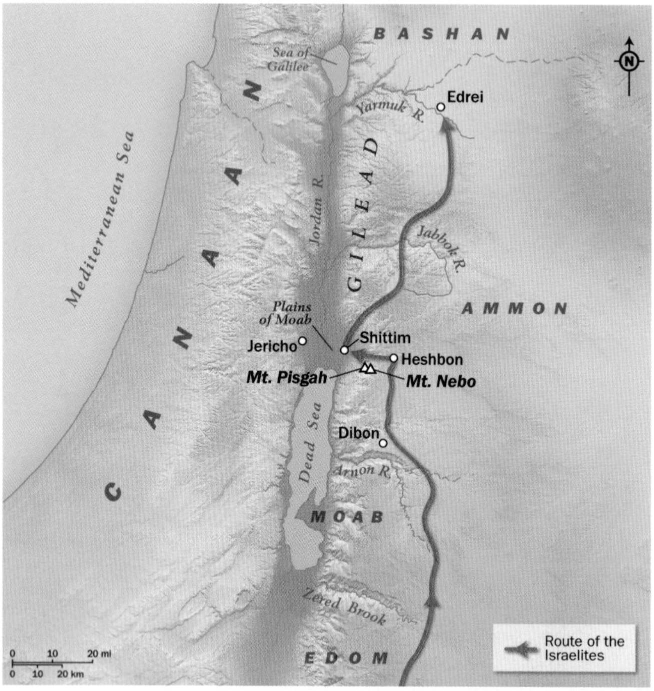

If a member of your community, whether a Hebrew man or a Hebrew woman, is sold to you

Map 8.1. Mount Nebo

and works for you six years, in the seventh year you shall set that person free. And when you send a male slave out from you a free person, you shall not send him out empty-handed. Provide liberally out of your flock, your threshing floor, and your wine press, thus giving to him some of the bounty with which the LORD your God has blessed you. *Remember that you were a slave in the land of Egypt, and the LORD your God redeemed you; for this reason I lay this command upon you today.* (Deut. 15:12–15; emphasis added)

Notice that both male and female slaves were to be set free after six years of service. And when they were freed, Israel was to "provide liberally" for them out "of the bounty with which the LORD your God has blessed you." Deuteronomy's emphasis on memory and especially on remembering its own experiences of slavery, oppression, and divine deliverance can be seen in many other passages:

- "Remember that you were a slave in Egypt, and diligently observe these statutes" (16:12).
- "Remember that you were a slave in Egypt and the Lord your God redeemed you from there; therefore I command you to do this" (24:18).
- "Remember that you were a slave in the land of Egypt; therefore I am commanding you to do this" (24:22).

The message here is that the Israelites were to remember that they used to be slaves and therefore commit themselves to living lives of obedience and mercy. This practice of remembering the past was intended to shape the ethical life of the community.

A Ritual of Memory and Offering

This practice of memory and obedience was integrated into Israel's worship life. Deuteronomy 26:1–11 describes a liturgy the Israelites were to recite as they brought the annual offering and left it at the altar. Notice the way the personal pronouns develop from "he" to "we" to "I":

When the priest takes the basket from your hand and sets it down before the altar of the LORD your God, you shall make this response before the LORD your God: "*A wandering Aramean was my ancestor; he went down into Egypt and lived there as an alien, few in number, and there he became a great nation, mighty and populous.* When the Egyptians treated us harshly and afflicted us, by imposing hard labor on us, we cried to the LORD, the God of our ancestors; the LORD heard our voice and saw our affliction, our toil, and our oppression. The LORD brought us out of Egypt with a mighty hand and an outstretched arm, with a terrifying display of power, and with signs and wonders; and he brought us into this place and gave us this land, a land flowing with milk and honey. *So now*

I bring the first of the fruit of the ground that you, O Lord, have given me."
(Deut. 26:4–10b; emphasis added)

The development from "he" to "we" to "I" shows how Israel's act of remembering its past with God played an important role in forming the people's identity as God's people. First, the ritual starts by describing the journey of an individual—"he." Israel recites a thumbnail version of the story of the ancestor Jacob—the "wandering Aramean" who "went down to Egypt" and "there . . . became a great nation." Second, the story evolves and becomes about the communal "us"—about our oppression and God's deliverance. The "Egyptians treated us harshly and afflicted us" but "the Lord brought us out of Egypt." Finally, the story develops further and becomes about "me"—about my own faith and obedience in worship. "So now I bring the first of the ground that you, O Lord, have given me." By reciting the story of the ancestor and the people and by connecting that story with his or her own story and practice, the ancient Israelite became part of the salvation history. Or rather, they let the salvation story become the story that defined faith and practice.

The Dynamic, Changing Nature of God's Law

Old Testament scholar Terence Fretheim has pointed out that a major feature of Deuteronomy is that God's "law is understood to be a dynamic rather than a static or fixed reality."[7] In Deuteronomy's narrative context, Moses speaks in the wilderness before Israel enters the land. But many of the laws that God gives through Moses look forward to a new, different context. These new contexts are often introduced by statements such as the following:

- "When the Lord your God has brought you into the land that he swore to your ancestors" (6:10)
- "When you cross the Jordan to go in to occupy the land" (11:31)
- "When the Lord your God enlarges your territory" (12:20)
- "When you have come into the land . . . [and God allows you to] set over [yourself] a king whom the Lord your God will choose" (17:14–15)
- "When you go out to war against your enemies" (20:1)

These examples are enough to show that Deuteronomy understands that God's will as expressed in the law changes over time. New circumstances require new laws.

The heart of God's law—God's "absolute law" in the Ten Commandments (5:6–21)—does not change over time. For instance, a law such as "observe the sabbath day and keep it holy" never changes. But what it means to keep the

Sabbath does change over time, in new circumstances. Keeping the Sabbath was not just about not working one day a week; it also included a Sabbatical principle in which every seven years, slaves were released from slavery. But notice how the practical release of slaves from slavery changed over time.

- In Exodus, which records the start of the wilderness years, only male slaves are freed on the seventh year: "When you buy a male Hebrew slave, he shall serve six years, but in the seventh he shall go out a free person, without debt" (21:2). But female slaves are not set free every seven years: "When a man sells his daughter as a slave, she shall not go out as the male slaves do" (21:7).
- In Deuteronomy's anticipation of life in the land, female slaves are included in the release: "If a member of your community, whether a Hebrew man or a Hebrew woman, is sold to you and works for you six years, in the seventh year you shall set that person free" (15:12).
- Deuteronomy adds another change. Not only does the person go out without debt, but the former owner must give them some start-up funds: "And when you send a male slave out from you a free person, you shall not send him out empty-handed. Provide liberally out of your flock, your threshing floor, and your wine press. . . . You shall do the same with regard to your female slave" (15:13–14, 17).

These examples could be multiplied, but this is enough to demonstrate that Deuteronomy understands God's law as changing to adapt to new times, new circumstances, new conditions, and new technologies.

Historical Interpretation

The Historical World behind the Text

As noted earlier in this chapter, there is very good reason to believe that the core section of Deuteronomy (4:44–28:68) was the book of the law that was found in the Jerusalem temple around 622 BCE, when the temple was being renovated during the reign of King Josiah. There is also very good reason to believe that this book of the law traced its own history through the Northern Kingdom of Israel.

The thesis is that when the kingdom split in 922 BCE after the death of King Solomon, priestly figures in both kingdoms preserved parts of the Mosaic legal and ethical traditions. The southern versions of these preserved traditions can be found in the set of laws in Exodus 20–23, and the northern version preserved traditions that can be found in Deuteronomy 4:44–28:68.

Box 8.6

Similar Laws in Exodus and Deuteronomy

Notice the many similar laws that are found in these two collections:

Exodus	Deuteronomy	
21:1–11	15:12–18	Slavery laws
21:12–14	19:1–13	Laws regarding violence and punishment
21:16	24:7	Kidnapping laws
22:16–17	22:28–29	Bride-price laws
22:21–24	24:17–22	Protections for widows, orphans, and foreigners
22:26–27	24:10–13	Loans and pledges
22:29–30	15:19–23	Appropriate meat for consumption and sacrifice
22:31	14:3–21	Dietary laws
23:1	19:16–21	Witness laws
23:4–5	22:1–4	Returning the animals and property of another
23:9	24:17–18	Treatment of foreigners
23:10–11	15:1–11	Provision for the poor
23:12	5:13–15	Sabbath regulations
23:13	6:13	Honoring the name of Yahweh
23:14–17	16:1–17	Sacred observances
23:19a	26:2–10	Firstfruits belong to Yahweh
23:19b	14:21b	Prohibitions around boiling a goat in its mother's milk

One view about the origin of the book of the law holds that when the Northern Kingdom fell to Assyria in 722/721 BCE, refugees from the north brought the book with them to Jerusalem. One reason to believe this is that there are clues that seem to indicate the book of the law reflects priorities that fit naturally within the Northern Kingdom. For example, Mount Sinai is consistently referred to as Mount Horeb in Deuteronomy—which was the north's name for that mountain. In addition, the core of Deuteronomy bears many similarities to the prophetic book of Hosea—who was a prophet in the Northern Kingdom in the decades immediately before that kingdom fell.

One of the more compelling reasons for considering northern origins for the core of Deuteronomy is the so-called law of the king in Deuteronomy 17. This important law establishes limits on royal authority. A king "must not acquire many horses for himself, or return the people to Egypt in order to acquire more horses, since the LORD has said to you, 'You must never return that way again.' And he must not acquire many wives for himself, or else his heart will turn away; also silver and gold he must not acquire in great quantity for himself" (17:16–17). Interpreters have noted this law seems to have King Solomon's royal excesses in mind: "King Solomon loved many foreign women" who "turned his heart away" (1 Kings 11:1a, 3b NJPS); "Solomon assembled chariots and horses. . . . Solomon's horses were procured from Mizraim [i.e., Egypt]" (1 Kings 10:26a, 28a NJPS).[8]

Box 8.7

Legal Revision

The chart in box 8.6 demonstrates that Exodus and Deuteronomy contain many similar laws. Close comparison of these two books reveals, however, that there are also significant legal differences that bear witness to scribal processes of legal revision. In America, there are several processes by which laws can be revised, including a process for the creation of amendments. On occasion, Israel also revised its legal codes to address changing times and circumstances.

One notable example of such a revision can be found in the legal material related to Passover. According to Exodus, Passover happens in a domestic setting, to the degree that the blood of the lamb slaughtered at twilight is put on the doorposts and lintels of the home (see, e.g., Exod. 12:1–17). For Deuteronomy, however, the Passover sacrifice may only take place in Jerusalem, which the book calls "the place the LORD will choose as a dwelling for his name" (Deut. 16:2). As if drawing attention to the fact that it is changing prior legislation, Deuteronomy 16:5–6 reiterates that the people are not permitted to offer the sacrifice in any of their towns but only in Jerusalem. Most interpreters assume that Deuteronomy's legal revisions are somewhat related to the centralizing policies of King Josiah (see 2 Kings 22–23).

If the world behind the core section of Deuteronomy reflects the Northern Kingdom, what of the world behind the beginning and end of Deuteronomy (1:1–4:43 and 29:1–34:12)? The matter is certainly complicated, because it is very possible that not all the material in these chapters hails from one time or one place. Some interpreters hold that all the material in these chapters dates back to Moses. Others think that some of the material—such as Moses's final song of blessing in chapter 33—is extremely ancient, while other sections date to later in Israel's history. Still others hold that the entirety of the beginning and end of Deuteronomy is a composition from much later in Israel's history. One view says that chapters 1–4 and 29–34 date to the time of Josiah's reformation in 622 BCE. This view says that if and when the core of Deuteronomy was discovered in the temple in 622, it was incorporated into a longer telling of Israel's history.

The Historical World in the Text

The book of Deuteronomy is presented as the farewell speech (in four parts) of Moses, who was not allowed to enter the promised land but was allowed to view it before he died. In recent decades, almost all secular scholars and many religious scholars have grown skeptical of the historicity of this recounting. Simply put, they do not credit the account of Moses giving a farewell speech as historical. Other biblical interpreters continue to accept the basic historicity of Moses, the exodus, the wilderness wandering, and the entrance into the land.

Some scholars take a middle road, holding that there was a historic Moses who led a community of Hebrew peasants or slaves out of Egyptian oppression. While they are skeptical of the view that the entire nation of Israel as presented in Deuteronomy was historically present on the plains of Moab, they do accept that a core set of the laws in Deuteronomy is ancient and goes back to Israel's earliest days. They conclude that the final form of the book of Deuteronomy is the result of an ancient set of laws that evolved, developed, and was edited over a long process that cannot be reconstructed with confidence.

FOR FURTHER READING: Deuteronomy

Brueggemann, Walter. *Deuteronomy*. Abingdon Old Testament Commentaries. Nashville: Abingdon, 2001.

Kline, Meredith G. *Treaty of the Great King: The Covenant Structure of Deuteronomy; Studies and Commentary*. Eugene, OR: Wipf & Stock, 2012.

Levinson, Bernard M. *Deuteronomy and the Hermeneutics of Legal Innovation*. New York: Oxford University Press, 1997.

Miller, Patrick D. *Deuteronomy*. Interpretation: A Bible Commentary for Teaching and Preaching. Louisville: John Knox, 1990.

Nelson, Richard D. *Deuteronomy: A Commentary*. Old Testament Library. Louisville: Westminster John Knox, 2002.

Olson, Dennis T. *Deuteronomy and the Death of Moses: A Theological Reading*. Overtures to Biblical Theology. Minneapolis: Fortress, 1994.

Thompson, Deanna A. *Deuteronomy*. Belief: A Theological Commentary on the Bible. Louisville: Westminster John Knox, 2014.

Tigay, Jeffrey H. *Deuteronomy: The Traditional Hebrew Text with the New JPS Translation*. JPS Torah Commentary. Philadelphia: Jewish Publication Society of America, 2003.

Part 3

STORIES OF LAND, LOSS, AND HOMECOMING

The Historical Books

Overview

The Historical Books of the Old Testament are the books that tell Israel's story from the death of Moses and the emergence of Israel in the promised land (ca. 1280–1220 BCE) to the end of the Old Testament period (ca. 433 BCE).

These books are marked by three important features. First, their primary genre of literature is narrative. There are songs, poems, lists of kings and judges, genealogies, and so on, but narrative dominates. Second, in the Christian Bible these books are organized in order to tell a roughly continuous story of Israel from around 1280 to 433 BCE. Third, the Historical Books include both source material and connecting material—that is to say, the authors of these books used a variety of older material. They then stitched that material together with their own words in order to create a continuous narrative. (It may be more accurate to speak of the authors of these books as "compilers" rather than "authors.") Biblical interpreters believe that they can often tell which passages in the Historical Books consist of older material and which passages are the composition of the historical compilers.

The Historical Books include the following:

Joshua	1–2 Chronicles
Judges	Ezra
Ruth	Nehemiah
1–2 Samuel	Esther
1–2 Kings	

Fig. 9.1. This illustration from the Visigothic-Mozarabic Bible of St. Isidore (960 CE) depicts the scene from 1 Kings 18 in which Elijah prays on Mount Carmel for Yahweh to be vindicated before the priests of Baal and fire falls from heaven.

Other Old Testament books, such as Exodus, Jeremiah, and Jonah, include historical narratives, but they are usually not considered among the Historical Books, per se, for two reasons. First, although books such as Exodus or Jeremiah include historical narrative passages, these historical narratives are not the main focus of these books. Second, a book such as Jonah is mainly narrative but was not originally part of the sets of books that the authors of the Historical Books stitched together—these books were collected and written by authors other than the compilers of the Historical Books.

Within the Historical Books, there are generally considered to be two main collections. The first of these is Joshua through 2 Kings (except for Ruth), and it also includes Deuteronomy. This collection, known as the Deuteronomistic History (abbreviated DH), takes its name from the book of Deuteronomy. (Note that Deuteronomy is considered part of both the Pentateuch and also the Deuteronomistic History.) In the Jewish tradition, the books of Joshua, Judges, 1–2 Samuel, and 1–2 Kings are called the Former Prophets—largely because the narratives in these books often involve prophetic figures.

The second collection in the Historical Books is composed of 1–2 Chronicles, Ezra, and Nehemiah. This complex of books is variously called the Chronistic History, the Chronicler's Work, or the Chronistic Books. Here, they

will be referred to as the Chronistic History (abbreviated CH). The
Deuteronomistic History tells the
story of Israel from the time of Israel's departure from Mount Sinai
(ca. 1280 BCE) to the destruction
of Jerusalem and the beginning of
the Babylonian exile (ca. 587–560
BCE). For the period of the divided

The Deuteronomistic History and the Chronistic History

Deuteronomistic History (DH)	Chronistic History (CH)
Deuteronomy	1–2 Chronicles
Joshua	Ezra
Judges	Nehemiah
1–2 Samuel	
1–2 Kings	

monarchy, the Deuteronomistic History narrates the fate of both the Northern
and the Southern Kingdoms. The CH begins with a series of genealogies starting with Adam but then spends most of its time retelling the story of Israel's
monarchic and exilic periods. At this time Jerusalem was rebuilt under the
leadership of the priest Ezra and the governor Nehemiah (ca. 450–433 BCE).
For the period of the divided monarchy, the CH tells only the story of the
Southern Kingdom of Judah.

Both the DH and the CH may have been authored or compiled not by one
person but by a "school" or team of scribes. For the sake of simplicity, in this
book we will use the singular—author, compiler, historian—to refer to the
agents responsible for putting together both the DH and the CH. Often we
will refer to the author/compiler of the DH as the Deuteronomic/Deuterono-
mistic Historian or the Deuteronomist and the author/compiler of the CH as
the Chronicler.

The remaining books in the Christian canon's group of Historical Books are
Ruth and Esther. These books will be discussed further in chapters 12 and 17.

Are the "Historical Books" Truly History Books?

Before turning to a discussion of each of these complexes of historical books,
we must address the important question of whether the so-called Historical
Books of the Bible are actually history books.

The term *history* is used in several different ways, and it can also be defined
in a number of ways. First, history can refer to "what actually happened" in the
past. Second, history can refer to the study of the past—to the study of "what
actually happened" and to developing methods of how to recover and learn
about the past. Third, history can refer to an account of what happened in the
past. These accounts can be written or verbal, or using modern technologies,
they can be video or audio accounts.

The Old Testament Historical Books are history in this third sense: they
offer a written, narrative account of what happened in Israel's past, Israel's
history. But two very important qualifications must be offered.

First, the Old Testament Historical Books do not meet the modern standards for "doing history." That is to say, modern historians have developed standard methods for producing accurate and responsible accounts about history. While there are many competing modern historical methods and no one method is universally accepted, the compilers of the Old Testament Historical Books did not have access to these modern methods.

Second, the writers of the Old Testament Historical Books—both the Deuteronomistic Historian and the Chronicler—were writing religious texts. They were doing theology. Both writers were writing to score theological points. Each believed that they knew important religious truths, and they were motivated to share these with other people. Their means of teaching these religious truths to others was to tell a part of Israel's story.

The Deuteronomistic History

Scholars believe that the books of the Deuteronomistic History were not written by one person but developed over time from many sources, as is the case with most books in the Old Testament. However, many scholars think we can deduce important things about the author, the contexts in which the books were written and compiled, and the purpose for which they were created.

Composition and Development

The most important clue to the identity of the Deuteronomic Historian and the reasons that motivated him to write can be deduced by looking at the closing verses of 2 Kings, the last book in the DH. Second Kings recounts that the Babylonian army had compelled the city of Jerusalem to surrender in 597 BCE and taken King Jehoiachin into exile in Babylon, along with many of Jerusalem's leading citizens (including the future prophet Ezekiel). The Babylonians then installed a new king, Zedekiah, who also rebelled against Babylon. The Babylonian army then totally destroyed Jerusalem in 586, resulting in the exile of many more citizens. The book of 2 Kings closes with these words:

> In the thirty-seventh year of the exile of King Jehoiachin of Judah [around 560 BCE], in the twelfth month, on the twenty-seventh day of the month, King Evil-merodach of Babylon, in the year that he began to reign, released King Jehoiachin of Judah from prison; he spoke kindly to him, and gave him a seat above the other seats of the kings who were with him in Babylon. So Jehoiachin put aside his prison clothes. Every day of his life he dined regularly in the king's presence. For his allowance, a regular allowance was given him by the king, a portion every day, as long as he lived. (2 Kings 25:27–30)

Working backward from this ending, scholars have concluded that the DH must have reached something like its final form after 560 BCE.

Historical sources. The Deuteronomistic Historian produced a coherent narrative of Israel's history by editing together stories, information, and poems from existing sources. He acknowledges some of these, especially when narrating stories about the period of the divided monarchy, when kings ruled the Northern Kingdom of Israel and the Southern Kingdom of Judah. Some of the sources that the Deuteronomistic Historian consulted are evident in passages that summarize the reign of each king. For example, note the references to the Book of the Acts of Solomon, the Book of the Annals of the Kings of Israel, and the Book of the Annals of the Kings of Judah:

> Now the rest of the acts of Solomon, all that he did as well as his wisdom, are they not written in the Book of the Acts of Solomon? The time Solomon reigned in Jerusalem over all Israel was forty years. Solomon slept with his ancestors and was buried in the city of his father David; and his son Rehoboam succeeded him. (1 Kings 11:41–43)

> Now the rest of the acts of Jeroboam, how he warred and how he reigned, are written in the Book of the Annals of the Kings of Israel. The time that Jeroboam reigned was twenty-two years; then he slept with his ancestors, and his son Nadab succeeded him. (1 Kings 14:19–20)

> Now the rest of the acts of Rehoboam, and all that he did, are they not written in the Book of the Annals of the Kings of Judah? There was war between Rehoboam and Jeroboam continually. Rehoboam slept with his ancestors and was buried with his ancestors in the city of David. His mother's name was Naamah the Ammonite. His son Abijam succeeded him. (1 Kings 14:29–31)

Unfortunately, these sources have all been lost to history. In addition to these explicitly named sources, scholars have sought to identify other sources that the Deuteronomic Historian used to create his history. For example, 1 Kings 1–2 offers a somewhat extended narrative about the political struggle between David's sons to see which of them would succeed their father on the throne (Solomon wins this struggle). Some biblical scholars have identified in this narrative a source that they call the Succession Narrative. First Samuel 4:1–7:2 narrates the tale of how the ark of the covenant was lost in battle to the Philistines but then later returned to Israel. Some biblical scholars believe that this account was once a separate source that they call the Ark Narrative. Scholars have thought to identify many other sources in the DH—with some success but rarely achieving consensus.

Contributions from the Deuteronomic Historian. In addition to editing together previously existing sources, the Deuteronomistic Historian wrote

Fig. 9.2. *Jeroboam Sacrificing to the Golden Calf* by Jean-Honore Fragonard

original material. His hand can be detected most clearly in the regnal formulas that begin and conclude the accounts of each king's reign in 1–2 Kings. The purpose of these regnal formulas is to assess the kings' reigns and their fidelity to God. Each king of the Northern Kingdom is measured against the negative model of King Jeroboam, the first king in the north. Jeroboam's great sin, in the eyes of the Deuteronomic Historian, was setting up golden calves in temples at Bethel and Dan. The purpose of these sanctuaries was to rival the Jerusalem temple (1 Kings 12:25–13:34). This sin was considered idolatry by the Deuteronomist, who wanted the kings of Israel to tear down these temples and return to worship at Jerusalem. When they did not, the Deuteronomist condemned them for walking in the sins of Jeroboam. All of the northern kings receive this condemnation. Here are the opening and closing regnal formulas for Ahab, whom the Deuteronomistic Historian regarded as among the worst kings of the Northern Kingdom:

idolatry The forbidden practice of worshiping images of deities fashioned by human hands.

> In the thirty-eighth year of King Asa of Judah, Ahab son of Omri began to reign over Israel; Ahab son of Omri reigned over Israel in Samaria twenty-two years. Ahab son of Omri did evil in the sight of the LORD more than all who were before him. And as if it had been a light thing for him to walk in the sins of Jeroboam son of Nebat, he took as his wife Jezebel daughter of King Ethbaal of the Sidonians, and went and served Baal, and worshiped him. He erected an altar for Baal in the house of Baal, which he built in Samaria. Ahab also made a

sacred pole. Ahab did more to provoke the anger of the LORD, the God of Israel, than had all the kings of Israel who were before him. (1 Kings 16:29–33)

So the king died, and was brought to Samaria; they buried the king in Samaria. . . . Now the rest of the acts of Ahab, and all that he did, and the ivory house that he built, and all the cities that he built, are they not written in the Book of the Annals of the Kings of Israel? So Ahab slept with his ancestors; and his son Ahaziah succeeded him. (1 Kings 22:37, 39–40)

The kings of Judah, on the other hand, are measured against the positive standard of King David and against the theological standard of the first commandment: "You shall have no other gods before me" (Exod. 20:3; Deut. 5:7). Negative assessments are not only reserved for the northern kings. Most of Judah's kings are also given negative or mixed evaluations. For instance, some are celebrated for walking in the ways of David but failing to remove the "high places": Asa (1 Kings 15:9–24), Jehoshaphat (1 Kings 22:41–50), Jehoash (2 Kings 12:1–21), Amaziah (2 Kings 14:1–22), Azariah/Uzziah (2 Kings 15:1–7), and Jotham (2 Kings 15:32–38). Only two are given unreservedly positive evaluations: Hezekiah (2 Kings 18:1–20:21) and Josiah (2 Kings 22:1–23:30). Here are the opening and closing regnal passages for Hezekiah:

In the third year of King Hoshea son of Elah of Israel, Hezekiah son of King Ahaz of Judah began to reign. He was twenty-five years old when he began to reign; he reigned twenty-nine years in Jerusalem. His mother's name was Abi daughter of Zechariah. He did what was right in the sight of the LORD just as his ancestor David had done. He removed the high places, broke down the pillars, and cut down the sacred pole. He broke in pieces the bronze serpent that Moses had made, for until those days the people of Israel had made offerings to it; it was called Nehushtan. He trusted in the LORD the God of Israel; so that there was no one like him among all the kings of Judah after him, or among those who were before him. For he held fast to the LORD; he did not depart from following him but kept the commandments that the LORD commanded Moses. (2 Kings 18:1–6)

The rest of Hezekiah's deeds and all his powerful acts—how he made the pool and the channel and brought water inside the city—aren't they written in the official records of Judah's kings? Hezekiah lay down with his ancestors. His son Manasseh succeeded him as king. (2 Kings 20:20–21 CEB)

Judah's one reigning queen, Athaliah (2 Kings 11:1–16), is not given an explicit evaluation, but the narrative of her reign suggests a negative evaluation by the Deuteronomistic Historian.

Some scholars who study the DH have also detected the hand of the Deuteronomistic Historian in a series of important speeches given by Israelite leaders at the end of their lives, as well as in several discourses provided by the narrator. These scholars identify a fixed theological ideology in the speeches, a perspective they ascribe to the Deuteronomistic Historian. These included speeches by the following:

Moses (Deut. 1–3)
Joshua (Josh. 23–24)
Samuel (1 Sam. 12)
Solomon (1 Kings 8)
Narrator—on why Israel fell (2 Kings 17)
"The prophets" and the "prophetess Huldah"—on why Judah fell (2 Kings 21:10–18; 22:14–20)

Origins and Editions

While there are many theories about the origins of the DH, the two most widely accepted are that the DH came into existence all at once in a single edition as the work of one "historian," or that it came into existence in two phases, with a first edition by one historian and then a second edition by the hand of a later writer.

Single-edition theory. Martin Noth was a German scholar who coined the term "Deuteronomistic History" for the narrative that runs from Deuteronomy through 2 Kings, arguing that the Deuteronomic Historian was not just an editor but an author.[1] Noth argued that the DH was compiled during the latter part of the Babylonian exile (after 560 BCE) in reaction to the destruction of Jerusalem in 586 and to explain why Jerusalem fell and its leaders were exiled.

Recall that many scholars believe that the core of the book of Deuteronomy (4:44–28:68; Noth considered the core to be 4:44–30:20) was at one point the independent Deuteronomic Book of Torah that was found in the Jerusalem temple in 622 BCE. According to this view, the newly rediscovered Book of Torah was presented to the reforming King Josiah ("I have found the book of the law in the house of the LORD," 2 Kings 22:8), and it became the basis of Josiah's religiously based reformation (622–609 BCE). But King Josiah was killed in 609 BCE, and the religious reformation that he started stalled. Judah's last few kings—Jehoahaz (609), Jehoiakim (609–598), Jehoiachin (598–597; then exiled to Babylon), and Zedekiah (597–587)—did not carry on this reformation.

The Deuteronomic Historian believed that if the Judean leadership and people had faithfully followed the law of God as set out in the Deuteronomic Book of Torah, then Judah, Jerusalem, and the Davidic kings would have been preserved by God. Writing during the exile, the Historian added 1:1–4:43 and chapter 34 to the core of Deuteronomy. Thus, the edited book of Deuteronomy

Box 9.2

Time Line of the Deuteronomistic History, Covering Events from the Time of Moses (ca. 1280 BCE) to the Exile (586-539 BCE)

Approximate Dates (BCE)	Events	Relevant Biblical Texts
1280	Life of Moses	Deuteronomy
1200	Conquest/emergence in the land	Joshua/Judges
1025–922	United monarchy (Saul, David, Solomon)	1 Samuel–1 Kings 11
922–722/721	Divided kingdom, ending with destruction of Northern Kingdom	1 Kings 12–2 Kings 17
721–586	Southern Kingdom	2 Kings 18–25
560–540	Deuteronomistic History edited/compiled	*Based on Noth's theory of composition*

then became the first book of the DH. Regarding the purpose of the DH, Noth writes: "[The Deuteronomic Historian] did not write his history to provide entertainment in hours of leisure or to satisfy a curiosity about national history, but intended it to teach the true meaning of the history of Israel from the [entrance of the people into the promised land in Joshua] to the destruction of [Jerusalem]. The meaning which he discovered was that God was recognizably at work in this history, continuously meeting the accelerating moral decline with warnings and punishments and, finally, when these proved fruitless, with total annihilation."[2]

Regarding Israel's future, Noth says the Deuteronomic Historian "expressed no hope for the future, not even in the very modest and simple form of an expectation that the deported and dispersed people would be gathered together."[3]

Dual-edition theory. Several scholars—most notably Abraham Kuenen, Julius Wellhausen, Frank Moore Cross, and Richard Nelson—assume that the Deuteronomic History was composed in two stages: stage one ended with the reign of Josiah (one of the rare monarchs whose reign is celebrated), and stage two concluded with the book's current ending in 2 Kings 25. Nelson has offered the most comprehensive argument for this dual-edition theory.

A complete summary of the dual-edition theory is beyond the scope of this chapter. But the most compelling textual argument for it is that the terminology and style of the concluding regnal formulas—the summary paragraphs of each king's reign—change significantly following the reign of Josiah. Nelson writes, "The historian's formulae, especially the verdicts upon the Judean kings, reflect a fascinating diversity, always made up of the same basic material of Deuteronomistic cliches and always with the same overall pattern, but never exactly alike. But the formulae of the exilic editor are carbon copies of each other with only the slightest differences. . . . The historian's verdicts for Judean kings are always supplemented by further information or at least by further cliches, but the exilic editor's are always limited to the bare formula itself, and even this is shorter than that of the historian."[4]

In addition to the single- and dual-edition theories regarding the development of the DH, there is a wide variety of other theories. These theories range from positing many editions and revisions of the DH, to rejecting the very idea of a DH, to arguing for a much later date for it.

Purpose of the Deuteronomistic History

Many interpreters believe that one of the primary motivations of the DH was to explain why God allowed Jerusalem to be destroyed, why God allowed the chosen people to go into exile, and what God's people should do next. To be more specific, many interpreters conclude that the Deuteronomic Historian believed God sent Israel and Judah into exile because they worshiped gods other than Yahweh. The Deuteronomist wanted the people, poised to return to the promised land at the end of the exile, to know that they must worship Yahweh faithfully or another such judgment would occur.

Noth believed the Deuteronomistic Historian had a very pessimistic purpose for writing—namely, that Israel and Judah were conquered and the people went into exile because the leaders and people failed to keep faith with God and his law. Many scholars have objected to this highly negative conclusion. Most famously, Noth's German contemporary Gerhard von Rad argued for some positive interpretations of the DH. He noted that the divine, unqualified promise to King David in 2 Samuel 7 and the characterization of David as both the ideal king of the past and the prototype for the perfect king to come run throughout the DH. In addition, the DH ends positively with King Jehoiachin released from prison and given a place of honor in the Babylonian court. Von Rad writes, "There can be no doubt, in our opinion, that we can attribute a special

honor The positive status that one has in the eyes of those whom one considers to be significant.

Box 9.3

Trauma and Literary Productivity

In the days after September 11, 2001, the streets and newspapers of New York City were inundated with poetry. Trauma had given birth to human creativity. Something similar happened with the Babylonian exile, and the Deuteronomistic History is just one example. There is a deep need within many human beings to respond to suffering by creating, whether through literature, art, or another form of expression. It is no accident that the Deuteronomistic History was not the only body of literature that emerged from the exile. In fact, it is not a stretch to say that nearly every book of the Old Testament was either written or edited in response to this traumatic event. For ancient Israelites, the most acute trauma was the exile; for the first followers of Jesus, it was the death of Jesus.

theological significance to the final sentences of the Deuteronomist's work"—there, "hinted at, and with great reserve," is the conclusion that "the line of David has not yet come to an irrevocable end."[5]

Literature in the Deuteronomistic History

Types of Literature

As with any large literary corpus within the Bible, the Deuteronomistic History includes many types of literature, including poems, psalms, prophecies, genealogies, and geographical descriptions. But far and away, the most dominant form of literature in the DH is narrative. Biblical narrative is different from other types of narrative in several respects. First, biblical narrative is theological. That is, biblical narrative assumes that God is active in the world and that God is at work in the present, shaping Israel's future.

Second, biblical narrative is historical, at least in the sense that it narrates the events of Israel's past. As noted above, the historical dimension of biblical narrative is not like much of modern history because it is not interested in trying to produce an objective report on the past. Rather, biblical historical narrative is interested in describing history in order to teach lessons about God and reflect on Israel's past and future.

Third, biblical narrative is distinctive because it has its own set of unique literary features. In the past half century, a great deal of research has been done on the literary features of biblical narrative. Of the many studies that have been published on this topic, the most influential has been Robert Alter's *The Art of Biblical Narrative*. The following brief discussion is adapted from Alter and several other important studies.[6]

Features of Biblical Narrative

Brevity. Hebrew narratives are concise, employing a minimum of words. The significance of each word is heightened by the text's brevity. This makes it all the more important for the reader to attend closely to everything that is in the text. A single word may greatly affect the meaning of a passage.

"Show" rather than "explain." Biblical narratives normally "show" a character's actions rather than "explain" a character's thoughts, motives, or feelings. The reader is very rarely told why a character does something. This results in narratives that invite the reader's active participation. In order to make sense of the text, the reader needs to supply hypothetical reasons why a character takes a certain action. It also results in a multiplicity of meanings, as readers supply varying motives to characters' actions.

Fig. 9.3. The story of King David's son Absalom revolting against and temporarily usurping his father is one of the longer stories in the books of Samuel (2 Sam. 14–19). Absalom is said to have been the most beautiful man in the kingdom—his wondrous hair is specifically noted (14:1–6). But his hair leads to his demise: while he is trying to escape after being defeated, his mount rides under a tree, and his hair is caught in the branches. His mount continues on, and Absalom is left helpless, hanging from a tree.

Symbolic wordplay. Biblical narrative is filled with symbolic wordplay. This may include the symbolism of a name, double meanings, puns, irony, parody, and the like. In addition to being aesthetically clever, such wordplays contribute to the meaning of a story by inviting the reader to ponder the significance of a given word or phrase. Such wordplay also can contribute to a passage having more than one clear meaning.

Repetition with variation. A very important aspect of biblical narrative is the repetition of key words or phrases. On the one hand, the repetition often signals the main meaning or theme of a passage. On the other hand, variation within the repetition is also important— slight changes in key phrases or themes can indicate narrative development.

Narrative gaps. A feature of biblical narrative that many modern readers find strange is the use of intentional narrative gaps—the withholding of key information when a narrative is recounted. These gaps might be about why a character does or says something, how old a character is when an event happens, where an event occurs, who hears or does not hear what is said, and so on. Sometimes a gap might be filled in later in a story. More frequently, however, a gap is left permanently open, and the reader is left to wrestle with ambiguity and accept that multiple interpretations of a story may be valid.

Juxtaposition. Biblical narrative often places smaller passages within their larger textual unit to achieve particular purposes. The placement of a given passage among adjacent passages or interrupting a longer passage can provide important developing elements of a larger story. Two adjoining passages that seem different can balance each other. Thus, continuity and discontinuity work together at times in biblical narrative.

The all-knowing, reliable narrator. From a literary perspective, the narrator of the biblical narrative is both omniscient and trustworthy. The narrator often reports knowledge regarding the inner thoughts of characters or about what is happening in the heavenly realm. How does the narrator know these things? The reader is not told. And yet the reader is expected to trust the narrator's account. This means that when the narrator reports something that happened or why it happened, the reader is to trust that information. But when a character says that something happened or why it happened, the reader can question whether a character's statements are trustworthy or not.

The Plot and Themes of the Deuteronomistic History

Plot and Development

As a literary complex, the Deuteronomistic History has a plot that runs through it. A plot can be described as a narrative problem to be solved, a literary mystery to be entertained, or a narrative question to be explored. In the DH, the problem or mystery is the failure of God's people—the fall and exile of the Northern Kingdom (Israel) with the destruction of Samaria in 722/721 BCE, and the fall and exile of the Southern Kingdom (Judah) with the destruction of Jerusalem in 586 BCE. As noted earlier in this chapter, Martin Noth viewed the purpose of the DH as being to explain the fall and exile of the people, while his German contemporary Gerhard von Rad believed that the work ends with hope—that the line of King David had not been extinguished and thus that there was still a future for the people because God's promises to David were trustworthy.

> **mystery** In the biblical world, something hidden that can be known only if and when it is revealed by God.

In this volume, we assume the plot of the DH is summarized in the speech given by Moses's successor, Joshua, at the end of the book of Joshua: Can Israel serve the Lord? Before Joshua enters the narrative, Moses renews the covenant between God and the people as they stand on the edge of the promised land; this is the book of Deuteronomy. Then in the book of Joshua, the new leader leads the people into the promised land. At the end of his life, Joshua also renews the covenant between God and the people. Joshua says, "Choose this day whom you will serve, whether the gods your ancestors served in the region beyond the River or the gods of the Amorites in whose land you are living; but as for me and my household, we will serve the LORD" (Josh. 24:15). The people respond, "We will also serve the LORD, for he is our God" (v. 18). But Joshua responds, "You cannot serve the LORD, for he is a holy God. He is a jealous God; he will not forgive your transgressions or your sins" (v. 19).

It is the contention here that this question—Can Israel serve the Lord?—provides the plot of the DH. More will be said about how this plot develops in the chapters dedicated to the books of Joshua, Judges, 1–2 Samuel, and 1–2 Kings.

Interpreters identify many different themes in the great literary complex of the DH. Four of the most prominent are mentioned here.

A cyclical and theological view of history. The DH views history as an arena in which the one God of Israel is the key actor. Because Israel's God chooses to be in a special relationship with the people of Israel, who often sin and turn their backs on him, their history often repeats itself in cycles of sin, judgment, repentance, deliverance, and peace. This cyclical view of history is especially evident in Judges. The same theological belief may also be applied to individual followers of God—individuals continue to sin, experience judgment, repent, receive deliverance, and experience peace . . . only to sin again and go through the cycle once more.

The importance of leadership. The DH places a special theological emphasis on leadership. When the people have faithful leadership—whether from judges, prophets, or kings—they do well. When the people have unfaithful leadership, they do poorly. The importance of leaders is especially evident in the major speeches given by important leaders.

God's faithfulness to the divine promise. Perhaps the most important theological theme in the DH is that of God's fidelity to his promises. The DH emphasizes that God chose Israel and remained faithful to his people in spite of their repeated infidelity. Most centrally, God promised to make Israel into a great nation and plant them in Canaan. These promises are made in the Pentateuch but fulfilled in the Deuteronomistic History. God chose David and his descendants to serve as kings of the people, and he selected Jerusalem to be the holy city where both God and David's line would rule.

Prophecy and fulfillment. Another critical theological theme in the DH is that of prophecy and fulfillment. God's word is ever present with the people through the ministries of "God's servants the prophets" (2 Kings 21:10). Through the prophetic word, God is active in history. Or, as von Rad writes, "What the Deuteronomist presents is really a history of the creative word. . . . It is only this word of [Yahweh] which gives continuity and aspiration to the phenomenon of history."[7]

The Open-Ended Conclusion of the Deuteronomistic History

The Deuteronomistic History ends with a strange yet tantalizing notice. As noted earlier, the text recounts that King Jehoiachin—who had been marched into exile in 597 BCE and replaced by Zedekiah, Judah's last king—was still alive in exile (2 Kings 25:27–30). He was released from prison and given a place of honor in the Babylonian emperor's presence—he was given "a seat above

Joseph and Jehoiachin

King Jehoiachin's story is similar to other narratives that recount the plight of Jews in the courts of foreign kings. The story of Joseph, for instance, contains a number of important parallels. Like Joseph, Jehoiachin is imprisoned (cf. Gen. 39), released from prison (cf. Gen. 41:14), given new clothing (cf. Gen. 41:42), and exalted to serve in the court of a foreign king (cf. Gen. 41:39–45). Similar parallels can also be found in books such as Daniel and Esther. The direction of influence is not clear. But what is clear is that, in every case, the Jewish protagonists are able to grow where they are planted and effect a positive future both for their people and for those around them.

other seats of the kings who were with him in Babylon," he dined with the emperor, and he was even given a living stipend for life. All of these are symbols of honor (compare 1 Kings 4:27).

What does this ending mean? More will be said about this in the chapter on 1–2 Kings, but here it is enough to note that the story goes on. The destruction of the kingdom and death of the last king, Zedekiah, was not the end of the line of King David. Jehoiachin lived and was free! As Terence Fretheim writes, this ending signals "a hopeful future"—a future in which God's promises to David (see 2 Sam. 7) and his presence with the descendants of Abraham and Sarah were still to be trusted. Fretheim writes, "At the end of Kings these words of promise are never retracted. With only words to hang on to, the future remains in the hands of the one who spoke them."[8]

This ending signals that the future of God's people did not end with the destruction of Judah and the death of King Zedekiah. The future of the people, according to the ending of the Deuteronomistic History, remained open.

FOR FURTHER READING: The Historical Books

Dutcher-Walls, Patricia. *Reading the Historical Books: A Student's Guide to Engaging the Biblical Text*. Grand Rapids: Baker Academic, 2014.

Fretheim, Terence E. *Deuteronomic History*. Interpreting Biblical Texts. Nashville: Abingdon, 1983.

Nelson, Richard D. *The Historical Books*. Interpreting Biblical Texts. Nashville: Abingdon, 1998.

Römer, Thomas C. *The So-Called Deuteronomistic History: A Sociological, Historical, and Literary Introduction*. New York: T&T Clark, 2005.

Trible, Phyllis. *Rhetorical Criticism: Context, Method, and the Book of Jonah*. Guides to Biblical Scholarship: Old Testament Guides. Minneapolis: Fortress, 1994.

Joshua

For modern readers of the Old Testament, perhaps no book is more troubling than the book of Joshua. The book poses disturbing theological, moral, and historical problems. Theological: The people of God wage a bloody campaign to wrest control of the promised land from the natives living there—and they do so, ostensibly, at God's command. (North American readers might be forgiven if they hear a bit of their own troubled history here.) Moral: God commands not only war but genocide. Historical: To make matters worse—or better?— the archaeological record in the Holy Land suggests that this great military campaign of command and conquest may never have happened. So what are modern readers, then, to make of this troubling book?

The book is named for the main human character in the book—Joshua son of Nun—who succeeded Moses as the leader of the people. But the sixth book of the Old Testament is not so much about Joshua as it is about the reentry of the chosen people into the land that God had, once upon a time, promised to Abraham, Sarah, and their descendants (see Gen. 12:1–3).

The book thus evokes many political and moral issues that are still relevant today in Israel and Palestine, as well as in any land or nation where past immigration has brought about conflict between natives and immigrants, or where present and future immigration is raising difficult questions. These questions include: To whom does a land belong? Who should be considered citizens of a country? How should competing populations interact with and regard each other? How are borders determined, controlled, and crossed? How should current countries regard past leaders who were once considered heroes in spite of (and even because of) atrocities that they committed during war? And many similar questions.

Background

Composition and Development

As is the case with most books of the Old Testament, the book of Joshua is anonymous. Its main human figure, Joshua, is identified in the Jewish Talmud as the author of the book that bears his name. Because of this, in Christian tradition he is also identified as its author. But nowhere in the biblical book itself is Joshua named as author, nor does the book include passages that might seem to indicate it was written by its main figure.

As early as the Reformation (1500s CE), readers began to conclude that, although the book contains material from sources that are quite ancient, the book itself was written much later. Most modern scholars consider Joshua to be a part of the longer Deuteronomistic History—a longer narrative arc comprising Deuteronomy, Joshua, Judges, 1–2 Samuel, and 1–2 Kings—which was edited together from a variety of older sources in or around the time of the Babylonian exile (586–539 BCE).

Genre

The book of Joshua is composed of two main types of literature: theological-historical narratives (chaps. 1–12, 22–24) and descriptions of the boundaries of tribal territories (chaps. 13–21).

Literary Interpretation

Introduction: Promise and exhortation to Joshua (Josh. 1). The book of Joshua begins with the Lord issuing Joshua both a promise and an exhortation. The promise is that "as I was with Moses, so I will be with you; I will never leave you nor forsake you" (1:5 NIV). The exhortation for Joshua is to be "strong and courageous" (1:2–9) as he assumes leadership of the people.

Preparations and entrance into the land (Josh. 2–5). Israel prepares to enter the land by sending two spies—or better, "scouts"—to Jericho, a fortified city just across the Jordan (chap. 2). The two scouts stay in the house of a prostitute,

---

Box 10.1

Outline

1. Introduction: Promise and exhortation to Joshua (1)
2. Preparations and entrance into the land (2–5)
3. Conquest of the land (6–12)
4. Division of the land (13–22)
5. Renewal of the covenant in the land (23–24)

Fig. 10.1. The Israelites escape from Egypt when Moses parts the sea and the people enter the wilderness. At the end of the wilderness wanderings, Joshua parts the Jordan and the people enter the land.

Rahab. The scouts are identified, and the king of Jericho orders their arrest. Rahab hides the two men and sneaks them out of the city, and she receives the promise that they will "deal kindly and faithfully" with her when Israel conquers the city. Joshua 3 describes Israel's crossing of the Jordan River into the land as a holy procession akin to that of a religious festival. Priests carry the ark of the covenant to the middle of the river, and in an echo of the miraculous deliverance of the people at the sea in Exodus 14, the river stops and the people walk across on dry land. After the people cross, the priests continue on, and the river resumes flowing. Twelve stone pillars—one for each tribe—are set up as memorials that the Lord parted the waters of the Jordan and brought the people into the land.

This miracle establishes Joshua as the divinely appointed successor to Moses—who had parted the waters of the sea. Having entered the land, all the males are circumcised, because circumcision had not been practiced during the wilderness years. The people then celebrate the Passover feast for the first time in the land. The descriptions of the rituals of circumcision and Passover are theologically important because they symbolize that the people are God's covenant people—in ritual good standing with both the Abrahamic covenant and the Mosaic/Sinaitic covenant.

A striking story that closes the first section of the book is worth special attention. Joshua has a vision of a man with a drawn sword. Joshua inquires, "Are you one of us, or one of our foes?" The man replies, "Neither. I am the commander of the armies of the Lord; now I come." The man then commands Joshua—in an echo of Moses before the burning bush—"Remove the sandals from your feet, for the place where you stand is holy" (5:13–15 AT). The story is striking because it does not associate the Lord specifically with Israel. The figure—either the Lord or an angel of the Lord—is neither Israelite nor Canaanite.

Conquest of the land (Josh. 6–12). According to the central section of the book of Joshua, Israel takes possession of the land by means of a violent military campaign. The narrative signals that the conquest of the land is not a human achievement but a divine action for which Israel itself can take no credit. First, Israel conquers Jericho (chap. 6). The story of the fall of Jericho's walls is also described as a priestly procession of the sort that one might have expected at an Israelite religious festival. Seven priests armed with trumpets—really shofars, hollow rams' horns—lead the ark of the covenant and the army in parading around the city for six days. On the seventh day, they march around the city seven times, then they blow their horns, all the people shout, and (in the words of the African American spiritual) "the walls came tumbling down." The Israelites are told to destroy the entire city, its residents, and all property, because they are "devoted to the LORD." The one exception is Rahab—who had dealt graciously with the scouts.

The narrative of conquest continues with the story of Achan's sin (chap. 7). Achan had taken a cloak, twenty weights of silver, and a bar of gold from Jericho as spoils of war. In doing so, he broke the commandment to destroy everything because it was devoted to the Lord. Joshua realizes someone had sinned when scouts whom he sends ahead to the city of Ai are defeated and flee in fear (that is, not being strong and courageous). Identified through God's revelation (by drawing lots) as the criminal, Achan confesses his sin and is executed. This story makes the point that Israel is not to go to war for reasons of greed and economic gain.

With the people cleansed of sin, Joshua urges them not to be dismayed and to defeat the city of Ai (chap. 8). He then leads the people to victory over Ai, which is totally destroyed—except this time the Lord allows them to keep the livestock of the city. Joshua again renews the covenant with the Lord. In Joshua 9, a people called the Gibeonites pretend to be travelers from a far country and present themselves at the Israelite camp as guests. Joshua, following the norms of the law, extends hospitality and makes a covenant of peace with them. When their trickery is known, Joshua abides by the covenant (thus disobeying the Lord's command to purge the land of foreign peoples), but he curses them verbally.

The conquest narrative continues with the dramatic story of the defeat of five kings who had allied themselves in order to defeat Israel. The foes clash at Gibeon, where "the LORD threw them into a panic" and "hurled huge stones on them from the sky" and caused the sun to stand still in the heavens (10:10–11 NJPS). The conquest story then climaxes as Joshua defeats city after city and king after king—first in the southern part of the land and then in the north, culminating with the city of Hazor. Joshua 12 lists the kings Joshua conquered, but chapter 13 describes the yet-unconquered parts of the land.

Division of the land (Josh. 13–22). Joshua 13–21 describes the division of the land among the tribes, with small sections of narrative interspersed. A few elements are of special note. First, the tribes of Reuben, Gad, and half of the tribe of Manasseh are assigned territories east of the Jordan River (the Transjordan). Second, a major fault line in the division of territories west of the Jordan is between Judah in the south (chaps. 14–15) and Ephraim in the north (chap. 16). This geographical division would later become a political

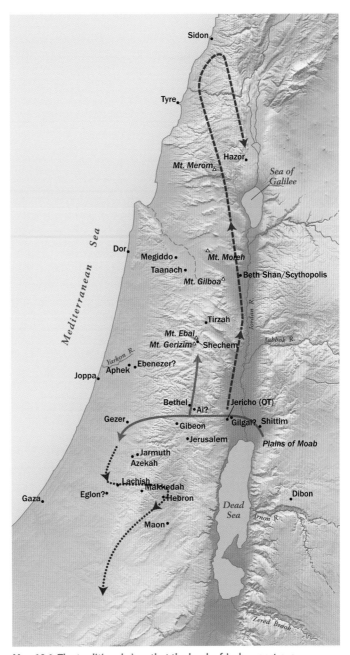

Map 10.1. The traditional view, that the book of Joshua portrays a three-forked invasion by Joshua of the land

and religious division. Third, chapters 20 and 21 describe the cities of refuge and the cities allotted to the Levites, respectively. The six cities of refuge were part of the judicial system—cities to which those accused of murder could flee to receive sanctuary until they could have a trial. Because the priestly

Map 10.2. Tribal divisions

tribe of Levi did not receive a tribal territory, they are allotted towns within the territories of other tribes. The Levites are divided into four groups. The descendants of Aaron served in and received cities within the tribes of Judah, Simeon, and Benjamin. The Kohathites served in and received cities within the tribes of Ephraim, Dan, and half of Manasseh. The Gershonites served in and received cities within the tribes of Isaachar, Asher, Naphtali, and half of Manasseh. And the Merarites served in and received cities within the tribes of Reuben, Gad, and Zebulun. In chapter 22, the Transjordanian tribes return to their territories.

Renewal of the covenant in the land (Josh. 23–24). The final section of the book of Joshua describes two national gatherings in which Joshua, now at the end of his life, leads the people in renewing the covenant and committing to serve the Lord. In the first gathering, Joshua exhorts the people to "be very steadfast to observe and do all that is written in the book of the law of Moses . . . so that you may not be mixed with these nations" (23:6–7) and "to love the LORD your God" (v. 11). In the second and more famous covenant renewal text, Joshua first reviews Israel's history in a long speech that is typical of the Deuteronomistic History. Then he challenges the people: "Choose this day whom you will serve . . . ; but as for me and my household, we will serve the LORD" (24:15).

The book ends with the reports of the deaths of Joshua and a Levite named Eleazar son of Aaron (a figure mentioned often in Joshua) and the report of the burial of Joseph's bones in the land. The report of the burial of Joseph completes the linking of the book of Joshua to the Pentateuch.

Box 10.2

The Plots of Joshua

Recall that in Genesis 12–18, God repeatedly promises Abraham and Sarah that their descendants would (1) become a great nation, (2) be blessed in order to bless other nations as God's priestly people, and (3) be given the land. At the start of the book of Joshua, the promise to become a great nation has been fulfilled. The second promise—being blessed to be a blessing—has been proven true several times. But the promise of the land, the third promise, is notably unfulfilled. At the end of the book of Deuteronomy, Moses and the people look across the Jordan River into the promised land. But Moses dies, and the book of Joshua begins with the people still on the verge of the Jordan River, still outside the promised land. Ominously, the promised land is filled with foreign peoples: Canaanites, Hittites, Hivites, Perizzites, Girgashites, Amorites, and Jebusites. From this perspective, one of the plots of the book of Joshua regards the fulfillment of the promise of the land—a land occupied by foreign peoples. Or, to put this a different way, a first plot of the book of Joshua regards God's faithfulness to the divine promises to his people.

A second plot of the book of Joshua involves the flip side of God's faithfulness—the ability of the people to be faithful to God. In the book of Numbers, the unfaithful exodus generation died out during the wilderness years and was replaced by the faithful wilderness generation. The question now arises in the book of Joshua whether the wilderness generation can be faithful to God as they enter and take possession of the land. This question ultimately leads to a gathering of all the people in Joshua 23–24 for what many interpreters describe as a covenant renewal ceremony.

The book of Joshua, as has already been noted, is about the entrance into and conquest of the promised land. At the start of the book, the people are still on the far side of Jordan. By the end, they have taken possession of much of the land—although it is important to note there are still Canaanites in the land. Most importantly, the Jebusites remain in possession of Jerusalem, from which Israel cannot dislodge them (15:63). In the process of taking the land, the people need help from a strange source—the Canaanite prostitute Rahab, who hid the two scouts sent to spy on Jericho. The Gibeonites trick the Israelites into a covenant of peace (chap. 9), and at times the people themselves sin and fail—such as Achan in chapter 7.

But the plot of Joshua is just as much about the obedience and disobedience of the people to the word of the Lord as it is about the conquest of the land. Will Joshua be strong and courageous in obedience, in leadership, and in not exhibiting fear? Will the people follow Joshua as they did Moses? What shape will their new life in the land take? Will it be centered on the Lord? As one reads the individual stories of Joshua, these plot elements are worth considering.

Theological Interpretation

God's Faithfulness to the Divine Promises

As noted earlier in this chapter, one of the main theological issues that the book of Joshua raises is God's faithfulness to his promises. In Genesis 12:1–3, the Lord promises Abraham three things: a land, many descendants who would be "a great nation," and that those descendants would be blessed to be a

Box 10.3

Can Israel Serve the Lord? Plots of the Deuteronomistic History

As was noted, the book of Joshua ends at the end of Joshua's life. Having succeeded—for the most part—in conquering and subduing the land, Joshua gathers the people at Shechem, when he was "old and well advanced in years," for what many readers call a ritual of covenant renewal (chaps. 23–24). Although the text itself does not call the ritual this, it does specify that "Joshua made a covenant with the people that day" (24:25). This covenant ritual marks the major turning point in the plot of the Old Testament narrative books.

Recall that in Genesis 12, the Lord promises Abram a land in which his descendants would become a great nation. From the end of the book of Genesis—when Jacob and his descendants had migrated to Egypt—through the book of Joshua, the major plotline is about the return of the people to the land that the Lord has promised Abraham. Left unresolved throughout the books of Exodus, Leviticus, Numbers, and Deuteronomy is the fulfillment of that divine promise of the land. The lengthy account in Joshua about the boundaries of the land and which tribes are to settle where is testimony to the resolution of that plotline. By the end of the book of Joshua, the plotline of the promised land has been resolved.

The ceremony of covenant renewal introduces a new plotline that dominates the rest of the narrative books in the Old Testament—Judges, 1–2 Samuel, 1–2 Kings, Ezra, Nehemiah, perhaps even 1–2 Chronicles—Can Israel, now a great nation settled in the promised land, serve the Lord?

Joshua, after having narrated the faithfulness of God to Israel and the long history of the Lord's saving acts for the people, puts this challenge to the people:

> Now therefore fear the Lord, and serve him completely and truthfully; put away the gods that your ancestors served beyond the River and in Egypt; serve the Lord. But if you are unwilling to serve the Lord, choose this day whom you will serve, whether the gods your ancestors served in the region beyond the River or the gods of the Amorites in whose land you are living; but as for me and my household, we will serve the Lord. (24:14–15 AT)

The people's answer is immediate and clear: "It is the LORD our God who brought us and our ancestors up from the land of Egypt, out of the house of slavery, and who did those great signs in our sight. . . . Therefore we also will serve the LORD, for he is our God" (vv. 17–18).

But then Joshua, having received the answer he had hoped to hear, responds in a most surprising way: "You can't serve the LORD, because he is a holy God. He is a jealous God. He won't forgive your rebellion and your sins." The people respond again, "No! The LORD is the one we will serve" (vv. 19, 21 CEB). Then Joshua replies, "You are witnesses against yourselves that you have chosen the LORD, to serve him." They answer, "We are witnesses" (v. 22).

The question in the coming books will be this: Can the people do what they have said? Can they be strong and courageous? Can they put away other gods and serve only the Lord? Can they obey the law of Moses, straying neither to the right nor to the left? Can they revere the Lord and thus not fear other threats? And if the people cannot—as Joshua said they could not—how will the Lord respond?

blessing to other nations: "In you all the families of the earth shall be blessed." Throughout the book of Genesis, these ancestral promises are repeated and renewed—over and over again. At the start of the book of Deuteronomy, Moses again reminds the people of that promise: "The LORD our God spoke to us at Horeb, saying, . . . 'See, I have set the land before you; go in and take possession of the land that I swore to your ancestors, to Abraham, to Isaac, and to Jacob, to give to them and to their descendants after them'" (Deut. 1:6, 8). God's promise of the land is a major theme in the first five books of the Bible.

As the book of Joshua begins, that promise is about to be tested and fulfilled. The "great nation" of Israel and its new leader, Joshua, stand on the verge of entering—or reentering—the promised land. God says to Joshua, "Every place that the sole of your foot will tread upon I have given to you, just as I promised to Moses" (1:3 ESV). By the end of the book, Israel has taken possession of the land—although many foreign families still reside in the land. The Canaanites have not been completely driven out.

God proves faithful to the promises made to Abraham and Sarah, Isaac and Rebekah, Jacob and Leah and Rachel, and Moses. Many, many, many years have passed since the first promise was made to Abraham. The people had left the land because of famine, had been enslaved, had been freed by the Lord, and had wandered in the wilderness. And now they are in the land. The Lord has proven faithful to the divine promises to Abraham and Sarah. But at what cost?

Fig. 10.2. A favorite story in Joshua is the fall of Jericho to the sound of the trumpet and the rescue of the sex-worker Rahab (Josh. 6). Rahab had offered refuge and escape to the spies whom Joshua had sent into the city (Joshua 2); in return for this act of deliverance, she is saved and becomes an ancestor of Jesus (Matt. 1:5).

Violence in God's Name and by God's Command

Many modern readers—especially readers who claim faith in the God of Abraham and Sarah—are deeply troubled by the violence in the Joshua narrative. In the book's opening verses, there is no explicit mention of violence, although God hints at what is coming when he says, "No one shall be able to stand against you" (1:5). But that soon changes.

Box 10.4

Violence in Joshua

The book of Joshua is a violent book from the outset. Chapter 1 begins with a divine speech in which Yahweh commands Joshua to take possession of land given to the Israelites (but currently occupied by others) and assures the newly appointed leader that no one will be able to stand against them (1:5). The book contains many other claims about the destructiveness of Joshua and the Israelites: "Joshua defeated the entire land, the hill country, the Negev, the Shephelah, the slopes, and all their kings; he left no survivors, but all that breathed he devoted to destruction, just as Yahweh the God of Israel commanded" (10:40 AT). If the contents of the book itself were not challenging enough, the history of the book's interpretation is also deeply troubling, especially when it has given sanction to religious violence.

As you read through the Old Testament, you will have many more opportunities to wrestle with difficult topics. We encourage you to do so with the following questions in mind: (1) Given its own historical context, what problems was the ancient text trying to address? (2) To whom was this text addressed, and what might it have communicated to them? (3) How is the text in tension with your own sensibilities as a reader? (4) If you do find yourself at odds with the biblical text, what do you think should be done about that?

The residents of the city of Jericho close their gates against the invading army of Israelites, and following the seven-day procession of trumpet-playing priests around the city, the Lord brings down the walls of Jericho in an act of divine violence: "The people shouted, the trumpets were blown, . . . and the wall fell down flat. And the people—down to each man—charged into the city and captured it. They devoted to destruction by the edge of the sword everyone who was in the city—men and women; young and old; oxen, sheep, and donkeys" (Josh. 6:20–21 AT).

Only the household of the prostitute Rahab, who had saved the two Israelite spies, is spared. She becomes part of the people and even an ancestor of King David and Jesus—she is mentioned in Matthew's genealogy of Jesus (Matt. 1).

Having committed and commanded violence at Jericho, the Lord then commanded that the violence continue at Ai (chap. 8), Hazor (chap. 11), and elsewhere. The book is explicit that God not only tolerated violence in his service but commanded it and even personally performed it.

The Land and Its Conquest

Closely related to the theme of divinely sanctioned violence in Joshua is the theme of the divinely blessed conquest of the land. As already noted, the book begins with the people standing on the verge of entering the promised land. By the end of the book, they occupy the land and move into the areas allocated

"The Ban" (Herem) in Joshua

Related to the broader theme of violence in the book of Joshua is the theological concept of "the ban"—which translates the Hebrew word *herem* (which is not the same as the English word *harem* and should not be confused with it). The word *herem* is difficult to translate, but it indicates a being or thing that is off limits to human beings because it is devoted to God alone. If a human sought to own or possess something that was *herem*—and therefore could only be owned by God—it would result in a devastating curse for both that person and his entire people. Exactly what persons and things were considered *herem* varies in the Old Testament, but the most extreme case occurred in the attack on Jericho, where everyone and everything in the city (except Rahab's household) were set aside as *herem*: "The city and everything in it are devoted to the Lord" (6:17 AT). Therefore, when the city was taken, every living thing was killed, and all the gold and silver went to the treasury of the Lord.

One possible rationale for this violence was to curb the desire for war. In the ancient world, a primary motive for war was to gain slaves and wealth—wealth in the forms of immediate spoils and ongoing taxation in the form of annual tribute. The biblical concept of *herem* seems aimed at this motive, since neither human slaves nor animals (in the case of Jericho) could be taken as spoils of war. Thus, the keeping of the *herem*—as rightfully horrifying as it seems to us—may have been seen as an act of the highest obedience to God and the relinquishment of selfish desires for profit in times of war.

to the individual tribes, with certain cities designated for refuge and for the Levites (chaps. 13–22).

The story of Joshua is told from the perspective of the people of Israel. From this perspective, the conquest of ancient Israel was the resettling of the promised land by the people to whom it justly belonged. But from the perspective of the Canaanites who were living in the land already, the story certainly would read very differently. As Richard Nelson writes,

> Modern readers experience discomfort with the notion of divinely directed conquest. We naturally read Joshua against the background of the Crusades, colonial conquests in the Americas, Africa, and Asia, and the physical and cultural destruction of indigenous peoples by aggressive outsiders. To us Joshua may sound like a theological justification for the forceful appropriation of land that rightfully belongs to others. Certainly a hermeneutic of suspicion is not out of place here, especially since the ideology of Joshua has been used to justify such policies in North America, South Africa, and the Middle East.[1]

But as Nelson also notes, the Israelites were almost always a small, vulnerable people, who were themselves constantly being invaded, enslaved, and oppressed: "It was most often Israel who was victimized as an indigenous people menaced by politically and technically superior outside forces."[2]

The issue of who has a right to live in and possess the promised land—or any land, for that matter—is an issue that resonates still today. But just to focus on

The Land and Modern Israel

The modern nation of Israel was constituted in 1948. Since that time, some people (including many native Palestinians) have viewed the land as territory occupied by an illegitimate power—namely, Israel. Many other people, however, believe that Israel has a right to exist as a Jewish state within its traditional boundaries. They view the migration of Jewish people to the land of Israel as a fundamental right—the right of a people to return to its original land. This complicated and multifaceted issue should be discussed with humility and with the recognition that slogans and headlines do not even come close to representing the current situation.

the issue of the land of Israel: Who has a right to live *there*? Following a revolt against Rome around 132 CE, Jews were barred from living in Jerusalem for a time. At the time, many Jews joined relatives who had already moved away from the land. Although a Jewish presence was always maintained in the promised land, over the centuries—especially during and after the Crusades—the Jews became a minority in the land. That reality started to shift in the 1800s, 1900s, and especially after World War II, when many Jews migrated to the land. But even how one describes this migration is fraught with tension. Were these modern Jewish migrants "returning to the land"? Or were they invading it? Do groups have rights to migrate across borders? If so, what gives them that right? Do nations have rights and responsibilities to control their borders? Who has the right to declare a border? These are difficult questions that persist into the present.

When people of faith take sides in these debates, they inevitably combine their theological and ethical perspectives with their political perspectives. We do not need to fear this reality, but we should be aware of how it shapes our conversations.

Leadership of God's People

The book of Joshua begins with the ominous words "After the death of Moses." These words may remind readers of what happened the last time the people were left without the leadership of Moses. In Exodus 32, when Moses is delayed from coming down from Mount Sinai, Aaron and the people panic. They forge a golden calf to represent the presence of the Lord and—in violation of the first commandment—worship the graven image of the calf as if it were the Lord.

A fundamental theme of the book of Joshua is leadership. In fact, leadership is a fundamental theme of the entire Deuteronomistic History. To oversimplify, when the people have good leadership, they thrive. When people have poor leadership, they suffer. For the Deuteronomistic History, good leadership is defined generally as adherence to the first commandment.

The importance of leadership is almost universally acknowledged today. There are myriad books, theories, conferences, schools, and coaches on leadership. One's commitments about what makes for good leadership are strongly influenced by one's political, philosophical, and economic ideologies. But theological commitments also influence one's views on leadership.

The book of Joshua is often seen as a story of leadership. According to the book's introduction, after the death of Moses, the Lord spoke directly to Joshua and commanded him to "be strong and courageous" in three different ways. First, Joshua was to be strong and courageous in leading the people to take "possession of the land" (1:6). Second, Joshua was "to act in accordance with all the law that my servant Moses commanded you; do not turn from it to the right hand or to the left" and to "meditate on it day and night" (vv. 7–8). And third, Joshua was to be strong and courageous by not being afraid (v. 9). At the end of Joshua 1, the people of Israel themselves also exhort Joshua to be strong and courageous (v. 16).

These three "be strong and courageous" exhortations to Joshua by the Lord contribute to the Deuteronomistic History's picture of a leader. Good leaders trust in God and therefore do not exhibit fear; they act in accordance with the law of Moses and do not turn from the law; and they trust in the promises the Lord made to Israel's ancestors.

The Need to Renew the Covenant

Another important theological issue in the book of Joshua is the need for the covenant with the Lord to be renewed from time to time—at least once each generation. Twice in the book, Joshua leads the people in a worship ritual that looks like a renewal of the covenant—although that language is not specifically used (to use this language is an act of theological interpretation). In Joshua 8:30–35, following the defeat and destruction of the city of Ai and acting in accordance with the law of Moses, Joshua builds an altar, writes a copy of the law on stones, and reads the entirety of it to the people. Then the Levitical priests bless the people. Again, at the end of the book and at the end of his life, Joshua calls the people to recommit themselves to following the Lord (chaps. 23–24). After gathering the people and narrating the long history of the Lord's saving acts on the people's behalf, Joshua calls the people to "choose this day whom you will serve . . . ; but as for me and my household, we will serve the Lord" (24:15).

It is often said that the people of God are always one generation away from extinction—meaning that if the people of God do not pass on their faith to their children and grandchildren, the community of faith can cease to exist within one or two generations. Perhaps no book of the Bible or story in the

Bible makes this point more clearly than the stories of the renewal of the covenant in Joshua 8 and 23–24. According to Joshua, the relationship between the Lord and the people requires renewal. Such renewal is an act of worship that includes blessing and offering, attending to the words of Scripture, and the articulation of commitment between the Lord and the people.

Historical Interpretation

The Historical World behind the Text

One way that historians read ancient stories such as Joshua is to ask, Although the story is set in 1240–1200 BCE, when was the story actually written down, for whom, and for what reasons? Readers may recall from the chapter introducing the Historical Books and especially the Deuteronomistic History that most scholars believe the DH was compiled (or completed) during the time of the Babylonian exile. That is to say, it was a story that was being told by and to a people who had suffered military defeat, whose cities and city walls had been destroyed, and who were themselves exiled in a foreign land—away from their land.

Interpreted against the background of the people's exile to Babylon, the story of Joshua urges the exiled Judeans to be "strong and courageous," to fear the Lord and maintain faith in the Lord, to obey the law of Moses and take heart that they would be returned to the promised land in due time, and, once they were back home, to be pure in their worship of Yahweh and (disturbingly) to drive out foreigners who do not worship Yahweh.

In this same context, the book may be interpreted to mean that obeying the law and trusting in God's promises would lead to a brighter future. It may have reminded the people that they had a long history of disobedience to the Lord—including the failure to wipe out the Canaanites, which later led to the people worshiping Canaanite gods. Richard Nelson's words are helpful in this regard:

> The audience of the final form of Joshua was looking back to a glorious past and hoping for a better future. This audience appears to match the situation of Jews of the exile or of the Persian period. The outcome of Israel's chronic disobedience had been defeat, exile, and loss of national independence. However, these readers continued to dream of a return to a situation where everything would be restored to the way things were when Joshua and the high priest Eleazar were co-leaders. . . .
>
> Joshua presents these exilic and postexilic readers with a glorious vision of the golden past as a reflection of what they hope might be true again. The community is offered hope for restoration of what has been lost and given a sense of connection with their pioneer ancestors who experienced God's mighty deeds.

Israel possesses all its land again, town by town, border by border, tribe by tribe.[3]

The Historical World in the Text

At the start of this chapter, it was noted that one of the factors that might make the moral issue of the conquest of the land less (or more?) problematic is that the archaeological record in the Holy Land provides no evidence that this great military campaign of command and conquest occurred, at least in the manner described in the book of Joshua.

There is no country on the planet that has been the subject of more archaeological investigation. The amount of literature on the archaeology and history of ancient Israel is immense and intimidating—and chock-full of strong disagreements between historians. There are debates about whether historians can use the biblical narrative at all to write history about ancient Israel. There are also debates about what the archaeological data are and how to interpret them. *The Quest for the Historical Israel: Debating Archaeology and the History of Early Israel* (by Israel Finkelstein and Amihai Mazar; edited by Brian Schmidt) and *The Rise of Ancient Israel* (by Herschel Shanks et al.) are good places to start to understand the huge intellectual challenges and the intensity of the debates.

Regarding the time period in which the book of Joshua is set (ca. 1240–1200 BCE), the evidence is mixed. On the one hand, it seems likely from the archaeological evidence that the cities of Jericho and Ai—whose destructions are detailed in chapters 6 and 8—were not occupied during the period. In addition, the archaeological record does not seem to support a mass conquest of the land by an invading army. On the other hand, the archaeological record

Fig. 10.3. A picture of the Merneptah Stele, with close-up of the "Israel is laid waste" section

Box 10.7

Three Models of the Emergence of Israel

Historians agree that through some series of events a distinct group of people emerged in the land of Canaan and that this people was eventually called "Israel." How this happened is somewhat unclear and open to significant amounts of interpretation, especially when the archaeological data are considered alongside textual materials. In general, three models are currently used:

Conquest: This model defends the overall picture found in Joshua. The assumption is that Canaan was invaded by an army of Israelites who dispossessed the Canaanites and seized their land.

Peaceful infiltration: Others have argued that nomadic bedouins infiltrated the land, peacefully settling in homes and towns in previously unoccupied portions of the land.

Revolution: Others have argued that the people called the Israelites were actually Canaanite peasants who rebelled against the tyranny of the city-states and formed a new identity as Israelites rather than Canaanites.

What seems most clear is that very little is clear. But one thing that cannot be reasonably disputed is that a people called Israel did emerge in the land during the historical era narrated in the book of Joshua.

does seem to show the emergence of distinctly Israelite towns and cities and the emergence in the land of an ethnically "Israelite" people. In addition, there are extrabiblical inscriptions, such as a monument by Pharaoh Merneptah in Egypt that bears witness to the existence of Israel in the land. In his monument, Pharaoh Merneptah (who reigned ca. 1213–1203 BCE) boasts that he defeated Israel and several Philistine cities: "Ashkelon is conquered, Gezer seized, Yanoam made nonexistent; Israel is wasted, bare of seed."[4]

FOR FURTHER READING: Joshua

Cottrill, Amy C. "Joshua." In *Women's Bible Commentary*, 3rd ed., edited by Carol A. Newsom, Sharon H. Ringe, and Jacqueline E. Lapsley, 103–8. Louisville: Westminster John Knox, 2012.

Creach, Jerome F. D. *Joshua*. Interpretation: A Bible Commentary for Teaching and Preaching. Louisville: John Knox, 2003.

Finkelstein, Israel, and Amihai Mazar. *The Quest for the Historical Israel: Debating Archaeology and the History of Early Israel*. Edited by Brian B. Schmidt. Archaeology and Biblical Studies 17. Atlanta: Society of Biblical Literature, 2007.

Hamilton, Victor P. *Handbook on the Historical Books: Joshua, Judges, Ruth, Samuel, Kings, Chronicles, Ezra-Nehemiah, Esther*. Grand Rapids: Baker Academic, 2008.

Nelson, Richard D. *Joshua: A Commentary*. Old Testament Library. Louisville: Westminster John Knox, 1997.

Shanks, Hershel, William G. Dever, Baruch Halpern, and P. Kyle McCarter Jr. *The Rise of Ancient Israel*. Washington, DC: Biblical Archaeological Society, 1992.

Judges

The professional basketball player Charles Barkley would often pronounce defiantly, "I am not a role model!" Barkley could well have spoken for some of the people we meet in the book of Judges. Not all characters are role models, and not all stories provide the reader with a pious moral meaning. For those readers who expect or hope to find holy characters and pious morality in the Bible, the book of Judges can be a confusing book. On the one hand, there are some stories that read like the heroic sagas of the founders of any given nation—the stories of Othniel, Ehud, Deborah and Barak, Jael, and Gideon might fit this bill. But on the other hand, the book of Judges retells stories that are troubling and even horrifying—and these stories are not just about Israel's Canaanite neighbors but about Israel itself—the stories of Abimelech, Jephthah and his daughter, Samson and Delilah, and the rape of the Levite's wife.

Just what-in-the-world kind of literature is this? The book of Judges is about two things. First, the book casts a narrative about the fallen-and-sinful human condition. The book describes what happens to human communities when they are left on their own without any rule of law or governing authority. What happens is chaos and anarchy. The book sums this up in its final verse: "In those days there was no king in Israel; all the people did what was right in their own eyes" (21:25).

Second, the book gives a partial answer to the question of whether Israel can serve the Lord. Recall that the book of Joshua ends with a covenant renewal ceremony in which Joshua urges the people to "choose this day whom you will serve . . . ; but as for me and my household, we will serve the LORD" (Josh. 24:15). The people reply enthusiastically, "We also will serve the LORD, for he is our God" (24:18). But then Joshua replies, "You cannot serve the LORD, for he is a holy God" (24:19). And the people respond again, "No, we will serve the Lord!" (24:21). Thus, the end of the book of Joshua sets up the plot for the narrative arc that spans from Joshua through 1–2 Kings.

The question is, Can the people serve the Lord? The book of Judges answers that question: When organized as a loose, tribal confederacy, led by charismatic judges, Israel cannot serve the Lord—at least not consistently. The book makes this argument by telling the story of a nation of people that is fairly healthy at the start of the book but descends into moral squalor by the book's end.

The book is named for the series of human characters who rise up to "judge" Israel. The word *judge* is a bit of a misnomer. The so-called judges who lead Israel are more often called "deliverer" or "savior." These leaders were primarily political and military figures, rather than legal figures. The verbal form of the word *judge* occurs often, but it is used more as a synonym for *rule* than as a technical term for making a legal decision. For example, of Othniel, the first judge, it is said, "The Spirit of the Lord came upon him, and he judged Israel; he went out to war, and the Lord gave King Cushan-rishathaim of Aram into his hand. . . . So the land had rest for forty years" (3:10–11). The word translated "judged" here could be replaced by "ruled" or "reigned."

During the years in which these judges ruled Israel, they doubtlessly would have had a legal function to mediate disputes and make judgments in legal matters. King Solomon is later described as making very wise decisions, and the story of one such case—when he judged between two women claiming to be the mother of the same child—is very famous. In the book of Judges, however, the judges are not shown in this role, with the exception of Deborah, who helps resolve disputes (4:4–6). In the one instance in which a crime is committed and an aggrieved party calls for judgment—the case of the rape and murder of the Levite's wife (chap. 19)—"all the people" heard the Levite's complaint and then declared the community of Gibeah guilty. In other words, the only time there is an actual judgment, a "judge" does not preside or make the legal decision.

Background

Composition and Development

As is the case with most books of the Old Testament, the book of Judges is anonymous. Judges is part of the long, narrative section of the Old Testament called the Deuteronomistic History (see chap. 9), which spans from Deuteronomy through 2 Kings (excluding Ruth). The compiler of this narrative—known as the Deuteronomistic Historian—is anonymous. He most likely worked around the time of Josiah's reformation (ca. 620 BCE) or during the period of the Babylonian exile (ca. 560 BCE). But he undoubtedly drew on sources that were ancient already by their time. These sources most likely included things such as

Outline

1. Failure to conquer the land (1)
2. Judgment; Joshua's death; Israel's infidelity (2:1–3:6)
3. The first set of judges: Othniel, Ehud, Shamgar, Deborah, Gideon (3:7–8:35)
4. Abimelech's attempt to reign as king (9)
5. The second set of judges: Tola, Jair, Jephthah, Ibzan, Elon, Abdon, Samson (10–16)
6. Anarchy, chaos, and injustice (17–21)

lists of Israel's judges; a variety of oral tradition stories and tales from different tribes and locales of ancient leaders; ancient psalm-like hymns, such as the "Song of Deborah" in Judges 5 (which may be the most ancient source in the Old Testament); and written sources that may have included narratives about ancient figures or descriptions of Israel's geography and which tribes settled where. The book of Judges most likely reached its final form during the exile.

Genre

The book of Judges is made up mostly of theological-historical narratives, but it also includes a prominent hymn (Judg. 5), as well as descriptions of the land and the tribes and the non-Israelites who lived within its borders (Judg. 1; 18).

Literary Interpretation

Failure to conquer the land (Judg. 1). The book of Judges begins by essentially contradicting one of the main narrative claims of the book of Joshua. If one reads Joshua naively, the sense is that—with the exceptions of the Gibeonites, Jebusites, and a few others—Israel's conquest of the land was virtually complete. Israel totally possessed the land, and almost all of the Canaanites were driven out or killed. Judges 1 calls that narrative into question. Beginning with the tribe of Judah, the chapter describes how the various tribes defeated some Canaanite tribes but not others. Note that there were many foreign people still in the land that Israel continued to struggle against. Some were defeated after Joshua; others were not. Particularly worth noting are all of the Canaanite tribes that persisted in the land even after the battles that followed Joshua's life:

- "The Benjaminites did not drive out the Jebusites" (Judg. 1:21).
- "Manasseh did not drive out the inhabitants of Beth-Shean and its villages, or Taanach and its villages, or the inhabitants of Dor and its villages, or

Comparing Joshua and Judges

Both Joshua and Judges depict the lengthy time period nestled between Israel's multigenerational journey out of Egypt and the establishment of the Israelite kingship depicted in 1 Samuel. But Joshua and Judges represent Israel's eventual settlement in very different ways. In particular, certain texts in Joshua seem to describe Israel's conquest of Canaan in absolute terms. Joshua 10:40, for instance, reads, "Joshua defeated the entire land, the hill country, the Negev, the Shephelah, the slopes, and all their kings; he left no survivors, but all that breathed he devoted to destruction, just as Yahweh the God of Israel commanded" (AT). When one turns to Judges, however, the land is full of non-Israelite neighbors, who were apparently not caught up in the conquest. The two are also very different theologically. The narrative in Joshua is primarily driven by the promises God had given to Israel to settle the land. Judges, however, is much more focused on depicting a dismal, nearly anarchic description of life under the leadership of charismatic judges, with an eye toward demonstrating the superiority of kingship.

the inhabitants of Ibleam and its villages, or the inhabitants of Megiddo and its villages; but the Canaanites continued to live in that land" (1:27).

- "Ephraim did not drive out the Canaanites who lived in Gezer; but the Canaanites lived among them in Gezer" (1:29).
- "Zebulun did not drive out the inhabitants of Kitron, or the inhabitants of Nahalol; but the Canaanites lived among them" (1:30).
- "Asher did not drive out the inhabitants of Acco, or the inhabitants of Sidon, or of Ahlab, or of Achzib, or of Helbah, or of Aphik, or of Rehob" (1:31).
- "Naphtali did not drive out the inhabitants of Beth-shemesh, or the inhabitants of Beth-anath, but lived among the Canaanites" (1:33).

Judgment; Joshua's death; Israel's infidelity (Judg. 2:1–3:6). Judges 3 contains a list of all the people that Israel did not drive out of the land: Philistines, Canaanites, Sidonians, Hivites, Hittites, Amorites, Perizzites, and Jebusites. Ominously, from the perspective of the book of Judges, "they took their daughters as wives for themselves, and their own daughters they gave to their sons; and they worshiped their gods" (3:6).

In familiar fashion, the book also begins with the death of the main character of the previous book—in this case, Joshua. Judges uses the death of Joshua to introduce a theologically laden, cyclical view of history: "The people served the LORD throughout the lifetime of Joshua and of the elders who outlived him and who had seen all the great things the LORD had done for Israel" (2:7 NIV). But then "another generation grew up who knew neither the LORD nor what he had done for Israel" (2:10b NIV). The book then describes a cycle of faithlessness, punishment, cries for help, divine deliverance, and peace that would happen during the period of the judges:

- "Then the Israelites did what was evil in the sight of the LORD and worshiped the Baals; and they abandoned the LORD" (2:11–12).
- "So the anger of the LORD was kindled against Israel, and he gave them over to plunderers who plundered them" (2:14).
- "Then the LORD raised up judges, who delivered them out of the power of those who plundered them. . . . Whenever the LORD raised up judges for them, the LORD was with the judge, and he delivered them from the hand of their enemies all the days of the judge" (2:16, 18).
- "But whenever the judge died, they would relapse and behave worse than their ancestors, following other gods, worshiping them and bowing down to them" (2:19).

The first set of judges (Judg. 3:7–8:35). The story of each judge follows the pattern described above. Sometimes there are no stories preserved about a particular judge. For example, regarding the judge Shamgar, the book simply states that he "struck down six hundred Philistines with an animal prod. He too rescued Israel" (3:31 CEB). Or, similarly, regarding the judges Tola and Jair:

> After Abimelech, Tola son of Puah son of Dodo, a man of Issachar, who lived at Shamir in the hill country of Ephraim, rose to deliver Israel. He judged Israel twenty-three years. Then he died, and was buried at Shamir.
> After him came Jair the Gileadite, who judged Israel twenty-two years. He had thirty sons who rode on thirty donkeys; and they had thirty towns, which are in the land of Gilead, and are called Havvoth-jair to this day. Jair died, and was buried in Kamon. (10:1–5)

The stories of other judges are also told briefly, without detail. An example of this is the first judge, Othniel, of whom it was said "the spirit of the LORD came upon him, and he judged Israel; he went out to war, and the LORD gave King Cushan-rishathaim of Aram into his hand" (3:10). For other judges, very long stories are told with significant detail. These include Ehud, Deborah, Gideon, Jephthah, and Samson.

Ehud is raised up to free Israel from the obese King Eglon of Moab. A lefty, Ehud straps a short sword to the inside of his right thigh. After delivering taxes to Eglon, he slips back in to see the king, takes out his sword, and thrusts it into the tyrant's belly. The king's fat swallows up the sword, and Ehud escapes.

During the period of the judges, according to one theory, when any of the tribes was threatened by a foreign people, a judge would sound a call to arms.

Fig. 11.1. This image depicts the triumph of Deborah and Barak over Jabin and Sisera (Judg. 4–5). The artist writes, "Deborah is depicted as an anthropomorphized palm tree. The text describes her as sitting under a palm tree where people came to her for judgment. She judges on the hills of Ephraim and is an Ephraimite. The palm tree in Jewish tradition is a symbol of beauty, fertility, and righteousness . . . and is also the tribal totem of Joseph" (Nahum HaLevi, *The Color of Conquest* [n.p.: Biblical Art Press, 2017], 29). Deborah is both a judge and a prophet.

All of the tribes were supposed to respond and unite to defend the people. When King Jabin of Hazor, which is in the northern part of the country, oppresses the people, Deborah of Ephraim—who was both a prophet and a judge—sounds the call to arms. The tribes of Zebulun and Naphtali, led by Barak, join Deborah, along with Ephraim, Benjamin, and Isaachar. But apparently the tribes of Reuben, Gad, Dan, and Asher do not respond. Judah and Simeon are not mentioned; some speculate this is because they were already at war with the Philistines. This is the tribal alliance at its best, and only some tribes respond. Deborah and Barak defeat Jabin's army. His general, Sisera, slips away and takes refuge in the tent of a Kenite woman named Jael. That night, Jael kills Sisera by driving a peg into his temple with a hammer.

Following the death of Deborah, the Midianites arise to oppress the Israelites. The Lord chooses Gideon of the western half tribe of Manasseh as judge and warrior. Gideon demands various signs as assurances that the Lord will be

Box 11.3

The Song of Deborah

The Song of Deborah in Judges 5:1–31 is widely considered to be one of the oldest texts in the Old Testament. It is a hymn that praises Yahweh for his victory over the enemies of Israel. The text begins by claiming that both Deborah and Barak sang this song but then presents the poem in the first person. In this way, the poem invites each of its readers to place themselves in the poem. Foremost in this poem is the theme of the Divine Warrior, who emerges from Edom ("Seir" is a synonym). Creation itself responds to the Divine Warrior's presence with earthquakes, rain, and clouds. The poem also praises Deborah, a "mother in Israel" (5:15), and Jael's slaying of Sisera (5:24–27). References in the poem to characters in the surrounding narratives invite comparison of the poetry and the prose. While there are clearly similarities, it is also clear that the editors who stitched together poetry and prose left some points of tension unresolved. The poem, for instance, makes no reference to Sisera sleeping, even though this is an important motif in the narrative (4:21).

with him. The most famous of these is the sign of the fleece—he leaves it on the ground overnight on a dry night, and it is full of dew in the morning; the next night he leaves it out when it is very dewy, and in the morning the fleece is dry. Gideon intends to go into battle with thirty-two thousand troops from Manasseh, Asher, Zebulun, and Naphtali. But the Lord decides Gideon has too many troops, so he commands that anyone afraid be sent home—twenty-two thousand depart. Still too many troops! The Lord commands that everyone drink from a spring. All the troops who scoop water into their mouths with their hands are sent home; those who humiliate themselves by lapping up water like dogs are allowed to stay—just three hundred remained. With those three hundred water-lapping soldiers, Gideon defeats the Midianites and pursues and slays their kings. Then the Israelites ask Gideon to "rule over us, you and your son and your grandson also." That is, they ask him to rule as king (8:22). Gideon refuses but asks each to contribute a golden earring. He forges the gold into an ephod (an object of clothing used to divine the will of God) and sets it up in his hometown. The Israelites eventually worship the ephod rather than the Lord.

Abimelech's attempt to reign as king (Judg. 9). Chapter 9 tells the story of Abimelech (whose name can mean "my father is king"), one of Gideon's seventy sons. Gideon had refused the kingship when it was proffered to him, but Abimelech slays sixty-eight of his brothers and is declared king by at least part of the tribe of Manasseh. Only the youngest of the seventy sons, Jotham, survives; he curses Abimelech and those who made him king. Civil war breaks out between Abimelech and his nobles, and when Abimelech besieges a tower, a woman throws down a millstone, killing him.

The second set of judges (Judg. 10–16). Jephthah of Gilead is a mighty warrior and bastard son of a man named Gilead by a prostitute. Jephthah's half brothers drive him away from home, where he becomes the leader of a band

Fig. 11.2. One of the most important roles of the judges is to lead Israel in battle. As the people of Israel emerge in the land, they often face military threats from neighboring peoples who seek mastery over them.

of outlaws. When the Ammonites oppress Israel, they ask Jephthah to deliver them. Jephthah agrees, so long as they receive him as their head should he be victorious. The text says that "the spirit of the LORD came upon Jephthah," bringing him to the edge of Ammon. There, he makes a rash vow to the Lord: "If you will give the Ammonites into my hand, then whoever comes out of the doors of my house to meet me, when I return victorious from the Ammonites, shall be the LORD's, to be offered up by me as a burnt offering" (11:29–31). The Lord gives Jephthah victory. When he returns, his daughter is the first person out the door. She asks for two months to "bewail my virginity" in the mountains with her friends. When she returns, Jephthah fulfills his vow. Nowhere in the story does it suggest the Lord approves of Jephthah's vow or expects him to fulfill it. During Jephthah's relatively short, six-year time as judge, civil war and dissension begin to break out within Israel.

Samson is the last judge, and the narrative of Judges 13–16 recounts his story. Born in the southeastern tribe of Dan to an unnamed woman during a time when the Philistines oppressed the Israelites, Samson is dedicated to the Lord as a Nazirite—a special class of worshipers whose vows include no alcohol and never cutting their hair.

Box 11.4

Jephthah's Daughter

The tragic account of Jephthah's unnamed daughter (Judg. 11:29–40) is among the most disturbing in the book of Judges. It is right up there with the narrative of the Levite's concubine (Judg. 19). What both of these stories share in common is the fact that women pay the price for unchecked violence and foolish patriarchal leadership. They are victims of a destructive culture that found itself again and again in the throes of violence and destruction. From the perspective of the book of Judges, these women are victims of a people without proper royal leadership. Jephthah's daughter dies because of a foolish oath offered up by Jephthah the Gileadite, who vows to sacrifice the first thing that comes out the door of his house, if God will only give him victory (11:30–31). The Lord never commands this; Jephthah offers it freely. And since Jephthah wins the battle, he is forced to reckon with the harsh reality of his vow. Unlike the story of Isaac, however, the Lord does not preserve the child from her brutal fate. Jephthah's daughter—like the Ammonite foes he vanquished—dies at the hands of her own father. But unlike the story of Isaac, the Lord also does not intervene to stop the father from sacrificing his child.

But intemperate violence and desire seem to guide Samson; he is described as killing many people and visiting a Philistine prostitute. He wants to marry a Philistine woman; his father objects but arranges the marriage anyway. At the wedding feast, Samson bets thirty Philistines that they cannot solve his riddle. The Philistines goad Samson's wife into coaxing the answer from Samson and thus are able to win the bet. In anger, Samson kills thirty men and uses the spoils to pay off the bet. His wife is given to Samson's companion, but he later returns for her. When her father refuses him, Samson sets fire to the Philistine city. War ensues. Samson is victorious and judges Israel.

Samson meets and falls in love with a woman named Delilah, who may have been either Philistine or Israelite. Their story has been recounted in drama by the British poet John Milton, in film by Cecille B. DeMille, and in song by the Grateful Dead. In these retellings, Samson is either a hero or a tragic figure. The Philistines bribe Delilah to discover the source of his seemingly inhuman strength—such that he cannot be kept in bonds, even when Delilah has Samson bound in the middle of the night. After several lies about how to bind him, he finally reveals that his uncut hair is the source of his strength. One night Samson falls asleep with his head in her lap. When he awakes, his hair has been shaved. He is bound and this time cannot break loose. The Philistines blind Samson and set him to hard service in bondage, turning a great millstone to grind grain. But his hair begins to grow back. They bring him out to be mocked at a great Philistine worship service celebrating his bondage. But his strength has returned, and he pushes down the pillars of the temple in which they are worshiping, killing himself and his Philistine captors.

Anarchy, chaos, and injustice (Judg. 17–21). Judges 17 tells the strange story of a man named Micah who steals silver from his mother. When she curses the

Photo © Osborne Samuel Ltd, London / Bridgeman Images

Fig. 11.3. *Samson and the Lion* by Cyril Edward Power

silver, he returns it to her. She then forges it into an idolatrous image, and he installs one of his sons—not a Levitical priest—as a priest. A Levite from Bethlehem comes to live with Micah, who assumes "the Lord will cause [him] to prosper now that the Levite is [his] priest" (17:13 AT).

Chapter 18 begins, "In those days there was no king in Israel." It tells how the tribe of Dan migrates from the southeastern portion of the land (perhaps to escape the Philistines, who lived nearby). Some Danites set out to find a new home, and along the way, they steal Micah's idol and persuade his priest to join them. Then the Danites travel to the far northwest portion of the land, where they settle and set up the idol.

Judges 19 recounts what may be the most terrifying of what the Old Testament scholar Phyllis Trible calls "texts of terror"—the rape of a Levite's concubine. (A concubine is a sexual partner who has legal status but not the

---

Box 11.5

The Judges and Their Tribes

The book of Judges does not provide a comprehensive look at everything that was happening in the land during the time of the judges. In fact, very few of the stories actually have all Israel in view. Most of the narratives focus on a particular tribe. Chapter 20 (which recounts a war against Benjamin, Saul's tribe) is one exception to this. The twelve judges named in the book represent the following tribes:

1. Othniel (Judah)
2. Ehud (Benjamin)
3. Shamgar (unnamed)
4. Deborah (Ephraim)
5. Gideon (Manasseh)
6. Tola (Issachar)
7. Jair (Manasseh)
8. Jephthah (Manasseh)
9. Ibzan (Zebulun)
10. Elon (Zebulun)
11. Abdon (Ephraim)
12. Samson (Dan)

As you work through Judges, pay careful attention to where events are happening and which tribes are involved. Doing so helps one appreciate the deeply fragmented nature of Israelite society, at least as it is depicted in the book of Judges.

Box 11.6

The Plots of Judges

There are several plotlines that run in, with, and through the book of Judges. As mentioned earlier, one of the overarching plotlines of the Deuteronomistic History is whether or not Israel can serve the Lord. Joshua had exhorted the people to serve the Lord but had also warned them that they could not do so. The book of Judges tells one piece of that larger plotline.

Specifically, Judges describes how Israel was not able to serve the Lord when they were led by judges and organized as a loose tribal confederation, lacking a central government. Without the spiritual character to remain true to God, the people lived in cycles of infidelity. This cycle spiraled downward until the society was lost in anarchy.

Within the book of Judges itself, there are at least three other major strands of plot, woven together so complexly that it is complicated to tease them apart. The first plotline concerns the moral and political disintegration of the people. The second plotline concerns Israel's serial disobedience to the Lord. The third concerns other threats to the Lord's direct reign over the people.

The disintegration of Israel. The first and most dominant plotline in Judges has to do with the complete disintegration of the people—morally and politically. As described earlier, the narrative premise on which the book begins is that Joshua left the people on a reasonably sound foundation both theologically (by choosing to serve the Lord) and politically (in possession of the promised land). But the plot thickens from the very beginning by listing all of the foreign people that had been left in the land, people who would be a political and theological snare.

Israel's serial disobedience. The book of Judges follows a downward cycle of doing evil in the sight of God, being handed over to a foreign oppressor, crying out to the Lord, being delivered by a judge, having peace during the judge's reign, and then . . . wash, rinse, repeat (so to speak). At the start of the book, the people's sins are fairly generic and the judges that God raises up lead well and are themselves faithful leaders—Othniel, Ehud, and Deborah.

Beginning with Gideon, things start to go a little wrong. Gideon leads well, but his setting up of a golden image is idolatrous. Things get worse under Jephthah, who kills his daughter to fulfill a rash vow. During his relatively short reign as judge, the people descend into political dissension. The story of Samson is one of a selfish man of intemperate appetites. He uses violence not in service of the nation or higher ideals but for personal purposes—such as gaining the funds to pay off a bet or seeking vengeance. The stories of Micah the thief and his idolatrous silver ephod and idol, of the migration of the tribe of Dan, and of the rape of the Levite's concubine demonstrate without relent the decline of the nation in every respect. The bloody civil war that follows and the unjust peace that is settled at the expense of six hundred innocent virgins bring the book to its tragic end, in which the complete depravity of the nation is exposed.

Who will rule the people? The theology of the Ten Commandments and of the Mosaic covenant held that the Lord was to rule directly as king over the people of Israel—the Lord was their sovereign, and they were to have "no other gods" or lords. But God's people also need human leadership. This is a reality that the narrative of the Old Testament underscores from the beginning. The book of Joshua emphasizes this reality by focusing on the "strong and courageous" leadership of Joshua. With Joshua's death, the mantle of leadership falls on a series of judges. The leadership theme of the Deuteronomistic History—as go the leaders, so goes the fate of the people—continues into the book of Judges. When there are good judges—which mostly happens toward the start of the period of Judges—the people fare well. When there are poor judges, the people fare poorly.

This question of rulership is made more complex in Judges by additional thematic strands. The first is that of idolatrous images—one made by Gideon, the otherwise faithful judge, who casts an ephod of gold that becomes a "snare" for the people when they are drawn to it rather than to the Lord. Similarly but more perniciously, Micah the thief casts an idol, ephod, and teraphim with the stolen-then-cursed silver.

The second theme that complicates the question of who will rule the people involves human beings who would claim leadership of the people. The most obvious are the series of foreign kings and lords—Cushan-rishathaim of Aram, Eglon of Moab, Jabin of Hazor, and the rest—who follow in ancient Pharaoh's footsteps and seek to claim lordship over the Lord's people. But even within Israel, some want a human king. Some try to enthrone Gideon. Gideon's son Abimelech seeks the crown for himself. Jephthah will only save the people if they will follow him.

But the most important thematic strand in the question of who will rule the people concerns the false gods of the Canaanites and other nations, to whom the Israelites stray. From the perspective of Judges, Israel's great vulnerability and sin was the remaining presence of foreign peoples in their midst—"They took their daughters as wives for themselves, and their own daughters they gave to their sons; and they worshiped their gods" (3:6). Periods of crisis and oppression were caused by Israel worshiping gods other than the Lord. For example, the text says they worshiped "the Baals and the Asherahs" (3:7), and they worshiped "the Baals and the Astartes, the gods of Aram, the gods of Sidon, the gods of Moab, the gods of the Ammonites, and the gods of the Philistines" (10:6). The word *worship* (Hebrew: *'abad*) means both "to worship" and also "to serve or be a slave." Thus, the term suggests that worshiping a god other than the Lord is a form of self-chosen servitude or slavery. For Israel, the danger of false gods in its midst meant not merely the allure to a theoretical unfaithfulness, the way modern people tend to think of religious choices. Rather, for Israel, the presence of the false gods meant the very real and constant temptation to step away from freedom and back into slavery.

full legal status of marriage.) The Levite and his concubine are on their way to his home in Ephraim when an old man extends them hospitality. They stay overnight at his home in the village of Gibeah in Benjamin. That night, a band of Benjaminites, described as "sons of perversion" (19:22 AT), demand that the priest be sent out so they can rape him. The priest throws his concubine out of the house, and the men rape her all night. In the morning, she dies. The Levite cuts her into twelve pieces, sends the pieces to the twelve tribes of Israel, and summons them to Mizpah for judgment. The tribes judge Gibeah guilty and go to war against Gibeah and the tribe of Benjamin. In the first battles, forty thousand Israelites and 25,100 Benjaminites die. Gibeah is utterly destroyed, and another twenty-five thousand Benjaminites are killed. The rest of Israel makes peace with Benjamin—but a strange and unjust peace. No one would give their daughters to any man in Benjamin as a wife. Instead, they capture four hundred virgins from the clan of Jabesh-gilead, which did not answer the summons to come to Mizpah. They then allow the Benjaminites to abduct two hundred young women going to Shiloh—where the ark of the covenant was kept—to dance in worship during the annual ceremony to the Lord. So the brutal gang rape of an innocent woman leads to a war in which there is great bloodshed. Then in order to forge a peace, six hundred more women are abducted.

The book of Judges ends with a brutal summation: "In those days there was no king in Israel; everyone did as he pleased" (21:25 NJPS).

Theological Interpretation

Can Israel Serve the Lord?

As has already been noted, the major plotline and theological question of the Old Testament narrative changes at the end of the book of Joshua. From the end of Genesis, the plotline has been if and when God would restore the people to the promised land. By the end of Joshua, that promise has been fulfilled. But in the covenant renewal ceremony at the end of Joshua, a new plotline is introduced—Can Israel serve the Lord? Israel had vowed to serve—that is, both to worship and to serve—the Lord, but Joshua had announced, "You cannot serve the Lord" (Josh. 24:19). The book of Judges, which covers the roughly two hundred years from 1220 BCE to 1020 BCE, demonstrates narratively that in spite of strong leadership from many judges, Israel was not able to serve the Lord. The narrative strongly suggests that Israel's own spiritual frailty and inveterate infidelity are to blame. Israel cannot stay faithful to the Lord—a theme that resonates throughout the Deuternonomic History (Deuteronomy–Kings).

Judges as Commentary on Human Nature

Most people expect all the Israelites in the Old Testament to be positive examples of the Israelite faith, but they are not. In addition, the first question that most people ask of a biblical text is, What does this text tell me to do or not to do? That is, most people read the Bible assuming that it is primarily an ethical text whose purpose is to instruct us in righteous living. While that is true of some parts of the Bible, such as the Ten Commandments, it is not true of all texts—including most of the stories in Judges and in the book as a whole.

The Bible is a powerful book because it is revelatory. Sometimes it reveals something about God. Sometimes it reveals something about creation. And sometimes—as in the book of Judges—it also reveals something about humanity. Better first questions to ask of biblical texts are, What does the text say? and What does the text mean?

So what does the book of Judges as a whole say? Overall, the story describes the massive disintegration and devolution of a relatively healthy and strong people to a completely unjust and unfaithful people. The repeated cycle—forsaking God, worshiping foreign gods, being given over to oppression, calling on the Lord, being delivered by a judge, and having peace during the judge's life—eventually devolves to the point that even during the judges' lives there isn't peace. The judges themselves bring violence inside Israel, in the cases of Jephthah and Samson. And after Samson, there are no more judges—just mass anarchy, injustice, infidelity, and violence.

The group rape of the Levite's concubine—in which he is himself complicit—and the ensuing civil war, followed by the abduction of six hundred more women is a story that sheds a brutal revealing light on the human condition. Human beings—even among God's people—are capable of great evil.

The human condition is one of being born into a broken and sin-dominated world. There is an old theological maxim that states, "It is not possible not to sin." Sin is inevitable. And where there is no law, where anarchy exists, sin will run wild. The situation within God's own "holy" people at the end of Judges is no better than it was in Genesis 6, when God saw that the inclination of the human heart was nothing but sin and violence, and God was sorry that he had created humanity.

At the end of the book, the reader is left to wonder: How will a God who promised not to destroy the world respond to his people when they are no better than humanity was before the flood?

The Condition of Women as the Health of Society

One compelling theological theme in the book of Judges deals with the condition of women, their role in society, and their overall welfare as a symptom of the health of society. Consider how the agency, status, and welfare of women deteriorate in Judges.

At the start of the book, women are in positions of status and power. They have strong agency in their own lives and in the life of Israel. They are relatively healthy and strong. Deborah is both a prophet and a judge. Even before she and Barak lead the people to military victory, she is a religious and political leader. The Kenite woman Jael, who drives a tent peg through the head of the oppressor general Sisera, also shows agency and can be seen as working to curb oppression. The Song of Deborah in Judges 5 praises Jael as "blessed of women . . . , of tent-dwelling women most blessed" (5:24).

But then the Song of Deborah turns to imagine "the mother of Sisera" (the enemy general) wondering why her son, the general, has delayed in returning home: "Why is his chariot so long in coming?" "Her wisest ladies" answer her,

Fig. 11.4. Abimelech is slain by a millstone that a woman drops off a tower. He dies, but not before he begs a soldier, "Draw your sword and kill me, so people will not say about me, 'A woman killed him'" (9:54). The would-be king, Abimelech, wishes to avoid the shame of being killed by a woman. The man in the background of this engraving, who is pointing upward, reminds the reader of the source of the millstone: the woman who slew Abimelech.

"Are they not finding and dividing the spoil?—A girl or two for every man" (5:28–30). Deborah's imagined scene of the Canaanite women is an ominous foreshadowing of the moral decline to come. Do not be misled by the euphemistic phrase "a girl or two for every man." The phrase means rape. In Deborah's imagination, the ladies in waiting explain that Sisera is late because his men are raping Israelite women. Total depravity. And foreshadowing.

The agency of women is again endorsed when a woman kills Abimelech by dropping a millstone on his head—an incredible feat of strength and courage. Perhaps Abimelech's sexist plea that he be run through with a sword so that it would not be said that he was killed by a woman is a sign that derogatory views of women are growing in Israel, or are at least present at the highest levels of power. The sacrifice of Jephthah's daughter is a sign that the welfare of women is slipping. Her father's rash and unjust vow led to her murder. She still retains some agency—she asks for and receives two months of life to mourn and be with her friends. But things are getting worse for women.

The conditions, welfare, and agency of women continue to decline. The Levite's concubine, the two hundred Gileadite women, and the four hundred worshipers of the Lord who are abducted show that, by the end of the book, Israelite society has deteriorated to the depraved conditions that the Song of Deborah had imagined in chapter 5 as the condition of society among the Canaanites.

In the modern world, we have learned that in order to improve the economic and social conditions of developing countries, one of the most effective and important steps that can be taken is to educate girls and young women. The narrative of Judges suggests that this wisdom was known in the ancient world too. When women are in leadership both religiously and politically, when women are allowed agency and strength in fields that are often only considered the domain of men, society is healthier. But when agency, leadership, and welfare are removed from women, society as a whole deteriorates.

Historical Interpretation

The Historical World behind the Text

If one reads the books of Joshua and Judges together, one might be surprised by the disappearance of Scripture within the narrative of Judges. Recall that Scripture played a large role in Joshua. In Joshua, the Lord commands Joshua to "be strong and very courageous, being careful to act in accordance with all the law that my servant Moses commanded you. . . . This book of the law shall not depart out of your mouth; you shall meditate on it day and night, so that you may be careful to act in accordance with all that is written in it" (1:7–8). Later, in Joshua 8, following the entrance into the land and the conquests of the cities of Jericho and Ai, Joshua gathers the people at Mount Ebal for a covenant renewal ceremony. At this ceremony, Joshua reads the entire "law of Moses" and carves a copy of the law of Moses on stones. At the end of Joshua, in the covenant renewal ceremony in Joshua 24, after the people vow to serve the Lord, "Joshua wrote these words in the book of the law of God" (24:26). At key moments, Scripture plays an important role in the book of Joshua. There is even a brief quotation from the lost Book of Jashar in the middle of the book (10:13).

By comparison, neither the law of Moses nor the book of the law are ever mentioned in Judges. Nor is there mention of any ancient portion of Scripture, nor even of a lost book such as the Book of Jashar. On the one hand, this difference suggests that the references to Scripture in Joshua may be anachronistic and from a much later date in Israel's history when sacred literature was more fully formulated. On the other hand, it also suggests that the Deuteronomistic Historian who wove the book of Judges together was true to his sources. If the written versions of Israel's founding laws and stories were not written down until later (after the time of the judges), it makes sense that they would not have played a role during the time of the judges. It is surprising that the Deuteronomistic Historian, who seems to have believed that Israel's great sin was failing to drive out the Canaanites and their gods from the midst of the land, did not continue the theme of the law of Moses from Joshua into Judges. But the reality that he did not do so suggests that he respected the integrity of the sources with which he worked.

The Historical World in the Text

As has already been noted in this chapter, the book of Judges begins by contradicting—or at least highly nuancing—the grandiose view in the book of Joshua of the land's complete conquest. Judges begins by claiming that after the death of Joshua there are still many tribes of foreign peoples left in the land. The tribes are described as separating to inhabit their allotted territories, where they in turn attempt to subdue the peoples that live in those respective areas. Israel is able to defeat some, but many others persist even a generation after Joshua. For the duration of the book, the tribes and judges struggle against a variety of internal and external peoples—and in the end, against other tribes.

As noted in the previous chapter, some historians have argued that these Israelites descended from bedouins who immigrated into the land and made homes and towns in areas that had previously been unoccupied. Other historians have argued that the people called the Israelites were actually Canaanite peasants who rebelled against overlords in the city-states of the Late Bronze Age and formed a people of a new identity: Israel. And still others support the narrative that Israel emigrated from Egypt in a grand escape from slavery. Perhaps the truth is quite complicated, and elements of all three models (and perhaps others) need to be combined in order to understand the historical process through which Israel emerged in the land. But what is clear is that Israel did emerge as a distinct people during the time of the judges.

Historians tend to be cautious thinkers. They tend to evaluate the historical value of written narratives, such as those in the book of Judges, with a generous amount of skepticism. For this reason, many historians are skeptical of drawing a straight line between what actually happened and how it is described in Judges. The hymn of Deborah in Judges 5 and the list of judges around which the narrative is woven both seem quite ancient. For this reason, those sources are given more weight when using the book to make historical judgments. Some historians do draw upon these sources to fashion an interpretation of the social contract of ancient Israel during this period. This social contract can be described as a tribal alliance led by charismatic judges and worship of a common God—Yahweh. That is to say, during this time there was no hereditary national leader of the people, nor was there a set way of choosing or identifying a national leader. One reason that there was no hereditary national leader or king was that the shared God—Yahweh—was understood as the people's ruler. When there was no military threat, each tribe ruled itself and governed its own concerns. When a military threat appeared, a judge arose to lead Israel against that threat. Those judges then held influence—they were said "to judge Israel" even after the military threat was subdued.

This social contract failed Israel toward the end of the period. It did not serve the increasing threat that arose from other nations, especially from the Philistines, nor did it serve the internal governance of the people.

FOR FURTHER READING: Judges

Biddle, Mark E. *Reading Judges: A Literary and Theological Commentary*. Reading the Old Testament. Macon, GA: Smyth & Helwys, 2012.

Matthews, Victor H. *Judges and Ruth*. New Cambridge Bible Commentary. Cambridge: Cambridge University Press, 2004.

McCann, J. Clinton. *Judges*. Interpretation: A Bible Commentary for Teaching and Preaching. Louisville: Westminster John Knox, 2011.

Schneider, Tammi J. *Judges*. Berit Olam: Studies in Hebrew Narrative and Poetry. Collegeville, MN: Liturgical Press, 2000.

Scholz, Susanne. "Judges." In *Women's Bible Commentary*, 3rd ed., edited by Carol A. Newsom, Sharon H. Ringe, and Jacqueline E. Lapsley, 113–27. Louisville: Westminster John Knox, 2012.

Webb, Barry G. *The Book of Judges.* New International Commentary on the Old Testament. Grand Rapids: Eerdmans, 2012.

Yee, Gale A., ed. *Judges and Method: New Approaches in Biblical Studies.* 2nd ed. Minneapolis: Fortress, 2007.

Ruth

The book of Ruth is one of the most charming and elegant stories in the Old Testament. The story is easy to follow, dramatic, entertaining, and meaningful. The narrative focuses on the relationship between two women: Ruth and her mother-in-law, Naomi. Both women take a remarkable journey together that begins with loss and famine but ultimately concludes with harvest, blessing, and security. It features a number of characters whose actions embody *hesed*—a Hebrew word that describes acts of loyalty and fidelity that go beyond what would otherwise be required or even imagined.

The book features four magnificent acts of *hesed*. The foremost example is Ruth's decision to bind herself to her mother-in-law—an act that is extravagant from the perspective of both law and custom. Second, when Naomi and Ruth return to Israel, an older man named Boaz shows *hesed* by both protecting and providing for Ruth, to whom he does not owe any obligation. Third, Ruth presents herself to this man for marriage. A final act of *hesed* is Boaz's act of bringing both Ruth and Naomi into his household as wife and mother-in-law. Altogether, the story may be the clearest narrative depiction of *hesed* in the Old Testament.

The book begins in a way that is recognizable to readers of Israel's ancestral stories: with a famine in the land (1:1; cf. Gen. 12:10; 26:1; 43:1; 47:13). The author designed this story to feel like the stories of old, elevating the narrative to the significance and grandeur of Israel's ancestors. What happens in the environment (famine) foreshadows what happens to the protagonists. The book of Ruth begins as Abram and Sarai's epic narrative does: with death and personal loss (1:1–5; cf. Gen. 11:31–32). Naomi loses her husband and then her two sons, Mahlon and Chilion, who are also the husbands of Ruth and

Orpah. This series of tragedies places Naomi and her two daughters-in-law in the vulnerable position of women without husbands.

Background

Composition and Development

The author of the book of Ruth is not known, and theories about authorship, dating, and compositional history vary widely. Some scholars think it comes from the time of the monarchy, and others see its origins in the exilic or postexilic period. Many scholars believe that the book was written sometime after the exile, drawing on older oral traditions. One reason for this is that the book is conscious that its audience might not know certain customs from earlier in Israel's history. For example, it says, "Now this was formerly done in Israel in cases of redemption or exchange: to validate any transaction, one man would take off his sandal and hand it to the other. Such was the practice in Israel" (4:7 NJPS).

The book is not considered part of the Deuteronomistic History, because it was written by a different community and in different circumstances. The story itself is set in the "days when the judges ruled" (1:1). This literary setting, what we have called the historical world within the text, is the primary reason why Protestant Bibles place the book between Judges and 1 Samuel. The Jewish Bible groups Ruth together with the Writings (Ketuvim), between the Song of Songs and Lamentations as part of the Megilloth.

Genre

The book of Ruth is a short story, a brief theological narrative comparable in style to the Joseph story (Gen. 37–50), the book of Jonah, or the prose narrative in Job 1–2. The book is a work of exceptional literary artistry, written by someone capable of rendering a narrative that is aesthetically pleasing, suspenseful, and an absolute delight to take in. Readers should approach it

---

Box 12.1

The Five Megilloth

The Five Megilloth ("scrolls") refers to a small collection of books in the Hebrew Bible: the Song of Songs, Ruth, Lamentations, Ecclesiastes, and Esther. While each of these books has its own compositional history, some Hebrew manuscripts include them as a collection, sometimes with varying sequences. Some reflect the liturgical calendar: Song of Songs (Passover); Ruth (Shavuot); Lamentations (Ninth of Av); Ecclesiastes (Sukkoth); Esther (Purim). Other manuscripts order these books chronologically.

Box 12.2

Outline

1. Loss: Widows in Moab (1:1–5)
2. Return: Naomi and Ruth's journey to Bethlehem (1:6–22)
3. Harvest: Ruth in Boaz's field (2:1–23)
4. Proposal: Encounter at the threshing floor (3:1–18)
5. Redemption: Boaz the kinsman-redeemer (4:1–12)
6. Marriage and birth: Boaz, Ruth, and the line of David (4:13–17)

appropriately—with sufficient care and deliberateness, keeping their eyes open for subtlety, drama, and layers of meaning.

Literary Interpretation

The story of Ruth is one of movement from loss to fullness, as the narrator traces the journeys of the book's main characters from Bethlehem to Moab and back.

Loss: Widows in Moab (Ruth 1:1–5). The story begins in Bethlehem, "the house of bread," where famine prompts Elimelech and Naomi to flee to Moab. Their sons marry Moabite women, Ruth and Orpah, but all three men die, leaving the women as widows.

Return: Naomi and Ruth's journey to Bethlehem (Ruth 1:6–22). When Naomi hears that the famine in Bethlehem has ended, she decides to return home. She urges her daughters-in-law to return to their mothers' houses for better chances at a future. After a tearful farewell, Orpah returns home. Ruth, however, "clung to her" (1:14). The author's choice of the word *clung* seems to purposefully echo Genesis 2:24: "Therefore a man leaves his father and mother and clings to his wife." Ruth's devotion to Naomi is akin to a husband's devotion to his wife. This is further emphasized by Ruth's moving pledge of loyalty:

> Do not plead with me to leave you,
> Or to turn away from following after you.
> Wherever you go, I will go;
> Wherever you lodge, I will lodge.
> Your people are my people,
> And your God is my God.
> Where you die, I will die;
> There will I be buried.
> May Yahweh do thus to me and more so,
> If death separates me from you. (1:16–17 AT)

Ruth's poetic pledge lyrically defines *hesed*: extravagant love and loyalty beyond what is required.

Box 12.3

The Plot of Ruth

The book of Ruth is a charming narrative with a sophisticated and thoughtful plot. The story moves from loss and scarcity to abundance and fertility. The term *fertility* is especially important when it comes to the book of Ruth. The story begins in the same way Abraham and Sarah's story does: with the onset of famine and the need to relocate in response to this crisis (Ruth 1:1; cf. Gen. 12:10). The state of the land parallels the state of the two protagonists, Ruth and Naomi, who in turn experience an interpersonal famine of their own in the loss of sons and husbands. But just as the land turns from famine to harvest, so their fates turn as well, especially with the introduction of Boaz, who will eventually marry Ruth. Their marriage produces a son, whose presence brings blessing and new life to his grandmother, Naomi (4:14–17).

The two women arrive in Bethlehem and are literally the talk of the town (1:19–22). Naomi takes on a new name to reflect her sorrow, calling herself Mara, meaning "bitterness." She left her homeland "full" and now returns "empty" (1:21). Naomi's words of despair hint at the reversal to come.

Harvest: Ruth in Boaz's field (Ruth 2:1–23). Chapter 2 introduces Boaz, described as a man of means and influence, along with significant familial connections to Naomi's deceased husband, Elimelech. Taking advantage of Israelite "welfare" law (Lev. 19:9; 23:22), Ruth gleans in the fields of Boaz in hopes that someone will "show [her] kindness" (2:2 AT). And someone does.

Philip Hermogenes Calderon / Yale Center for British Art, Gift of David Doret, Yale BA 1968, and Linda Mitchell

Fig. 12.1. Following the death of her husband and two sons, Naomi urges Ruth and Orpah to return to their "mothers' house." Orpah does so, but Ruth, like many biblical figures, sets out on a journey to a foreign country—where she has no family other than the aged Naomi.

Box 12.4

The Threshing Floor Scene

On many different levels, the threshing floor scene is intended to be climactic. The threshing floor is where crops are harvested, and in contrast to the beginning of the story, which finds our characters in famine, it represents the pinnacle of abundance. This scene also represents a climactic, dramatic, and even erotic turn in Ruth's relationship to Boaz. Modifying Naomi's instructions, Ruth takes the initiative and asks him to spread the hem of his garment over her—asking Boaz to marry her. The scene is also sexually suggestive. She goes to Boaz after he has been made more pliable by drink; the sexually charged verb "lie down" is used eight times in this chapter; she uncovers his "feet" (sometimes euphemistic for genitalia). While the story does not explicitly say that their encounter was sexual, the author clearly creates an erotic glow around the event.

Boaz comes to the field, greets his workers with a blessing (2:4), and almost immediately notices Ruth, asking, "Whose young woman is this?" (2:5 AT). He moves quickly to ensure that she does not glean in any other field but instead works exclusively in his. He arranges for her safety and comfort as she gleans.

He offers a short, admiring speech that applauds Ruth's *hesed* to Naomi and asks Yahweh to bless her: "May Yahweh repay your deed; may it be a full recompense from Yahweh the God of Israel, under whose wings you have come to take refuge" (2:12 AT). The Hebrew word for "wings" (*kanaf*) is important, because it will come up again in the next chapter. Boaz sends Ruth home to Naomi with a large gift of grain.

Proposal: Encounter at the threshing floor (Ruth 3:1–18). At Naomi's initiative, Ruth prepares herself for a late-night encounter with Boaz at the threshing floor after he had been celebrating the completion of the barley harvest, eating and drinking. When she arrives, Ruth takes the initiative. She startles him by uncovering his "feet" (sometimes a euphemism for male genitalia). Waking up to find a strange woman at his feet, Boaz asks her name, and she replies with what is effectively a marriage proposal that recalls Boaz's blessing in chapter 2. Ruth says, "Spread the hem of your garment [*kanaf*] over your handmaid because you are a kinsman-redeemer" (3:9 AT). The Hebrew word for "hem of your garment" is the same noun used in 2:12 (translated "wings" there) when Boaz blessed Ruth. Boaz accepts Ruth's proposal—he becomes the answer to his own prayer! Here, Boaz experiences Ruth's *hesed*: "May you be blessed by Yahweh, my daughter; this latter example of your *hesed* is even better than the former example" (3:10 AT). Both of them are *hesed* to each other.

Boaz agrees to marry Ruth, but there is one problem—a relative who is more closely related to Naomi has the responsibility and right to marry her before Boaz has the right. This may seem odd to modern readers, but this was the custom—the possessions of Naomi's deceased husband are involved. Because Naomi's husband, Elimelech, had died, the closest male relative now has the right to acquire his field—but with that right comes the responsibility to care for Naomi and Ruth, including providing a male heir for Naomi by marrying or procreating with Ruth. There is one relative, called a "kinsman-redeemer" (3:12 AT) or "guardian-redeemer" (NIV), more closely related to Naomi than Boaz is. The Hebrew term *go'el* really means something like "a kinsman who fulfills family responsibility to a relative in need."

Changes in the agricultural environment remain an important literary device. Ruth meets Boaz at the climax of harvest and fertility when the crop is being winnowed and threshed. For the people of the ancient Near East, fertility in the land and the fertility of the womb were interconnected theological realties. They were ultimately a sign of divine blessing. As the land bears its fruit, that reality of blessing is reflected in the formerly desolate lives of Ruth and Naomi whose fortunes are about to change.

Redemption: Boaz the kinsman-redeemer (Ruth 4:1–12). Boaz goes to the city gate and convenes ten elders. He explains Ruth's situation and defers to the "kinsman-redeemer" (*go'el*) who is more closely related. This *go'el* wants the field but does not want Naomi and Ruth. Ironically, this man, called only "the *go'el*," says, "I am not able to act as *go'el* without corrupting my lineage" (4:6 AT), thus making way for Boaz to act as *go'el* and marry Ruth.

The people at the gate and the elders offer a moving blessing that links the story of Ruth to those of the other great matriarchs of Israel: "May Yahweh make the woman entering your house like Rachel and Leah, who built the house of Israel. . . . May your house be like the house of Perez, whom Tamar bore to Judah" (4:11–12 AT).

Marriage and birth: Boaz, Ruth, and the line of David (Ruth 4:13–17). The prayers of the people also come true when Yahweh gives Boaz and Ruth a son named Obed, the grandfather of King David (4:17). The birth of Obed is also a reversal of fortunes for Naomi. The women say to her, "Blessed be Yahweh, who did not hold back a redeemer for you this day. May his name be proclaimed in Israel. He will restore life to you and sustain you in your old age, for he is born to your daughter-in-law who loves you, who is better to you than seven sons" (4:14–15 AT).

Theological Interpretation

Famine, Scarcity, and the Abundance of Creation

Given its minimal references to God, the book of Ruth may seem to say little about theology. But careful attention to the text as a work of literary artistry reveals that the book pulses with theological life.

To begin with, the book generally moves from desolation to fertility. Chapter 1 begins with a famine in the land and the loss of Naomi's husband and two

Box 12.5

Fertility in the Ancient World

As noted earlier, fertility is a widespread and important motif in all the cultures of the ancient Near East. This is not surprising given that ancient peoples were vulnerable to environmental vagaries: drought, floods, natural disasters, destructive insects, and so on. In a way that differs from many modern societies, life itself was tied to the health of the natural world. Fertility theology is explicitly expressed in texts like Psalm 104, which claims that all of creation flourishes when God sends forth the powers of life, and it is implicit in the book of Ruth, where Ruth's own life closely follows the agricultural seasons, moving from famine to abundance.

sons, one of whom is Ruth's husband. The peak of the story—Ruth's encounter with Boaz at the threshing floor in chapter 3—takes places during the climax of the agricultural season: harvest. And the story ends with the birth of a child, Obed. For the ancient Israelites, the God of Israel was also a God of fertility, abundance, and blessing. To recognize the fruits of fertility in Ruth is to recognize the presence and work of God.

The Moabite Ruth as an Israelite Ancestress

The book of Ruth ends with a genealogy, which might seem strange to the modern reader. But this genealogy is deeply significant for specifically theological reasons. It links Ruth (a Moabite) to the lineage of King David, the king whose dynasty Yahweh chose to rule in perpetuity (2 Sam. 7). Much later, the New Testament begins with another genealogy: "This is the genealogy of Jesus the Messiah the son of David" (Matt. 1:1 NIV). In this genealogy, Ruth is one of four named women, all foreign—"Boaz [was] the father of Obed, whose mother was Ruth" (1:5b)—the others being Tamar, Rahab, and "Uriah's wife" (i.e., Bathsheba, who may have been Israelite but was married to a Hittite foreigner; 1:6b NIV).

messiah A word meaning "anointed one"; it designated a promised and expected deliverer of the Jewish people; when capitalized, it refers to Jesus.

The author of Ruth consistently emphasizes Ruth's foreign identity by calling her such things as "Ruth the Moabite" or "the young Moabite woman" (see 2:2, 6; 4:5, 10). The blessing that the people of the village and their elders offer also emphasizes the lineage of foreign women in Israel's history, which Ruth now shares—it asks that Ruth's house be like the house of Perez, whom Tamar the Canaanite bore to Judah. This is important, because in ancient Israel there were some who thought that Israel's bloodlines should remain pure. The books of Kings blame Solomon's many foreign wives for turning his heart away from Yahweh (1 Kings 11:1–8). Following the exile, the high priest Ezra led the restored community of Judah to drive out foreign wives and to make a vow not to "give your daughters to [foreigners'] sons and not to take their daughters for your sons" (Ezra 9:12). The book of Ruth, by contrast, emphasizes the fidelity (*hesed*) of "Ruth the Moabite" and celebrates the role she and women such as Tamar the Canaanite play in the lineage of kings and eventually the Messiah.

Fig. 12.2. Ruth gleans in Boaz's field, gathering leftover grain that had been passed over by the harvesters. Biblical law demands that harvesters leave such leftovers for the poor to gather.

Care for the Vulnerable

Ruth encounters Boaz because she is taking advantage of an ancient Israelite welfare system, which allowed the destitute to glean from what the harvesters leave behind (see, e.g., Lev. 19:9–10; Deut. 24:19–20). As noted above, one of the most important themes of Ruth is *hesed*. This is demonstrated in multiple ways throughout the story, such as in Ruth's generous loyalty to Naomi, and also here in Boaz's willingness to let Ruth glean in his field and in his offer of protection and hydration. The *hesed* of God is manifest in the *hesed* of Boaz.

The God Who Blesses

God's agency in Ruth is primarily portrayed as active in blessing. Yahweh is explicitly mentioned on several occasions but most especially in words of blessing. Naomi blesses her daughters-in-law with these words: "May Yahweh show you exceptional fidelity [*hesed*], just as you have done with the dead and also with me" (1:8 AT). Unbeknownst to Naomi, who saw herself as the recipient of divine misfortune (1:13, 21), this blessing would also come true for her. Boaz's words are also full of divine blessing (2:4, 12; 3:10). As mentioned above, his blessing to Ruth in 2:12 ("May Yahweh repay your deed; may it be a full recompense from Yahweh the God of Israel, under whose wings you have come to take refuge," AT) would ultimately be fulfilled by Boaz himself.

Chapter 4 contains two blessings. In the first case, after Boaz announces his forthcoming acquisition both of Ruth and of Elimelech's property, the people at the gate and the elders make explicit the connections that the story to this point had only implied: "May Yahweh make the woman entering your house like Rachel and Leah, who built the house of Israel" (4:11 AT). Naomi was not only an exemplar of *hesed*, but she was also a matriarch of Israel. Second, a group of women offers a blessing for Naomi that indicates the profound reversal she experienced: "Blessed be Yahweh, who did not hold back a redeemer for you this day. May his name be proclaimed in Israel. He will restore life to you and sustain you in your old age, for he is born to your daughter-in-law who loves you, who is better to you than seven sons" (4:14–15 AT). We never hear Naomi's response. The only indication we have is that this was a future she fully embraced (4:16).

Historical Interpretation

The Historical World behind the Text

It is clear both from the reference in Ruth 4:7 to the ancient legal practice and from the setting of the story "in the days when the judges ruled" (1:1) that the book was written down many centuries after the action in the story took place. But the book does not contain any reference to a definitive date for the book's composition, much less any information about the author(s). Many themes could potentially connect to a wide range of historical experiences: the return of Naomi after wandering in a foreign land, famine and drought, marriage to foreigners, Davidic lineage, and so on. None of these themes provide a strong enough connection to a particular moment in Israel's history to allow for a sure dating. Scholars often use studies of linguistic forms in a biblical book to date the book. Such studies of Ruth place the book somewhere between the earlier Pentateuch and Deuteronomistic History and the later texts of Ezra-Nehemiah, Ecclesiastes, and Chronicles. In other words, a date just after the exile might tentatively be assigned.

If this tentative date for the writing down of the story is accepted, one can imagine the story of Ruth as part of a vigorous conversation about the influence of foreign people on the faith life of the Judean people. On the one hand, as already noted, both the Deuteronomistic History (which may have been slightly older than Ruth) and the Chronicles-Ezra-Nehemiah narrative (which may have been later than Ruth) express suspicion about the influence of foreign women on the nation. Contrary to these views, the book of Ruth expresses appreciation and even validation of the contribution that foreign women made to the people of Israel.

A key verse in this line of interpretation is the response of the unnamed "redeemer" (*go'el*), who says, "I am not able to act as *go'el* without corrupting my lineage. You redeem it, for I cannot" (4:6 AT). The word translated here as "lineage" implies that the so-called redeemer (who ironically does not redeem) is unwilling to serve as redeemer because the offspring he would sire with Ruth would be corrupted because Ruth is a Moabite. Over against this xenophobia, Boaz is willing to marry and procreate with Ruth because she has shown *hesed* to Naomi and has joined herself to Israel and the Lord, saying, "Your people shall be my people, and your God will be my God" (1:16 AT).

The Historical World in the Text

Ruth is a curious book from the perspective of history. The book takes history with the utmost seriousness, as evidenced by the fact that it ends with a genealogy directly linking Ruth to King David. One of its primary goals is to establish a historical connection to the family of Israel's most well-known monarch. While some modern critics are skeptical of the historicity of the narrative, others find it credible, especially its central historical claim that a Moabite woman was the great-grandmother of David.

The book also offers insight on cultural practices that were ancient even by the time the story was written down, such as the responsibility of the nearest male relative (the *go'el*) to be responsible for the widow and daughter-in-law of Elimelech if he wanted to purchase the dead man's land. Accordingly, the book fleshes out for historians how some aspects of Israel's kingship-based society functioned. The book also offers a rare glimpse into how certain legal matters were conducted, as indicated in chapter 4: "Now this was the custom in earlier days concerning redeeming and exchanging—to establish any matter, a person took off their sandal and gave it to their neighbor. This was the manner of attesting in Israel" (4:7 AT).

FOR FURTHER READING: Ruth

Eskenazi, Tamara Cohn, and Tikva Frymer-Kensky. *Ruth: The Traditional Hebrew Text with the New JPS Translation*. JPS Bible Commentary. Philadelphia: Jewish Publication Society of America, 2011.

Koosed, Jennifer L. *Gleaning Ruth: A Biblical Heroine and Her Afterlives*. Studies on Personalities of the Old Testament. Columbia: University of South Carolina Press, 2011.

Lee, Eunny. "Ruth." In *Women's Bible Commentary*, 3rd ed., edited by Carol A. New-som, Sharon H. Ringe, and Jacqueline E. Lapsley, 142–49. Louisville: Westminster John Knox, 2012.

Sakenfeld, Katharine Doob. *Ruth*. Interpretation: A Bible Commentary for Teaching and Preaching. Louisville: John Knox, 1999.

Schipper, Jeremy. *Ruth: A New Translation with Introduction and Commentary*. Anchor Yale Bible 7D. New Haven: Yale University Press, 2016.

1–2 Samuel

The books of 1–2 Samuel are named in Protestant and Catholic Christian Bibles after the prophet and judge Samuel (Orthodox Christian Bibles call these books 1–2 Kingdoms). Samuel, however, is only the main character in 1 Samuel 3–8. Samuel's mother, Hannah, is the main character in 1 Samuel 1–2, and Samuel shares center stage in 1 Samuel 9–15 with Saul, the first king of Israel. Saul and David, the second king of Israel, are the main characters in 1 Samuel 16–2 Samuel 1. And David alone is in the spotlight in 2 Samuel 2–24. In truth, the two books might have been more accurately titled after Saul and David. Or, maybe, simply after David. The Septuagint quite appropriately refers to 1–2 Samuel as 1–2 Reigns, emphasizing their focus on the establishment of Israel's monarchy.

The books of 1–2 Samuel narrate the introduction of kingship to Israel and explore the next, obvious question in the plotline of the Deuteronomistic History: When organized as a kingdom, with one monarch and a centralized government, could Israel serve the Lord?

Background

Composition and Development

As with most books of the Old Testament, the books of 1–2 Samuel are anonymous. They are part of the long narrative portion of the Old Testament called the Deuteronomistic History, which spans from Deuteronomy through 2 Kings (excluding Ruth).

The author of this narrative—known as the Deuteronomistic Historian—is anonymous. He most likely was actively writing and editing this history around 620 BCE in Jerusalem, with a second edition of history completed during the period of the Babylonian exile, probably around 560 BCE. But the Deuter-onomistic Historian certainly drew upon sources that were ancient already by the time he was writing and editing. For 1–2 Samuel, these sources most likely included the Ark Narrative (1 Sam. 4:1–7:1; 2 Sam. 6:1–19), the narrative of David's rise (1 Sam. 16:14–2 Sam. 5:12), and the Succession Narrative (2 Sam. 9–20, and continuing in 1 Kings 1–2). In addition, the books clearly include ancient stories preserved at least in part through oral tradition, some ancient hymns such as the Song of the Bow in 2 Samuel 1 (a song that David himself may have composed upon the death of his friend Jonathan),[1] and other written sources that might have included narratives about Saul and David.

Genre

The books of 1–2 Samuel are made up mostly of theological-historical narra-tives, but they also include a few prominent hymns (1 Sam. 2; 2 Sam. 1; 22–23). Some scholars consider these books as among the first historical books on record. The label "historical books" is somewhat appropriate for several rea-sons: the main literary genre in 1–2 Samuel is historical narrative; the books chronicle events that putatively took place around 1020–960 BCE; and the books are written in such a way that they are clearly reflecting on the past and incorporating older source material as they tell Israel's story.

While the books are historical narrative, they are not "history" in the modern sense of the term, because the aim of the author was not simply to describe the past as accurately and objectively as possible. Rather, 1–2 Samuel might more accurately be labeled "theological narrative" or "symbolic narrative," because the aim of the author was to draw on the past in order to communicate theo-logical and ethical truths about God, about God's relationship with Israel, and about how to follow God.

Literary Interpretation

Hannah and the birth of Samuel (1 Sam. 1–2). Similar to the book of Exodus, the book of 1 Samuel begins with the story of a woman whose faithful actions lead to the birth of a national deliverer. In Exodus, it was the two righteous (and barren) Hebrew midwives, Shiphrah and Puah, who resisted Pharaoh's command to kill all male Hebrew babies because they feared God. Thus, the deliverer Moses was born and survived Pharaoh's genocidal command. In 1 Samuel, the reader meets a woman named Hannah. Hannah, like many other important women in the Bible, is barren. She prays for children and promises to dedicate her firstborn son to the Lord as a Nazirite (a special class of people consecrated to the Lord's service). Samuel is born, and he becomes a man who serves in

Outline

1. Hannah and the birth of Samuel (1 Sam. 1–2)
2. Samuel, the last judge; Israel demands a king (1 Sam. 3–8)
3. The rule of Saul, Israel's first king (1 Sam. 9–15)
4. The rise of David and decline of Saul (1 Sam. 16–31)
5. The rule of David, Israel's second king (2 Sam. 1–24)
   a. David succeeds Saul (2 Sam. 1–4)
   b. David's reign and God's covenant (2 Sam. 5–7)
   c. David's troubled reign (2 Sam. 8–20)
   d. The end of David's reign (2 Sam. 21–24)

the place of a national deliverer for Israel. He is also a prophet and Israel's last judge.

Samuel, the last judge; Israel demands a king (1 Sam. 3–8). First Samuel 3 begins with the ominous note that "the word of the LORD was rare in those days," and it tells the well-loved story of the call of the boy Samuel, who has been dedicated as a Nazirite and is being raised by the elderly priest, Eli, at the tabernacle in Shiloh. The Lord calls the boy Samuel in the night, but Samuel thinks it is Eli calling. Eli instructs him to respond to God's call by saying, "Speak, LORD, for your servant is listening" (3:9). When Samuel does, the Lord reveals to him that he is dismissing the house of Eli as his servants. Samuel then replaces Eli. First Samuel 4 tells how the Philistines—a people often in violent conflict with Israel in those days—capture the ark of the covenant and kill Eli's sons Hophni and Phinehas. The ark, which symbolized the presence and power of the Lord, responds to God's will. Wherever it is taken by the Philistines, it brings calamities and curses. The Philistines finally return the ark to Israel, where it is stored in the Judean village of Kiriath-jearim.

Prophets and Kings

Throughout the Old Testament, prophets are often paired with kings. Samuel anoints and advises Saul and David; Nathan serves as David's court prophet; Elijah is a prophetic thorn in the sides of Ahab and his wife Jezebel; Isaiah serves Hezekiah; and the prophetess Huldah prophesies to Josiah. In each of these cases, the prophets are called upon to speak Yahweh's words to the king. They are divine messengers of the heavenly king sent to communicate with Yahweh's earthly regent. Sometimes their words are supportive, and sometimes they are correctional and demanding.

The deep connection between prophets and kings persists until the Davidic monarchy ends in 586 BCE. The demise of the monarchy, however, does not mark the end of prophecy. Like so many other ancient Israelite institutions, prophecy adapts to the changing situations.

Samuel serves as Israel's last judge, but he is also a prophet. When Israel demands a king, God commands Samuel to anoint Saul as king, even though by asking for a human king, Israel was rejecting the Lord as its king. Samuel first warns Israel that kings will rule over them, impose taxes and forced labor, and draft their sons and daughters. Sometimes God's judgment is to give God's people exactly what they want.

The rule of Saul, Israel's first king (1 Sam. 9–15). The next several chapters recount the anointing of Saul as king and his rule. Because Israel was divided into different tribes, Saul is announced and received as king several times in different locales. In 1 Samuel 12, Samuel delivers his farewell speech—this is one of several speeches that occur at key locations in the Deuteronomistic History. In this speech, a key leader looks backward to narrate Israel's history with God and then looks forward to warn Israel: "If you will fear the LORD, worship him, obey him, and not rebel against the LORD's command, and if both you and the king who rules over you follow the LORD your God—all will be well" (1 Sam. 12:14 CEB).

Saul and his son Jonathan lead the people to victories over the Philistines. But Saul—like the judge Jephthah before him—makes a rash vow that should have resulted in the death of his son, but the people refuse to let Jonathan be put to death. Saul

Fig. 13.1. The call of Samuel is also the dismissal of Eli. Because Eli's sons are scoundrels and Eli does not discipline them, Eli and his sons are dismissed and replaced by Samuel. When Samuel reports this to Eli, the old man says, "He is the Lord; may he do that which is good in his sight" (3:18 AT).

proves to be a victorious king, but according to 1 Samuel 15 he did not follow God faithfully, and the Lord rejects him as king.

The rise of David and decline of Saul (1 Sam. 16–31). The second half of 1 Samuel recounts the rise of David, the decline of King Saul, and how conflict and enmity inevitably grew between the two kings. Samuel anoints David in 1 Samuel 16, although David is only a young boy. David joins Saul's court, where his skill at playing music on the lyre eases Saul "whenever an evil spirit sent from God" plagues him (16:23 AT). First Samuel 17 tells the well-known story of David and Goliath.

The chapters that follow relate David and Saul's fractious and complicated relationship. David becomes best of friends with Saul's son Jonathan and marries Saul's daughter Michal. But Saul, jealous of David's increasing fame and success and perhaps suffering from mental illness, tries to kill David. Jonathan

Box 13.3

David's Anointing

The anointing of David as king in 1 Samuel 16 is a well-loved story. In the story, Samuel is sent to anoint one of Jesse's sons as the new king of Israel to replace Saul. Samuel is told to listen to God for who is to be anointed, but instead he looks with his eyes. When the eldest son, Eliab, who was tall and fair, passes before Samuel, the prophet thinks, "Surely the LORD's anointed is now before the LORD" (v. 6). God's response is a shutdown for the ages: "Do not look on his appearance or on the height of his stature, because I have rejected him; for the LORD does not see as mortals see: they look on the outward appearance, but the LORD looks on the heart" (v. 7). Jesse then trots out Abinadab and Shammah to see if they are royal material. "Neither has the LORD chosen this one" (v. 8). Jesse brings four more sons forward, but none of them are the future king either. "Don't you have any more sons?" asks Samuel. "One more," says Jesse, "but he's too young, he's out shepherding the sheep" (v. 11 AT). At this point in the story, ancient audiences would have laughed. In the ancient Near East, the shepherd was universally a symbol of the king. Ancient audiences would have laughed to note that the child David is already fulfilling his future vocation as king: he is shepherding the flock. When David is brought forth, the Lord says, "Rise and anoint him; for this is the one" (v. 12).

Two key words in this story are *see* and *listen*. Samuel is told to listen to God's divine revelation, but instead he sees with his human vision. In 1 Samuel 16:3, Samuel is commanded: "You shall anoint for me the one whom I name to you." But in each case when Eliab, Abinadab, Shammah, and David are presented, Samuel looks with his eyes. When dealing with matters of God's actions and will, human sight is an inadequate tool. "The LORD does not see as mortals see; they look on the outward appearance, but the LORD looks on the heart" (v. 7).

and Michal help David escape. At one point, David flees to the Philistines, where he acts insane in order to avoid incarceration or death. At another point, he takes refuge in Moab. In one famous story (1 Sam. 24), Saul enters a cave where David is hiding. As Saul urinates, David spares his life—but cuts off a piece of Saul's cloak as a trophy. Later, David marries a second wife and spares Saul's life a second time. David serves for a time with the Philistines in Gath. He takes vengeance on an Amalekite army that had destroyed the city of Ziklag and had taken women and children captive, including David's two wives. David rescues the captives and distributes the spoils of wars in a wise manner. The book ends by describing how the Philistines defeat Saul and how Saul and his sons—including Jonathan—are put to death.

The rule of David: David succeeds Saul (2 Sam. 1–4). Second Samuel begins with David receiving the report of a messenger about the death of Saul and Jonathan. David then sings a lament—the Song of the Bow (2 Sam. 1:19–27)—at the loss of his friend. The next chapters recount a struggle for the succession of the throne. At first, David is crowned king by Judah in the south, and Ishbaal, a son of Saul, is hailed as king by some of the northern tribes. After a two-year struggle, David prevails and is king of all Israel.

Fig. 13.2. The story of David and Jonathan is one of the only stories in the Bible about friendship. Jonathan's love for David is so great that he helps him escape when his father, Saul, attempts to kill him. When Jonathan is killed in battle, David tears his clothes, weeps, and sings a dirge in his memory.

The rule of David: David's reign and God's covenant (2 Sam. 5–7). Having consolidated his rule, David captures the independent mountain city of Jerusalem from the Jebusites and makes it his capital—"the city of David" (2 Sam. 5:7). David then recovers the ark of the covenant from its storage in Kiriath-jearim. With ceremony and dancing, he brings it to Jerusalem—symbolically and religiously placing the Lord God at the center of the kingdom. The move to a new capital unifies the two split sections of the nation—the south led by the tribe of Judah and the north led by the tribe of Ephraim and others. David builds himself a palace and fathers many children with his multiple wives and concubines.

Second Samuel 7 tells one of the most important stories in the entire Old Testament—the account of the Lord's covenant with David. Having built himself a palace (one kind of "house") and fathered many children (another kind of "house"), David decides to build a temple (a third kind of "house") for God. But the Lord refuses. Speaking through the prophet Nathan, the LORD declares to David, "The LORD will make you a house. . . . I will raise up your offspring after you. . . . He shall build a house for my name, and I will establish the throne of his kingdom forever. I will be a father to him, and he shall be a son to me. When he commits iniquity, I will punish him. . . . But I will not take my steadfast love from him" (2 Sam. 7:11–15).

The rule of David: David's troubled reign (2 Sam. 8–20). The next chapters tell the long and troubled story of David's reign: his ups and downs, victories and defeats. Second Samuel 8 especially tells of David's wars and gives a sense of the expanse of his kingdom. David is often successful in war and foreign policy but unsuccessful domestically. Most dramatic are two episodes. In the first, David commits adultery with Bathsheba, the wife of one of his captains, Uriah. When

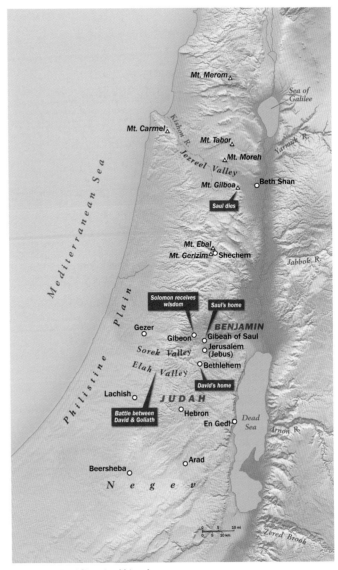

Map 13.1. David's united kingdom

Bathsheba reports to David that she is pregnant, David tries to cover up the affair. Eventually, he has Uriah and his unit abandoned in the midst of battle, where all the men die. David then marries Bathsheba. The prophet Nathan confronts David with his sins—and although David repents, his child with Bathsheba dies.

In a second dramatic episode, one of David's sons, Amnon, rapes David's daughter Tamar (Amnon's half sister). David refuses to punish Amnon because he loves him, so Tamar's full brother Absalom has Amnon killed. Absalom flees, and David has him exiled for three years because again he cannot punish

Nathan's Parable of the Sheep

When readers of the Bible think about parables, they usually think about Jesus in the Gospels. The parables of the sower and of the prodigal son are among the most widely recognized. But parables are found in both Testaments. One of the most famous Old Testament parables is given by the prophet Nathan in 2 Samuel 12. The parable follows immediately upon David's adulterous affair with Bathsheba and his cover-up murder of her husband, Uriah (2 Sam. 11). In this harrowing story of royal corruption, David lives up to the very worst fears about kingship—that it is a fundamentally extractive institution (see 1 Sam. 8). Like other parables, Nathan's is intended to entrap its listener, David, by making him identify with the victim, at least initially. But this is only a rhetorical ruse, however, since Nathan eventually turns the tables on David and exposes him as a victimizer.

his son. Upon his return, Absalom plots a revolt against David. The revolt is at first successful, and David is forced to flee Jerusalem. Later, David regains his strength and reconquers his kingdom, and Absalom is killed during the conflict. David laments his rebellious son's death: "O my son Absalom, O Absalom, my son, my son!" (2 Sam. 19:4).

The rule of David: The end of David's reign (2 Sam. 21–24). The final chapters of 2 Samuel detail more of David's ups and downs, including his final benediction, a sin David commits by taking a census of the people, and how he averts punishment for the sin by means of an offering. The death of David is narrated in 1 Kings 1.

Theological Interpretation

Tracking God's Agency

The figure of God must always be taken into account when considering the meaning of a book of the Bible. Although God's agency is less directly apparent in 1–2 Samuel than in books such as Genesis or Exodus, he is nevertheless strongly present. The narrative most clearly reveals the agency of God through the ark of the covenant and the prophets Samuel and Nathan.

When the ark of the covenant, which was the earthly manifestation of the Lord's power and presence, is captured in the Ark Narrative (1 Sam. 4–6), it seems to have a will of its own. The ark embodies God's will—wherever the Philistines take it, disaster strikes. When David later moves it to Jerusalem in a celebratory occasion, the ark exhibits the power of death and life. One of the drivers of the cart carrying the ark reaches out to steady the ark and is struck dead. David, fearing that the curses associated with the ark would fall upon him, leaves it at the home of Obed-edom for three months, during which time "the Lord blessed Obed-edom and all his household" (2 Sam. 6:11).

Box 13.5

The Plots of 1–2 Samuel

The main plot of 1–2 Samuel serves the overall plot of this portion of the Deuteronomistic History: Can Israel serve the Lord? The books of 1–2 Samuel organize the narrative under the leadership of its three main human characters: Samuel, Saul, and David. Each of these is the main figure in a portion of 1–2 Samuel. Each character is called by God and commissioned for service. Each man's service and life is a mixed bag of faithfulness and unfaithfulness—none more so than David.

Samuel is both a prophet and a judge. Although his death is not reported until 1 Samuel 25, the lion's share of his work takes place in 1 Samuel 1–8. In a time when the word of God is rare, his birth is a miracle of divine intervention and grace—for the entire nation and not just for his mother, Hannah, who sings,

> There is no rock like our God. . . .
>   The foes of the Lord shall be scattered;
>   He will thunder against them in the heavens.
>   The Lord will judge the ends of the earth.
>   He will give power to His king. (1 Sam. 2:2c, 10 NJPS)

This testimony seems strange in its immediate context, as Israel has no king, but since Samuel will be commissioned to anoint kings in Israel, the verse makes sense in its broader narrative context.

Samuel is Israel's last judge. As noted earlier, he is commissioned to replace Eli, whose wicked sons do not follow in their father's ways. Ironically, Samuel's own sons are corrupt and do not follow in his ways. He is the last judge, and he anoints Israel's first two kings. He is also the first in a new brand of prophet—a prophet who speaks the word of God to, with, and against kings. There have been prophets before—Abraham, Moses, Miriam, Deborah—but the rise of monarchy will require a separation of powers, as it were, a system of checks and balances to counter the influence of kings.

Saul is Israel's first king. His story line covers 1 Samuel 9–31, with the main portion of his narrative unfolding in chapters 9–15. Although kingship is presented in 1 Samuel 8 and 10 as rebellion against God and rejection of the Lord as Israel's king, Saul's anointing as king in 1 Samuel 9 is seen as God's merciful response to the people's suffering (similar to the sending of Moses in the exodus): "He shall save my people from the hand of the Philistines; for I have seen the suffering of my people, because their outcry has come to me" (1 Sam. 9:16).

Saul is successful as a military leader, but the narrative presents him as having several problems. He falls into frenzies from time to time, making people wonder, "Is Saul too among the prophets?" This wondering was not seen as a compliment. Saul fails to follow God's commandment and offers a major sacrifice on his own, rather than waiting for Samuel. He also offers a rash oath similar to Jephthah in the book of Judges, and he ignores the Lord's commandments against taking the spoils of war. Perhaps most significantly, Saul develops paranoia concerning David and devolves into mental illness—plotting against David and more than once trying to kill him. For some or all of these reasons, the crown was removed from Saul and his family. Saul achieved some military success and partially united the nation, but on the whole, the narrative presents him as a failure.

David is the second king of Israel. His name occurs more often in the Bible than any other human figure (even Jesus!), and his story encompasses more narrative space than any other (with the possible exceptions of Moses, Jesus, and Paul, depending on how one counts). No biblical figure is more complicated or more difficult to make sense of from a narrative point of view.

On the one hand, 1–2 Samuel make no effort to cover up David's most unsavory qualities and deeds. David is a violent military leader with a seriously checkered resume. The refrain grows up around David that "Saul has killed his thousands, but David his ten thousands" (1 Sam. 21:11). His story can be legitimately interpreted as showing that he is disloyal to Saul. He is anointed king while Saul still reigns, and he serves and takes refuge among the Philistines, Israel's enemies (1 Sam. 21:10–15; 27:1–12; 29:1–11). After Saul's and Jonathan's deaths, David wages a successful bid for the crown against Ishbaal, Saul's son. David's affair with Bathsheba and subsequent murder of Uriah and his squad show David as a desirous, scheming, murdering king of the very kind that Samuel warned the people against (1 Sam. 8). His weaknesses as a father results in a kingdom-wide rebellion, during which common men and women pay for the king's personal weaknesses. The fact that 2 Samuel ends by describing one last sin of the king and how national punishment is narrowly escaped by means of a ritual sacrifice suggests that the narrative views the king very critically.

On the other hand, the narrative casts David as among the most successful and positive characters in the Bible. He unifies the twelve tribes, conquers Jerusalem, and centers the governance and faith of the people there in "the city of David." If the list of his military conquests can be taken at face value, he briefly raises Israel's national status until it is on a par with more powerful neighbors. When challenged to his face by a righteous prophet, he swallows his pride and admits his sin. Although his personal weakness with Absalom leads to national rebellion, he is able to overcome the revolt and reestablish equilibrium in the kingdom. He leaves the kingdom better off than when he came on the scene and sets the stage for peace in the next generations. The Deuteronomistic History remembers him as the most faithful king and measures all later kings against him—most likely because he brings the ark to Jerusalem and does not promote the worship of other gods. For example, King Hezekiah—judged by the same historians to be among Judah's more faithful kings—is described as follows: "He did what was right in the sight of the LORD just as his ancestor David had done. He removed the high places, broke down the pillars, and cut down the sacred pole" (2 Kings 18:3–4). From a New Testament perspective, the covenantal promise that the Lord made to David in 2 Samuel 7—that one of his descendants would forever reign as king of God's people—became one of the most important texts that set the stage for later hopes that God would one day send a Messiah to save God's people.

These brief incidents symbolize that the ark—and thus God—is not a mere object to be hidden away and brought forth at will. Rather, the Lord remains the God of the Great Commandment—the one whom Israel is to love above all other things. The incidents also symbolize the power of the Lord to curse and to bless—or, as Hannah sang in her song when Samuel was born, "The

LORD kills and brings to life; he brings down to Sheol and raises up" (1 Sam. 2:6). When David learns that the Lord has blessed Obed-edom, he continues the journey to bring the ark to Jerusalem, singing and dancing and celebrating before the ark as it rolls toward its new home. The placement of the ark at the center of the people in Jerusalem symbolizes several things: the memory of the exodus and Sinai, where God revealed plans for the ark; the power and presence of the Lord; David's commitment that God be central; and God's blessing of David and his kingdom.

Kingship and the People of God

In 1 Samuel 8, Israel demands a king. The entire story is worthy of a close reading, because it marks a major change in the theological understanding of who the "people

Paul Cézanne

Fig. 13.3. The story of the affair between David and Bathsheba, which led David to murder Bathsheba's husband, has been depicted by many artists. The history of this art shows how the patriarchal tradition consistently portrayed Bathsheba as a seductress—even though the text offers no support for such an interpretation—thereby attempting to shift sin in the story from David to Bathsheba. But the text is clear—David's sins are the center of this story.

Sheol The underworld, or place where all the dead dwell; called Hades in the New Testament, where it sometimes appears to be synonymous with hell.

of God" are. Since the time of the exodus until this point in the story, for Israel to be the people of God meant that the Lord was directly their king. The good news of what Jews call the second word of the Decalogue and Christians call the first commandment—"I am the LORD your God . . . ; you shall have no other gods"—was that the Lord was Israel's ruler, and they never had to serve any human as their sovereign; they never had to serve another pharaoh. Why would Israel want to serve a human when they could serve the Lord, who was "compassionate and merciful, very patient, full of great loyalty and faithfulness" (Exod. 34:6 CEB)? And Israel alone, out of all the nations, was God's chosen people.

But Israel wanted a king, "like the other nations." In 1 Samuel 8, the people make their demand of Samuel because they do not want his corrupt sons to lead them. The foolish irony of the request should be obvious. Samuel is a human prophet and judge. He is righteous, but his sons are not. Therefore, Israel

God's Dangerous Power

In ancient Israel, God's power was not only awe inspiring; it was also danger-ous. The Ark Narrative in 1 Samuel 4–6 manifests this life-threatening power of God, especially against Israel's enemies and their gods. One famous story re-counts the ark's toppling of the Philistine idol Dagon (1 Sam. 5:1–12). Like other divine contest stories (e.g., 1 Kings 18; see also Bel and the Dragon, which is an extra story in Daniel that is included in Catholic and Orthodox Bibles), the idols of the nations are shown to be nothing more than material objects made with human hands. The dangerous nature of God's presence is often a difficult concept for modern readers to grasp, but it was a fundamental belief for an-cient Israel and one of the chief reasons the priesthood was so important. The rituals they taught and practiced allowed a holy God to live among God's people in a way that was both beneficial and safe for frail human creatures.

The voice of God through the prophets Samuel and Nathan also shows that the will and actions of God can bring both judgment and salvation. In a time when the word of the Lord was rare in the land (1 Sam. 3:1), these two prophets represent God's enduring commitment and faithfulness to the stiff-necked people who "cannot serve the Lord," as the book of Judges so thoroughly dem-onstrated. Even when they reject the Lord's direct reign over them by demand-ing a human king, the Lord remains faithfully present through the words of these two prophets. Even when the kings are unfaithful so that first Saul must be set aside and later David must be chastised, the Lord does not walk away from the people but remains steadfast. The final story of 2 Samuel, in which David sins but offers a sacrifice to avert national punishment, says more about God's charac-ter as a loving and faithful God than it does about David's character as a sinner.

demands a human king. Would a human king be any more likely to be righteous than a human judge? Would even a righteous king's sons be any more likely to be righteous than a human judge? And a king would have much more power than a judge! Later, Israel and Judah would learn the folly of their ancestors' decision.

The people's demand displeases Samuel, but the Lord declares, "They have not rejected you, but they have rejected me from being king over them" (1 Sam. 8:7). Samuel is commanded to anoint a king for Israel, but first, at God's com-mand, he warns them what kings are like:

These will be the ways of the king who will reign over you: he will take your sons and appoint them to his chariots and to be his horsemen, and to run before his chariots; and he will appoint for himself commanders of thousands and com-manders of fifties, and some to plow his ground and to reap his harvest, and to make his implements of war and the equipment of his chariots. He will take your daughters to be perfumers and cooks and bakers. He will take the best of your fields and vineyards and olive orchards and give them to his courtiers. He will take one-tenth of your grain and of your vineyards and give it to his officers and his courtiers. He will take your male and female slaves, and the best of your

Fig. 13.4. Second Samuel 21 tells the grisly story of David's vengeance on behalf of the Gibeonites, who are slain by Saul. David gives seven sons and grandsons of Saul over to the Gibeonites, who impale them and leave them hanging. Rizpah, the mother of two of Saul's sons, protects their bodies from the scavengers for months, until David properly buries the bones of Saul and Jonathan. This African American rendering of the story calls to mind the many unjust lynchings and murders that African Americans have suffered and the lamentations of their mothers (see 2 Sam. 3:7; 21:1–14).

cattle and donkeys, and put them to his work. He will take one-tenth of your flocks, and you shall be his slaves. (1 Sam. 8:10–17)

What are human kings good for? Taxes, armies, wars, drafts, and oppression. And Israel replies, "We demand a king, so that we might be like other nations!" Israel was willing to surrender its unique, chosen status as the only people over whom God reigned directly in order to be like other people.

The Lord's Covenant with David

If we follow the order of the narrative, the people's demand for a king required a significant theological reworking of the relationship between the Lord and Israel. This is most clearly seen in the covenant relationship between God and the people. There are several important covenants in the Old Testament, and in terms of Israel's relationship with God, there have been two major covenants to this point. Each includes promises and requirements and signs. In the covenant with Abraham, God promised Abraham and Sarah many descendants, a land for those descendants, and that they would be blessed to be a blessing. The sign and requirement for the covenant was the circumcision of the male children. In the covenant with Moses, God promised Israel that the Lord would be their God (and king). The sign of the covenant was the keeping of the Sabbath. The requirement of the covenant was faithfulness to the stipulations of the covenant as expressed in the Ten Commandments and the various case laws.

The introduction of human kingship—along with the resulting replacement of the Lord as the direct sovereign of the people—requires adjustments to the existing covenants. Or, rather, it requires a new covenant—this one directly with the king, in this case, King David.

The covenant with King David in 2 Samuel 7 is one of the more important passages in the Old Testament for Christian theologians. The story is built around the various, rich meanings of the Hebrew word *bet*, the basic meaning of which is "house." As in English, the Hebrew word for house can mean at least four different things: (1) a physical house or building, (2) a human household or family, (3) a temple or house of worship, and (4) a royal dynasty, as in the House of Windsor. The story in 2 Samuel 7 plays on all these meanings. David, having moved to Jerusalem and fathered a household of children (a *bet*), and having built himself a palace (a *bet*), decides to build a temple (a *bet*) for the Lord: "Now when the king was dwelling in his house [*bet*], and the Lord had given him rest from all his enemies around him, the king said to the prophet Nathan, 'See now, I am dwelling in a house [*bet*] of cedar, but the ark of God dwells in a tent.' Nathan said to the king, 'Go, do all that is in your heart; for the Lord is with you'" (2 Sam. 7:1–3, modified).

The king and prophet shared power, but they had split roles. The prophet spoke for God. The king—even when seeking to do something generous for God, such as build a temple—had to seek the will of God by asking permission from the prophet before taking a significant action. The prophet was then supposed to seek God's will. Assuming that God would be pleased by the decision to build a temple for the ark of the covenant, the prophet Nathan immediately says yes, without even seeking God's will. And note that David does not even spell out what he is going to do, but only says, "I am dwelling in a house of cedar, but the ark of God dwells in a tent." Apparently, merely noting this disparity is enough for the prophet to give the go-ahead to "do all that is in your heart." But this is not the end of the story. That night, the Lord speaks to the prophet:

> Go and tell my servant David: "Thus says the Lord: Are you the one to build me a house [*bet*] to live in? I have not lived in a house since the day I brought up the people of Israel from Egypt to this day, but I have been moving about in a tent and a tabernacle. Wherever I have moved about among all the people of Israel, did I ever speak a word with any of the tribal leaders of Israel, whom I commanded to shepherd my people Israel, saying, 'Why have you not built me a house of cedar?'" (2 Sam. 7:4–7)

The Lord interrupts the plans of both prophet and king and says that he will build a house for David, rather than the other way around.

Now therefore thus you shall say to my servant David: "Thus says the LORD of hosts: . . . I will make for you a great name, like the name of the great ones of the earth. And I will appoint a place for my people Israel. . . . Moreover the LORD declares to you that the LORD will make you a house [bet]. When your days are fulfilled and you lie down with your ancestors, I will raise up your offspring after you, who shall come forth from your body, and I will establish his kingdom." (2 Sam. 7:8–10, 11b–12)

Lord of Hosts A title given to Yahweh, describing his command over heavenly armies.

The Lord here says to David, "You will not *build me a house* [meaning a temple]. Quite the reverse, I will *build you a house* [meaning a dynasty]." But notice also that the language placed in God's voice directly echoes the vocabulary and content of the covenant with Abraham. Like Abraham, the Lord promises David "a great name" (compare Gen. 12:2). And whereas God had promised Abraham "a land" (Gen. 12:1), here God promises "a place" where they will be planted and from which they will be "disturbed no more." Thus, two of the central promises of the Abrahamic covenant are called out and repeated to David in this new covenant.

There is more. In Genesis 12:7, Abraham was promised, "To your offspring [literally: seed] I will give this land." David's "offspring" is given both a promise and a command: "He shall build a house for my name, and I will establish the throne of his kingdom forever. I will be a father to him, and he shall be a son to me. When he commits iniquity, I will punish him with a rod such as mortals use, with blows inflicted by human beings. But I will not take my steadfast love from him, as I took it from Saul, whom I put away from before you. Your house and your kingdom shall be made sure forever before me; your throne shall be established forever" (2 Sam. 7:13–16). God's promise to David here cannot be emphasized strongly enough. Several aspects are crucial.

First, as part of this new Davidic covenant, God promises David an eternal dynasty: "I will establish the throne of his kingdom forever." And also: "Your house and your kingdom shall be made sure forever." This means that one of David's descendants would forever rule as king of God's people. Because the Hebrew word for "anointing" a king was *mashah*, the king was at times called "God's anointed"—God's *mashiah* or God's messiah. From this term and the promise in this covenant, Israel later came to hope for the coming messiah to fulfill this promise after Israel's kings were no more.

Second, God promises, "I will be a father to him, and he shall be to me a son." With respect to Israel's theological understandings, subtle differentiations are at work here. The human king is not a god or divine, but he is a "son of God"—God is the king's father. (Many centuries later, when Jesus addressed God as "Father," he may have been making a messianic claim.) Throughout the Old Testament, references to the king as God's son can be found, such as in Psalm 2, "You are my son; today I have begotten you" (v. 7), or in the reference to the king in Isaiah 9, "For a child has been born for us, a son given to us" (v. 6). The human king, in this way, is seen not as God but as God's representative and chosen viceroy. Earlier in the Old Testament, all Israel was understood as God's "seed" and firstborn son. Moses was commanded in Exodus to say to Pharaoh, "Thus says the LORD: 'Israel is my firstborn son.' I say to you, 'Let my son go that he may worship me'" (4:22–23). While the corporate understanding of the people as God's firstborn child continues in Israel, it is fair to say that it is displaced by the individual notion that the king is God's son.

Third, although the promise regarding the kingship (and sonship) of David's descendants is absolute—"I will not take my steadfast love from him, as I took it from Saul"—the requirement for the king to keep God's laws is nevertheless in place. When the king sins, he will be punished: "When he commits iniquity, I will punish him." Similar to this, when Psalm 89 describes the Davidic covenant, it says, "If his sons forsake my law . . . , I will punish their sin with the rod . . . ; but I will not take my love from him" (vv. 30, 32–33 NIV).

Thus, the Davidic covenant was understood to be absolute, like the Noahic covenant—meaning God's promises were guaranteed forever, without the requirement placed upon human beings. But it also had conditional elements similar to the covenants with Abraham and Moses, meaning that obedience to the law was required, and when sins were committed, punishment would occur, and repentance and forgiveness would be required. David himself learns this after his affair with Bathsheba and his murder of Uriah.

The rise of kings in Israel also elevated the importance and role of the prophets. Once a human king was given such great power and authority, it was required that an office exist that could speak to the king regarding his sins and unrighteous actions—the prophet.

(It should also be noted that according to the prophet's directions, David's son would build the Lord a house. Apparently, God was not totally against the idea of a temple.)

Historical Interpretation

The Historical World behind the Text

As has been noted repeatedly in this book, the Deuteronomistic History (Deuteronomy through 2 Kings, except for Ruth) was likely compiled shortly before and/or during the exile, from older source materials. Historians often try to identify and use the older sources—such as the Ark Narratives in 1 Samuel—in order to help reconstruct the world behind the text. In addition, historical critics read the entirety of 1–2 Samuel against the experience of the exile. Read against the exile, 1–2 Samuel can be seen as a mourning over and longing for a golden age of national independence with strong kings and prophets.

The Historical World in the Text

The rise of kingship. In the previous section, Israel's demand for a king was analyzed from a theological and narrative perspective. There, the demand was seen as a rejection of the Lord as Israel's direct sovereign, as the result of the ethical failure of Samuel's sons to be righteous as he was, and as a result of Israel's desire to be like the other nations, most of whom had kings. In that light, Israel's demand for a king is seen mainly as unfaithfulness to God. But when analyzed from a historical perspective, it may be that the demand for a king is both more understandable and also less unfaithful.

As has been established in previous chapters, historians are confident that a people called Israel emerged in the land (the Levant) in the last quarter of the second millennium BCE (ca. 1250–1220). The texts of Joshua and Judges tell us that during this period, Israel was a loose confederation of tribes not governed by a king. The evidence from archaeology matches this assertion—there are no signs of central government, such as massive monumental architecture like palaces or temples. Israel does not appear to have had kings during this time.

Both the biblical text and archaeological findings show that at some point kingship was introduced to Israel. From a historical perspective, the questions can be asked, When and why did this change occur? There are many ways of answering these questions, and much ink has been spilled over them using various historical methods. For example, some approaches involve developing complicated sociological models based on population size and other evolving factors. Some historical approaches discount the Bible as a source for drawing historical conclusions, while others value the biblical text as a historical source. Some are based on highly complicated models for interpreting archaeological findings. And so on. All of them are controversial. For the purposes of this introductory book and the question of when kingship was introduced in Israel, we will pursue just one angle of inquiry on which the Bible and archaeology seem to agree. And we will trust the Bible and archaeology in ways some historians might consider naive. The angle of inquiry involves the Philistines.

Judges and 1–2 Samuel suggest that at roughly the same time Israel was emerging as a people in the hill country of Judah, another people—known to us as the Philistines—was also emerging to the west, on the coastal plains of the Mediterranean Sea. The Philistines endured as a people for the entire span of the kingdoms of Israel and Judah. They are also known from the writings of both Egypt and Assyria. Most likely, the Philistines were a sea people who relocated to the eastern edge of the Mediterranean, where they inhabited the cities of Gaza, Ashkelon, Ashdod, Ekron, and Gath. They may have been refugees from Crete or from the area of the Aegean Sea, and they brought with them a distinctive form of material culture that set them apart from the indigenous populations of ancient Canaan.

According to Judges and 1–2 Samuel, there was significant conflict between the Philistines and the Israelites. In much of this conflict, the Philistines were victorious (cf., e.g., the apparent superiority of the Philistines at the time of the story of David and Goliath and also in the deaths of Saul and Jonathan). One reason for their success may be that they had superior military technology, but they may also have had superior organization.

The beginning of 1 Samuel 8 stresses that Israel demanded a king because of the corruption of Samuel's sons. However, at the end of the chapter, the people add a new note: "No! We are determined to have a king for ourselves, so that we also may be like other nations, and that our king may judge us and go out before us to fight our battles!" (1 Sam. 8:19–20 AT). Then, in 1 Samuel 9:16, when Saul is identified as king, the text reads, "You shall anoint him to lead my people Israel. He shall save my people from the hand of the Philistines, for I have seen the suffering of my people."

From a strictly historical perspective, it may be that the mounting military pressure from the Philistines—and perhaps from other local nations such as the Ammonites (1 Sam. 11) and the Amalekites (1 Sam. 15)—demanded that Israel's social structure evolve to a more centralized governance (namely, monarchy). The reality may simply have been that a loose confederation of tribes, lacking a centralized government and a central leader, could not withstand the military threats from more powerful and centrally organized neighbors.

The kingdom of David and Solomon. A surface reading of the stories of David and his son Solomon (Solomon's story is told in 1 Kings 1–11) suggests that for a brief period, Israel as a nation reached near superpower status. The biblical narrative recounts that David not only successfully unified Israel and pacified her most war-like neighbors, such as the Philistines, but also extended Israel's control over such neighboring nations as Moab, Edom, Ammon, Syria, and Aram (see the description of David's conquests in 2 Sam. 8). First Kings goes on to describe how Solomon married one of Pharaoh's daughters and received a pomp-and-circumstance, dignitary visit from the queen of Sheba. Those chapters also describe how Solomon built up the nation through military and government expansion. For all of these reasons, the era of the kingdom of David and Solomon has been described as either "the golden age" of Israel or an era of grand enlightenment.

As with most historical analysis of the Old Testament, some modern historians have cast doubt on the historicity of these narratives. There may be no historical question regarding the Old Testament about which there is currently more intensive debate than that of the kingdom of David and Solomon. Some historians have gone so far as to question and even deny that David ever existed. As can be expected, many others defend the historicity of the biblical account. And, of course, many historians take some sort of moderating, middle view.

From the viewpoint of extrabiblical archaeological and inscriptional (written) evidence, there are reasons both to question the biblical account and also to support it. The most important extrabiblical sources are themselves issues of controversy, unfortunately. So not only are there few pieces of key evidence on which to base conclusions; those pieces of evidence are themselves points of conflict and debate.

As noted in previous chapters, it is clear historically that a people called Israel emerged in the promised land sometime late in the second millennium (ca. 1200 BCE)—the period addressed by the books of Joshua and Judges. Further, it is agreed that by the ninth century BCE, the kingdoms of Israel and Judah were established in the north and south of the land. So the question from a historical perspective is, What came between the emergence of Israel and the kingdoms of Israel and Judah? A people named "Israel" existed in the land during the period described by 1–2 Samuel and 1 Kings 1–11. Can these books be used as a historical source to reconstruct what happened in those years? Was there a Davidic kingdom? What do the archaeological sources contribute to the discussion?

There are many complicated ways in which historians come to decisions about what happened historically and how to interpret evidence. For the purposes of this chapter, we will look only at a few important extrabiblical sources and briefly comment on the biblical narrative.

The Tel Dan Stele. Perhaps the most important inscription that mentions David is the Tel Dan Stele. A stele is an inscribed stone monument, usually erected for some national purpose. The Tel Dan Stele was erected at the command of King Hazael of Aram (Syria), probably around the end of the ninth century BCE. While a few critics doubt the authenticity of the inscription, it is almost universally accepted as authentic because it was discovered in a controlled archaeological dig and photographed *in situ* (meaning while it was still being carefully unearthed). In the inscription, the Aramean king boasts of having defeated an unnamed king of Israel and makes reference to the "house of David."

Fig. 13.5. The Tel Dan Stele, which was discovered in a controlled archaeological dig in 1993–94 that was led by Avraham Biran, contains the oldest known extrabiblical reference to the house of David. The stele dates to the ninth century BCE. One very important detail of the inscription is the very clear reference to "the house of David"—the Davidic dynasty that ruled in Jerusalem. While even here there is controversy and some deny that the Aramaic consonants *bytdwd* (*bet-david*) should be translated as "house of David," the majority of scholars accept both the authenticity of the stele and of the translation "house of David."

The Moabite Stone. A second important ancient inscription is known either as the Moabite Stone (based on the nation of its origin) or the Mesha Stele (the king who erected the stone). This monument was erected around 840 BCE by King Mesha of Moab to commemorate his successful rebellion, overthrowing the subjugation of the king of Israel. The inscription will be discussed again later in this book, but here it is enough to note that the stele mentions "Omri king of Israel" and "his son [who] succeeded him." The stele may also contain a reference to the "house of David" in line 31, although that section of the inscription is highly damaged. Recent studies have argued for and against the reading of "house of David" in the stele. Israel Finkelstein and Thomas Römer argue that the text refers to the ancient "King Balak" of Moab (see Num. 22–24), while Michael Langlois—who used advanced computer technology to examine the inscription closely—confirms the reading "house of David."[2]

The invasion of Pharaoh Shishak. Although slightly outside the texts under consideration here, it is also worth noting that according to 1 Kings 11:40, the pharaoh who ruled Egypt at the end of Solomon's life was Shishak. According to 1 Kings 14:25–28, after Solomon's death, Shishak attacked and forced the capitulation of Solomon's son Rehoboam in Jerusalem. The biblical Shishak has been correlated with Pharaoh Sheshonq I of Egypt, who erected monuments commemorating his invasion of Israel.

There are other correlations between the biblical narratives of 1–2 Samuel, 1 Kings 1–11, and archaeology. For example, while the temple that Solomon is said to have built was destroyed in 587 BCE when the Babylonians conquered Jerusalem, almost every aspect of the intricate description of the temple in 1 Kings 6–7 has been confirmed by archaeological discoveries of temples in the same time period and region. First Kings 9 describes a series of nationalistic

---

Box 13.7

The Text of the Tel Dan Stele

The inscription has been partially broken and lost, but lines 2–9 of the inscription, as restored and translated by Biran, read as follows:

2. my father went up [against him when h]e fought at [. . .]
3. and my father lay down, he went to his [ancestors (viz. became sick and died)]. And the king of I[s-]
4. rael entered previously in my father's land, [and] Hadad made me king,
5. And Hadad went in front of me, [and] I departed from the seven [. . .]
6. s of my kingdom, and I slew [seve]nty kin[gs], who harnessed th[ousands of cha-]
7. riots and thousands of horsemen (or: horses). [I killed Jeho]ram son [of Ahab]
8. king of Israel, and [I] killed [Ahaz]iahu son of [Jehoram kin-]
9. g of the House of David, and I set*

* A. Biran and J. Naveh, "The Tel Dan Inscription: A New Fragment," *Israel Exploration Journal* 45 no. 1 (1995): 1–18.

building and military projects initiated by Solomon, such as fortifications to the walls of Jerusalem, Hazor, Gezer, and Megiddo; storage cities and cities for his chariots and his cavalry; and a fleet of ships. Some archaeologists believe that they have found evidence of these imperial building projects at Hazor, Megiddo, and Gezer. Other archaeologists acknowledge that the discoveries do indicate imperial activity, but they say the findings date from a later period in Israel's history.

Making historical judgments about the historicity of the Bible's description of the kingdoms of David and Solomon is extremely difficult. The inherent difficulty in drawing conclusions from complicated data is made even more challenging by religious and political entanglements that come into play. Beyond the importance of David for both Judaism and Christianity, the figure of David and the city of Jerusalem are even more important for the modern nation of Israel and its foes. For some in Israel, establishing that David lived and moved his capital to Jerusalem in 1000 BCE is important because it gives modern Jews a historical claim to the land and especially to the city of Jerusalem. For the same reason, it is politically important to others to question the historicity of the David story.

FOR FURTHER READING: **1–2 Samuel**

Alter, Robert. *The David Story: A Translation with Commentary of 1 and 2 Samuel*. New York: Norton, 1999.

Anderson, A. A. *2 Samuel*. Word Biblical Commentary 11. Dallas: Word, 1989.

Brueggemann, Walter. *First and Second Samuel*. Interpretation: A Bible Commentary for Teaching and Preaching. Louisville: Westminster John Knox, 2012.

Gilmour, Rachelle. *Representing the Past: A Literary Analysis of Narrative Historiography in the Book of Samuel*. Supplements to Vetus Testamentum 143. Leiden: Brill, 2011.

Hackett, Jo Ann. "1 and 2 Samuel." In *Women's Bible Commentary*, 3rd ed., edited by Carol A. Newsom, Sharon H. Ringe, and Jacqueline E. Lapsley, 150–63. Louisville: Westminster John Knox, 2012.

Halpern, Baruch. *The First Historians: The Hebrew Bible and History*. San Francisco: Harper & Row, 1988.

Klein, Ralph W. *1 Samuel*. 2nd ed. Word Biblical Commentary 10. Nashville: Thomas Nelson, 2000.

McCarter, P. Kyle. *2 Samuel: A New Translation with Introduction, Notes, and Commentary*. Anchor Yale Bible 9. New York: Doubleday, 1984.

14

1–2 Kings

The books of 1–2 Kings in the Jewish and Christian Bibles are named for the series of kings of Israel and Judah around whom the narrative is structured. In the Greek version of the Old Testament and in Orthodox Christian traditions, the books are called 3–4 Kingdoms or Reigns. In the Christian Bible, they are considered part of the Historical Books, but in Judaism they are considered part of the Former Prophets because of the important role that certain prophetic figures play. In contrast to 1–2 Samuel, which feature Samuel, Saul, and David, the books of 1–2 Kings have many significant characters and cover a much longer time period (960–586 BCE).

As noted in previous chapters, although considered "historical" in the Christian Old Testament and "prophetic" in the Jewish Bible, the literary genre contained in these books is not properly understood as either history or prophecy. The term *history* is still somewhat apt, because the narrative does tell the stories of Israel and Judah between approximately 960 and 586 BCE. While the books are historical narrative, they are not "history" in the modern sense of the term. The authors (or editors) of 1–2 Kings were not attempting to describe the past as accurately and objectively as possible. Rather, they were engaged in a highly theological project. They were attempting to draw on the stories of the past in order to explain why Israel and Judah fell, to recognize God's purpose with Israel and Judah, and to understand God's future for the people. For this reason, the genre of 1–2 Kings may be more accurately described as "theological narrative" or "symbolic narrative."

Background

Composition and Development

As with most books of the Old Testament, the books of 1–2 Kings are anonymous. They are part of an extended narrative portion of the Old Testament spanning from Deuteronomy through 2 Kings (except for Ruth) that many scholars call the Deuteronomistic History (see chap. 9).

The editors of this narrative—known as the Deuteronomistic Historian—are anonymous. In the book, we follow the thesis that there were at least two editors/authors of 1–2 Kings. The first author was most likely active around 620 BCE, working in Jerusalem; this author was responsible for the bulk of the Deuteronomistic History. A second author, working in the Babylonian exile around 560 BCE, brought the work up to date and finished 2 Kings. The Deuteronomistic Historian certainly drew upon sources that were ancient already by the time they were writing and editing. Scholars who work closely with this portion of the Old Testament have identified certain of these sources through a variety of methods. These older source materials include the Succession Narrative, in which Solomon inherits the throne from David (1 Kings 1–2); "the Book of the Annals of Solomon" (1 Kings 11:41 AT); the Book of the Annals of the Kings of Israel (e.g., 1 Kings 14:19; 15:31); the Book of the Annals of the Kings of Judah (e.g., 1 Kings 14:29; 15:7); and other implied sources, such as narratives about the prophets Elijah and Elisha (1 Kings 17–2 Kings 13). In addition, 1–2 Kings include older source material that was passed down through either oral tradition or other written sources, such as ancient lists of Solomon's servants (1 Kings 4:7–19), the negative evaluation of Solomon in 1 Kings 11, or the letter from the Assyrian leader Rabshakeh and the subsequent prayer of King Hezekiah in 2 Kings 19.

Genre

As already noted, 1–2 Kings is made up mostly of theological narratives or symbolic narratives. But the books also include prayers, hymns, prophecies, and most importantly for these books, regnal formulas at the start and end of the narrative about each king. Special attention is given to these regnal formulas below.

Literary Interpretation

The death of David and succession of Solomon (1 Kings 1–2). Similar to the books of Joshua and Judges, 1 Kings starts by reporting the death of the main character of the previous book—in this case, King David. And similar to Exodus and 1 Samuel, 1 Kings also launches its own narrative with the actions of a strong woman—in this case, Bathsheba, one of David's wives. David had fathered sons by many women. As David is dying, one of his sons—Adonijah, the son of Haggith—plots to succeed his father. He is next in line to the throne after his older brothers Amnon and Absalom, who had died. (Another older son, Chileab, is mentioned in 2 Sam. 3:3, but he is never mentioned again.) Able to secure the support of some key power players in the kingdom (but not all), Adonijah is crowned and acknowledged by some leaders as king.

The prophet Nathan alerts Bathsheba of Adonijah's plans, and the two go to King David on his deathbed. Bathsheba convinces David to reiterate an earlier promise to bequeath the throne to her son, Solomon: "As the Lord lives, who delivered my life from every crisis, and as I vowed to you by the Lord, your son Solomon will reign as king after me" (1:29–30 AT). So Solomon is also crowned king and acknowledged by some but not all—but Solomon sits on the throne. Adonijah apparently sues for peace with King Solomon, but Solomon detects falsehood in his plots and has Adonijah put to death. Solomon then secures the throne through a series of actions, and 1 Kings 2 concludes: "The kingdom was now established in Solomon's hands" (NIV).

The reign of Solomon (1 Kings 3–11). The reign of Solomon can be described in three sections. The first section, 1 Kings 3–4, portrays the young king as wise. When God appears to him in a vision, Solomon asks not for wealth or long life but for the wisdom to rule justly. God gives Solomon the wisdom he sought, and Solomon proves wise in cleverly judging between two women who each claim a baby as her son (1 Kings 3:16–28). Following this judgment, the narrative says, "All of Israel . . . revered the king, because they saw that the wisdom of God was in his heart to execute justice" (v. 28 AT). And in 1 Kings 4:29–30, the text concludes, "God gave Solomon wisdom and very great discernment, and wideness of heart as vast as the sand of the seashore. . . . He was wiser than every other human" (AT).

The second section, 1 Kings 5–8, describes Solomon's building and dedication of the temple. The building of the temple is described as fulfilling the will of God, who had declared to David in 2 Samuel 7 that his son would build a temple for God's name. The temple is magnificent in splendor, but the narrative notes the incredible cost and how much forced labor Solomon conscripted (1 Kings 5:13–18). All told, the narrative says that hundreds of thousands of people were forced to work on the project (although it may be that the term translated "thousand" had a different meaning). The narrative is clear that

Fig. 14.1. The most famous story regarding Solomon's wisdom is the account of two women who both claim to be the mother of a baby boy. Solomon orders the child to be cut in half, with each woman to receive a half. One agrees, but the other says, "Oh, my lord, give her the living child, and by no means put him to death" (1 Kings 3:26 ESV). Solomon wisely identifies the second woman as the true mother of the boy.

the amount of forced labor was extreme and subtly refers back to Samuel's early warning about the exploitative tendencies of monarchs (1 Sam. 8). The theological high point of this section is in 1 Kings 8 with the dedication of the temple. After describing the temple at great length, the narrative reports Solomon's opening declaration: "The Lord said he dwells in darkness. I have built you an exalted house, a place for you to dwell forever" (8:12–13 AT). Later

The Theology of the Temple

The temple in Jerusalem is one of ancient Israel's most significant and powerful institutions. What was said in Exodus 25 of the tabernacle is true for the house of the Lord: "Have them make a sanctuary for my sake, so that I might dwell among them" (Exod. 25:8 AT). The temple exists because Yahweh desires to live among the people of Israel. But the God of Israel is also holy, and if not properly approached, that holiness can be dangerous (see, e.g., Lev. 10). The priesthood was charged with mediating between God and Israel through rituals, sacrifices, instruction, and so on.

The temple was organized into three major sections: the vestibule, the nave, and the inner sanctuary. As one moved closer to the inner sanctuary, the holiness of the space was reflected in the quality of the materials used to make the utensil (gold as opposed to bronze, for instance). Among other things, the temple was a place where Israel obeyed its God, expressed gratitude, received forgiveness, and remembered its past.

he says, "But will God truly dwell on the earth? Even heaven and the highest heaven cannot contain you, let alone this house that I have built. Now turn toward the prayer of your servant . . . so that your eyes may be open toward this house day and night" (8:27–29 AT). God responds to Solomon, "I have answered your prayer and your request. . . . I have consecrated this temple you built by making it my permanent home; I will be constantly present there" (9:3 NET). Solomon's temple in Jerusalem remains the focal point of the Southern Kingdom until its destruction in 586 BCE.

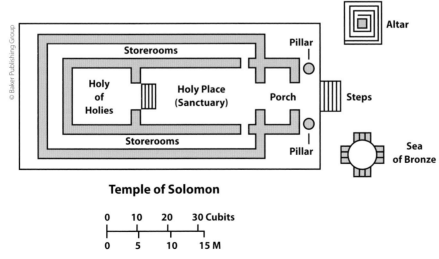

© Baker Publishing Group

Temple of Solomon

Fig. 14.2. The layout of the temple

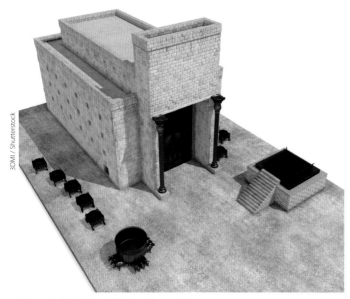

Fig. 14.3. Depiction of Solomon's temple

In the third section of Solomon's story (1 Kings 9–11), the king reaches the height of his glory . . . and then declines into folly. In 1 Kings 9, God appears to Solomon again, reassuring him of the Davidic covenant: "I shall establish your royal throne over Israel forever, as I said to your father David" (9:5 AT). Solomon's other building projects are then described (9:15–28), with pains again taken to note the forced labor that Solomon used for his kingdom building. The apex of Solomon's glory is narrated with the elaborate account of the queen of Sheba's visit (1 Kings 10). Solomon's glory is then summarized: "Thus, King Solomon was greater than all the kings of the earth in wealth and in wisdom. The whole earth sought the presence of Solomon to hear his wisdom, which God had given his heart" (10:23–24 AT).

Solomon's rapid rise to glory is matched by an equally rapid decline into folly. Having already indicated the folly and suffering caused by the king's imperial building projects, the narrative says, "King Solomon loved many foreign wives. . . . And his wives turned his heart away [from God]" (11:1, 3 AT). Solomon follows foreign gods, such as Astarte, Milcom, Chemosh, and Molech, and builds places of worship for them (11:5–8). In spite of two personal appearances from the Lord, "Solomon didn't do what the Lᴏʀᴅ commanded" (11:10 CEB). Toward the end of his life, enemies arise against Solomon from both outside and inside his kingdom. From outside, threats arise from Edom, Aram, and Egypt. From inside, a man named Jeroboam from the northern tribe of Ephraim rebels against Solomon. Jeroboam escapes by fleeing to Egypt, where he takes shelter until Solomon's death in 922 BCE.

The kingdoms of Israel and Judah (1 Kings 12–2 Kings 17). The story of the rebellion of the northern tribes is told as a tale of adolescent, male folly. Following Solomon's death, his son Rehoboam succeeds to the throne. The northern rebel Jeroboam returns from his exile in Egypt and gathers the northern tribes at Shechem. There, they demand that Rehoboam lower the heavy taxes and reduce the heavy forced labor that Solomon had inflicted on the people. Rehoboam's elder counselors advise him to lower the burden, but the younger counselors urge him to say, "My little finger is thicker than my

Fig. 14.4. Solomon gives a banquet for the queen of Sheba.

father's loins!" (12:10; the phallic insult is obvious). Rehoboam listens to the young men and threatens to raise the people's taxes even further. As a result, the northern ten tribes secede, saying, "What share do we have in David?" (12:16). Thus, the descendants of Abraham and Sarah split into two kingdoms. The northern ten tribes form the kingdom of Israel, with Jeroboam as its first king. The southern tribe of Judah forms its own kingdom of Judah, with Rehoboam continuing as king. (The twelfth priestly tribe of Levi had no land; its priests were dispersed around both kingdoms.) Because the Southern Kingdom had both Jerusalem and Solomon's temple—the spiritual center

---

Box 14.3

"Here Are Your Gods, O Israel, Who Brought You up out of the Land of Egypt"

In 1 Kings 12:25–33, Jeroboam establishes alternative worship sites at Dan and Bethel, designed to compete with the temple at Jerusalem, the capital city of David and Solomon. Jeroboam creates two golden calves and then provocatively declares, "Here are your gods, O Israel, who brought you up out of the land of Egypt" (12:28). For those familiar with the book of Exodus, this story sounds ominously familiar. A very similar declaration is also found in Exodus 32:4, only there the declaration issues from the mouth of Aaron, who is describing a single golden calf. It is not clear which of the two stories is influenced by the other, or if they are perhaps influenced by a third, unknown source. Either way, both Aaron and Jeroboam are clearly depicted in highly negative terms as idolatrous worshipers who lead God's people astray.

Map 14.1. Divided kingdom

of the people—Jeroboam sets up two golden calves to represent the Lord, with the words "Here are your gods, O Israel, who brought you up out of the land of Egypt" (12:28). He sets up one in a temple in Bethel and another in a temple in Dan so that his subjects would not make pilgrimage to Jerusalem.

The rest of the book of 1 Kings and the majority of the book of 2 Kings are organized according to the dates when the various kings of Israel and Judah ruled. The normal pattern is that the reign of a king is announced and evaluated in highly formulaic language; various events from that king's reign are recounted; and the death of the king is recounted, along with a summary judgment regarding his value as king. Then the reign of the next king is announced and the pattern repeats. The description of the reign of King Omri of Israel illustrates the pattern:

> In the thirty-first year of King Asa of Judah, Omri began to reign over Israel; he reigned for twelve years, six of them in Tirzah.
> He bought the hill of Samaria from Shemer for two talents of silver; he fortified the hill, and called the city that he built, Samaria, after the name of Shemer, the owner of the hill.
> Omri did what was evil in the sight of the LORD; he did more evil than all who were before him. For he walked in all the way of Jeroboam son of Nebat, and in the sins that he caused Israel to commit, provoking the LORD, the God of Israel, to anger by their idols. Now the rest of the acts of Omri that he did, and the power that he showed, are they not written in the Book of the Annals of the Kings of Israel? Omri slept with his ancestors, and was buried in Samaria; his son Ahab succeeded him. (1 Kings 16:23–28)

divided kingdom A reference to the Northern and Southern Kingdoms, which split shortly after Solomon's death.

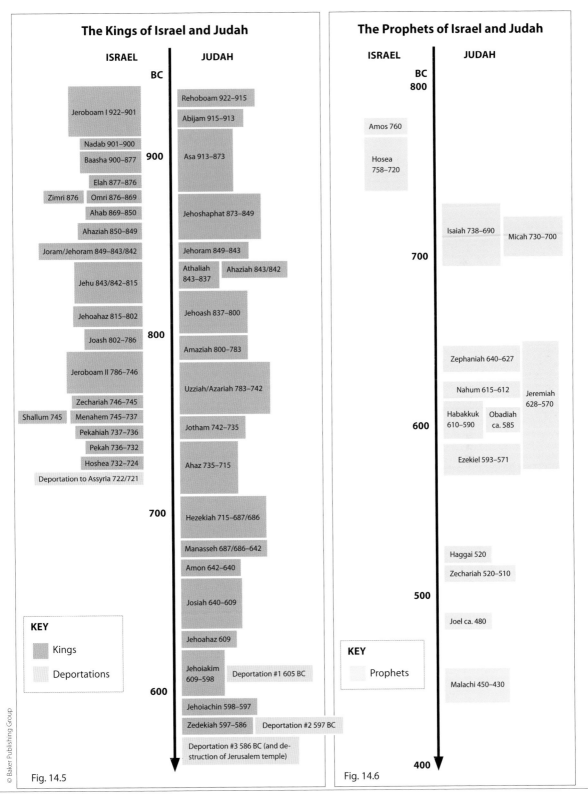

The Kings of Israel and Judah

ISRAEL | JUDAH

BC

Jeroboam I 922–901

Rehoboam 922–915

Abijam 915–913

Nadab 901–900

Baasha 900–877

900

Asa 913–873

Elah 877–876

Zimri 876 | Omri 876–869

Ahab 869–850

Ahaziah 850–849

Jehoshaphat 873–849

Joram/Jehoram 849–843/842

Jehoram 849–843

Athaliah 843–837 | Ahaziah 843/842

Jehu 843/842–815

Jehoahaz 815–802

Jehoash 837–800

Joash 802–786

800

Amaziah 800–783

Jeroboam II 786–746

Uzziah/Azariah 783–742

Zechariah 746–745

Shallum 745 | Menahem 745–737

Pekahiah 737–736

Jotham 742–735

Pekah 736–732

Hoshea 732–724

Ahaz 735–715

Deportation to Assyria 722/721

700

Hezekiah 715–687/686

Manasseh 687/686–642

Amon 642–640

Josiah 640–609

Jehoahaz 609

KEY

Kings

Deportations

Jehoiakim 609–598 | Deportation #1 605 BC

600

Jehoiachin 598–597

Zedekiah 597–586 | Deportation #2 597 BC

Deportation #3 586 BC (and destruction of Jerusalem temple)

Fig. 14.5

The Prophets of Israel and Judah

ISRAEL | JUDAH

BC
800

Amos 760

Hosea 758–720

Isaiah 738–690 | Micah 730–700

700

Zephaniah 640–627

Nahum 615–612

Jeremiah 628–570

Habakkuk 610–590 | Obadiah ca. 585

600

Ezekiel 593–571

Haggai 520

Zechariah 520–510

500

Joel ca. 480

KEY

Prophets

Malachi 450–430

400

Fig. 14.6

© Baker Publishing Group

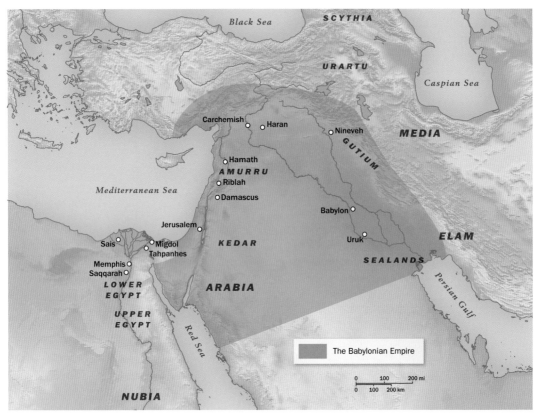

Map 14.2. Babylonian Empire

The stories that occur in these chapters also feature many prophets, because the prophets often played the role of checking the king's power and calling him to faithfulness. For example, stories of the prophets Elijah, Micaiah, and Elisha dominate the narrative from 1 Kings 17 through 2 Kings 8. These prophetic figures play such an important role in these books that the Jewish Bible considers 1–2 Kings part of the Former Prophets in its organizational structure.

The books of 1–2 Kings tell the fate of both nations, the Northern Kingdom of Israel and the Southern Kingdom of Judah. The books tell of the prophets' attempts to call the nations to faithfulness, of acts of divine intervention that they performed, of the roles played by faithful kings who lead the people well, of the roles played by unfaithful kings who lead the people poorly and away from God, and of international events such as wars and famines.

During the eighth century BCE, the Assyrian Empire, which was centered in the Tigris-Euphrates valley, was expanding its reach across the ancient Near East. The book of 2 Kings recounts that the Assyrians forced Israel to become a vassal state within their empire. The kingdom of Israel revolts unsuccessfully several times, and eventually the Assyrians launch a three-year siege of Samaria, Israel's capital city, and finally destroy the city and defeat the kingdom

Box 14.4

The Rise of the Assyrian Empire

The Assyrian Empire shaped ancient Israel's history in fundamental ways, beginning especially in the ninth and eighth centuries BCE when Assyria began to expand farther west. While there had been incursions into the west by earlier Assyrian kings (e.g., Tiglath-pileser I, 1114–1076 BCE; Assur-bel-kala, 1073–1056 BCE), the pace of incursions increased significantly in the ninth century under Assurnasirpal II (883–859 BCE) and his more expansionistic son, Shalmaneser III (859–824 BCE). The Assyrian monarch Tiglath-pileser III (745–727 BCE) was a vigorous warrior, campaigning, securing tribute, and putting down riots. Eventually, he even wore the dual crown of both Assyria and Babylon. He innovatively implemented a provincial system, whereby regions would become integrated into Assyria itself, resulting in a more direct form of Assyrian rule. The Northern Kingdom's capital of Samaria, for instance, was integrated into the Assyrian provincial system.

in 722/721 BCE (2 Kings 17:5). Assyria forces many of Israel's citizens into exile in Mesopotamia and simultaneously resettles in Israel exiles from other conquered vassal states—Babylon, Cuthah, Avva, Hamath, and Sepharvaim (2 Kings 17:24).

The kingdom of Judah (2 Kings 18–25). At the same time that the Assyrian Empire destroys the kingdom of Israel, it also attempts to conquer the kingdom of Judah. However, Judah, under the leadership of King Hezekiah, with the support and guidance of the prophet Isaiah, is able to resist. The invading Assyrians, led by King Sennacherib, besiege Jerusalem around 701 BCE but are not able to conquer it (2 Kings 18–20). Hezekiah is remembered by the Deuteronomistic Historian as an effective and faithful king.

Following Hezekiah's death, his son Manasseh ascends to the throne. Manasseh is judged by the Deuteronomistic Historian to be Judah's most unfaithful king and the primary cause of the exile: "He did evil in the eyes of the Lord, according to the abominations of the nations. . . . He set up altars to Baal, made a sacred pole as King Ahab of Israel had done, worshiped the hosts of heaven, and served them" (2 Kings 21:2–3 AT). In addition, "Manasseh also shed very much innocent blood, until he had filled Jerusalem with it from one end to the other" (2 Kings 21:16a AT). His son Amon succeeds him, and his rule is similar to his father's.

Manasseh's grandson Josiah, however (like Hezekiah a century earlier), is recalled as a faithful king who leads the nation in a political, moral, and religious reformation. Second Kings 22–23 recounts the story of Josiah's reformation. At the king's orders, the temple is to be renovated. As renovations begin, the high priest Hilkiah reports, "I have found the book of the law in the house of the Lord" (2 Kings 22:8). The discovery of the lost (or hidden) "book of the law" leads Josiah to initiate a moral and religious reformation, the details of which are recorded in 2 Kings 23.

Box 14.5

The Plots of 1–2 Kings

Can Israel serve the Lord as a united kingdom or in divided kingdoms? As has been discussed in earlier chapters, the main plot of the second portion of the Deuteronomistic History (Josh. 24–2 Kings 25) answers the question, Can Israel serve the Lord? Joshua led the people in a renewal of the covenant, during which he charged them to choose either to serve the Lord or to serve another god. When the people responded that, like Joshua, they would serve the Lord, Joshua responded, "You cannot serve the Lord" (24:19 AT). Having already narrated that the people could not serve the Lord when led by charismatic judges and organized by tribes (Judg. 1–1 Sam. 8) and that they could not do so when led by one king as a united kingdom (1 Sam. 9–1 Kings 11), the books of 1–2 Kings take up the question of whether either the Northern Kingdom or the Southern Kingdom could serve the Lord.

As noted earlier in this chapter, the story is organized around the reign of each king. Each king is evaluated according to whether he did evil in the eyes of the Lord, and each is given a summary judgment as the end of his reign is reported. For the northern kings, every one of them is condemned with the notice that he did evil in the eyes of the Lord, especially following the sin of Jeroboam, who set up the two golden calves in Bethel and Dan—a sin that is seen as proof that the Northern Kingdom and its kings did not serve the Lord faithfully. But some northern kings—especially King Ahab—are noted for being even worse than the rest.

In the case of the southern kings, the evaluation is less uniform—and, in keeping with the complicated legacies of David and Solomon, much more complicated for both the Deuteronomistic Historian and the modern reader to decipher. For example, Rehoboam and his son Abijam are judged as unfaithful because their hearts were not true to the Lord (see 1 Kings 15:1–8). By way of contrast, their successors Asa and Jehoshaphat are judged as mostly faithful, for they removed the male temple prostitutes from the temple and limited worship of Asherah. But the narrative also notes that they did not take down the "high places," where the worship of Baal and Asherah and associated destructive worship practices took place (see 1 Kings 15:9–15; 22:41–46). Most of the Judean kings are judged as partially or mostly faithful, but two later Judean kings are particularly singled out for their faithfulness: Hezekiah (1 Kings 18:1–8; 20:20–21) and Josiah (1 Kings 22:1–2). Several kings—Manasseh, Amon, Jehoahaz, Jehoiakim, Jehoiachin, and Zedekiah—are evaluated as uniformly unfaithful to the Lord. The combined legacy is complicated, therefore, but the overall trend and resulting fall of the Southern Kingdom lead to the conclusion that while individual kings and leaders are capable of serving the Lord with partial faithfulness, in the end the nation as a whole was not capable of serving the Lord.

Meanwhile, on the international scene, the nascent Babylonian Empire rises and replaces the Assyrians as the dominant international empire. King Josiah is killed in battle by the Egyptians and replaced by Jehoiakim, who serves as

Box 14.6

The High Places

A "high place" (Hebrew: *bama*) refers to an elevated area (natural or constructed) that is dedicated to worship or sacrifice. In 1–2 Kings, the term frequently appears in its plural form (*bamot*) and is typically used in a derogatory manner for worship that takes place outside Jerusalem (1 Kings 3:3; 11:7; 12:30–32). When used polemically, the "high places" represent the presence of idolatrous, foreign worship that threatened Yahweh's singularity and exclusive presence in Jerusalem. It is for this reason that the destruction of high places is attributed to the kings that the Deuteronomistic Historian respects most deeply (e.g., Hezekiah and Josiah).

vassal of Egypt until submitting to the Babylonians as their vassal for three years. His son Jehoiachin replaces him on the throne and rebels against Babylon.

In 597 BCE, Babylon forces Jehoiachin and Jerusalem to surrender. When the city capitulates, it is stripped of its wealth, and Jehoiachin and many other leading citizens are forced into exile in Babylon in a first deportation.

The Babylonians place Jehoiachin's uncle Zedekiah on the throne, and he reigns for ten years as Judah's last king. When he rebels against the Babylonians, they besiege the city until they finally make a breach in the wall. The king and his soldiers attempt to flee but are caught—Zedekiah's sons are executed, his eyes are put out, and he is taken into exile. The Babylonians destroy the city's walls and buildings—including the temple—and deport a second wave of leading citizens into exile.

Second Kings ends with the notice that "in the thirty-seventh year of the exile of King Jehoiachin of Judah" (25:27; around 560 BCE), the king was released from prison in Babylon, given new clothing, and offered a seat of honor at the table of the Babylonian emperor. In this description, the narrative hearkens back to the story of Joseph, who is similarly exalted from prison and clothed with new, honorific garb (Gen. 41:37–45).

The prophets and literary interpretation of 1–2 Kings. As has also already been noted, prophetic figures play a major role in the books of 1–2 Kings—so much so that these books are considered part of the Former Prophets in the Jewish Bible. As is the case with the kings, not all of the prophets are faithful figures. While most are, there are also false or unfaithful prophets. Some of them serve false gods—such as the 450 prophets of Baal and four hundred prophets of Asherah in 1 Kings 18. Other unfaithful prophets purportedly serve the Lord, but do not do so in truth—such as King Ahab's four hundred Yahwistic court prophets in 1 Kings 22. Nor are all of the prophets in 1–2 Kings major figures. For example, there is an unnamed "man of God" and a similarly unnamed prophet in 1 Kings 13. An otherwise unknown prophet named "Shemaiah the man of God" appears to Rehoboam after the split of the nation to warn him not to go to war against the rebellious tribes, "because this matter is from [God]" (1 Kings 12:24 AT). The prophet Jonah is also mentioned in 2 Kings

Box 14.7

Prophets and Kings in 1–2 Kings

Prophet	King/Kings	Nation	Chapters
Nathan	Solomon	United	1 Kings 1 (also in 2 Samuel)
Elijah	Ahab, Ahaziah	Israel	1 Kings 17–19; 2 Kings 1–2
Micaiah	Ahab	Israel	1 Kings 22
Elisha	Joram, Jehu, Jehoahaz	Israel	2 Kings 2–13
Isaiah	Hezekiah	Judah	2 Kings 19–20
Huldah	Josiah	Judah	2 Kings 22

14:25. The prophetess Huldah, however, played a significant role in the Josianic reformation in 2 Kings 22.

Three major aspects about the prophets as literary characters in the books of 1–2 Kings stand out. First, the prophets are often figures who are played off against the royalty—kings, queens, and royal servants. When the king is a faithful character—such as Hezekiah or Josiah or even Solomon—the prophet and king work together. But when the king is an unfaithful character—such as Ahab, Ahaziah, or Jehu—the prophet and king are pitted against each other.

Second, although we know historically that prophets were present throughout the historical period under investigation, it is interesting that prophets are often absent from the literary stage in the narrative. After Elisha, the narrative has no major prophetic figures in the Northern Kingdom. Indeed, the known literary prophets of that time period, Amos and Hosea, do not appear in the narrative. Similarly, in the narrative about the Southern Kingdom, there are no major prophetic figures after Hezekiah and Isaiah other than Huldah. And again, known historic literary prophets, such as Jeremiah and Habakkuk, do not appear as characters in the narrative.

Third, the agency of God in 1–2 Kings is in part taken up by the prophetic figures. The prophets speak for God and their pronouncements enact the will of God. For example, when the narrative introduces Elijah, it reports, "Elijah the Tishbite, an inhabitant of Gilead, said to Ahab, 'As the LORD lives, the God of Israel whom I serve, there will be no dew or rain except at my bidding'" (1 Kings 17:1 NJPS). After this announcement, there is no rain in the land until Elijah calls for rain in a confrontation with 450 prophets of Baal at Mount Carmel (1 Kings 18).

Theological Interpretation

Tracking the Agency of God

In the books of 1–2 Kings—where the focus of agency is so strongly on each human king—a reader may wonder how the agency of God is being presented. In

Fig. 14.7. Elijah runs from the chariot of Ahab.

the books of 1–2 Samuel, the agency of God was most clearly revealed through the ark of the covenant and the prophets Samuel and Nathan. In 1–2 Kings, the prophets continue to be the major locus through which the will and agency of God are communicated—specifically Nathan, Elijah, Micaiah, Elisha, Isaiah, Huldah, other anonymous "men of God," and other named prophets.

Recall again that when the prophet Samuel was born, the narrative reports that the word of God was rare and visions were not widespread. Then Samuel receives his inaugural vision from God in 1 Samuel 3, after which he continues to receive the word of God, and all Israel receives the word through him. The narrative of 1–2 Kings continues the literary trajectory along which the will and word of God are communicated through the prophets.

When evaluating the theological nature of God's word as spoken through the prophets in 1–2 Kings, one can say that it functions alternatively as "law" and "gospel" (good news). At times, God's word is law—calling Israel to faithfulness, warning against unfaithfulness, naming and condemning sin, announcing condemnation or judgment, and bringing about punishment. At other times, God's word is gospel—pronouncing blessing and permission, announcing forgiveness, bringing healing and even resurrection, giving guidance and provision.

The recurring appearance of anonymous characters who are called "man of God" in the Deuteronomistic History (but especially in 1–2 Kings) illustrates this point. These men of God announce condemnation on various figures. In contrast

resurrection The reanimation of dead human bodies; this teaching is generally understood to be a later theological development in Judaism and Christianity that is based on core understandings of the Old Testament God as a deity who saves from death.

Fig. 14.8. Elisha succeeded Elijah as prophet in the Northern Kingdom in the ninth century BCE. He is typically depicted as bald because of the account of the forty-two boys who bully him, calling him "baldy." The text says two "she bears" charged out of the woods and mauled the boys (2 Kings 2:23–24).

to the "man of God" in Judges 13, who is an angelic figure announcing the birth of Samson, the men of God who appear in 1–2 Samuel and 1–2 Kings appear to represent human characters—prophets who announce judgment. In 1 Samuel 2—just before the boy Samuel's inaugural vision and call—a "man of God" appears and announces to the priest Eli that because of the sins of his sons Hophni and Phinehas, God is judging his house with the death of his sons; the "man of God" also promises that God would "raise up a faithful priest . . . who shall go in and out before my anointed one." In 1 Kings 13, after Jeroboam I of Israel sets up his two golden calves, a "man of God" appears and announces judgment against him; he also says that one day "a son shall be born to the house of David, Josiah by name," who will atone for Jeroboam's sins (1 Kings 13:2). But the narrative notes that "Jeroboam did not turn from his evil way" (v. 33). In 1 Kings 20, a "man of God" appears to Ahab (among Israel's most unfaithful kings) and pronounces blessings on his wars against the neighboring nation of Aram (Syria).

These brief appearances of anonymous prophetic figures illustrate concisely how the prophetic figures speak into existence God's judgment (law) and promise (gospel). It could also be noted that in 2 Kings 17, the narrative articulates the reasons that the kingdom of Israel fell to Assyria by saying, "Indeed the Lord warned Israel and Judah by the hand of every prophet and every seer, saying, 'Repent from your evil ways and keep my commandments, . . . which I have sent to you by the hands of my servants the prophets'" (v. 13 AT).

In 1–2 Kings, the agency of God is also realized more directly as God simply acts miraculously through such things as nature, other nations, and disease. An example occurs in the reign of King Jehoahaz of Israel, reported in 2 Kings 13: "[Jehoahaz] did what was evil in the eyes of the Lord, and followed the sins of Jeroboam son of Nebat, through which he led Israel to sin; he did not turn from them. The anger of the Lord was kindled against Israel, so that he gave them into the hand of King Hazael of Aram, and into the hand of Ben-Hadad son of Hazael. But Jehoahaz prayed to the Lord, and the Lord heard him, for he saw the oppression of Israel, how the king of Aram oppressed them. And the Lord gave Israel a deliverer" (vv. 2–5a AT).

Israel and Judah's Sin

Perhaps the most dominant theological theme in the books of 1–2 Kings is the sin or sins that Israel and Judah committed, which led to their downfall. Although the books of 1–2 Kings present a complicated narrative regarding the sin, judgment, and fall of the two kingdoms, the predominant theme is the idolatry to which both countries—led by their kings—fall prey. It is not a stretch to say that 1–2 Kings is a narrative and theological exposition on the fate of the first commandment in Israel's long monarchic history.

This theme is most clearly evident in the narrative's repeated indictments, such as the condemnation of "the sins of Jeroboam that he committed and that he caused Israel to commit" (1 Kings 15:30)—that is, the setting up of the golden calves as idols to represent the Lord at Bethel and at Dan. As noted earlier, the narrative presents Jeroboam's setting up of the idols as a sin equivalent to the forging of the golden calf by Aaron in Exodus 32. In addition, Jeroboam set up "high places"—rural worship sites where syncretistic worship practices took place, mixing elements of Canaanite religion with those of Israelite religion. The Deuteronomistic Historian and other biblical authors believed that the worship practices that occurred at these sites included practices such as child sacrifice.

As the Deuteronomistic History evaluates the kings of Israel, it judges them harshly for continuing in the sin of Jeroboam. In addition to whatever sins or evils that the particular kings committed individually, each of them is charged with participating in the sin of Jeroboam by not removing the golden calves or taking down the high places. For example, King Baasha "did what was evil in the sight of the LORD, walking in the way of Jeroboam and in the sin that he caused Israel to commit" (1 Kings 15:34). And Omri, who was not a descendant of Jeroboam, nevertheless "walked in all the way of Jeroboam son of Nebat, and in the sins that he caused Israel to commit, provoking the LORD, the God of Israel, to anger by their idols" (1 Kings 16:26). Even King Jehu, who "wiped out Baal from Israel" by destroying his temple, "did not turn aside from the sins of Jeroboam son of Nebat, which he caused Israel to commit—the golden calves that were in Bethel and Dan" (2 Kings 10:28–29). And so on.

Second Kings 17 reports the sack of Samaria (the capital of the Northern Kingdom) and the fall of Israel at the hands of the Assyrians. It recounts how the city was besieged and then sacked, how the Israelites were exiled to Assyria and other places, and later how foreign populations were forcibly resettled in Israel. The judgment of the Deuteronomistic Historian is then reported:

> It was because of the sins of the people of Israel against the LORD their God, who had brought them up out of the land of Egypt, from under the power of Pharaoh the king of Egypt. They worshiped other gods and walked in the ways of the people that the LORD drove out before the people of Israel, and in the ways that the kings of Israel made. The people of Israel secretly did things that were not right against the LORD their God. They built for themselves high places . . . ; they set up for themselves pillars and sacred poles . . . ; they made offerings on all the high places, as the nations did whom the LORD carried away before them. They did wicked things, provoking the LORD to anger; they served idols, of which the LORD had said to them, "You shall not do this." Yet the LORD warned Israel and Judah by every prophet and every seer, saying, "Turn from your evil ways and keep my commandments. . . ." They would not listen but were stubborn, as their ancestors had been, who did not believe in the LORD their God. . . . They made for themselves cast images of two calves; they made a sacred pole, worshiped all the host of heaven, and served Baal. They made their sons and their daughters pass through fire; they used divination and augury; and they sold themselves to do evil in the sight of the LORD, provoking him to anger. (2 Kings 17:7–17, modified)

And thus, according to the Deuteronomistic History, Israel's defeat and fall result from its idolatry—the result of the sin of Jeroboam son of Nebat.

The foreign peoples whom the Assyrians resettle in Israel—people from "Babylon, Cuthah, Avva, Hamath, and Sepharvaim"—bring with them their false gods and their idolatrous worship practices, which included child sacrifice (2 Kings 17:31). These new people start to worship the Lord but continue to worship their gods; thus, syncretistic practices continued in the land.

The narrative then relates that Judah also sinned against God and worshiped false gods, though it never participates in the sin of Jeroboam because it has Jerusalem with the Solomonic temple as its capital. Judah nevertheless falls prey to idolatry. Following the fall of Israel, two kings who are rated highly in the eyes of the Deuteronomistic Historian reign in Judah—each one doing what was right in the eyes of the Lord and following in the ways of his ancestor David: Kings Asa and Hezekiah. The narrators credit their faithfulness to the Lord in part for their success in rebelling against and fending off the Assyrians. After Hezekiah, however, comes a son who does not follow in his father's or David's steps: Manasseh "did what was evil in the eyes of the LORD, following the abominable practices of the nations." He rebuilds the high places, makes altars for Baal and Asherah, worships the host of heaven, and even makes "his son pass through the fire"—child sacrifice (2 Kings 21:6). According to the Deuteronomistic Historian, it is for the sins of Manasseh that God judges Judah in such a way that it falls to Babylon in 586 BCE. While King Josiah's political and religious reform delayed God's judgment of Judah, in the end, the sins of Manasseh—idolatry and its concomitant injustices—result in Judah's judgment.

Can Israel Serve the Lord? If Not, What Then?

The main plotline from Joshua 24 to the end of 2 Kings has been the question, Can Israel serve the Lord? In Joshua 24, Joshua asserts, "You cannot serve the Lord." The people respond, "No, we will serve the Lord!" And Joshua then concludes, "You are witnesses against yourselves that you have chosen the Lord. . . . So put away the foreign gods that are among you, and turn to the Lord" (vv. 19–23).

The book of Judges shows that when organized as a tribal league and led by judges, Israel cannot serve the Lord. The narrative of 1 Samuel 1–1 Kings 11, the story of the united monarchy, shows that Israel is not able to serve the Lord when organized as one nation under God, with one human king to rule them all. Solomon is portrayed to some extent as a new pharaoh, breaking the "law of the king" in Deuteronomy that states Israel's king "must not accumulate horses for himself or allow the people to return to Egypt to do so. . . . Furthermore, he must not marry many wives lest his affections turn aside, and he must not accumulate much silver and gold. . . . Then he will not exalt himself above his fellow citizens" (Deut. 17:16–17, 20 NET). Solomon does exactly that, returning the people to their condition back in Egypt—serving a greedy king; he also imports many foreign wives and their gods. Thus, even though Jeroboam sinned by "departing from David," the splitting of the united monarchy into two nations is nevertheless said to be God's will—"This matter is from me" (1 Kings 12:24 AT).

The verdict of the narrative is that when led by one king as one nation, Israel cannot serve the Lord. And 2 Kings concludes that neither the kingdom of Israel nor the kingdom of Judah was able to "put away the foreign gods that are among you" and serve the Lord. Thus, both nations went into exile, according to the will of the Lord.

But the narrative of 2 Kings ends with the hopeful note that King Jehoiachin—who had gone into exile in the first deportation in 597 BCE—was released from prison in the thirty-seventh year of his exile and given a place of honor in the Babylonian emperor's court (2 Kings 25:29–30). This open-ended, unresolved conclusion leaves hope for Judah and its monarchy. God's promise to David that one of his descendants would forever be king of Israel was not extinguished, for the king and his royal line lived. Yes, Israel cannot serve the Lord—whether organized as a tribal alliance led by judges or as a nation led by kings. But is that the last word? No—not necessarily. The question with which the narrative leaves the reader then is, What will the Lord do with the people? What will the Lord do with this chosen-and-promised people who cannot serve him, but to whom he is committed?

Historical Interpretation

The Historical World behind the Text

When it comes to analyzing the historical world in the text and comparing it with the historical world behind the text, 1–2 Kings is interesting in that the distance between the two is as close as any other book in the Deuteronomistic History. The end of 2 Kings recounts Josiah's promising reformation, his murder and the disappointing turn away from reformation that then occurred, the destruction of Jerusalem, the exile of leading citizens, and the king's release in exile. That narrative of those tragic events in the text matches the historical events behind the text and occurred close to simultaneously with the writing of the Deuteronomistic History. The exiled Judeans hoped for the return to their home and the restoration of king and country.

The Historical World in the Text

In order to make historical judgments, one needs sources. When it comes to biblical books, the question is always, Does this book contain material that is a valid source for drawing historical conclusions or for writing history? For all but the most skeptical historians, the answer to this question with respect to the books of 1–2 Kings is yes. Along with other Old Testament books that date to the time of the kingdoms of Israel and Judah (e.g., the prophetic books of Amos, Hosea, Isaiah, Micah, Jeremiah, Nahum, Habakkuk, and Zephaniah, as well as certain psalms), the books of 1–2 Kings do have value as historical sources. If that positive judgment is accepted, the obvious next question is, What materials and data within 1–2 Kings are valid historical sources? And, inevitably, on that question there is less agreement.

At a minimum, the list of kings and the basic outline of the years of their reigns is generally to be trusted (although the length and years of the reigns are not always perfectly accurate or trustworthy). In addition, the major human historical events narrated in the books—such as invasions, wars, and coups—can be trusted. Those events line up well with extrabiblical written sources from the time of the divided monarchy and with archaeological evidence. Two of those written sources were discussed in chapter 13—the Tel Dan Stele and the Moabite Stone.

The Tel Dan Stele, which dates to the end of the ninth century BCE, is an Aramean inscription in which the Aramean king boasts that he defeated

Fig. 14.9. The Assyrian emperor Sennacherib boasted of his campaign against Hezekiah and Judah in art that he had inscribed on the walls of his palace. Sennacherib claimed that he destroyed forty-six of Hezekiah's fortified cities, along with many smaller settlements, and that he shut Hezekiah up in Jerusalem "like a caged bird." Sennacherib leaves out that he was not able to conquer Jerusalem.

"[Jeho]ram son [of Ahab] / king of Israel, and [I] killed [Ahaz]iahu son of [Jehoram kin-] / g of the House of David." The stele also mentions "Omri king of Israel" and "his son [who] succeeded him." These kings and their reigns are recounted in 1 Kings and are known figures. The mention of "Omri king of Israel" is especially noteworthy. The kingdom of Israel did not enjoy political stability in the same way that Judah did, where a single line of Davidic descendants reigned for the duration of the kingdom. In Israel, dynasties were ended by various coups and murders, and then a new short-lived dynasty would begin. According to 1 Kings 16, Elah murdered Baasha around 876 BCE; he reigned seven days before he was killed and replaced by a general named Omri. Omri succeeded in establishing a dynasty that lasted four generations and around half a century. It was Omri who moved Israel's capital to Samaria, which was a ruin that he rebuilt and established as a new center of power (similar to David moving the united monarchy's capital to Jerusalem). Omri and his son Ahab were strong, capable political and military leaders.

The Moabite Stone, or Mesha Stele, mentions Ahab. In the inscription, King Mesha of Moab says that King Omri oppressed Moab, and Israel occupied part of Moab's territory for forty years. The stele then boasts how Mesha was able to rebel. The incident lines up well with an event narrated in 2 Kings 3.

Beginning around 911 BCE, the Mesopotamian kingdom of Assyria began to reassert its power and establish an empire. This empire, commonly known as the Neo-Assyrian Empire, is usually dated from 911 to 609 BCE, when it was defeated by the rising Babylonian Empire. As the Assyrians rose in power, their armies and emperors began asserting themselves southward along the eastern shore of the Mediterranean Sea—eventually imposing themselves on the kingdom of Israel and then on the kingdom of Judah (along with all the other small kingdoms along the coast).

The various Assyrian emperors left many written sources that at times align with the narrative of 1–2 Kings and shed light on the history of ancient Israel. One of the most important sources is the Black Obelisk of Shalmaneser. Shalmaneser III (858–824 BCE) was an Assyrian emperor who conquered many nations along the Mediterranean. In 853 BCE, Shalmaneser fought a battle against the combined armies of eleven kingdoms—this coalition included forces under King Jehu of Israel. Later, Shalmaneser forced Jehu to submit and become his vassal. A panel on the Black Obelisk shows a figure believed to be Jehu prostrating himself in front of Shalmaneser. The obelisk includes the inscription "The tribute of Jehu, son of Omri, I received." The image is believed to be the oldest image of any biblical figure. It is worth noting that while Jehu was not a descendant of Omri—having led a coup against Omri's descendant and established a new dynasty—he is nevertheless called "son of Omri," which is what all Israelite kings were called in Assyrian inscriptions.

Two important sets of inscriptions that bear upon the history of the kingdoms of Israel and Judah are the royal inscriptions of the Assyrian emperors and the annals of the Neo-Babylonian emperors. The most famous of these may be the annals of the Assyrian king Sennacherib (705–681 BCE), who campaigned along the Levant in the late eighth century. The books of 2 Kings, Isaiah, and Micah all lend biblical perspective on Sennacherib's invasions, but 2 Kings 18–19 especially recounts them. Following the defeat of the Northern Kingdom in about 722/721 BCE, the kingdom of Judah was an Assyrian vassal state. But King Hezekiah of Judah rebelled. As part of his religious and political reformation of Judah, he had fortified many Judean cities and prepared for the inevitable Assyrian invasion. The invasion occurred in 701 BCE. Sennacherib was able to subdue most of Judah but was unable to capture Jerusalem or force the submission of Hezekiah.

In 609 BCE at the battle of Carchemish, the rising Neo-Babylonian Empire defeated the armies of the waning Neo-Assyrians and Egyptians. There was a new hegemonic power dominant in the ancient Near East. The battle is known from King Nebuchadnezzar's annals as well as from the book of Jeremiah. Not long after his victory, Nebuchadnezzar forced Jerusalem to surrender (597 BCE), and the first deportation of exiles to Babylon occurred—a group that included King Jehoiachin. Judah's last king, Zedekiah, later rebelled. Following a siege of the city, Jerusalem was completely destroyed, and the second deportation occurred in 587 BCE. Nebuchadnezzar's account of his victory corresponds both to the biblical account in 2 Kings and also to some Judean ostraca (writing on pottery shards) from the city of Lachish, which shed light on the human suffering from Sennacherib's invasion.

ostraca Shards of pottery, sometimes used as small tablets for writing.

The purpose of this chapter is not to recount a full history of the kingdoms of Israel and Judah—a task that literally fills many books—but to give a brief sense of the historical dimensions involved with reading 1–2 Kings. The Deuteronomistic History is not a history in the modern sense—that is, it is not an attempt to write an objective and accurate historical narrative of those kingdoms and their times. Rather, it is a theological narrative written by scribes to explain why both the kingdoms of Israel and Judah failed, and why the fall of those kingdoms was according to the will of their God.

FOR FURTHER READING: 1–2 Kings

Bright, John. *A History of Israel*. With an introduction and appendix by William P. Brown. 4th ed. Louisville: Westminster John Knox, 2000.

Brueggemann, Walter. *1 & 2 Kings: A Commentary*. Smyth & Helwys Bible Commentary. Macon, GA: Smyth & Helwys, 2000.

Hens-Piazza, Gina. *1–2 Kings*. Abingdon Old Testament Commentaries. Nashville: Abingdon, 2006.

Howard, Cameron B. R. "1 and 2 Kings." In *Women's Bible Commentary*, 3rd ed., edited by Carol A. Newsom, Sharon H. Ringe, and Jacqueline E. Lapsley, 164–79. Louisville: Westminster John Knox, 2012.

King, Philip J., and Lawrence E. Stager. *Life in Biblical Israel*. Library of Ancient Israel. Louisville: Westminster John Knox, 2001.

Leuchter, Mark, and Klaus-Peter Adam. *Soundings in Kings: Perspectives and Methods in Contemporary Scholarship*. Minneapolis: Fortress, 2010.

Miller, J. Maxwell, and John H. Hays. *A History of Ancient Israel and Judah*. 2nd ed. Louisville: Westminster John Knox, 2006.

Sweeney, Marvin A. *1 & 2 Kings: A Commentary*. Old Testament Library. Louisville: Westminster John Knox, 2007.

Wray Beal, Lissa M. *1 & 2 Kings*. Apollos Old Testament Commentary 9. Downers Grove, IL: IVP Academic, 2014.

15

1–2 Chronicles

The books of Genesis through Kings form a kind of primary history, beginning with creation and ending with the exile. Throughout that process, the people of Israel begin with a barren couple (Abraham and Sarah), grow into a populous people while in Egypt, are freed from slavery, settle in Canaan, establish a monarchy, and are ultimately defeated by the Babylonians. This history closes on the hopeful note that in exile, the last Davidic king has been released from prison and given a place of honor at the emperor's table.

In the wake of Jerusalem's fall and the exile, a new history was constructed. We call this history the Chronistic History (CH), and it is composed primarily of the books of 1–2 Chronicles (sometimes more simply called Chronicles) and also includes Ezra-Nehemiah (see chap. 16).

The books of Chronicles cover a similar time period as Genesis through Kings, beginning with Adam and ending with Cyrus's decree allowing Jewish exiles to return to their land, where he would fund the rebuilding of the temple of Yahweh (2 Chron. 36:22–23). The books pass over seminal events such as the exodus, Sinai, and the conquest of Canaan. They also omit the history of the Northern Kingdom completely, focusing instead on the descendants of David and the Southern Kingdom.

Even though 1 Chronicles begins with Adam in a lengthy genealogy (1 Chron. 1:1), the primary concern is reinterpreting and recasting the narrative of Samuel-Kings from the time of King Saul's death (1 Chron. 10) and King David's anointing (1 Chron. 11). The first nine chapters are primarily genealogical lists, followed by a selection of narrative material, much of which is similar to Samuel-Kings.

With all that said, it would be wrong to approach Chronicles with the expectation that it is simply a repeat of Samuel-Kings. Far from it. Chronicles is a highly sophisticated work of theological history that significantly alters how important characters, events, and institutions are understood. The result is something akin to the synoptic problem in the Gospels. The three Synoptic Gospels (Matthew, Mark, and Luke) contain a significant amount of shared material, but that material is often reworked to accomplish the individual evangelist's various literary and theological ends. Something similar is at work in Chronicles. Many of these features will be described in the paragraphs below.

Background

Composition and Development

The compositional history of Chronicles is a fascinating topic given the book's obvious but complex relationship to Samuel-Kings. Scholars date the book as early as the Persian period (539–333 BCE) and as late as the Hellenistic period (333–63 BCE). It is unclear whether Chronicles is the work of an individual or a number of authors and editors. For the sake of simplicity, we will refer to the author of Chronicles as "the Chronicler." The book neither names nor suggests any authors. Beginning in the nineteenth century, interpreters argued that Chronicles had the same author as Ezra-Nehemiah, due to common content and linguistic similarities. That theory has largely been set aside, however, in favor of seeing Chronicles as a composition independent of Ezra-Nehemiah.

Chronicles' unique emphasis on David and the temple may provide some clues as to its authorship. These literary and theological emphases suggest that the history was written around the dedication of the second temple under the leadership of Zerubbabel (a descendant of David). If this is the case, then Chronicles functions alongside Haggai and Zechariah to support the temple restoration project undertaken around 520–515 BCE.

Genre

The books of Chronicles are a lengthy historiographic narrative containing a wide variety of genres. On the whole, the books provide a narrative account that begins with Adam (1 Chron. 1:1) and ends with Cyrus's decree (2 Chron. 36:22–23). In between is a range of genres, including genealogies, poetic speeches, narratives, legends, annalistic material, and prophetic oracles. As with the Deuteronomistic History, the books of Chronicles are not history in the modern sense. They are, rather, theological history, a narrative of Israel designed to make a theological argument. The books contain many forms of literature, including a nine-chapter-long genealogy (1 Chron. 1–9) and important hymns. But the majority of Chronicles is theological narrative.

Box 15.1

Literary Interpretation

The books of 1–2 Chronicles cover familiar ground from the material in Samuel-
Kings, but they have different emphases
and offer a different perspective. Instead
of repeating material we have already
covered in looking at Samuel and Kings,
we will highlight Chronicles' unique literary contributions.

Genealogies (1 Chron. 1–9). Chronicles begins with nine chapters of genealogy. But these are not chapters to skip over out of boredom. Just as in Genesis
and Matthew, the genealogies are not simply (or even primarily) about record
keeping; they are about theology. Some of the genealogical material echoes
material found elsewhere in the Old Testament, and some of it is entirely
original to Chronicles.

Genealogies are important for a number of reasons. First, the genealogies of
David and his tribe Judah are given special attention (1 Chron. 3:1–4:43), along
with the priestly descendants of Levi (6:1–81). After the exile and the restoration of the temple, both the priesthood and the Davidic identity of Zerubbabel
(the postexilic descendant of David) were important and influential factors in
the new community. Second, the genealogical section concludes with part of
the Benjaminite genealogy (found also in 8:1–40), thereby serving as a useful
literary pivot to Saul the Benjaminite in chapter 10.

The genealogies begin in more or less the same place as the book of Genesis—
with the first man, Adam (1 Chron. 1:1). Unlike Genesis, however, the genealogical material is not interrupted by narratives. These chapters are largely just
genealogical lists. Chapter 1 begins with Adam and then turns to the history
of Israel/Jacob in chapter 2. Significant attention is given to Judah's ancestry
(2:3–4:23), no doubt because David belongs to this lineage (3:1–24). The descendants of Reuben and Gad are listed in 5:1–22.

Significant space is also given to Levi (6:1–81), which is not surprising given
the tribe's association with ritual service of the temple and the fact that after
the exile the priesthood played an increasingly significant role in leading the
people. Samuel, for instance, is included under the "sons of Levi" (see 6:28),
which is surprising since he is understood in 1 Samuel to be an Ephraimite
(1 Sam. 1:1). This alteration in Samuel's lineage is part of Chronicles' larger
tendency to bring the actions of Israel's historical figures into conformity with
Mosaic law, which reserves cultic service for the Levites. Chapter 7 narrates the
genealogies of Issachar, Benjamin, Naphtali, Manasseh, Ephraim, and Asher.

Chapter 8 surprises the reader with a second Benjaminite genealogy. This final genealogy sets the stage for the narrative of Saul, who is a Benjaminite.

The reign of Saul (1 Chron. 10). In contrast to 1 Samuel, which spends a considerable amount of time on Saul's ascendency, rule, and eventual death (1 Sam. 9–31), 1 Chronicles dedicates only a single, fourteen-verse chapter to the ill-fated monarch. And that chapter basically only covers the death of Saul, his sons, and his entire house (1 Chron. 10:4–6). In keeping with its particular theology of judgment, the narrative states that Saul died because he did not fulfill Yahweh's commands, consulted a ghost, and did not seek Yahweh's advice. As a result, "he [Yahweh] transferred the kingdom to David son of Jesse" (1 Chron. 10:13–14 AT). The brief story of Saul is a clear illustration of why the books of Chronicles are just as interesting for what they leave out as for what they include.

The reign of David (1 Chron. 11–29). This section focuses on the reign of David, and its chapters are among the most interesting in the entire book, especially if one is familiar with the depictions of David in 1–2 Samuel. On the whole, David is portrayed in a far more positive light than he is in 1–2 Samuel, with emphasis placed on his influence as a unifying leader, a military victor, an obedient servant of Yahweh, and a divinely appointed monarch. Most of the unflattering stories about David—such as the sexual exploitation of Bathsheba, murder of Uriah and the rebuke of the king by Nathan, his son Amnon's rape of his daughter Tamar, Absalom's murder of Amnon and later rebellion against David—are omitted. The story of his unauthorized census of Israel, though, which was "evil in the sight of God," is included (1 Chron. 21). On the whole, the David of Chronicles has been burnished so that he is presented in a far more favorable light than he is in Samuel. This provides a significant insight into the book's commitments.

Box 15.2

Satan

According to 1 Chronicles 21:1, "Satan rose up against Israel and incited David to take a census of Israel" (NIV). This narrative is also told in 2 Samuel 24:1, but that verse says something quite different: "The anger of Yahweh again was stoked against Israel and he incited David against them, saying, 'Go and number Israel and Judah'" (AT). The Chronicler engages in creative theological editing by removing Yahweh's anger from the equation and replacing it with "Satan"—a term that may refer to a kind of semidivine figure of temptation or may simply refer to a human adversary. Both texts still recognize that David's demand for a census—whether "incited" by God or "Satan"—is a sinful one. Not even the books of Chronicles spare David from this bit of dirt. But from the Chronicler's perspective, at least the God of David comes out without a stain.

Fig. 15.1. Chronicles plays up David's role as a musician and psalmist. For example, following David bringing the ark to Jerusalem, 1 Chronicles 16 presents a lengthy psalm that is composed of sections of Psalms 105, 95, and 106.

The narrative of Chronicles is also interested in associating David with the Jerusalem cult and the eventual completion of Yahweh's first Jerusalem temple under his son Solomon. First Chronicles 22–29, for instance, narrates David's preparations for the construction of the temple. These accounts have no parallel in Samuel or Kings. In contrast to Samuel-Kings, the temple is a father-son project, prepared by David and finished by Solomon.

The reign of Solomon and completion of the temple (2 Chron. 1–9). Chronicles also depicts the reign of Solomon more favorably than does Samuel-Kings, emphasizing the king's piety and his association with the construction of the temple. The description of the temple's construction is altered in 2 Chronicles 3:1–5:1 so that it conforms more closely to the tabernacle of Moses in the Pentateuch. This reflects the book's concern to bring history into conformity with Torah.

The end of Solomon's reign is significantly different from what one finds in Kings. First Kings 11:29–40, for instance, blames Solomon for the division of the two kingdoms because of his love for foreign women, disobedience, high taxes, forced labor, and false worship. It also says that Solomon sought to kill Jeroboam but failed to do so. None of this tarnishing material is included in Chronicles. The narrative of Solomon's reign in Chronicles ends with a description of the queen of Sheba's visit, a catalog of his immense wealth, and a neutral report of his death.

The reigns of the kings of Judah (2 Chron. 10–36). The last section of Chronicles narrates the history of the divided kingdom up to the destruction

cult Every aspect of a given group's worship life, including its practices, sacred spaces, personnel, implements, etc.

of Jerusalem at the hand of Babylonian armies. While much of this material is drawn from the books of Kings, the Chronicler also tells this story in his own way, using seemingly original material, and in ways that significantly change the narrative found in 1–2 Kings.

For example, the depiction of Manasseh in 2 Kings is completely negative. In fact, the book blames Manasseh for the Babylonian exile (2 Kings 21:10–15), even though he lived several generations prior to the tragic events. According to 2 Kings, his infractions have primarily to do with violations of the first commandment and excessive bloodshed (2 Kings 21:1–9). Second Chronicles, however, has a different view of Manasseh's reign, apparently driven by a theology of divine judgment that emphasizes the responsibility of the individual. In Chronicles, Manasseh is exiled to Babylon, where he repents of his sins and humbles himself before the God of Israel (2 Chron. 33:10–13). After being restored to his position, he continues his repentance by enacting sweeping cultic reforms (2 Chron. 33:14–17). In 2 Kings, Manasseh is the primary cause of the Babylonian destruction of Jerusalem, while in Chronicles he is a model of penitence.

The Chronicler, however, places the bulk of the blame for the exile on Zedekiah (Judah's last king), the leaders of the priests, and the people. Zedekiah is blamed for ignoring Jeremiah (36:12), refusing to submit to Nebuchadnezzar (36:13), and stubbornness (36:13). The leaders of the priests and the people

---

Box 15.3

The Plot of 1–2 Chronicles

In so many ways, the plot in Chronicles closely parallels that of Samuel-Kings. Where it diverges from Samuel-Kings is where we can discern Chronicles' unique contributions to the biblical canon and also gain some understanding of the problems its creators were trying to address.

In scope, Chronicles proposes to be an expansive history, beginning with Adam (1 Chron. 1:1) and concluding with Cyrus's decree that he would rebuild the temple and allow exiled Jews to return to their homeland (2 Chron. 36:22–23). Seen in this way, the plot of Chronicles proposes to include the entirety of the time covered from Genesis to Kings, sometimes called the "Enneateuch" or Israel's "Primary History."

The fact that Chronicles concludes with Cyrus's decree is the first clue as to this postexilic book's primarily concern: the reconstructed temple in Jerusalem and the attendant priesthood. As you will see below, many of the most distinctive literary and theological themes in Chronicles revolve around how the temple is built and dedicated during the reigns of David and Solomon. The book's distinct emphasis on the temple suggests that Chronicles is somehow addressing the building of the second temple under the Persians. Like so many examples of historiography, Chronicles is just as much about its author's current circumstances as it is about the past.

historiography
"The writing of history"; a written work that offers a particular representation of historical events.

were unfaithful and guilty of committing the same practices undertaken by the "nations" (36:14). Theologically, Chronicles seems to show some discomfort with the notion of "generational sin," whereby sins of the ancestors are visited upon the children (cf. Exod. 20:5–6; Deut. 5:9–10). Chronicles insists, instead, that the consequences of sin fall upon sinners and not upon future generations.

Second Chronicles departs significantly from 2 Kings in its conclusion. Whereas 2 Kings ends with the release of King Jehoiachin of Judah from prison in Babylon, Chronicles ends with the decree of Cyrus of Persia, allowing the exiles to return to the land and charging them to rebuild the temple (36:22–23). Both books arguably end on a hopeful note. For Chronicles, however, that hope is focused on the restoration of the temple.

Theological Interpretation

Modern readers often have a bias against copycats, knockoffs, and rip-offs. It is thought that derivative literature, as secondary, has lesser value. The books of Chronicles often get treated this way—as a less-interesting, abbreviated version of Israel's primary history (Genesis–Kings). But by writing off Chronicles in this way, we lose the opportunity to encounter one of Israel's richest works of theological narrative. These books are a rich trove of theological reflection and provide insight into early Jewish theology.

Theological Diversity

As a starting point, the mere presence of 1–2 Chronicles in the Old Testament indicates that the canon memorializes theological diversity and disputation. Keep in mind that 1–2 Chronicles and 1–2 Kings do not simply provide alternative perspectives on Israelite history. They provide competing and, in some cases, mutually exclusive interpretations of the same events. For example, they disagree on who is responsible for the exile, details about David's life, and how the temple was constructed. As noted above, the interpretive challenges posed by 1–2 Kings and 1–2 Chronicles are analogous to the challenges posed by the Synoptic Gospels (Matthew, Mark, and Luke).

But the presence of theological diversity is not a problem to be solved or papered over. It is a reality to be accounted for and wrestled with. In the same way that Jesus's life, death, and resurrection provoked a range of responses, God's work among ancient Jews provoked a variety of interpretations. One of the reasons Scripture is so powerful is because of its ability to speak in many different ways and at many different times.

The Role of David and His Descendants

David is a singular character in both the Deuteronomistic History (Joshua–2 Kings) and in Chronicles. He is, without doubt, Israel's most famous king and the recipient of divine, covenantal promises that forever link his dynasty with the reign of Yahweh, the Israelite God (2 Sam. 7; 1 Chron. 17). It is Yahweh who plucks David from the pasture and makes him ruler (1 Chron. 17:7–10); Yahweh gives him victory (v. 10); Yahweh will build a "house" (i.e., dynasty) for David and his descendants (vv. 10–11); and Yahweh promises that this dynasty will last in perpetuity (v. 14).

The Chronicler's favoring of David also has implications for how he depicts non-Davidic monarchs. Saul's narrative, for instance, is diminished to less than a single chapter (1 Chron. 10:1–14). Those verses, moreover, depict Saul in a deeply denigrating way. While on the run from the Philistines, Saul kills himself. The Chronicler is careful to note that his sons died as well, bringing an end to Saul's house and any potential threat to David's dynasty (10:6).

The Temple

The temple is central to Chronicles' theology. For the Chronicler, Yahweh's temple demonstrates his supremacy over all other gods. In a communication to King Huram of Tyre, Solomon says that he intends to build a house for his God, because "our God is greater than all other gods" (2 Chron. 2:5). The book additionally amplifies the temple's prestige in several ways. First, it reconstrues the narrative of David in ways that allow him to contribute to the temple's construction, elevating the status of both the king and the temple. In contrast to 1–2 Kings, which make Solomon the chief temple-builder, 1–2 Chronicles clearly make David a cofounder of the original Israelite temple in Jerusalem. Additionally, the books conclude with reference to the temple's restoration, making its reestablishment the climax of the Chronicler's history.

It can be difficult for American Christians (and especially American Protestants) to appreciate the degree to which a building could occupy such a valuable space in Israel's history and imagination. The sacredness of space and location is deemphasized in Protestant Christianity in a way that is not true of Judaism or some other forms of Christianity. But in order to understand properly the important role of the temple in 1–2 Chronicles and elsewhere, one must appreciate the Old Testament's conviction that while God's presence is everywhere, God chooses to be especially available in particular places and through particular means. Above all else, the place God is most present and available is the temple.

Sacred History

Finally, 1–2 Chronicles has a unique, sacred view of history and history-writing. The book seems to view history-writing as part of the prophetic vocation. The prophet Nathan, for instance, is said to have written down Solomon's deeds in a history (2 Chron. 9:29), and Isaiah is depicted as a historian of Uzziah (2 Chron. 26:22; cf. 12:15; 13:22). Both the history itself and the act of authoring that history are sacred. All of this suggests that the Chronicler saw his task as a prophetic one. By offering an account of Israel's history from Adam to Cyrus, the Chronicler preserves for the world a word of God.

Jean Fouquet

Fig. 15.2. Construction of the temple during the reign of Solomon. In 1–2 Chronicles David is seen as a cofounder of the temple, and the Chronicler's history concludes with the temple's reestablishment.

Historical Interpretation

The Historical World behind the Text

The author (or authors) of Chronicles was clearly situated within the Persian period, but the exact nature of their circumstances remains something of a mystery. The clear emphasis on the temple might suggest that the Chronicler's massive literary accomplishment was somehow done in support of the rededication of the temple or the reestablishment of its significance among the returnees. Even still, a temple-centric work such as Chronicles might have proven necessary at many points in either the Persian or the Hellenistic periods. Open questions include whether Chronicles was composed by a single author or set of editors, or whether it was composed in blocks or even in layers. Also unknown is whether it was composed in stages and, if so, what prompted the composition of these additional materials. Apart from a major discovery, these questions will remain unanswered.

The Historical World in the Text

When it comes to the events narrated in the book—beginning with Adam and ending with Cyrus—1–2 Chronicles raises more historical questions than one

Box 15.4

The Second Temple Period

The Second Temple period is a span of time after the dedication of the second temple in 515 BCE. The "first temple" refers to the sacred worship center built by Solomon and destroyed by the Babylonians. Many scholars believe that Chronicles' emphasis on the temple in its retelling of Israelite history is directly related to the books' historical context in the Persian period, when the second temple was constructed. This would have been a time of increased interest in the temple and of its social and religious function within ancient Judah. The construction of the second temple is particularly emphasized in books like Ezra-Nehemiah, Haggai, and Zechariah. The Second Temple period ended in 70 CE when the Romans destroyed the temple.

can deal with in a single chapter. This is especially true when considering the complicated relationship between 1–2 Chronicles and parallel material from other biblical books, such as 1–2 Samuel, 1–2 Kings, Isaiah, Jeremiah, and so on. With all that said, a number of the more consequential questions are highlighted below.

The books were clearly written and edited late in Israel's history, at the end of the exile or later. As a result, the author(s) had access to a version of books like 1–2 Samuel and 1–2 Kings and most likely to the final form of the Pentateuch. But what exactly is the compositional relationship between 1–2 Chronicles and its sources? The books of Chronicles clearly contain material that cannot be found elsewhere in biblical books. What were those sources, and what happened to them? Or did the author compose them without reference to sources? Most of these questions cannot be answered with any level of certainty given the dearth of data.

A number of parallel accounts (texts common to both Samuel-Kings and 1–2 Chronicles) contain contradictory details. For example, the accounts of Hezekiah portray him in positive terms. He is among the great kings of Israel like David and Josiah. Just as in 2 Kings 18–19 and Isaiah 36–39, the Assyrian king Sennacherib lays siege to the city of Jerusalem during Hezekiah's reign (2 Chron. 32:1–33), but the three accounts differ in some details. For example, in 2 Chronicles, after Sennacherib lays siege to the city, Hezekiah musters a large force to fortify the city and prevent the Assyrian army from having easy access to water. He then offers a rousing, pious speech that urges his people to "be strong and courageous" because the Lord was with them (32:7–8 AT). These verses in Chronicles contrast with the less-flattering account in 2 Kings 18, in which Hezekiah surrenders to the king of Assyria and offers tributary gifts from Yahweh's temple (vv. 13–16). The books of Chronicles turn a fragile-looking king into a stalwart of faith and trust.

To be sure, discrepancies like this can cause significant problems for historians, who are tasked with exploring the relationship between textual witnesses and historical events. But such discrepancies also raise important theological questions. Why was it important theologically for a Persian-period author to emphasize the temple? Why were David and Solomon so important to a people that were no longer under the authority of a Judahite monarchy? Why did the Chronicler deemphasize negative accounts about David known from the Deuteronomistic History? It is clear that Chronicles has something significant to say about the God of Israel, the temple, and the future of the exiles. The precise nature of that message is most easily discernible in sections where the Chronicler has altered received material.

FOR FURTHER READING: **1–2 Chronicles**

Boda, Mark J. *Commentary on 1–2 Chronicles: From the Baker Illustrated Bible Commentary*. Ebook Short Series. Grand Rapids: Baker Books, 2019.

Endres, John C., William R. Millar, and John Barclay Burns, eds. *Chronicles and Its Synoptic Parallels in Samuel, Kings, and Related Biblical Texts*. Collegeville, MN: Liturgical Press, 1998.

Japhet, Sara. *1 & 2 Chronicles: A Commentary*. Old Testament Library. Louisville: Westminster John Knox, 1993.

Klein, Ralph W. *1 Chronicles*. Hermeneia. Minneapolis: Fortress, 2006.

Krüger, Thomas. *2 Chronicles*. Hermeneia. Minneapolis: Fortress, 2012.

McKenzie, Steven L. *1 & 2 Chronicles*. Abingdon Old Testament Commentaries. Nashville: Abingdon, 2004.

Throntveit, Mark A. *When Kings Speak: Royal Speech and Royal Prayer in Chronicles*. Society of Biblical Literature Dissertation Series 93. Atlanta: Scholars Press, 1987.

Tuell, Steven S. *First and Second Chronicles*. Interpretation: A Bible Commentary for Teaching and Preaching. Louisville: Westminster John Knox, 2001.

Ezra-Nehemiah

At first glance, it might seem strange to consider Ezra and Nehemiah together. English translations usually treat them as separate books. But the separation of Ezra and Nehemiah is a later phenomenon. Ancient Hebrew and Greek manuscript evidence indicates that Ezra and Nehemiah were considered a single work. Christians in the third century CE were the first to separate the books into two segments. Following the ancient sources, this book will treat them as a single composition.

Ezra-Nehemiah is set in the Persian period and deals with the plight of Jews who returned from exile with the support of Cyrus of Persia (Ezra 1:1–4; cf. 2 Chron. 36:22–23). The book narrates the story of their homecoming, the restoration of the temple and its attendant rituals, and various conflicts in the new community.

On the whole, Ezra-Nehemiah wrestles with important social and theological questions related to the negotiation of identity, the establishment of community boundaries, and the restoration of ancient institutions.

Background

Composition and Development

The composition of Ezra-Nehemiah has been a matter of debate for some time. Important questions include the following: What is the relationship between Ezra-Nehemiah and 1–2 Chronicles? Was Ezra-Nehemiah written by a single author or compiled separately and only brought together at a later point? What role did the two protagonists, Ezra and Nehemiah, play in the composition of the book, and most especially of the memoirs (the Ezra Memoir in Ezra 7–8;

9–10; Neh. 8; and the Nehemiah Memoir in Neh. 1:1–7:72; 11:1–2; 12:31–43; 13:4–31)? How should our understanding of Ezra-Nehemiah's compositional history be influenced by alternative versions of the narrative found outside the typical boundaries of Protestant Bibles (e.g., 1 Esdras)? Which figure came first, Ezra or Nehemiah? As is often the case with biblical interpretation, there are not always clear answers.

Ezra-Nehemiah is clearly composed of multiple literary elements, some of which had an independent life outside the book. The various letters and lists of returnees are examples. When those once-independent elements were combined into the current form of the text—whether all at once or in stages—remains something of a mystery. The events described in Ezra-Nehemiah are primarily from the fifth century BCE. However, the latest Persian king mentioned (Darius II, cf. Neh. 12:22) reigned from 423 to 405 BCE, suggesting that the book was compiled after that point.

Genre

Ezra-Nehemiah is a compilation of genres including memoir, historical narrative, list, letter, confession, and archival material. Various sources were woven together into a narrative that recounts the return of exiles, the establishment of a community in Jerusalem, the restoration of the temple and of worship, the reconstruction of the city wall, the casting out of foreign wives and children, and the activities of Ezra and Nehemiah.

Ezra-Nehemiah is also linguistically interesting because it is a bilingual body of literature. Most of the text is written in Hebrew, but there are large sections (primarily administrative communications) written in Aramaic (Ezra 4:8–6:18; 7:12–26).

Literary Interpretation

Ezra-Nehemiah describes and interprets one of the most significant inflection points in Judean history. After suffering military defeat and forced deportation at the hands of the Babylonians, exiled Jews were offered an opportunity under the Persians to return to their ancestral lands, restore their traditional

---

Box 16.1

Outline

1. Return of the exiles and rebuilding of the temple (Ezra 1–6)
2. Ezra's return and reforms (Ezra 7–10)
3. Nehemiah's return and rebuilding of the wall (Neh. 1–12)
4. Nehemiah's departure, second return, and reforms (Neh. 13)

Box 16.2

The Aramaic Sections of Ezra-Nehemiah

Ezra-Nehemiah is a bilingual book, with sections written in both Hebrew and Aramaic. For example, Ezra 4:8–6:18 is written in Aramaic, as is Artaxerxes's letter deploying Ezra on his mission (7:12–26). In the Persian period, Aramaic was a *lingua franca*—a common language that allowed especially elites to communicate with one another.

Ezra-Nehemiah is not unique in this regard. The book of Daniel also contains a large section of Aramaic text (Dan. 2:4b–7:28). It is no accident that these Aramaic sections cover the life of Daniel and his friends in the highly cosmopolitan royal courts of various Mesopotamian kings. As a language, Aramaic is similar to Hebrew. Both are Semitic languages and therefore closely related to languages such as Arabic, Akkadian, Moabite, and Edomite.

worship practices, and rebuild their community. It is a moving story of defeat and homecoming. But it is also a story of the struggle to reestablish a landed identity after living for decades in a foreign land. Like the greatest of human stories, Ezra-Nehemiah is marked by hope, pain, conflict, and renewal.

Return of the exiles and rebuilding of the temple (Ezra 1–6). The narrative of Ezra-Nehemiah begins in the same way that 2 Chronicles ends: with the edict of King Cyrus of Persia allowing exiled Jews to return home and rebuild the temple of the Lord (Ezra 1:1–4; cf. 2 Chron. 36:22–23). Both texts connect this momentous event to the prophetic ministry of Jeremiah (Ezra 1:1; 2 Chron. 36:22), who prophesied a period of homecoming and restoration on several different occasions (cf. Jer. 25:1–14; 29:1–33).

Box 16.3

Who Was Ezra?

Ezra is not only a protagonist within the narrative complex of Ezra-Nehemiah; he is also one of the most important religious figures for later Judaism, on up to the present day. As both a priest and a scribe, he was a public teacher and promoter of Torah, making him a Moses-like figure. His story is primarily recorded in Ezra 7–10 and Nehemiah 8–9. He was among those who returned under the Persian king Artaxerxes. Ezra's return to Jerusalem was accompanied by an official letter in Aramaic (Ezra 7:11–26), granting him official status and authority to govern Judah and Jerusalem according to the laws of the "God of heaven."

One of the more troubling events in Ezra's career is recorded in Ezra 9–10. An accusation is brought that some among Israel had not "separated themselves from the people of the lands" (9:1), whose abominable practices resembled those of the Canaanites, Hittites, Perizzites, Jebusites, Ammonites, and so on. The primary issue is intermarriage and the ethnic corruption of their descendants (9:2). After public confession and prayer, it is decided to expel the offending women and children (10:1–4). The terrifying effects of this policy are all the more troubling when one considers the patriarchal social structure and the deep vulnerability women would have had apart from the provision and protection of a man.

Fig. 16.1. Ezra reads the law.

Chapter 2 contains a list of returnees, beginning with significant leaders such as Zerubbabel (the Davidic descendant), Jeshua, and Nehemiah. The sum total of returnees is 42,360. Upon arriving, some of the clan chiefs make a freewill offering to support the rebuilding of the temple (2:68–69), foreshadowing what was to come.

Ezra 3–4 narrates the resumption of temple sacrifices and rituals under the leadership of Jeshua son of Jozadak and Zerubbabel son of Shealtiel: "They set up the altar on its foundation. . . . And they kept the festival of booths" (3:3–4). In the second year of their return, they lay the foundation of the temple and celebrate. "But many of the older priests and Levites and heads of families, who had seen the first house, wept aloud when they saw the foundation of this house, although many others shouted loudly with joy. No one could distinguish the sound of the joyful shout from the sound of the people's weeping, because the people rejoiced very loudly. The sound was heard at a great distance" (3:12–13 CEB).

All of this activity around the new temple stirs up tension between the returnees and local populations, referred to as "the adversaries of Judah and Benjamin" (4:1). They offer to help with the rebuilding project and claim to be Yahweh worshipers who had been forcibly relocated to the area under the Assyrian king Esarhaddon (4:2; cf. 2 Kings 17). Zerubbabel, Jeshua, and other leaders deny the request, resulting in a long period of escalation and delay in the building project (4:4–24).

Construction on the temple resumes in Ezra 5–6, this time during the reign of the Persian king Darius. According to chapter 5, these events are also associated with the prophetic ministries of Haggai and Zechariah (5:1). The completion and dedication of the temple is met with joy by the returnees (6:16). Priests and

Box 16.4

The People of the Land

A group of people known as the "people of the land" or the "adversaries of Judah and Benjamin" appear in Ezra to undermine and disrupt the building of the temple (4:1–7). Earlier in the story, the people of the land are a cause for fear and a primary reason for the establishment of an altar (3:3). According to the narrative, this group of inhabitants is successful in their attempts, at least until the second year of Darius's reign, under whom the work is completed (5:1–2). The identity of this group of people is somewhat ambiguous. According to 4:2, they claim to have been settled in the land during the reign of Esarhaddon (a seventh-century Assyrian king) and to worship the God of the returnees.

Despite these claims, it is also possible that local Judeans—those who had not been exiled to Babylon—were among the "people of the land." It turns out, then, that the various conflicts that emerge between the returnees and the people of the land may not have been simply an insider-outsider conflict. Inner-Judean dynamics were likely also at play.

Levites are appointed for the service of God according to the law of Moses, and a celebration of the festival of Passover follows (6:19–22).

Ezra's return and reforms (Ezra 7–10). At this point in the narrative, Ezra joins his fellow returnees in Jerusalem. The account begins with a lengthy genealogy establishing that Ezra is a descendant of Aaron, the chief priest (7:1–5), and is a scribal expert in Moses's teaching. Chapters 7–10 along with Nehemiah 8–9 are often called the Ezra Memoir, because they reflect on Ezra's attempts to help lead the fledgling community of returnees and to instruct them in the law of Moses.

Within these chapters, Ezra engages in a flurry of activity. Before even arriving, he proclaims a fast by the Ahava River and appoints twelve priests who will be charged with the temple vessels and the contributions made to the rebuilding effort (8:21–30). Upon arrival in Jerusalem, the vessels and precious metals are weighed out in the temple, and the returnees make burnt offerings to Yahweh.

The final chapters of Ezra fixate on an intermarriage crisis. According to chapter 9, the people of Israel, including the priests and the Levites, had not separated themselves from the people of the land whose practices were akin to those of the Canaanites and foreigners (9:1–2). Having taken their daughters as wives, "the holy seed has mixed itself" with the people of the surrounding lands (9:2). Following the example of King Josiah (2 Kings 22:11–13), Ezra is so deeply troubled by this situation that he rends his garments, tears hair out of his head, and enters a state of mourning. At the time of the evening sacrifice, he ends his mourning and offers a public prayer of confession and repentance (9:5–15).

Ezra's own public acts of sorrow and repentance inspire members of the community to do similarly. In an action that is shocking to modern readers, the community resolves to make a covenant with Yahweh to expel their foreign wives along with the children born of the union (10:3–4). The chapter ends with

Who Was Nehemiah?

Nehemiah is the other protagonist in the Ezra-Nehemiah literary complex. Like Daniel or Esther, Nehemiah is an exiled Jew who finds himself serving in the court of a foreign king. In particular, we are told that he was the cupbearer (Neh. 1:11). His personal access to the king affords him the opportunity to advocate on behalf of Jerusalem, whose ruins he mourns (1:4–11). King Artaxerxes notices Nehemiah's distress and inquires as to the reasons. After a brief exchange about the ruinous state of Jerusalem, the king agrees to send Nehemiah to Jerusalem to oversee repairs on the city and its defenses. The king not only provides for Nehemiah's protection but also commits to providing him with supplies for the work ahead. Many of the details of his life and mission are contained within the Nehemiah Memoir (Neh. 1:1–7:72a; 11:1–2; 12:31–43; 13:4–31).

a list of those who had married foreign women. It is noted that four leaders—Jonathan, Jahzeiah, Meshullam, and Shabbethai—oppose the sending out of the foreign wives and children.

Nehemiah's return and rebuilding of the wall (Neh. 1–12). Nehemiah 1 continues the restoration work started in Ezra, only this time with a distinct emphasis on the rebuilding of Jerusalem's walls. Like Ezra himself, Nehemiah is in exile at the story's beginning. He serves as cupbearer to the Persian king. When he hears about the dilapidated state of Jerusalem's walls (Neh. 1:1–3), his response echoes that of Ezra's to the news of intermarriage. He weeps, mourns, fasts, and prays (1:4–11).

In an act of foreshadowing, the narrative introduces Sanballat the Horonite, Tobiah the Ammonite, and Geshem the Arab. They represent the significant opposition that Nehemiah and his colleagues will face in the coming chapters. These three mock the work of Nehemiah, saying, "What is this that you are doing, rebelling against the king?" (Neh. 2:19). They assume that rebuilding the walls of Jerusalem is an act of war. Just as Ezra's project was met with opposition from the people of the land, so will Nehemiah's efforts be opposed.

Nehemiah initiates the rebuilding of the walls. That project faces opposition on several occasions. Sanballat and his companions are the face of the adversary. Their machinations stir the people toward both piety and pragmatism—offering up prayers to Yahweh and setting up watchmen day and night (3:36–38; 4:1–3).

But Nehemiah's mission is interrupted not only by external threats. Internal issues also demand his attention. Economic demands pushed some Jews to take loans against their lands. Angered by the situation, Nehemiah chides those who are taking advantage of their brethren and calls on them to abandon their claims on the debt and to return the property (5:10–11). In an act of solidarity and integrity, Nehemiah refuses the governor's food allowance (a tax on the people) for twelve years in order to avoid burdening the people (5:14–15).

Despite opposition, Nehemiah completes the wall (6:15–19) and appoints guards to protect it (7:1–3). His next step is to assemble the people and register them according to their families. He is aided by a genealogical record of people who returned from exile (7:4–72).

Chapters 8–10 shift away from matters of rebuilding and registration to that of liturgy and piety. Ezra appears and begins reading "the scroll of the Torah of Moses" before the Water Gate (Neh. 8:1 AT). As the scroll is read, some are charged with interpreting the text and making it accessible to the audience. Out of obedience, the people celebrate the festival of booths (8:13–18) and offer a communal confession (9:1–37), followed by the making of a covenant (10:1–40).

The book continues with a series of lists (11:1–12:26) and a narrative about the dedication of the wall (12:27–43).

Fig. 16.2. The leaders of Judah (Yehud), a province of the Persian Empire, are not allowed to undertake major projects without imperial permission. Nehemiah seeks and receives the emperor's blessing to rebuild the walls of Jerusalem—which some local leaders assume is an act of rebellion.

Box 16.6

The Plots of Ezra-Nehemiah

Ezra-Nehemiah contains several interwoven plotlines that center on the two protagonists and their fellow Jewish returnees. Taken as a whole, the books deal with the challenges of returning from exile, rebuilding a collapsed society, and forging a renewed identity. The narrative is initiated by King Cyrus's decree that he has been called to rebuild the temple in Jerusalem, allowing exiled Jews to return and encouraging those who remain to support the renovation project (Ezra 1:1–4). This initiating event creates both possibilities and problems that are explored throughout Ezra-Nehemiah.

Two specific problems are explored in detail. First, Cyrus's exhilarating and hopeful announcement motivates large numbers of Jews to return to their homeland and rebuild the temple and Jerusalem's protective walls. Their efforts, however, are not universally welcomed, and opposition arises from several quarters. The plot explores the question, What should the returnees do when they encounter opposition to their arrival and to the various projects they are trying to undertake? Second, obedience to the Torah is of supreme importance. This is especially evident in the character of Ezra, who is an expert in the Torah and a descendant of the priestly line of Aaron (Ezra 7:1–6). The book, in turn, wrestles with what faithfulness looks like for the returnees attempting to forge a new identity as a covenant community that centers its life on the Torah.

Box 16.7

The Role of the Lists

Ezra-Nehemiah contains several different lists. These lists record a number of things, including who returned from exile (Ezra 2:1–67; 8:1–14; Neh. 3:1–32; 7:6–72) and who settled in Jerusalem and Judah (Neh. 11:1–24, 25–36). They describe who intermarried (Ezra 10:15–44) and who agreed to a covenant of faithfulness to divine commands (Neh. 10:1–40). And finally, they verify the identities of the priests, Levites, and temple gatekeepers (Neh. 12:1–26).

Literarily, these lists answer questions that are important to many human communities: Who helped found this community of returnees? What connection do those returnees have to previous generations? Who can officially serve in the cult? Who has committed themselves to a faithful life? Who has violated the community's code of conduct?

Nehemiah's departure, second return, and reforms (Neh. 13). Ezra-Nehemiah concludes with additional material prohibiting intermarriage (13:1–9, 23–31), the renewal of tithing (13:10–14), and a narrative about Sabbath violations (13:15–22). Its final words are a prayer in which Nehemiah asks God to remember how the priesthood was defiled and how Nehemiah cleansed it from foreign influence. He petitions God (and perhaps also the reader): "Remember me, my God, for good" (13:31).

Theological Interpretation

Ezra-Nehemiah is an important theological witness. Some of it may inspire and some of it may disturb. Whatever the case, Ezra-Nehemiah reflects theologically on one of the most significant moments in Judah's history, when many Jews returned from exile, restored the temple, and renovated the city's defenses.

This set of circumstances created a context in which important theological questions needed to be answered: What kind of community would the returnees need to form in order to survive? Where had the community gone astray? How could it make things right? How was God involved in all of these events?

Promise and Fulfillment

Ezra-Nehemiah claims to describe an age of prophetic fulfillment: "In the first year of King Cyrus of Persia, in order that Yahweh's word from the mouth of Jeremiah might be fulfilled, Yahweh stirred up the spirit of King Cyrus of Persia, so that he dispatched a herald and a declaration throughout his entire kingdom" (Ezra 1:1 AT). These words claim that Yahweh had given Cyrus dominion over the earth and had charged him with rebuilding the temple in Jerusalem (1:2). Cyrus also allowed any of "his [Yahweh's] people" to return to Jerusalem to participate in the rebuilding efforts (1:3). The book elsewhere

Fig. 16.3. Many scholars believe that the entire Torah (Pentateuch) reached its final form during the exile and that this is what is meant by the "law of Moses" in Ezra 3:2 and the "scroll of Moses" in Nehemiah 13:1. In addition, many historians hold the view that the first synagogues were built in the period following the exile.

claims that Yahweh was involved in disposing the heart of the king toward the Jews (Ezra 6:22).

The promise-fulfillment theme is further supported by the prophetic ministries of Haggai and Zechariah. While Ezra-Nehemiah does not provide many details on the nature of their ministries, the books named after them clearly lift up themes of both promise and fulfillment.

Ezra himself operates as a Mosaic, priestly figure in the new community. By pedigree, he is part of the priestly line, and by training, he is a scribal expert in the law (Torah) of Moses (Ezra 7:1–6). Both elements come together to make him an ideal leader for the fledgling community that was hoping to restore temple functions, reestablish a community in their ancestral lands, and maintain piety to their ancient faith.

Torah Observance

Divine law is a central feature of Ezra-Nehemiah. Obedience to the law is emphasized with such urgency that one gets the impression that the community's fragile new existence is entirely dependent on adherence to divine command.

To name just a few examples, the altar of Yahweh is built "as it is written in the law of Moses the man of God" (Ezra 3:2 AT). After building the altar, the people celebrate the festival of booths, followed by the regularly required offerings, and eventually dedicate the newly renovated temple (6:13–18). The entire intermarriage crisis is framed in terms of a violation of divine law (9:14; 10:2, 10). And exile itself is the result of disobedience.

Both Ezra and Nehemiah are depicted as pious, Torah-observant leaders, modeled in many cases after Israelite heroes such as Moses, Aaron, and Josiah. Both function as the conscience of the community, admonishing, instructing, and inspiring it according to the perceived needs of the moment. In the case of Ezra, his role is specifically as both a teacher and a fervent scribal expert: he "had set his heart on the study of the Torah of Yahweh and to do it and to teach the statues and ordinances in Israel" (Ezra 7:10 AT). In the case of both characters, the external restoration of the temple and city is paralleled by a social and religious restoration centered on the Torah.

Restoration of the Temple

The restoration of Yahweh's temple is a significant theme throughout Ezra-Nehemiah, especially in the first six chapters of Ezra and the last two chapters of Nehemiah. This strong emphasis on the temple and its practices may seem strange to twenty-first-century Americans. But for ancient Israel, the temple of Yahweh was his dwelling place (or the place that God's name dwelled). Cyrus's decree in Ezra 1 calls the temple the "*house* of Yahweh, the God of Israel" (1:3, modified). There was no contradiction between the belief that God dwelled both in heaven and in the temple. The temple was seen as the central point of contact between the two realms. The temple was where Yahweh made himself available to Israel to receive their gratitude, hear their prayers, offer forgiveness, confer blessing, and so on. The book of Exodus makes clear that the temple and especially the altar and the priesthood are ritual and architectural expressions of Yahweh's desire to be among the people. The restoration of the temple and its attendant rituals expresses the return of Yahweh's favor to his people.

Historical Interpretation

Ezra-Nehemiah purports to narrate one of the most significant moments in Israelite-Jewish history, when the disaster of the exile began to recede. The edict of Cyrus presented them with new opportunities for returnees to renegotiate their communal identity, reaffirm their covenantal obligations to Yahweh, and rebuild institutions that once structured worship and life. A number of important questions are raised by a historical study of Ezra-Nehemiah.

The Historical World behind the Text

For a long time, scholars have debated the historical chronology of Ezra-Nehemiah. The key question is whether Ezra preceded Nehemiah or vice versa.

The Bible clearly places Ezra's mission prior to that of Nehemiah, but this sequence is not without problems. While the Bible closely links their two missions, it is strange that neither protagonist seems to have any knowledge of the other. Nehemiah 8:9 mentions both figures, but it is widely understood to be a scribal harmonization—an acknowledgment of the problem we are describing here. Whatever the case may be, the chronological issues surrounding Ezra-Nehemiah point to the larger challenge of using theological texts like Ezra-Nehemiah in the reconstruction of history.

Due to its focus on returnees, Ezra-Nehemiah does not talk much about the Jews who stayed behind. But the truth is that many Jews did not return with Zerubbabel, Ezra, and Nehemiah but stayed in Mesopotamia. Others had fled the destruction of 586 BCE by relocating to such places as Egypt and other parts of Africa, Damascus, Asia Minor, Greece, and elsewhere in Europe. Most of these people also did not return to the land. To historians, this is known as the diaspora—the dispersion of the people among the nations.

The Historical World in the Text

Tensions between returnees and the "people of the land." Reading only Ezra-Nehemiah might give the impression that the exiled Judeans were returning to a land full of non-Jews, as if all Jews were sent into exile. For example, in one of the chapters about intermarriage, Ezra 9:1 compares the "people of the land" to the Canaanites, Hittites, Perizzites, Jebusites, Ammonites, Moabites, Egyptians, and Amorites. But we know from other biblical books that a significant Jewish population remained in Judah after the Babylonian defeat of Jerusalem. Some went into exile and others did not (2 Kings 25:22). If that is true, then what was Ezra-Nehemiah trying to accomplish by minimizing the presence of Jews who had not been exiled? What sorts of divisions might have existed within the community of returnees itself?

The fact that the returnees met resistance from the people of the land when they started to rebuild the temple and the walls of Jerusalem should not surprise anyone. If one grants that it was mainly the elites who were taken into exile—and thus it was the elites who were returning—one can easily imagine why those who had been left behind were less than enthusiastic about their return. They interpreted the move to rebuild the temple and the walls as acts likely to lead to war once again.

Cyrus the Great of Persia. Cyrus plays an important—and largely positive—role elsewhere in the Old Testament (see, e.g., 2 Chron. 36:22–23; Isa. 45:1–7). This positive depiction of the king is maintained in Ezra-Nehemiah as well and expanded to include Artaxerxes, who grants Nehemiah's request to return to Jerusalem (Neh. 2:1–9). We know from the Cyrus Cylinder, an extrabiblical historical source, that Cyrus generally followed a policy of allowing repatriated deportees to rebuild their home sanctuaries.

The benevolent depiction of these powerful dictators suggests that the author of Ezra-Nehemiah saw significant benefits in living under their reign. But emperors do not typically show benevolence without good cause. What benefit did they see in supporting the work of restoring the temple and the city? The answer to this question is no doubt complicated, but one can assume with a high degree of probability that the kindness shown to the returning exiles was calculated to benefit the empire in one way or another.

From Israelites to Jews—a changed identity. For most of the Old Testament, the people within the narrative are Israelites and later Judeans. Speaking in broad generalities, Israelites and Judeans were members of a holy nation, with a holy king, a holy land, and a holy space (the temple). Following the exile, the people's identity profoundly changed. They were now a holy people (the Jews), with a holy book ("the scroll of the law of Moses"), a holy law, and led by a holy priesthood. They were no longer a nation but a province (Yehud) of the Persian Empire.

This profound change in the identity of the people cannot be overstated. The people in the narrative of Ezra-Nehemiah are Second Temple Jews (as opposed to Israelites). Many Old Testament scholars believe that the document that the priest Ezra reads out loud was the final form of the Pentateuch (the Torah). For the most part, the people would no longer live as an independent nation with its own king. Rather, they would take on a primarily religious identity—following the holy laws of the Torah under the leadership of priests.

FOR FURTHER READING: **Ezra-Nehemiah**

Berquist, Jon L. *Judaism in Persia's Shadow: A Social and Historical Approach*. Eugene, OR: Wipf & Stock, 2003.

Eskenazi, Tamara Cohn. *In an Age of Prose: A Literary Approach to Ezra-Nehemiah*. Society of Biblical Literature Monograph Series 36. Atlanta: Scholars Press, 1988.

Fensham, F. Charles. *The Books of Ezra and Nehemiah*. New International Commentary on the Old Testament. Grand Rapids: Eerdmans, 1983.

Redditt, Paul L. *Ezra-Nehemiah*. Smyth & Helwys Bible Commentary. Macon, GA: Smyth & Helwys, 2014.

Shepherd, David, and Christopher J. H. Wright. *Ezra and Nehemiah*. Two Horizons Old Testament Commentary. Grand Rapids: Eerdmans, 2018.

Southwood, Katherine. *Ethnicity and the Mixed Marriage Crisis in Ezra 9–10: An Anthropological Approach*. Oxford Theological Monographs. Oxford: Oxford University Press, 2012.

Throntveit, Mark A. *Ezra-Nehemiah*. Interpretation: A Bible Commentary for Teaching and Preaching. Louisville: Westminster John Knox, 1992.

Williamson, H. G. M. *Ezra-Nehemiah*. Word Biblical Commentary 16. Waco: Word, 1985.

17

Esther

The book of Esther tells the story of an exiled Jewish woman who marries the Persian king (Ahasuerus), uncovers a plot to kill the Jewish people, and cleverly maneuvers her foe into a trap with the help of her uncle Mordecai. The book now stands at the center of the Jewish festival known as Purim, which celebrates Esther's actions, features a reading of the book, and is often accompanied by carnivalesque and comedic dress and behavior.

Despite its serious subject matter, the book of Esther is a deeply humorous book. Its bumbling, gullible, and easily manipulable king is the most frequent target of the author's humor. While studying Esther, readers should keep their eyes open for literary devices like irony, absurdity, exaggeration, sexual humor, caricature, farce, and slapstick.

Like other books set in exile or written from the perspective of diaspora, it also deals with the dynamics of forced relocation, including the negotiation of multiple cultural identities, external threats to the group's survival, and imperial domination.

Background

Composition and Development

The book of Esther is set in the Persian period, and most scholars think it was composed during the same time. We know nothing about the author or the circumstances under which the book was written. The name of the Persian king (Ahasuerus) is fictional and cannot be confidently associated with any particular Persian king (sometimes Xerxes I or Artaxerxes is suggested).

Jacopo Robusti Tintoretto

Fig. 17.1. One of the most popular scenes from the book of Esther for artists to depict is the moment when Esther faints before King Ahasuerus as she intercedes for the Jewish people. This story is not in the Hebrew manuscript tradition—and thus is not in Jewish or Protestant Bibles—but it is in Orthodox Bibles and has traditionally been in Catholic Bibles (since the Council of Trent in 1546 confirmed the authority of the verses): "Then having passed through all the doors, she stood before the king, who sat upon his royal throne, and was clothed with all his robes of majesty, all glittering with gold and precious stones; and he was very dreadful. Then lifting up his countenance that shone with majesty, he looked very fiercely upon her: and the queen fell down, and was pale, and fainted, and bowed herself upon the head of the maid that went before her. Then God changed the spirit of the king into mildness, who in a fear leaped from his throne, and took her in his arms, till she came to herself again, and comforted her with loving words" (Add. Esth. 15:6–8 KJV).

The book of Esther has one of the most interesting compositional histories of all the Old Testament books. Two distinct traditions of Esther exist—one in Hebrew and the other in Greek. The Greek tradition itself can be broken into two different versions, often called the Old Greek and the Alpha versions. The Greek versions of Esther contain additional material and reflect different concerns. For instance, the Septuagint (LXX) includes characters' prayers and makes explicit mention of God. The Hebrew Masoretic Text makes no explicit reference to God. Common translations like the New International Version or the English Standard Version use the Masoretic Text as a basis for translation. English translations of the additional Esther material can be found in the Apocrypha section of the New Revised Standard Version. Our commentary below is based on the Hebrew Masoretic Text (and so without the additions).

Genre

The book of Esther is a theological narrative that can be classified more specifically as a court tale, a genre known elsewhere in the ancient Near East. In these stories, Jews find themselves in service to foreign kings and often in positions of power and influence. While there, they encounter conflict among the king's officials, and the stories describe the Jews' response to such difficulties and, typically, recount their success, as well as the superiority of their God over the gods of the foreign nations.

The book of Esther, along with the first six chapters of Daniel, tells such a tale. In Daniel, "certain Chaldeans" step forward to slander "the Jews" (Dan. 3:8), resulting in the fiery trial of Shadrach, Meshach, and Abednego. That conflict nearly kills the three Jewish youths. In the book of Esther, Haman launches an attack against all the Jews in the kingdom of Persia for the pettiest of reasons: Mordecai refused to bow in deference to him (Esther 3:6, 13). Haman's intended atrocity is farcically disproportionate to the social slight he receives from Haman and is part of the book's larger attempt to mock the murderous Haman.

> **Box 17.1**
>
> ## *Outline*
>
> 1. Ahasuerus hosts a banquet (1)
> 2. Esther becomes queen; Mordecai reports a plot to kill the king (2)
> 3. Haman plots to destroy the Jews (3)
> 4. Esther resolves to rescue the Jews (4)
> 5. Esther hosts a banquet (5)
> 6. Ahasuerus honors Mordecai (6)
> 7. Haman is destroyed (7)
> 8. Esther saves the Jews (8)
> 9. The Jews defend themselves; Purim is established; Mordecai is exalted (9–10)

Chaldean An alternative term for "Babylonian."

Esther is an astonishing literary achievement. Readers should prepare themselves to be shocked, entertained, amused, provoked, and disturbed. The book's heavy use of farce, exaggeration, and humor does not mean, however, that the book lacks seriousness. To the contrary, the book of Esther uses humor to confront directly some of the weightiest issues in Jewish history, including threats of annihilation, the danger of publicizing one's national and religious identity, and the complexities of navigating life under foreign rule.

Literary Interpretation

Ahasuerus hosts a banquet (Esther 1). Chapter 1 sets the scene in a characteristically absurd way. The Persian king Ahasuerus hosts a banquet that lasts 180 days—a full half year!—culminating in a seven-day feast in the king's garden. Everyone drinks and does whatever their hearts desire (1:8). On the last day, the drunk king orders Queen Vashti to appear before him so he can show off her beauty to his guests (1:10–12). Vashti refuses the king, throwing his merry mood out of balance.

Not knowing how to respond to the queen's rebuff, the king seeks the counsel of his courtiers and advisors in what will become a familiar pattern. In an obvious moment of farcical humor, one of the advisors concludes that Vashti's act is not only a personal matter for the king, but it also threatens national security and domestic tranquility (1:18).

Absurdity begets absurdity, and the king decides that the best response to Vashti's disruptive behavior is to issue a kingdom-wide royal edict that bans her from his presence. According to his advisors, this edict will not only banish Vashti, but it will also guarantee that "all the wives will give honor to their husbands, great and small alike" (1:20 AT).

Esther becomes queen; Mordecai reports a plot to kill the king (Esther 2). Chapter 2 addresses the king's next problem: he is queenless. His advisors—always full of ideas—propose that he select a new queen via a contest of beautiful virgins. When the king agrees, virgins from around the kingdom are brought to the fortress of Susa, where they undergo twelve months of beauty treatments in preparation for their one-night "turn" with King Ahasuerus.

Esther is favored and so receives special treatment from other members of the court (2:9; cf. Gen. 41:37–45; Dan. 1:9). Esther also finds favor in the eyes of Ahasuerus, who loves her more than the other women and crowns her queen in place of Vashti. Throughout all these events, Esther does not reveal her identity as a Jew, in keeping with the urging of her uncle, Mordecai (2:20).

Haman plots to destroy the Jews (Esther 3). Chapter 3 introduces the villain, Haman. He is a descendant of Agag the Amalekite—whose people attacked Israel as it left Egypt (Exod. 17). These intertextual connections foreshadow the reemergence of the ancient conflict in Haman's actions toward the Jewish nation. Haman is promoted above all other officials (3:1). Mordecai, however, refuses to kneel or bow to him, a slight that angers Haman so much that he decides to do away with all the Jews throughout the empire.

Taking advantage of the king's gullibility, Haman convinces Ahasuerus that a "certain people" are disobeying him and should be punished with extermination. In a full-blown demonstration of ineptitude and irresponsibility, the king agrees and simply hands executive authority over to Haman.

Esther resolves to rescue the Jews (Esther 4). Hearing about this threat, Mordecai urges Esther to approach the king and intercede on behalf of their people. Despite the fact that she is the queen, she cannot simply march into the throne room; to do so would put her life at risk (4:10–11). At this point,

---

Box 17.2

"Vashti Was Right," by Debbie and John Orenstein

In the Old Testament, foreign rulers such as Pharaoh, the Babylonian emperor, or King Ahasuerus are not typically role models. They are often depicted committing sin or doing evil. The composers Debbie and John Orenstein capture this truth in their song, "Vashti Was Right—or—Book of Zeresh (A Purim Spiel)." In part of the song, they write:

> "Tell that creep he can come to me." Vashti was right. . . .
>
> Vashti was right. Vashti was right.

Mordecai offers her that famous line of encouragement: "Who knows? Perhaps you arrived at royalty for such a time as this" (4:14 AT). Esther asks Mordecai to initiate a community-wide fast on her behalf and announces, "Then I will go to the king, though it is against the law, and if I perish, I perish" (4:16 ESV).

Esther hosts a banquet (Esther 5). Esther courageously approaches the king, wins his favor, and invites both him and Haman to a feast that she will prepare. At the feast, the king offers to grant her a request of "up to half the kingdom" (5:6 NIV). Instead of protesting Haman's genocidal policy, she invites both Ahasuerus and Haman to another feast the next day. Haman leaves the banquet happy, until he sees Mordecai. He returns home, where he, his wife, and his friends plot to kill Mordecai the next day (5:9–14).

Ahasuerus honors Mordecai (Esther 6). The story continues with the king unable to sleep. The chosen remedy is reading the king his royal annals—the royal version of counting sheep. These records were probably about as interesting as going through your old files, and that is precisely the point. But in the process of hearing the annals read, the king realizes that Mordecai had saved his life (2:21–23) but had never been rewarded. Just as the king decides to honor Mordecai, Haman is approaching the palace to advocate for Mordecai's execution.

The king asks Haman what should be done for "the man whom the king really wants to honor?" (6:6 CEB). Thinking that the honor would fall to no one but himself, Haman recommends that the honoree be given a garment worn by the king and a crowned horse that the king has ridden and that he be attended by a royal official. The man should then be paraded around the city with heraldry.

These rewards, however, fall not to Haman but to Mordecai. In a complete turning of the tables, Haman is chosen as the royal official to lead Mordecai

---

Box 17.3

Feasts in Esther

Feasts play an important role both in the book of Esther and in the annual performance of the book during the feast of Purim. There are ten feasts in Esther:

1. Ahasuerus's royal feast (1:2–4)
2. Ahasuerus's feast for the men of Susa (1:5–8)
3. Vashti's banquet for the women (1:9)
4. Esther's enthronement feast (2:18)
5. Haman and Ahasuerus's feast (3:15)
6. Esther's first feast (5:4–8)
7. Esther's second feast (7:1–9)
8. The feast of the Jews (8:17)
9. The feast of Purim (9:17)
10. The second feast of Purim (9:18)

throughout the city square, heralding his enemy's accomplishments and honored status. Heavy with shame, Haman goes to Queen Esther's second banquet.

Haman is destroyed (Esther 7). The story comes to its climax in chapter 7, and everything that was once hidden now comes to light: Esther's true identity, her plans to protect her people, and the plot of Haman to destroy the Jewish people. Upon learning these things, the king is literally speechless. He leaves the room and returns to find Haman prostrate before Esther, begging for his life. The king has Haman executed on the very same gallows he intended for Mordecai.

Esther saves the Jews (Esther 8). Esther receives Haman's property, and Mordecai is honored again by King Ahasuerus. But the royal edict against the Jews remains a problem, since royal edicts could not be revoked (8:8; cf. 1:19). A new decree is crafted that allows Jews to defend themselves and plunder the possessions of their assailants, but only on a single day, the thirteenth day of the twelfth month (8:9–14). This results in tremendous joy among the Jewish population (8:15–17).

The Jews defend themselves; Purim is established; Mordecai is exalted (Esther 9–10). The Jewish people muster in their respective towns and fend off their assailants. They win an overwhelming victory. The text uses the occasion to describe the establishment of the feast of Purim to commemorate the occasion (9:20–32). Purim is to be celebrated by feasting, sending gifts of food, and providing presents for the poor (9:22). The word *Purim*, which means "lots," is explained: "Haman son of Hammedatha the Agagite, the enemy of all the Jews, had plotted against the Jews to destroy them, and had cast Pur—that is 'the lot'—to crush and destroy them" (9:24).

casting lots A divination practice akin to "drawing straws" and used to select a person for a given task; lots were marked stones similar to dice (see Jon. 1:7; Acts 1:26).

Box 17.4

Esther as Serious Humor

The book of Esther is full of humor, as is the annual performance of the book at the festival of Purim. As the outlandish size of his feasts and whims suggest, the king is a royal fool. As such, he is both dangerous and manipulable. But this humor, far from being a mere laughing matter, is a serious form of truth telling. As the philosopher Peter Berger has written, "The comic experience provides a distinctive diagnosis of the world. It sees through the facades of ideational and social order, and discloses other realties lurking behind the superficial ones."*

Dictators do not like humor and often have oppressed the Jews. Adolf Hitler banned the celebration of Purim in Nazi Germany. During the Nazi era, many atrocities were carried out against Jews on Purim. In 1944, Hitler declared that if the Nazis were defeated, the Jews would celebrate "a second Purim." In an ironic twist, another dictator who persecuted Jews, Joseph Stalin, suffered a cerebral hemorrhage on Purim in 1953 and died shortly thereafter.

* Peter Berger, *Redeeming Laughter: The Comic Dimension of Human Experience* (Boston: De Gruyter, 2014), 34.

The book closes by relating King Ahasuerus's mighty deeds and reporting that Mordecai was "second only to King Ahasuerus" (10:3 CEB) and was beloved among his people for seeking their welfare.

Theological Interpretation

The Absence and Presence of God in Esther

Esther poses a unique challenge to readers interested in theological questions: the Hebrew version of the book lacks any mention of God. (This may be the reason that Esther is the only book that has not been found among the Dead Sea Scrolls.) Even when the story describes dramatic reversals, astounding acts of deliverance, or remarkable coincidences—instances where one might expect divine activity—Yahweh is not invoked. Given the pervasive presence of God in other Jewish literature from the same period, the book of Esther is truly remarkable.

But the absence of any mention of Yahweh does not necessarily indicate divine absence from the story. This is especially important if one considers the theistic culture in which the book was written. The idea of an atheistic or godless cosmos simply did not exist. It is reasonable to conclude that even though the Hebrew version of Esther does not contain explicit references to God, the author who wrote it almost certainly assumed divine involvement of some sort, even if that involvement is hidden behind the scenes.

However, divine involvement may be implied at several points throughout the story. For instance, after learning about Haman's plot to kill all the Jews in the kingdom, Mordecai approaches Esther with a plan to counteract this existential threat. After they exchange messages, Mordecai finally convinces her with these words: "For if you keep quiet at such a time as this, relief and deliverance will emerge for the Jews from elsewhere, but you and your father's house will perish. Who knows? Perhaps you arrived at royalty for such a time as this" (4:14 AT). Mordecai's statement is ambiguous and does not make explicit reference to God. But the operative question is this: What animates Mordecai's hope and grounds his confidence if not his hope in the God of Israel?

Finally, as noted above, the Greek versions of Esther contain many references to God, including prayers. This version of Esther is read as canonical Scripture by many Christians around the world.

Esther and Vocation: "For Such a Time As This"

One important theological theme that interpreters have seen in Esther is the theme of vocation (or "calling"). Mordecai's famous statement to Esther that

Fig. 17.2. The text describes how Esther makes the most of her environment—in this case, the king's harem. She impresses Hegai, the royal eunuch in charge of the harem, who gives her the best treatment, as depicted here. Esther later wins the love of Ahasuerus and is named queen. Through intelligence and courage, she emerges from a position of powerlessness to one of power.

she may have "arrived at royalty for such a time as this" (4:14 AT) makes the point that a public "office" has been bestowed on Esther—she is the queen. With this office comes a divine calling to use her position for the welfare of the neighbor—in this case, her people.

The Reformer Martin Luther said that all people of God are called and that everyone is given a vocation by God—not just prophets and priests. Luther wrote:

How is it possible that you are not called? You have always been in some state or station; you have always been a husband or wife, or boy or girl, or servant. Picture before you the humblest estate. Are you a husband, and you think you have not enough to do in that sphere to govern your wife, children, domestics, and property so that all may be obedient to God and you do no one any harm? Yea, if you had five heads and ten hands, even then you would be too weak for your task, so that you would never dare to think of making a pilgrimage or doing any kind of saintly work.[1]

Luther's point is actually that all people have many vocations or callings, each of which is important to God. A woman might be a banker, a wife, a mother, a sister, and a citizen. A man might be a teacher, a son, a friend, and a neighbor. All of these are divine callings.

Historical Interpretation

The World behind the Text

Esther is a tricky book from the perspective of history. The book is clearly set in the Persian period (539–333 BCE) and during the reign of a Persian king. Unlike similarly situated books like Daniel, Ezra, or Nehemiah (see Dan. 1:1; Ezra 1:1; Neh. 1:1–2), Esther does not provide specific chronological data. The name Ahasuerus seems to be a Hebraized version of Xerxes (486–465 BCE). The Greek versions assume it is Artaxerxes. Additionally, neither Queen Esther nor the events associated with her are found anywhere in extrabiblical Persian and Hellenistic sources.

Such historical problems can lead to a variety of conclusions. It is at least possible that the events in Esther are historical—or partially so—but simply have no extrabiblical evidence to verify their claims. More likely, in our view, is that the book of Esther tells truth but does so in a fictional way. There are many absurdities in the book. These include the 180-day feast of Ahasuerus, the king's buffoon-like behaviors, the seventy-five-foot gallows that Haman prepares for Mordecai but on which he himself dies, and so on. These absurdities suggest that the book is satire and should be read as such. The book can also be read as protest or resistance literature. It may have been written during a time when diaspora Jews were facing oppression by another empire or kingdom. As such, it may have functioned to strengthen the spirits of those being persecuted.

The book of Esther is a powerful and inspiring tale about how a small number of Jews rescued their kinsfolk from certain doom, using guile, courage, and perhaps even some understated divine help.

The World in the Text

The book of Esther is read in the synagogue at the festival of Purim, and the story itself describes the establishment of the festival. Some interpreters think that the story and Purim may have originated separately, being joined together in order to allow diaspora and Second Temple Jews to celebrate an originally non-Jewish festival. Others find no tension between the foundation of the festival and the great celebration that the Jews experienced when they defeated those who tried to destroy them in chapter 9. These scholars accept the story as the origin of Purim. Either way, the story of Esther and the festival of Purim are now joined together in Jewish life.

Purim is the one night of the year when Jews are encouraged to drink to excess. The book of Esther establishes the festival as "days of drinking and rejoicing" (9:22 AT). In the Talmud, Rabbi Rava declares that one should drink until "one cannot tell the difference between *'arur Haman* ('cursed be Haman') and *baruk Mordecai* ('blessed be Mordecai')" (*Megillah* 7b). The reading of the story in the synagogue takes on a festive, almost vaudevillian atmosphere. People dress in satirical and colorful costumes. When the name of the villain Haman is read (fifty-four times), people sound noisemakers and rattles in order to blot out his name. When the hero Mordecai's name is read (fifty-eight times), the group erupts in cheers. Because the main character is a woman, women participate in leading the reading in all but the most conservative synagogues. Charitable gifts are expected of the faithful, and a festive meal is celebrated.

FOR FURTHER READING: **Esther**

Crawford, Sidnie White. "The Book of Esther." In *The New Interpreter's Bible*, 3:853–941. Nashville: Abingdon, 1999.

———. "Esther." In *Women's Bible Commentary*, 3rd ed., edited by Carol A. Newsom, Sharon H. Ringe, and Jacqueline E. Lapsley, 201–7. Louisville: Westminster John Knox, 2012.

Fox, Michael V. *Character and Ideology in the Book of Esther*. 2nd ed. Grand Rapids: Eerdmans, 2001.

Levenson, Jon D. *Esther: A Commentary*. Old Testament Library. Louisville: Westminster John Knox, 1997.

Part 4

POETIC
COLLECTIONS

18

Poetry, the Poetic Books, and Wisdom

The poetic books of the Christian Old Testament are a set of books that consist completely or mainly of poetry. In Jewish Bibles, these books are in the third part of the Jewish canon—the Writings (Ketuvim).

These books are distinguished by several important features. First, they are dominated by the genre of Hebrew poetry. Second, they are not organized in historical order. The book of Job does not fit into the biblical story at all but is about "a man in the land of Uz whose name was Job" (Job 1:1)—a time is not given for the story, nor is the location of the land of Uz known. The books of Psalms and Proverbs are anthologies of compositions by many different authors from a wide range of centuries. Song of Songs and Ecclesiastes also do not contribute to the story of Israel in any narrative sense.

There is also a great deal of biblical poetry outside the poetic books. Most of the prophetic books (the Latter Prophets in the Nevi'im section of the Jewish canon) consist of poetry, and poems and hymns are interspersed throughout other Old Testament books. Calculations vary, but approximately 35 percent of the Old Testament is biblical poetry. Because biblical (Hebrew) poetry functions differently than Western or modern poetry, it is helpful to understand its basic features when reading these books.

> **Box 18.1**
>
> ### *The Poetic Books*
>
> Job
> Psalms
> Proverbs
> Ecclesiastes
> Song of Songs (or Song of Solomon)
> (Wisdom—Roman Catholic and Orthodox Bibles)
> (Sirach—Roman Catholic and Orthodox Bibles)

Building Blocks of Biblical Poetry

Hebrew poetry is both like and unlike poetry in other languages. In what follows, we discuss some of these similarities and differences in order to understand better how the biblical authors communicated through poetry.

The Line

In order to define and understand poetry, it is helpful to distinguish between poetry and prose (narrative). In both English and Hebrew, the basic units of prose are the sentence and the paragraph. Sentences can be almost any length an author might choose—short, medium, long, or very long. (The same is true in Greek; Eph. 1:3–14 is actually one very long Greek sentence!) In prose, series of sentences form paragraphs. In English, we separate paragraphs by using spaces between them. For example, consider the layout and the length of sentences in this chapter. This written organization of prose is a way to capture visually how people actually speak. People's everyday speech is in sentences and paragraphs.

By contrast, in both Hebrew and English, the basic units of poetry are the line and the stanza or the poem. Poetry was actually first a spoken phenomenon. For certain occasions and reasons, people have chosen at times to speak or sing poetically. Although the definition of poetry is contested, it is agreed that poetry consists of speech or writing that has a number of short lines, which do not have to be complete sentences and which are usually about the same length. These lines are combined together—either orally or visually—to form stanzas. Consider the opening four lines of poetry from John Donne's "Holy Sonnet 6" and from Psalm 111:

> Death, be not proud, though some have called thee
> Mighty and dreadful, for, thou art not so,
> For those whom thou think'st, thou dost overthrow,
> Die not, poor death, nor yet canst thou kill me.[1]

> [aleph] I will give thanks to the Lord with my whole heart,
>   [bet] in the company of the upright, in the congregation.
> [gimel] Great are the works of the Lord,
>   [dalet] studied by all who delight in them. (Ps. 111:1–2)

It is clear from the beginning of these two poems that the basic building block of each is the line. In English, Donne's poetic lines have similar length, a common meter, and an ABBA end-rhyme scheme. In Psalm 111, the lines are clear because each starts with a successive letter of the Hebrew alphabet—aleph (a), bet (b), gimel (g), dalet (d), and so on.

Poetic lines are joined together to form poetry—or verse. Sometimes Hebrew poems, such as Psalms 34 and 111, were composed as unified poems without subdivisions. In other cases, such as Psalms 2, 46, or 114, Hebrew poems were composed to have two or more stanzas that act as subdivisions. In Hebrew, the length of a poetic line is usually between two and six words. When translated into English, however, the line usually requires more words to convey the sense of the Hebrew. Thus, in English translations of Hebrew poetry, lines usually consist of between seven and twelve words.

The line in Hebrew poetry has been called by a confusing variety of terms, including colon (plural: cola), verset, stich (plural: stichoi), half-line, half-verse, and "A" (or "B," etc.). Here we will refer to "the line." When two lines are combined, they form a verse. Here is the first verse of Psalm 111, consisting of two lines of poetry:

> [*aleph*] I will give thanks to the LORD with my whole heart,
> [*bet*] in the company of the upright, in the congregation.

Sometimes, there are three lines in a verse; these infrequent verses (less than 5 percent of poetic verses in the Old Testament) are often called triplets or tricola. Here is one example:

> As the mountains surround Jerusalem,
> so the LORD surrounds his people,
> from this time on and forevermore. (Ps. 125:2)

Parallelism (or Pairing)

A second basic feature of Hebrew poetry is parallelism, the pairing of words, lines, verses, stanzas, and even entire psalms. Although the phenomenon of parallelism is ancient, the term itself was coined by Robert Lowth in 1787 in his *Lectures on the Sacred Poetry of the Hebrews*. Lowth spoke of three ways in which Hebrew lines were in parallel with each other: (1) synonymous (the second line says essentially the same thing as the first); (2) antithetical (the second line says essentially the opposite thing as the first); (3) synthetic (everything that does not fit the first two categories).

In recent decades, this approach has been thoroughly critiqued. As should be obvious, when a catch-all category such as "synthetic" is needed to capture everything that does not fit anywhere else, the categories are probably inadequate and unhelpful. James Kugel concluded that Lowth's categories had "disastrous effect on subsequent criticism."[2] The rich, multidimensional ways in which Hebrew words, lines, and verses relate to one another was reduced to three. In truth, the ways in which the words, lines, and verses relate to one another are extensive. The point is not to define those ways but to experience them and get caught up in the wonder and liveliness of the poetic play.

In the following examples, note how words, lines, and verses are paired (that is, are in parallel).

Pairing Words within a Line

At the smallest unit, biblical poetry often pairs words within a line:

> The LORD is my light and my salvation. (Ps. 27:1a)
> You have turned my mourning into dancing. (Ps. 30:11a)
> O LORD, my rock and my redeemer. (Ps. 19:14c)
> Surely goodness and mercy shall follow me. (Ps. 23:6a)
> Love and faithfulness will greet each other. (Ps. 85:10a AT)
> Righteousness and peace will kiss each other. (Ps. 85:10b)
> I will pour out my spirit on all flesh. (Joel 2:28b)

These examples could be multiplied many times over. Here notice the pairs of words: light and salvation, mourning and dancing, goodness and mercy, love and faithfulness, righteousness and peace. Sometimes both words describe the subject (light and salvation). Sometimes they are the subject (love and faithfulness; righteousness and peace). Sometimes they are titles (rock and redeemer). Sometimes the first is transformed into the second (mourning into dancing). Sometimes one is the object (my spirit) and one the recipient (all flesh). It is especially common in Hebrew poetry to pair an abstract concept (salvation, mourning, redeemer) with a more concrete object or action (light, dancing, rock).

Pairing Lines

At the most important level, biblical poetry almost always pairs lines of poetry. To put it more precisely, there is almost always parallelism between the two or three lines of poetry that make up a verse of biblical poetry. Consider these examples:

> A Love and faithfulness will greet each other,
> B righteousness and peace will kiss each other. (Ps. 85:10 AT)

> A I will pour out my spirit on all flesh;
> B your sons and your daughters shall prophesy. (Joel 2:28b–c)

> A Ill-gotten wealth is of no avail,
> B But righteousness saves from death. (Prov. 10:2 NJPS)

> A Do not answer fools according to their folly,
> B or you will be a fool yourself. (Prov. 26:4)

At the most basic level, the energy of biblical poetry is generated from the ways in which the two lines—A and B—interact (are in parallel) with each other. In the first example, the two lines mirror each other tightly. God's characteristics of love, faithfulness, righteousness, and peace are depicted as messengers who meet and kiss one another. In the second example, line A speaks of God's action using a pair of nouns (pouring out his spirit on all flesh); line B speaks of the result of that action using another pair of nouns (sons and daughters will prophesy). In the third example, line A speaks a negative truth (crime doesn't pay), and line B counters with a positive (righteousness saves). In the last example, line A offers advice (Do not argue with a fool), and line B gives the reason for the advice (you will prove yourself a fool). These examples illustrate the most basic levels of energy between the lines—there is much more there to be discovered.

But it is worth saying again: the parallelism that occurs between the two (or three) lines that make up a verse is the most important level of biblical poetry.

Pairing Verses

In biblical poetry, two verses are often paired to form a slightly larger unit of parallelism. Consider these examples:

> A Love and faithfulness will greet each other,
> righteousness and peace will kiss each other.
> B Faithfulness will sprout up from the ground,
> and righteousness will look down from the sky. (Ps. 85:10–11 AT)

> A Where can I go from your spirit?
> Or where can I flee from your presence?
> B If I fly to heaven, you are there;
> if I lie in my bed in Sheol, you are there. (Ps. 139:7–8 AT)

> A Do not answer fools according to their folly,
> or you will be a fool yourself.
> B Answer fools according to their folly,
> or they will be wise in their own eyes. (Prov. 26:4–5)

For the purposes of this introductory chapter, we will just touch the surface of analysis. In the first example, notice how in verse A, four of God's qualities—love, faithfulness, righteousness, and peace—are imagined as human messengers who do two things: greet and kiss. In verse B, two of those four qualities are imagined as things from nature: faithfulness is a plant that grows up from the ground; righteousness is the sun that shines down (notice the pairing of up and down). In the second example, couplet A repeats a rhetorical question by pairing two verbs (where can I go and flee?) with two nouns (from your spirit and presence).

Fig. 18.1. Psalm 85 depicts the divine characteristics of love, faithfulness, righteousness, and peace as messengers going before God, as plants growing from the ground, and as sunlight shining down. John August Swanson interprets the poem visually by drawing on the scenery of his rural Mexican background.

Couplet B answers the rhetorical question by pairing two opposite verbs (fly and lie in bed) with two opposite places (heaven and Sheol—the places of life and death). To paraphrase: "If I fly to the place of life, you are there! If I lie down in the place of death, you are there too!"

In the third example, the book of Proverbs offers two contradictory "rules for living." In couplet A, we are told, "If you argue with a fool, you just prove yourself a fool." But in couplet B, we are told, "If you don't argue with a fool, he (and others) will conclude he is wise." So which one is correct? Sometimes A and sometimes B, depending on the time, person, and place. How do we know when to apply the first rule and when to apply the second rule? It takes wisdom!

Combining Verses to Create Stanzas and Poems

The next unit of size in biblical poetry is the stanza. Some poems have only one stanza, and some of these are short, such as Psalm 134:

> Come, worship the Lord, all you servants of the Lord,
>   who stand by night in the house of the Lord!

Lift up your hands to the holy place,
    and worship the Lord.
May the Lord, maker of heaven and earth,
    bless you from Zion. (AT)

Other short, one-stanza poems include Psalms 117, 121, 131, and 133. But there are longer one-stanza poems, including Psalms 111 and 112 (which will be discussed shortly) and each of the five chapters of Lamentations. Many prophetic messages consist of one stanza, either long or short.

Most of the poems in the Old Testament, however, have at least two stanzas. Sometimes these stanzas are similar in length. But more often the various stanzas in a poem are unequal in length.

Parallelism between Stanzas and between Poems

In rare cases, parallelism functions between stanzas of a poem and even between poems themselves. For example, the first two stanzas of Psalm 139 clearly function in parallel to each other—the first stanza describing God's omniscience (knowing everything) and the second describing God's omnipresence (being present everywhere).

O Lord, you have searched me and known me.
You know when I sit down and when I rise up;
    you discern my thoughts from far away.
You search out my path and my lying down,
    and are acquainted with all my ways.
Even before a word is on my tongue,
    O Lord, you know it completely.
You hem me in, behind and before,
    and lay your hand upon me.
Such knowledge is too wonderful for me;
    it is so high that I cannot attain it. (Ps. 139:1–6)

Where can I go from your spirit?
    Or where can I flee from your presence?
If I ascend to heaven, you are there;
    if I make my bed in Sheol, you are there.
If I take the wings of the morning
    and settle at the farthest limits of the sea,
even there your hand shall lead me,
    and your right hand shall hold me fast.
If I say, "Surely the darkness shall cover me,
    and the light around me become night,"
even the darkness is not dark to you;
    the night is as bright as the day,
    for darkness is as light to you. (Ps. 139:7–12)

In a few cases, entire poems are arranged next to each other and clearly meant to be heard in parallel with one another. Psalms 111 and 112 are both alphabetic acrostic poems—poems in which each successive line begins with a subsequent letter of the Hebrew alphabet. The topic of the first poem concerns the qualities of God; the topic of the second concerns the qualities of God's righteous followers.

Praise the LORD!
I will give thanks to the LORD with my whole
   heart,
     in the company of the upright, in the
      congregation.
Great are the works of the LORD,
   studied by all who delight in them.
Full of honor and majesty is his work,
   and his righteousness endures forever.
He has gained renown by his wonderful deeds;
   the LORD is gracious and merciful.
He provides food for those who fear him;
   he is ever mindful of his covenant.
He has shown his people the power of his
   works,
     in giving them the heritage of the nations.
The works of his hands are faithful and just;
   all his precepts are trustworthy.
They are established forever and ever,
   to be performed with faithfulness and
     uprightness.
He sent redemption to his people;
   he has commanded his covenant forever.
   Holy and awesome is his name.
The fear of the LORD is the beginning of
   wisdom;
     all those who practice it have a good
      understanding.
   His praise endures forever. (Ps. 111)

Praise the LORD!
   Happy are those who fear the LORD,
     who greatly delight in his commandments.
Their descendants will be mighty in the land;
   the generation of the upright will be
   blessed.
Wealth and riches are in their houses,
   and their righteousness endures forever.
They rise in the darkness as a light for the
   upright;
     they are gracious, merciful, and righteous.
It is well with those who deal generously and
   lend,
     who conduct their affairs with justice.
For the righteous will never be moved;
   they will be remembered forever.
They are not afraid of evil tidings;
   their hearts are firm, secure in the LORD.
Their hearts are steady, they will not be afraid;
   in the end they will look in triumph on their
   foes.
They have distributed freely, they have given to
   the poor;
     their righteousness endures forever;
     their horn is exalted in honor.
The wicked see it and are angry;
   they gnash their teeth and melt away;
   the desire of the wicked comes to nothing.
(Ps. 112)

Each psalm begins with "Praise the LORD!" Psalm 111 ends with "The fear of the LORD is the beginning of wisdom" and Psalm 112 takes up that theme in verse 1 with "Happy are those who fear the LORD." Other poems that occur in parallel are Psalms 103 and 104, Psalms 105 and 106, and Job 38–39 and Job 40–41.

Other Aspects of Biblical Poetry

There is much more to biblical poetry than the line and parallelism.[3] Those who have studied poetry in other languages will recognize that many features of biblical poetry are also common in poetry of those other languages.

Brevity and Concision

Poetry is typically briefer and more concise than prose. Whereas prose tends to be more comprehensive, poetry tends to be more compressed. Think, for example, of the Japanese haiku, which has just three lines of five, seven, and five syllables. The poems are short, but they can evoke tremendous emotion and insight. The Western sonnet is slightly longer—fourteen lines—but still relatively short compared to most prose compositions. The brevity and concision of biblical poetry are evident in the shortness both of each line and of the poems overall. Psalm 131 is a good example of a concise poem that evokes emotions and insight:

> O Lord, my heart is not lifted up,
>   my eyes are not raised too high;
> I do not occupy myself with things
>   too great and too marvelous for me.
> But I have calmed and quieted my soul,
>   like a weaned child with its mother;
>   my soul is like the weaned child that is with me.
> O Israel, hope in the Lord
>   from this time on and forevermore.

Metaphor and Simile

Because poetic compositions are generally shorter than prose, they rely more on metaphor and simile than prose does. These figures of speech occur often in prose, of course. Jesus uses them to teach the disciples and the crowds. He teaches that the kingdom of God is like a man who scatters seed on the ground, or a woman who adds yeast to dough, or a thief that comes in the night. The

kingdom of God / kingdom of heaven Phrases that describe the phenomenon of God ruling, wherever and whenever that might be; sometimes the phrases refer to a more precise manifestation of God's reign (e.g., in heaven or at the end of time).

Box 18.2

Metaphors and Similes for God

The God of the Old Testament is incomparable. Paradoxically, therefore, the Old Testament compares God to many things. Here is a partial list of metaphors and similes for God in Old Testament poetry:

- shepherd
- agriculturalist
- rock
- refuge
- fortress (stronghold)
- light
- fire
- lion

- protective wings
- cup
- king
- rescuer
- guardian (keeper)
- thunderstorm
- provider
- parent

- warrior
- sun
- shade
- shield
- banquet host
- city
- potter

apostle Paul also frequently uses metaphor and simile. But poetry often makes metaphor and simile central features of the composition. In the example above from Psalm 131, the poet first describes herself as humble using the metaphorical expression "My eyes are not raised too high." Then she describes herself as having a calm soul "like the weaned child that is with me." With that, the poem closes by exhorting Israel to "hope in the LORD."

Because biblical poetry is a form of ancient Near Eastern poetry, the metaphors and similes that it draws on come from the ancient Near Eastern world of thought. Most of these are from the natural world, but many also come from the human experience during the Iron Age—especially from the domains of war, family life, religion, and the political sphere.

Human beings are likewise described with a rich array of metaphors. Imagery is used for the poets, the poets' enemies, the poets' friends, and so on. The poets use comparisons to describe danger, sin and judgment, and mercy and forgiveness.

The high frequency of similes and metaphors makes engaging with biblical poetry both easy and difficult. It is easy because the imagery is so accessible to people—people have experiences of sun, shade, light, rocks, and wings. But understanding the imagery can be more complicated, since the meaning an image evoked for someone in Iron Age Israel may be different than for someone today. It can take work and imagination to understand and engage the poetry of the Bible.

It seems fitting to conclude this introductory chapter on biblical poetry with the first poem in the book of Proverbs, which consists of a poetic invitation to the poetry of Israel's wisdom tradition:

> For learning wisdom and discipline;
>> For understanding words of discernment;
> For acquiring the discipline for success,
>> Righteousness, justice, and equity;
> For endowing the simple with shrewdness,
>> The young with knowledge and foresight.
> —The wise man, hearing them, will gain more wisdom;
>> The discerning man will learn to be adroit;
> For understanding proverb and epigram,
>> The words of the wise and their riddles. (Prov. 1:2–6 NJPS)

FOR FURTHER READING: Poetry, the Poetic Books, and Wisdom

Alter, Robert. *The Art of Biblical Poetry*. Rev. ed. New York: Basic Books, 2011.

Berlin, Adele. *The Dynamics of Biblical Parallelism*. Rev. ed. Biblical Resource Series. Grand Rapids: Eerdmans, 2008.

Brown, William P. *Character in Crisis: A Fresh Approach to the Wisdom Literature of the Old Testament*. Grand Rapids: Eerdmans, 1996.

Fokkelman, J. P. *Reading Biblical Poetry: An Introductory Guide*. Translated by Ineke Smit. Louisville: Westminster John Knox, 2001.

Gillingham, S. E. *The Poems and Psalms of the Hebrew Bible*. Oxford Bible Series. New York: Oxford University Press, 1994.

Goh, Samuel T. S. *The Basics of Hebrew Poetry: Theory and Practice*. Eugene, OR: Cascade Books, 2017.

Kugel, James L. *The Idea of Biblical Poetry: Parallelism and Its History*. Baltimore: Johns Hopkins University Press, 1981.

Murphy, Roland E. *The Tree of Life: An Exploration of Biblical Wisdom Literature*. 3rd ed. Grand Rapids: Eerdmans, 2002.

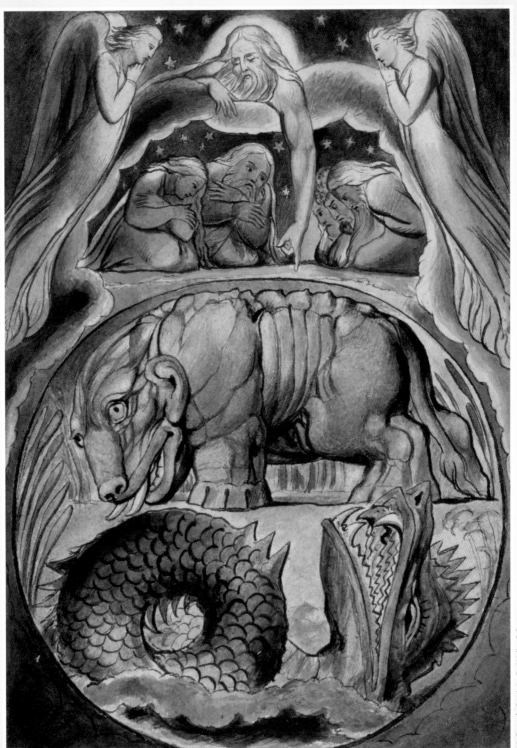

Job

The book of Job is about suffering, God's involvement in human suffering, and how humans react to suffering—both their own and their neighbor's. One of the most elegant yet inscrutable books in the Old Testament, Job both attracts and repels readers. The poetry of the body of the book is beautiful, yet it can be frustratingly ambiguous. The prose of the book's beginning and ending is concise and clearly communicates a fundamental theological problem about suffering. The interactions between Job and his friends—as well as between Job and God—are highly charged and tense. The book of Job is a masterpiece of theological composition and a spiritual treasure.

The book is named for its central character, Job, who is the paragon of the wise and prosperous life. In the book's own words, he is "the greatest of all the people of the east" (1:3). The implication is that Job is wealthy and great because he is righteous. Job also has a large family. But then Job is made to suffer—with God's permission. Job is often said to be a book about the suffering of the innocent, but Job is about the suffering of the righteous. The book wrestles with a central conundrum: Why do the righteous suffer? It gives special attention to God's role in Job's plight. At first, God gives permission that allows "the Satan" to torment Job. Job questions God. In the end, God shows up and answers Job's questions (although many interpreters find his response less than satisfying). The book has inspired many works of art, music, and literature, including those by Georg Friedrich Handel, Ralph Vaughan Williams, Neil Simon, William Blake, John Milton, Fyodor Dostoevsky, Franz Kafka, Carl Jung, Archibald MacLeish, and Elizabeth Brewster.

Background

Composition and Development

The man Job is mentioned twice by the prophet Ezekiel (14:14–20), who lived during the Babylonian exile. Ezekiel refers to Job, along with Noah and Daniel, as an exceedingly righteous man. Thus, one may conclude that the story of Job is older than the exile. But whether part or all of the book is older than the exile is a matter of debate. Many scholars believe that the entire book of Job dates from after the exile. In older scholarship, some argued that the poetic body of the book (3:1–42:6) is older than the exile, while the prose frame (1–2; 42:7–17) was composed and added to the older section sometime after the exile. More recently, based on the vocabulary, style, and syntax of the book, many scholars have concluded that most of the book of Job was written by a single author at some point after the exile (with the exception of the Elihu speech in chaps. 32–37, which most scholars regard as a later addition because Elihu is mentioned in neither the prologue nor the epilogue). It is clear that the author of Job went to some extent to make the poetry of the body seem older by adding archaic features. But there is plenty of evidence to regard the composition of the poetry as contemporaneous with the prose.

The author is anonymous. The main author is obviously a Judean who worked with an older legend and put it to verse. As C. L. Seow concludes, "Despite its setting [in the east], the book is most at home between the very late sixth century and the first half of the fifth century and in Yehud [Judah]."[1]

Genre

As already mentioned, the book of Job consists of a prose frame (chaps. 1–2; 42:7–17) around a poetic body (3:1–42:6). The poetic section is a series of dialogues between Job and his three friends (chaps. 3–31), before a previously unnamed fourth friend, Elihu, offers a monologue (chaps. 32–37); then God and Job exchange words (chaps. 38–42). These poetic exchanges form the longest sustained poetic discourse in the Bible.

Within the poetry are several genres, such as lament, prayer for help, covenant lawsuit, and wisdom discourse. Several genres have been suggested for the book as a whole, including drama, epic, and exemplary-sufferer narrative. Seow best summarizes the complexity: "The book is one of a kind in form, though it employs a rich variety of genres . . . , which together contribute to the theological conversation encapsulated in the book."[2]

One more thing must be said about the genre. The book of Job is not history in any sense. The narrative takes place "in the east" in an unknown "land of Uz." No historical dates, figures, events, or known places are named. Job is literally a "timeless" book. Further, the ease with which the narrative in chapters 1–2 moves in and out of heaven is unlike anything else in the Bible and suggests that this book is to be read as an extended parable, with a series of deeply theological dialogues about suffering. Theologically speaking, many scholars regard as a hypothetical parable the idea that God would allow "the Satan" (literally, "the accuser") to torment a righteous person in order to see if the man would curse God to his face—"Imagine this, if you will . . ." These scholars argue that the rest of the Bible is at odds with the idea that God would do such a thing.

Literary Interpretation

Introduction: Job's righteousness and suffering (Job 1–2). Job is introduced as a man who is so righteous that the day after his children throw a feast, he offers an extravagant sacrifice for each of them in case one of them may have sinned and "cursed God in their hearts" (1:5). In heaven, the Lord brags to "the Satan"—a member of his heavenly court whose role is to bring charges against sinners, something like an attorney general—that Job perfectly "fears God and turns away from evil" (1:8). The Satan responds that Job is only righteous and fears God because God has been so good to him; take away all he has and "he will

Box 19.1

Outline

1. Introduction: Job's righteousness and suffering (1–2)
2. First cycle of speeches (3–14)
   a. Job (3)
   b. Eliphaz (4–5)
   c. Job (6–7)
   d. Bildad (8)
   e. Job (9–10)
   f. Zophar (11)
   g. Job (12–14)
3. Second cycle of speeches (15–21)
   a. Eliphaz (15)
   b. Job (16–17)
   c. Bildad (18)
   d. Job (19)
   e. Zophar (20)
   f. Job (21)
4. Third cycle of speeches (22–27)
   a. Eliphaz (22)
   b. Job (23–24)
   c. Bildad (25)
   d. Job (26–27)
5. Wisdom speech (28)
6. Job's final speech (29–31)
7. Elihu's speech (32–37)
8. God's response (38:1–42:6)
   a. God's first speech (38–39)
   b. God's second speech (40–41)
   c. Job speaks (42:1–6)
9. Prose conclusion (42:7–17)

curse you to your face" (1:11). The Satan is given permission to attack Job's possessions—but not his body—and departs from God's presence. Calamity befalls Job. In one day, all his flocks and herds, his servants and house, and all his children are destroyed. Job responds, "The LORD has given; the LORD has taken away; bless the LORD's name" (1:21 CEB).

Back in heaven, the Lord again brags to the Satan that Job is "a blameless and upright man who fears God and turns away from evil. He still persists in his integrity" (2:3). The Satan responds that Job is only righteous because he has his health; attack that and "he will curse you to your face" (2:5). Given permission to attack Job's health—but not take his life—the Satan again departs from the presence of the Lord. Job is stricken with disease but says to his wife, "Shall we receive good from God, and shall we not receive evil?" (2:10 ESV).

Job's three friends—Eliphaz, Bildad, and Zophar—come in order to "console and comfort him" (2:11). Upon seeing his suffering, they weep, tear their clothes, throw dust in the air, and sit silently with him for seven days. Up to this point, the friends provide genuine comfort.

First cycle of speeches: Job (Job 3). After sitting on an ash heap for seven days, "Job opened his mouth and cursed the day of his birth" (3:1)—about as close to "cursing God" as one can get without explicitly doing so! But Job

---

Box 19.2

The Plots of Job

There is more than one way to think about the plot of the book of Job. On the surface, the plot is whether the Satan can get Job to curse God to his face. The Satan is allowed to attack Job's family and property, but Job does not curse God. The narrator adds, "In all this Job did not sin or charge God with wrongdoing" (1:22). The Satan is then allowed to attack his health, but again Job does not curse God. But the narrator adds a subtle difference, saying, "In all this Job did not sin with his lips" (2:10). Job does not praise God, and the narrator seems to allow room for the possibility that Job curses God in his heart.

Another way of thinking about the book's plot emerges from the dialogues between Job and his friends. Following the destruction of Job's life, Job and his counselors engage in a conversation that occupies most of the book. Job complains, asserts his innocence, challenges his accusers, bemoans his suffering, asserts that wickedness often is unpunished, challenges God to answer, and finally defends himself at length. Job's friends assert that the righteous do not suffer and that suffering is a sign of guilt; they urge him to repent, defend God against Job's challenges, assert Job deserves his punishment, accuse him of undermining faith in God, and claim no mortal can be righteous before God. The plot question that runs through these dialogues is whether any satisfying answers or lasting truth about why the righteous suffer can be found at all.

Fig. 19.1. While the New Testament refers to "the patience of Job" (James 5:11 KJV), the book of Job actually spends most of its time on the suffering and lamenting of Job. Artistic depictions of his agony, such as here by Xavier Cortada, remind interpreters that the book of Job does not romanticize or gild Job's suffering.

does not ever curse God, let alone to his face. Job's initial lament for all he has lost contains no accusation against God but is simply a lament that would be at home in the book of Psalms or Lamentations: "Why is light given to one in misery? . . . I am not at ease, nor am I quiet; I have no rest; but trouble comes" (3:20, 26).

First cycle of speeches: Eliphaz (Job 4–5). Eliphaz responds cautiously, "If one ventures a word with you, will you be offended?" (4:2). He offers a careful argument based on tradition and experience: "Think now, who that was innocent ever perished?" (4:7). Then he hesitantly claims to have experienced a vision from God in which he heard the words, "Can mortals be righteous before God?" (4:17). He urges Job to cry out to God: "As for me, I would seek God, and to God I would commit my cause. . . . For he wounds, but he binds up; he strikes, but his hands heal" (5:8, 18).

First cycle of speeches: Job (Job 6–7). Job renews his lament—"The arrows of the Almighty are in me" (6:4)—and then turns his ire on his friends: "My companions are treacherous like a torrent-bed. . . . [Have I said], 'Teach me, and I will be silent; make me understand how I have gone wrong?'" (6:15, 24).

Box 19.3

Job's Friends

One of the most fascinating aspects of the book of Job is the characterization of Job and his friends. How is the reader meant to understand the character of the friends? At the end of the book, God judges Job's three friends: "After the Lord spoke these words to Job, the Lord said to Eliphaz the Temanite, 'My anger burns against you and your two friends, because you have not spoken to me as is right, as my servant Job has done'" (42:7 AT). Because of this divine judgment, many scholars have been dismissive of the speeches of Job's three friends (and of the fourth friend, Elihu).

More recently, however, a more appreciative approach to these speeches has begun to emerge. As Seow writes, "The theologies of Job's friends are similarly thoughtful. The friends are indeed able theologians who offer keen insights that are part of the larger theological conversation in the book. Hence, despite divine judgment of the friends in the Epilogue, early and medieval interpreters found much that they had to say genial. In fact, some like Aquinas and Calvin were rather naturally drawn to the theology of the friends more than the virulent posture of Job."*

The task of the generous reader is to appreciate the friends' attempt to comfort Job and dialogue with him and then also consider the best of the friends' theologies—but also to sniff out what in their theological formulations deserves divine judgment.

Gustave Doré / Lebrecht History / Bridgeman Images

Fig. 19.2. Job's friends are more than literary foils for his suffering. At least in their early conversations with Job, they offer sophisticated and thoughtful reflections on suffering, sin, and salvation.

* C. L. Seow, *Job 1–21: Interpretation and Commentary*, Illuminations (Grand Rapids: Eerdmans, 2013), 96.

Then Job addresses God: "Remember that my life is a breath. . . . I loathe my life; I would not live forever. . . . Why do you not pardon my transgression and take away my iniquity?" (7:7, 16, 21).

First cycle of speeches: Bildad (Job 8). Prompted by Job's weighty lament and ignoring his prayer for forgiveness, Bildad responds, "How long will you say these things? . . . Does God pervert justice?" (8:2–3). Bildad then urges Job to repent:

> If you will seek God
> > and make supplication to the Almighty,
> if you are pure and upright,
> > surely then he will rouse himself for you
> > and restore to you your rightful place. (8:5–6)

First cycle of speeches: Job (Job 9–10). Job acknowledges the truth of what his friends have said—"Indeed, I know that this is true. But how can mere mortals prove their innocence before God?" (9:2 NIV). He continues with words of praise and awe for the Creator, before reasserting his innocence: "Though I am innocent, I cannot answer him; I must appeal for mercy to my accuser" (9:15). Job turns again to God, "I loathe my life. . . . Let me alone, that I may brighten up, before I go, never to return" (10:1, 20–21, modified).

First cycle of speeches: Zophar (Job 11). Zophar is outraged by Job's "babble" and cries out, "You say, 'My conduct is pure, and I am clean in God's sight.' But O that God would speak. . . . Know then that God exacts of you less than your guilt deserves" (11:4–6). Zophar insists that God's ways are unknowable for human beings, for God is transcendent: "Can you find out the deep things of God? Can you find out the limit of the Almighty? It is higher than heaven— what can you do? Deeper than Sheol—what can you know?" (11:7–8). He then urges Job to repent.

First cycle of speeches: Job (Job 12–14). In an extended response, Job answers the charge that he babbles and claims to know too much about God by accusing his friends of the same two things: "I have understanding as well as you; I am not inferior to you" (12:3). Job then acknowledges God's strength and wisdom (12:13). In the second movement of his speech, Job's anger with his friends grows: "All of you are worthless healers. If you would be silent indeed, it would count to you as wisdom" (13:4–5 AT). Then comes a very serious charge: "Will you speak falsely for God, and speak deceitfully for him?" (13:7). Job then turns to God in prayer: "Remove your hand far from me, and do not let dread of you terrify me. Call, and I will indeed answer! Or I will speak and you respond to me!" (13:21–22 AT). Job concludes by meditating on the brevity of human life: "You prevail against them forever and they pass on" (14:20 AT).

Second cycle of speeches: Eliphaz (Job 15). In Eliphaz's second speech, he approaches from a new angle and accuses Job of undermining faith: "But you are destroying piety and hindering prayer before God" (15:4 AT). Foreshadowing God's later speech, Eliphaz asks, "Were you brought forth before the hills? Have you listened in the council of God?" (15:7–8). He then recalls the wisdom of the ancient sages, saying that "the wicked writhe continually in pain all their days" (15:20, modified).

Second cycle of speeches: Job (Job 16–17). Job responds, "Miserable comforters are you all" (16:2). Then he renews his powerful lament: "My spirit is broken, my days are extinguished; it is the graveyard for me" (17:1 AT).

Second cycle of speeches: Bildad (Job 18). Bildad explodes in fury, "Why are we regarded as beasts? Why are we stupid in your eyes?" (18:3 AT). He follows this outburst with a speech, borrowing from Proverbs, that asserts that the wicked are to blame for their suffering, because "they are sent into a net by their own feet" (18:8, modified). The implication is that Job has brought his own suffering upon himself.

Second cycle of speeches: Job (Job 19). Job rejects Bildad's implication—"Are you not ashamed to wrong me?" (19:3)—and turns his complaint back on God: "Know then that God has put me in the wrong, and closed his net around me" (19:6). Then, in what is the most famous passage in the book, Job laments:

> O, then, that my words were written!
>   O, then, that they were inscribed in a scroll!
> O, with an iron stylus and with lead,
>   carved forever into a rock!
> For I know that my redeemer lives,
>   and at the last he will arise over the dust;
> and after my skin has been thus destroyed,
>   in my flesh I shall see God. (19:23–26 AT)

Second cycle of speeches: Zophar (Job 20). In Zophar's second speech, he turns Job's language back on him, suggesting that the wicked may "mount up high as the heavens" for a while but eventually "will lie down in the dust" (20:6, 11). He concludes that "the heavens will reveal their iniquity" (20:27).

Second cycle of speeches: Job (Job 21). Job, based on his own experience, utterly rejects Zophar's assertions. He asks, "Why do the wicked live on, reach old age, and grow mighty in power?" (21:7). The wicked reject God but live in prosperity. He concludes, "How then will you comfort me with vanity? There is nothing left of your answers but unfaithfulness" (21:34 AT).

Third cycle of speeches: Eliphaz (Job 22). Eliphaz, whose first speech was thoughtful, now turns and accuses Job of wickedness: "Is not your wickedness great? There is no end to your sins!" (22:5, modified). Again, he calls for Job to repent: "If you return to the Almighty, you will be restored" (22:23).

Third cycle of speeches: Job (Job 23–24). Job responds that he wishes he could lay his case before God: "Would that I knew where to find him. . . . I would lay out my case before him; I will fill my mouth with proofs!" (23:3–4 AT). Job again asserts both his innocence and his contention that the most wicked often prosper.

Third cycle of speeches: Bildad (Job 25). In a short speech, Bildad asks, "How then can a mortal be righteous before God?" (25:4).

Third cycle of speeches: Job (Job 26–27). Job responds, "I hold fast my righteousness, and will not let it go" (27:6). (It is not clear who speaks the long passage in 27:7–23; it does not fit Job's voice, and since Zophar does not give a third speech, it may be these are Zophar's words.)

Wisdom speech (Job 28). Chapter 28 is usually thought of as a wisdom poem that serves as an interlude. It is unclear whether the speech reflects Job's words or those of a narrator who inserted them into the dialogues at this point. The poem's primary concern is where wisdom can be found, concluding, "Truly, the fear of the Lord, that is wisdom" (28:28).

Job's final speech (Job 29–31). In his lengthy final speech, Job longs for the days of his prosperity (chap. 29), laments his suffering (chap. 30), and belabors his innocence (chap. 31). Job 31:5–40 consists of what Matitiahu Tsevat calls "the most terrible oath in the Bible."[3] In this extended oath, Job swears upon his integrity and risks all in order to be judged by God: "Let me be weighed in a just balance, and let God know my integrity" (31:6). As Tsevat says, "Job throws caution to the winds. Over and over he explicitly calls upon himself every conceivable punishment if what he says is not true."[4] After Job's oath, the text notes, "The words of Job are ended" (31:40).

Elihu's speech (Job 32–37). A fourth friend, Elihu, who is mentioned in neither the prologue nor the epilogue, then appears and speaks. Elihu is said to be "angry at Job because he justified himself rather than God; he was angry also at Job's three friends because they had found no answer" (32:2–3). Elihu introduces himself by saying, "I am young in years . . . ; therefore I was timid and afraid to declare my opinion to you" (32:6). Scholars who believe the Elihu chapters are a later addition to the book hear in these words the voice of the later, "younger" scribe who added his contribution to the book. Elihu alone addresses Job by name: "Hear my speech, O Job, and listen to all my words" (33:1). Elihu argues that God speaks to people in visions ("in a dream, in a vision of the night"; 33:15) and also through chastisement ("They are also chastened with pain"; 33:19). "Then [the sufferer] prays to God, and is accepted by him" (33:26). Elihu insists that "according to their deeds he will repay them. . . . God will not do wickedly" (34:11–12). He concludes that Job's "answers are those of the wicked" (34:36). Then, anticipating God's speeches to come, Elihu concludes, "Hear this, O Job; stop and consider the wondrous works of God. Do you know how God lays his command upon them?" (37:14–15).

God's response: God's first speech (Job 38–39). Earlier, Job had expressed his desire to lay his case before God. He finally gets his wish when God speaks to him: "Then the LORD answered Job out of the whirlwind: 'Who is this

Fig. 19.3. God's appearances to humans, called theophanies, are often accompanied by dramatic supernatural phenomena, including fire, earthquakes, lightning and thunder, and darkness. These phenomena communicate both the power of the divine and the mystery of divine-to-human communication.

that darkens counsel by words without knowledge? Gird up your loins like a man, I will question you, and you shall declare to me'" (38:1–3).

In the Lord's first speech, he takes Job on a long rhetorical tour of creation and asks if he knows how any of it was created or how it works: "Where were you when I laid the foundation of the earth? Tell me, if you have understanding" (38:4). Job visits the earth, the sea, the heavens, the atmosphere, the wilderness of the wild animals, the mountains, and the air in which birds fly. The Lord concludes, "Shall a faultfinder contend with the Almighty? Anyone who argues with God must respond" (40:2).

God's response: God's second speech (Job 40–41). Despite his desire to confront God, Job is apparently cowed by the Lord's powerful presence and argument, and he refuses to speak: "I am of small account; what shall I answer you? . . . I will not answer" (40:4–5). The Lord repeats his challenge: "I will question you, and you declare to me. Will you even put me in the wrong?" (40:7–8). Then the Lord invites Job to consider Behemoth and Leviathan, which may refer to the hippopotamus and crocodile or perhaps simply two mythological beasts; either way, they symbolize the chaotic forces that militate against the creative will of God. The Lord contends that humans are terrified of these creatures, but to him they are just creatures that he has made, "just as I made you" (40:15).

God's response: Job speaks (Job 42:1–6). Job's final words are the source of much debate. He begins clearly enough, acknowledging the Lord's power, purpose, and knowledge. He also recognizes his own limitations. "I know[5] that you can accomplish all things. . . . I have uttered what I did not understand, things too wonderful for me, which I do not know" (42:2–3 AT). Job confesses, "I had heard of you by the hearing of the ear, but now my eye sees you" (42:5).

Then follows a key verse in the book (42:6), which (unfortunately) is obscure and unclear. Here is a standard translation and a new proposal from scholar William Brown:

Therefore I despise myself,
    and repent in dust and ashes. (NRSV; cf. NIV)

Therefore, I relent
    and am comforted over (or concerning) dust and ashes.[6]

The traditional approach views Job's last statement as one of repentance. Challenged by God, he humbles himself and repents of his charge against God. Job withdraws his case, acknowledges that a mere human being cannot comprehend or judge God's ways, repents, and thus seeks God's forgiveness.

Many scholars argue against this traditional translation and interpretation. Brown, for example, agrees that Job withdraws the formal case he has made against God but interprets the Hebrew verb *naham* differently. The verb can mean "to be sorry or regret" (as in Gen. 6:6). But it can also mean "to comfort or be comforted." Brown notes that the verb occurs six other times in Job, always with the meaning of comfort. Most importantly, Job's three friends come to him with the intention to "comfort him" (2:11). But Job later says, "Miserable comforters are you all" (16:2), and he asks, "How then will you comfort me with vanity?" (21:34 AT). According to this reading, Job finally receives comfort when the Lord speaks to him, and he is afforded the chance to see creation through God's eyes.

Prose conclusion (Job 42:7–17). In the conclusion to the book, God rebukes Job's three friends and instructs them to ask Job to pray for them, "for you have not spoken of me what is right," or "for you have not spoken to me as is right" (the translation is disputed). Job does so, and the Lord accepts his prayer. God then restores to Job twice as much wealth as he had lost; he also has seven more sons and three more daughters.

Theological Interpretation

Is There True Piety among Humans?

As noted earlier, the prose introduction to the book frames the plot around the questions of Job's motivation for being righteous (that is, pious). God brags about Job's righteousness, but the Satan scoffs that Job is only righteous and fears God because God has been so good to him—but take away all he has, and "he will curse you to your face" (1:11). As Matitiahu Tsevat writes,

> Job is the pious man, if there is one. The problem is: is there one? Which is secondary to the main problem: is there piety? Which is, as the accuser insists: is there disinterested piety? He claims that Job behaves according to standards of religion only as long as he finds it useful, whereas piety begins where usefulness ends. God accepts the challenge as proposed by the accuser and on his terms,

Carol Newsom on the Translation of Job 42:6

Old Testament scholar Carol Newsom illustrates the ambiguity of Job 42:6 by identifying several legitimate translations of the verse:

(1) "Therefore I despise myself and repent upon dust and ashes" (i.e., in humiliation; cf. NRSV; NIV);

(2) "Therefore I retract my words and repent of dust and ashes" (i.e., the symbols of mourning);

(3) "Therefore I reject and forswear dust and ashes" (i.e., the symbols of mourning);

(4) "Therefore I retract my words and have changed my mind concerning dust and ashes" (i.e., the human condition);

(5) "Therefore I retract my words, and I am comforted concerning dust and ashes" (i.e., the human condition).

With a slightly different understanding of the grammar, the [Tanakh (Jewish American translation)] translates, "Therefore, I recant and relent,/ Being but dust and ashes."*

* Carol A. Newsom, "Job," in *The New Interpreter's Bible* (Nashville: Abingdon, 1996), 4:629.

and this acceptance determines the meaning of piety for the rest of the book. From now on, he who performs an action in expectation of material reward is not to be credited with religious or moral behavior.[7]

God and the Suffering of the Righteous/Innocent

A second theme of the book, as important as the first, is the problem of God and the suffering of the righteous (or the innocent). Tsevat argues that having come face-to-face with God, Job "gained knowledge about God and thus indirectly about the world in general. . . . Job's misinterpretation of God and the world was due to his conceptions which were by and large those of Israelite tradition."[8] This misinterpretation of God is the misconception that "the world is founded on justice, i.e., *quid pro quo*, reward and punishment, . . . the principle of retribution."[9] God's interrogation of Job teaches Job that he does not accurately perceive the nature of creation or God's governance of creation. Job and his friends both believe in a tight causal connection between moral righteousness/unrighteousness and one's fate in the material world—that God and creation work by rewarding righteousness and punishing unrighteousness. God's speeches show that neither Job nor his friends accurately understands how God and creation function. "Justice is not woven into the stuff of the universe nor is God occupied with its administration."[10]

Why do the innocent and even righteous suffer if God is a good God? Creation has been fashioned in such a way that the genuinely dangerous forces of chaos (represented by Behemoth and Leviathan) are permitted to roam the earth. As the divine speeches make clear, these creatures are beyond human capacity to subdue or control. They endanger human life and yet are an integral part of God's creation. Job has to learn that part of living the wise life is recognizing that human beings share creation with more powerful creatures. The fabric of creation is not made of a tight moral weave in which deeds automatically result in morally equivalent consequences. What's more, God does not intrude to reward the righteous and punish the unrighteous. You may ask, "But should not God do so?" The book of Job responds, "Were you there when God created the universe?"

God's Speeches to Job

The poetic portion of the book reaches its climax in the divine speeches. Job demands an audience with God and offers him two options: "Call, and I will indeed answer! Or I will speak, and you respond to me!" (13:22 AT). God chooses the first option: "I will question you, and you shall declare to me" (38:3). God then asks Job a series of rhetorical questions about whether Job was present when God created the universe, whether he knows the way creation functions, whether he understands the nature of creation, and whether he is able to do any of what God has done and continues to do. Job's unspoken answer to all of God's questions can only be, "No, I was not there, I do not understand, and I

Laurent de La Hyre

Fig. 19.4. The gift to Job of a new fortune and the birth of new children symbolizes the restoration of his relationship with God, but it leaves open the question of the injustice surrounding his original loss. His new daughters (all exceptionally beautiful) are given whimsical names—Jemimah ("dove"), Keziah ("cinnamon"), and Qeren-Happuch ("box of eye shadow")—and are even granted inheritances, perhaps a sign that Job has come to see the world through a more just and moral perspective. Job has changed.

doctrine A belief or set of recognized beliefs held and taught by a religious group.

Box 19.5

Tsevat's Illustration of the Doctrine of Just Retribution

Tsevat imagines the theological problem of the book of Job as an equilateral triangle: "At the three vertexes we have G standing for God Who turns His face to man and is accessible to him, J for Job, the upright man, and R for the philosophy of retribution or justice in the world. The Book of Job, then, tells of an attempt to maintain these ideas simultaneously—an attempt which ends in failure."*

One cannot have all three corners of the triangle. Job's friends choose God and the doctrine of retribution—and therefore maintain that Job must have sinned to have experienced suffering. Job chooses his own righteousness and the doctrine of retribution—and therefore maintains that God is at fault. God turns to Job and maintains Job's righteousness—and therefore rejects the doctrine of retribution: God does not govern the universe by rewarding righteousness and punishing unrighteousness.

* Matitiahu Tsevat, "The Meaning of the Book of Job," *Hebrew Union College Annual* 37 (1966): 104–5.

am unable to do what you do." In the end, Job admits, "I have uttered what I did not understand, things too wonderful for me, which I did not know" (42:3 ESV).

Human Response to Suffering

Another issue that the book of Job raises regards how humans should respond to suffering—both their own and that of loved ones. A clue to the answer comes in God's judgment against Eliphaz and his two friends. God's words to Eliphaz are usually translated, "For you have not spoken of me what is right, as my servant Job has" (42:7; see NRSV, NIV, NJPS, etc.). However, the preposition translated here as "of me" is more naturally translated "to me." In fact, the NRSV translates every other occurrence of the verb "speak" followed by this preposition in the Old Testament (Hebrew: *dibber + el*) as "speak to." Thus, a more natural translation would be "For you have not spoken to me as is right, as my servant Job has." This translation also eliminates an apparent contradiction in the text. On the one hand, God had accused Job of speaking "words without knowledge" (38:2). If Job 42:7–8 is translated as "spoken of me what is right," God would be contradicting his own words.

Box 19.6

Are God's Speeches Satisfying?

Do God's speeches offer a compelling answer to Job's questions? Do they offer compelling answers to our questions about God and the suffering of the righteous and innocent? The author of the book of Job thought so, which is why Job either receives comfort from God or repents of his accusations—depending on what interpretation of 42:6 one favors.

How do the divine speeches offer such an answer? As noted earlier, they demonstrate to Job that he and his friends do not understand the nature of creation. Kathryn Schifferdecker argues convincingly that the Job speeches are profoundly "non-anthropocentric." She writes, "The creation theology implicit in the divine speeches . . . is unique in the Bible in its radical non-anthropocentricity. In other biblical texts, particularly in Genesis and Psalms, humanity is the crown of creation, its master or at least its caretaker. . . . In the divine speeches, though, humanity has almost no place except for passing references." She continues, "The author of the divine speeches, by removing human beings from the center of the created world, enlarges Job's (and the reader's) vision of that world. When Job was happy and prosperous, he was the center of his universe."* In the end, she concludes that "the order God establishes in creation is neither what the friends believed it was, nor what Job in his despair feared it was. The world is not a safe place, but it is indeed an ordered one."†

Job is invited to see creation through God's eyes—and to delight with God in the vast amount of space in which humanity has no presence at all. This world is free, often dangerous, and of as much value to God as is humanity.

* Kathryn Schifferdecker, *Out of the Whirlwind: Creation Theology in the Book of Job*, Harvard Theological Studies 61 (Cambridge, MA: Harvard University Press, 2008), 123.
† Schifferdecker, *Out of the Whirlwind*, 125.

But if the more natural translation is followed, there is no contradiction—Job can speak inaccurately about God yet also speak faithfully because Job is *speaking to God*. In fact, in the entire book, Job's friends never pray to God on Job's behalf; they only argue with Job's theology. Job, however, both argues with his friends and also argues with God in prayer. Thus, with respect to how people should respond to their own suffering, the book urges them to argue with God—lament, complain, accuse, question, yell; it is all acceptable. God can take it. And with respect to how people should respond to others' suffering, the book suggests spending time with them, comforting them with one's presence, praying to God on their behalf, bringing food and other gifts (Job's brothers and sisters "ate bread with him in his house; they showed him sympathy and comforted him for all the evil that the LORD had brought upon him; and each of them gave him a piece of money and a gold ring"; 42:11)—but never, never trying to fix their theology. When someone is suffering, it is not the time to debate doctrine.

Historical Interpretation

The view of the authors is that the story of Job was not intended to be understood as being about a historical figure. As noted earlier, this conclusion seems likely because the introductory verses place Job "in the east" in an otherwise unknown "land of Uz," with no historical dates, figures, events, or known places named. As for the historical world behind the text, scholars vary in their assessment. The book is very difficult to place and somewhat difficult to date.[11] It is likely that the book reached its final form in the Levant sometime after the exile. There is little to nothing in the book that can help historians better understand the historical world of the Levant at that time.

FOR FURTHER READING: **Job**

Balentine, Samuel E. *Job*. Smyth & Helwys Bible Commentary. Macon, GA: Smyth & Helwys, 2006.

Janzen, J. Gerald. *Job*. Interpretation: A Bible Commentary for Teaching and Preaching. Atlanta: John Knox, 1985.

Newsom, Carol A. "Job." In *The New Interpreter's Bible*, 4:319–637. Nashville: Abingdon, 1996.

Schifferdecker, Kathryn. *Out of the Whirlwind: Creation Theology in the Book of Job*. Cambridge, MA: Harvard University Press, 2008.

Seow, C. L. *Job 1–21: Interpretation and Commentary*. Illuminations. Grand Rapids: Eerdmans, 2013.

Psalms

The book of Psalms, also called the Psalter, contains some of the most well-known and best-loved passages in the Old Testament. When people of faith experience crisis and need to hear a word of consolation from the Bible, they often turn to Psalms. There they hear promises such as "The LORD is my shepherd, I shall not want" (Ps. 23:1), or "The LORD is my light and my salvation, whom shall I fear?" (Ps. 27:1). Many Christian hymns and worship songs take some or all of their lyrics from Psalms. Some people pray and read Psalms daily. Indeed, the book of Psalms is a treasury of biblical, spiritual poetry.

Background

The word *psalm* comes from a Greek word meaning "song"; thus, the book of Psalms is a book of songs. The Hebrew title of the book is *Tehillim*, meaning "praises," "praise," or "praise songs." By chapter, Psalms is the longest book in the Bible; according to the current division into different poems, it contains 150 psalms.[1] These psalms were written by many different authors over many different centuries and from many different locations.

Composition and Development

Davidic Authorship

Many psalms begin with what is called a superscription (more on this later). Because many of these superscriptions include phrases such as "a psalm of David" or simply "of David," the tradition grew that David wrote many or all of the psalms. The New Testament often quotes a portion of a psalm and attributes it to David, sometimes even when a psalm does not bear his name in its superscription.[2] The Talmud also credits David with the whole collection: "David composed the Book of Psalms through ten elders: Adam, Melchizedek, Abraham, Moses, Heiman, Yedutun, Asaph, and the three sons of Korah."[3]

Today, many critical scholars do not believe that David wrote even those psalms that bear the superscription "of David." There are several reasons for this. First, many of these psalms make reference to the temple, which was built after David died. For example, Psalm 27:4: "One thing I asked of the LORD . . . : to live in the house [temple] of the LORD all the days of my life, . . . and to inquire in his temple." Second, the phrase "of David" in Hebrew is *ledavid*, literally "to David" or "for David." It need not be understood as meaning "written by David." Third, the spelling, syntax, and lexicography of the text of most psalms indicate that most or all of them were written later than David lived (1000 BCE).

A likely interpretation of the psalms that bear "of David" at their head is that they belonged to groups of psalms that were collected for use in the temple at Jerusalem, the "City of David." Some of these psalms include what scholars call a historical superscription—one that connects the psalm with a particular event in David's life. Most prominently, Psalm 51—a plea for forgiveness—begins with the words, "A Psalm of David, when the prophet Nathan came to him, after he had gone in to Bathsheba." Scholars who deny that David wrote the psalms view these historical superscriptions (indeed all of the superscriptions) as early additions to the text—the first indication of how the psalm was interpreted and how it is to be understood and used. Some of these scholars believe that David may have written some of the older psalms in the Psalter or in 2 Samuel (such as 2 Sam. 2:19–27; 2 Sam. 22:2–51 // Ps. 18; 2 Sam. 23:1–7; Ps. 68). Other scholars maintain that David wrote every psalm that bears the superscription "of David"; they view the New Testament citations and the historical superscriptions as evidence for this conclusion.

Box 20.1

Martin Luther on the Psalms

The sixteenth-century Reformer Martin Luther wrote that the book of Psalms "might well be called a little Bible. In it is comprehended most beautifully and briefly everything that is in the entire Bible."* By this he meant that it contains a "book of examples" of the entire life of faith. The 150 poems in the book of Psalms sing praises from the mountaintops, shout cries of despair "out of the depths" (Ps. 130:1), cry prayers of repentance after sin, sing songs of thanksgiving after deliverance, whisper words of trust in the midst of crisis, and preach proclamations of promise about the future.

* Martin Luther, "Preface to the Psalter," in *Word and Sacrament I*, Luther's Works 35 (Philadelphia: Fortress, 1960), 254.

Whether David wrote the psalms or not, however, the point of preserving and gathering them remains the same: to preserve these prayers and praise songs so that the people of faith in all generations could pray and sing them; to preserve, in Luther's words, this "little Bible" of examples of the life of faith.

A Collection of Collections

It is clear that the Psalter developed over time. Not only were the individual psalms written over many centuries, but the smaller collections that make up the book were also brought together and slowly edited into the final form of the Psalter. Some of these smaller collections can be identified by their superscriptions, such as the Psalms of Asaph, the Psalms of the Korahites (literally "sons of Korah"), and the Psalms of Ascents.

Fig. 20.1. "I will lift up mine eyes unto the hills" (Ps. 121:1 KJV).

Other smaller collections have been identified by scholars, such as the Elohistic psalter (Pss. 42–83, which prefer "Elohim" to "Yahweh") and the enthronement psalms (Pss. 93–99, which celebrate the Lord's reign).[4] Other psalms have been identified by Jewish tradition, such as Psalms 113–18, which are known as the Egyptian Hallel.

As the psalms were edited together, phrases and even verses seem to have been added to some psalms, especially to the ends (e.g., see Pss. 2:12; 51:18–19). This editing happened over a long period of time in a process that cannot be reconstructed. But it is helpful to recognize that our book of Psalms is a collection of smaller collections that were brought together for later use.

Genre

As noted, the book of Psalms is a collection of 150 songs. For the past century, the dominant approach to the study of these songs has been a literary approach known as form criticism. This approach was developed by German scholar Hermann Gunkel and has been furthered in a variety of ways by many scholars. The approach is based on the assumption that common life situations generate common "forms" of prayers. For example, in our contexts, the life situation of a shared meal has generated the "before-meal prayer." From the life situation

form criticism An academic approach that classifies literary materials by type or genre and identifies the purposes for which such materials were intended.

of putting children to bed comes the "bedtime prayer." In some cultural contexts, the common life situation of death has generated the "lament-for-the-dead prayer." The idea is that these common forms of prayer share similar elements. By studying these common elements in the psalms, Gunkel and others have reasoned backward to imagine the life situations for which various psalm forms were generated. Prior to form criticism, it was most common to read a psalm and try to place it at some historical point in the life of David or some other biblical character.

Most Psalms scholars recognize a relatively small set of psalm forms: prayers for help (or laments), hymns of praise, psalms of trust, and songs of thanksgiving. These categories will be further explored below in the summary of the book of Psalms.

Box 20.2

Outline

As the Psalter was edited, the scribes divided it into five books by inserting four doxologies into the completed text. The purpose of these doxologies was most likely to present the Psalter as the five books of David—to correspond with the five books of Moses (the Pentateuch). The Psalter can thus be outlined as follows, with the doxologies included. Note the editorial remark after the doxology that concludes Book 2 of the Psalter: "The prayers of David son of Jesse are ended."

doxology A hymn or group of words that expresses praise to God.

1. Book 1: Psalms 1–41
   Blessed be the LORD, the God of Israel,
     from everlasting to everlasting.
   Amen and Amen. (41:13)

2. Book 2: Psalms 42–72
   Blessed be the LORD, the God of Israel,
     who alone does wondrous things.
   Blessed be his glorious name forever;
     may his glory fill the whole earth.
   Amen and Amen. (72:18–20)

   The prayers of David son of Jesse are ended.

3. Book 3: Psalms 73–89
   Blessed be the LORD forever.
     Amen and Amen. (89:52)

4. Book 4: Psalms 90–106
   Blessed be the LORD, the God of Israel,
     from everlasting to everlasting.
   And let all the people say, "Amen."
     Praise the LORD! (106:48)

5. Book 5: Psalms 107–50

Box 20.3

Anatomy of a Psalm

Number. Psalm numbers are a later addition to the poem. No one set out to write Psalm 89. In the Septuagint, the Greek version of the Old Testament, the numbering of the psalms is different.

Title. Many English versions of the Psalms include editorial headings or titles that are not original to the poem. These titles are often helpful, meant to guide the understanding of or reading of the psalm, but they should not be mistaken as a part of the Bible.

Superscription. In many of the psalms there is a superscription, a title that is a part of the text of many of the oldest versions of the Psalms, but which most scholars believe to have been added after the psalm was composed. Superscriptions contain several pieces of information: (1) There may be a person with whom the psalm is associated: here it is Ethan the Ezrahite; various psalms are attributed to David, the Korahites, Asaph, and others. (2) Numerous difficult Hebrew terms may indicate a type of psalm: Psalm 89 is called a *maskil*, and other examples are *miktam*, *shiggaion*. (3) Such terms may have something to do with musical or liturgical setting, such as "according to lilies" (Ps. 80), "at the time of anger" (Ps. 22), "for the leader" (Ps. 36). (4) Or they may refer to specific instrumentation for the performance of the psalm, such as "on the *gittith*," "on the *sheminith*," and so forth.

Verses. Verse numbers are a later addition to the poetry of the psalms. Different versions and translations have different numbering. In English, the fairly standard modern numbers were first used in the Geneva Bible of 1560. Verse numbers are useful primarily for reference and do not necessarily have much to do with what and how the psalm means.

Psalm 89 "God's Covenant with David"

¹ *A Maskil of Ethan the Ezrahite.*

I will sing of your steadfast love, O LORD, forever;
  with my mouth I will proclaim your faithfulness to all generations.
² I declare that your steadfast love is established forever;
  your faithfulness is as firm as the heavens.
³ You said, "I have made a covenant with my chosen one,
  I have sworn to my servant David:
⁴ 'I will establish your descendants forever,
  and build your throne for all generations.'" *Selah*

Verses 5–51

⁵ Let the heavens praise your wonders, O LORD,
  your faithfulness in the assembly of the holy ones.
. . . .
⁵⁰ Remember, O LORD, how your servant is taunted;
  how I bear in my bosom the insults of the peoples,
⁵¹ with which your enemies taunt, O LORD,
  with which they taunted the footsteps of your anointed.
⁵² Blessed be the LORD forever. Amen and Amen.

Body. The bulk of a psalm is made up of verses, which contain two and sometimes three lines. The break between the lines of a verse is clearly marked in the Hebrew and is often indicated in English translations by a semicolon and/or indentation for a new line. References are often made to lines within a verse, such as Psalm 89:50a, "Remember, O LORD, how your servant is taunted"; and 89:50b, "how I bear in my bosom the insults of the peoples." Psalms can be short (117 has 2 verses) or long (119 has 176 verses).

Unknown words. In many psalms we find the word *Selah* at the end of a verse. Scholars are not entirely sure what this means, but it may indicate a pause in the psalm or mark important divisions in the psalm. In Psalm 89 *selah* occurs at the ends of verses 4, 37, 45, and 48. Another example of an unknown word in the middle of a psalm is *higgaion*, at the end of 9:17.

Closing additions. Many of the psalms have had material added to them, often at the end, either to connect them to a psalm that follows or to mark a major division in the Psalter. Thus Psalm 89:52 has been added to close both the psalm itself and Book III of the Psalter—in this case voicing doxology, or praise of the Lord.

From Rolf A. Jacobson and Karl N. Jacobson, *Invitation to the Psalms: A Reader's Guide for Discovery and Engagement* (Grand Rapids: Baker Academic, 2013), 30.

Literary Interpretation

The poets of the book of Psalms adapted the various psalm forms in many ways. This means that while most psalms fit a general category, not all psalms include every major element that characterizes a particular form. In what follows, the most common forms of psalms are explained and illustrated by way of one psalm that typifies the category.

Prayer for Help (Lament Psalm): Psalm 13

The most common form of psalm in the Psalter is the prayer for help. These psalms are often called lament psalms, but this term is not really accurate, since a lament is technically a cry of mourning after hope is lost—for instance, after the death of a loved one. A prayer for help is a prayer uttered in the midst of a crisis while there is still hope for a good ending. The elements of a prayer for help are a situation of crisis, an address to God, a complaint, a request for help, an expression of trust, and a promise to praise.

Situation of crisis. The prayer for help comes out of the psalmist's crisis. In Psalm 13, the exact nature of the crisis is vague—probably intentionally so, in order that generations of people could pray this prayer in the midst of a variety of crises.

Address to God. The prayer for help is rooted in the belief that the Lord has the power to transcend any crisis and bring deliverance. Psalm 13 is addressed "O Lord" and later "O Lord my God." This is typical of the prayers for help. These prayers are not simply complaints to an unhearing universe; they are prayers to a personal God with whom the psalmist has a relationship.

Box 20.4

Psalm 13

How long, O Lord? Will you forget me forever?
  How long will you hide your face from me?
How long must I bear pain in my soul,
  and have sorrow in my heart all day long?
How long shall my enemy be exalted over me?

Consider and answer me, O Lord my God!
  Give light to my eyes, or I will sleep the sleep of death,
and my enemy will say, "I have prevailed";
  my foes will rejoice because I am shaken.
But I trusted in your steadfast love;
  my heart shall rejoice in your salvation.
I will sing to the Lord,
  because he has dealt bountifully with me.

Complaint. In the prayers for help, there are always complaints—expressions of the crises from which the prayers are cried. Scholars point to three types of complaints: the "I complaint," the "you complaint," and the "they complaint." The "I complaint" is the personal dimension of the crisis. In Psalm 13, the psalmist cries, "How long must I bear pain in my soul, and have sorrow in my heart all day long?" (v. 2). The "you complaint" is the theological dimension of the crisis. The psalmist of Psalm 13 complains, "How long, O LORD? Will you forget me forever? How long will you hide your face from me?" (v. 1). The "they complaint" is the social dimension of the crisis. In Psalm 13, the psalmist cries, "How long shall my enemy be exalted over me?" (v. 2).

Request for help. The most important part of each prayer for help is the request for help. These prayers are prayed in the belief that the Lord can change the situation in which the psalmist is stuck, can "deliver from evil," so to speak. In Psalm 13, the psalmist asks, "Give light to my eyes, or I will sleep the sleep of death" (v. 3). In other psalms, those who are suffering cry, "Deliver me" (3:7), "Answer me" (4:1), "Lead me" (5:8), and "Save my life" (6:4). As part of the request for help, the psalmists often offer motivating reasons—rational arguments for why God should answer the prayer. In Psalm 13, the psalmist says, "And my enemy will say, 'I have prevailed'; my foes will rejoice because I am shaken" (v. 4).

Expression of trust. In most prayers for help, the psalmist not only prays to the Lord for help but also expresses trust that the Lord will deliver. In Psalm 13, the psalmist confesses, "But I trusted in your steadfast love" (v. 5). In other psalms, the psalmists say things such as "You are the holy one, enthroned. You are Israel's praises. Our ancestors trusted you—they trusted you and you rescued them" (22:3–4 CEB), or "O my God, in you I trust" (25:2).

Promise to praise. A final element of the prayer for help is the promise to praise. The psalmist ends by saying, "I will sing to the LORD, because he has dealt bountifully with me" (v. 6). In other psalms, the sufferers say things such as "I will give to the LORD the thanks due to his righteousness, and sing praise to the name of the LORD, the Most High" (7:17), or "in the great congregation I will bless the LORD" (26:12). These promises are not attempts to bargain with God, as they are sometimes misinterpreted. Rather, they are another side of the expression of trust. They are promises made in faith.

Box 20.5

Lament Psalms and the Spirituals

In much of Western Christianity, the lament psalms have been largely ignored. But one social location in which they have been embraced is the African American Christian tradition. There, in spirituals such as "Poor Wayfaring Stranger," "Nobody Knows the Trouble I've Seen," and "Sometimes I Feel Like a Motherless Child," the lament tradition has played a vital role.

Prayers for help most often come from individuals, as in Psalm 13, but they also appear less commonly in a communal form (see, e.g., Ps. 44). The elements of a prayer for help do not always occur in the same order; nor do they all occur in every example. Additionally, there are several subtypes of these psalms, including prayers of confession (also called penitential psalms, such as Ps. 51), prayers asserting innocence (Ps. 17), and the imprecatory psalms (psalms that ask God to punish one's enemies; see Ps. 137).

Hymn of Praise: Psalm 113

The hymn of praise is the second most common type of psalm in the Psalter. Typical elements in these psalms are a situation of worship, a call to praise, and reasons for praise (also called an unfolding praise testimony).

Situation of worship. The hymn of praise assumes a time of public worship and celebration. The community comes together to praise God. Theologically, praise is both testimony (telling others who God is and what he has done) and worship (giving oneself to God in love).

Call to praise. Most hymns begin and end with a call to praise. The most characteristic form of this call is the one found at the beginning of Psalm 113, the Hebrew phrase *halelu yah*, which literally means "Praise Yah(weh)!" ("Praise

---

Box 20.6

Psalm 113

Praise the LORD!
Praise, O servants of the LORD;
   praise the name of the LORD.

Blessed be the name of the LORD
   from this time on and forevermore.
From the rising of the sun to its setting
   the name of the LORD is to be praised.
The LORD is high above all nations,
   and his glory above the heavens.

Who is like the LORD our God,
   who is seated on high,
who looks far down
   on the heavens and the earth?
He raises the poor from the dust,
   and lifts the needy from the ash heap,
to make them sit with princes,
   with the princes of his people.
He gives the barren woman a home,
   making her the joyous mother of children.
Praise the LORD!

Fig. 20.2. The Psalms have been central to the worship life of many communities of faith. Whether chanted in a plain-song style (as above), sung in metric paraphrase (such as "All Creatures That on Earth Do Dwell"), or sung in a modern praise-song style, the Psalms are beloved by worshipers.

the LORD!"). There are several other calls to praise: "Bless the LORD!" (103:1); "Rejoice in the LORD!" (33:1); "Make a joyful noise to God!" (66:1); and "Sing to the LORD!" (98:1). The point is to call a community of worshipers to offer praise testimony to God.

Reasons for praise. This second major feature of the hymn of praise often forms the body of the psalm. The body of each hymn contains unfolding praise of God that offers reasons for praise, but that are best understood as a testimony about who God is and what he has done. In Psalm 113, the psalmist says, "The LORD is high above all nations, and his glory above the heavens" (v. 4)—and yet God's way of being in the world is to act in the lowest, most earthy places—"who looks far down . . . [and] raises the poor from the dust, and lifts the needy from the ash heap" (vv. 6–7). God is high above yet reaches down to touch the lowliest of creatures!

Other hymns declare that the Lord "provides food for those who fear him" (111:5), "has established the world" (93:1), "is faithful in all his words, and gracious in all his deeds" (145:13), and "forgives all your iniquity, . . . heals all your diseases" (103:3). Sometimes the hymns praise God in the second person ("You are great") and sometimes in the third person ("God is great"). In most hymns, the song switches between the two forms.

There are several subtypes of the hymn of praise, including the creation psalm (Pss. 8; 104), the historical psalm (Ps. 136), and the Torah psalm (Ps. 119).

Psalm of Trust: Psalm 23

Recall that in prayers for help, the sufferers usually express trust in God at the same time as calling for God's help. Similar expressions of trust often form their own complete psalms. These psalms are often favorite psalms (Pss. 23; 27; 46; 121). Like the prayer for help, the psalm of trust can be spoken by a community or an individual. Psalm 23 is a good example of a psalm of trust; it implies a situation requiring trust and includes expressions of trust, descriptions of troubles, and descriptions of God's care.

Situation requiring trust. The psalm of trust can be prayed in almost any situation, but the language of this psalm form implies a situation of crisis—either a present crisis, as in Psalm 46 ("God is our refuge and strength, a very present help in crisis" [v. 1, modified]), or a future crisis, as Psalm 121 implies with its expression that "the LORD will keep your going out and your coming in from this time forth and forevermore" (v. 8 ESV). In Psalm 23, references to the "darkest valley" and "the presence of my enemies" make it clear that the psalmist faces a crisis. But these prayers are prayed in all types of situations, whether those of severe crisis or those of daily life.

Box 20.7

Psalm 23

The LORD is my shepherd, I shall not want.
  He makes me lie down in green pastures;
he leads me beside still waters;
  he restores my soul.
He leads me in right paths
  for his name's sake.
Even though I walk through the darkest valley,
  I fear no evil;
for you are with me;
  your rod and your staff—
  they comfort me.
You prepare a table before me
  in the presence of my enemies;
you anoint my head with oil;
  my cup overflows.
Surely goodness and mercy shall follow me
  all the days of my life,
and I shall dwell in the house of the LORD
  my whole life long.

Expressions of trust. The psalms of trust express confidence in God's presence and in his ability to save. In Psalm 23, the psalmist confesses, "You are with me; your rod and your staff—they comfort me" (v. 4), and "You prepare a table before me in the presence of my enemies" (v. 5). In Psalm 46, a communal psalm of trust, the community says, "The LORD of hosts is with us; the God of Jacob is our refuge" (vv. 7, 11). Psalm 27 confesses, "Whom shall I fear?" (v. 1), and Psalm 16 says, "I shall not be moved" (v. 8).

Descriptions of trouble. Also typical of the language of the psalms of trust are vivid descriptions of trouble and crisis. As noted above, the psalmist of Psalm 23 speaks of "walk[ing] through the darkest valley" and being in "the presence of my enemies." Psalm 46 describes how "the mountains shake in the heart of the sea" and "the nations are in an uproar, the kingdoms totter" (vv. 3, 6 AT). Other psalms of trust speak of the presence of enemies that threaten (23:5; 42:1–4), the reality of death (16:10), the dangers of war (27:3), and the awful conditions of illness (91:6).

Descriptions of God's care. Central to the psalms of trust are powerful descriptions of God's presence and care. Psalm 23 confesses, "You are with me" (v. 4). Psalm 46 says, "The LORD of hosts is with us" (vv. 7, 11). Psalm 16 expresses confidence that "the LORD [is] always before me" (v. 8). The psalms of trust use powerful metaphors to express the presence and care of God: the Lord is shepherd (23:1), light (27:1), shelter (27:5), portion and cup (16:5), refuge (46:1), rock and fortress (62:2), strong tower (61:3), dwelling place (90:1), and protector (121:5). These metaphors are not decorations that adorn the limbs of the tree; they are part of the tree itself.

These psalms also describe God's care by describing his characteristic activities. In Psalm 23, the shepherd-Lord "leads me beside still waters" and "leads me in right paths" (vv. 2–3) and "prepare[s] a table before me in the presence of my enemies" (v. 5). In Psalm 91, the psalmist speaks promises on behalf of God:

> Those who love me, I will deliver;
>> I will protect those who know my name.
> When they call to me, I will answer them;
>> I will be with them in trouble,
>> I will rescue them and honor them.
> With long life I will satisfy them,
>> and show them my salvation. (vv. 14–16)

These promises are not to be interpreted in some naive, rigid sense. Rather, they are general descriptions of the type of help that God provides in the midst of life's dangers. For the psalmists, these promises are characteristic of God's saving help.

Song of Thanksgiving: Psalm 30

The song of thanksgiving shares aspects in common with the hymn of praise. Like the hymn of praise, these songs tell who God is by telling what he has done; the difference is that rather than tell what God has done in the distant past, the authors of the songs of thanksgiving sing about what God has done for them in the present. In this sense, the song of thanksgiving is addressed primarily to other humans and secondarily to God.

The song of thanksgiving also shares things in common with the prayer for help. Whereas the prayers for help, sung in the midst of crisis, promise to thank

---

Box 20.8

Psalm 30

I will extol you, O Lord, for you have drawn me up,
  and did not let my foes rejoice over me.
O Lord my God, I cried to you for help,
  and you have healed me.
O Lord, you brought up my soul from Sheol,
  restored me to life from among those gone down to the Pit.

Sing praises to the Lord, O you his faithful ones,
  and give thanks to his holy name.
For his anger is but for a moment;
  his favor is for a lifetime.
Weeping may linger for the night,
  but joy comes with the morning.

As for me, I said in my prosperity,
  "I shall never be moved."
By your favor, O Lord,
  you had established me as a strong mountain;
you hid your face;
  I was dismayed.

To you, O Lord, I cried,
  and to the Lord I made supplication:
"What profit is there in my death,
  if I go down to the Pit?
Will the dust praise you?
  Will it tell of your faithfulness?
Hear, O Lord, and be gracious to me!
  O Lord, be my helper!"

You have turned my mourning into dancing;
  you have taken off my sackcloth
  and clothed me with joy,
so that my soul may praise you and not be silent.
  O Lord my God, I will give thanks to you forever.

God later, the songs of thanksgiving are the giving of that promised praise, sung after the crisis has passed.

Psalm 30 offers an excellent example of the song of thanksgiving—in this case, the song of an individual who has survived a crisis. It demonstrates the elements of the song of thanksgiving: a situation of worship after a crisis, a call to praise, a report of the crisis and request for help, a report of the delivery, and renewed praise.

Situation of worship after a crisis. As noted above, the song of thanksgiving is situated after God has delivered a sufferer from a crisis. Like the hymn of praise, the location assumed by the song of thanksgiving is a place of communal worship, where the singer both offers testimony to others about God and also gives praise to God.

Call to praise. Like the hymn of praise, the song of thanksgiving begins with a call to praise. Here the psalmist sings personal praise first: "I will extol you, O Lord, for you have drawn me up, and did not let my foes rejoice over me. O Lord my God, I cried to you for help, and you have healed me" (Ps. 30:1–2). Then the psalmist calls others to join the praise: "Sing praises to the Lord, O you his faithful ones, and give thanks to his holy name" (v. 4).

Report of crisis and request for help. The crisis reported in Psalm 30 is generic; it might be any crisis. This is intentional so that individuals in many different types of crises can pray these psalms. The past crisis in Psalm 30 is described with a variety of language: "foes [who] rejoice over me" (v. 1); nearly going "down to the Pit" (v. 3); God's "anger" and "weeping . . . [throughout] the night" (v. 5). This language evokes a range of possible crises. In other songs of thanksgiving, these crises are described with words such as: "The cords of death encompassed me; the torrents of perdition assailed me" (18:4); "My body wasted away. . . . My strength was dried up" (32:3–4); "We went through fire and through water" (66:12).

The report also includes the prayer for help that the psalmist prayed. In Psalm 30, the singer says, "I cried to you for help" (v. 2), and "To you, O Lord, I cried, and to the Lord I made supplication" (v. 8). Psalm 107 is a longer and more generic psalm that describes four different types of people who were in crisis—those who "wandered in desert wastes" (v. 4), prisoners who "sat in darkness and in gloom" (v. 10), those who "were sick" (v. 17), and travelers who "went down to the sea in ships" (v. 23). The psalm reports that each of these groups of sufferers "cried to the Lord in their trouble" (vv. 6, 13, 19, 28).

Report of the delivery. The heart of these psalms is the description of the help received. The psalmists desire that others know the saving help of the Lord. They wish for others to know that help is available for those who cry "to the Lord in their trouble." Psalm 30 describes that the singer was "drawn"

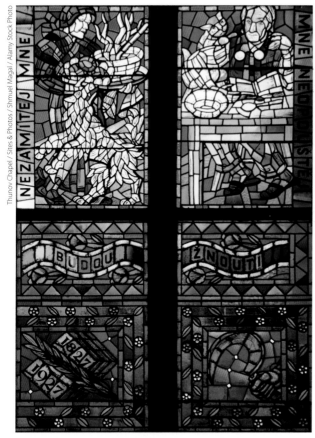

Fig. 20.3. The Psalms have often been presented visually for worshipers in stained glass windows and other art. Here the art portrays Psalm 126:5–6: "May those who sow in tears reap with shouts of joy."

up (v. 1), healed, "restored . . . to life" (v. 3), and in a stunning poetic turn of phrase, "clothed . . . with joy" (v. 11).

Renewed praise. There is often renewed praise in the songs of thanksgiving. Psalm 30 ends with the psalmist's statement "O LORD my God, I will give thanks to you forever" (v. 12). The Hebrew language of the Old Testament does not have a word for "thanks" or "thanksgiving." The word that is often translated as "thanks"—as in Psalm 30:12 and in Psalm 107:1, "O give thanks to the LORD"—actually means something more like "testify" or "confess." Thus, praise is testimony to others about what God has done for the individual or the community.

Other Psalm Forms

Most Psalms scholars identify other forms of psalms, including wisdom psalms (Pss. 1; 14; 37; 53; 73; 90; 119), royal psalms (Pss. 2; 18; 20–21; 45; 72; 89; 110; 132), historical psalms (Pss. 78; 105–6; 135–36), creation psalms (Pss. 8; 19; 34; 104; 139), and other small forms, such as entrance liturgies (Pss. 15; 24) and blessings (Pss. 67; 134). The first four types—wisdom, royal, historical, and creation—are not really "forms" of psalms but thematically similar psalms. In all four cases, psalms with these themes actually occur in several different forms. For example, royal psalms—which are about the Judean, *human* king and God's work through him—occur as a song of thanksgiving (Ps. 18), a prayer for help (Ps. 20), a coronation liturgy (Ps. 2), a lament after the destruction of the king's reign (Ps. 89), a wedding psalm (Ps. 45), and more.

Theological Interpretation

Because the book of Psalms has the most chapters of any book in the Bible (150 chapters or psalms), and because its poems were penned by many different hands over many years and in many places, some scholars argue that

The Faithfulness of the Lord

A central theme of the Psalter is the faithfulness of the Lord:

> For great is his loving faithfulness toward us,
> and the truthfulness of the Lord endures forever. (117:2 AT)

> Lord, where is your loving faithfulness of old,
> which you swore to David by your truthfulness? (89:49 AT)

> Let your face shine upon your servant,
> in your loving faithfulness, save me! (31:16 AT)

> I am like a thriving olive tree in the house of God;
> I trust in the loving faithfulness of God forever. (52:8 AT)

> [God] has magnified the deliverance of his king;
> he has shown loving faithfulness to his anointed one. (18:50 AT)

> Praised be God, who has not rejected my prayer
> or taken his loving faithfulness from me! (66:20 AT)

> Many are the woes of the wicked person,
> but the one who trusts in the Lord is surrounded by loving faithfulness. (32:10 AT)

> Let them thank the Lord for his loving faithfulness,
> for his wonderful works to humanity. (107:8, 15, 21, 31 AT)

there can be no theology of the Psalms. To say otherwise would be either reductive (flattening and reducing the rich variety of theological expression in the Psalter) or impracticable (taking up far too many pages). Both points have merit, but a few things may be briefly said here by way of introduction to a huge topic.

First, it must be noted that every psalm names God and is about God. This is not true of every Old Testament book, many of which have chapters that do not mention God. In fact, the entire book of Esther does not refer to God! God is the central reality of the book of Psalms.

In particular, God's faithfulness can be said to be a—perhaps even *the*—central theme in the book of Psalms. The psalms were collected, preserved, and passed down through the generations because faithful scribes believed that the Lord God of Israel was faithful to his beloved creation, as well as to the promises he had made to Abraham and Sarah and later to Moses and David and then to the descendants of those promises—both in the synagogue and in the church. The theme of faithfulness runs throughout the Psalter.

Faithfulness and the Hymns of Praise

The hymns of praise tell who God is by telling what God has done. The basic witness of those hymns is that God is faithful. Consider the shortest of all the hymns, Psalm 117:

> Praise the LORD, all you nations!
>> Worship him, all you peoples!
>> *Because God's faithful love toward us is strong,*
>> the LORD's faithfulness lasts forever!
> Praise the LORD! (117:1–2 CEB, italics added)

If the hymnists of the Psalter had only one thing to say, this would be it: "His faithfulness is great unto us!" A close examination of all the hymns of praise shows two areas in which the Lord consistently proves faithful: creation and history.

The Lord's Faithfulness in Creation

For the psalmists, the Lord is the creator of all. The earth is not the result of a violent conflict between gods (as in some creation myths of Israel's neighbors) but a beloved act of a faithful God,

> who made the heavens through understanding,
>> for his loving faithfulness endures forever;
> who spread out the earth on the water,
>> for his loving faithfulness endures forever;
> who made the great lights,
>> for his loving faithfulness endures forever. (136:5–7 AT)

Indeed, creation is a place of order. The Lord has "set a boundary that [the forces of chaos] may not pass" (104:9). This order in turn encompasses time, which has a daily and a seasonal rhythm: "You have made the moon to mark the seasons; the sun knows its time for setting" (104:19). The daily rhythm allows for human and animal life to live mutually: "When the sun rises, [the wild animals] withdraw. . . . People go out to their work and to their labor until the evening" (104:22–23). The seasonal rhythm allows for the harvests that sustain God's creatures: "You cause the grass to grow for the cattle, and plants for people to use, to bring forth food from the earth" (104:14). God's faithfulness is known through this order.

Creation is also a place of wonder. The author of Psalm 139, reflecting on how God "knits" each child together in the mother's womb, says, "I praise you, for I am fearfully and wonderfully made. Wonderful are your works; that I know very well" (v. 14). This wonder and beauty of creation bear the fingerprints of the Lord's faithfulness.

The Lord's Faithfulness in History

According to the Psalms, history is also an arena of God's faithfulness. Within history, God has proven faithful by being faithful to Abraham and Sarah's descendants:

> It is he who remembered us in our low estate,
>> for his loving faithfulness endures forever;
> and rescued us from our foes,
>> for his loving faithfulness endures forever. (136:23–24, modified)

The Psalms view Israel's history with God as the long and sad story of how Israel consistently proved unfaithful to God: "They did not remember the greatness of your loving faithfulness" (106:7 AT); "They were rebellious in their intentions" (106:43 AT). Yet the Lord was faithful and forgiving: "For their sake he remembered his covenant, and showed compassion according to the greatness of his loving faithfulness" (106:45, modified). Why did God forgive? Because it is God's nature to be faithful.

According to the Psalms, God's faithfulness often took the form of wondrous acts. These acts include the promises God made to Abraham and Sarah and the actions he took to be faithful to those promises: "the covenant that he made with Abraham, his sworn promise to Isaac" (105:9). In theological terms, this action is referred to as *election*—God's act of choosing Abraham and Sarah and their descendants (see 105:12–15). Because of this election, God proved faithful to Abraham, Sarah, and their descendants in many other wondrous acts of deliverance and rescue. The Lord "remembered his holy promise, and Abraham, his servant" (105:42).

The Lord's Faithfulness and the Prayers for Help

The prayers for help in the Psalter are based on two fundamental assumptions. First, the prayers are the petitions and complaints of those who understand themselves to be in a covenantal relationship with a faithful God. Second, the psalmists believe that God has the ability to alter the situation of crisis in which they find themselves.

Sometimes, the psalmists' crises are the result of enemies' oppression. In these cases, they insist that their only hope is the faithfulness and steadfast love of the Lord: "Wondrously show your loving faithfulness, O savior of those who seek refuge from their adversaries" (17:7, modified; see also 31:16; 40:1; 44:26; 69:13; 109:26). At other times, people can be their own worst enemies and commit significant sins that land them in trouble with both the human and divine authorities. At these times, once again, the psalmists claim their only hope is the faithfulness of God, and they plead for forgiveness: "Be mindful of your mercy, O Lord, and of your faithfulness, for they are from old. Do not remember the sins of my youth or my transgressions; according to your loving faithfulness, remember me, for the sake of your goodness, O Lord" (25:6–7, modified; see also 51:1–2).

Fig. 20.4. Psalm 100, known as "Old Hundreth" because of the well-known musical setting of the psalm as "All People That on Earth Do Dwell," is a favorite psalm. The psalm depicts the literal fulfillment of the Psalms' admonition that all people of all lands worship the Lord with joy and song.

The Lord's Faithfulness and the Psalms of Trust

In the psalms of trust, spoken in crisis yet from a posture of faith, the psalmists completely throw themselves into the arms of the Lord's faithfulness. As Psalm 52 expresses, "I am like a thriving olive tree in God's house; I trust in the faithfulness of God forever and ever" (52:8 AT). Drawing richly from the symbolic world available to them, the psalmists use powerful metaphors to describe their dire circumstances—"the valley of the shadow of death" (23:4 KJV); "evildoers [who] assail me to devour my flesh" (27:2); "the mountains [that] shake in the heart of the sea" (46:2). They also use metaphors to speak of God's faithful presence and help—"Your faithfulness reaches to the skies" (57:10 AT); "my shepherd" (23:1); "my light and my salvation" (27:1); "our refuge and strength" (46:1).

A brief prayer near the end of Psalm 90 offers a fitting summary of this major theme: "Satisfy us in the morning with your steadfast love, so that we may rejoice and be glad all our days" (v. 14).

Historical Interpretation

As noted earlier in the chapter, there are historical psalms—psalms that narrate or elaborate on certain parts of the history of Israel and Judah. These psalms include 78, 105–6, and 135–36. In addition, many other psalms are useful to historians as they seek to reconstruct the history of the Old Testament or various aspects of daily life and the worship life of ancient Israel. For the vast majority of people, however, the poetry and spirituality of the Psalms has been more important.

FOR FURTHER READING: **Psalms**

Brueggemann, Walter. *The Psalms and the Life of Faith*. Edited by Patrick D. Miller. Minneapolis: Fortress, 1995.

DeClaissé-Walford, Nancy L. *Introduction to the Psalms: A Song from Ancient Israel*. St. Louis: Chalice, 2004.

Jacobson, Rolf A., and Karl N. Jacobson. *Invitation to the Psalms: A Reader's Guide for Discovery and Engagement*. Grand Rapids: Baker Academic, 2013.

McCann, J. Clinton, Jr. *A Theological Introduction to the Book of Psalms: The Psalms as Torah*. Nashville: Abingdon, 1993.

Miller, Patrick D. *Interpreting the Psalms*. Philadelphia: Fortress, 1986.

Wenham, Gordon J. *Psalms as Torah: Reading Biblical Song Ethically*. Studies in Theological Interpretation. Grand Rapids: Baker Academic, 2012.

Proverbs

Every culture generates proverbs—short, pithy statements that contain essential wisdom about life, the world, and truth. Coaches, teachers, parents, and others authority figures are often the source of these nuggets of wisdom. One coach says, "Focus on what you can control." A grandparent says, "Measure twice, cut once." A boss says, "All the excuses in the world are not worth the smallest result." Through these types of sayings, the tradition and wisdom of the past are handed down to the next generations.

The book of Proverbs is the Old Testament's collection of such wisdom. The Hebrew name for the book, *Mishle*, can be translated as "proverbs" or "wise sayings." In the Jewish canon, the book is part of the Writings; in the Christian Old Testament, it is situated between Psalms and Ecclesiastes. Proverbs is part of a larger collection of biblical wisdom texts, including Job, Ecclesiastes, and some of the Psalms. Wisdom literature is concerned with questions such as, What is the good life? What is wisdom? What can we know about this world? How should we deal with challenges? How should we interact with people in society?

Background

Composition and Development

According to tradition, the author of Proverbs is Solomon, remembered for his great wisdom. The first verse of the book reads, "The proverbs of Solomon son of David, king of Israel." But the book contains other attributions as well. Two sections begin by saying, "The words of the wise" (22:17) and "These also belong to the wise" (24:23 AT). Proverbs 25 begins, "These are the

Fig. 21.1. The Gutenberg Bible was the first major book published using a movable-type printing press. The first page of its second volume, containing the opening of the book of Proverbs, includes a tall *P* into which an image of King Solomon was fashioned. The ornate birds and monkey in the margins are merely for decoration. A massive investment was required to print such a huge and ornate book, and Gutenberg went broke on the project. Perhaps he was comforted by Proverbs 22:2: "The rich and the poor have this in common: the Lord is the creator of all of them" (AT).

proverbs of Solomon that the men of King Hezekiah of Judah copied" (v. 1 AT). Chapter 30 contains "the words of Agur son of Jakeh" (v. 1), and chapter 31 has "the words of King Lemuel; a pronouncement that his mother taught him" (v. 1 AT).

So it is clear that the book of Proverbs is a collection of subcollections that grew over time in a manner that cannot be reconstructed. Many scholars doubt that the collection originated with Solomon, although many of the proverbs are undoubtedly ancient. The collections in chapters 10–30 are likely more ancient. The vocabulary and style of chapters 1–9 and 31 suggest that these chapters were among the last sections added to the more ancient material—perhaps as late as 300 BCE.

Genre

Despite the book's title, it is much more than a mere collection of short sayings. Proverbs is an anthology of wisdom material that includes poems, pithy axioms, and lengthy discourses. While the material is organized into units, these sections are not sequentially arranged. This structural insight should shape how a reader approaches the book. In the words of Ellen Davis, "Read straight through, they are tedious and they run together in the mind, for there is no plot, no consistent development of a logical argument or a moral theme. But it is a quite different thing when one encounters them as they are meant to be *heard* (and not, in the first instance, read). Proverbs are meant to be pondered, one at a time."[1]

Whatever its literary forms, the book features relatable truths about life, which can be learned from careful observation of the world. For Proverbs, the world is ordered in such a way that those who pay attention to it will, in general, fare better than those who do not. The book contains general truths that are applicable in some but not all cases.

Box 21.1

Humor and Truth Telling in Proverbs

Humorous proverbs are not only more memorable; they also can be more poignant. Reinhold Niebuhr notes that the "intimate relation between humor and faith is derived from the fact that both deal with the incongruities of our existence."* Humor is a form of truth telling. It can work by pointing out the absurdities of life in such a way that we laugh at them but also learn from them. Just think—a gold ring in a pig's snout! A dog eating its own vomit! Yes, some people are sort of like those things.

* Reinhold Niebuhr, *Discerning the Signs of the Times: Sermons for Today and Tomorrow* (New York: Scribner's Sons, 1946), 112.

Proverbs often communicate truth through humor. But the humor itself is not the point—proverbs that are humorous are not jokes told simply to make one laugh. They use humor in order to teach wisdom. The proverbial use of humor has several dimensions. First, because some proverbs are funny, they are more memorable and therefore more effective. Consider a couple of humorous proverbs:

> Like a dog that returns to its vomit,
>   so is the foolish man who takes his own advice. (26:11 AT)

> Like a gold ring in a pig's snout,
>   so is a beautiful woman without sense. (11:22 AT)

> As a door turns on its hinges,
>   so the lazy man turns in his bed. (26:14 AT)

> The constant dripping of a rainy day
>   and a bickering wife are alike. (27:15 AT)

These proverbs are also true of bickering husbands, beautiful but senseless men, and lazy or foolish women. The sheer humor of these proverbs makes them memorable.

The social context of the book of Proverbs is more difficult to determine. It seems likely that traditional wisdom material was taken from a variety of social contexts (e.g., the family, daily life, the royal court) and then integrated

Box 21.2

Outline

1. The proverbs of Solomon (1–9)
2. Additional proverbs of Solomon (10:1–22:16)
3. The words of the sages (22:17–24:34)
4. Additional proverbs of Solomon, copied by men of King Hezekiah (25–29)
5. The words of Agur (30)
6. The admonitions of King Lemuel's mother; the woman of substance (31)

into what we now call the book of Proverbs. This book was most likely curated for the use of young men who were trained to serve in the courts of the rulers.

Literary Interpretation

Proverbs is poetry. This fact should shape how readers approach the book. The choice to convey wisdom via poetry was a significant one on the part of Israel's scribes. Proverbial texts are typically short, but that does not mean that we should read them quickly. As readers wade into Proverbs, they should treat the task of reading the book with the same care and intention that went into writing it.

The proverbs of Solomon (Prov. 1–9). The book of Proverbs begins with sayings from Israel's most famous sage, King Solomon. This section opens with a prologue (1:1–7) that introduces the entire book. It tells the reader why the book exists and how it should be used. For example, Proverbs is "for the knowing of wisdom and instruction, for comprehending words of discernment, to take in prudent instruction—righteousness, justice, and equity," and so on (1:2–3 AT). The prologue wants the reader to understand that "fear of the Lord is the beginning of knowledge" and that "wisdom and instruction are despised by fools" (1:7 AT).

Chapters 1–9 read as a coherent sequence. They feature an imaginative scenario in which a father instructs his son in how to live wisely. The reader (i.e., "you") is to receive his words and obey them as the final word on the workings of the world. These chapters also prominently feature Woman Wisdom and Woman Stranger. Woman Wisdom augments the authoritative voice of the father, and she declares to the son that wisdom alone brings true happiness (1:20–33; 8:1–9:6). Her value is greater than material riches (3:13–18). She is a "tree of life" (3:18) to those that cling to her. Woman Wisdom's association with the creation of the world (8:22–31) makes her a mythic, even goddess-like figure, granting her added authority when addressing the son. Woman Stranger, on the other hand, tempts young men with smooth and tantalizing words (2:16–19; 5:1–23; 6:20–35; 7:1–27). But according to the father, the sweetness is only temporary. Woman Stranger's

---

Box 21.3

Ellen Davis on the Poetry of Proverbs

Ellen Davis notes, "Poetry is the kind of language best suited to probing the inexhaustible mystery of the human situation *in its entirety*, and that is exactly what wisdom seeks to explore. Prose is the tool of analysis, of explanation, of scientific and academic research. But poetry looks at phenomena whole. . . . [It is] language that is primarily designed to engage the imagination."*

* Ellen F. Davis, *Proverbs, Ecclesiastes, and the Song of Songs*, Westminster Bible Companion (Louisville: Westminster John Knox, 2000), 19.

words lead one to death and destruction (7:26–27).

Carol Newsom draws attention to the fact that these chapters are deeply and uncritically shaped by the discourse of the patriarchal family.[2] Within that ecosystem, maleness is normative, making "woman" the primary symbol of otherness and, in the case of Woman Stranger, a symbol of threat. While both Woman Wisdom and Woman Stranger are personifications of women that stem from stereotypes projected by men, Christine Roy Yoder writes, "Personified wisdom refuses to remain captive to female stereotypes. . . . Wisdom strides with increasing boldness across time, texts, and testaments, captivating the imaginations of many and taking on a robust life of her own."[3]

Titian

Fig. 21.2. Woman Wisdom is portrayed here in her heavenly role as one created at the beginning of creation (8:22) and as one who mediates divine instruction (8:32).

Additional proverbs of Solomon (Prov. 10:1–22:16). The second collection of proverbs is also attributed to Solomon, but it reads very differently from Proverbs 1–9. Rather than being a coherent sequence, the collection's coherence comes from the nature of the collection itself. The texts in this section represent what most people think about when they hear the word *proverb*. A proverb is a pithy and poetic maxim about various aspects of human life. The sayings in Proverbs 10:1–22:16 reflect a variety of life situations, but they generally steer the reader away from foolishness and in the direction of the wise life. Consider the following examples:

> He who loves instruction loves knowledge,
>   but he who hates correction is stupid. (12:1 AT)

> He who works his soil will have enough food;
>   but he who chases worthless things is devoid of sense. (12:11 AT)

> He who guards his mouth preserves his life;
>   he who opens wide his lips receives ruin. (13:3 AT)

> Commit your deeds to Yahweh,
>   and your plans will be established. (16:3 AT)

Proverbs 22:17–24:22 and the Instruction of Amenemope

Proverbs 22:17–24:22 parallels an Egyptian wisdom collection, the Instruction of Amenemope, in both structure and content. A few examples will illustrate the point.

> Give your ears and hear what is said,
>   give your mind over to their interpretation:
> It is profitable to put them in your heart,
>   but woe to him that neglects them!
> Let them rest in the shrine of your belly
>   that they may act as a lock in your heart. (Instruction of Amenemope)*

> Incline your ear and hear words of wisdom;
>   and set your heart to my instruction.
> For it is pleasing that you keep them deep within you;
>   they are prepared on your lips. (Prov. 22:17–18 AT)

> Do not displace the surveyor's marker
>   on the boundaries of the arable land,
> nor alter the position of the measuring line. (Instruction of Amenemope)†

> Do not move an ancient boundary
>   that was made by your ancestors. (Prov. 22:28 AT)

The close relationship between these texts bears witness to the widespread use of wisdom literature in the broader ancient Near East.

* Christopher B. Hays, *Hidden Riches: A Sourcebook for the Comparative Study of the Hebrew Bible and Ancient Near East* (Louisville: Westminster John Knox, 2014), 298.
† Hays, *Hidden Riches*, 300.

The words of the sages (Prov. 22:17–24:34). The proverbs in 22:17–24:22, attributed to "the wise," are typical maxims about the virtuous and disciplined life. One troubling and well-known parable states, "Do not refrain from disciplining a boy. . . . If you strike him with a rod, you will save his life from Sheol" (23:13–14 AT). Proverbs 24:23–34 is a small section attributed simply to "the sages" (24:23). The first part of the collection is made up of typical maxims focused especially on speech and honest living (24:23–29). The section closes with a short didactic narrative about the dangers of the lazy life (24:30–34).

Additional proverbs of Solomon, copied by men of King Hezekiah (Prov. 25–29). Solomon is also associated with the collection of Proverbs in chapters 25–29, but in this case, the proverbs are said to be copied by men of King Hezekiah (25:1). The unit contains a variety of sayings to address different scenarios. Special emphasis is placed on behavior in the royal court (25:2–7), and several sections use comparison as a pedagogical device:

Like golden apples in settings of silver is a well-put phrase. (25:11 AT)

Like the fastening of a stone in a sling is giving honor to a fool.
(26:8 AT)

As a door turns on its hinges, so the lazy man turns in his bed.
(26:14 AT)

The words of Agur (Prov. 30). The next section is titled "The words of Agur son of Jakeh." The chapter contains an assortment of seemingly unrelated poems and statements. Verses 1–6 contain a strange first-person poem that appears to value piety over wisdom. Verses 7–10 are also in the first person and offer a pious prayer in which the supplicant asks to be given only what he needs, lest his satisfaction lead him to renounce Yahweh. Verses 11–14 reflect on the types of men who bring curses down upon their ancestors. They are marked by delusion, haughtiness, and disregard for the poor. Finally, verses 15–31 contain a variety of sayings, some of which are marked by a typically Semitic, numerical way of introducing and remembering a saying:

> There are three things that are too wonderful for me,
> and four that I cannot comprehend:
> the way of the eagle in the heavens,
> the way of the snake on a rock,
> the way of a ship upon the sea,
> and the way of a man with a woman. (30:18–19 AT)

The admonitions of King Lemuel's mother; the woman of substance (Prov. 31). Chapter 31 is made up of two units (vv. 1–9 and vv. 10–31). Verses 1–9 contain the admonitions of the mother of an unknown King Lemuel, and verses 10–31 extol and describe the "woman of substance."[4] Both units feature the words and actions of exceptional women occupying traditional roles: mother and wife. Proverbs begins with admonitions from the father (chaps. 1–9) and here ends with reflections from a mother and about a woman of substance.

Verses 10–31 warrant special comment given their long history of (mis)interpretation and (mis)appropriation. Structured as a Hebrew acrostic poem, these verses poetically extol the "woman of substance." She and her household lack nothing because she is an effective and energetic manager of her household's operations, goods, and holdings. She is an economic force! She buys and sells fields, plants a vineyard, markets merchandise, manages a staff, and produces products. Her work is so fruitful that it is compared to an entire fleet of ships (v. 14). The woman of substance is generous toward the poor (v. 20) and has no fear of the future because of her diligent work (vv. 20–21). She herself speaks

Fig. 21.3. The woman of substance is undoubtedly an idealized depiction, but there is no reason to believe that women in ancient Israel could not operate in society as she does. This stained-glass portrayal of the woman of substance captures the ways in which she enters the economic sphere and leads her household.

and utters wisdom (v. 26). The poem provides a suitable end to Proverbs when it lauds the woman's fear of the Lord:

> Grace is deceitful,
>   and beauty is meaningless.
> A woman who fears Yahweh,
>   she is worthy of praise. (31:30 AT; cf. 1:7)

Theological Interpretation

Proverbs is a rich work of theology. From beginning to end, the authors' and editors' reflections on daily life were grounded in a number of important theological convictions about how the world actually works. Because Proverbs lacks references to many of Israel's most important theological traditions—such as the covenants with Abraham, Moses, and David; the royal theology of Jerusalem and its temple; major themes such as sin, judgment, forgiveness, and restoration; or the prophetic insistence on both justice and hope—some interpreters used to think of Proverbs as nontheological. But this mistaken notion misses that Proverbs does theology in a different key.

A Discernible Creation

Proverbs emphasizes God's work in creation. The world is created with Woman Wisdom (3:19–20), who is herself a transcendent and mythic figure. In stark contrast to Ecclesiastes (see chap. 22, "Ecclesiastes"), Proverbs is confident in the human ability to comprehend the patterns and rhythms of God's creation. Woman Wisdom stands on the busy streets of this world crying out in search of eager pupils (1:20–21). The path to the "good life" is accessible to all who have an open ear and a humble heart. The path to wisdom is also apparent. Those willing to use their minds, submit to the teaching of the past, and avoid temptation will find themselves on the clear path of wisdom.

But God's work in creation is not limited to the originating act. God is active in the world and in ways that should lead to trust in his goodness (3:5–6; 16:20; 22:19; 28:25; 29:25). For Proverbs, trust in God is the source of true riches and joy (16:20; 28:25).

Despite the clear theological convictions of Proverbs, the book is devoid of references to important Israelite narratives, such as the exodus, the wilderness years, and Mount Sinai. Apart from references to specific kings like Solomon or Hezekiah, we hear basically nothing about Israel's national story as related in Genesis–Kings or Chronicles. These stories often feature Yahweh's revelations about Israel's legal obligations and responsibilities. For Proverbs, however, revelation about the world emerges as a consequence of human reason, experience, and reflection, not divine disclosure.

Fear of the Lord

The book of Proverbs repeatedly exhorts its readers to fear the Lord (1:7; 3:7; 8:13; 9:10; 10:27; etc.). The word *fear* might seem like a strange choice of words in this context. What does it mean to fear the Lord? In the context of Proverbs, one should not associate fear with words like *terror* or *dread*.

Fig. 21.4. Solomon teaching proverbs to the people.

Instead, fear manifests itself in a willingness to receive correction, instruction, and admonishment. A person who fears the Lord is an attentive learner and a diligent student. The fear of the Lord is about willingness to be shaped by voices and traditions from the past.

Historical Interpretation

Even though Proverbs is short on historical references, the book nonetheless highlights important issues in Israelite history and culture. The book is self-consciously an anthology of collected writings and sayings. These individual components emerged from a variety of social settings, including family life, commerce, scribal circles, and the royal court. While it is difficult to provide details beyond these generalizations, Proverbs as a whole offers a glimpse into how individuals and communities were shaped through traditional ideas and artfully crafted teachings.

We will probably never know the degree to which Solomon's reputation as a sagely king corresponds to the historical reality. But we can know with certainty that his reputation and the teachings associated with him had an immense impact on generations of Jews and Christians seeking to live a wise life, up to the present day. Proverbs is similar to other ancient Near Eastern wisdom texts. This is nowhere more apparent than in Proverbs 22:17–24:22, which has clearly been influenced by the Egyptian Instruction of Amenemope (see above). The precise method of transmission is unknown. We do know, however, that wisdom literature and the scribal culture that preserved it were cosmopolitan in nature.[5] Scribal texts and ideas were transmitted across cultures and languages on a seemingly regular basis. The fact that Proverbs contains material that so clearly echoes other ancient Near Eastern texts bears witness to the lively exchange of ideas and texts that likely took place among scribal circles.

FOR FURTHER READING: **Proverbs**

Davis, Ellen F. *Proverbs, Ecclesiastes, and the Song of Songs.* Westminster Bible Companion. Louisville: Westminster, 2000.

Fox, Michael V. *Proverbs 1–9: A New Translation with Introduction and Commentary.* Anchor Bible 18A. New York: Doubleday, 2000.

———. *Proverbs 10–31: A New Translation with Introduction and Commentary.* Anchor Yale Bible 18B. New Haven: Yale University Press, 2009.

Murphy, Roland E. *The Tree of Life: An Exploration of Biblical Wisdom Literature.* 3rd ed. Grand Rapids: Eerdmans, 2002.

Newsom, Carol A. "Woman and the Discourse of Patriarchal Wisdom." In *Reading Bibles, Writing Bodies: Identity and the Book*, edited by Timothy K. Beal and David M. Gunn, 116–31. Biblical Limits. London: Routledge, 1997.

Perdue, Leo G. *Wisdom Literature: A Theological History.* Louisville: Westminster John Knox, 2007.

Stewart, Anne W. *Poetic Ethics in Proverbs: Wisdom Literature and the Shaping of the Moral Self.* New York: Cambridge University Press, 2016.

Yoder, Christine Roy. *Proverbs.* Abingdon Old Testament Commentaries. Nashville: Abingdon, 2009.

Ecclesiastes

The Hebrew title of the book of Ecclesiastes is *Qohelet*, which means "one who assembles" or "one who instructs." This title is taken from the first verse of the book: "The words of Qohelet, son of David, king in Jerusalem" (1:1 AT). "Ecclesiastes" (meaning "assembly") is how the Greek Septuagint translates *Qohelet*. The title is appropriate insofar as the book presents itself as the word of a particular sage who offers discourses on a wide variety of topics.

Ecclesiastes belongs to the larger collection of Wisdom literature, which includes Proverbs and Job (and some of the Psalms). As such, Ecclesiastes seeks to understand the world and determine how best to live in it. The book shares many assumptions with its wisdom counterparts, including its beliefs that the world was created by God and that human beings can explore that world with varying degrees of success.

While the book squarely fits within the category of Wisdom literature, there are also ways in which Ecclesiastes stands on its own. The book reaches a unique set of conclusions about the world that we will explore in greater detail below. Many of these conclusions will seem strange and maybe even unsettling. Ecclesiastes can be a frustrating book, especially for readers who are used to more optimistic literary fare. Be patient with the book, and you will find that it offers a thought-provoking way of navigating a deeply uncertain world.

Ecclesiastes reminds us that the biblical corpus does not speak with one voice on all matters. There is diversity in the canon, even among bodies of literature like Wisdom literature, which approach the world with similar questions.

Background

Composition and Development

The authorship of Ecclesiastes has traditionally been assigned to an aged Solomon, in accordance with the book's superscription: "The words of Qohelet, son of David, king in Jerusalem" (1:1 AT). Even though Solomon is never mentioned by name and the title "son of David" may refer to any king of Davidic lineage (including Jesus; see Matt. 1:1), tradition held that Solomon wrote most of the book of Ecclesiastes.

Several pieces of evidence suggest, however, that Ecclesiastes was written during the Persian period (539–333 BCE) or the Hellenistic period (333–63 BCE), long after the time of Solomon. The most convincing pieces of evidence are linguistic in nature. The book contains loan words from both Aramaic and Persian. For example, Ecclesiastes 2:5 uses the Persian word *pardes* ("orchard"). Persian loan words are particularly important since Israelites did not have any significant encounters with Persia until the sixth century BCE, hundreds of years after Solomon lived. The presence of Aramaic terminology also points to a later date when Aramaic was more prominent.

If the book was written later, then it was authored pseudonymously. Pseudonymity is the act of writing a text under the name and persona of someone else. This phenomenon might seem strange to modern readers, who are accustomed to the realities of intellectual property law. In the ancient world, however, pseudonymous authorship was not uncommon. Using the name of an ancient person from the past granted the text an air of authority that a contemporary author simply could not command. Given Solomon's reputation for wisdom (see 1 Kings 3), it is not surprising that he would be chosen as the authorial voice of a book on wisdom.

pseudonymity The practice of ancient authors attributing their own writings to other people, such as a revered teacher or prominent church leader who had influenced their thinking, using a pseudonym ("false name").

pseudonymous author An author who uses a pseudonym (fictitious name); the author of a pseudepigraphic text.

Box 22.1

Two Types of Israelite Wisdom

Scholars identify two types of wisdom in Israel's theological tradition. First, there is the positive or optimistic strain, which includes Proverbs and many psalms. In this strain, the authors view both the world and God as trustworthy, understandable, and sensible. Everyday life should be guided by common sense, a dedication to God, and a commitment to order and following the law. A second strain is negative or pessimistic, and it includes Job, Ecclesiastes, and other psalms. These writings call into question the simplistic assumptions of the positive strain. They question God's justice, the fairness of the world order, and the trustworthiness of creation. The fact that both strains of wisdom literature are present in the Old Testament bears witness to the complexity with which the Old Testament views life.

Genre

Ecclesiastes does not belong to any particular genre but includes elements from several different types of literature, including proverbs, sayings, autobiography, and narrative elements. However, the book should be read as a literary whole, not broken into independent parts. The journey from chapter 1 to chapter 12 is meandering but meaningful. Throughout the text, the author engages in a variety of experiments. He reflects on those experiments and reaches conclusions. Some of these conclusions persist and others are replaced.

Literary Interpretation

Ecclesiastes is demanding literature for any reader. It is meandering and exploratory, rather than sequential and straightforward, forcing the reader to slow down and remain attentive to the text. In addition to its challenging literary features, Ecclesiastes offers potentially disturbing answers to many of life's most nettlesome questions.

The book itself is loosely framed by the phrase "'Vanity of vanities,' says Qohelet" (1:2; 12:8 AT). Although it would be wrong to say that "vanity" is the singular message of the entire composition, it is nonetheless an important touchstone that the author returns to over and over again.

Superscription and prologue (Eccles. 1:1–11). Ecclesiastes begins with an introduction of Qohelet and some of the book's most persistent themes: the futility of pursuing gains in life, the cyclical nature of the cosmos, the assertion that nothing truly new ever happens, and the claim that even memory itself fades.

Part 1: Quest for wisdom (Eccles. 1:12–18). The book then pivots to describe Qohelet's attempts to seek and search out "by wisdom all that is done beneath the heavens" (1:13 AT). In this quest to study the world, he acquires tremendous wisdom (1:16). In the process, however, he learns two important lessons: (1) the pursuit of knowledge is "chasing after the wind" (1:17 AT), and (2) the pursuit of wisdom invites vexation and pain (1:18).

> ### Box 22.2
>
> ## Outline
>
> The structure of Ecclesiastes is difficult to determine with certainty. This outline is tentative at best.
>
> 1. Superscription and prologue (1:1–11)
> 2. Part 1—Life is toil and vanity, yet a gift from God (1:12–6:12)
>   a. Quest for wisdom (1:12–18)
>   b. Achievement, pleasure, and toil (2:1–26)
>   c. Seasons and times (3:1–22)
>   d. Human relationships (4:1–16)
>   e. Foolishness and wisdom (5:1–7)
>   f. Wealth and labor (5:8–6:12)
> 3. Part 2—The future is unknown, so enjoy the gift of life (7:1–10:20)
>   a. Maxims and reflections on wisdom (7:1–29)
>   b. Boundaries of wisdom (8:1–17)
>   c. Reflections on mortality (9:1–18)
>   d. Miscellaneous proverbs (10:1–20)
> 4. Part 3—Life is short, so enjoy and recall youth (11:1–12:8)
> 5. Epilogue: Fear God (12:9–14)

Part 1: Achievement, pleasure, and toil (Eccles. 2:1–26). Qohelet then turns to reflect on pleasure, achievement, and the futility of work. His methodology of exploration changes somewhat in chapter 2. Here he engages in what are effectively experiments. For example, he says to himself, "I explored in my mind if it was possible to tempt my flesh with wine—my mind guiding me with wisdom—and how to apprehend folly, until I see what is good for humans to do under the heavens during the few days of their lives" (2:3 AT). After a lifetime of acquiring and achieving, Qohelet concludes that all of it was "vanity and a chasing after wind" (2:11). His reflection on life and its labors leads him to despair (2:20) and ultimately to conclude that there is nothing good for a person but to "eat and drink and find satisfaction in their own toil" (2:24 NIV).

Part 1: Seasons and times (Eccles. 3:1–22). Ecclesiastes 3 begins with these famous words: "For everything there is a season, and a time for every delight under heaven" (3:1 AT). What follows is a list of binaries, each of which begins with the phrase "a time to . . .": "A time to be born and a time to die, a time to plant and a time to uproot plants" (3:2 AT). God is explicitly said to be the one who set this system into place: "He [God] has made everything fitting in its time; what's more, he has placed eternity into their minds, without humanity ever discovering what God has done from beginning to end" (3:11 AT). Even as Qohelet unveils the mysteries of creation, he acknowledges limitations to that knowledge.

Box 22.3

A Time for Everything

A beautiful poem in Ecclesiastes 3 may be the most famous passage in the book. Legendary folk singer Pete Seeger wrote a famous song based on the chapter, "Turn! Turn! Turn!" The poem illustrates the whole of life through a series of contrasts:

> For everything there is a season, and a time for every delight under heaven:
>
> a time to be born, and a time to die;
>   a time to plant, and a time to uproot plants;
> a time to kill, and a time to heal;
>   a time to break down, and a time to build up;
> a time to cry, and a time to laugh;
>   a time to mourn, and a time to dance;
> a time to throw stones, and a time to gather stones;
>   a time to hug, and a time not to hug;
> a time to seek, and a time to lose;
>   a time to keep, and a time to throw away;
> a time to tear, and a time to sew;
>   a time to be quiet, and a time to speak;
> a time to love, and a time to hate;
>   a time for war, and a time for peace. (3:1–8 AT)

God's involvement in creation raises questions about the presence and persistence of evil in the world and about human mortality: "I saw still more under the sun: in place of justice, wickedness was there, and in place of righteousness, wickedness was there" (3:16 AT). Both the righteous and the wicked will be judged, each in their own time (3:17). Finally, Qohelet observes that the animals and human beings will have the same future. Both breathe the same air and share the same fate. What are the implications of this finding? "There is nothing better than each should enjoy his work, for that is his inheritance" (3:22 AT).

Part 1: Human relationships (Eccles. 4:1–16). Ecclesiastes 4 contains a set of observations about human relationships and activities. The oppressor's cruel misuse of power means that the happiest members of humanity are those who are either dead or unborn (4:2–3). In Qohelet's estimation, enterprise and skilled labor emerge out of one person's envy for another and are futile. He notes the futility of a person's work to amass wealth and goods if there is no meaningful community with whom to enjoy the fruits of this labor. Companionship is a superior way. The reward for joint toil is greater, and companions can help one another in time of need. The final observation concerns the superiority of a poor, wise youth over an old, foolish king. The former can ascend from a prison, but the latter's foolishness can bring him to ruin. Yet even in the case of the poor man who becomes a king, this is still futility, because his accomplishments were never known to generations past, and they will be forgotten by the generations of the future. Whatever name he might make for himself will be erased from memory.

Part 1: Foolishness and wisdom (Eccles. 5:1–7). The next section offers advice on interacting with God and avoiding zealous or otherwise foolish behavior. Akin to other wisdom literature, these verses pay particular attention to dangers of the tongue. Qohelet urges his readers to "not be reckless with your mouth, nor let your heart be quick to speak a word before God; for God is in the heavens and you are upon the earth. Therefore let your words be few" (5:2 AT).

Part 1: Wealth and labor (Eccles. 5:8–6:12). According to conventional wisdom, those who voraciously acquire wealth and resources may seem to be in a better position than those without such advantages. But according to Ecclesiastes, abundant wealth does not necessarily translate into good living and is in fact another futile venture (5:8–20). The rich are never satisfied (5:10), and

---

Box 22.4

Ecclesiastes in Popular Culture

Ecclesiastes has had a wide influence in literature and culture. Shakespeare's Sonnet 59 cites Ecclesiastes 1:9. Ernest Hemingway's famous novel *The Sun Also Rises* (which was made into a movie) takes its title from Ecclesiastes 1:5. Edith Wharton's *The House of Mirth* takes its title from Ecclesiastes 7:4, and Laura Lippman's *Every Secret Thing* draws from Ecclesiastes 12:14.

Fig. 22.1. Qohelet finds purpose in one good thing: "to eat and to drink and to find enjoyment in all of his toil that he toils under the sun the few days of the life that God gave him" (5:18 AT).

they so fear losing their wealth that sleep escapes them. All their exertions are for naught, since the rich will leave this world in the same way that they came into it: naked and empty-handed (5:15). Qohelet finds only one good thing for the rich and the poor alike: "to eat and to drink and to find enjoyment in all of his toil that he toils under the sun the few days of the life that God gave him—for this is his lot" (5:18 AT). Eunny Lee writes, "Qohelet's notion of enjoyment entails an authentic experience of the world that recognizes both its tragic limitations and its joyous possibilities of good."[1]

Ecclesiastes continues its teaching on wealth and labor in chapter 6. The emphasis on the futility of gathering wealth is maintained, illustrated by the tragic situation in which God permits a stranger to enjoy another person's riches. All of the time spent accumulating wealth is futile, since neither the rich person nor the kinship group will have access to it. In such a case, an unburied stillborn is more fortunate (6:3). Qohelet then ponders whether there is any advantage at all in being wise or foolish, rich or poor (6:7–9).

At this point, Qohelet reveals his sense of humanity's boundaries, not only in terms of agency but also in terms of epistemology. Human action is futile because "whatever has happened has already been named" (6:10 AT), and humanity is not strong enough to resist (6:11). With regard to epistemology, Qohelet argues that it is impossible to determine what is good for mortals, given the limited amount of time in their fleeting lives (6:12).

Part 2: Maxims and reflections on wisdom (Eccles. 7:1–29). In the second major part of the book, Qohelet reflects on the uncertainty of the future and therefore the need to enjoy the gift of life. These reflections begin with a collection of proverbial statements (7:1–10) that compare superior and inferior things: the "day of death" is superior to the "day of birth" (7:1); it is better to go to the "house of mourning" than to the "house of feasting" (7:2), and "the heart of the wise is in the house of mourning" (7:4); both death and mourning are the common end of all living things, and "better is the end of a thing than its beginning" (7:8).

The second part of chapter 7 offers a meditation on wisdom itself (7:11–29). This section begins with laudatory language. Wisdom offers protection and gives life (7:12), but the world is not entirely predictable, and wisdom cannot always protect against the vagaries of history. Qohelet admits that the righteous perish and the evil prolong their life (7:15). The incomprehensibility of the world places limits on human inquiry: "All this I have tested with wisdom. I said, 'I will be wise,' but it was far from me. That which is far off and exceedingly deep—who can discover it?" (7:23–24 AT). Wisdom comes in knowing the limits of human reasoning.

Part 2: Boundaries of wisdom (Eccles. 8:1–17). Chapter 8 continues to emphasize the limits of wisdom. Within the context of a royal court, Qohelet observes that obeying the king's command as if it were the absolute authority is a wise decision to make (8:1–5). But there are limits even to this wisdom, since not even a king can hold back death: "No one has authority over wind [spirit] in order to restrain it or authority over the day of death" (8:8 AT).

The chapter also explores the limits of wisdom in making sense of the cosmos's moral fabric. Traditional wisdom suggests that positive consequences result from wise or righteous deeds, and similarly that foolishness and evil beget negative consequences. Qohelet's observation of the world says otherwise (8:9–14). All of this is vanity. Instead, he reiterates his earlier conclusion that "there is nothing better for human beings under the sun, except to eat, drink, and enjoy themselves" (8:15 AT).

Part 2: Reflections on mortality (Eccles. 9:1–18). Mortality plays an important role in Qohelet's teaching about wisdom and the world. Whether for the righteous or wicked, animal or human, the same fate awaits every living thing. Yet even given this dismal destination of the living, the dead have it worse: they have nothing to look forward to. They are forgotten and have nothing to live for (9:4–6). So Qohelet again urges his readers to eat and drink in gladness

(9:7), wear fresh and washed clothes (9:8), enjoy life with the woman you love (9:9), and toil at whatever work you can find, because in Sheol there is neither work nor wisdom (9:10).

Part 2: Miscellaneous proverbs (Eccles. 10:1–20). The second part of Ecclesiastes concludes with a collection of miscellaneous proverbs about wisdom, foolishness, the moral fabric of the cosmos, and rulers. Some proverbs draw on themes from other chapters, and others employ new language.

Part 3—Life is short, so enjoy and recall youth (Eccles. 11:1–12:8). Beginning in chapter 11, Qohelet offers one of his strongest appeals to live fully into the moment because "you do not know what disaster may come upon the land" (11:2 NIV). Spending too much time trying to predict the future prevents a person from doing the important work of sowing and reaping (11:4–6). We can only be certain of death and the nothingness it represents (11:8). He urges the young to enjoy life while they are young, for it quickly dissipates (it is "vanity," 11:10), but to do so knowing that God will one day hold them to account (11:9). The young should do this because the days of sorrow and death are coming (12:1–8).

Epilogue: Fear God (Eccles. 12:9–14). The book concludes with an epilogue that may, at first glance, feel out of sync with the preceding materials. The last verses of the book mark the end of Qohelet's first-person discourses and describe him in the third person (cf. 1:1). Verses 9–11 describe Qohelet as one who taught others by seeking out, studying, and recording wise sayings. Verses 12–14 attempt a summary of Qohelet's work using the pious language of traditional Wisdom literature: "Fear God and keep his commandments, for this is everything for all humanity" (12:13 AT). This summary may not be

---

Box 22.5

All That Is Vanity

The book of Ecclesiastes famously begins, "'Vanity of vanities,' says Qohelet, 'vanity of vanities, all is vanity'" (1:2 AT). The word translated "vanity" literally means "smoke" or "vapor"—that which is inherently illusive, ungraspable, insubstantial. Qohelet says all the following things are vanity:

- wisdom (1:16–18; 2:15–16)
- pleasure (2:1–11)
- work (2:18–23)
- success and envy (4:4–6)
- individuality (4:7–8)
- dreams (5:7)
- love of money (5:11–20)
- achievement without joy (6:1–6)

- wanton desire (6:7–9)
- laughter of fools (7:6)
- vain praise (8:10)
- unjust reward/punishment (8:14)
- the future (11:8)

as discordant with earlier chapters as one might initially think, since Qohelet elsewhere urges fear of God (5:7; 7:18; 8:12, 13).

Theological Interpretation

Ecclesiastes offers some of the most thought-provoking theology in all of the Old Testament. Many readers will find that it is unsatisfying, disturbing, and pessimistic. Its view of death as the ruthless leveler of all living things will no doubt raise eyebrows among those who hold to a future resurrection. Even if a reader ultimately rejects some of Qohelet's claims, his work ought to engender respect as a rigorous attempt to make sense of a complicated world. In that sense, Qohelet is a model of critical and reflective inquiry.

Human Limitations

Qohelet is keenly aware of the limits placed on human beings as creatures of this world. People may set their minds to understand the world, acquire wealth, and build a name, but ultimately they will bump up against the inertial forces of time, history, and finitude. Time limits our lifespans. History's cyclical nature means that nothing truly novel will ever exist. The human capacity to learn and reason is limited by the often-unpredictable world we inhabit. There are seasons for everything, which means there are temporal limits on all activities under the sun. Events are also limited by God's will: "Whatever has happened has already been named" (6:10 AT). The book of Ecclesiastes encourages its readers to respect the limitations placed on humanity.

The book also attempts to create a deep sense of humility in the human quest to understand how the world works. This is especially true when it comes to understanding the moral fabric of creation. As Qohelet sees it, deeds do not necessarily correspond to consequences—at least not in a way that is perceptible: the wicked often go unpunished; no one can foresee when doom will strike; and sometimes the righteous are treated like the wicked (8:5–14).

Futility

For the book of Ecclesiastes, many things in this life are futile or "vanity": the acquisition of wealth, chasing after renown, achieving great things, and so on. Qohelet would no doubt look at many of our dreams, aspirations, and anxieties and call them vanity. But none of this means that Qohelet is calling us to run out the clock in a joyless march to the grave. Instead, for Qohelet, "the gift of enjoyment and the futility of gain are two sides of the same coin."[2] Qohelet's despair does not lead him to nihilism. Instead, it leads him to enjoy and embrace the gifts of this world—especially those experienced around the table.[3] It is there that relationships are built, love is kindled, and the gifts of creation are enjoyed.

Qohelet would make a terrible graduation speaker. His views of the world sit uncomfortably alongside the typical optimism of high school and college graduates. Whereas the typical graduation speaker might say, "Go and change the world," Qohelet would say, "Your ability to understand this world and to impact it are limited. Whatever efforts you make will quickly be forgotten after you join every other living creature in the ground. Instead, fulfill your responsibilities, respect your limitations, and enjoy the gifts life offers you."

Historical Interpretation

Even though Ecclesiastes is not specifically about historical events, it raises important historical questions. Unfortunately, most of those questions do not come with easy answers. For example, if Ecclesiastes is pseudonymously authored, then what can we know about the real author? Why did the author choose to use Solomon—Qohelet—as his voice? For whom was the book written? What can we know about the community the book purports to address? Does Ecclesiastes represent a conventional or critical voice within the broader wisdom tradition?

We know very little about the circumstances surrounding the authorship and production of Ecclesiastes, apart from some very general facts. If the dating posited earlier in the chapter is correct, then the book was written during a generally tumultuous period when domination of the ancient Near East changed hands multiple times and when the postexilic community struggled to reestablish itself under difficult circumstances. Despite the tumult, this period proved to be one of the most fruitful periods in Jewish history. It saw the completion of remarkable texts like Chronicles, Ezra-Nehemiah, and many other canonical and noncanonical works. Ecclesiastes belongs to this period of exceptional literary creativity.

FOR FURTHER READING: **Ecclesiastes**

Bartholomew, Craig G. *Ecclesiastes*. Baker Commentary on the Old Testament Wisdom and Psalms. Grand Rapids: Baker Academic, 2009.

Brown, William P. *Ecclesiastes*. Interpretation: A Bible Commentary for Teaching and Preaching. Louisville: John Knox, 2000.

Fox, Michael V. *A Time to Tear Down and a Time to Build Up: A Rereading of Ecclesiastes*. Grand Rapids: Eerdmans, 1999.

Heim, Knut Martin. *Ecclesiastes: An Introduction and Commentary*. Tyndale Old Testament Commentaries. Downers Grove, IL: IVP Academic, 2019.

Seow, Choon-Leong. *Ecclesiastes: A New Translation with Introduction and Commentary*. Anchor Bible 18C. New York: Doubleday, 1997.

Song of Songs

Here is a delightful bit of trivia about the Song of Songs: No book of the Bible was commented upon more in medieval monasteries than the Song. The Song of Songs is the title of a book that is also known as the Song of Solomon, Canticles, or simply the Song. The title "The Song of Solomon" reflects the ancient tradition that King Solomon wrote the book. The Hebrew title, *Shir hashirim*, means "the song of songs" or even "the greatest of songs," like other superlative formulations in Hebrew (see "Lord of lords," Deut. 10:17; "king of kings," Dan. 2:37). As this title indicates, the book is an incomparable composition, and it is also one of the most intriguing books in the Old Testament.

The Song of Songs is a unique collection of poetic exchanges that explore the amorous relationship between two unnamed lovers. These exchanges are augmented by a third set of voices, the "daughters of Jerusalem," who offer commentary on the lovers' relationship. Song of Songs is not a story or a narrative. It is best understood as a collection of lyric poems organized according to a repeating cycle of absence and presence. The poems, in turn, reflect the lovers' sense of longing, desire, and delight.

The Song of Songs is also unique in its depiction of mutuality between the female and the male lover. Neither partner dominates the other. They both pursue, desire, and enjoy one another. This depiction of human romantic love stands in stark contrast to how male-female relationships are described elsewhere in the Old Testament, leading some to argue that the Song of Songs may have been written by a woman.

Whatever the case, the Song of Songs is one of the greatest poetic achievements of the Old Testament. It is worthy of careful study and consideration. Religious communities often express discomfort with erotic representations of human sexuality, especially when those representations place such heavy

Fig. 23.1. Although God's name never appears in the Song of Songs, the book was nevertheless the most commented upon book in the medieval period, as this page from the twelfth-century Winchester Bible exemplifies. It was interpreted allegorically as a love story between God and his people.

emphasis on desire and enjoyment. Studying the Song of Songs offers an opportunity to consider the importance of human sexual desire, erotic longing, and the power of love, which the book asserts "is strong as death" (8:6).

Background

Composition and Development

Very little is known about the compositional history of the Song of Songs. The text does not leave any clues regarding its authorship or historical circumstances. The reference to Solomon in 1:1 ("concerning/for/about/by Solomon") is as much an indication of authorship as the phrase "concerning David" is in the Psalter (e.g., Pss. 3; 4; 11; 13; see discussion in chap. 20, "Psalms"). Such titles are ambiguous and say little about the text's composition history. The fact that Solomon is mentioned elsewhere in the text (e.g., 1:5; 3:7, 9, 11; 8:11–12) is sparse evidence from which to develop a theory of composition.

We also know little to nothing about the two lovers themselves. The male lover is depicted as a royal figure (1:4, 12), but that is all we know about his station in life. This level of ambiguity may be intentional. The lovers' voices and their words receive greater emphasis than their identities. Rhetorically, this ambiguity invites readers to see themselves in the poems. Historically, readers are left with little solid ground on which to build a theory of composition.

Genre

The Song of Songs is a collection of erotic love poetry. This genre is known elsewhere in the ancient Near East, in Egypt and Mesopotamia. The Song of Songs is the sole representation of this genre in the Old Testament. Unfortunately, we know little about how well the genre was represented in ancient Israelite and Jewish culture. It is possible that the poems emerged out of some form of popular literature, but this is purely speculative. How the book was used and why it was written remain open questions.

The description of the power and joy of love in some passages suggests that the Song should be considered part of the wisdom tradition of the Old Testament (see, e.g., 3:10–11; 8:6–7). Wisdom literature prizes the discernible order in creation, which can be studied and understood. In that vein, the Song of Songs teaches that love— including erotic expressions of love between committed lovers—is a gift from God.

Fig. 23.2. In the ancient Near East, agricultural images were often used in erotic poetry because of the comparison between human sexuality and natural fertility. Here an illuminated manuscript from the fifteenth century CE captures some of the agricultural imagery in the Song of Songs.

In contrast to this view, however, there is a long history of reading the Song allegorically as describing the covenantal relationship between God and his people. This approach considers the Song part of the biblical tradition of comparing God's relationship with his people to marriage (see Hosea, Ezekiel, and so on).

Literary Interpretation

Title and dedication to Solomon (Song 1:1). As noted above, the book begins by connecting the Song to Solomon, though the nature of this connection is unspecified.

Box 23.1

Outline

1. Title and dedication to Solomon (1:1)
2. Dialogue 1: The lovers speak (1:2–2:7)
3. Dialogue 2: The woman searches for her lover (2:8–3:11)
4. Dialogue 3: The man praises the woman's beauty (4:1–5:1)
5. Dialogue 4: The woman longs for her lover; the daughters of Jerusalem speak (5:2–6:3)
6. Dialogue 5: The man again praises the woman's beauty (6:4–8:4)
7. Conclusion: The lovers, the daughters of Jerusalem, and others speak (8:5–14)

Dialogue 1: The lovers speak (Song 1:2–2:7). The first unit includes brief exchanges between the woman and the man. In the Song of Songs, the woman is the first and the last to speak; the book begins and ends with her expressions of longing for her lover: "May he kiss me with the kisses of his mouth. . . . Hurry, my beloved!" (1:2; 8:14 AT). After these initial expressions of longing, the woman describes herself using an ambiguous phrase: "dark and lovely," or "sunburned yet beautiful" (1:5 AT). The translation of this verse is contested: Is she lovely despite being dark? Is she lovely alongside being dark? Is she lovely because she is dark? The text can bear multiple understandings. The next verse suggests that she is swarthy because she has spent significant time in the sun guarding the vineyards and neglecting herself. However we interpret these verses, the woman's beauty is praised unequivocally elsewhere.

The dialogue continues until 2:7. After initial inquiries about where to find one another, the lovers praise each other's beauty, drawing luxuriously on images from creation and society. They praise each other as singularly wonderful: "Like a lily among the thorns, so is my lover among the maidens. Like an apple among the trees of the forest, so is my beloved among the young men" (2:2–3 AT). The dialogue includes a well-known verse: "He brought me to the house of wine, and his banner over me was love" (2:4 AT).

The unit ends with a phrase that is repeated throughout the book: "I admonish you, daughters of Jerusalem, by the gazelles or the does of the field: do not stir or arouse love until it pleases" (2:7 AT; cf. 3:5; 8:4). The meaning of this is unclear. Given the book's claim that love is as strong as death (8:6), however, it may simply be a warning about the profound power of love.

Dialogue 2: The woman searches for her lover (Song 2:8–3:11). The next dialogue begins with the voice of the woman describing the man leaping over mountains and bounding over hills. She longs to run away with him now that "winter is past" and new growth is starting to occur (2:11). The woman's longing is made all the more poignant by her lover's absence: "Let me see your face, let me hear your voice" (2:14).

Fig. 23.3. The woman in the Song of Songs describes herself as "dark and lovely" as a result of having been sent to work in the sun. This imagery is controversial. It is important to be aware of the racial, ethnic, and gendered biases readers bring with them to the Song of Songs.

The scene shifts to the night, when the woman searches after her lover in what feels like something of a dream sequence. She seeks but does not find (3:1). When she does find her love, she clings to him in hopes of avoiding the burden of distance and separation again. The unit ends with a poem about the wedding of Solomon, emphasizing his military might, wealth, and royal dignity (3:7–11).

Dialogue 3: The man praises the woman's beauty (Song 4:1–5:1). Chapter 4 is a lengthy poem that lauds the beauty of the woman's body and the sweetness of her love. Images from creation and society are used to describe

---

Box 23.2

"Arise, My Love"

The second dialogue includes a famous and powerful expression of the renewing power of love:

> Arise, my love, my fair one,
>   and come away;
> for now the winter is past,
>   the rain is over and gone.
> The flowers appear on the earth;
>   the time of singing has come,
> and the voice of the turtledove
>   is heard in our land.
> The fig tree puts forth its figs,
>   and the vines are in blossom;
>   they give forth fragrance.
> Arise, my love, my fair one,
>   and come away. (2:10–13)

the woman: her eyes are like doves, her hair is like a flock of goats, her teeth are like ewes, her neck like the tower of David, and so on. The man is smitten by her and claims that her love is better than wine (4:10). In keeping with themes of hiddenness, presence, and accessibility, he refers to her as a locked garden and a sealed spring (4:12). An invitation is issued in verse 16 for the man to "come to his garden." Some kind of consummation is reported in 5:1, when the man responds, "I have come into my garden, my sister, my bride!" (NIV).

Dialogue 4: The woman longs for her lover; the daughters of Jerusalem speak (Song 5:2–6:3). In another dream-like sequence, the woman awakens, stirred from sleep by the voice of her lover at the door. But the encounter is fleeting, and by the time she opens the door, her lover is gone. Again, the themes of presence, absence, and longing are emphasized: "I sought him out but did not find him; I called out to him, but he did not answer me" (5:6 AT). In this case, however, the watchmen, who are supposed to keep citizens safe, assault the woman on her quest for her lover (5:7).

Echoing the man's laudatory poem in chapter 4, the woman praises the body and charms of her lover to the maidens of Jerusalem in 5:10–16. His head is gold, his locks are curled, his eyes are like doves, his cheeks a bed of spices— "He is utterly desirable" (v. 16 AT). Her audience offers to help the woman find him. She responds with a metaphorical description of a sexual encounter and a declaration of their mutual belonging: "My beloved has gone down to his garden. . . . I am my beloved's and my beloved is mine" (6:2–3).

Cylinder Seals

A cylinder seal was a small barrel-shaped device that was used to make an impression on clay or other soft substances, which then hardened to form a seal on a document or other surface. These seals often served to validate or authenticate documents or to indicate property or relationship.

© 2014, Baker Publishing Group. Courtesy of the British Museum, London, England.

Fig. 23.4. Cylinder seal.

Box 23.4

How to Read the Song of Songs

As a piece of literary artistry, the Song of Songs is worth careful study. Despite its brevity, it is not the kind of book that can be digested quickly. The poem uses poetic devices such as metaphor, parallelism, and repetition.

The primary skill that enables one to appreciate great poetry is patience. With the Song of Songs, the reader needs it in abundance. A few guidelines will help you appreciate the poetry of the Song of Songs.

First, pay careful attention to the voices. Who is speaking? If this question cannot be answered, then consider how the poem is intentionally using ambiguity. This is easier to see in Hebrew, where masculine and feminine second-person pronouns ("you") have different forms—thus, some study Bibles will mark when the male or the female is speaking.

Second, in poetry silence and emptiness are often just as important as filling lines with words. Pay careful attention to what is said and what is not said.

Third, do not limit the metaphors by reducing them to one meaning or by explaining them away. Rather, "entertain" them. Let them roll around in your imagination and consider various meanings. It is commonplace in interpretation to say that every metaphor is both true and untrue. The woman says, "I am a rose." Is that true? Well, yes and no. Be attentive to where the metaphor connects and where it begins to break down. The metaphors are from an ancient agricultural culture, which may seem strange to modern ears (e.g., "Your eyes are doves," 4:1; "Your teeth are like a flock of ewes," 6:6).

Fourth, pay attention to the themes of distance and proximity. These are fundamental to how the Song of Songs creates a sense of longing, desire, and mystery.

Dialogue 5: The man again praises the woman's beauty (Song 6:4–8:4). The man returns to his praises of the woman's beauty (6:4–9; 7:1–7), drawing on metaphors from nature and society. He regards her as singularly magnificent among all women, acclaimed by even the most powerful and regal of women (6:9). In the second poem (7:1–9), he begins with praise of her feet and moves up toward the head. The woman responds in verses 10–13, claiming that she belongs to her beloved and is the object of his desire (7:10). She calls for him to join her in the vineyards where she will give her love to him (7:12). The passage ends with the familiar refrain, "I adjure you, O daughters of Jerusalem, do not stir up or awaken love until it is ready!" (8:4).

Conclusion: The lovers, the daughters of Jerusalem, and others speak (Song 8:5–14). The book concludes with a poem about the woman's love and desire for the man (8:5–6), a statement about love's power (8:6–7), and brief speeches by the woman, her brothers, and the women of Jerusalem (8:8–14). The woman's poem about love is worth special consideration. She says:

> Set me like a cylinder seal upon your heart,
> like a seal upon your arm.
> For love is as strong as death,
> passion as relentless as Sheol.

> Its flashes are flashes of fire,
>   a divine flame.
> Many waters are unable to quench love;
>   floodwaters cannot drown it.
> If someone were to give all the wealth of his house in exchange for love,
>   it would be utterly despised. (8:6–7 AT)

This is not the only place in which the author speaks of love as an abstraction. The author elsewhere warns the young women of Jerusalem against arousing love too early (2:7; 3:5; 8:4), suggesting that it is a force to be treated with caution and concern. Love is as strong as death, which overtakes all human life, provokes fear in human hearts, and consistently demands our respect. The references to unquenchable fire also suggest that love is not only powerful but potentially dangerous. Despite these dangers, it is of such great value that the greatest riches in the world are worthless in comparison.

Theological Interpretation

God in the Song of Songs

Readers of the Old Testament naturally wonder whether the Song of Songs has anything to say about matters of religious or theological import. On its face, the book has nothing explicit to say about God, Israel's election, the divine commandments, the temple, and other prominent Old Testament topics. Yet there is a long and robust tradition of interpreting the Song of Songs theologically. Given its inclusion in a religious book like the Bible, none of this is surprising.

There are several places where the text may refer to the divine in subtle terms. In chapter 2, the woman says, "I admonish you, daughters of Jerusalem, by the gazelles or the does of the field: do not stir or arouse love until it pleases" (2:7 AT). The Hebrew phrase translated "by the gazelles or the does" sounds vaguely like part of an ancient Near Eastern (and biblical) oath formula, a religious vow in which the speaker invokes witnesses to their promise (see, e.g., Deut. 32:1; Isa. 1:2). The noun in the phrase "by the gazelles" (*bitsva'ot*) is *tseva'ot*, which also means "hosts," as in the divine title "LORD of hosts" (cf. 1 Sam. 1:3, 11; 4:4; 2 Sam. 5:10, etc.). The use of this word could thus be a subtle, behind-the-scenes reference to God.

The poem in 8:6–7 depicts love as a cosmic force as powerful as death, and it too may contain a subtle reference to the divine name, hence the translation "divine flame."

> For love is as strong as death,
>   passion as relentless as Sheol.

Its flashes are flashes of fire,
a divine flame. (8:6 AT)

These are subtle references to God at best, and none gives much indication of an underlying theology. But when combined with the Song's place in Israel's Wisdom literature, they help support the conclusion that erotic and amorous relationships are a gift from God to be treasured and treated reverently.

The Song of Songs as an Allegory about the Divine-Human Relationship

The fact that the book says nothing explicit about God has not stopped Jewish and Christian interpreters from reading the book theologically. In general, a number of interpretive paths have been followed. Some interpret the Song of Songs as a poetic depiction of Israel's marital relationship with Yahweh and, by inference, as an allegory for the triune God's relationship with the church. References to Israel as the wife of Yahweh are not difficult to find, especially in the prophetic literature (see, e.g., Jer. 2:1–2; Ezek. 16; 23; Hosea 1–3). Christian interpreters, in turn, see the church as the bride or lover of Christ, whose words are represented by the man. The book has also been read as Christ's words to individual Christian believers.

Fig. 23.5. In both Judaic and Christian mysticism, the Song of Songs has been an important source text. However, the Song's influence has been felt far beyond the boundaries of just the mystic traditions. It has greatly influenced spirituality, music, monasterial life, and more.

allegory A type of figurative speech in which the elements or characters that make up a story signify concepts or other entities in the real world.

The Power and Gift of Love

Even scholars who deny that the Song of Songs can be interpreted as a book about God still recognize that it has something to say about the life of faith. The book luxuriously celebrates human erotic love. The abundance of creational language suggests that human sexuality is part of God's good creation—intended to be enjoyed and celebrated. Throughout its history, Christianity has shown a distinct discomfort with human sexuality—perhaps recognizing, as the author of the Song did, that love is powerful (8:6–7). But if the Song of

The Song of Songs as Allegory

In recent years, the Christian systematic theologian Robert Jenson offered a commentary on the Song of Songs in the tradition of allegorical interpretation.* While granting that the "overt meaning" of the text relates to a human erotic relationship, Jenson reads the text allegorically on several grounds, including that such a reading (as an allegory for God's love for God's people) was one of the reasons the book was included in the Christian canon. Jenson concludes that the Song of Songs "portrays the love between the Lord and his people as *desire*. With his immensely influential *Agape and Eros*, Anders Nygren persuaded three generations of theologians and exegetes that self-giving love, *agape*, and desire, *eros*, are two incompatible sorts of love, and that only the former characterizes the relationship between the biblical God and his people; no allegory plausibly solicited by the Song can agree."[†] In other words, interpreted allegorically, the Song teaches that the biblical God *desires* his people with the passion of a lover and God's people are to return that passion.

* Robert W. Jenson, *Song of Songs*, Interpretation: A Bible Commentary for Teaching and Preaching (Louisville: John Knox, 2005).
[†] Jenson, *Song of Songs*, 12.

Songs has anything to say about it, that power is not to be ignored or feared but rather to be reverenced, longed for, and enjoyed.

Historical Interpretation

The Song of Songs raises important historical questions, but it yields very few straightforward answers. For example, who are the two lovers, and why are their identities veiled? How should we think about the historical Solomon's relationship to the book? Apart from several explicit references to Solomon (1:1, 5; 3:7, 9, 11; 8:11–12), there are not any identifiable historical events, customs, or circumstances that would allow us to place the book within a specific historical framework—to say nothing about whether the book is contemporaneous to Solomon himself.

Who wrote the Song of Songs, and from what social location? Was this a priestly figure? A court scribe? Some other highly literate author or authors? Given the prominence of the female lover's voice, some have wondered if a woman wrote the book. That is possible. Additionally, seemingly late linguistic features suggest to some that the book was written relatively late in Israel's history. But linguistic evidence alone is a fragile basis on which to build a theory of composition.

A related set of historical issues concerns the social location of the Song of Songs. As noted above in our conversation about genre, erotic love poetry is found elsewhere in the ancient Near East, but it is difficult to determine how and by whom it was used. Was this kind of literature popular? Was it widespread in Israelite society, or was it consumed only by the elite? Was the Song of Songs performed in any way, and did it have ritual significance?

These questions are among many others that biblical scholars have wrestled with for millennia.

FOR FURTHER READING: Song of Songs

Davis, Ellen F. *Proverbs, Ecclesiastes, and Song of Songs*. Westminster Bible Companion. Louisville: Westminster John Knox, 2000.

Exum, J. Cheryl. *Song of Songs: A Commentary*. Old Testament Library. Louisville: Westminster John Knox, 2005.

Fishbane, Michael. *Song of Songs*. JPS Bible Commentary. Philadelphia: Jewish Publication Society, 2015.

Jenson, Robert W. *Song of Songs*. Interpretation: A Bible Commentary for Teaching and Preaching. Louisville: John Knox, 2005.

Keel, Othmar. *The Song of Songs: A Continental Commentary*. Translated by Frederick J. Gaiser. Minneapolis: Fortress, 1994.

Part 5

PROPHETIC
LITERATURE

Prophecy and the Prophetic Books

The category of prophetic books in the Christian Old Testament refers to sixteen books that bear the names of Old Testament prophets and contain either stories about those prophets or the messages they delivered. In Jewish Bibles, the same books are called the Latter Prophets (the Former Prophets make up the Deuteronomistic History; see chap. 9, "The Historical Books").

These books are marked by three important features. The first relates to their content, which, for the most part, consists of the prophetic messages (or oracles) that the biblical prophets delivered. There are also brief narratives about the prophets. Second, these books primarily appear in poetic form. Within this poetic form are common prophetic genres of songs, visions, poems, and oracles (see chap. 18, "Poetry, the Poetic Books, and Wisdom"). This is not to say that narrative is absent (see, e.g., Jonah), but simply that poetry tends to dominate this large collection of texts. Third, as a group these books accompany the longer history of Israel as told in 2 Kings through Ezra-Nehemiah—the time period from roughly 760 to 433 BCE (see fig. 14.6, "Prophets of Israel and Judah," in chap. 14).

The prophetic books include the Major Prophets and the Minor Prophets. These terms refer to the length of the books, not their importance. In the ancient world, the four so-called Major Prophets each took up one long scroll, while the twelve Minor Prophets were all contained on a single scroll, the Book of the Twelve.

The Major Prophets

Isaiah	[Lamentations]*	Daniel
Jeremiah	Ezekiel	

The Minor Prophets

Hosea	Jonah	Zephaniah
Joel	Micah	Haggai
Amos	Nahum	Zechariah
Obadiah	Habakkuk	Malachi

* The book of Lamentations follows Jeremiah in the biblical canon because it was traditionally believed to have been written by Jeremiah. Lamentations is not a prophetic book but a book of lament prayers. In the Jewish Bible, Lamentations is included among the Writings (Ketuvim).

There were many other prophets alive and active during the same years as the prophets whose words and actions came down to us in the books that bear their names. Some of these other prophets were regarded as "false prophets" by the editors of the Old Testament. Even though some of these prophets worshiped Yahweh, they were nevertheless considered false prophets, similar to the prophets of Baal against whom Elijah struggled (see 1 Kings 18). The "prophets of peace" that Jeremiah regularly denounced and struggled against are examples of those prophets—the prophet Hananiah son of Azzur is singled out in Jeremiah 28.

There were also many other "faithful prophets" whose words were not recorded and saved for posterity. The prophet Huldah, for instance (2 Kings 22), is an example of such a prophet, as is "Uriah the son of Shemaiah," whom Jeremiah regarded as a fellow faithful prophet prophesying "in words like those of Jeremiah" (Jer. 26:20 ESV). King Jehoiakim sought to silence him. At first, he was able to escape to Egypt, but he was forcibly retrieved and put to death by the king. Why did Jeremiah escape the same fate? Because he had influential friends: "The hand of Ahikam the son of Shaphan was with Jeremiah so that he was not given over to the people to be put to death" (26:24 ESV).

Prophets: Messengers from God

Prophets have been defined in different ways, but at the most basic level, they were divine messengers. As God's messengers, the prophets delivered many different types of messages. Many of these dealt with the future, and for this reason, some people came to believe that a prophet's primary job was to predict or announce the future. But the more basic understanding of the prophets as messengers emerges from careful analysis of the Scriptures.

In the ancient Near East, where few people could read or write, most messages were delivered verbally. Consider the following story, in which Jacob sends a messenger to his brother, Esau:

> Jacob sent messengers before him to his brother Esau in the land of Seir, the country of Edom, instructing them, "Thus you shall say to my lord Esau: Thus says your servant Jacob, 'I have lived with Laban as an alien, and stayed until now; and I have oxen, donkeys, flocks, male and female slaves; and I have sent to tell my lord, in order that I may find favor in your sight.'" (Gen. 32:3–5)

The phrase "thus says [Name]" is known as the messenger formula. The messenger would journey to the person to whom the message was addressed, state the messenger formula, and then speak the message in first person. Notice in the above story from Genesis, messengers announce, "Thus says your servant Jacob, 'I have lived with Laban as an alien . . .'"—speaking in the first person.

In the prophetic books, the messenger formula occurs before, after, or during a prophetic message, and it appears in many different variations. For example, the following occur just in the book of Amos:

- "Thus says the LORD" or "Thus says the Lord GOD" (1:3; 5:3)
- "Hear this word that the LORD has spoken" (3:1)
- "Says the LORD" or "says the Lord GOD" (4:6; 3:13)
- "The Lord GOD has sworn" (6:8)
- "This is what the Lord GOD showed me" (7:1)
- "The LORD said to me" (8:2)
- "The LORD has sworn" (8:7)

In addition to seeing the biblical prophets as divine messengers, people have understood them in other ways. Gene Tucker provides a list: (1) mystics or visionaries; (2) literary giants or poets; (3) great theologians or religious philosophers; (4) social reformers or ethical radicals; (5) seers or predictors; and (6) preachers of repentance.[1] Bryan Bibb offers additional possibilities: (1) ecstatic revealer; (2) messianic predictor; (3) religious genius; and (4) political functionary.[2] While there is some validity to each of these views, none of them captures the essence of what the biblical prophets were as clearly as the simple category of God's messengers.

Finally, it is worth noting that prophets were active elsewhere in the ancient Near East. The role of prophet was not unique to ancient Israel. Prophetic functionaries served alongside other diviners to provide people—often rulers—with

Prophecy in the Ancient Near East

Prophecy was present throughout the ancient Near East in a wide variety of forms and settings, in everything from administrative records to omen lists. Conceptually, prophecy is best understood to be a subset of the mantic or divinatory disciplines. While "divination" can have a negative connotation in some circles, the term simply refers to discovering (i.e., divining) the will of the gods. Sometimes this involved interpreting dreams, and at other times it meant interpreting natural phenomena such as sheep livers or astrological events. The prophets, for their part, were understood to be communicators of divine messages.

While the Old Testament is the largest collection of prophetic texts from the ancient Near East, other collections have been found elsewhere. The uniqueness of Old Testament prophecy can only be appreciated when the biblical phenomenon is compared to the prophetic activity of its contemporaries.

insight into the divine will. While we do have some literary records of prophets, especially from the Neo-Assyrian period, Israel's prophets are unique for the extensive literary record that survives them.

Prophetic Creative License

The prophets took enormous creative license in their charge to deliver God's messages in ways that both communicated ideas and also changed hearts and minds. The biblical prophets could not change the content of the messages that God entrusted to them, but they had vast freedom in how they communicated those messages. Consider the following examples:

- Amos sings a message in the form of a "lamentation for the dead," telling the Israelites that their nation had died (Amos 5:1–2).
- Amos imitates a "call to worship" that summons worshipers not to praise God but to come and sin (Amos 4:4–5).
- Hosea uses his marriage to an unfaithful woman and the names of his children—"Not-shown-mercy" and "Not-my-people"—to condemn the people and their religious leaders for ethical and faith violations. He later changes the names to "Shown-mercy" and "My-people" to proclaim hope (Hosea 1:6, 9; 2:23).
- Isaiah sings a message in the form of a "love song" from the perspective of God the lover, whose beloved practices injustice (Isa. 5:1–7).
- Isaiah walks about Jerusalem naked for three years to announce that those who trust in military alliances to save them from Assyria will be led away without clothing (Isa. 20).

- Isaiah gives his children symbolic names to communicate his messages: "A-remnant-shall-return" and "The-spoil-speeds-the-prey-hastens" (Isa. 7–8).
- Jeremiah smashes clay pots, waves around a dirty loin cloth, wears the harness of an ox, refuses to marry or father children, and buys property that was occupied by an invading army—all to get his messages across (Jer. 13; 16; 19; 27; 32).
- Joel calls the people to a national fast (Joel 1–2).
- Haggai and Malachi take on new names—"My-festival" and "My-messenger," respectively—to communicate their messages (Hag. 1:1; Mal. 1:1).

In short, the prophets exhibit great zeal to deliver God's messages effectively. The German Old Testament scholar Gerhard von Rad writes that the prophets "showed no hesitation in availing themselves of all manner of forms in which to clothe their message. Nothing, whether secular or sacred, was safe from appropriation as a vessel for the discharge of his task by one prophet or another. What these men wanted to do, of course, was to attract attention: indeed sometimes, as when, for example, they laid violent hands on some time-hallowed, holy form of expression, their express intention was to shock their audience."[3]

Prophetic Authority

According to the biblical text, the prophets' authority came solely from God. It did not derive from the nation or king they served, from the money they were paid, from any characteristic they bore (such as being naturally mystical), from any ritual they performed, from where they performed the ritual, from the sign action they carried out, or from any chemical agent—such as a hallucinogen or alcohol—they might take to spark a vision.

There were others—kings and professional prophets—who thought the authority of a prophet derived from one or more of these sources. The prophet Amos, for example, complains that the people made the prophets drink wine (Amos 2:12)—apparently to induce prophetic visions. When Amos preaches against the king at Bethel, the high priest Amaziah orders him to stop prophesying there and to "go back to the land of Judah. Earn your bread there and do your prophesying there. Don't prophesy anymore at Bethel, because this is the king's sanctuary and the temple of the kingdom" (7:12–13 NIV). Amos responds that his authority does not come from the king or the temple but was strictly a matter of his call from God: "The LORD took me from following the flock, and the LORD said to me, 'Go, prophesy to my people Israel'" (7:15). Similarly, the prophet Jeremiah wears the harness (yoke) of an ox to symbolize

Fig. 24.1. Christ with the twelve minor prophets. The continuing significance of the Hebrew prophets for Christianity is manifest in this twelfth-century illustration from a commentary on Ecclesiastes by St. Jerome. The prophets surrounding Christ (who, of course, is central) are Hosea, Joel, Amos, Obadiah, Jonah, Micah, Nahum, Habakkuk, Zephaniah, Haggai, Zechariah, and Malachi.

that the nation of Judah must serve Babylon. The prophet Hananiah grabs the harness and smashes it—apparently believing there was power in the very act of smashing the harness—and announces, "I am breaking the harness of the king of Babylon" (Jer. 28:2 AT). Jeremiah mocks him in response, announcing that the truth of the word of the Lord was the only thing that made a prophet's words authoritative.

For many prophets—especially those entrusted with messages of judgment and calls for repentance—their vocation was dangerous and burdensome. As noted earlier, King Jehoiakim of Judah puts the prophet Uriah to death for his condemnatory messages (Jer. 26:20–23). As often happens with human leaders, many Israelite and Judean kings "blame the messenger" for the messages they receive. In 1 Kings 22, King Ahab of Israel complains about the prophet Micaiah: "I hate him, for he never prophesies anything favorable about me, but only disaster" (v. 8). After then receiving a negative prophecy from Micaiah (who warned him against going to war), the king has him locked up in jail and fed only a ration of bread and water.

In another example, King Balak of Moab hires the seer Balaam to curse the people of Israel (Num. 22–24), "for I know that whomever you bless is blessed and whomever you curse is cursed" (Num. 22:6 CEB). What follows is a comic story in which King Balak takes the prophet up a mountain to curse Israel. Balak sacrifices seven bulls and seven rams on prepared altars—apparently hoping that the expense of the offering will influence God. But God instead sends Balaam a message of blessing for Israel. Balak tries another place for a sacrifice, and then another, but the message from God is the same: blessing for Israel. Balak decides not to pay Balaam for his service, and Balaam responds, "Didn't I tell your messengers, whom you sent to me, 'If Balak would give me his house full of silver and gold, I wouldn't be able to break the LORD's command for good or ill by my own will. I'll say whatever the LORD says'?" (Num. 24:12–13 CEB).

Some modern interpreters have tried to explain the prophets' authority using categories more at home in a scientific age. For example, the prophets had more morally evolved consciences than others. Some interpreters in the mid-twentieth century saw the prophets as people with great physical and moral courage. One of the most famous attempts to ground prophetic authority in some modern sensibility came from the great Jewish biblical scholar Abraham Heschel, who notes that the prophets' "breathless impatience with injustice may strike us as hysteria" and that "the vastness of their indignation and the vastness of God's anger" might strike us as disproportionate.[4] He then argues that it is precisely the prophets' ability *to feel* that is the ground of their authority: "The prophet is a man who feels fiercely. God has thrust a burden upon his soul. . . . God is raging in the prophet's words."[5] The prophet hears cries and feels pains that are imperceptible to the masses. The prophet also loves humankind more fiercely than others. Moreover, the prophet is able to feel God's emotions more acutely than others: "The prophet is overwhelmed by the grandeur of divine presence. . . . There is an interaction between man and God which to disregard is an act of insolence."[6] Heschel bases this supposed superiority of feeling on the biblical idea that the prophets were able to receive God's word, in part, because they had "voice but not vote" in the parliamentary assembly of heaven. The prophets are depicted as observing God's deliberations in the council of heaven. Consider these passages:

Micaiah said, "Therefore hear the word of the LORD: I saw the LORD sitting on his throne, with all the host of heaven standing beside him to the right and to the left of him. And the LORD said, 'Who will entice Ahab, so that he may go up and fall at Ramoth-gilead?' Then one said one thing, and another said another, until a spirit came forward and stood before the LORD, saying, 'I will entice him.' 'How?' the LORD asked him. He replied, 'I will go out and be a lying spirit in the mouth of all his prophets.' Then the LORD said, 'You are to entice him, and you shall succeed; go out and do it.' So you see, the LORD has put a lying spirit in the mouth of all these your prophets; the LORD has decreed disaster for you." (1 Kings 22:19–23)

In the year that King Uzziah died, I saw the Lord sitting on a throne, high and lofty; and the hem of his robe filled the temple. Seraphs were in attendance above him; each had six wings: with two they covered their faces, and with two they covered their feet, and with two they flew. And one called to another and said:

"Holy, holy, holy is the LORD of hosts;
   the whole earth is full of his glory."

The pivots on the thresholds shook at the voices of those who called, and the house filled with smoke. And I said: "Woe is me! I am lost, for I am a man of unclean lips, and I live among a people of unclean lips; yet my eyes have seen the King, the Lord of hosts!"

Then one of the seraphs flew to me, holding a live coal that had been taken from the altar with a pair of tongs. The seraph touched my mouth with it and said: "Now that this has touched your lips, your guilt has departed and your sin is blotted out." Then I heard the voice of the Lord saying, "Whom shall I send, and who will go for us?" And I said, "Here am I; send me!" (Isa. 6:1–8)

> Surely the Lord God does nothing,
>> without revealing his secret
>> to his servants the prophets. (Amos 3:7)

Thus says the Lord of hosts: Do not listen to the words of the prophets who prophesy to you; they are deluding you. They speak visions of their own minds, not from the mouth of the Lord. They keep saying to those who despise the word of the Lord, "It shall be well with you"; and to all who stubbornly follow their own stubborn hearts, they say, "No calamity shall come upon you."

> For who has stood in the council of the Lord
>> so as to see and to hear his word?
> Who has given heed to his word so as to proclaim it? (Jer. 23:16–18)

In all of these passages, the true prophet is one who listens in on the divine deliberation in the "council of the Lord" and then delivers the word to those for whom it is intended. Heschel draws from this to posit that the prophets were those of superior feeling—his word for this is *pathos*. The prophet was able to feel God's pathos—the prophet has "a *sympathy with the divine pathos*, a communion with the divine consciousness which comes about through the prophet's reflection, or participation in, the divine pathos."[7]

Heschel's construal of prophetic authority as vested in their sympathy with the divine pathos is just one modern attempt to translate prophetic authority in modern terms or sentiments. It is offered here by way of one influential example. Another popular example contemporaneous with Heschel was that of Gerhard von Rad, who saw the prophets more as theologians, each of whom received an inherited theological witness and then, in turn, adapted the tradition as they bore witness to what they considered God's continuing activity in the world. As von Rad writes, the Old Testament bears witness to the "continuing divine activity in history."[8] In both of these examples, however, it is worth noting that the prophetic authority is vested in something inherent to the prophets themselves—their capacity either for sympathy or for reworking tradition theologically.

The biblical text itself would object to these suggestions, insisting that prophetic authority derives solely from the God who called the prophets and communicated his messages to and through them. The sticking point for some is the question of revelation—the means by which God communicated messages to the prophets. The prophets themselves report a variety of means by which they received divine messages. In the end, any attempt to rationalize the revelatory claim of the prophets will find itself in some tension with the texts themselves, which understand the prophetic word to originate outside the prophets.

The Literature of the Prophetic Books

Several literary forms are found in the prophetic books. Most broadly, one can distinguish between prose narratives about the prophets and poetic messages (many scholars use the term *oracle* to describe prophetic messages, while some prefer just *message*) spoken by the prophets. While this distinction fails at many points, it offers at least a basic point of departure. The prose narratives about the prophets are very similar to the narrative portions of the books of 1–2 Samuel and 1–2 Kings that depict the actions of prophets such as Samuel, Nathan, Elijah, Elisha, Micaiah, and Isaiah. In fact, Isaiah 36–39 is largely identical to 2 Kings 18:13–20:19; both recount stories about Isaiah and King Hezekiah of Judah. The books of Jeremiah, Ezekiel, Daniel, and Jonah also devote large sections to narratives about the prophets. For more on the interpretation of Old Testament narrative, see chapter 9, "The Historical Books."

With respect to the poetic messages spoken by the prophets, one can again use a simple distinction as a point of departure. The prophetic messages basically fall into one of two categories: good news or bad news. The "good news" messages are often called messages of salvation, while the "bad news" messages are generally called messages of judgment.[9] Once again, the simple distinction between good news and bad news fails, because there are messages—such as the prophetic "call story"—that fall into neither category. But as a basic point of reference, the distinction is helpful. Within these two broad categories, as noted earlier, the prophets display an exhilarating range of creative license. In what follows, several of the most frequent forms of literature are described.

Prophetic Call Stories

Some of the prophets report their call stories. The most important of these are Isaiah (Isa. 6), Jeremiah (Jer. 1), Ezekiel (Ezek. 1:1–3:15), and Amos (Amos 7:14–15). One also thinks of the call stories of Moses (Exod. 3), Samuel (1 Sam. 3), and Gideon (Judg. 6:11–27). Many of these stories share common elements. First, the word or presence of God calls the prophet to ministry—Isaiah and Ezekiel see visions, while Jeremiah and Samuel hear the voice of God. Second, the prophet offers an excuse—Moses offers three different excuses, including, "Who am I

Fig. 24.2. Three of Israel's major prophets: Jeremiah, Isaiah, and Ezekiel.

that I should go to Pharaoh?" and "What is [your] name?" (Exod. 3:11, 13); Isaiah says, "I am a man of unclean lips" (Isa. 6:5); Jeremiah says, "I am only a boy" (Jer. 1:6); and so on. Third, God offers reassurance—he reveals his name to Moses; he forgives Isaiah's sins; he assures Jeremiah, "Do not say, 'I am only a boy'" (Jer. 1:7). Fourth, sometimes the prophet is symbolically endowed with the word of God—a seraph touches Isaiah's lips with a burning coal; the Lord touches Jeremiah's mouth and says, "Now I have put my words in your mouth" (Jer. 1:9); Ezekiel is given a scroll to eat, and "it tasted as sweet as honey" (Ezek. 3:3 AT). Fifth, the prophet is given a commission—Moses is to free the people, Isaiah is to preach judgment, Jeremiah is to preach both good and bad news, and so on.

Messages of Judgment

When most people think of the message of the Old Testament prophets, they think of judgment. The initial words of some messages of judgment signal a call for repentance or an announcement of judgment. These messages often take the following forms:

- *Summons to hear.* These messages are introduced by expressions such as "Woe to you," "Ah, sinful nation," "Ah, you who . . . ," "Hear the word of the Lord," "Alas for those who . . . ," and the like. A specific audience for the message is identified or implied.

- *Messenger formula.* The most common form of the messenger formula is "Thus says the Lord," and it can occur before, in the middle of, or after a message.
- *Description of sins or grievances.* These messages characterize the people's sins into two broad categories: failure to love God (idolatry and blasphemy) and failure to love the neighbor (injustice and unrighteousness).
- *Announcement of punishment or call to repent.* A word such as "therefore" often occurs just before a punishment is announced or a call to repent is sounded.

Consider this short example from the prophet Amos:

> Hear this word, you cows of Bashan
> > who are on Mount Samaria,
> who oppress the poor, who crush the needy,
> > who say to their husbands, "Bring something to drink!"
> The Lord GOD has sworn by his holiness:
> > The time is surely coming upon you,
> when they shall take you away with hooks,
> > even the last of you with fishhooks.
> Through breaches in the wall you shall leave,
> > each one straight ahead;
> > and you shall be flung out into Harmon,
> > > says the LORD. (Amos 4:1–3)

The audience here is the wealthy women of Samaria, here called "cows of Bashan" (the most desirable and costly cattle in the land). They are summoned to "hear this word." Their sins include oppressing the poor and crushing the needy, while living in wealthy indifference. The consequence, which is introduced here with the words "The Lord GOD has sworn," is that they will be captured and taken away when the city walls fall. The messenger formula is added at the end. Not all the prophetic messages of judgment call for repentance, but in many cases a call for repentance is implied. Sometimes, however, the prophet announces that the time for repentance has passed, and judgment is now inevitable.

As noted earlier, these messages of judgment take many different forms: a song of lamentation, a love song, a mock courtroom scene (the "prophetic lawsuit"), symbolic prophetic sign actions, symbolic names for children, taunt songs, mock calls to worship, mock praise songs, prophetic rants, wisdom-like sayings, and so on. There was no form of communication—either sacred or secular—that the prophets were afraid to borrow to get their messages across.

Messages of Salvation

Although the Old Testament prophets are often considered messengers of doom and judgment, their messages actually contain a great deal of hope and good news. In fact, it can be argued that one should think of the biblical prophets primarily as preachers of hope. The message of salvation usually begins with the words "fear not" and then offers promises of God's beneficent actions. The story of the prophet Isaiah bringing good news to King Ahaz of Judah when he was facing an attack from the combined forces of the nations of Israel and Aram (Syria) is a classic example of a message of salvation:

> The LORD said to Isaiah, Go out to meet Ahaz—you and your son "A-remnant-shall-return"—at the end of the channel of the upper pool on the highway to the Fuller's Field. Say to him, Take heed! Be still! Do not fear! Do not let your heart be faint because of these two smoldering sticks of firewood, because of the fierce anger of Rezin and Aram and the son of Remaliah. Because Aram—with Ephraim and the son of Remaliah—has plotted evil against you, saying, Let us go up against Judah and cut off Jerusalem and conquer it for ourselves and make the son of Tabeel king in it; therefore thus says the Lord GOD:
>
> > It shall not stand,
> >   and it shall not come to pass. . . .
> > If you do not stand firm in faith,
> >   you shall not stand at all. (Isa. 7:3–7, 9b, modified)

Notice the signal of the message of salvation: "Take heed! Be still! Do not fear!" Following this is the description of the threat and the promise of deliverance: "It shall not stand!" What shall not stand? The enemies' plan to march up against Judah and conquer it. The name of Isaiah's son—"A-remnant-shall-return"—is the promise that only a remnant of the invading armies' troops will survive to return to their lands.

Similar to the messages of judgment, the messages of salvation could take many forms, such as the names of children, a praise hymn, a simple announcement, or an elaborate message. They often also include an exhortation to hope and to keep faith, as in the message above: "If you do not stand firm in faith, you shall not stand at all."

Messages against the Nations

By some counts, roughly 30 percent of the prophetic corpus consists of a message form known as the messages/oracles against the nations. For example, Amos 1–2, Isaiah 13–23, Jeremiah 46–51, and Nahum 2–3 are all primarily such messages. When reading these denouncements, one must distinguish between the rhetorical or "fictive" audience of the message and the actual or physical audience. The prophet Isaiah, as noted above, often preached directly to the kings in Jerusalem—to Ahaz and Hezekiah, for example. However, he often addressed messages against other nations and other kings, including Babylon (13:1–22), the king of Babylon (14:3–21), Assyria (14:24–31), Moab (chaps. 15–16), Damascus (chap. 17), Ethiopia (chap. 18), Egypt (19:1–15), Tyre (23:1–12), and Samaria (28:1–8). We can imagine that the prophet literally spoke these words in the presence of the Judean kings or other officials. Sometimes these messages against the nations were good news for Jerusalem, as in the story of Isaiah and Ahaz. The news that the invading enemy nation would be struck down was good news for the invaded land; bad news for our enemies is good news for us. Such is the case with the messages against Assyria and Babylon, as well as the message against Samaria in Isaiah 28:1–8. On the other hand, if the foreign nation that is condemned was a military ally on which Judah was depending, then the condemnation of the foreign nation was bad news; bad news for our friends is bad news for us. This was the case when Isaiah condemned Ethiopia and Egypt, upon whom Judah was relying in its war against Assyria.

Theology of the Prophetic Books

During Israel's monarchic period (tenth–sixth centuries BCE), the vocation of the prophet was often closely linked to the vocation of the king. Samuel's prophetic ministry is illustrative. Early in the monarchy's history, he begrudgingly anoints Saul as king over all Israel (1 Sam. 8–10). In response to the new king's disobedience, however, Samuel rebukes Saul and then oversees the transfer of royal power to David (1 Sam. 16). Samuel's role in these events foreshadows the important role prophets would play vis-à-vis Israel's kings.

For the Old Testament, true prophets were not simply sycophantic bolsterers of royal policies. They were first and foremost messengers of Yahweh, Israel's heavenly sovereign. It was their responsibility to communicate Yahweh's words, whether of hope or doom, rebuke or restoration. This often put them at odds with their earthly sovereigns. Isaiah, for instance, urges King Ahaz to trust in Yahweh's ability to save him during the Syro-Ephraimite crisis. The king ultimately refuses (Isa. 7:1–17) and relies instead on the power of Assyria (cf. 2 Kings 16:7–9). Jeremiah famously sends a scroll of threats and warnings to King Jehoiakim in hopes of persuading him to turn from his evil ways (Jer. 36:1–4). Jehoiakim not only rejects Jeremiah's words, but he also cuts up the scroll and burns it (36:21–25). Many other illustrations could be added. Even when the prophets were not directly in contact with kings, their oracles were often directed toward rulers, priests, and other holders of power.

Royal Theology

In the Southern Kingdom of Judah, the prophets and monarchy shared a set of theological premises commonly called a royal theology or a Zion theology. Royal theology had three basic beliefs: (1) The Lord had chosen ("elected") David and his descendants as his appointed kings and the temple on Mount Zion in Jerusalem as his dwelling place—this is called the "double election." Because God chose David and Zion, (2) he would protect both the Davidic king and the city of Jerusalem. But (3) because the Lord will not dwell in a morally corrupt community, he would also hold both the Davidic kings and the people of Jerusalem accountable when they sinned. The royal theology is expressed well in both 2 Samuel 7 and Psalm 89. In Psalm 89, the Lord says,

> I have made a covenant with my chosen one,
>   I have sworn to my servant David:
> "I will establish your descendants forever,
> and build your throne for all generations." . . .
>
> If his children forsake my law
>   and do not walk according to my ordinances,
> if they violate my statutes
>   and do not keep my commandments,
> then I will punish their transgression with the rod
>   and their iniquity with scourges;
> but I will not remove from him my steadfast love,
>   or be false to my faithfulness.
> I will not violate my covenant. (vv. 3–4, 30–34)

Every prophet except Hosea (who was from the Northern Kingdom) interacts with and develops this theology in some way.

Even after the demise of the monarchy, the experience of the exile, and then the diaspora and return from exile, royal theology continues in various ways. The exilic and postexilic prophets are among the most important preservers and innovators of royal theology in all of Israel's long history. The exilic prophet of Isaiah 40–55, for instance, reinterprets the Davidic covenant so that it includes not only the house of David but his entire Judean audience (Isa. 55:3–5). He also speaks to the exiles in Babylon and reminds them that they are still "Jerusalem" even though they are no longer living there (meaning the promises of royal theology still hold; Isa. 40). Other prophets preserve the hope of a coming Davidic ruler who will restore Judah's independence and return a son of David to the throne in Jerusalem (e.g., Ezek. 34:23–31). Christian messianic faith is a downstream effect of the prophetic tradition's persistent reinterpretation of Davidic royal ideology.

Creation

The Old Testament bears witness to a rich and multifaceted creation theology, and the prophetic books are no exception. Animating this theology is the assumption that Yahweh, the God of Israel, is the creator and ruler of the cosmos. In the words of the book of Isaiah, it is "Yahweh who created the heavens and stretched them out, who spread the earth and what she produces, who gave breath to its inhabitants and spirit to those who walk on it" (Isa. 42:5 AT). As divine messengers, the prophets give voice and expression to Yahweh's deep and abiding care for the welfare of creation—human and nonhuman alike. Creation crops up in the prophetic books in many different ways.

Creation funds the poetry of the prophets. Even a cursory survey of prophetic literature reveals that its author-poets drew heavily on creational imagery. In 2002, William Brown wrote a book titled *Seeing the Psalms*, about metaphor in the Psalms. A similarly titled book could be written about the Prophets. Metaphors involving creation describe everything from Yahweh's actions to the terrors of human violence. Skillful readers of the Prophets must learn to "see" the Prophets and be attentive to how metaphor is deployed not only for rhetorical effect but also to shape theological claims.

Elements of creation also often serve as agents of Yahweh, both for weal and for woe. Echoing the book of Exodus, Joel 1 describes an actual plague of locusts that afflict Judah's agricultural fields (Joel 1:4–5). This army is later identified as Yahweh's army (2:25). In the richly ironic and humorous book of Jonah, Yahweh appoints a fish to swallow Jonah and ultimately set him back on the path to Nineveh (2:1–10). Many other examples could be named. Suffice it to say that creation is not merely a stage on which God's acts of redemption play out; creation contributes to the divine drama.

God's Sovereignty

For the prophets, Yahweh is not only creator of the cosmos, but he is also the king of creation. Like ancient Near Eastern kings, Yahweh has a throne room with an entourage (e.g., Isa. 6:1–13), goes to war against oppressors and enemies (Jer. 21:4–6), receives tribute from vassal kingdoms (Isa. 60), defeats the forces of chaos to ensure the fertility and prosperity of the land (Ezek. 34:1–31), and issues judgments and edicts against nations under his authority (see all the oracles against foreign nations). Within this theological framework, the prophets were understood to be Yahweh's messengers delivering oracles, judgments, and edicts from the deity's heavenly throne room. Israel's and Judah's human kings were merely God's viceroys or regents on earth—they owed as much (or more) obedience to Yahweh as did the prophets, the priests, or the commoners.

The Kingship of Yahweh

Even though Israel clearly understood its God to be a cosmic king, there is still significant debate about the nature of Yahweh's rule. How did he influence historical events? To what degree were actions in history determined or even predetermined by him? How did Yahweh actually accomplish things in the world? Is the future open to human influence? How was Yahweh involved in historical tragedies such as the destruction of the Northern Kingdom or the Babylonian exile? For ancient Israel, these are not merely theoretical questions. They are life and death questions. If Yahweh is as deeply involved in history as the Old Testament suggests, then one must reckon with his involvement in disasters and tragedies.

These questions are made all the more difficult by the fact that many of them—especially those related to election and predestination—have been deeply influenced by Christian theological debates, none of which has been resolved. The reader of the Old Testament should also be aware that how one answers these questions may depend on what text is being read.

predestination The concept or doctrine that some or all events are predetermined by God or that individual and national destinies may likewise be predetermined.

Ethics of the Prophets

As noted earlier, from the prophets' perspective, there are two broad types of sin: failure to love the Lord God (idolatry and blasphemy) and failure to love one's neighbor as oneself (injustice and unrighteousness). In this, the prophets are of one voice with both Jesus Christ and the apostle Paul. When asked which is the greatest commandment, Jesus replies, "The first is, 'Hear, O Israel: the Lord our God, the Lord is one; you shall love the Lord your God with all your heart, and with all your soul, and with all your mind, and with all your strength.' The second is this, 'You shall love your neighbor as yourself.' There is no other commandment greater than these" (Mark 12:29–31). Similarly, Paul writes that "the whole law is summed up in a single commandment: 'You shall love your neighbor as yourself'" (Gal. 5:14). Jesus and Paul stand proudly and faithfully in the same tradition as the prophets. These commandments are simple, but very hard to keep. They are straightforward, but there are many subtle and complex ways in which people violate them.

Failure to Love God (Idolatry and Blasphemy)

For the biblical prophets, the major sin of the people is failure to love God, and this failure is the root of all other ethical failings. Failure to love the Lord takes many forms, but most broadly its forms are idolatry (worshiping a false god) and blasphemy (worshiping the true God in a false way).

The most blatant manifestation of this sin is the literal worship of other deities—those false gods, idols, and "lies" of Israel's neighbors: Baal, Asherah, Molech, and so on. The prophet Hosea condemns the people of the Northern

Kingdom for worshiping Baal, Asherah, and the idols corresponding to those gods: "My people consult a piece of wood, and their divining rod gives them oracles. For a spirit of whoredom has led them astray, and they have played the whore, forsaking their God" (Hosea 4:12). Hosea also says, "The more I [God] called them, the more they went from me; they kept sacrificing to the Baals, and offering incense to idols" (Hosea 11:2). Jeremiah accuses the Southern Kingdom of the same sin: "The rulers transgressed against me; the prophets prophesied by Baal, and went after things that do not profit" (Jer. 2:8).

From the prophets' perspective, when people worship idols, it is not just a sin against God. Idolatry inevitably leads to other sins; the prophets believe that when people start to worship false gods, the neighbor will always suffer in the end. They regularly condemn the practices of worshiping idols, citing especially the human sacrifice and the self-harm/flagellation that they see in those cults. Jeremiah says, "They built the high places of Baal in the valley of the son of Hinnom, to offer up their sons and daughters to Molech, though I [God] did not command them, nor did it enter my mind that they should do this abomination, causing Judah to sin" (Jer. 32:35; see also Ps. 106:37–41; Isa. 57:5; Jer. 19:5; Ezek. 23:37).

The prophets also consider worship of the true God in false ways as failure to love God properly. There are many ways in which the people do this. Amos accuses the people of insincere, rote worship of God (Amos 5:21–24). Isaiah accuses them of trying to worship the Lord with blood on their hands (Isa. 1:12–17). The prophets condemn the Northern Kingdom's "sin of Jeroboam," in which Jeroboam had two golden calves forged and placed in temples in Bethel and Dan in order to rival the temple in Jerusalem (see 1 Kings 12:28–30). Hosea condemns such idolatry: "And now they keep on sinning and make a cast image for themselves, idols of silver made according to their understanding, all of them the work of artisans. 'Sacrifice to these,' they say. People are kissing calves!" (Hosea 13:2). In a similar vein, the prophets condemn all nonorthodox worship of the Lord that was occurring at the various "high places" throughout the Northern Kingdom. The prophets also condemn the people for not offering the full tithe as a sacrificial gift to the Lord and for forcing prophets to drink wine in order to spark a vision or prophetic word. Other prophets, such as Joel, call the people back to worship and proclaim a fast and a time of repentance.

The prophets with almost one voice condemn the kings and the religious leaders of the land for trusting in themselves rather than the Lord. When the political leaders make political alliances with other nations, for example, the prophets see this as a violation of the commandment to trust God. Isaiah warns the kings in his time against trusting in military alliances with Egypt and Ethiopia (Isa. 18–20), instead urging them to trust in the Lord. When the Judean king makes a political alliance with Egypt against the Assyrians, Isaiah calls it "a covenant with death" and announces, "Your covenant with death will be annulled, and your agreement with Sheol will not stand" (Isa. 28:15, 18). Isaiah says that the religious leaders who encourage these alliances are false:

> The priest and prophet reel with strong drink,
>> they are confused with wine,
>> they stagger with strong drink;
> they err in vision,
>> they stumble in giving judgment. (Isa. 28:7)

The prophets also believe that political leaders' failure to consult God ("seeking the Lord's counsel") when making important decisions is failure to trust God. So Isaiah preaches,

> Oh, rebellious children, says the LORD,
> who carry out a plan, but not mine;
> who make an alliance, but against my will,
>> adding sin to sin;
> who set out to go down to Egypt
>> without asking for my counsel,
> to take refuge in the protection of Pharaoh. (Isa. 30:1–2)

Similarly, Hosea condemns the northern dynasty that had usurped the throne in a coup: "They made kings, but not through me; they set up princes, but without my knowledge" (Hosea 8:4). For the prophets, an ultimate act of unfaith was not only to disregard the messages they brought from the Lord but also to silence the prophets by force. Hosea announces,

> The days of punishment have come,
>> the days of recompense have come;
>> Israel cries,
> "The prophet is a fool,
>> the man of the spirit is mad!"
> Because of this great iniquity,
>> the judgment will be great. (Hosea 9:7, modified)

Similarly, Amos laments, "You . . . commanded the prophets, saying, 'You shall not prophesy'" (2:12).

Failure to Love the Neighbor (Injustice and Unrighteousness)

From the perspective of the prophets, failure to love and obey God always leads to failure to love the neighbor. If failure to love God can be described

HOSEA.   JOEL.   AMOS.   OBADIAH.

Fig. 24.3. Christian appreciation for the Hebrew prophets is evident on screens displayed in the Bristol Cathedral in the United Kingdom. The prophets on this screen are Hosea, Joel, Amos, and Obadiah.

broadly as the sins of idolatry and blasphemy, failure to love the neighbor can be described as the sins of injustice and unrighteousness.

In the prophetic vision, those who love and follow the Lord practice justice and righteousness. The prophet Amos expresses this vision of the godly life: "Let justice roll down like waters, and righteousness like an ever-flowing stream" (Amos 5:24). Human nature being what it is, Israel is consistently unable to live up to this standard. The prophet Isaiah complains, "How the faithful city has become a prostitute! She that was full of justice, righteous dwelled in her—but now murderers" (Isa. 1:21, modified). Isaiah says that the Lord "expected justice, but saw bloodshed; righteousness, but heard an outcry" (Isa. 5:7, modified).

Under the broad umbrella of injustice and unrighteousness, the prophets see all the usual human violence and crimes. Both Hosea and Jeremiah offer a summary of the Ten Commandments to enumerate Israel's injustice: "Swearing, lying, murder, stealing and adultery burst forth; bloodshed follows bloodshed" (Hosea 4:2 AT); "Will you steal and murder and commit adultery and swear falsely, and sacrifice to Baal, and follow other gods whom you have not experienced?" (Jer. 7:9 NJPS). The prophets complain about those in power, mostly the kings and government officials, who use their power to gobble up the land and threaten the vulnerable.

There is a small set of spheres in which the prophets see consistent injustice: the government, the marketplace, the courtroom, the religious centers.

The government. The government draws the most consistent and passionate prophetic ire. The government causes unjust wars. The rulers tax the people unjustly, gathering wealth from the poor for those who are in power ("You trample the poor and take levies of grain from them"; Amos 5:11 AT). It supports idolatry by building temples for false gods or importing the worship of false gods into the Lord's temple.

The government hoards land. The land produces the means of survival, so its unjust acquisition draws Isaiah's ire: "Ah, you who join house to house, who add field to field, until there is room for no one but you" (Isa. 5:8). Who is it who joins house to house? The story of King Ahab and Queen Jezebel murdering a man named Naboth in order to acquire his property, which the king coveted, shows how those in power grab up the land (see 1 Kings 21). Isaiah complains,

> Your princes are rebels
>   and companions of thieves.
> Everyone loves a bribe
>   and runs after gifts.
> They do not defend the orphan,
>   and the widow's cause does not come before them. (Isa. 1:23)

Micah sees the seats of government as the centers from which injustice emanated: "What is the transgression of Jacob? Is it not Samaria? And what are the shrines of Judah? Are they not Jerusalem?" (1:5 AT).

The marketplace. The marketplace is a special location in which the prophets see injustice. Because the Lord values a fair marketplace, many of the prophets preach against those who cheat others: "Can I forget the treasures of wickedness in the house of the wicked, and the scant measure that is accursed? Can I tolerate wicked scales and a bag of dishonest weights?" (Mic. 6:10–11). Amos criticizes merchants who say to themselves,

> When will the new moon be over
>   so that we may sell grain;
> and the sabbath,
>   so that we may offer wheat for sale?
> We will make the ephah small and the shekel great,
>   and practice deceit with false balances,
> buying the poor for silver
>   and the needy for a pair of sandals,
>   and selling the sweepings of the wheat. (Amos 8:5–6)

The economy in ancient Israel was based on trading in measures of volume (an ephah was about 35 liters) and measures of weight (a shekel was about 11 grams). But the weights and measures were not standard from city to city, town to town, or merchant to merchant, so cheating was commonplace. "Selling the sweepings of the wheat" refers to the inclusion of the discardable portion of the wheat in what was sold.

The courtroom. The legal courtroom (called "the gate") is another venue in which the prophets notice injustice. Amos complains that "they hate the one who reproves in the gate, and they abhor the one who speaks the truth," and he also calls out those "who afflict the righteous, who take a bribe, and push aside the needy in the gate" (Amos 5:10, 12). Isaiah also preaches against those "who acquit the guilty for a bribe, and deprive the innocent of their rights" (Isa. 5:23). Micah condemns "rulers [who] give judgment for a bribe" (Mic. 3:11).

The religious centers. The prophets reserve their most intense ire for their fellow religious leaders—those who should be teaching the people to live justly and righteously but who instead lead them into sin. Micah rails, "Its priests teach for a price, its prophets give oracles for money" (Mic. 3:11). Hosea blasts priest and prophet:

> Yet let no one contend,
>   and let none accuse,
>   for with you is my contention, O priest.
> You shall stumble by day;
>   the prophet also shall stumble with you by night,
>   and I will destroy your mother.
> My people are destroyed for lack of knowledge;
>   because you have rejected knowledge,
>   I reject you from being a priest to me.
> And since you have forgotten the law of your God,
>   I also will forget your children. (Hosea 4:4–6)

Hosea goes on to say that the more priests and prophets there are, the more sin (rather than righteousness) increases! Amos ridicules the religious leaders at important religious centers, such as Bethel, Gilgal, and Beer-sheba: "Seek me and live; but do not seek Bethel, and do not enter into Gilgal or cross over to Beer-sheba" (Amos 5:4–5).

Vision of a Just World

The prophetic vision for justice includes special care for the most vulnerable portions of the population: widows, orphans, refugees, sojourners, the poor, the oppressed. Isaiah exhorts the people to "learn to do good; seek justice, rescue the oppressed, defend the orphan, plead for the widow" (Isa. 1:17), even while he laments those "who legislate sinful laws . . . to turn aside the needy from justice, to rob the poor of my people of justice, to cheat widows" (10:1–2 AT). The special concern for the most vulnerable leads the prophets to champion the cause of the needy and confront those in power.

But the prophets also have visions of God's preferred future, a future in which nations will stream to Jerusalem to learn the Lord's ways—the ways of peace in which "nation shall not lift up sword against nation, neither shall they learn war any more" (Isa. 2:4). That vision of God's preferred future is most vividly cast by the prophet Isaiah, who sees a vision of what is often called "the peaceable kingdom":

> The wolf shall live with the lamb,
>   the leopard shall lie down with the kid,
> the calf and the lion and the fatling together,
>   and a little child shall lead them.
> The cow and the bear shall graze,
>   their young shall lie down together;
>   and the lion shall eat straw like the ox.
> The nursing child shall play over the hole of the asp,
>   and the weaned child shall put its hand on the adder's den.
> They will not hurt or destroy
>   on all my holy mountain;
> for the earth will be full of the knowledge of the LORD
>   as the waters cover the sea. (Isa. 11:6–9)

FOR FURTHER READING: Prophecy and the Prophetic Books

Blenkinsopp, Joseph. *A History of Prophecy in Israel*. Rev. ed. Louisville: Westminster John Knox, 1996.

Brueggemann, Walter. *The Prophetic Imagination*. 40th anniversary ed. Minneapolis: Fortress, 2018.

Dempsey, Carol J. *The Prophets: A Liberation-Critical Reading*. Minneapolis: Fortress, 2000.

Heschel, Abraham J. *The Prophets*. Perennial Classics. New York: HarperCollins, 2001.

Limburg, James. *The Prophets and the Powerless*. Minneapolis: Augsburg, 1977.

Nissinen, Martti. *Ancient Prophecy: Near Eastern, Biblical, and Greek Perspectives*. Oxford: Oxford University Press, 2017.

Sharp, Carolyn J. *The Old Testament Prophets for Today*. Louisville: Westminster John Knox, 2009.

von Rad, Gerhard. *Old Testament Theology*. Vol. 2, *The Theology of Israel's Prophetic Traditions*. Translated by D. M. G. Stalker. Old Testament Library. Louisville: Westminster John Knox, 2001.

Weems, Renita J. *Battered Love: Marriage, Sex, and Violence in the Hebrew Prophets*. Overtures to Biblical Theology. Minneapolis: Fortress, 1995.

Isaiah

The book of Isaiah is one of the most influential Old Testament texts for Christian theology and history. According to the United Bible Society's *The Greek New Testament*, the New Testament contains more than four hundred references to the book of Isaiah.[1] Isaiah's popularity in the New Testament is rivaled only by Deuteronomy and Psalms. And Isaiah is similarly prominent in rabbinic literature.

The book of Isaiah also poses serious interpretive challenges. Readers can be forgiven if going through the book induces literary motion sickness. Often without warning or transition, the text shifts from one genre to the next, or from one topic to the next, leaving the reader with questions such as, Who is the speaker? Is this the beginning of a new poem or the end of the last one? To a large extent, the to-and-fro of Isaiah is a result of its complex compositional history, which we will talk about below.

As one wades into this masterpiece of Hebrew prophetic literature, it is helpful to keep two things in mind. First, the book requires patience. Isaiah is the kind of book that can be fruitfully studied over an entire lifetime. Isaiah is not a narrative like Jonah, and while it has important organizing features, the book resists summarization. Second, it is helpful to remember that most of Isaiah is poetry. The poets responsible for Isaiah were not just good prophets; they were excellent poets. Appreciating the book's artistry and significance requires treating it as art—worthy of care and consideration.

Background

The book of Isaiah begins by introducing itself as "the vision of Isaiah son of Amoz" (1:1). We know about the prophet Isaiah from the book that bears his name, from 2 Kings 19–20, and from 2 Chronicles 26:20. Isaiah had an incredibly long prophetic ministry. According to Isaiah 6:1, he received a call to prophetic ministry "in the year that King Uzziah died," which was 738 BCE. Isaiah's death is not recorded anywhere in the Bible, but he was alive and active as a prophet at least as late as 701 BCE. There is significant reason to believe that he lived and prophesied until 690 or later.

Isaiah apparently came from a priestly family, since he was in the inner temple during his call experience (6:1). He was married to a prophetess (8:3), with whom he had at least two sons and maybe three. He and his wife gave their sons symbolic names in order to communicate his prophetic messages (more on this below).

Isaiah lived and prophesied in Jerusalem, often in the presence of the kings who ruled during his ministry: Jotham (ca. 738–735 BCE), Ahaz (735–715 BCE), and Hezekiah (715–687 BCE). He was apparently on good terms with Hezekiah, at least early in Hezekiah's reign, but was on less favorable terms with Ahaz, whose policies Isaiah opposed. He was creative as a prophet. For example, he employed a love song at one point to get his message across (5:1–7), and at another time he walked around Jerusalem "naked and barefoot for three years" in order to dissuade King Hezekiah from joining a revolt against Assyria, warning him that anyone who did so would be led away naked into exile (20:3).

Historical Context

The historical context of the book of Isaiah is a complicated subject, in part because there is difference of opinion among scholars about whether the entire book contains the words of "Isaiah son of Amoz" (1:1), whose ministry spanned from around 738 to 690 BCE. For the purpose of introducing the book here, we will focus only on the historical context of this eighth-century Isaiah.

Four massive events shook Jerusalem to its core during Isaiah's life. Many of Isaiah's datable prophetic messages can be linked to one of these crises.

The Syro-Ephraimite crisis (735–732 BCE). In 735 BCE, the Northern Kingdom of Israel joined forces with the nation of Aram and waged war on Judah. They, along with other nations, had decided to rebel against the Assyrian Empire, of which they were vassal states. Judah, the Southern Kingdom, was not an Assyrian vassal at the time and understandably declined to join the revolt (see 2 Kings 16:5–9). In order to gain Judah's compliance, Israel and Aram tried to

Box 25.1

The Assyrian Impact on Israelite History

The Assyrians were an Akkadian-speaking people located in northern Mesopotamia, primarily within the borders of modern-day Iraq. Though eventually unified by culture, geography, and language, several different local and nomadic groups made up Assyria. The Assyrian Empire entered a new era of regional domination in the eighth century BCE. As the Assyrians pushed father west, their actions had a powerful impact on the historical trajectories of both the Northern and Southern Kingdoms. The Northern Kingdom met its end at the hands of Assyria, and the Southern Kingdom bore its own share of scars from the encounter. Books such as Isaiah, Nahum, and Jonah bear special witness to this formative time in Israel's history.

topple King Ahaz and replace him with a puppet king they could control. The invasion failed, but Ahaz voluntarily became a vassal of Assyria, journeying to Damascus to submit to the Assyrian king Tiglath-pileser III.

The fall of Samaria and the exile of the Northern Kingdom (722/721 BCE). The Northern Kingdom became an Assyrian vassal around 745 BCE. They rebelled against the Assyrian kings several times, but when King Hoshea rebelled and allied with Egypt, the Assyrian king Shalmaneser had had enough. He invaded Israel and besieged its capital city, Samaria, for three years. In 722/721 BCE, Samaria fell. Many leading citizens of the Northern Kingdom were killed or taken into exile, but a substantial number fled south and joined the kingdom of Judah.

The campaigns of Sargon II (720–710 BCE). For about a decade, various nations along the eastern edge of the Mediterranean Sea rebelled against Assyria. The Assyrian king Sargon responded by marauding up and down the

oncenawhile, CC BY-SA 3.0 / Wikimedia Commons

Fig. 25.1. This image of King Sennacherib is a wall relief in his palace at Nineveh. Note that the face of Sennacherib has been chipped away. This was likely done by invaders who intentionally marred his likeness.

coast, putting down rebellions. Isaiah steadfastly warned Ahaz and Hezekiah against joining these rebellions.

The invasion of Sennacherib (701 BCE). When Sargon was killed in battle in 705 BCE and his body was not recovered, Hezekiah rebelled against Assyrian rule. Sargon's son Sennacherib invaded Judah in 701 to reconquer the kingdom. This invasion is known both from the biblical sources and from Sennacherib's annals, where he boasts that he destroyed many of Hezekiah's fortified cities and confined Hezekiah in Jerusalem "like a caged bird." Although Sennacherib was unable to conquer Jerusalem, the devastation and death caused by the revolt and subsequent war were enormous. Sennacherib may have invaded Judah again around 690 BCE—if so, that invasion also failed to capture Jerusalem.

Composition and Development

The authorship, composition, and development of the book of Isaiah are deeply contested by scholars. Yet Isaiah provides some of the clearest evidence of how prophetic books developed over generations—even over centuries. There are many different theories about how the book came to us in its present form, none of which needs to be delineated in great detail here. In what follows, we offer some guidelines for understanding the different approaches to the book.

First, there is a distinction between the book called Isaiah and the prophet called Isaiah.[2] This is always the case with books named after their authors: there is Matthew the evangelist and Matthew the book, Amos the prophet and Amos the book, and so on.

Second, centuries of interpretation have led many scholars to conclude that the book of Isaiah is the product not of a single author but rather of a multigenerational group of disciples and scribes. According to this view, the book reflects the following components:

1. First Isaiah: Most of the prophetic messages in chapters 1–35 were spoken by the prophet "Isaiah son of Amoz" in Jerusalem at various times between the years 738 and 690 BCE.

2. Historical interlude: The historical narrative in chapters 36–39 is borrowed from portions of 2 Kings 18–20. Recall that 2 Kings is part of the Deuteronomistic History (see chap. 9, "The Historical Books"), which dates to approximately 620–560 BCE. This implies that these chapters in Isaiah were added to the older collection of messages sometime after 620 BCE.

3. Second Isaiah: The messages that occur in chapters 40–55 do not identify their author, location, or date. But these chapters seem to assume a location in the Babylonian exile and three times mention "Cyrus" (44:28;

45:1, 13)—presumably the Persian king Cyrus, who defeated Babylon in 539 BCE and sent the Judean exiles home to rebuild Jerusalem and its temple (Ezra 1:2–8; 6:1–14). These texts are very hopeful about a return to Jerusalem.

4. Third Isaiah: In chapters 56–66, the mood changes from hope to disappointment, and the perceived location shifts from exile in Babylon to Jerusalem. These differences lead some interpreters to view this final section as later than Second Isaiah and thus the work of a supposed Third Isaiah.

Scholars who take this view believe that there was an original prophetic corpus of literature from the ministry of Isaiah son of Amoz. These texts were assembled, edited, updated, and added to over the course of centuries, from 738 to 490 BCE and beyond. Scholars who take this view regard the entire book of Isaiah as the work of generations and centuries.

The most important body of evidence for Isaiah being a multigenerational work is the set of texts whose contents assume fundamentally different historical contexts than those of the historical prophet Isaiah. As just noted, several explicit references are made to the sixth-century Persian king, Cyrus II (Isa. 44:28; 45:1, 13). The historical Isaiah was active as a prophet around 738–690 BCE, well over 130 years prior to Cyrus II's reign. Still other texts assume Jerusalem's destruction (see, e.g., Isa. 44:26; 51:3; 52:9; 58:12), which occurred in 587 BCE. Still others assume Judah's exile, which happened around the same time (Isa. 43:5; 49:5; 56:8).

According to this approach, none of these texts makes sense in an eighth-century, Judean setting. They do make sense, however, if one recognizes that the book of Isaiah—like other ancient Near Eastern texts—was edited, arranged, and compiled over a long period of time. Books like Isaiah, in other words, are the product of scribal culture.[3]

With this information in mind, many scholars speak of three sections of Isaiah, each roughly corresponding to a historical period: First Isaiah (chaps. 1–39, eighth century BCE), Second Isaiah (chaps. 40–55, sixth century BCE), and Third Isaiah (chaps. 56–66, sixth–fifth centuries BCE). Alternatively, one can also categorize these according to the dominant imperial powers of the time: First Isaiah (Assyria), Second Isaiah (Babylon), and Third Isaiah (Persia). Some scholars are less confident about dividing chapters 40–55 from chapters 56–66, and yet even these scholars assume that all these chapters were written after the destruction of Jerusalem at the hands of the Babylonians.

There are many scholars, however, who dispute this threefold division of the book of Isaiah. Some conservative scholars hold to a unified composition of the entire book. They argue that the book mentions only one prophetic author,

"Isaiah son of Amoz" (1:1; 2:1; 13:1). They also point to many similarities that span the entire book, such as the use of the title "the Holy One of Israel" (which occurs twelve times in chaps. 1–39, fourteen times in chaps. 40–66, and only six times in the rest of the entire Old Testament). Perhaps the strongest argument in favor of a unified composition is the fact that the threefold view of authorship requires the existence of otherwise anonymous prophets to write chapters 40–55 and chapters 56–66. They argue that prophets with such great influence and skill would have been known and mentioned elsewhere in the Bible. More liberal scholars doubt any correspondence at all between Isaiah son of Amoz and the book itself. They posit that the book's long, complex history of composition and development cannot be recovered.

This is only the roughest summary of the various views of Isaiah's authorship and composition. The book underwent a lengthy and complicated developmental process—as is witnessed at the very least by the insertion of 2 Kings 18–20 as chapters 36–39. The fact that Isaiah's words were preserved and reinterpreted indicates the prophet's profound influence and significance. It might seem disrespectful to say that later generations altered Isaiah's work, but nothing could be further from the truth. Concepts of authorship were different in the ancient world, where "intellectual property" and "copyright" were not active in the way they are today.

Genre

Like many prophetic books, Isaiah is a collection of texts about a wide range of topics, such as the fate of the nations, the sins of God's people, Jerusalem's future, politics, and divine grace. The book includes many genres: a call story, a love song, taunt songs, coronation songs, visions, oracles against

---

Box 25.2

Outline

1. First Isaiah of Jerusalem (1–35)
   a. Introduction, early polemics, Isaiah's calling, and promises (1–12)
   b. Prophecies about the nations (13–23)
   c. Prophecies about the eschatological future (24–27)
   d. Later prophecies about Judah's final days (28–33)
   e. Prophecies about restoration (34–35)
2. Historical interlude: Assyria threatens Judah (36–39)
3. Second Isaiah of the exile: Prophecies about Judah's suffering, judgment, restoration, and return (40–55)
4. Third Isaiah of the return: Prophecies about returning, tensions and divisions, and a renewed Zion (56–66)

the nations, and so on. The book is predominantly made up of poetry, but there are exceptions (see, e.g., chaps. 36–39). David Petersen helpfully divides the poetic material into three types of discourse: polemical, promissory, and liturgical.[4] Polemical literature includes everything from judgment oracles to disputations. Promissory material describes God's commitments to the future, for Israel, the nations, and creation. Liturgical material has its setting in the worship life of Israel.

Literary Interpretation

A lengthy and complicated book such as Isaiah can be divided in a number of different ways. The discussion that follows is largely organized according to dominant literary and theological themes.[5]

First Isaiah of Jerusalem: Introduction, early polemics, Isaiah's calling, and promises (Isa. 1–12). The first chapter of Isaiah is designed as an introduction, apparently to the entire sixty-six-chapter book. After the historical notice (1:1), the book moves into a poem that calls the cosmos as witnesses against God's rebellious "children" (1:2). The sin of God's people has left "daughter Zion" vulnerable to the same forces of chaos and judgment that leveled the infamous cities of Sodom and Gomorrah (1:7–9). Zion will burn, but out of the ashes will emerge a new city (1:26–27). This first chapter foreshadows much of what is to come.

Chapters 2–12 deal with the fate of Judah and Jerusalem. Judgment and hope are interwoven (see, e.g., chaps. 2–4). Chapter 5 contains the famous "Song of the Vineyard," in which the prophet takes on the guise of a vineyard planter/lover whose hard and careful work on behalf of the vineyard is met

---

Box 25.3

Sixty-Six Chapters, Sixty-Six Books?

Some readers of the Bible notice that the book of Isaiah has sixty-six chapters and wonder if there is some significance to the fact that the Protestant Bible also has sixty-six books. While this numerical coincidence is interesting, it seems unlikely that it is anything more than a coincidence. The division of the biblical books into chapters/verses is a very late phenomenon (thirteenth century CE). It happened a long time after the biblical books were written. What's more, only Protestant Christian Bibles have sixty-six books. Catholics and Orthodox Christians have more expansive canons, making the observation of only relative significance to global Christianity.

Because the Old Testament is sacred literature and considered by many to be inspired by God, it is understandable that readers anticipate finding meaningful and even hidden connections throughout the canon. The Bible itself, after all, is a book full of stories about divine mysteries and revelations. When such connections are made, however, it is important to weigh and consider them with great care and with an eye toward evidence.

Fig. 25.2. Seraphim purifying the lips of Isaiah. See Isa. 6:6–7.

Bridgeman Images

with disappointment (5:1–7). God desires justice from his people, but receives only bloodshed.

Chapter 6 describes a heavenly vision in which the prophet receives a commission from Yahweh, to which he famously responds, "Here am I; send me!" (6:8). Isaiah receives the dreary news that his words will not enlighten or effect change, but rather will "dull" the minds of God's people and "blind" their eyes (6:10). Hope will reside in a holy remnant—a stump containing a "holy seed" (6:13).

Isaiah 7–8 is related to an event called the Syro-Ephraimite crisis in 735 BCE. King Ahaz of Judah refused to join a multinational alliance against the king of Assyria. In response, Damascus and Israel (the Northern Kingdom) attacked Judah with the intention of replacing Ahaz with a more agreeable monarch. The prophet urges King Ahaz to trust that Yahweh will deliver him. Ahaz chooses instead to appeal to none other than the king of Assyria himself, Tiglath-pileser III, for rescue—willingly becoming a vassal of Assyria. Ahaz's lack of trust in Yahweh starkly contrasts with the response of Hezekiah, who faces a similar situation under a different Assyrian king but chooses to trust in Yahweh's saving power (see chaps. 36–37).

Chapters 9–12 contain powerful descriptions of the coming, ideal Davidic descendant, who will conquer foes, administer justice, and usher in a new age of peace (9:1–7; 11:1–16). These texts may have been composed for the coronation of King Hezekiah (ca. 715 BCE). After a brief indictment of those who exploit the needy (10:1–4), chapter 10 includes a lengthy series of poems in which Assyria is understood to be both the agent and object of Yahweh's wrath (10:5–34). The poem is carefully designed to subversively mimic the propagandistic rhetoric of the Neo-Assyrian Empire.[6] The section concludes with a psalm of thanksgiving (chap. 12).

First Isaiah of Jerusalem: Prophecies about the nations (Isa. 13–23). Isaiah 13–23 is a collection of oracles concerning foreign nations. The announcements are directed at nations such as Babylon, Moab, Damascus, and Egypt. In most cases, these oracles are polemical in nature, though there are some exceptions (see, e.g., 19:16–24). While these oracles address foreign nations, their audience was domestic—God's own people. The underlying theological conviction of the oracles is that Yahweh, God of Judah, is also king of the nations.

Box 25.4

Children with Prophetic Names

Several children in Isaiah 7–8 are given special names to convey divine messages: Shear-jashub ("A-remnant-shall-return," 7:3), Immanuel ("God-with-us," 7:14), and Maher-shalal-hash-baz ("The-spoil-speeds-the-prey-hastens," 8:1–4). In various ways, these names communicate Yahweh's demands and promises to Isaiah's audiences.

The New Testament's Gospel of Matthew cites Isaiah 7:14 in connection with the miraculous birth of Jesus by the virgin Mary (Matt. 1:23). The Immanuel child of Isaiah 7 clearly had a contemporary prophetic role in Isaiah's own place and time, and this meaning should be recognized and appreciated. But Christians also recognize that the same God was at work in the life of Jesus and that these Old Testament stories might in some ways foreshadow God's work through Jesus the Messiah.

The book of Isaiah is not the only prophetic book to use children's names as billboards of divine intentionality. In the book of Hosea, the prophet is commanded to give children names that are prophetically significant. Hosea's wife, Gomer, gives birth to a daughter who is given the name Lo-ruhamah, which means "not shown mercy." When Gomer has a son, he is named Lo-ammi, which means "not my people."

First Isaiah of Jerusalem: Prophecies about the eschatological future (Isa. 24–27). Chapters 24–27 are enigmatically fascinating. They have sometimes been called "proto-apocalyptic" and assigned a very late date. But this label is problematic, since features typical of apocalyptic literature are absent. Many scholars consider them part of Second Isaiah due to thematic, theological, and linguistic similarities with chapters 40–55. Christopher Hays argues for dating these chapters to the seventh century and to the reign of Josiah in particular. Major themes include the epic destruction and desolation brought upon creation. The world is a mess. Destruction brings about the end of the "ruined city" and the establishment of Yahweh's reign at Zion. A hymn of praise (25:1–5) is followed by a feast of victory, in which Yahweh will "swallow up death forever" (25:8). Chapter 26 contrasts the two cities—Zion and the "lofty city" (26:5)—and celebrates Yahweh's establishment of peace. In chapter 27, Yahweh commits to watching over his vineyard to protect it against all adversaries, reversing the earlier imagery of the Song of the Vineyard in chapter 5. Yahweh appeals to the exiled Northern Kingdom, hoping that they will set aside their idolatrous worship and instead worship in Jerusalem, Yahweh's holy city.

First Isaiah of Jerusalem: Later prophecies about Judah's final days (Isa. 28–33). An eclectic collection of texts can be found in chapters 28–33. The oracles tend toward the polemical, taking aim at the sins of both Israel and Judah, and portend the last days of Judah. And yet hopeful themes exist alongside judgment. Many of these oracles seem to be prophecies that Isaiah son of Amoz had spoken early in his ministry (perhaps at the time of the Syro-Ephraimite war) and then reworked and extended later in his ministry (perhaps when Sennacherib invaded Judah in 701 BCE). While God's people might be tempted

Immanuel A Hebrew name meaning "God with us," first used in Isaiah 7:14 and later applied to Jesus in Matthew 1:23; sometimes spelled *Emmanuel* in the New Testament.

apocalyptic literature A genre of heavily symbolic, eschatologically oriented literature that displays distinctive literary characteristics and claims to unveil the truth about the world as viewed from a dualistic and deterministic perspective.

to trust in foreign alliances with countries like Egypt or in swift war horses (see 30:1–5), the prophet urges them to trust instead that "[God] will surely show you grace at the sound of your cry; when he hears it, he will answer you" (30:19, modified). When Yahweh's people return to him, "Assyria will fall by a sword, not of man; a sword, not of a human, will devour him" (31:8, modified). The prophet accuses Judah of having made a "covenant with death" (28:15, 18), meaning that they have made a worthless alliance with Egypt—but God promises to overturn their covenant with death. Isaiah 32 begins with a poem about a righteous king, whose eyes will be unsealed and whose ears will listen (cf. 6:9–10). It then quickly shifts to an oracle condemning Jerusalem's corrupt women, followed by an abrupt transition to an oracle about salvation and about the transformation of the wilderness by God's Spirit. Chapter 33 concludes the section with a lengthy prayer (33:2–9), a divine response (33:10–16), and hopeful descriptions of Zion's future (33:17–22).

First Isaiah of Jerusalem: Prophecies about restoration (Isa. 34–35). Chapters 34–35 begin with a furious address to all nations and peoples (34:1–2). Quickly, however, the poem directs its ire toward Edom. The Old Testament leaves hints that there was a long and troubled history between Israel and Edom. According to Genesis, the Edomites are descendants of Esau (see Gen. 36), with whom Jacob was in frequent conflict from birth (see Gen. 25:19–34; 27:1–41). Apart from these troubled memories, Edom apparently did harm to his "brother" during the Babylonian conquest of Judah (see, e.g., Ps. 137; Obad.). Isaiah 35 turns in a decidedly different direction and reads much like some oracles in chapters 40–55. The wilderness is miraculously transformed (35:1–3, 7), the physically disabled are healed (35:5–7), and the exiled return home on secured paths (35:8–10).

Historical interlude: Assyria threatens Judah (Isa. 36–39). The bulk of the narrative material in Isaiah is found in chapters 36–39. These chapters are very similar to 2 Kings 18–20 and narrate Sennacherib's invasion of Judah in 701 BCE. This is one of the most heavily documented military campaigns in biblical history. Not all of the sources agree, but there is an abundance of relevant sources, both within the Bible and outside of it. In contrast to King Ahaz, King Hezekiah trusts in Yahweh's words through Isaiah, and his city is saved as a result. Chapter 38 contains a narrative about a time when Hezekiah is healed after falling ill.

Chapter 39 is of particular importance to the larger structure of the book. In this short narrative, envoys from the Babylonian king Merodach-baladan visit King Hezekiah. In an attempt to impress his guests, Hezekiah shows them his wealth and weaponry (39:2). Upon hearing about this, Isaiah prophesies that one day the entire contents of Hezekiah's royal house will be carried off to Babylon, including some of his own sons (39:6–7). Hezekiah seems to misunderstand the severity of Isaiah's oracle and simply notes that "there will be peace and reliability in my days" (39:8 AT). He may experience peace, but his legacy—his dynastic name—was under threat.

The narrative foreshadows the Babylonians' plunder of Jerusalem under Nebuchadnezzar (see, e.g., 2 Kings 24:13), but unlike the books of Kings and Jeremiah, Isaiah contains no description of the event itself. Turn the page to Isaiah 40, and the text assumes that the Babylonian conquest of Judah and the exile have already happened. The event was so powerful and so traumatic that it could be felt without being explicitly named.

Second Isaiah of the exile: Prophecies about Judah's suffering, judgment, restoration, and return (Isa. 40–55). The Protestant Reformer Martin Luther observed that upon turning to chapter 40 one enters Isaiah's "second book."[7] Luther was not primarily making a point about composition (who wrote the book) but rather about content. The portion of Isaiah that begins with chapter 40 definitely feels like the work of another author.

Chapters 40–55 are predominantly words of promise and comfort to exiled Judahites, living in the wake of the violent Babylonian defeat of their homeland. This point is apparent from chapter 40's opening lines:

> Comfort, comfort my people, says your God;
>> speak to Jerusalem's heart,
>>> and cry out to her
>> that her battle is over,
>>> that her transgression is pardoned,
>>>> that she has taken from Yahweh's hand double in exchange for her
>>>> sins. (Isa. 40:1–2 AT)

Throughout chapters 40–55, Yahweh addresses his people's fear with words of promise (see 41:10, 13–14; 43:1, 5; 44:2, 8; 51:7). In addition to comfort, Isaiah 40–55 contains a number of other significant themes: the return of exiled Judeans to Judah, the ministry of a mysterious "servant," and God's use of Cyrus as a delegated agent in his plan to restore Israel.

At the heart of Isaiah 40–55 is the hope of return. A gentle shepherd to distressed sheep, Yahweh promises to gather his scattered flock (40:10–11) and make a way through the desert, just as he once made a way through the sea in the exodus (43:1–7, 16–21). Creation transforms in response to God's decree: difficult terrain is flattened (40:3–4); water emerges in desiccated wilderness (41:17–20; 43:19–21; 44:3–4). Like Abraham and Sarah, who also made a long journey from Mesopotamia, Judah would make its way back to a restored Zion under the protection of Yahweh's promises (51:1–3).

Isaiah 40–55 contains a number of passages that mention a "servant" of Yahweh. Four of these passages have traditionally been called Servant Songs

(42:1–9; 49:1–7; 50:4–11; 52:13–53:12), although the word *servant* occurs in other passages in chapters 40–55 (41:8; 42:19; 43:10; 44:1, 21; etc.). These four passages were first identified as the Servant Songs by Bernhard Duhm in an 1892 commentary, but it is unlikely that the author of Isaiah 40–55 thought of these passages as a unit or intended readers to think about Yahweh's "servant" separately from the many other passages in which the servant is mentioned. The identity of the servant in these songs or throughout chapters 40–55 is unclear. Suggestions include Israel itself (see 44:1 and 49:3, which refer to Jacob/Israel explicitly as a servant), some unnamed Judean exile, Jeremiah, the author of chapters 40–55, and even King Cyrus of Persia. Others suggest that some of these texts are purposefully ambiguous, inviting readers to identify the servant with a variety of historical figures. At times, the servant seems to be an individual who has a mission to Israel; at other times, "the servant" clearly refers to a collective: the nation Israel. In the second Servant Song, both of these are the case: "He said to me, 'You are my servant, Israel, in whom I will be glorified'" (49:3 ESV), and "[He] formed me from the womb to be his servant, to bring Jacob back to him; . . . It is too light a thing that you should be my servant to raise up the tribes of Jacob" (49:5, 6 ESV). It could be that the author did not intend any one person or group of persons to be identified as *the* servant. Whatever the case may be, Yahweh's servant (or servants) is an agent of God and helps bring about God's work in the world.

Cyrus plays an important role in Isaiah 40–55. He is mentioned by name several times (44:28; 45:1, 13) and in all cases positively. Yahweh refers to him as "my shepherd" and the one who will "fulfill my entire purpose" (44:28 AT). In Isaiah 45:1, he is called Yahweh's messiah / anointed one. Yahweh pledges Cyrus support in order to grant him success and victory (45:1–3), and all "for the sake of my servant, Jacob, and Israel my chosen one" (45:4, modified).

Box 25.5

The Suffering Servant

Isaiah 52–53 contains the most well-known of the Servant Songs, especially among Christians. In memorable language, the poem describes him as someone who is widely despised, rejected, and reviled (53:3). Most significantly for Christians, however, is the claim that the servant suffered for "our" sake: "Surely he has borne our infirmities" and "carried our illnesses" (53:4 AT); he was "wounded for our sins," and "by his wounds we receive healing" (53:5 AT). Given Jesus's own suffering, it is no accident that Christians see the ministry of their Messiah in these descriptions of the suffering servant (cf. Acts 8:26–40). It is important that Christians learn to read against two horizons: (1) the horizon of the text's historical audience (sixth-century Judean exiles) and (2) the horizon of Jesus's messianic ministry. Both allow us to interpret the texts in ways that resonate for faithful readers.

Third Isaiah of the return: Prophecies about returning, tensions and divisions, and a renewed Zion (Isa. 56–66). Chapters 56–66 are similar to chapters 40–55 in many ways. These final chapters also assume a historical context subsequent to the exile. It seems to be assumed that some exiles have returned, but that the experience had been disappointing. The prophet speaks of hope regarding the restoration of Zion, the transformation of creation, and the imminent manifestation of divine salvation. Yahweh's promises of salvation in these chapters (e.g., 56:1) are more clearly tied to obedience than they are in chapters 40–55, though Isaiah 60–62 are exceptional in this regard. These three chapters contain some of the most glorious promises about Zion and about God's "servant," but they are not tied to obedience in the way that others in 56–66 are.

These chapters have a number of distinct features. First, they adopt a more polemical tone toward members of the community whose actions are considered unfaithful and destructive (see 56:9–57:13; 58:1–14; 59:1–21; 65:1–7). Many scholars interpret these texts as evidence of fracturing and division within the postexilic community. Second, Sabbath observance is also prioritized in a way not found elsewhere in the book (56:2, 4, 6; 58:13). Finally, there is an emphasis on the construction and operation of the temple (56:1–8; 60:7; 66:1–4; see also 44:28), perhaps reflecting a context in which the temple is being restored.

Theological Interpretation

Given its size and scope, Isaiah raises a great number of theological questions. Several are particularly prominent: What is proper worship before the Holy One of Israel? In times of crisis, whom should God's people trust? What kind of future can God's people and God's city (Jerusalem) expect? How should Isaiah be interpreted in light of Jesus?

Faithful Worship

The issue of proper worship pervades the book of Isaiah. In a stunning introduction, Yahweh belts out this screed:

> What to me are your hordes of sacrifices? says Yahweh.
> I have had enough of your offerings of rams
> and the fat of well-raised animals.
> In the blood of bulls, lambs, or goats I take no pleasure. . . .
> Your new moons and your designated times my very being hates.
> They burdened me greatly.
> I tire of bearing them.
> When you spread your hands,
> I will hide my eyes from you;

> Even though you multiply prayers,
>> I will not listen—
> your hands are brimming with blood. (1:11, 14–15 AT)

But God does not give his people the silent treatment. He offers them a way back to proper worship and proper relationship with him:

> Bathe, make yourself clean;
>> get the evil of your deeds out of my face;
>>> stop the evil!
> Learn to do good,
>> chase justice,
>>> correct oppression,
> do justice for the orphan,
>> contend on behalf of the widow. (1:16–17 AT)

Christians have frequently (and quite incorrectly) assumed that these verses denounce Israel's sacrificial system as empty ritual and call instead for a religion of the heart; anti-Catholic sentiments often lurk behind this critique. But nothing could be further from the truth. The point is not that God despises rituals. After all, he commands them in Exodus–Numbers. The point is that God is repulsed by hypocritical worship. God hates it when worshipers harm their neighbors and then assume they can approach God as if nothing ever happened. The problem is not the ritual but the practitioners.

Faith and Unbelief

Themes of trust and distrust loom large in Isaiah. In the first part of the book (chaps. 1–39), the reader is presented with two royal figures, Ahaz (7:1–8:23) and Hezekiah (36:1–37:38), both of whom face significant military threats. Ahaz chooses not to trust God's assurances through Isaiah. Hezekiah, however, does. In Isaiah 40–55, the prophet offers extravagant promises as he urges Judahites to cast off fear and trust in the efficacy of God's words (40:6–8; 55:8–13). Trauma, military defeat, and exile have eroded the bonds of love and trust between God and Israel. Isaiah 40–55 is, to a very large extent, designed to repair these connections and forge a new path into the future.

The Future

The book of Isaiah has much to say about the future and most especially the future of Jerusalem. Jerusalem (often called Zion) is at the center of Isaiah's eschatological gaze. Eschatology refers to the future that Yahweh promises. Jerusalem was the capital of the Southern Kingdom, where David and his ancestors ruled and where Yahweh's temple stood. In the future, nations will stream to Zion, where they will learn and behold the ways of peace (2:3–4; 11:1–9; 60:18), experience the rule of a righteous king (11:1–5), and offer their tribute (chap. 60). Foreigners will no longer threaten Zion's walls but will instead rebuild them (60:10). Zion will literally be a shining example of Yahweh's just and righteous reign over the earth (60:19–21; 62:2).

Fig. 25.3. *Lion and the Lambs, 1984.* Perhaps the best-known (but wrongly remembered) image from the book of Isaiah is the iconic vision of lions and lambs lying down together in peace. Actually, the prophet speaks of wolves and lambs lying down together—the lions lie down with calves (11:6; see also 65:25).

Yahweh, King of the World

Related to Isaiah's vision of the future, the book of Isaiah emphasizes God's sovereignty over all creation and especially over the nations of the earth. This is evident throughout the book but is especially clear in the oracles concerning foreign nations (chaps. 13–23). In these decrees, King Yahweh makes sovereign declarations of judgment and promise about the past, present, and future of these kingdoms. As noted above, these same nations will one day bring their devotion, adoration, and tribute to Jerusalem, which serves as the center of Yahweh's earthly rule. Yahweh's royal status is also clear in Isaiah's famous "call narrative" (chap. 6), where the prophet depicts Yahweh seated on a lofty throne and garbed in the finery of a king. Isaiah, as a prophet, is understood to be a herald of Yahweh's royal court.

eschatology The study or focus on "last things," such as the restoration of Jerusalem, the return of Christ, final judgment, or other phenomena associated with the end times.

The Fifth Gospel

Throughout church history, Christians have perceived the work of Christ in the words of Isaiah (see Luke 4:14–21; Acts 8:26–40). For this reason, Isaiah has often been called "the fifth Gospel."[8] Yet understanding Christ's relationship to the Old Testament is no easy matter. The New Testament authors frequently interpret Jesus's existence as the messianic fulfillment of Old Testament promises (see, e.g., Matt. 1:22–24, citing Isa. 7:14; Matt. 12:15–21, citing Isa. 42:1–4). It should come as no surprise that early Christians reinterpreted received traditions in light of new experiences of salvation.

Acts 8 provides an interesting example of early Christian messianic interpretation of the Old Testament. Philip encounters an Ethiopian eunuch reading Isaiah 53:7–8. The eunuch asks a question that scholars still grapple with today: "Tell me, about whom does the prophet say this—himself or someone else?" (Acts 8:34 AT). Upon experiencing the power of Jesus's life, death, and

eunuch A castrated male who typically served in royal courts.

resurrection, Christians could not help but reinterpret their received Scriptures. In our view, one need not feel compelled to choose only one answer to the eunuch's question. If one thing is clear from Isaiah, it is that theological traditions from the past can be fruitfully reinterpreted in light of present needs.

When the authors of the New Testament reinterpreted the Old Testament in light of Jesus's life, death, and resurrection, they were engaging in a common interpretive practice—one already present in the pages of the Old Testament. Old Testament authors frequently interpreted new events in light of old ones. In the book of Isaiah itself, for example, the return from exile is compared not only to the exodus (43:16–21) but also to the days of Noah (54:9–10). Jeremiah similarly uses God's judgment of Sodom and Gomorrah as a prophetic symbol of his own age (Jer. 23:14–15; cf. 49:17–18).

But that isn't the whole story. It is also important to understand that the Old Testament was a true word of God to Israel in its own time, quite apart from the later Christian understanding that Jesus was the Messiah. Hezekiah, for instance, was offered a word of God from Isaiah during Sennacherib's incursion into Judah in the late eighth century BCE. Understanding how that word shaped Hezekiah's response and therefore impacted Judah's history says something profoundly significant about God, faith, and the world.

Two things can be true at the same time: Christians can, on the one hand, recognize Jesus's messianic ministry in the texts of the Old Testament. On the other hand, Christians can also recognize that those same texts had deep significance for Israel in earlier centuries. These dual hermeneutical horizons attest to the potency of the Old Testament tradition and to its flexibility and resiliency in the face of changing circumstances.

Historical Interpretation

Some of the most fascinating historical questions raised by the book of Isaiah relate to its compositional history, which we discussed above. The book of Isaiah is a book whose writing took several hundred years and spanned three major Near Eastern empires. And we cannot even begin to say how many scribes were involved in the process! But these historical factors also have theological significance. What does it mean to call a book like Isaiah—with its complex compositional history—the Word of God? How can one, on the one hand, affirm the deeply human and historical processes that produced the book of Isaiah and, on the other hand, call that book Holy Scripture? These are not easy questions, but they are important ones. What is more, they apply to every Old Testament book, all of which have undergone some kind of lengthy editorial process.

The book of Isaiah is also deeply shaped by Judah's experiences with the aforementioned imperial powers: Assyria, Babylon, and Persia. Judah never achieved parity with these powers. It could offer various forms of resistance, but it could never truly compete with them. Unlike the United States, Judah was never in a position to dictate international policy, wield overwhelming military force, or command the cultural heights. Judah was often forced to rely on other political entities to help it in times of crisis. In the Syro-Ephraimite crisis, for instance, Judah leaned on Tiglath-pileser III to ensure its safety. At other times, Egypt filled that role. The point is that Judah's geopolitical vulnerability sometimes forced it to depend on others for its safety. This geopolitical dependence no doubt informs the book's theological emphasis on trust in Yahweh.

Finally, in the process of trying to subjugate Judah, several emperors saw fit to secure obedience through military domination. Sennacherib's siege of Jerusalem (701 BCE) and Nebuchadnezzar's destruction of Jerusalem (586 BCE) are two major examples. The latter was particularly destructive and resulted in the forced deportation of an unknown number of Judahites to Mesopotamia. A key question emerges: How did the bitter social forces of defeat, societal collapse, economic exploitation, religious disruption, and forced relocation leave their mark on the pages of Isaiah—or any other Old Testament book for that matter? Given the Bible's central and esteemed role in American culture, it is easy to forget that the Old Testament was shaped by traumatic human experiences of loss, destruction, and grief. The book of Isaiah is just one example of how the brutal meat grinder of history fundamentally influenced the creation of biblical texts.

FOR FURTHER READING: Isaiah

Barker, Margaret. *Isaiah*. Eerdmans Commentary on the Bible. Grand Rapids: Eerdmans, 2003.

Blenkinsopp, Joseph. *Opening the Sealed Book: Interpretations of the Book of Isaiah in Late Antiquity*. Grand Rapids: Eerdmans, 2006.

Brueggemann, Walter. *Isaiah*. 2 vols. Westminster Bible Companion. Louisville: Westminster John Knox, 1998.

Childs, Brevard S. *The Struggle to Understand Isaiah as Christian Scripture*. Grand Rapids: Eerdmans, 2004.

Goldingay, John. *The Theology of the Book of Isaiah*. Downers Grove, IL: IVP Academic, 2014.

Hanson, Paul D. *Isaiah 40–66*. Interpretation: A Bible Commentary for Teaching and Preaching. Louisville: John Knox, 1995.

Seitz, Christopher R. *Isaiah 1–39*. Interpretation: A Bible Commentary for Teaching and Preaching. Louisville: John Knox, 1993.

Tull, Patricia K. *Isaiah 1–39*. Smyth & Helwys Bible Commentary. Macon, GA: Smyth & Helwys, 2010.

MAGNA
EST
ENIM
VELUT

MARE
CONTRI
TIO

...UA
...HREN
...TI.5

Jeremias

Jeremiah

The book of Jeremiah is a collection of poetic and narrative texts about the prophet Jeremiah son of Hilkiah. By word count, Jeremiah is the longest book in the Bible. The book is well known for its moving (and sometimes disturbing) portrayals of Yahweh. Jeremiah proclaims a God who does not judge his people as a disinterested judge. Instead, God's rage over the people's sin mingles with divine sorrow. Jeremiah is not merely about the violation of divine commandments; it is about the fracturing of a covenantal relationship.

But there is also hope and possibility for this broken relationship—in the opportunity to repent, for instance. When repentance can no longer change the course of events, then Yahweh offers to accompany his people through the disaster in exile and eventually return them to their land. As chapter 1 indicates, the prophet's mission is "to uproot and to break down, to destroy and to overthrow, to build and to plant" (1:10 AT).

Background

The Prophet Jeremiah

The prophet Jeremiah son of Hilkiah is known mostly from the book that bears his name, which contains many of his messages and also many stories about him. Jeremiah came from a priestly lineage; he descended from the line of Abiathar, a chief priest in David's time. After David's death, Abiathar supported David's older son Adonijah for the throne, rather than Solomon, so Solomon banished Abiathar to Anathoth—a village in the hill country of Benjamin, north of Judah. Jeremiah was born in Anathoth.

Fig. 26.1. This Persian or Iranian art apparently depicts Jeremiah 24, in which God shows Jeremiah a basket of good figs and a basket of bad figs. The good figs symbolize the Judeans who were sent into exile in what is now Persia/Iran, whom God would regard as good, "for they shall return to me" (24:7). The bad figs represent King Zedekiah and his officials in Jerusalem and those in Egypt: "I will make them a horror," symbolized by the half-dead donkey (24:9). Paradoxically, Jeremiah himself was forcibly taken into exile in Egypt by his followers.

Jeremiah experienced a call to prophetic ministry as a young boy, and his ministry was long, from as early as 628 BCE to as late as 570 BCE. Jeremiah never married or fathered children because, he said, "the children who are born" in Jerusalem during his days would die or go into exile (16:3 CEB). Jeremiah's words were recorded and preserved by his faithful scribe and disciple, Baruch. Near the end of Jeremiah's life, his supporters took him to Egypt, where he most likely died.

Jeremiah fiercely criticized the rulers of his day, accusing them of false worship, violence against the vulnerable, and foolish foreign-policy decisions. As a result, he faced a fair amount of resistance, which came in the form of social isolation, imprisonment, and various kinds of peril. The book offers a deeply personal portrayal of Jeremiah's suffering. He expresses anger and anguish toward his opponents and even toward God, who called him into his vocation.

Historical Context

The prophet lived through a series of dramatic historical events, including the most tragic events in ancient Judah's history: the Babylonians' destruction of Jerusalem and the temple and the subsequent exile of Judeans to Mesopotamia. Biographically, Jeremiah lived and ministered before, during, and after this seminal set of events. These and other key events shaped Jeremiah's ministry.

Josiah's reformation (620 BCE). According to 2 Kings 22–23, King Josiah launched a massive reformation of Judah's religious life around 620 BCE. The book of 2 Kings reports that this reformation was sparked by the discovery of a Torah scroll (perhaps containing the core of Deuteronomy) found in the temple when it was being remodeled at the king's command. Based on the instructions of the Torah scroll, the king removed all the elements of pagan deities that had been introduced in and around Jerusalem, tore down high places (worship sites) throughout the land, drove out male and female temple prostitutes, and reinstituted the celebration of the Passover festival. Josiah was killed in battle with the Egyptians in 609 BCE. The book of Jeremiah is surprisingly silent about Josiah's reforms, despite the fact that there would seem to be significant theological overlap between Jeremiah's theology and the reforms of Josiah—at least as they are reported in the book of Kings.

First deportation (597 BCE). During Jeremiah's life, the Babylonian Empire under Nebuchadnezzar overcame the Assyrian Empire and ruled the ancient Near East. In 597 BCE, the Babylonians forced Jerusalem to submit. They stripped the city of much of its wealth and deported many of its leading citizens into exile, including King Jehoiachin, placing his uncle Zedekiah on the throne. Jeremiah was not deported.

Fall of Jerusalem and second deportation (586 BCE). Following a rebellion by Zedekiah, the Babylonians returned to Jerusalem, besieging and conquering it in 586 BCE. The walls were torn down, the city razed, and the temple

---

Box 26.1

Waves of Exiles

It is common for authors and teachers to refer simply to the Babylonian exile as if it were a single, decisive event. In fact, the term refers to a prolonged series of events that ultimately resulted in the conquest of Jerusalem, the destruction of Yahweh's temple, the dethroning of multiple Judean rulers, and the forced deportation of many Judeans to Mesopotamia. This left Judah in a state of economic, political, and social collapse. While decisive moments certainly existed, the crisis was a slow-boiling one. The impacts of that crisis, moreover, were felt differently at different strata of society. Deported elites, for instance, were forced to live outside their homeland, under circumstances foreign and perhaps even hostile toward them. Those who remained—largely poor agriculturalists—found themselves contributing to the Babylonian tribute coffers.

destroyed. A second deportation of leading citizens occurred. Judah was incorporated into the empire as a province, with Gedaliah as its governor. Once again, Jeremiah was not deported, perhaps because he steadfastly opposed rebelling against Babylon.

Assassination of Gedaliah and flight to Egypt (582 BCE?). Gedaliah the governor was assassinated by rebels. Although Jeremiah commanded the people to stay in Judah, many fled to Egypt in fear of Babylonian wrath. Jeremiah and Baruch were forced to relocate with them.

Composition and Development

Like many of the Old Testament prophetic books, the book of Jeremiah has a complicated, largely opaque compositional history. While many of the oracles undoubtedly trace back to the historical prophet Jeremiah, the book itself has undergone a significant amount of editing and redaction.

Evidence of this complex compositional history becomes apparent in a comparison of the Hebrew version of Jeremiah (the Masoretic Text) and the Greek version of Jeremiah (the Septuagint or LXX). English translations of the Old Testament (e.g., NRSV, NIV, ESV, CEB) within the Protestant tradition

Fig. 26.2. Baruch, the disciple of Jeremiah and probable author of much of his book.

are based on the Masoretic Text. The
Masoretic Text of Jeremiah is not only
longer than the Septuagint's text, but
its chapters are also ordered differently.
For instance, in the Masoretic Text, the
oracles against foreign nations are found
in chapters 46–51, but in the Septuagint
these texts are in chapters 25–31 in a
different sequence. Adding to the in-
trigue is the fact that both editions of
Jeremiah—the Masoretic Text and the
Septuagint—are represented among the
Dead Sea Scrolls.

The book itself also seems to contain the fragments of earlier endings. Jeremiah 51, for instance, concludes, "Up to this point are the words of Jeremiah"
(51:64 AT). Immediately after this notice is an entire chapter that largely dupli-
cates 2 Kings 24:18–25:30. The implication is that these chapters from 2 Kings
were added to a version of Jeremiah that ended with chapter 51 in order to
provide an external witness to the fulfillment of Jeremiah's predictions.

The book of Jeremiah uniquely highlights the relationship between prophets
and scribes. While the role of scribes in the preservation and editing of prophetic
literature is widely assumed, the scribes themselves are not typically found in the
texts. In the book of Jeremiah, however, the scribe Baruch is featured (see, e.g.,
chaps. 32, 36, 45). Chapter 36 in particular bears witness to the important role
scribes could play in the preservation, publication, and expansion of prophetic
literature. First, Jeremiah dictates words for Baruch to record (36:4). Second,
Baruch is asked to speak Jeremiah's words in the temple (36:6–8). Third, after
King Jehoiakim destroys the original scroll, Jeremiah secures another and dictates the words of the original scroll to Baruch; the text then claims, "Many
similar words were added to them" (Jer. 36:32). While the precise details of
the account may be fictional, the role of scribes in recording and transmitting
texts is known throughout the ancient Near East.

Genre

Like most of the Prophets, the book of Jeremiah is a collection of both narrative and poetic materials. It includes oracles of judgment, laments, prophecies
against foreign nations, reports of symbolic acts, and epistolary material. As
with many other prophetic books, the process by which these various texts were
composed and brought together is largely unknown. What's more, the book
does not follow a strictly chronological sequence. Rather, its primary concern

is wrestling with the catastrophe of the Babylonian exile—a traumatic event that marks Judaism up to the modern day.

Literary Interpretation

Introduction, call, doom, and lamentation (Jer. 1–10). The central interest of the book of Jeremiah is reflecting theologically on the most definitive and devastating event of Jeremiah's time: the Babylonian exile. After a historical notice (1:1–3) and a narrative about Jeremiah's calling (1:4–19), the book immediately jumps into Jeremiah's oracles to Jerusalem and Judah, accusing them of sin, urging repentance, and warning of potential disaster. The ferocity and pointedness of Jeremiah's oracles no doubt contributed to the modern-day term *jeremiad*.

Jeremiah's laments (Jer. 11–20). More than other prophetic books, the book of Jeremiah fixates on the prophet's conflicts with his opponents, himself, and even God. In the past, some of these texts have been called Jeremiah's confessions, based on rough comparisons to Augustine's *Confessions*. It is more accurate, however, to refer to these texts as laments, since they share far more in common with the book of Psalms than they do with the writings of Augustine. Like the Psalms, Jeremiah's laments mix both anger and sorrow as the prophet mourns divine judgment, complains about his enemies, and even argues with God.

Oracles to Jerusalem's upper class (Jer. 21–24). Chapters 21–24 are largely directed toward Jerusalem's rulers and elites. Sometimes Jeremiah calls out individuals, and at other times he simply calls out the house of David. Jeremiah blames these ruling elites for the Babylonian exile. They have abandoned the covenant with Yahweh and mistreated those in their charge. With characteristic intensity, Jeremiah tells the leaders of Jerusalem that "I myself [God] will go

---

Box 26.3

Augustine's Confessions *and Jeremiah's Laments*

Jeremiah's laments have often been called his confessions, an intentional comparison to St. Augustine of Hippo's most famous book, *The Confessions*, which he started writing in 396 CE. At the heart of Augustine's work is the restless human heart, which finds its content and joy in God alone. *The Confessions* is best understood as spiritual autobiography. This is especially true of books 1–9, which begin with Augustine's birth and end with his conversion to Christianity and the death of his mother, Monica. In our view, the comparison between Augustine and Jeremiah breaks down rather quickly. The laments of Jeremiah are best understood in the context of the larger lament tradition, which is especially present in books like Psalms and Lamentations.

to war against you with an outstretched hand and a mighty arm" (21:5 AT). The only hope of survival, Jeremiah argues, is in surrendering to the Babylonians (21:8–9). The "mighty arm" of Yahweh—once directed against the oppressive powers of Pharaoh—is now being directed against Jerusalem.

Jeremiah's policy toward Babylon (Jer. 25–29). In chapters 25–29, Jeremiah advocates for submission to Babylon. He says Yahweh had granted Babylon authority over the earth for a period of time (27:6–7), but even Babylon's reign would come to an end. The nations of the earth would serve Babylon for seventy years (25:11), after which Babylon would cease to be the agent of judgment and would become instead the object of judgment. It is no surprise that Jeremiah's message was controversial. Not only was submission economically diminishing, but it also wounded national pride.

Words of hope and comfort (Jer. 30–33). Jeremiah's calling is summarized in the first chapter of the book: "See I have appointed you this day over the nations and over the kingdoms, to uproot and to break down, to destroy and to overthrow, to build and to plant" (1:10 AT; cf. 31:28).

Fig. 26.3. This contemporary depiction of Jer. 29:1–7, entitled *New Roots*, illustrates Jeremiah's word to the exiles in Babylon: "Build houses and live in them; plant gardens and eat what they produce. Take wives and have sons and daughters. . . . Seek the welfare of the city . . . , for in its welfare you will find your welfare" (29:5–7). The exiles should not resist Babylon but seek its welfare!

In the first thirty chapters of the book, most of the emphasis has been on the destructive elements of the prophet's calling. In this section, however, the book turns toward hope. The prophet looks forward to a time of restoration when the yoke of oppression will be broken, wounds will be healed, and the people of God will return to the land. This new age of redemption will be marked by the establishment of a new covenant (31:31). What's new about this covenant is not the contents of its demands, which remain the same, but rather the people's ability to keep those commandments. God's commands will be inscribed on their hearts. It will no longer be necessary for people to be taught about the Lord, because "they will all know me [Yahweh], from their least to their greatest" (31:34 AT). The section concludes with Yahweh insisting that nothing in heaven or on earth can break his covenant with the house of David.

Judah's demise (Jer. 34–45). Chapters 34–45 describe Judah's demise under Babylonian aggression, reinforce why it is happening, and offer descriptions of life after Jerusalem's fall. The unit begins with Nebuchadnezzar's armies at the gates of Jerusalem and Lachish (34:1–7). Not surprisingly, blame for the destruction is placed squarely at the feet of Judah's rulers and especially its kings. Even when presented with opportunities to turn aside from judgment, the kings demonstrate that they are fully responsible for the disaster to come (see especially chap. 36). In an attempt to silence Jeremiah and prevent him from disheartening the people, a group of officials throw the prophet in prison (38:6). The unit also describes how Jeremiah was forced to relocate to Egypt, despite his warning against just such an action (chaps. 42–44).

Oracles concerning foreign nations (Jer. 46–51). Chapters 46–51 include oracles the prophet speaks concerning foreign nations. In such oracles, the God of Israel through the prophet addresses Israel's neighbors (Egypt, Philistia, Moab, Babylon, etc.). The theological assumption of these oracles is that Yahweh is king of the world. As such, he has the right to address these nations in the way that any monarch would address his subjects. Similar collections are found in Isaiah 13–23 and Ezekiel 25–32.

Jerusalem's destruction (Jer. 52). The book of Jeremiah concludes with a historical narrative describing Jerusalem's destruction. The chapter closely follows 2 Kings 24:18–25:30, and as a conclusion to the book, the passage legitimizes Jeremiah's predictions about Jerusalem, thereby demonstrating that he was a true prophet (cf. Deut. 18:15–22).

Theological Interpretation

The book of Jeremiah is not for the faint of heart. It is a fierce, combative, impassioned collection of texts that meditate on ancient Judah's most painful national disaster: the destruction of Jerusalem and the exile of God's people to Babylon. Given Jeremiah's theological assumptions, it would have been impossible to imagine a disaster like this apart from divine involvement. Jerusalem, after all, was Yahweh's holy city. The Judeans were Yahweh's holy people, and the temple in Jerusalem was the center of Jewish religious life.

A Broken Covenant

At the heart of Jeremiah's message is the strained covenantal relationship between Yahweh and his people. The relationship was under significant stress and both parties suffered as a result. Chapter 2 puts it this way:

> I remember your youthful loyalty,
>> your bridal love.
> You followed after me in the wilderness,
>> in an unsown land.
> Israel was holy to Yahweh,
>> the firstfruits of his harvest.
> All who ate of it were guilty,
>> disaster befell them,
>>> declares Yahweh. (2:2–3 AT)

The prophet goes on to blame this grim situation on priests, teachers/guardians of the law, rulers, and prophets. The issue is not simply that rules had been broken. According to Jeremiah, the source of life itself had been forfeited in favor of death and destruction:

> For my people have committed two evils:
>> they have abandoned me,
> the fount of living waters,
> in order to hew out for themselves cisterns,
>> fractured cisterns that cannot hold water. (2:13 AT)

But idolatry for Jeremiah is not simply a matter of improper worship. Neglecting the first commandment ("You shall have no other gods before me," Exod. 20:3; Deut. 5:7) inevitably spills over into neglecting the neighbor. Love of God and love of neighbor are intertwined. In chapter 19, for instance, Jeremiah breaks an earthenware jug as a sign of impending divine judgment and declares Yahweh's judgment is necessary: "I am about to bring disaster against this place that will cause the ears of all who hear of it to tingle, because they have abandoned me and profaned this place, making sacrifices in it to other gods, whom neither they nor their ancestors or the kings of Judah knew. They filled this place with the blood of the innocents. They built high places of Baal to burn their sons with flame as burnt offerings to Baal" (19:3–5 AT). Violating sacred space is intertwined with violating the innocent. This theme holds true throughout Jeremiah.

Shocking Imagery

In his attempts to criticize the leaders, Jeremiah employs some of the sharpest, most vitriolic rhetoric in the Old Testament. Like other prophets of Israel, Jeremiah fills his oracles with metaphors, some of which are disturbing in the modern day, where sensibilities have evolved, especially around matters of gender. Most notably, Jeremiah makes extensive use of the marriage metaphor, in which Yahweh is described as Israel's husband. When that metaphor is mapped onto Jeremiah's accusations of idolatry, the result looks something like Jeremiah 2:20:

> For long ago I broke your yoke,
>   I tore off your shackles.
> But you said, "I won't serve!"
> Indeed, upon every high hill,
>   and under every verdant tree,
>   you sprawled—a whore! (AT)

The language was shocking in Jeremiah's time, and it is shocking in our own, especially because these words are placed in the mouth of God. Every modern reader of Jeremiah needs to wrestle with the implications of such metaphors, which are found elsewhere in the Old Testament prophets as well (see, e.g., Hosea 2; Ezek. 16; Nah. 3). Whenever reading ancient texts (Scripture or otherwise), it is important to keep several things in mind. Modern readers cannot simply leave their own perspectives aside and try to read the text in an objective or neutral way, nor should they. Some of the most generative and important theological thinking happens when people of faith raise questions about Scripture. The book of Psalms, for instance, would not exist in its current form if its authors had not been willing to ask God bold questions, like, Why? or How long?

But it is also important to understand the text as a product of its own time and place. It is useful to consider how and why a text was composed and how it compares to other texts, concepts, and ideas in its broader culture. Approaching a text in this manner is difficult, due in large part to the fact that reading the Bible is itself a cross-cultural experience; its authors, compilers, and even most of its culture no longer exist. And yet, in order to understand these texts more deeply, the attempt can and should be made.

Box 26.4

Prophecy and Rhetoric

Jeremiah's rhetoric grabs the attention. Sometimes it is moving, and sometimes it is shocking. In almost all cases, it is memorable. The prophets were not simply passing along divine messages, as if they were divine stenographers. Drawing on human creativity and ancient tradition, they crafted their messages in ways that would help them accomplish their goals to announce, persuade, judge, and so on. As such, their oracles should be studied not only to determine *what* they say but also to appreciate *how* they say it. Study Bibles and commentaries can be particularly helpful in this regard. They are often generated by scholars and experts who specialize in helping readers understand more deeply the nuances of the text. In the end, study of prophetic books like Jeremiah will only benefit from careful reflection on these texts both as divine messages and as products of human culture.

The Interior Life of the Suffering Prophet

More than any other prophetic book, the book of Jeremiah reflects on the interior life of the prophet, who endured great suffering. This is especially the case in chapters 11–20. When the prophet's difficult message produced a strong, even violent, reaction from many of his contemporaries, they took it out on Jeremiah. He laments his suffering, calling himself a "docile lamb led to the slaughter" (11:19 AT). Like the psalmists, the prophet does not hesitate to protest Yahweh's role in his suffering and in the suffering of his people: "Why does the way of the wicked prosper? Why do the treacherous thrive? You plant them and they take root; they go forth and produce fruit. You are near their mouths but far from their hearts" (12:1–2 AT).

Jeremiah 11–20 concludes with a legend about Jeremiah's persecution followed by several moving laments. After hearing Jeremiah prophesy, a priest named Pashhur son of Immer had Jeremiah flogged and imprisoned (20:1–3). What follows this event are some of the most impassioned laments in the Old Testament. The prophet accuses Yahweh in no uncertain terms:

> You have deceived me and I was deceived!
> You are stronger than I am and you prevailed.

Box 26.5

The Suffering of God

Jeremiah is not the only one who suffers. The book named for him insists that God suffers as well. No interpreter has probed this issue more deeply than Terence Fretheim, who highlights the joint suffering of both the prophet and his God.* We already broached this topic above in our discussion of Yahweh's strained relationship with Judah. Jeremiah insists on placing Yahweh's judgment and fierce rage in the context of fractured faithfulness, betrayed trust, and overt neglect.

Yahweh's suffering comes to the fore in texts like Jeremiah 4:19:

> My anguish, my anguish;
>   I'm bent over in pain.
> The walls of my heart,
>   my heart groans to me;
>   my heart will not be silent;
> for a trumpet sound my soul hears,
>   a battle cry! (AT)

The statement is surrounded by divine speech, making it difficult to determine whether the speech comes from God or from the prophet.† This ambiguity may in fact be purposeful: the suffering of God is embodied in the suffering of the prophet.

* Terence E. Fretheim, *The Suffering of God: An Old Testament Perspective*, Overtures to Biblical Theology (Philadelphia: Fortress, 1984), 156–62.
† Fretheim, *Suffering of God*, 160.

I became a thing of mockery all the day;
    everyone ridicules me. (20:7 AT)

With honesty and fervor, Jeremiah accuses God of tricking him into his prophetic calling. The tone of lament shifts into confidence, however, as Jeremiah lays his case before Yahweh and expresses trust in his ability to enact justice (20:11–13).

Glimmers of Hope

The predominant tone of the book of Jeremiah is doom and accusation. Nonetheless, the book is not without hope and comfort. As the prophet's call narrative indicates, Yahweh has commissioned him "to uproot and to break down, to destroy and to overthrow, to build and to plant" (1:10 AT). Jeremiah bore a message of both judgment and promise. The promises are primarily concentrated in chapters 30–33, and they emphasize the return from exile, God's faithfulness to Israel, the restoration of fortunes, and the establishment of a "new covenant" (see especially 31:31–37).

Rembrandt / Everett Collection / Shutterstock

Fig. 26.4. This painting by Rembrandt is the classic image of a troubled Jeremiah. The suffering of the prophet is one of the most memorable aspects of Jeremiah's ministry and may have contributed to comparisons with Jesus (see Matt. 16:14).

Historical Interpretation

The primary historical events that concern the book of Jeremiah are the destruction of Jerusalem and the subsequent deportation of many Judeans to Mesopotamia. The historical prophet warned about these events, experienced them, and survived. The book leaves a slew of historical questions in its wake. How extensive was the damage inflicted upon Jerusalem by the Babylonian armies? What was Jeremiah's relationship with the Babylonians, given his support of surrender? What are the circumstances of the prophet's death?

Additionally, as already noted above, the book's compositional history remains something of a mystery. Why do we have two Jeremiah traditions—one preserved in the Masoretic Text and the other in the Septuagint? What does this teach us about how the book was transmitted and preserved over the centuries? As people of faith, what does it mean to call Jeremiah "Holy Scripture" when there are multiple versions of the book preserved over the centuries?

Finally, according to the superscription in Jeremiah 1:1–3, Jeremiah prophesied during the reign of Josiah. This monarch is remembered as a king who pleased the Lord and followed in the ways of David (a compliment!) (2 Kings 22:2). In fact, 2 Kings 23:25 says that no other king turned back to the Lord in the way Josiah did, with all of his heart, soul, and might. And yet there is very little available evidence that connects Jeremiah's prophetic ministry to the reign of Josiah, to say nothing of his reforms. The relationship between Jeremiah and Josiah remains a mystery.

FOR FURTHER READING: Jeremiah

Allen, Leslie C. *Jeremiah: A Commentary*. Old Testament Library. Louisville: Westminster John Knox, 2008.

Brueggemann, Walter. *A Commentary on Jeremiah: Exile and Homecoming*. Grand Rapids: Eerdmans, 1998.

Clements, R. E. *Jeremiah*. Interpretation: A Bible Commentary for Teaching and Preaching. Louisville: John Knox, 1988.

Fretheim, Terence E. *Jeremiah*. Smyth & Helwys Bible Commentary. Macon, GA: Smyth & Helwys, 2002.

O'Connor, Kathleen M. *Jeremiah: Pain and Promise*. Minneapolis: Fortress, 2012.

Lamentations

The book of Lamentations follows Jeremiah in Protestant and Catholic Bibles, due to the traditional attribution of the book to Jeremiah, and is thus part of the prophetic corpus.[1] In Jewish Bibles, Lamentations is part of the five Megilloth (scrolls) and is thus part of the Writings (Ketuvim). The book contains five chapters of lament over the destruction of Jerusalem in 587 BCE. The destruction of Jerusalem by the Babylonian Empire forms the historical background of the book.

Background

Composition and Development

According to tradition, the prophet Jeremiah—known as the "weeping prophet"—wrote Lamentations. The ancient Greek translation of the book begins with the attribution of the volume to Jeremiah: "It happened after Israel was taken into captivity and Jerusalem was made desolate, that Jeremiah sat weeping and lamented this lamentation over Jerusalem" (AT). Many scholars still credit Jeremiah with the authorship of Lamentations, because the prophet was alive and present in Jerusalem when it was destroyed and because the book of Jeremiah has seven sections of lament (11:18–23; 12:1–6; 15:10–21; 17:14–18; 18:18–23; 20:7–12, 14–18). Other scholars point out that the older Hebrew manuscript tradition does not name Jeremiah as the author and that there are major stylistic differences between Jeremiah's complaining prayers and the lamentations in this book. They also note the books' theologically different perspectives with respect to the destruction of Jerusalem. These scholars conclude that Lamentations was most likely written by an anonymous Judean, who—like Jeremiah—survived the city's sack by the Babylonians. As F. W. Dobbs-Allsopp summarizes, "The internal evidence for a sixth-century date [soon after the 586 BCE destruction of Jerusalem] is certainly compatible with such a dating and general setting."[2]

Genre

Lamentations represents a particular type of song known as the city-lament genre, in which the city is personified as a woman and mourned. According to Dobbs-Allsopp,

> The city-lament genre is best known from ancient Mesopotamia, where it undoubtedly originated. It consists of five classic compositions ("Lamentation over the Destruction of Ur," "Lamentation over the Destruction of Sumer and Ur," "Nippur Lament," "Eridu Lament," "Uruk Lament"). . . . The five classic compositions depict the destruction of particular cities and their most important shrines. The destruction, brought about as a result of the capricious decision of the divine assembly and the subsequent abandonment of the city by its chief gods, is typically carried out by the chief god. . . . The city's chief goddess is usually the other major actor in these poems. She is portrayed as challenging the assembly's decision and then bewailing the destruction of the city.[3]

Scholars assume that these poetic compositions were used in cultic ceremonies, perhaps related to the restoration of sanctuaries. In such a context, the city laments were apotropaic, protecting the structure and its people from the anger of the gods and any future disasters.

According to Dobbs-Allsopp, Lamentations exhibits nine features in common with the Mesopotamian city laments:

- subject and mood
- structure and poetic technique

- divine abandonment
- assignment of responsibility
- divine agent of destruction
- destruction
- weeping goddess
- lamentation
- restoration and return of the gods[4]

In Lamentations, each of these features is thoroughly transformed theologically. For example, theologically, the people are held responsible for the destruction because of their sin. Jerusalem itself is portrayed as a woman, since it did not have a patron goddess. The theme of the return of the gods is, of course, missing; in its place is a concluding plea for restored relationship with God: "Restore us to yourself, O LORD, that we may be restored! Renew our days as of old—unless you have utterly rejected us, and you remain exceedingly angry with us" (5:21–22 ESV).

Fig. 27.1. An oil painting from the 1880s depicts a Jewish man praying at the Western Wall in Jerusalem. This section of the wall dates back to the first century CE, when the second temple was destroyed.

Literary Interpretation

Lamentations is a collection of poems that meditate on the horrifying destruction of Jerusalem at the hands of the Babylonians. In modern Bibles, each poem is assigned a chapter. In general, Hebrew poetry does not have meter, but Lamentations is exceptional in this regard. It adopts the *qinah* meter, which is reserved for poems of mourning, lament, and sorrow. Similar to music played in a minor key, the *qinah* meter conveys a sense of mourning, loss, and even protest. The book utilizes other literary features such as "acrostics" throughout the book. Most of these features, however, often remain invisible due to the limits of translation.

First and second acrostic laments (Lam. 1–2). In the first two chapters, Jerusalem is personified as a woman, "daughter Zion" or "daughter Jerusalem." In the Mesopotamian city laments, in the context of polytheistic religions, the chief goddess of the cities mourns and demands justice. In the monotheistic context of Judean religion, the city itself—personified as a woman—weeps and mourns, transforming the weeping goddess image into the city. These initial chapters give full vent to Jerusalem's bitter grief, along with her recognition that their ruin is the result of divine judgment and wrath. God's involvement is not veiled or moderated. In Lamentations, the Lord has become "like a foe" (2:5) bent on destroying the city.

Third acrostic lament (Lam. 3). Chapter 3 turns to the lament of an unnamed survivor who is afflicted by Yahweh. In Lamentations, Israel's God is no longer a protective shepherd but a menacing predator bent on destruction. The light of hope briefly breaks through this thick cloud of despair when the author calls to mind that the "kindnesses of Yahweh are never ending" (3:22 AT). Chapter three pivots to repentance and self-reflection (3:40–47) before concluding with appeals to Yahweh to hear his appeal, vindicate him, and destroy his enemies (3:55–66).

Fourth acrostic lament (Lam. 4). In the fourth chapter, Lamentations describes the grizzly siege against Jerusalem in wrenching lyric lines. The bitter forces of scarcity and violence transform human solidarity into cruelty. If the poem were not so clearly grounded in ancient history, one might mistake this chapter for a postapocalyptic, dystopian hellscape.

Fifth (nonacrostic) lament (Lam. 5). Lamentations concludes with a communal lament and appeal for Yahweh to "remember, Oh Yahweh, what has happened to us" (5:1 AT) and "restore us to yourself" (5:21). Several things are clear from a reading of Lamentations: Jerusalem has suffered a horrifying disaster, the author(s) of Lamentations believe that this disaster is Yahweh's judgment, and they believe that Yahweh alone is their source of hope. But these convictions are communicated in the dense and highly creative form of Hebrew poetry. As a reader, you would do well to take it in slowly, thoughtfully, and patiently.

Theological Interpretation

The Judgment of the City

In spite of the deeply emotional expression of lamentation and pain, the poet of Lamentations is in agreement with most of the Old Testament in seeing the Lord as the agent who destroyed Jerusalem and deported its leading citizens into exile. The poet also agrees with the rest of the Old Testament that the Lord was righteous in this judgment. Perhaps because of its lamentation form, the book does not develop this theological theme or name specific sins. Tantalizing statements such as "I have rebelled against his word" (1:18) and "I

Box 27.3

Lamentations as Lament and Acrostic

The first four chapters of the book of Lamentations take the form of the Hebrew *qinah*, a lament or lamentation. The lament was a genre of song to be sung over the death of a loved one or, in this case, over the destruction of a city. The *qinah* is the only form in biblical poetry that had a defined meter (two lines that have a 3 + 2 stress pattern). An example of an individual singing a *qinah* upon the death of a loved one is David after the death of Jonathan (the Song of the Bow, 2 Sam. 1:17–25). In Amos 5:1–3, the prophet sings a *qinah* in a prophetic satire, singing derisively over the death of "maiden Israel"—the nation.

The first four chapters of Lamentations are also alphabetic acrostic poems (see also Pss. 9–10; 25; 34; 111; 112; 119; 145; Prov. 31). The poems in chapters 1, 2, and 4 each consist of twenty-two verses, and each verse begins with a successive letter of the Hebrew alphabet. The poem in chapter 3 consists of sixty-six verses, with each letter of the Hebrew alphabet starting three verses. Chapter 5 also consists of twenty-two verses, but it does not continue the alphabetic-acrostic structure.

The significance of the alphabetic acrostics is debated. The form certainly indicates that the poems are careful scribal or priestly compositions, not unconstrained emotional outbursts. At the very least, the form makes poems more easily memorized and thus more readily used liturgically to mourn the destruction of the city and the temple. Dobbs-Allsopp is insightful:

> The poet has chosen language as his means of consolation and there is no better symbol of the power and potential of language than the alphabetic acrostic, modeled most likely on the simple abecedaries that were commonplace in scribal schools. The alphabet stands as the paradigmatic symbol of culture and civilization in the ancient Near East, and thus its prominence in these poems profoundly reasserts the values of civilization and culture even in the face of utterly devastating and dehumanizing suffering.*

* F. W. Dobbs-Allsopp, *Lamentations*, Interpretation: A Bible Commentary for Teaching and Preaching (Louisville: John Knox, 2002), 4.

called to my lovers" (1:19) suggest that idolatry and blasphemy were of major concern. The leading citizens of the city are particularly targeted: "The visions of your prophets were false and worthless; they did not expose your sin" (2:14 NIV), and "It happened because of the sins of her prophets and the iniquities of her priests" (4:13 NIV). The Lord's righteousness is reason both to accept the judgment and to repent and turn to the Lord in hope of restoration: "Let us examine our ways and test them, and let us return to the Lord. Let us lift up our hearts and our hands to God in heaven" (3:40–41 NIV).

Lamentation

It is helpful to distinguish between two similar types of prayer found in the Bible—the prayer for help and the lamentation. Many scholars use the term "lament" to encompass both types of prayer, but they are different. The prayer for help is offered when a favorable outcome is still possible. The lamentation is prayed after the unfavorable outcome has already occurred. When a loved one lingers on the edge of death, for instance, one prays a prayer for help. After the loved one has died, one laments.

The theological power of lamentation comes in several forms. First, the lamentation as a public song calls the community together to share one another's pain. Second, the lamentation expresses the most painful emotions and articulates the deepest suffering in such a way that God's presence is also demanded. The lamentation implicates God in the pain and attempts to transfer that pain to God in order to resolve (or at least diffuse) it. Third, the lamentation calls for compassion. In some instances, the only help that can be offered to one lamenting is compassion and empathy.

Hope in the Character of the Lord

In the textual center of the book of Lamentations—the middle section of the middle poem—the poet lights a small flame of hope in the dark night of despair: Lamentations 3:21–39. It is too long to quote in its entirety here, but the central expression of hope is as follows:

> I call all this to mind—
>   therefore, I will wait.
>
> Certainly the faithful love of the LORD hasn't ended;
>   certainly God's compassion isn't through!
> They are renewed every morning.
>   Great is your faithfulness. (3:21–23 CEB)

This shred of hope places Zion's confidence not in itself—not in its ability to repent or change behavior in any lasting way—but in the character of the Lord, who is a God of steadfast love, enduring mercy, and everlasting faithfulness. There are flickers of hope elsewhere in the book in appeals for restoration and punishment for Judah's enemies (especially Edom; see 4:21–22).

It is important not to ignore the immense suffering and pain in Lamentations and run too quickly to these hopeful middle verses. After this encouraging section, the book returns to its main theme of lamentation, pain, and suffering. If these verses of hope are all one knows of Lamentations, the book is being ignored at best and misread at worst. However, to deny that the book of Lamentations literally places hope in the center of the book is also to misread the book. The hymn writer Thomas Chisholm drew on this passage to compose the beloved hymn "Great Is Thy Faithfulness," which expresses hope in the midst of hopeless times and reflects on God's faithfulness in the long haul. The hymn faithfully interprets the hope that the anonymous poet of Lamentations expressed.

Historical Interpretation

The book of Lamentations is not epic poetry; it does not tell a story or develop any narrative themes. Its main contribution to historical approaches to the Old Testament is that it offers a glimpse into the songs of those who survived the destruction of Jerusalem in 586 BCE. Although we cannot know for sure how these songs were used following that devastation, it is safe to conclude that the poems were

Fig. 27.2. William Brassey Hole depicts Judah's greatest tragedy, the fall of Jerusalem at the hands of the Babylonians. This devastating event inspired several biblical books, including Lamentations, as well as many works of art.

composed and first used in the midst of the ruins of Jerusalem. The book gives a powerful sense of the people's emotions and trauma, and it offers a report of how they experienced and interpreted the horrors of that event.

FOR FURTHER READING: Lamentations

Allen, Leslie C. *A Liturgy of Grief: A Pastoral Commentary on Lamentations*. Grand Rapids: Baker Academic, 2011.

Berlin, Adele. *Lamentations: A Commentary*. Old Testament Library. Louisville: Westminster John Knox, 2002.

Dobbs-Allsopp, F. W. *Lamentations*. Interpretation: A Bible Commentary for Teaching and Preaching. Louisville: John Knox, 2002.

Goldingay, John. *The Book of Lamentations*. New International Commentary on the Old Testament. Grand Rapids: Eerdmans, 2022.

———. *Lamentations and Ezekiel for Everyone*. Louisville: Westminster John Knox, 2016.

O'Connor, Kathleen M. "Lamentations." In *Women's Bible Commentary*, 3rd ed., edited by Carol A. Newsom, Sharon H. Ringe, and Jacqueline E. Lapsley, 278–82. Louisville: Westminster John Knox, 2012.

William Brassey Hole / Lebrecht History / Bridgeman Images

ՄՆեսին եկեկեայե․ վարգասխեն գաբ եսեա․ ինէ խումաբ գեոմյ
և կատեսաբ եսեա գեստաս ։

28

Ezekiel

The book of Ezekiel is one of the most challenging pieces of literature in the Bible. The book provokes a wide array of responses, including shock, confusion, anger, and wonder. The prophet was apparently an ecstatic, which makes interpreting some of his visions challenging and even disturbing. Even in ancient days, many rabbis were cautious about the book. According to Jewish tradition passed down from the Jewish philosopher Maimonides, people were not to study the opening chapters of Ezekiel until they were forty years old.

Background

The Prophet Ezekiel

Little is known about Ezekiel. He is not mentioned outside of the book that bears his name and is only mentioned by name twice within the book—the rest of the time he is normally called "son of man" (meaning "mortal"). He was a Zadokite priest who would have served in the Jerusalem temple prior to the Babylonian exile, and he was among the Judeans who went with the first deportation into exile in 597 BCE—probably as a boy. In Babylon, he experienced a call to prophetic ministry (chaps. 1–3). In exile, he lived in Tel-abib along the river Chebar (3:15). He was married, but "the delight of [his] eyes" died (24:15–18). He often acted strangely when communicating his prophetic messages, and this strange behavior apparently confused people. Because of his visions and ecstatic behavior, some consider him the father of Jewish mysticism.

Historical Context

As already indicated, the major historical events that shaped Ezekiel's life were those that marked the onset of the Babylonian exile.

First deportation (597 BCE). During Ezekiel's life, the Babylonian Empire under Nebuchadnezzar overcame the Assyrian Empire and ruled the ancient Near East. In 597 BCE, the Babylonians forced Jerusalem to submit. They stripped the city of much of its wealth and deported many of its leading citizens into exile, including King Jehoiachin, placing his uncle Zedekiah on the throne. Ezekiel was among those exiled in the first deportation. In exile, he experienced his prophetic call and warned against a second rebellion. After the first deportation, there were Judean communities both in Jerusalem (where Zedekiah was king and Jeremiah prophesied) and in Babylon (where King Jehoiachin lived and where Ezekiel started to prophesy).

Fall of Jerusalem and second deportation (586 BCE). Following a rebellion by Zedekiah, the Babylonians returned to Judah. They besieged Jerusalem and finally conquered it in 586 BCE, tearing down the walls, razing the city, and destroying the temple. They also deported a second group of leading citizens. The exile was of particular importance to a priest like Ezekiel whose calling and vocation were tied up in temple service. When the temple was destroyed by Nebuchadnezzar's armies (2 Kings 25:8–17), it was impossible for Ezekiel to perform the mandates of priestly service.

Composition and Development

Very little is known about how the book of Ezekiel was composed. The abundance of first-person material may suggest that Ezekiel himself played a significant role in writing the book. But where the work of Ezekiel ends and that of an editor begins is difficult to determine with any level of certainty. Readers would do well to keep in mind that "authorship" as a concept was understood quite differently in the ancient world. In contemporary America, it would be strange for a book to be written by multiple authors without acknowledging the work of each contributor. In the ancient world, however, it would have been quite commonplace for a work to be written, edited, and compiled by multiple scribes, without any of them feeling a need to claim authorship over the work.

Genre

Ezekiel is a prophetic book containing a variety of literary genres, including narratives, vision reports, prophetic sayings, oracles against foreign nations, and reports of symbolic acts. Many of the unique aspects of Ezekiel are due to the fact that he operates as both a prophet and a priest. Both elements of his identity find expression in the various texts that make up the book.

The book of Ezekiel stands out among the Prophets in several ways. First, it is predominantly prose, not poetry. Most other prophetic books are dominated by poetic oracles. Second, Ezekiel is generally organized chronologically, giving it a coherence and consistency unseen in most other prophetic books. This chronological arrangement is created with a sequence of date formulas that mark significant turning points in the book (see, e.g., 1:1–3; 8:1; 20:1; 24:1; 26:1; 29:1, 17). These dates also provide a structure for the book that covers twenty years of Ezekiel's life (593–571 BCE)—the normal period of time for a priest's career (see Num. 4:1–4, 21–24, 29–33). Ezekiel's ministry began before the destruction of Jerusalem and the temple, and his messages from this period consist of warnings and judgment. Following the fall and the second deportation, messages of consolation and restoration are more numerous.

Fig. 28.1. Stained glass depiction of Ezekiel's visions, including both the chariot throne and four hybrid creatures. Hybrid creatures and deities are common in ancient Near Eastern iconography, from Egypt to Mesopotamia. Interpreters of Ezekiel should keep this in mind when attempting to understand the bizarre creatures in Ezekiel 1.

Literary Interpretation

Ezekiel's calling and opening visions (Ezek. 1–7). The first seven chapters of Ezekiel feature the prophet's initial visionary experiences. They are set "in the thirtieth year" (1:1), when Ezekiel was among the exiles near the Chebar River. In these chapters, Yahweh appears to Ezekiel with rich and complex imagery that is reminiscent of the temple and especially the holy of holies where the ark was kept. Four composite, human-like creatures accompany the vision of "the appearance of the likeness of the glory of Yahweh" (1:28, modified). This awkward phrase appears frequently in Ezekiel and demonstrates the prophet's respect for the transcendent glory of Yahweh.

Yahweh calls and commissions Ezekiel to the rebellious people of Israel (2:1–3:15). In these initial chapters, we first encounter Ezekiel's moniker, "mortal" (Hebrew, *ben 'adam*). After consuming a scroll as sweet as honey (3:1), he is told to address the recalcitrant house of Israel. Yahweh calls Ezekiel a "watchman" (3:17 NIV, NJPS), entrusted with a grave and weighty responsibility: to warn people about threats to their lives. If he does not warn them, then the prophet himself will be held responsible.

Ezekiel's messages are not always spoken. Like other prophets of Israel, he engages in symbolic actions. Chapters 4–5 contain some of these "sign acts." For example, Yahweh commands Ezekiel to make a model city and "set up a siege against her" (4:1–3 AT). This was to serve as a "sign" for the house of Israel (4:3).

Chapters 1–7 end with a word of doom: "Doom! Doom is coming upon the four corners of the land" (7:2 NJPS). A day of Yahweh's wrath has arrived, when Yahweh will judge his people according to their ways. Nothing will be able to save from the horrors of this day. For Ezekiel, Yahweh's judgment is not the arbitrary act of a capricious deity. He will treat them according to their own "way" and in line with "their own judgments" (7:27).

Box 28.2

Monstrous Creatures in the Bible

The books of Ezekiel, Daniel, Job, and Revelation are well known for their bizarre monsters. Ezekiel 1 describes four living creatures with four faces and four wings. They have the feet of a calf, skin that sparkles like bronze, and even human hands. Their faces are those of a human, lion, ox, and eagle.

What are we to make of these bizarre creatures? While some might wonder if Ezekiel was visited by aliens, the more likely explanation is in the art and literature of the ancient Near East, which has a vast collection of hybrid creatures. These monstrous figures often exhibit normal elements of everyday creatures fashioned into something truly extraordinary.

Box 28.3

Valley of Dry Bones

The hand of the Lord was on me, and he brought me out by the Spirit of the Lord and set me in the middle of a valley; it was full of bones. He led me back and forth among them, and I saw a great many bones on the floor of the valley, bones that were very dry. He asked me, "Son of man, can these bones live?" I said, "Sovereign Lord, you alone know." Then he said to me, "Prophesy to these bones and say to them, 'Dry bones, hear the word of the Lord! This is what the sovereign Lord says to these bones: I will make breath enter you, and you will come to life. I will attach tendons to you and make flesh come upon you and cover you with skin; I will put breath in you, and you will come to life. Then you will know that I am the Lord.'"

So I prophesied as I was commanded. And as I was prophesying, there was a noise, a rattling sound, and the bones came together, bone to bone. I looked, and tendons and flesh appeared on them and skin covered them, but there was no breath in them. Then he said to me, "Prophesy to the breath; prophesy, son of man, and say to it, 'This is what the sovereign Lord says: Come, breath, from the four winds and breathe into these slain, that they may live.'"

So I prophesied as he commanded me, and breath entered them; they came to life and stood up on their feet—a vast army. Then he said to me: "Son of man, these bones are the people of Israel. They say, 'Our bones are dried up and our hope is gone; we are cut off.' Therefore prophesy and say to them: 'This is what the sovereign Lord says: My people, I am going to open your graves and bring you up from them; I will bring you back to the land of Israel. Then you, my people, will know that I am the Lord, when I open your graves and bring you up from them. I will put my Spirit in you and you will live, and I will settle you in your own land. Then you will know that I, the Lord, have spoken, and I have done it, declares the Lord.'"

—Ezekiel 37:1–14 AT

Artist unknown

Fig. 28.2. This depiction of Ezekiel's dry-bones vision in chapter 37 is from the synagogue at Dura-Europas.

Judgment and divine departure (Ezek. 8–24). Chapters 8–24 continue the theme of divine judgment, with particular emphasis on Yahweh's departure from the temple (see especially chaps. 8–11). For Ezekiel, Yahweh's people are not the only ones who go into exile: Yahweh himself also goes into exile with the people—or at least he is able to reach them in exile in order to bring them home. The temple has been defiled with false worship and must be purged before it can be reestablished as sacred space worthy of God's holy presence. Yahweh's presence will not return to Jerusalem until chapter 43.

Using symbolic actions, allegory, and prophetic reports, the remaining chapters (12–24) reflect in various ways on Jerusalem's destruction and the exile of Yahweh's people. These chapters also introduce the topic of false prophecy (see especially chaps. 13–14). False prophets are degenerate and operate out of their own imaginations. They convince God's people that they live in a season of peace (13:10), when in fact they stand on the edge of disaster. The texts contained in this section are often violent and, in some cases, deeply troubling in their depictions of women (see especially chaps. 16 and 23). We will address these issues later in the chapter.

Oracles concerning foreign nations (Ezek. 25–32). As already discussed, many prophetic books contain a collection of oracles directed toward the foreign nations of the world (cf. Isa. 13–23 and Jer. 46–51). Ezekiel's oracles are in chapters 25–32. These prophecies assume that Yahweh is over the nations and is not simply a national deity. There is no indication that these oracles were ever delivered to the nations addressed. Instead, they were written for domestic consumption to assure Ezekiel's audience of Yahweh's power.

Words of hope and restoration (Ezek. 33–48). The book of Ezekiel comes to a dramatic conclusion in chapters 33–48. Chapter 33 emphasizes Ezekiel's role as a prophetic watchman for Israel. As part of his calling, Ezekiel is required to warn of impending disaster. If he fails to do so, then the blame will fall on him (33:1–9). This is followed by a report about the fall of Jerusalem (33:21–22).

According to chapter 34, the shepherds of Israel—that is, its leaders—have failed in their charge to care for Yahweh's flock. Instead of tending the sheep of Israel, they attend only to themselves and neglect the needs of the vulnerable members of the fold (34:2–5). Yahweh will not allow his flock to be abandoned, so he promises to appoint over them a Davidic shepherd who will "graze them and be their shepherd" (34:23 AT). This new ruler will be Yahweh's appointed agent on earth, and this new era will be marked by a "covenant of peace," security, blessing, and fertility (34:25–31).

This section of Ezekiel also features one of the most well-known Old Testament prophetic texts: Ezekiel's vision of the valley of dry bones (37:1–14). This vision symbolizes the resurrection of Israel. The text says, "These bones are the entire house of Israel" (37:11 AT), and at Ezekiel's command, the divine breath animates and lifts them out of their graves. The core of the promise is a return to the land (37:12), where Yahweh's temple will be restored. The section concludes with oracles against Gog and Magog—figures that represent Israel's foreign enemies (chaps. 37–39).

With the defeat of Israel's enemies, the book reaches its climax in chapters 40–48. In these detailed chapters, Yahweh's glorious presence returns to the temple. Through visionary journeys, Ezekiel visits Jerusalem on Yom Kippur (the Day of Atonement), the holiest day of the year. The prophet receives instructions on restoring the temple and preparing for the return of Yahweh's presence. The temple envisioned is not a replica of any previous holy structures, such as Solomon's temple or the wilderness tabernacle. Although it resembles these, Ezekiel's temple is something new. The temple is the seat of Yahweh's cosmic rule and the center of creation. Water flows from it and brings abundant life wherever it goes.

Finally, Ezekiel receives instructions on how to reestablish the land itself. Special attention is paid to the land's boundaries, as tribes are allotted portions in a symbolic north–south arrangement.

Theological Interpretation

Ezekiel is a singularly interesting book among the Prophets. As a result, it raises many theological questions for modern readers. Drawing deeply from the wells of priestly theology and ritual, Ezekiel interprets the exile theologically. In line with other prophets, Ezekiel believes that the exile was an act of divine judgment. But God's involvement in judgment also gives Ezekiel hope that the temple and the land will be restored.

The theological elements of Ezekiel are complicated and laden with layer upon layer of background knowledge. We encourage readers to consult a commentary or study Bible while reading Ezekiel.

Ezekiel's Priestly Identity

A crucial starting place is understanding and appreciating Ezekiel's relationship to Israel's priesthood. Ezekiel is a Zadokite priest. According to Numbers, priestly service begins either at age thirty (Num. 4:3) or twenty-five (Num. 8:23–25). In either case, retirement comes at age fifty. The date formulas at the beginning (1:1–3) and end (40:1) indicate that the book's internal timeline spans twenty years—the entire career of a priest if one follows Numbers 4:3. Given the temple's destruction and his own exile to Babylon, Ezekiel was unable to fulfill his normal role as a priest in Jerusalem. The editors apparently want us to conclude that Ezekiel nonetheless figured out a way to fulfill his priestly commitments, even under circumstances that his education did not prepare him for. Ezekiel's priestly background informs everything from the symbolism in his visions to his interpretation of judgment in terms of land purgation and sacrifice.

The crisis of the exile is the animating theological issue for Ezekiel. He draws deeply from the wells of priestly theology and ritual in his interpretation of this crisis. As a priest, he believed that Yahweh not only created the world but also ruled it. He understood the world in categories such as holy and profane, clean and unclean, faithful and idolatrous. In line with the other prophets, Ezekiel's theological priors led him to assume that Yahweh was involved in Jerusalem's destruction and the subsequent exile of his people. But that same rich theological tradition also included topics such as restoration, covenant, and forgiveness, all of which allow Ezekiel to assert that judgment is not the end of the story.

Priestly theology is also clearly on display in Ezekiel's visions of the restored temple (chaps. 40–48). Ezekiel's temple theology deserves special attention, especially given the outsized influence Ezekiel has on the New Testament book of Revelation. As noted above, although Ezekiel's temple is similar to Solomon's temple and the wilderness tabernacle, the temple in Ezekiel is something new, bearing witness to the remarkable imagination of the authors who gave us Ezekiel 40–48. Theologically, the temple is the location of Yahweh's divine presence. Proximity to that holy presence is proximity to life-giving powers signified by the water that flows out from the temple. Like the Priestly account of creation in Genesis 1:1–2:3, Ezekiel's restored world is one that is teeming with life.

Box 28.4

Texts of Terror

The phrase "texts of terror" comes from Phyllis Trible's book by the same title.* In that groundbreaking collection of essays, Trible deals with narratives that depict profoundly disturbing and lamentable stories of violence against women—in particular, against Hagar (Gen. 16; 21), Tamar (2 Sam. 13), the Levite's unnamed concubine (Judg. 19), and Jephthah's daughter (Judg. 11). Trible's important insights apply to poetic and prophetic texts as well. Many of the poems we read in the Prophets—and especially Ezekiel, Jeremiah, and Hosea—are rightly called a "land of terror from whose bourn no traveler returns unscarred."† There are risks involved in journeying to this land, but as centuries of diverse readers attest, there are also rewards for those willing to study this jagged and dangerous terrain.

* Phyllis Trible, *Texts of Terror: Literary-Feminist Readings of Biblical Narratives*, Overtures to Biblical Theology (Philadelphia: Fortress, 1984).
† Trible, *Texts of Terror*, 2.

Fig. 28.3. William Blake depicts the prophet Ezekiel kneeling at the deathbed of his wife. In Ezekiel 24, the prophet is told that Yahweh will take away the "delight of your eyes" and that he is not to mourn her (24:15–18).

Reading Disturbing Texts

The book of Ezekiel contains some of the most horrific and disturbing texts in the Old Testament. Chapter 16, for instance, is infamous for its depictions of Jerusalem as a wife turned salacious whore. Undergirding this extended metaphor is the image of Jerusalem as Yahweh's wife. According to chapter 16, Yahweh rescues her as a child on the verge of death. At the time of marriage, Yahweh takes her as his own (16:8). But according to Ezekiel, Jerusalem uses Yahweh's gifts to engage in adulterous behavior (i.e., unfaithfulness to Yahweh). As punishment, Yahweh promises to strip her naked in front of her lovers and "direct bloody and impassioned fury against [her]" (16:38 NJPS). The chapter ends with the promise that Jerusalem will feel shame for her deeds and that Yahweh will forgive her (16:59–63).

The modern reader cannot but cringe at these descriptions, and rightfully so. These texts depict a scene that can only be described in terms of violent sexual assault. The texts are all the more painful in the context of a faith tradition that sees the Bible as a faithful (even authoritative) source for theological reflection.

As twenty-first-century readers, we have several responsibilities when reading difficult ancient texts. First, we have a responsibility to our own ethical and theological compasses. Like Abraham or Moses, we should speak up when God's words demand an objection (cf. Gen. 18:16–33; Exod. 33:9–14; Num. 14:11–19). The God of the Bible is a God of dialogue, even when that dialogue is harsh, critical, or pained. The book of Psalms is masterful in showing us how to do this. Second, we also have a responsibility to read ancient texts as artifacts of their own time and to evaluate them on these terms.

Historical Interpretation

Ezekiel experienced one of the most catastrophic events in Israel's history: defeat and exile at the hands of the Babylonians. This event left Judah in a state of societal collapse with an uncertain future. Ezekiel bears witness to this historic moment and tries to make theological sense of it, drawing on prophetic experiences, priestly theology, and inherited literary forms. Scholars have recently employed the analytical frameworks of "trauma theory" to understand biblical texts such as Ezekiel more fully. Given Ezekiel's own experience of traumatic events, this approach has shed light on the book's attempts to address the trauma in the prophet's own community.[1] The book of Ezekiel does not give us unmediated access to the mind of the prophet, but it is nonetheless a literary artifact that emerged out of traumatic experiences and in many ways attempted to address it. The recent integration of trauma theory into biblical studies demonstrates the fruitfulness of interdisciplinary inquiry into the Bible.

But Ezekiel is not alone in providing a response to the traumas of exile. The prophet was roughly contemporaneous with other prophets, including the author of Isaiah 40–55, Jeremiah, Daniel, Obadiah, and Habakkuk. If we expand our inquiry beyond the prophetic books, an even larger body of literature emerges, including books like Lamentations and 1–2 Kings. Looking at the broader landscape, it becomes clear that Ezekiel is but one among many responses to the exile. These responses are diverse in every possible way. They differ in how they talk about Yahweh's involvement in the disaster. They analyze the causes differently. When they express hope, they do so in unique ways. Creative productivity often follows in the wake of human disasters, and this was certainly the case for ancient Judah. Fruitful historical inquiry can emerge from study of the various exilic texts with a view toward understanding their responses to the experience of exile.

FOR FURTHER READING: **Ezekiel**

Blenkinsopp, Joseph. *Ezekiel*. Interpretation: A Bible Commentary for Teaching and Preaching. Louisville: John Knox, 1990.

Carvalho, Corrine L. *The Book of Ezekiel: Question by Question*. Question by Question Bible Study Commentary. Mahwah, NJ: Paulist Press, 2010.

Carvalho, Corrine L., and Paul V. Niskanen. *Ezekiel, Daniel*. New Collegeville Bible Commentary, Old Testament 16. Collegeville, MN: Liturgical Press, 2012.

Lapsley, Jacqueline E. "Ezekiel." In *Women's Bible Commentary*, 3rd ed., edited by Carol A. Newsom, Sharon H. Ringe, and Jacqueline E. Lapsley, 283–92. Louisville: Westminster John Knox, 2012.

Odell, Margaret S. *Ezekiel*. Smyth & Helwys Bible Commentary. Macon, GA: Smyth & Helwys, 2005.

29

Daniel

The book of Daniel is named after its chief protagonist—a faithful Jewish exile known for revealing mysteries, educating kings, and receiving apocalyptic revelations. The book places Daniel and his companions in the reigns of various ancient Near Eastern conquerors: Nebuchadnezzar, Belshazzar, Darius, and Cyrus. These are only the named kings; many other unnamed monarchs, conquerors, and tyrants also had a profound influence on the book, as we will see below (e.g., Alexander the Great and Antiochus IV Epiphanes).

Caught up in the great power struggles of their day (Dan. 1:1–3), Daniel and his companions are forced to negotiate their Jewish identities in the context of imperial domination and violence. From within these adversarial conditions, a number of critical questions emerge: What does it mean to be faithful to the Torah when doing so invites royal ire and even death (e.g., chaps. 3, 6, 10–12)? How does one negotiate two different—and in some cases antithetical—identities? What are the implications of the book's claim that Daniel's people are suffering, at least in part, because of their own sin (1:1–2; 9:3–19)?

In the Christian canon, Daniel is the fourth of the "Major Prophets"—meaning the longer prophetic books. In the Jewish canon, however, Daniel is part of the "Writings." The reason for this is most likely because Daniel is very different from Isaiah, Jeremiah, and Ezekiel. Those prophetic books contain both narratives about the prophets and collections of their prophetic messages. Daniel, by contrast, contains mostly narratives about the prophet.

Background

The Character Daniel

The New Testament refers to Daniel as a prophet in one place, where it cites language from two of his apocalyptic visions (Matt. 24:15). In some ways, Daniel is very much like the prophets, in that he communicates messages from heavenly sources and serves in the royal court, as many other prophets did. But in other ways, Daniel is quite different from the prophets, most notably in the fact that he is the recipient of apocalyptic visions—a kind of revelatory experience that is distinct from what one finds in the prophetic literature. Additionally, Daniel (like Joseph) is a keen interpreter of dreams, a wise administrator, and a cunning politician. When all this is taken together, Daniel is best understood to be a hybrid figure whose characterization in the book cannot be easily labeled.

Historical Context

As is the case with many other biblical books, a distinction must be made between the historical period in which the story is set and the historical period in which the story was initially composed. In the case of Daniel, situating these texts historically is immensely complicated.

The book's literary setting is the sixth-century-BCE exile. During this time, many faithful Jews faced the challenges of how to negotiate and maintain their Jewish identity and Yahwistic faith in foreign contexts. As the singer of Psalm 137 asks, "How could we possibly sing the Lord's song on foreign soil?" (v. 4 CEB). There is no reason to doubt that some of the chapters of Daniel—especially the stories in chapters 1–6—emerge from this period of time, perhaps originally in oral form.

There is strong evidence, however, that the book was also deeply influenced by events in the second century BCE, especially from the time of Antiochus IV Epiphanes. Antiochus IV Epiphanes was a member of the Seleucid dynasty, named after its founder, Seleucus, who served under Alexander the Great. The influence of Antiochus IV Epiphanes on the book of Daniel cannot be overstated. He enacted a number of policies that militated directly against Judaism's most treasured institutions: Sabbath observance and circumcision were forbidden, and the Jerusalem temple itself was desecrated and then dedicated to Zeus. The book's connections to these events will be explored in greater detail below.

Composition and Development

The issue of Daniel's compositional development has several challenges. First, the book itself does not make any authorship claims. What's more,

Box 29.1

An Account of the Persecution

Not long after this, the king sent an Athenian senator to compel the Jews to forsake the laws of their ancestors and no longer to live by the laws of God; also to pollute the temple in Jerusalem and to call it the temple of Olympian Zeus, and to call the one in Gerizim the temple of Zeus-the-Friend-of-Strangers, as did the people who lived in that place.

Harsh and utterly grievous was the onslaught of evil. For the temple was filled with debauchery and reveling by the Gentiles, who dallied with prostitutes and had intercourse with women within the sacred precincts, and besides brought in things for sacrifice that were unfit. The altar was covered with abominable offerings that were forbidden by the laws. People could neither keep the sabbath, nor observe the festivals of their ancestors, nor so much as confess themselves to be Jews.

On the monthly celebration of the king's birthday, the Jews were taken, under bitter constraint, to partake of the sacrifices; and when a festival of Dionysus was celebrated, they were compelled to wear wreaths of ivy and to walk in the procession in honor of Dionysus. At the suggestion of the people of Ptolemais a decree was issued to the neighboring Greek cities that they should adopt the same policy toward the Jews and make them partake of the sacrifices, and should kill those who did not choose to change over to Greek customs. One could see, therefore, the misery that had come upon them. For example, two women were brought in for having circumcised their children. They publicly paraded them around the city, with their babies hanging at their breasts, and then hurled them down headlong from the wall. Others who had assembled in the caves nearby, in order to observe the seventh day secretly, were betrayed to Philip and were all burned together, because their piety kept them from defending themselves, in view of their regard for that most holy day.

—2 Maccabees 6:1–11

there are several versions of Daniel, some in Hebrew and some in Greek. The Greek versions contain extra material, sometimes called the Additions to Daniel (Prayer of Azariah, Bel and the Dragon, and Susanna). The version of Daniel used by Protestants is based on Hebrew manuscripts, meaning that Protestants have a smaller collection of Danielic texts than other segments of Christianity.

Adding to this complexity, the book divides into two major sections, one dominated by the genre of court tales (chaps. 1–6) and the other by apocalypses (chaps. 7–12). Most scholars agree that these two sections have independent origins, each section dealing with kings who literally lived hundreds of years apart. Daniel 1–6 features sixth-century kings like Nebuchadnezzar (ruled 605–562 BCE), and Daniel 7–12 is marked by symbolic but unmistakable references to Antiochus IV Epiphanes (ruled 175–164 BCE) and, in particular, to his stunning acts of religious persecution against Jews (see, e.g., 8:8–14; 9:27; 11:30–35).

The book of Daniel is also bilingual, half of it written in Hebrew (1:1–2:4; 8:1–12:13) and half in the related language of Aramaic (2:4–7:28). The reason

Apocalypse

An apocalypse is a distinctive literary genre of ancient Jewish and Christian revelatory literature. Almost all proposed definitions of the genre include the following features:

1. Apocalypses purport to describe a revelatory experience received by a human being.
2. The revelatory experience is expounded in the form of a story that includes information about the visionary and his experience.
3. The revelation requires assistance from a heavenly being, often an angel, who provides interpretation, guidance, or challenge to the visionary.
4. The revelation discloses an alternative reality, whether in the heavenly realms or a future worldly state, that transcends the present phenomenal order.*

* Greg Carey, "Apocalypses," in *The Oxford Encyclopedia of the Books of the Bible* (Oxford: Oxford University Press, 2011), 39–55.

for the sudden and unexpected shift from Hebrew to Aramaic in Daniel 2:4 is unclear, as is what this shift reflects about the book's history of composition.

These characteristics indicate a complicated process of composition and editing. What seems most likely is that some of the court tales (chaps. 1–6) go back to the sixth century BCE, when Jews were first exiled to Mesopotamia. Some of these narratives may have existed at one time in oral form. However, most of the apocalyptic revelations seem to be associated with the traumatic persecution under Antiochus IV Epiphanes in the second century BCE.

Genre

As noted, Daniel divides into two major genres. Daniel 1–6 is a series of court tales, a genre known elsewhere in the Bible (e.g., the book of Esther) and the ancient Near East. In such stories, Jews serve in foreign royal courts, often in positions of power and influence. In this environment, the Jews encounter conflicts but typically prevail over their foreign counterparts and/or enemies. In the first six chapters of Daniel, Daniel and his friends deftly navigate the dangers of life in the palace of Mesopotamian monarchs.

Daniel 7–12 is a collection of apocalypses, a distinctive genre of revelatory literature. In apocalyptic literature, a human receives a vision or other revelatory experience and requires divine assistance to understand it. Daniel has four such experiences in the second half of the book (chaps. 7, 8, 9, and 10–12).

Despite the generic divide between the two sections of the book of Daniel, several literary and theological assumptions link them together. These will be explored in greater detail below.

Outline

1. Court tales in exile (1–6)
   a. Daniel and his friends in the royal court (1)
   b. Nebuchadnezzar's dream about a great statue (2)
   c. Shadrach, Meshach, and Abednego in the fiery furnace (3)
   d. Nebuchadnezzar's dream about a great tree (4)
   e. Belshazzar's feast and the writing on the wall (5)
   f. Daniel in the den of lions (6)
2. Apocalyptic visions of the future (7–12)
   a. A vision of four beasts (7)
   b. A vision of a ram and a goat (8)
   c. A visionary reinterpretation of a prophecy (9)
   d. A vision of history and the final days (10–12)

Literary Interpretation

Court tales in exile: Daniel and his friends in the royal court (Dan. 1). The first chapter of Daniel introduces the fragile status of its protagonists in a foreign royal court and highlights one of the book's most important theological claims—that earthly kings have power because God grants it to them. Nebuchadnezzar did not conquer Jerusalem's king; "The Lord *gave* Jehoiakim king of Judah into [Nebuchadnezzar's] hand" (1:2 AT). The relationship between divine sovereignty and human sovereignty lies at the heart of the book.

Although his power is derived, Nebuchadnezzar has great capacity to influence the lives of Daniel and his friends. This reality makes them vulnerable to the king's responses to small decisions, such as what they eat. Daniel and his friends navigate their new environment with skill and become exemplary

Daniel and Humor

The book of Daniel is deeply humorous. It shares this characteristic with other biblical books like Esther and Jonah. This is not to say that the book lacks seriousness. Quite the opposite: it uses humor to engage serious topics like imperialism, royal arrogance, and faithfulness.* While interpreting humor cross-culturally is challenging, there is strong evidence that the stories in Daniel use humorous devices both as a strategy of resistance and as a way to strengthen community cohesion.

In Daniel, the humor is primarily directed toward the king and, in the case of Daniel 3, toward the king's bureaucracy. Readers should be prepared to encounter comedic devices such as irony, exaggeration, caricature, and slapstick.

* See, e.g., Daniel Valeta, *Lions and Ovens and Visions: A Satirical Reading of Daniel 1–6* (Sheffield: Sheffield Phoenix, 2008); Michael J. Chan, "*Ira Regis*: Comedic Inflections of Royal Rage in Jewish Court Tales," *Jewish Quarterly Review* 103, no. 1 (2013): 1–25.

members of the royal court, showing themselves to be "ten times" better than all the other royal mantic experts.

Court tales in exile: Nebuchadnezzar's dream about a great statue (Dan. 2). In Daniel 2, Nebuchadnezzar has a disturbing dream and summons his mantic experts to interpret it. In a surprising move, he demands they also tell him *what* he dreamed (2:2–12). When they protest that no one can fulfill his request except the "gods, whose dwelling is not with flesh" (2:11 AT), the king explodes. He orders the execution of all his courtiers, including Daniel and his friends. The Jewish exiles seek God's help, and God reveals the mystery to Daniel (2:19–23).

The narrator builds suspense by hiding the details of the dream until Daniel himself discloses them to the king: The king saw a large, awesome statue, with a head of gold, chest and arms of silver, belly and hips of bronze, legs of iron, and feet of iron and pottery (2:31–33). A rock struck the statue at its feet and destroyed it. All that remained was the rock, which became an enormous mountain. Daniel explains to the king that the dream concerns the rise and fall of kingdoms, including his own. Sometime in the future, God will set up another kingdom that will persist throughout the ages.

Nebuchadnezzar bows before Daniel, confessing that Daniel's God is "God of gods" and "Lord of kings" (2:47). This acknowledgment marks the first chapter in Nebuchadnezzar's education, an important narrative element through chapter 4.

Court tales in exile: Shadrach, Meshach, and Abednego in the fiery furnace (Dan. 3). In chapter 3, the temperature gets turned up in more ways than one. This court tale features Daniel's three friends, Shadrach, Meshach, and Abednego, who face an extreme test of religious faithfulness: the king requires that the assembled subjects bow before a golden image he has erected (3:4–7). Failure to do so results in a swift and fiery death (3:6). The three young men refuse to comply, and "certain Chaldeans" report their defiance to the king. Given a second chance to bow down, the Jews tell the king that, whether or not their God chooses to save them, "we will not serve your gods, and to the golden image that you have erected we will not bow down" (3:18 AT).

The king responds with an outburst of face-twisting royal rage, the heat of which is matched only by the temperature of the furnace, increased to such a degree that it kills the king's servants. After the three Jews are cast into the furnace, a fourth man who looks like a god appears. The king is astonished that the men in the fire are unscathed. Nebuchadnezzar again learns the supremacy of the Jewish God, even over his own royal power.

Court tales in exile: Nebuchadnezzar's dream about a great tree (Dan. 4). Chapter 4 concerns another ominous dream of Nebuchadnezzar, recounted in a literarily unique way. The story is told in the first-person voice of the king and functions as a sort of testimony to all the peoples of the earth (4:1–3). Nebuchadnezzar recounts a dream of a gigantic tree at the center of the earth. Adorned with beautiful foliage and abundant fruit, it feeds all the creatures of the earth (4:10–12). Then a heavenly being chops down the tree and declares that "he" (Nebuchadnezzar) would be transformed—body and mind—into an animal and driven from human society. All this will happen so everyone would know that the Most High has authority over "all kingdoms on earth" (4:17 NIV).

Fig. 29.1. The eighteenth- and nineteenth-century artist William Blake dramatically depicted Nebuchadnezzar's foray among the beasts in this stunning painting.

William Blake

After a twelve-month delay between the declaration and the fulfillment—perhaps to give Nebuchadnezzar time to repent (see 4:27)—the judgment comes to pass at the very moment the king boasts about his royal accomplishments. He is driven into the realm of beasts, where his body is transformed into a composite creature, not unlike the monsters that appear in the apocalyptic visions in Daniel 7–8. In the end, Nebuchadnezzar acknowledges the authority of God and states that "[God] humbles those who walk proudly" (4:37 AT).

Court tales in exile: Belshazzar's feast and the writing on the wall (Dan. 5). Daniel 5 shifts to the reign of Belshazzar, who hosts a great feast and calls for the temple vessels brought from Jerusalem by Nebuchadnezzar (see 1:1–3). These vessels were reserved for cultic purposes. While the king and his guests drink from them and praise an array of gods, a great hand appears, writing the mysterious phrase "MENE, MENE, TEKEL, and PARSIN" (5:25). As in earlier stories, only Daniel is able to interpret both the words and their significance. Ultimately, Daniel concludes that Belshazzar is being condemned for failing to learn the lessons of his father, Nebuchadnezzar (5:22–23). Belshazzar, unlike Nebuchadnezzar, never confesses wrongdoing, nor does he otherwise show signs of repentance—arrogance for which, the text says, he was killed that very night (5:30).

Court tales in exile: Daniel in the den of lions (Dan. 6). Daniel 6 is the last and most famous court tale. Like Daniel 3, this story features jealous courtiers who use royal decrees to destroy their "enemy." Unable to find any wrongdoing on Daniel's part, they conspire to weaponize a royal decree against him. They

Box 29.5

"Mene, mene, tekel, and parsin"

Daniel, interpreter of mysteries, reads and explains the Aramaic words inscribed on the plaster wall by a mysterious human hand: "*Mene:* God has numbered the days of your reign and brought it to an end. *Tekel:* You have been weighed on the scales and found wanting. *Peres:* Your kingdom is divided and given to the Medes and Persians" (5:26–28, modified).

Even with this interpretation, the message is something of a mystery. Each of the words refers to a particular weight: *tekel* = a shekel, *mina* = sixty shekels, and *peres* = two half minas. But understanding the individual words does not make the meaning obvious.

Daniel's interpretation includes intricate wordplay, especially with respect to the final word, *parsin*. In Aramaic, the word is plural. In his interpretation, Daniel uses the singular noun, *peres*, and thereby accomplishes a double wordplay. First, he says that "your [Belshazzar's] kingdom will be divided [*perisat*]," and then he says it will be "given to the Medes and the Persians [*paras*]."

Fig. 29.2. Rembrandt famously depicted the ominous scene in Daniel 5, in which a mysterious human hand composes a riddle for Belshazzar.

convince the king to issue a thirty-day ban on all supplication to anyone but himself. In an (ironically) unflattering depiction of the king, the king signs the decree into law without even a peep of protest.

The king is dismayed to discover that Daniel violates the law, and he attempts to rescue him. In a farcical reflection on royal power, the great king is actually a weak character, manipulated by his own courtiers and incapable of reversing his own decree.

Daniel's punishment is being thrown into a den of lions. Despite its long history of artistic interpretation, the story focuses more on the anxiety of the king than it does on Daniel's night among the beasts. Early in the morning, the king rushes to the lions' den and finds Daniel unharmed. Daniel says an angel with him in the pit preserved him from death; the text says Daniel's trust in God had preserved him (6:23).

In a reversal of fortunes, the king condemns Daniel's enemies to the same death they had designed for him, and like Nebuchadnezzar before him, Darius learns some important lessons. This God rules an indestructible dominion, does signs and wonders in the heavens, and delivers from death.

Apocalyptic visions of the future: A vision of four beasts (Dan. 7). In Daniel's first terrifying vision, he sees four beasts—a lion with wings; a devouring bear; a four-headed, winged leopard-like creature; and a fourth horrific beast with powerful iron teeth and ten horns (7:2–8). From its horns sprout a "little horn" with a big mouth, speaking "arrogantly" (7:8). Interrupting this arrogant speech, the Ancient of Days takes his throne and condemns the beast to a fiery fate. "One like a human being" then appears to receive "dominion, glory, and rulership" from the Ancient of Days (7:14 AT).

A heavenly attendant announces to Daniel that the beasts represent human kingdoms, but they do not ultimately win the day. The "holy ones" (7:18) will receive an everlasting kingdom but only after they suffer severely under "the horn." The vast majority of scholars assume that "the horn" refers to Antiochus IV Epiphanes, whom we discussed above.

Apocalyptic visions of the future: A vision of a ram and a goat (Dan. 8). Daniel's second vision also features beasts and horns: a dominating ram, a

---

Linking Daniel 1–6 and Daniel 7–12

The court tales of Daniel 1–6 follow the plight of Daniel and his friends, Hananiah, Mishael, and Azariah. Reflecting their newly acquired dual identity, the Jewish youths are given court names that reflect their new identities as members of a Mesopotamian royal court: Belteshazzar, Shadrach, Meshach, and Abednego (Dan. 1:7). In these chapters, Daniel and his friends navigate the various challenges posed by life in the court of a foreign king. Sometimes those challenges originate from a royal dilemma (see, e.g., Dan. 2; 4; 5), and at other times, the challenges emerge from malicious members of the court set on doing harm (Dan. 3; 6). In all cases, Daniel and his friends demonstrate their exceptional gifts and extraordinary faithfulness to God.

Chapter 7 marks the beginning of the apocalyptic section of Daniel (chaps. 7–12). While these chapters make a distinct switch in genre, many of the same questions are addressed: What is the relationship between God's kingdom and earthly kingdoms? How is God involved in human history? Who determines the rise and fall of royal powers? How does God call the faithful to live under the shadow of imperial domination? What strategies of resistance are available to the victims of imperial rule? How and to whom does God reveal heavenly mysteries?

furious goat, and several horns, including a "small horn" that wars against the hosts of heaven. As with the first vision, the imagery of this vision also portrays earthly rulers, several of which are explicitly named (Media/Persia and Greece). The ancient Jewish readers addressed by this text understood that the small horn was Antiochus IV Epiphanes, who, despite his notable strength and vigor, would ultimately be destroyed (8:25).

Apocalyptic visions of the future: A visionary reinterpretation of a prophecy (Dan. 9). It is not often that we find Old Testament characters explicitly interpreting other Old Testament texts, but Daniel 9 is one such instance: "I, Daniel, perceived in the books the number of years that, according to Yahweh's word to Jeremiah the prophet, are to pass for the ruins of Jerusalem—seventy years" (9:2 AT). Daniel's understanding prompts a prayer of confession (9:4–19), in which he acknowledges Israel's sin and especially their rejection of the prophets (9:6, 10). Israel, he confesses, is not primarily the victim of Babylonian imperial violence; it is the recipient of divine judgment. Daniel appeals to God's tender mercies (9:15–19): "Incline your ear, O my God, and hear. Open wide your eyes, and see our desolations and the city that is called by your name; for it is not because of our righteousness that we make our appeals before you, but because of your great compassion" (9:18 AT).

While Daniel is still praying, Gabriel appears with a counterintuitive interpretation of Jeremiah's "seventy years" prophecy. According to Gabriel, "seventy weeks of years" (not merely seventy years) had been determined for Daniel's people and their city. A cascading sequence of disasters will unfold until finally the "desolater" himself is brought to an end.

Apocalyptic visions of the future: A vision of history and the final days (Dan. 10–12). The last three chapters of Daniel form a single unit. Daniel has a vision of a magnificent man and falls into a trance, undone by the sight (10:2–9). An angelic mediator tells him about a conflict in the heavens among various heavenly "princes" assigned to the people/regions of Persia, Greece, and Israel (10:10–21; cf. Deut. 32:8–9). He then gives Daniel a sophisticated and veiled recounting of history, focused primarily on the Seleucid dynasty ("king of the north") and Ptolemaic dynasty ("king of the south"), both of which arose in the wake of Alexander the Great's death. For the second-century-BCE author of Daniel 10–12, history contains patternable and revelatory insights into the cosmic order of the world. But these insights into the past also grant him credibility to make claims about events in his own time, during the terrorizing reign of Antiochus IV Epiphanes.

But the author does not stop with the present. In chapter 12, he presses into the future, predicting a time of trouble but also a time of deliverance (12:1). This chapter is the first biblical text to imagine individual resurrection followed by the separation of those who will awake to eternal life and those who will awake to reproach and contempt (12:2). This theology of resurrection was used to oppose Antiochus IV's violent program of persecution. The earthly ruler Antiochus was able to leave destruction and death in his wake. But the heavenly ruler Yahweh was able to raise the dead and either reward them with eternal life or punish them to eternal "reproach and everlasting contempt" (12:2 AT).

Theological Interpretation

Faithfulness, Accommodation, and Resistance

The book of Daniel is literature of the defeated (1:1–2). Both its court tales (chaps. 1–6) and apocalypses (chaps. 7–12) assume an environment of domination and even oppression by several Near Eastern and Mediterranean powers. As a result, much of Daniel deals with navigating the landscape of conquest: forcible deportation, seizure of wealth and goods, and conscription into royal service. How does one exercise faithfulness in such an environment? How can one be faithful in service to both an earthly king and a heavenly king?

Upon their arrival at the Babylonian court, Daniel and his friends receive Babylonian names (Belteshazzar, Shadrach, Meshach, Abednego; 1:7). This common practice of renaming foreign courtiers bespeaks the dual identity that Daniel and his friends have to negotiate in their exilic context. Many of the stories in chapters 1–6 explore this idea, often spinning humor-laced stories about the challenges of navigating between compliance and resistance.

Although not monolithic in their depictions of kings, chapters 7–12 approach royal power differently. In these chapters, the kings are not the textured—even if cartoonish—characters known from the court tales. Instead, they are ferocious and destructive actors in a symbolic drama. The monarchs in Daniel 1–6 were certainly threatening (see especially chaps. 2, 3, and 6), but they also had the ability to learn and to change. One could imagine living a faithful life under the rule of these kings, even if at times they forced their subjects to make difficult—and sometimes compromising—decisions.

Not so with the kings of Daniel 7–12, the most notorious of which was Antiochus IV Epiphanes. He is acrimoniously described as the one who makes war

Fig. 29.3. Shadrach, Meshach, and Abednego cast into the furnace by Nebuchadnezzar, as depicted in the Visigothic-Mozarabic Bible of St. Isidore, 960 CE.

against the holy ones (7:20–21), takes away the regular burnt offering (8:11–12), and even considers himself greater than any god (11:36). Daniel 7–12 summons its readers to courage in the midst of terror and desolation. That courage is to be grounded in understanding and trust. The reader understands that, while God permits monstrous forces to rule for a time (see, e.g., 7:11–14), in the end earthly empires will be replaced with an empire of "everlasting righteousness" (9:24; cf. 7:21–22). Hope was grounded in the fact that their suffering, though acute at times, was finite (12:1).

Who Is the True King?

The book of Daniel claims that the Israelite God reigns over history. This single claim—that the God of the Jews is also the "Lord of kings" (2:47)—is the central lesson that Nebuchadnezzar must learn (see chaps. 2–4). The various kings of the earth struggle to understand that their power is delegated to them by God for a time and a season.

Every ancient Near Eastern king readily recognized that their authority was granted by the gods. In fact, in official texts kings often boasted about their chosen and privileged status in the eyes of their deities. But the book of Daniel is up to something different. In Daniel, the king not only must recognize his own dependence, but he also must confess that his sovereignty derives from the god of a defeated, subject people. This God, Nebuchadnezzar confesses, has a kingdom that endures over the generations (4:34).

The book of Daniel recognizes the intoxicating and dangerous effects of royal power, along with the need for kings to learn humility, lest they face judgment. In Daniel 5, for example, pride morphs into blasphemy when Belshazzar uses the temple vessels at a drunken feast to celebrate gods of "gold and silver, bronze, iron, wood, and stone" (5:4). The story unflinchingly claims that Nebuchadnezzar had learned humility before God (5:20–21), thereby admitting that royal power—thought inherently dangerous—can be wielded competently and fruitfully. Because Belshazzar failed to absorb this insight, his reign—not to mention his life—was cut off abruptly (5:30).

According to the book of Daniel, the Jewish people will not always be subjects under foreign rule. The long nights of domination will end, sometimes after a period of intense suffering (7:21–22; 8:23–25; 9:25–27). Several texts imagine a time when sovereignty will be granted to faithful members of the community (7:13–14, 21–22, 27).

Mystery and Revelation

Daniel is a book about secrets, mysteries, and revelations. As Nebuchadnezzar proclaims, "Truly, your God is God of gods and Lord of kings, and a revealer of mysteries, for you [Daniel] have been able to reveal this mystery" (2:47 ESV). The supremacy of the Hebrew God is demonstrated in his ability to disclose hidden realities and lay bare what is shrouded in mystery. God's favor toward Daniel is manifest in his ability to interpret such hidden realities to those around him, and most especially to those in authority.

Daniel's role as mediator of divine mysteries also forms an important literary and theological bridge between chapters 1–6 and chapters 7–12. In these latter chapters, Daniel is not an interpreter of divine mysteries but a recipient of apocalyptic revelations. As is typical of apocalypses, interpretation is undertaken by a heavenly figure who helps Daniel make sense of the visions he receives (7:15–28; 8:15–27). Common to both sections of the book, however, is the assumption that the God of the Hebrews is a God who both reveals and conceals.

In all of this, the unique position of the reader should not be overlooked. Several verses enjoin Daniel to "seal" the contents of the book because they concern the future (8:26; 12:4). But the content of these visions, along with their meaning, is known to readers, who have been observing Daniel's visions throughout. In other words, like Daniel, the reader is in the know, having privileged access to cosmic mysteries. Knowledge of history's violent but ultimately hopeful conclusion is meant to strengthen readers and allow them to endure until the end (12:11–13).

God, History, and Judgment

The book of Daniel shares a key conviction with many other Old Testament books: the events of history must be interpreted theologically. This claim is already present in the book's introductory verses: "In the third year of the rule of Jehoiakim king of Judah, Nebuchadnezzar king of Babylon came to Jerusalem and laid siege against it. And *the Lord gave Jehoiakim king of Judah into Nebuchadnezzar's hand*, along with some of the vessels of the house of God" (1:1–2 AT). For the book of Daniel, it is insufficient to say that the fall of Jerusalem was simply a consequence of Babylonian imperialism. God was caught up in all of it. Historically, the book is situated in an age of empire. Theologically, it was in an age of judgment.

This potentially disturbing conviction also nourishes the book's most profound expressions of hope:

> [God] changes times and seasons,
>   deposes kings and sets up kings;
> he gives wisdom to the wise
>   and knowledge to those who have understanding.
> He reveals deep and hidden things;
>   he knows what is in the darkness,
>   and light dwells with him. (2:21–22)

Consistent throughout Daniel is the assumption that kings and earthly powers ultimately derive their power from God (1:2; 2:47; 3:26–30; 4:1–3, 25; 7:27). While earthly rulers may at times operate outside the bounds of their delegated authority—even in profoundly monstrous ways—God eventually puts them in check, ensuring that their destructive behavior is limited (7:11–14; 8:8–14, 25; 9:24–27).

Historical Interpretation

The book of Daniel presents the reader with a number of interesting and challenging historical questions. First, the book's composition spans hundreds of years and is likely the work of many different scribal hands. Some of the court tales likely have roots in the sixth-century-BCE Babylonian exile, when they may have circulated as independent stories before being integrated into a larger Danielic collection. The apocalypses, however, are much later. While chapter 7 is somewhat unique, chapters 8–12 show strong connections to the violent events of 167 BCE. When all is said and done, the book of Daniel is properly understood as the work of generations.

Related to this last point is the fact that the Hebrew-Aramaic book of Daniel does not contain the entirety of Danielic literature. So called "additions" to Daniel exist in Greek. These include Bel and the Dragon, the Prayer of Azariah, the Song of the Three Jews, and Susanna. It is possible that these additions at one time existed in Hebrew or Aramaic, but evidence of such is nonexistent.

Box 29.7

An Excerpt from Bel and the Dragon

"Bel and the Dragon" refers to two court tales written in Greek, both of which concern the protagonist, Daniel. The shorter of the two is included below:

Now in that place there was a great dragon, which the Babylonians revered. The king said to Daniel, "You cannot deny that this is a living god; so worship him." Daniel said, "I worship the Lord my God, for he is the living God. But give me permission, O king, and I will kill the dragon without sword or club." The king said, "I give you permission."

Then Daniel took pitch, fat, and hair, and boiled them together and made cakes, which he fed to the dragon. The dragon ate them, and burst open. Then Daniel said, "See what you have been worshiping!"

When the Babylonians heard about it, they were very indignant and conspired against the king, saying, "The king has become a Jew; he has destroyed Bel, and killed the dragon, and slaughtered the priests." Going to the king, they said, "Hand Daniel over to us, or else we will kill you and your household." The king saw that they were pressing him hard, and under compulsion he handed Daniel over to them. (Bel 1:23–30)

Whatever the case may be, the collection of Danielic literature is much larger than the book of Daniel found in Protestant Bibles. These additions point to the canonical diversity within the global Christian church. Many other Christian groups (e.g., the Catholic and Eastern Orthodox churches) do include these additions in their canon.

There are also a number of chronological and historical problems that have exercised interpreters throughout the centuries. For example, 1:21 states that Daniel remained in the court until "the first year of King Cyrus." Then we learn that Daniel is still in Mesopotamia in "the third year of King Cyrus of Persia" (10:1). While explanations for this apparent discrepancy exist, the fact remains that some kind of explanation is needed. The figure of "Darius the Mede" (5:31) is also difficult to identify. While some attempts have been made to associate this figure with known historical figures (e.g., Ugbaru/Gubaru/Gobryas), most suggestions have ultimately proven unconvincing.

FOR FURTHER READING: Daniel

Davis, Dale Ralph. *The Message of Daniel: His Kingdom Cannot Fail*. The Bible Speaks Today. Downers Grove, IL: IVP Academic, 2013.

Longman, Tremper, III. *How to Read Daniel*. Downers Grove, IL: IVP Academic, 2020.

Lucas, Ernest C. *Daniel*. Apollos Old Testament Commentary 20. Downers Grove, IL: InterVarsity, 2002.

Newsom, Carol A., and Brennan W. Breed. *Daniel: A Commentary*. Old Testament Library. Louisville: Westminster John Knox, 2014.

Pace, Sharon. *Daniel*. Smyth & Helwys Bible Commentary. Macon, GA: Smyth & Helwys, 2008.

Seow, C. L. *Daniel*. Westminster Bible Companion. Louisville: Westminster John Knox, 2003.

Hosea

Hosea is the first book in a collection of books known as the Book of the Twelve or the Minor Prophets. As discussed earlier, the prophetic books include the Major Prophets and the Minor Prophets, with "Major" and "Minor" referring to the length of the books, not their importance. In the ancient world, the Major Prophets (Isaiah, Jeremiah, Ezekiel, Daniel) each took up one long scroll, while the twelve Minor Prophets were all contained on a single scroll, so also called the Book of the Twelve (or just the Twelve).

Like other prophetic books, Hosea contains accusations of unfaithfulness, promises of reconciliation, and oracles of judgment. But several characteristics make it stand out among other prophetic books. First, most prophetic figures in the Old Testament are associated with the Southern Kingdom of Judah, centered in Jerusalem. Hosea is a northern, Israelite prophet. Some scholars even argue that the book of Hosea reflects a northern dialect of Hebrew.

Hosea's relationships with one (or perhaps two) women and his children also set the book apart among the prophetic books more broadly. These relationships function symbolically and are integrated into the prophet's mission, acting as a billboard of the messages he is trying to convey. While such things are not entirely out of the norm for prophetic literature (see, e.g., Isa. 7:1–17; 8:1–4; 9:6; Ezek. 24:15–27), they take on added theological and literary significance in Hosea.

The book of Hosea is challenging. As we will see below, God's treatment of "adulterous" Israel is shocking to the modern ear. Some readers struggle to read the text with even a modicum of appreciation. Others interpret the book as a powerful statement of God's compassion and love for Israel, despite its history of unfaithfulness. These challenges will be discussed further below.

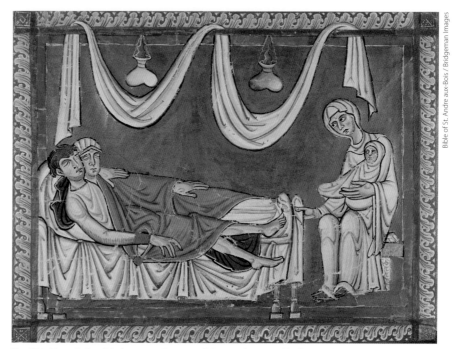

Fig. 30.1. The relationship between Hosea and Gomer dramatically depicted the troubled relationship between Yahweh and Israel, understood to be his bride.

Background

The Prophet Hosea

As with many of the prophets, we know nothing about Hosea other than what can be gleaned from the book that contains his prophetic messages. Hosea was a native of the Northern Kingdom of Israel and was called to prophesy to it. He must have been fairly young when he was called to prophetic ministry, and he had a relatively long career.

The most well-known, but least understood, aspect of the prophet's life was his marriage to "Gomer daughter of Diblaim." Gomer is called in Hebrew an *'eshet zenunim*, which is translated as "a wife of whoredom" in the NRSV and "a promiscuous woman" in the NIV (1:2). The precise meaning of the phrase is highly disputed. Older interpreters understood Gomer as either a common prostitute or a cultic prostitute (see 2 Kings 23:7)—and to make things more confusing, there are differing interpretations of what a cultic prostitute was or was not. More recent interpreters argue that Gomer was merely a promiscuous woman; whether Hosea knew this from the start or only discovered it over the course of time is also debated. In any event, Hosea's marriage and the naming of their three children became symbolic acts through which he communicated his messages of judgment and repentance.

Historical Context

Hosea lived and prophesied during a turbulent and ultimately destructive time in Israel's history. During his lifetime, seven different kings ruled from Samaria: Jeroboam II (786–746), Zechariah (746–745), Shallum (745), Menahem (745–737), Pekahiah (737–736), Pekah (736–732), and Israel's last king, Hoshea (732–724). Four of these kings—Zechariah, Shallum, Pekahiah, and Pekah—were murdered by their successors. Samaria was sacked by the Assyrians, who deported most of Israel's leading citizens into exile. That traumatic disaster was the culminating historical event of Hosea's life. His death is not reported, but it is possible that he fled south and took refuge in Judah at the end of his life.

During Hosea's life, the Neo-Assyrian Empire arose and exerted its violent influence along the eastern edge of the Mediterranean Sea. In 745 BCE, King Menahem paid tribute to Tiglath-pileser III in order to help establish his reign (2 Kings 15:9).[1] He lived through the Syro-Ephraimite crisis, when Israel and Aram attempted but failed to depose the Davidic king in order to place a puppet on the throne who would support their rebellion against Assyria. That revolt was also unsuccessful.

Composition and Development

According to the book's opening verse, Hosea's prophetic ministry occurred under the Judean kings Uzziah, Jotham, Ahaz, and Hezekiah, as well as the Northern Kingdom's monarch Jeroboam son of Joash. Scholars have often wondered about this dual regnal formula and especially why only one northern king is mentioned. With regard to the Judean kings, their mention seems to be an attempt to make Hosea's ministry coterminous with the ministry of Isaiah of Jerusalem; the regnal formula in Isaiah 1:1 is identical. Similarly, the reference to Jeroboam II would seem to connect Hosea's ministry with the prophet Amos, who apparently also operated at the same time (see Amos 1:1). All of this suggests that the historical Hosea worked during the second half of the eighth century BCE, prior to the Northern Kingdom's fall to the Assyrians in 722/721 BCE.

There is no reason to doubt that a core of material from the book of Hosea originated in some manner from the historical prophet of the same name. Like many other prophetic books, it is almost certain that Hosea was edited and reworked by anonymous editors, until it reached its current form as the first book of the Twelve.

Outline

1. Superscription (1:1)
2. Symbolic actions depicting Israel's unfaithfulness (1:2–3:5)
3. Oracles of judgment, hope, and a call to repentance (4–14)

Genre

The book of Hosea is a remarkable and complicated piece of literature. Broadly speaking, it is a prophetic collection containing a wide range of genres. The book conveniently alternates between chapters dominated by prose (Hosea 1 and 3) and chapters dominated by poetry (Hosea 2, 4–14). The book contains reports of symbolic actions (1:2–11; 3:1–5), along with a variety of prophetic proclamations, including threats of judgment, indictments, and promises of reconciliation (4:1–14:9). These oracles are primarily directed at the Northern Kingdom. Hosea 12:2–6, however, addresses "Judah," the name of the Southern Kingdom.

Literary Interpretation

As noted above, the book of Hosea can be divided into two main sections, chapters 1–3 and chapters 4–14. Chapters 1–3 have received the greatest amount of attention. This is primarily because of their focus on Hosea's relationship(s) with women and secondarily because of their focus on his children. These chapters are exceptionally challenging for modern readers whose ethics around sexuality differ significantly from those of the authors of Hosea. We will take up the ethical and theological challenges posed by these texts in the following section.

Superscription (Hosea 1:1). The book of Hosea opens, as many prophetic books do, with a superscription identifying the prophet and detailing his historical context. As noted above, Hosea is a native of the Northern Kingdom, Israel, but his context is given in terms of Judean kings (Uzziah, Jotham, Ahaz, and Hezekiah), as well as the king of the Northern Kingdom (Jeroboam son of Joash). Hosea's ministry was coterminous with the ministry of Amos in the north (Amos 1:1) and Isaiah of Jerusalem in the south (Isa. 1:1).

Symbolic actions depicting Israel's unfaithfulness (Hosea 1:2–3:5). The first portion of Hosea contains the bulk of the book's narrative. God commands Hosea to "go take for yourself a wife of whoredom and have children of whoredom, because the land whores itself away from the Lord" (1:2 AT), introducing the governing metaphor of chapters 1–3: Israel as Yahweh's unfaithful wife. The various marital, sexual, and parental images in these chapters illustrate Israel's scandalous betrayal of her marital relationship to Yahweh, her husband.

Box 30.2

Hosea's Marriage

God's command that Hosea marry a "wife of whoredom" is shocking for many readers. There is no doubt that it would also have been shocking to the people of Hosea's time. Would the God of Israel really issue such a command to a prophet? We will never know for sure. What we do know about the prophets is that they frequently used visible, public signs in support of their prophetic messages. No doubt provoking a similar level of shock, Isaiah is commanded by God to walk around naked for three years as a prophetic sign for Egypt and Nubia (Isa. 20:1–6). Jeremiah is commanded to purchase a loin cloth and hide it in the cleft of a rock near the Euphrates River (Jer. 13:1–11). We will probably never know if the events behind the prophet's marriage in the first chapters of Hosea reflect historical reality. However, they do reflect a commonplace prophetic practice found throughout the canon.

Hosea's threats of judgment and vision of restoration are also depicted in the context of the marriage relationship. With volcanic force, Hosea lobs this sharp rhetorical projectile:

> Contend against your mother, contend!
> For she is no wife of mine,
>   and I am no husband of hers.
> Let her put away her whorings from her face
>   and her adultery from between her breasts,
> lest I strip her bare
>   and make her as on the day she was born,
> make her like a wilderness,
> turn her into a parched land,
>   and kill her with thirst. (2:2–3 AT)

The language is violent and brutal, especially when viewed from a modern perspective—spousal abuse is now rightly and completely condemned. From the author's eighth-century-BCE perspective, Yahweh's actions were intended to prompt repentance, return, and reconciliation:

> Then she shall say,
>   "I will go and return to my first husband,
>   for it was better for me then than now." (2:7 ESV)

This last poetic line summarizes how the chapter thinks about divine judgment. Its purpose is to cause sufficient discomfort and adversity to provoke Israel to abandon its false gods and return to its true God—the one who brings fertility and blessing.

Oracles of judgment, hope, and a call to repentance (Hosea 4–14). Chapter 4 takes up a more direct form of accusation, using legal language to lay out Yahweh's case against Israel: "Yahweh has a case again the inhabitants of the land. There is no truthfulness or faithfulness, no knowledge of God in the land" (v. 1 AT). This sin has far-reaching and devastating consequences for creation itself:

> Therefore the land mourns,
>> and all its inhabitants languish;
> the beasts of the field,
>> the birds of the heavens,
> and even the fish of the sea are taken away. (4:3 AT)

For Hosea, Israel's ancient call to govern creation as God's image on earth (Gen. 1:26–28) has taken a dystopian turn. Whereas God created a world teeming with life, Israel's rulers undid that work, leaving only death and destruction in their wake.

Chapter 5 addresses Israel's leadership directly—the "priests," the "house of Israel," and the "royal house" (v. 1), condemning them for their faithlessness (vv. 3, 7). Israel sought help for its sickness from Assyria but found only empty promises (v. 13). Yahweh will become like a ferocious predator, attacking his people until they turn from and seek his face (v. 15).

In chapters 6–7, an unnamed voice urges repentance and asks his audience to consider that Yahweh's attack also contains a promise: "He has torn us in order that he may heal us" (6:1 AT). Yahweh's judgment is not arbitrary rage but is directed toward a particular aim: healing and reconciliation. Yahweh does not discipline Israel and Judah in a disinterested manner. Their unfaithfulness is a source of pain:

> What shall I do with you, O Ephraim?
>> What shall I do with you, O Judah?
> Your faithfulness is like a morning cloud,
>> and like dew that hastens away early. (6:4 AT)

The remaining verses detail in various ways the iniquities of God's people, describing the people as criminals, an adulterous spouse, and senseless doves. Israel again puts its hope in both Egypt and Assyria but to no avail (7:11–13, 16). To place their hope anywhere other than Yahweh is to invite destruction and death.

Chapter 8 further elucidates the reasons for Yahweh's judgment and also emphasizes the need for sacrifice to be paired with obedience: "Though they offer choice offerings and eat flesh, Yahweh does not accept them" (v. 13 AT; cf. 6:6). The chapter ends with a double-barreled condemnation of both the Northern and the Southern Kingdoms, both of whom will be objects of Yahweh's judgment (8:14).

Fig. 30.2. Both Assyria and Egypt were powerful nations in part because they were riverine civilizations. Easy access to abundant water resources allowed them to flourish in ways that other civilizations could not.

Chapter 9 returns to the marriage metaphor with full force:

> Do not rejoice, O Israel;
>   do not be glad like the peoples,
> for you have whored, abandoning your God.
>   You have loved a harlot's reward
>   on all threshing floors. (9:1 AT)

Unfaithfulness to Yahweh is again construed in terms of marital betrayal, but the rhetoric is sharpened by the insistence that God's people not only found another lover, but they also sold themselves for a "harlot's reward." As a consequence, Israel will be judged and also sent packing back to Egypt: "They will not reside in the land of Yahweh, but Ephraim will return to Egypt, and in Assyria they will eat unclean food" (9:3 AT). The exodus—Israel's paradigmatic narrative of liberation—will be reversed. Israel's unfaithfulness opens wide the doors of death and bondage. A sure sign that Israel is the source of its own demise is the way it treats its prophets—as animals to be snared (vv. 7–8). Hosea's words are true to history: the Northern Kingdom of Israel was taken into exile by the Assyrians in 721 BCE.

In Hosea 9:9, the oracle shifts to reflect on Israel's history. The prophet compares Israel's current unfaithfulness and the "days of Gibeah"—a reference to a harrowing tale of violent rape in Judges 19–20. Yahweh recalls how, "like grapes in the wilderness" and like "first fruit on the fig tree," he found Israel; but then Israel came to "Baal-peor," where the people dedicated themselves to a "shameful thing" (9:10, modified). "Baal-peor" is shorthand for a set of narratives in Numbers 25, where the text closely associates the adoption of foreign worship practices with whoring. A third historical incident is something that occurred at Gilgal (v. 15). The allusion is ambiguous but may have to do with the initiation of the Israelite monarchy itself (1 Sam. 11:14–15). According to Hosea, "All of their evil is at Gilgal, for there I hated them" (9:15 AT). By linking these three incidents—Gibeah, Baal-peor, and Gilgal—the prophet demonstrates that God is patient and that Israel's faithlessness is long-standing. God's fierce anger is not caused by a momentary loss of temper but rather erupts after the slow, grinding buildup of anger fueled by generations of betrayal and heartache.

Agricultural imagery is present throughout Hosea, but chapter 10 places it front and center. The poem refers to Israel as a luxuriant, fruitful vine (v. 1), but the increase in blessing and prosperity results in increased idolatry. The inhabitants of the Northern Kingdom do not "fear the LORD" (v. 3), but rather "tremble" for the "calf of Beth-aven" (v. 5)—Hosea's derogatory designation for the idolatrous cult at Bethel. Because of this, Israel will be carried into exile in Assyria. The false places of worship will be turned into ruins, and the nations will gather together in opposition to Israel (vv. 8–10).

The prophet proclaims that sowing righteousness will result in a harvest of "steadfast love." In response to breaking up the ground and preparing it for harvest, Yahweh commits to raining "righteousness" down upon his people

---

Box 30.3

The Marriage Metaphor

Hosea 1–3 heavily utilizes the metaphor of marriage. The metaphor provides a conceptual map onto which Hosea can locate actions such as (un)faithfulness, judgment, and repentance. This potent imagery adds layers of texture to Hosea's accusations and promises. Idolatry, in Hosea's understanding, is not simply a matter of breaking a commandment; it is about a fractured marital relationship.

Feminist authors have noted the deeply patriarchal patterns of these chapters, especially when it comes to how Yahweh proposes to punish his wayward wife: stripping her naked (2:5, 12); abandoning her to die in the wilderness (2:5); disavowing their children (2:6); isolating her from the world (2:8). Only after severe punishment is reconciliation offered, when Yahweh woos her back home (2:16–17). Hosea is not alone in utilizing this imagery (see, e.g., Jer. 2:1–3:5; Ezek. 16:1–63).

(v. 12). Ultimately, however, chapter 10 ends not with the hope of repentance but with a declaration of doom: "At dawn, the king of Israel will be utterly ruined" (v. 15 AT).

Chapter 11 is one of the most well-known and moving chapters in the book, no doubt because of its emphasis on redemption, reconciliation, and homecoming. These themes have appeared elsewhere (see, e.g., 1:10–11; 2:14–23; 3:5), but not with the same force or emphasis. Here they draw more on parental metaphors than on the marital metaphor. The chapter begins with a painful recollection of the past:

> When Israel was a child, I loved him,
>   and out of Egypt I called my son.
> The more I called them,
>   the more they walked away from me,
>   sacrificing to the Baals,
>   and offering to graven images. (11:1–2, modified)

Yahweh's relationship to Israel is that of a parent to a child, but like many such relationships, this one is complicated and strained. The will of the parent is resisted and discarded by the child, whose loyalty is unruly and fickle. In one of the Bible's tenderest images of the God-Israel relationship, Yahweh recalls, "It was I who taught Ephraim [i.e., Israel] to walk, . . . took them up in my arms; . . . I healed them. I led them . . . with bands of love. . . . I bent down to them and fed them" (vv. 3–4). But Yahweh's compassionate provision was met with rejection, sparking threats of judgment.

But then something new and unexpected happens when Yahweh alters course, much in the same way that a heated argument between parent and child turns to tears and reconciliation. He breaks down with a stream of questions: "How can I give you up, Ephraim? How can I hand you over, O Israel?" (v. 8). Ultimately, despite his anger over Israel's infidelity, he cannot give up on his child.

In chapters 12–13, the book returns to the war drum, announcing judgment against God's people for their sins. Israel is a contentious people, like its ancestor Jacob (12:3–4). It uses false scales, demonstrating that it "loves to oppress" (12:7). Then the accusations turn to Israel's idolatrous worship of Baal. Once God tenderly cared for Israel as it emerged from Egypt and began its dangerous wilderness journey (13:4–6), but now he is a predator that threatens his people's journey (13:7–8).

The book ends with a message of hope that rests on Israel's repentance and Yahweh's forgiveness (14:1–3). Repentance opens a path to healing, new growth, and a fruitful future (14:4–8). The wise and prudent take note of the lessons learned (14:9).

The Meanings of the Names of Hosea's Children

Hosea gave his children symbolic names. Initially, the meaning of these names was a message of judgment; later, he reinterprets the names as words of promise.

The name Jezreel, given to the first son, means "he sows." Jezreel was a place where the founding member of King Jeroboam's dynasty had committed an atrocity—thus it was a call for judgment: "On that day I will break the bow of Israel in the valley of Jezreel" (1:5). Later, perhaps as late as the fall of Samaria, Hosea reinterprets the name to mean "I will sow him for myself in the land" and "great shall be the day of Jezreel" (2:23; 1:11).

The name Lo-ruhamah, given to Hosea's daughter, means "not shown mercy." At first, this was a message of judgment: "I will no longer have pity on the house of Israel or forgive them" (1:6). Later, Hosea renames her Ruhamah, which means "shown mercy": "I will have pity on Lo-ruhamah" (2:23).

The name Lo-ammi, given to Hosea's second son, means "not my people": "For you are not my people and I am not your God" (1:9). Later, Hosea renames him along with his daughter: "Say to your brother, Ammi, and to your sister, Ruhamah . . ." (2:1), and "I will say to Lo-ammi, 'You are my people'; and he shall say, 'You are my God'" (2:23).

Theological Interpretation

Patriarchy and Sexism in Hosea

The book of Hosea raises a number of significant and challenging theological questions. Many of these go to the core of theological discourse—namely, how to describe God's character and actions. Related questions include the following: How should one deal with descriptions of God that modern readers find archaic and off-putting? What should believing readers do with texts in which women are depicted in demeaning and brutalizing ways? What should one make of the marriage metaphor, especially in the way chapter 2 seems to legitimize abuse of women by their husbands? What should one do with the fact that these texts provoke such a wide range of responses, including everything from reverence to repulsion?

Many readers feel uncomfortable criticizing God's word. They might ask themselves, "Who am I to protest sacred speech?" This pious (but ultimately misguided) objection ironically fails to note that the human protestation of divine speech is not only normal, but it is also *biblical*. It is not unusual for biblical characters to argue with God (see, e.g., Gen. 18:16–33; Exod. 3:1–4:17; Jer. 1:4–19), demand that God pay attention (Ps. 13), and even disagree with God outright (Exod. 32:1–14; Num. 14; cf. Matt. 15:21–28). Through narratives like these, readers are invited into a dialogical relationship with God. Conflict with God is part of the biblical journey of faith. When readers raise objections to Hosea's demeaning and violent portrayal of women, they find themselves wearing the mantle of Jacob, Moses, and the Canaanite woman, all of whom challenged divine words.

Reading across Cultures and Centuries

Part of the interpretive task involves considering that Hosea was written thousands of years ago, by people who belong to a different culture and time. Reading the Bible is always a cross-cultural experience.[2] In the same way that a person might experience culture shock when traveling to a foreign country with radically different customs and practices, one might experience shock when reading the Bible. The difference, however, is that for many religious people, the Bible is not merely a cultural artifact; it represents a collection of sacred texts. The Bible is somehow and in some way a "word of God."

Students of the Bible should engage Hosea both honestly and critically. No questions or methods of textual interpretation are out of bounds. But one should also interact with historical texts empathetically, with an eye toward what the authors were trying to accomplish in their own times and with the intellectual and theological resources at their disposal. It is possible to acknowledge the cultural chasm between today's reader and Hosea, while also appreciating the prophet's attempt to name the evils and wrongs of his time and work toward a future that more clearly reflects God's abounding love for creation.

Idolatry, Unfaithfulness, Decadence

With these qualifications in mind, the prophet Hosea perceives several problems in his own time: foreign influence, idolatrous unfaithfulness, and decadence. The contents of Hosea are not unique within the broader prophetic corpus, but the manner in which he presents them certainly is, both for better and for worse. Hosea invites its modern readers to consider what (un)faithfulness looks like in our own time. What does it mean to have an idol? Hosea grounds these problems in what he called "lack of knowledge" (4:6; cf. v. 1): because the people did not know Yahweh or his ways, they went astray after idols and false gods, such as Baal and Asherah. For this lack of knowledge, he especially blames the

Fig. 30.3. The goddess Asherah is depicted here as a source of fertility, abundance, and blessing. For Hosea, faithful worshipers should attribute such benefits to Yahweh alone.

religious leaders, the priests, and prophets who were entrusted with the care and education of the people. He says they were actually greedy for the people to sin because then the people would pay them to receive forgiveness (4:8).

Creation in Hosea

Finally, Hosea lifts up important creational themes. In chapter 4, the prophet indicts Israel for lacking faithfulness and knowledge of God and for other sins like stealing, adultery, and bloodshed (4:1–2). But Hosea contends that these sins actually cause the land and its inhabitants to mourn, alongside wild animals, birds, and fish (4:3). For Hosea, the well-being of creation hinges upon human obedience. Texts such as these can help stir people to think more comprehensively about the impact of human behavior on the natural world.

Historical Interpretation

Hosea is a fascinating book from the perspective of history. It is part of a small collection of prophetic texts that focus on the Northern Kingdom of Israel (see, e.g., Amos and the narratives of Elijah and Elisha in 1–2 Kings). Most of the prophetic books focus on the Southern Kingdom of Judah and its capital, Jerusalem. This is due, at least in part, to the fact that only the Southern Kingdom survived in a recognizable way. While the book of Hosea does not say explicitly that the prophet is a citizen of the Northern Kingdom, this is a strong possibility, given the book's overall emphasis. Despite this northern association, scribes in the Southern Kingdom clearly considered the book worth preserving and even editing. Whether Judean scribes are responsible for the book's references to the Southern Kingdom (e.g., 1:7, 11; 3:5; 5:5, 10, 14–15) is uncertain.

Many of Hosea's texts describe judgment and destruction of the Northern Kingdom in general and of Samaria in particular. Samaria was in fact defeated in 722 BCE, perhaps under Assyrian kings Shalmaneser V or Sargon II, or both. The precise fate of the capital city of Samaria is uncertain, since archaeological evidence does not indicate the city's destruction. According to 2 Kings 17, the inhabitants of Samaria were deported and new inhabitants were brought in; such a forced relocation of populations is certainly within the realm of possibility.

FOR FURTHER READING: **Hosea**

Fretheim, Terence E. *Reading Hosea–Micah: A Literary and Theological Commentary.* Macon, GA: Smyth & Helwys, 2013.

Goldingay, John. *Hosea–Micah*. Baker Commentary on the Old Testament Prophetic Books. Grand Rapids: Baker Academic, 2021.

Lim, Bo H., and Daniel Castelo. *Hosea*. Two Horizons Old Testament Commentary. Grand Rapids: Eerdmans, 2015.

Mays, James Luther. *Hosea: A Commentary*. Old Testament Library. Philadelphia: Westminster, 1969.

Sherwood, Yvonne. *The Prostitute and the Prophet: Hosea's Marriage in Literary-Theoretical Perspective*. Journal for the Study of the Old Testament Supplement Series 212. 1996. Reprint, London: Continuum, 2004.

Wolff, Hans Walter. *Hosea: A Commentary on the Book of the Prophet Hosea*. Hermeneia. Minneapolis: Fortress, 1988.

Yee, Gale A. *Poor Banished Children of Eve: Woman as Evil in the Hebrew Bible*. Minneapolis: Fortress, 2003.

Joel

The book of Joel is crisis literature. In this brief but forceful prophetic book, Jerusalem and Judah face a variety of threats to their well-being and existence. Some of these threats are happening in the present, and others are on the horizon. But disaster is only part of the story. In response to communal complaints and petitions for help, Yahweh responds with compassion for his Jerusalem, his children, and the land. Days of restoration are coming for Jerusalem and for Judah. These coming days will not only see a restoration of safety and fertility; they will also bear witness to the gathering of the nations across the earth, where Yahweh's people have been scattered.

Versification in Joel differs depending on the translation used. Most Christian translations (e.g., NRSV, NIV) divide Joel into three chapters (1:1–20; 2:1–32; 3:1–21), whereas most translations used in Jewish communities (e.g., NJPS) divide the book into four chapters (1:1–20; 2:1–27; 3:1–5; 4:1–21). We will use the versification system adopted by the NRSV and NIV. Recall that the addition of verse numbers in the biblical text was a practice adopted by Christians in the medieval period.

Background

The Prophet Joel

Almost nothing is known about the prophet Joel son of Pethuel. He is not mentioned outside the book of Joel, and very little can be deduced about him from the book. Given his positive views of ritual and worship (unlike Amos or Isaiah), he may have been a priest. He also reflects a positive perspective on

Jerusalem and the temple, suggesting he may have been associated with either the Southern Kingdom of Judah or the postexilic Persian province of Yehud.

Historical Context

The book of Joel has no dating formula and is almost impossible to date with certainty. While it describes various disasters (e.g., locusts, invasion), these are sufficiently ambiguous to prevent identifying them with specific historical events. The latter half of the book contains a higher concentration of hopeful oracles, but these do not help provide any evidence on which to establish a historical setting.

The book's position as second in the Book of the Twelve suggests that the ancients understood Joel to be a preexilic contemporary of Amos and Hosea. However, most modern scholars place him sometime in the postexilic era, either in the fifth or fourth century BCE. One reason for this late date is that the book seems to know traditions and texts from other books of the Old Testament, such as Isaiah and Micah (3:10), Amos (3:16), Zephaniah (2:1–2), and Obadiah (chap. 3). The book also makes no reference to kings, which fits the postexilic era. The book's main crisis regards an invasion of locusts. If taken as a metaphor for an invading human army, the book fits better before the exile because prior to the exile Judah experienced many military invasions. But if taken literally, it better fits the postexilic time period. After the exile, while it was a province of the Persian Empire, military threats were less common. In addition, we know from other books such as Haggai and Zechariah that famine (sometimes resulting from plagues such as locust) were quite common. The strongest piece of evidence linking Joel to later periods in Judean history is found in 3:6, which mentions the Ionians/Greeks.

Composition and Development

The same evidence that prevents us from dating the book also makes it difficult to say anything about how the book developed as a literary collection. What can be said is that the book of Joel was at some point intentionally integrated into the Book of the Twelve and placed into its second position after Hosea.

Genre

Like other prophetic books, Joel contains a variety of genres. The book begins didactically, calling on the "inhabitants of the land" to listen and learn from unprecedented events. The book contains poems describing national disasters, summons to mourn and lament, calls to repent, promises of judgment against Judah's enemies, and oracles promising forgiveness and restoration. Joel shares with other prophetic books a general movement from disaster and judgment to forgiveness and restoration.

Literary Interpretation

Superscription (Joel 1:1). The book of Joel begins with a superscription attributing the book to "Joel son of Pethuel" (1:1). Nothing is known of this person, including the historical circumstances of his life. All we know is that he has received a word from Yahweh. The terse introduction complements the book's deep sense of urgency; it has a point to make, and it wants to get there quickly.

The plague of locusts and a call to repentance (1:2–2:17). After the superscription, the book urges its readers to teach their children about an unprecedented locust plague (1:2–3). Many questions have been raised about this plague of locusts. Is verse 4 describing an actual plague of locusts afflicting

Nuremburg Chronicle

Fig. 31.1. Locust plagues in the Bible are most typically associated with the book of Exodus, as shown here in the Nuremburg Chronicle, but a plague of locusts also plays an important role in the book of Joel, where it represents the ravages of divine judgment.

Judah, or are the locusts metaphorical or symbolic of a foreign army? Do they perhaps foreshadow an invasion to come when the "day of the Lord" finally arrives? Four different Hebrew words are used to describe the locusts ("cutter," "locust," "grub," "hopper," in English). Could each term represent a different nation, king, or event? Perhaps they represent different stages of the locusts' development? Perhaps the use of four different words simply underscores the completeness with which the locusts devastated the land? These questions are made even more difficult by the book's lack of a concrete historical setting.

These are important questions, but what is often overlooked in studying the identity of the locusts is how they fit into the larger constellation of creational forces and imagery present in Joel 1–2. Taken as a whole, these chapters depict acts of judgment and salvation that are cosmic in scope, involving the entire natural order—from the stars in the sky to the very soil itself. The locusts in 1:4 are only one part of that larger picture. Enemy invaders are described metaphorically with the "teeth of a lion" (1:6 AT), and they devastate agricultural growth (1:7). The country is severely decimated, causing the ground to mourn alongside the priests (1:9–10). Wine, oil, and other agricultural products are destroyed (1:10–12; cf. 1:16–17), and joy itself has "dried up" among the population (1:12 AT). The failure of the crops means that storage areas are empty, like the stomachs of the people and the animals (1:17). Creational sorrow and human sorrow are deeply interconnected.

The animals respond as well with groaning and bewilderment (1:18), because fire consumes their feeding areas and eliminates their sources of hydration. Having nowhere else to turn, the animals "pant" after Yahweh as they would for water (1:20 NIV).

Even the world's light is diminished. The day of the Lord will be one of "darkness and gloom" (2:2), because a violent horde scorches the earth, leaving behind a desolate wasteland (2:3–5). The power of this army is so great that creation

<hr />

Box 31.2

Creation and Judgment

The book of Joel is not the only biblical book in which God employs the non-human creation to enact his will, either to judge or to save. In fact, this is one of the Bible's most persistent motifs. The book of Exodus is perhaps the most famous example, with its numerous creation plagues, including blood, frogs, locusts, lice, and pestilence. God uses the created things of this world to oppose the death-dealing actions of Pharaoh. But God also employs the wind to help save Israel from certain death at the Red Sea (also known as the Sea of Reeds). He drives back the sea with a strong east wind, thereby making a way for his people (Exod. 14:21). These texts say something about how Yahweh acts in the world. They demonstrate that the God of Israel tends to act through created means—human and nonhuman alike.

will tremble from ground to sky (2:10). The astral entities themselves—sun, moon, and stars—will lose their ability to illuminate the cosmos and effect growth on the earth. But the cries of Yahweh's people are heard (2:15–17) and the deity's compassion is stirred up on behalf of "his land" (2:18). Just as Yahweh's judgment brought desolation upon the earth, so his salvation will cause new life to grow in the form of "new grain," "new wine," and "new oil" (2:19 AT). Yahweh addresses the soil and the animals directly, telling them to "fear not" (2:21–22), for he would bring the rains followed by an overflowing harvest. With a final nod back to the locusts, Yahweh promises to "repay" Judah the years devoured by the destructive plague (2:25).

Unfortunately, there is no answer key at the back of the book to tell us the precise identity of the locusts. One thing is clear, however: the destructive deeds of the locusts need to be interpreted in light of the larger cosmic and creational drama that preoccupies Joel 1–2. They are but one element of a larger creational upheaval that occurs at Yahweh's direction. The locusts are, as 2:25 indicates, Yahweh's own "great army."

The devastation wrought by the locusts provokes a call to lament (1:8–20). Everyone, from the priest to the farmer, is called upon to mourn and fast in response to the desolation that is upon them. This, in turn, is followed by a terrifying poetic description of "the day of the LORD" (2:1–11), in which the Lord himself stands at the head of a devastating army from whom no one can escape (2:3). Most terrifying of all is the fact that Yahweh himself stands at the head of the army (2:11).

But this most terrifying of claims also stands at the book's theological and literary fulcrum. When the battle reaches its peak, the book's tone changes from terror to tenderness. Yahweh's roar of terror (2:11) becomes a call to return: "Yet even now, says Yahweh, come back to me with all your heart—with fasting, weeping, and lamentation" (2:12 AT). It is Yahweh's character that gives the prophet confidence:

> Return to Yahweh, your God:
>> for he is gracious and compassionate,
> slow to anger and abounding in loyalty,
>> and he relents from disasters. (2:13 AT)

Fig. 31.2. This bronze sculpture of Joel rending his garments is located in the Biblical Gardens of the Moshav Yad HaShmona in the Judean Hills, near Jerusalem. Rending one's garments was a dramatic act of grief or repentance—many people only had one garment and every garment was hand produced. The prophet Joel said, "Rend your hearts and not your clothing. Return to the LORD, your God, for he is gracious and merciful" (2:13). Joel had a deeper and more meaningful grief and repentance in mind.

For Joel, the world turns on the compassion of God. The hope of his compassion also stirs up a call to gather the people, young and old alike (2:15–17), to seek reprieve from the disaster.

Promise of deliverance, the Spirit, and the day of the Lord (2:18–3:21). Yahweh responds with compassion. Fertility returns, shame retreats, and the assaulting army will depart (2:19–20). Creation itself is addressed and welcomed into the celebration:

> Do not be afraid, oh soil;
> > rejoice and be happy,
> > because Yahweh has done incredible things!
> Do not be afraid, beasts of the field,
> > because the pastures of the wilderness have greened,
> > > a tree has borne its fruit,
> > > fig and vine have given their abundance. (2:21–22 AT)

Creation was entangled in the consequences of the initial crisis, and the same would be true of the restoration. Yahweh promises to bring rain and abundance (2:23–24) and to "repay you the years" devoured by the locust plague (2:25 AT). Where Judah was once afflicted by desolation and defeat, it would eat abundantly and be free of shame (2:26–27).

The text then promises that "I [Yahweh] will pour out my *spirit* [breath/wind] on all flesh," resulting in prophecy, dreams, and visions (2:28, italics added). Signs will appear in the heavens in anticipation of "the great and terrible day of Yahweh" (2:31 AT), and on that day, "Everyone who calls upon the name of Yahweh will be delivered" (2:32 AT).

In the final chapter, Yahweh gathers the nations of the earth and judges them for abusing his people and his land (3:1–3). For the book of Joel, violence begets violence and war begets war (3:4–8, 13). When the seeds of violence finally come to fruition, it will be a dark day felt across the cosmos (3:14–16). For Judah's enemies, it will be a day of terror, but Judah itself will find refuge in its God.

Theological Interpretation

Creation in Joel

Creation plays an important theological role in the book of Joel. As we said above, the crisis depicted in Joel is not only detrimental to human life, but it also negatively impacts creation. The locusts devour, cut, and decimate; in the words of 1:10, "Dirt is devastated, soil languished" (AT). The future day of the Lord would also wreak havoc on both flora and fauna. Agriculture suffers, wilderness pastures are devoured by fire, and water sources dry up (1:15–20).

Creation Theology in the Prophets

The Prophets of the Old Testament are best known for their fierce oracles of judgment and for their powerful poetry. Recently, biblical interpreters interested in ecotheology have begun turning to the Prophets for their insights into creation. Those concerned with the perils of climate change will find that Joel also saw an ecological disaster on the horizon for his people. This disaster would turn Eden into a wasteland (2:3). While Joel did not tie that disaster to global warming or to fossil fuels, he did think that humans contributed to the disaster and that they also had the ability to correct their course.

Even the cosmic elements of creation respond to the horde that tramples the earth on the day of the Lord:

> Before them the earth trembles,
>   heavens shake;
> sun and moon go dark,
>   and stars withhold their brightness. (2:10 AT)

All of creation is caught up in the impacts of violence and sin.

But creation also responds to Yahweh's saving grace. In the wake of divine compassion, life reemerges from the dystopian hellscape of the first half of the book: new wine, new oil, fruit-bearing trees, early rain, and an abundant harvest (2:19, 22–25). These are but the firstfruits of Judah's restoration, which will climax in chapter 3, where its fortunes are restored and the foreign nations are judged.

Jerusalem and Zion

Like so many books of the Old Testament, Joel is preoccupied with the fate of Jerusalem and the land of Judah. For a book so concerned with judgment on a cosmic scale, it might seem strange that Joel is firmly fixated on one particular location: "my holy mountain" (2:1). But Jerusalem/Zion is not just any city. It is Yahweh's city—a chosen city, within a chosen land, whose inhabitants are a chosen people. The interplay between the cosmic and the particular does not pose an irreconcilable contradiction. Yahweh's election of a particular people (Abraham and Sarah's offspring, the Jews) is for the sake of the entire human family (Gen. 12:1–3). The particular serves the universal.

The Promise of the Spirit

The most famous section of the book of Joel comes near the end of chapter 2:

> I will pour out my Spirit on all flesh;
> your sons and your daughters shall prophesy,

Pentecost The Greek term for the Jewish harvest festival called the Feast of Weeks, situated chronologically between Passover and the Feast of Tabernacles.

> your old men shall dream dreams,
> and your young men shall see visions.
> Even on the male and female servants
> in those days I will pour out my Spirit. (2:28–29 ESV)

Considered against the background of the Old Testament and the ancient Near East, the promise of the Spirit's coming is stunning in its inclusivity. The Spirit will be poured out on all flesh—male and female, young and old, slave and free: "Even on the male and female servants in those days I will pour out my Spirit."

Throughout the Old Testament there were female prophets—Miriam in the exodus, Deborah in the days of the judges, Isaiah's wife in the eighth century BCE, and Huldah near the end of the kingdom of Judah. Nevertheless, the promise that the Spirit would send visions and dreams and the gift of prophecy to all flesh is astounding.

Historical Interpretation

We have already broached the book's most nettlesome historical questions: When was the book written? How and when was the book edited? When was it added to the Book of the Twelve? To which historical disaster(s) does the book refer? Are the locusts to be understood literally? Metaphorically? Symbolically? Perhaps all of the above? Joel is famously reticent about its origins and even about its namesake, "Joel son of Pethuel" (1:1), leaving scholars with only the scantest evidence from which to discern a historical setting.

The book of Joel reminds modern readers just how little we actually know about the origins of biblical books. Joel is certainly an extreme example, but every other biblical book faces similar questions to varying degrees.

FOR FURTHER READING: Joel

Barton, John. *Joel and Obadiah: A Commentary*. Old Testament Library. Louisville: Westminster John Knox, 2001.

Claassens, L. Juliana M. "Joel." In *Women's Bible Commentary*, 3rd ed., edited by Carol A. Newsom, Sharon H. Ringe, and Jacqueline E. Lapsley, 309–11. Louisville: Westminster John Knox, 2012.

Collins, John. *Joel, Obadiah, Haggai, Zechariah, Malachi*. New Collegeville Bible Commentary. Collegeville, MN: Liturgical Press, 2013.

Fretheim, Terence E. *Reading Hosea–Micah: A Literary and Theological Commentary*. Macon, GA: Smyth & Helwys, 2013.

Goldingay, John, and Pamela J. Scalise. *Minor Prophets II*. New International Biblical Commentary. Peabody, MA: Hendrickson, 2009.

Limburg, James. *Hosea–Micah*. Interpretation: A Bible Commentary for Teaching and Preaching. Atlanta: John Knox, 1988.

Nogalski, James. *The Book of the Twelve: Hosea–Jonah*. Smyth & Helwys Bible Commentary. Macon, GA: Smyth & Helwys, 2011.

O'Brien, Julia M. "Joel." In *Theological Bible Commentary*, edited by Gail R. O'Day and David L. Petersen, 265–66. Louisville: Westminster John Knox, 2009.

Stuart, Douglas. *Hosea–Jonah*. Word Biblical Commentary 31. Waco: Word, 1987.

Amos

A retired colleague of ours, Mark Hillmer, would often quote his professor Sheldon Blank from Hebrew Union College: "If you like the prophet Amos, you don't understand him." Professor Blank's witty remark well captures the creative yet acerbic nature of the prophet Amos. His prophetic messages of judgment are often profound and humorous. But if you find yourself laughing at his prophetic wit, you probably do not realize that the prophet would also think that you, too, in the words of the apostle Paul, "have sinned and fall short of the glory of God" (Rom. 3:23).

Background

The Prophet Amos

The superscription to the book introduces it as containing "the words of Amos, who was one of the shepherds from Tekoa" (1:1 AT), which was a village in the Southern Kingdom of Judah. Later in the book, Amos is quoted as saying of himself, "I am not a [professional] prophet, nor a disciple of a prophet; rather, I am a cattle herder and a picker of sycamore figs. But the Lord took me from going after the flock and said to me, 'Go, prophesy to my people Israel'" (7:14–15 AT). Some commentators assume from these verses that Amos may have been poor or uneducated, but such conclusions betray urban prejudices. Amos may have been a relatively poor farmhand, but he may also have been a prosperous and privileged farm owner. It is impossible to say. But one thing seems sure: Amos was not a professional court prophet who earned his living offering prophecies for pay. He was a layperson from the Southern Kingdom of

Judah who was called by the Lord to deliver messages of warning and judgment to the people and rulers of the Northern Kingdom of Israel.

Historical Context

The superscription and narratives of the book place Amos as interacting with King Jeroboam II of Israel, who reigned from 786 to 746 BCE. Because the introductory formula says that his messages were delivered "two years before the earthquake," many scholars conclude that he may only have prophesied for a single year (760?) and then either returned to Tekoa or perhaps been arrested and killed by Jeroboam. It is uncertain. What does seem certain is that the kingdom of Israel was relatively peaceful and prosperous during the reign of Jeroboam. But Amos believed the peace and prosperity were only surface deep—that underneath the peace and prosperity, the kingdom was morally and spiritually corrupt.

Composition and Development

As is the case with most of the prophetic books of the Old Testament, the book of Amos consists of various prophetic messages that the prophet delivered, and it also may contain material that was added later by editors or copyists. Amos's prophetic messages were most likely written down by some of his disciples and then brought south to Jerusalem, where they were saved and eventually edited into the book that now bears the prophet's name. The book was likely edited in more than one stage. For example, a series of five very similar visions in chapters 7–8 is interrupted once by a narrative about the priest Amaziah that explains the third vision and again by a collection of judgment messages after the fourth and fifth visions.

Genre

The book of Amos is made up almost entirely of prophetic messages, or oracles. The majority consist of judgment speeches. Amos uses many different genres to get his messages across: numerical sayings, a funeral dirge, a mock call to

---

Box 32.1

Outline

1. Superscription (1:1)
2. Judgment of Israel's neighbors and Israel (1:2–2:16)
3. Collection of judgment messages (3:1–6:14)
4. Five visions and the Amaziah narrative (7:1–9:4)
5. Concluding messages (9:5–15)

worship, and the like. The book also includes a few messages of salvation, which are interspersed throughout the book in key locations. These include Amos 3:12, three hymnic fragments (4:13; 5:8–9; 9:5–6), and a conclusion that promises a future beyond judgment (9:7–15).

Literary Interpretation

Superscription (1:1). The opening superscription places Amos during the reigns of Jeroboam II of Israel (786–746) and Uzziah of Judah (783–742). This places him as a near contemporary of the prophet Hosea.

Judgment of Israel's neighbors and Israel (Amos 1:2–2:16). The book of Amos begins by sounding the keynote message of the book:

> And [Amos] said,
> "From Zion the Lord roars!
> From Jerusalem he raises his voice!
> The pastures of the shepherds wither,
> and the top of Carmel dries up!" (1:2 AT)

The twice-emphasized note that the Lord speaks from Zion and from Jerusalem establishes in no uncertain terms that the secession of the northern tribes from the southern tribes may have been a political reality, but it did not change the theological reality that all twelve tribes of Israel still had one and only one God: the Lord. Amos says the Lord "roars"—a verb that often describes the voice of a lion (see, e.g., Judg. 14:5; Isa. 5:29). The image of the lion was associated with images in the temple in Jerusalem, thus strengthening the sense that God's judgment emanates from Jerusalem. And God's judgment is far-reaching. Mount Carmel is at the extreme northwest tip of Israel. God roars in Jerusalem and Mount Carmel dries up. The phrase "the pastures of the shepherds" may refer to the kings of Israel enthroned in Samaria, because "shepherd" was often a metaphor for kings throughout the ancient Near East.

Amos 1:3–2:16 needs to be read as one unit. In this section, one can imagine the prophet from Judah arriving in the Northern Kingdom and starting to preach to a gathered crowd. Amos starts by naming the sins of Israel's neighbors and pronouncing God's judgment. In each case, the message culminates with "I will send [kindle] a fire."

First, Aram is condemned for the sin of having "thresh[ed] Gilead with threshing sledges of iron" (1:3). Gilead was a border territory that Israel and Aram often fought over. We can imagine the crowd cheering; a prophetic judgment message for one's enemy was good news. Second, the Philistines are condemned for enslaving people. More cheering. Third, Tyre is condemned for trading slaves and for breaking "the covenant of kinship" with Israel (1:9). Fourth, Edom is condemned because "he pursued his brother with the sword" (1:11). More cheering and some rage. Fifth, Ammon is condemned "because they have ripped open pregnant women in Gilead in order to enlarge their territory" (1:13). More rage and more cheering. Sixth, Moab is condemned for having desecrated the body of Edom's king. More cheering. Seventh, Israel's fellow Yahweh-worshiping neighbor, Judah, is condemned "because they have rejected the law of the LORD, and have not kept his statutes, but they have been led astray by the same lies" (2:4). Note that while the sins of Israel's neighbors are general sins against humanity, Judah's sins are specifically against the Lord's law; being "led astray by the same lies" refers to worshiping idols ("lies") rather than the Lord. More cheering.

Then, having whipped up the crowd, the prophet turns his prophetic tongue on Israel: "For three transgressions of Israel, and for four, I will not revoke the punishment" (2:6). The cheering crowd goes silent. He then lays out Israel's sins at length and in direct quotation of the law of the Lord (more on this later in the chapter).

Collection of judgment messages (Amos 3:1–6:14). The next four chapters contain numerous short messages of judgment. Unlike chapters 1–2, these chapters are not constructed as a coherent unit but as a collection. Some illustrate the powerful rhetoric and creative voice of the prophet Amos (more on this below).

When reading each short passage, the reader must try to discern who the original audience was and what sins the prophet is calling out. Some messages are directed to the nation as a whole. For example, in 3:1–2 the prophet cries against the "people of Israel" and addresses the entirety of their sins. This short message can be considered the theme verse for chapters 3–6. Other messages are directed to the women of the capital Samaria (4:1–3), to those who come to worship at the temples in Bethel and Gilgal (4:4–5), to those who make legal judgments in the courts (5:10–17), to the priests who lead worship (5:21–24), and to the leaders of Judah and Israel (6:1–7).

The overall message of this section can be summarized as follows: At every level of society, Israel has failed to love the Lord its God and to love the neighbor in many, many ways. For all these sins, the Lord will punish Israel. Although the Lord has already punished Israel through famine and disease, the climactic verse of this section names a new vehicle of the Lord's judgment: "Indeed, I will raise up against you a nation, house of Israel, says the LORD God of heavenly forces, and they will oppress you from Lebo-hamath to the desert ravine" (6:14 CEB). That nation was Assyria.

Five visions and the Amaziah narrative (Amos 7:1–9:4). The five visions that the prophet reports in 7:1–9:4 are meant to be read as a coherent unit, although several smaller sections are often excerpted to be read and preached in Christian churches. For example, the Amaziah narrative (7:10–17) and the visions of the "plumb line" and the "summer fruit" occur as appointed readings in the Revised Common Lectionary (a system of assigning readings for Christian worship that many congregations follow).

In the first vision, the prophet sees a swarm of locusts descending on the land at harvest time. The prophet pleads for the Lord to forgive and relent, and he does. In the second vision, the prophet sees a shower of fire devouring the land. The prophet pleads for the Lord to stop, so the Lord relents. In the third vision, the prophet sees the Lord standing beside a wall being built, and the Lord is holding what most translations call a "plumb line"—we are not sure exactly what this word means, but it appears to be a tool to measure whether a wall is being built "true" (straight and right). The Lord then holds the plumb line in the middle of the people, and the prophet announces that this time the judgment will not "pass them by" but that "sanctuaries of Israel shall be laid waste, and I will rise against the house of Jeroboam with the sword" (7:9)—meaning that the king of Israel himself would be judged and would die.

© Lisle Gwynn Garrity

Fig. 32.1. Martin Luther King Jr. is well known for his use of the prophet Amos's famous words, "Let justice roll down like waters, and righteousness like an ever-flowing stream." He explicitly quotes Amos 5:24 in his famous 1963 "Letter from a Birmingham Jail." In that missive, he rhetorically asks, "Was not Amos an extremist for justice?" The image "God of Justice" illustrates the prophetic vision for freedom and justice for the captive and the oppressed.

The next passage describes how the priest Amaziah of Bethel (the main temple in the Northern Kingdom) confronts Amos and tells him to leave the land because his preaching offends the king. This narrative was likely inserted into the series of visions to describe the prophetic judgment against King Jeroboam. Amos refuses to leave, insisting that the Lord had sent him to proclaim the prophetic word. Amos then announces that the priest Amaziah will be exiled and die in a foreign land.

The series of visions resumes with the fourth vision. The prophet sees a basket of "summer fruit" and announces "the end" is coming (8:1–2). The

Box 32.2

Amos's Creativity

Prophets are messengers of God. This is evident from the fact that their oracles often begin with phrases such as, "Thus says Yahweh." Part of their calling was to relay messages that they had seen, heard, or discerned. But the prophets were not merely stenographers. They were also interested in moving and convincing their audiences; they were literary and hortatory artists. Careful study of prophetic texts—especially in their original languages—shows an immense amount of creativity in the construction and delivery of their words. This is nowhere more apparent than in the book of Amos, which uses powerful rhetorical and literary devices to capture the reader's attention, provoke them to think more deeply, and ultimately move them toward faithfulness.

The prophet Amos was capable of delivering a very simple and straightforward message of judgment. Consider his announcement that just as a shepherd might rescue "two legs, or a piece of an ear" from a lion's mouth, "so shall the people of Israel who live in Samaria be rescued" (3:12). In other words, judgment is coming, and only a small portion of the population of the city will be rescued. But note the creativity. The prophetic message is harrowing, as the audience envisions only being able to rescue a couple of legs or "a piece of an ear" from the lion's mouth! Notice, too, how this short message of judgment recalls the keynote verse: "From Zion the Lord roars" (1:2 AT).

Amos copied forms of speech and ways of singing in order to get his message across. There was probably no literary genre from which he was not willing to borrow, no line of decorum that he was not afraid to cross, in order to get Yahweh's message across to Israel. For example, notice how in this short passage the prophet borrowed the "call to worship" genre (compare Ps. 100) from Israel's worship life:

> "Come to Bethel, and transgress;
>   to Gilgal, and multiply transgression;
> bring your sacrifices every morning,
>   your tithes every three days;
> offer a sacrifice of thanksgiving of that which is leavened,
>   and proclaim freewill offerings, publish them;
>   for so you love to do, O people of Israel!"
>   declares the Lord God. (4:4–5 ESV)

The call to worship would have been sung at the start of a worship service, especially one of the three pilgrimage festivals of the year, at which Israelite males were to bring

Hebrew words for "summer fruit" and "end" sound very much alike—especially in the northern accent. Amos pokes fun at their accent and also announces God's judgment.

A series of short judgment messages is then inserted into the series of visions, giving the reason for God's judgment on Israel. The people "trample on the needy," cheat in the marketplace with "false balances, buying the poor for silver" (meaning enslaving people for financial debts), and worship false gods such as "Ashimah of Samaria"—therefore, the entire nation will suffer from famine and go into exile (8:4–6, 14). The fifth and final vision is the harshest.

offerings to one of the central worship sites, such as Bethel or Gilgal. But notice how Amos lays violent hands on the literary form and mocks the worshipers. They are to "come to Bethel" not to praise God but to "transgress" and "multiply transgression"! He piles on the sarcasm.

Rather than bring in their offerings once a month or their tithes three times a year, they should bring their offerings "every morning" and their tithes "every three days"! This the literal translation. The translators of the NIV miss the prophet's sarcasm and change his words to "bring . . . your tithes every three years." The NIV knows that a person cannot possibly tithe—give 10 percent of one's wealth—every three days, so they presume to change the prophet's words. But that is precisely the prophet's point! Even if the Israelites could tithe every three days, they still would not please God, because in their worship they only multiply their sins: "for so you love to do, O people of Israel!" We can imagine the prophet showing up at Bethel or Gilgal or other worship centers and singing this "call to worship" as an announcement of the people's sins.

A similar example is found in Amos 5, where the prophet borrows the genre of the funeral dirge or lament—the song sung over the corpse of a loved one. The prophet sings:

> Hear this word that I take up over you,
>   O house of Israel, a dirge [lament]:
> "Fallen, never again to rise,
>   is the virgin Israel,
> forsaken on her land,
>   with no one to lift her up.
> For thus says the Lord,
>   'The city that marches out a thousand
>   shall only receive a hundred back;
> and the one that sends out a hundred,
>   only ten shall return among the house of Israel.'" (5:1–3 AT)

The reader can imagine the prophet lifting up his voice in the call to mourn. In ancient Israel, people were likely buried the day they died, so we can envision citizens hearing the call and wondering, Who died? The prophet then sings his truth to the people: "You, O virgin Israel, have died." The reader is invited to discover similar examples of prophetic creativity throughout the book.

The prophet sees the Lord "standing beside the altar," announcing the destruction of the people (9:1).

Concluding messages (Amos 9:5–15). The book of Amos concludes with three short passages. The first is a hymn to the Lord, celebrating his universal reign: "He who touches the earth, . . . who builds his upper chambers in the heavens, . . . the LORD is his name" (9:5–6). This hymn serves as the exclamation point on the judgment messages of Amos. The judgment Amos preaches comes not from himself but from the Lord, who rules heaven and earth.

The second passage may be the most theologically intriguing in the book (9:7–10). Here the Lord claims that just as he brought Israel out of Egypt, so also he brought the Ethiopians, Philistines, and Arameans out of other lands in similar exodus-like deliverances. Then the Lord promises, "I will not utterly destroy the house of Jacob" (meaning the Northern Kingdom; 9:8).

The final verses of the book may have been added to the end of the book during the exile, because the vocabulary sounds very much like that of Isaiah 40–55 (so-called Second Isaiah). But if so, the message here is consistent with that of the eighth-century-BCE prophet Amos. Though a time of judgment comes, the passage offers a vision of new life in which "the mountains shall drip sweet wine, and all the hills shall flow with it. I will restore the fortunes of my people Israel. . . . I will plant them upon their land" (9:13–15).

Theological Interpretation

There Are Really Only Two Sins—Idolatry and Injustice

As noted several times already, the biblical prophets see only two types of sin: idolatry and injustice—or, to put it more plainly, failure to love the Lord and failure to love the neighbor. The prophet Amos would agree with this flat assessment, but he might add, "These two simple sins come in an infinite number of complex forms and disguises."

Amos considered the root of Israel's sin its failure to love the Lord its God, who had rescued the people from Egypt and planted them in the promised land. The prophet first highlights what the Lord had done for Israel: "You only have I known of all the families of the earth" (3:2); "Also I brought you up out of the land of Egypt, and led you forty years in the wilderness, to possess the land of the Amorite" (2:10); and "Did I not bring Israel up from the land of Egypt?" (9:7). Yet Israel had strayed into worshiping the false gods of her neighbors: "They have been led astray by the same lies [false gods] after which their ancestors walked" (2:4); "You have lifted up the shrine of your king, the pedestal of your idols, the star of your god—which you made for yourselves" (5:26 NIV); and "Those who swear by Ashimah of Samaria, and say, 'As your god lives, O Dan,' . . . they shall fall, and never rise again" (8:14). Samaria and Dan refer to the alternative—and from Amos's perspective, apostate—shrines established by the Northern Kingdom of Israel.

Israel's failure to worship the Lord was not complete abandonment of the Lord for other gods. Amos likely believed that many in Israel were guilty of syncretism—worshiping other gods in addition to the Lord and corrupting their worship of the Lord by including some practices of idol worship. These inclusions may have been as extreme as child sacrifice. In Amos's thinking, failure to worship the Lord exclusively led many in Israel (and Judah) to stray from keeping the law of the Lord. Thus, in chapters 1–2, when Amos turns his sights on Judah and then Israel after having first condemned the surrounding nations, he first mentions Judah's failure to keep the law:

> For three transgressions of Judah,
>   and for four, I will not revoke the punishment;
> because they have rejected the law of the LORD,
>   and have not kept his statutes. (2:4)

Then, turning to Israel's failure to keep the law, Amos gets explicit about some of the laws that the people had failed to keep:

> For three transgressions of Israel,
>   and for four, I will not revoke the punishment;
> because they sell the righteous for silver,
>   and the needy for a pair of sandals—
> they who trample the head of the poor into the dust of the earth,
>   and push the afflicted out of the way;
> father and son go in to the same girl,
>   so that my holy name is profaned;
> they lay themselves down beside every altar
>   on garments taken in pledge;

Fig. 32.2. Amos and other prophets and some laws condemn the use of high taxes to control and oppress the poor. Amos proclaimed, "Because you trample the poor and take from them taxes of grain, you shall not live in the houses of cut stone that you have built" (5:11 AT).

and in the house of their God they drink
wine bought with fines they imposed. (2:6–8)

For each of these violations of the law, there are not necessarily direct stat-utes in the pentateuchal law that one can quote, but there are passages that shed light on Amos's interpretive thinking. To "sell the righteous for silver, and the needy for a pair of sandals" was to enslave people for their debts, even the smallest debts (see Exod. 21:7–11). To "trample the head of the poor . . . and push the afflicted out of the way" was not just to ignore the needs of the poor (see Deut. 15:7–11) but especially to deny the poor equal rights in legal matters (see Amos 5:10–11, 15; Exod. 23:6). For a "man and his father to go into the same maiden" (AT) violated the law's prohibition both on incest and other sexual-boundary violations (see Lev. 18:8; 20:12). To "lay themselves down beside every altar on garments taken in pledge" violated a statute from the Covenant Code: "If you take your neighbor's cloak in pawn, you shall restore it before the sun goes down; for it may be your neighbor's only clothing to use as cover" (Exod. 22:26–27). To make the Nazirites, a special class of disciples, "drink wine" was to force them to violate one of their holy vows (see Num. 6:3).

In addition to this catalog of legal violations, the prophet names specific acts of injustice—failure to love the neighbor—of which the people were guilty:

- violence and robbery (3:10)
- taxing the poor by imposing on them "levies of grain" (5:11)
- taking bribes in lawsuits, especially against the poor (5:12)
- living lives of luxury in Samaria while disregarding the poor (4:1–5; 6:4–7)
- cheating in the marketplace with "false balances" and "selling the sweep-ings of the wheat" (8:5–6)

While the prophet specifically judged Judah and Israel for having strayed from the Lord's revealed law in the Pentateuch, his condemnation of the sur-rounding nations for sins such as war, slavery, and murder of women and their unborn children reveals his belief in a basic "natural law." Such a standard is available to all humans, simply as a matter of human nature. There are basic tenets of law and ethics to which every person is accountable, whether they are a worshiper of the Lord or not.

A Dim View of Israel's Worship and Theology

Anyone who hates going to worship—especially to long, somber worship services—will find a kindred spirit in the prophet Amos, who complains, "I hate, I despise your festivals, and I take no delight in your solemn assemblies"

(5:21). But Amos is not speaking just for himself. He is also speaking for God. The prophet does not despise worship itself, but the rote, going-through-the-motions worship in which the worshipers praise God and give offerings but are never transformed by God's love into people of justice and of love for the neighbor.

Thus, the prophet announces that Israel's offerings are in vain (4:4–5), that both their offerings and their praise are rejected: "Take away from me the noise of your songs; I will not listen to the melody of your harps" (5:23). Amos condemns those who grudgingly observe the monthly new moon and weekly Sabbath services but really long to get back to their dishonest daily lives:

> They say, "When will the new moon be over
>   so that we may sell grain;
> and the sabbath,
>   so that we may offer wheat for sale?
> We will make the ephah small and the shekel great,
>   and practice deceit with false balances,
> buying the poor for silver
>   and the needy for a pair of sandals,
>   and selling the sweepings of the wheat. (8:5–6)

The prophet also calls out the practice of journeying to a holy site in order to "seek" the will of the Lord—that is, to ask a temple priest or prophet whether a particular course of action will be blessed by the Lord. For those who engage in such practices the prophet offers this blunt word:

> Seek me and live;
>   but do not seek Bethel,
> and do not enter into Gilgal
>   or cross over to Beer-sheba;
> for Gilgal shall surely go into exile,
>   and Bethel shall come to nothing.
>
> Seek the LORD and live,
>   or he will break out against the house of Joseph like fire,
>   and it will devour Bethel, with no one to quench it.
> Ah, you that turn justice to wormwood,
>   and bring righteousness to the ground! . . .
>
> Seek good and not evil,
>   that you may live;
> and so the LORD, the God of hosts, will be with you,
>   just as you have said.
> Hate evil and love good,
>   and establish justice in the gate;

Box 32.3

Prophetic Critique and Antiritual Theologies

Amos is clearly critical of the worshipers of his time. He despises their hypocrisy. On the one hand, they "worship" Yahweh with the prescribed rituals but disregard the well-being of their neighbors. For Amos, faithfulness to God and faithfulness to neighbor are intrinsically connected. One cannot neglelct one without also violating the other. Amos is not alone in this critique. In Isaiah 1:14, Yahweh rails against ancient Judah with these words: "Your new moons and your appointed feasts my soul hates; they have become a burden to me; I am weary of bearing them" (ESV).

There is a long history of (mis)interpretation related to these verses, especially among Protestants. Some interpreters assume that Amos and Isaiah see the cult itself as the problem—as if Israel's worship practices are nothing more than "dead" religious rituals standing in the way of true and authentic faith. In some cases, these faulty assumptions have tragically fueled the flames of anti-Catholic and anti-Jewish sentiment. Contemporary readers should be aware of the interpretive traditions they inhabit and how those traditions both illuminate and distort the texts they are reading.

> it may be that the LORD, the God of hosts,
> will be gracious to the remnant of Joseph. (5:4–7, 14–15)

The message is clear: You do not need to go to a holy site to seek God's will. You already know it: do "good and not evil," "establish justice in the gate," and, in the most famous passage from the book of Amos, "let justice roll down like waters, and righteousness like an ever-flowing stream" (5:24).

Amos has a special contempt for Israel's belief in the goodness of the coming day of the Lord. The day of the Lord may originally have been associated with the Year of Jubilee (see Lev. 25:8–55). In the Year of Jubilee, which occurred every fifty years, all debts were forgiven, all land was returned to its original family, and slaves were set free in order to return to their families. Because the Year of Jubilee began by sounding the trumpet on "the tenth day of the seventh month—on the day of atonement" (Lev. 25:9), some interpreters believe that the "day of the LORD" was originally the fiftieth year to which so many in Israel looked forward. At some point, however, the term came to stand roughly for "that day in the future when the Lord will act decisively on Israel's behalf to save her from her enemies." To this, Amos says, "No!" The Lord would act decisively and soon, but it would not be on Israel's behalf: "Alas for you who desire the day of the LORD! Why do you want the day of the LORD? It is darkness, not light; as if someone fled from a lion, and was met by a bear" (5:18–19).

The Sovereignty of the Lord

At the very heart of the prophet's theology is a deep belief in the universal sovereignty of Israel's Lord. Amos believes and proclaims that the Lord is the creator and sustainer of everything. This is evident throughout the book and specifically in the three hymnic passages (4:13; 5:8–9; 9:5–6), each of which confesses God as creator of all and includes the phrase "the LORD is his name." Even if these hymnic fragments are later additions by an editor, they nevertheless are consistent with the prophet's theology as expressed throughout the book. The prophet also believes that the Lord's agency in history is thorough enough that both judgment and salvation could come from the same God.

Amos also believes that the Lord's reign over creation extends to history and nature. The prophet, for example, on many occasions announces that the Lord's punishment of Israel will include drought, pestilence, and famine: "I also withheld the rain from you when there were still three months to the harvest"; "I struck you with blight and mildew; I laid waste your gardens and your vineyards; the locust devoured your fig trees and your olive trees" (4:7, 9). Likewise, the Lord is sovereign over history and capable of raising up the Assyrian Empire as the rod of his punishment: "An adversary shall surround the land, and strip you of your defense; and your strongholds shall be plundered" (3:11). The threatening promise of judgment that Israel would go into exile (5:5; 6:7; 7:17) needs an executing agent, which is the unnamed nation of Assyria: "I am raising up against you a nation, O house of Israel, says the LORD, the God of hosts, and they shall oppress you from Lebo-hamath to the Wadi Arabah" (6:14). Tantalizingly, the prophet also believes that the Lord's saving action is not limited to Israel. In a final portion of chapter 9, the prophet asserts that the Lord performed exodus events for the Philistines, the Ethiopians, and the Arameans. The universal reign of God is not simply one of judgment but also one of salvation (9:7).

The Prophetic Word and the Promise of God's Faithfulness

For all of his negativity about the value of Israel's worship, the prophet Amos deeply believes in the power of the prophetic words. One of Israel's greatest sins, in the prophet's eyes, is that Israel prevented the prophets from delivering their words of warning and judgment (2:12; 7:16; etc.). Amos believes that those who hear the word can turn from the path of destruction and that the prophets who proclaim this word are God's very servants:

> Surely the LORD God does nothing
>> without revealing his secret
>> to his servants the prophets.
> A lion has roared;
>> who will not fear? (3:7–8 CEB)

In the series of visions in chapters 7–9, the prophet also plays the role of intercessor, praying to the Lord on behalf of the people, like Moses in Exodus 32.

He pleads, "O Lord GOD, forgive, I beg you! How can Jacob stand? He is so small!" (7:2). Twice these intercessions are heeded by God. Then the priest commands Amos not to prophesy any longer, and there are no more intercessions. Is the danger of commanding the prophet to be silent that he can no longer intercede on the people's behalf?

Yet even after judgment, the prophet promises that the Lord will be faithful to Israel's remnant, that God will gather the people again and replant them on the land. Throughout the book, Amos speaks as if total destruction will come—and it did come for the nation; in the end, the nation was destroyed and its tribes went into exile, becoming the ten lost tribes of Israel. But Amos also promises throughout the book that a remnant shall remain—ten out of a hundred, a hundred out of a thousand—and that the Lord will be faithful to this remnant: "The eyes of the Lord GOD are upon the sinful kingdom, and I will destroy it from the face of the earth—except that I will not utterly destroy the house of Jacob" (9:8).

Historical Interpretation

In terms of historical issues, there is little of controversy when it comes to interpreting the book of Amos. A small minority of scholars assert that the entire book is a fiction drafted many centuries after its purported author lived, but most scholars accept that the prophet lived and was active during the reign of Jeroboam II of Israel and that the messages contained in the book come from his mouth. These scholars believe that a group of disciples—known as "sons of the prophet" (see 7:14)—wrote down, collected, and preserved the prophet's words for future generations.

The book is useful for understanding various historical practices and artifacts. For example, the "beds of ivory" mentioned in 6:4 are most likely wooden beds with ivory inlays, like those that have been unearthed in archaeological digs. Similarly, the book reinforces things known elsewhere in Scripture about the Nazirites or the day of the Lord. But the primary historical value of the book is that it gives us the concrete words of the prophet Amos—a strong prophetic word spoken by an irascible, tenacious servant of the Lord.

FOR FURTHER READING: **Amos**

Carroll R., M. Daniel. *The Book of Amos*. New International Commentary on the Old Testament. Grand Rapids: Eerdmans, 2020.

———. *The Lord Roars: Recovering the Prophetic Voice for Today*. Grand Rapids: Baker Academic, 2022.

Erickson, Amy. "Amos." In *Women's Bible Commentary*, 3rd ed., edited by Carol A. Newsom, Sharon H. Ringe, and Jacqueline E. Lapsley, 312–18. Louisville: Westminster John Knox, 2012.

Fretheim, Terence E. *Reading Hosea–Micah: A Literary and Theological Commentary.* Macon, GA: Smyth & Helwys, 2013.

Goldingay, John. *Hosea–Micah*. Baker Commentary on the Old Testament Prophetic Books. Grand Rapids: Baker Academic, 2021.

Jeremias, Jörg. *The Book of Amos: A Commentary.* Translated by Douglas W. Stott. Old Testament Library. Louisville: Westminster John Knox, 1998.

Limburg, James. *Hosea–Micah*. Interpretation: A Bible Commentary for Teaching and Preaching. Atlanta: John Knox, 1988.

Mays, James Luther. *Amos: A Commentary.* Old Testament Library. Philadelphia: Westminster, 1969.

Stuart, Douglas. *Hosea–Jonah*. Word Biblical Commentary 31. Waco: Word, 1987.

Obadiah

The book of Obadiah is the shortest book in the Old Testament, and it is the fourth book in the Book of the Twelve. It appears near the books of Amos and Hosea, which date to the eighth century BCE, but the dates of the prophet Obadiah and the book named for him are debated. The fact that the book falls immediately after Amos suggests that the scribes who ordered the canon may have thought it could be dated to as early as the eighth century BCE. However, the book's superscription simply states, "The vision of Obadiah," without a regnal date formula.

Background

The Prophet Obadiah

Nothing is known of the prophet Obadiah other than what can be gleaned from the book of Obadiah. The book gives no date formula and makes no mention of Obadiah's lineage or hometown. Obadiah means "servant of the Lord" and is not an uncommon name in the Old Testament. The content of the book suggests that the prophet was of Judean descent and had inherited a version of the theology of Zion, namely that the Lord had elected Jerusalem and specifically Mount Zion as his dwelling place and the descendants of Jacob as his people. It also seems clear that Obadiah had experienced the trauma of Jerusalem's destruction. The location from which he prophesied is unknown.

Because of the similarity between the book of Obadiah and Jeremiah 49:7–22, which is cast as Jeremiah's words from the land of Egypt, it may be that Obadiah was among the remnant of Judeans who fled to Egypt after the destruction of

Obadiah and Jeremiah 49:7–22

The similarities between these two texts are notable, especially in the first seven verses of Obadiah. Both texts are explicitly directed against the Edomites, whose land was southeast of the Dead Sea (cf. Obad. 1; Jer. 49:7). Esau is explicitly mentioned in both texts (Obad. 6; Jer. 49:8, 10). Additionally, the descriptions of Yahweh's judgment against Edom are similar (Obad. 5–6; Jer. 49:9–10).

It is clear that the two texts share a great deal in common, but it is not clear whether they are somehow dependent on one another. One possibility is that the common subject matter (Edom's participation in the destruction of Jerusalem) resulted in similar content. Whatever the case may be, these two prophetic texts demonstrate that the survivors of the exile held deep resentment toward this people group, who may have been distant family members.

Jerusalem and the assassination of the governor Gedaliah—but this conclusion is tentative at best.

Historical Context

Determining the date of Obadiah involves at least two elements. Primarily, it is a matter of dating the incident to which the book is responding. Obadiah 1 states, "Thus says the Lord God concerning Edom," a nation to Israel's east. Obadiah 10–14 describes "the slaughter and violence" that Edom committed against the people of Judah. The dating of the book depends on correlating these verses with one of two events narrated elsewhere in the Old Testament. One option is to relate them to the Edomite rebellion during the reign of Jehoram (849–843/842 BCE; see 2 Kings 8:20–22). If this is the event that verses 10–14 describe, then the prophet lived at the same time as Elijah and Elisha; he may even have been the same Obadiah who appears in 1 Kings 18:2–16. A second option is to relate these verses with the fall of Jerusalem in 587/586 BCE, in which the Edomites, who had been Judah's allies, joined with the Babylonians. According to Psalm 137:7, they betrayed Judah and cried out, "Tear it down! Tear it down! Down to its foundations!" (see also Jer. 49:9–16; Lam. 4:21–22). If this is the event described, Obadiah was a contemporary of the prophets Jeremiah and Habakkuk.

A secondary way of dating the book is based on its vocabulary and spelling—a process known as linguistic dating. Based on both these factors, and especially based on the distinctive similarity between Obadiah verses 1–9 and Jeremiah 49:7–22, almost all scholars opt for the later date, sometime soon after the destruction of Jerusalem in 587/586 BCE.

Assuming this later date, the historical context of the book of Obadiah is just after the last years of the kingdom of Judah. The reforming King Josiah carried out his ambitious religious and political reformation (see 2 Kings 22–23) and then was killed in battle against the Egyptians in 609 BCE. In the short years that remained for the kingdom of Judah, a series of kings reigned—Jehoahaz, Jehoiakim, Jehoiachin, and Zedekiah. These kings rebelled against foreign empires, were dethroned, defeated, and exiled. In 597 BCE, King Jehoiachin surrendered to the Babylonians and was exiled to Babylon. The Babylonians replaced him with his uncle Zedekiah. Zedekiah in turn rebelled and was defeated by the Babylonians in 587/586; his sons were killed in front of him, his eyes were put out, and he also was exiled to Babylon. The city and its temple were razed to the ground, and many of its citizens were slaughtered, exiled, or scattered. Apparently, the Edomites joined Babylon in the destruction of Jerusalem, or at the very least, they exalted in Jerusalem's suffering. Into this reality, the prophet Obadiah spoke.

Composition and Development

Little can be known about the composition and development of the book of Obadiah, in part because it is so short. There is little reason to doubt that the book contains the words of a prophet named Obadiah who lived in or near Jerusalem.

Genre

The book of Obadiah consists of a single message of judgment against the nation of Edom for its participation in the destruction of Jerusalem in 587/586 BCE, and then it offers a hopeful vision (from Judah's perspective) of an idealized future in which the Lord rescues the scattered remnants of the people.

It is helpful to distinguish between the "fictive audience" of Obadiah's message and the "actual audience." On the fictive level, the message is directed to the nation of Edom and condemns it using second-person vocabulary: "I will surely make you least among the nations" (v. 2). To that audience, the book is a message of judgment and punishment. The actual audience, however, is the exiled people of Judah. To that audience, the book is a message of redemption and hope.

Fig. 33.1. In the nineteenth century, a chocolatier in France included "prophet cards" (similar to baseball cards) with their boxes of candy. This one displayed the prophet Obadiah issuing a dire warning. The text translates, "The pride of your heart seduced you because you dwell in the clefts of the rocks" (see Obad. 1:3).

Box 33.2

Outline

1. Superscription (1a)
2. Judgment of Edom (1b–9)
3. Edom's guilt and sin (10–16)
4. God's promised, ideal future (17–21)

Literary Interpretation

Superscription (Obad. 1a). The book of Obadiah opens simply, stating, "The vision of Obadiah. Thus says the Lord GOD concerning Edom." It includes no information about the prophet himself or the historical context of his message.

Judgment of Edom (Obad. 1b–9). In verses 1b–9, the prophet announces the Lord's judgment of Edom. In this section, he says the Lord "will surely make you least among the nations." The prophet continues, "Your proud heart has deceived you"—apparently a reference to Edom's decision to join in the destruction of Jerusalem. Then he adds, "You say in your heart, 'Who will bring me down to the ground?'" (v. 3). This reference to what the Edomites say "in [their] heart" is very similar to language that occurs frequently in the psalms of lament, in which the psalmists complain about their oppressors' inner beliefs. Consider these examples from Psalm 10:

> For the wicked boast of the desires of their heart,
> > those greedy for gain curse and renounce the LORD.
> In the pride of their countenance the wicked say, "God will not seek it
> > out";
> > all their thoughts are, "There is no God." . . .
>
> They think in their heart, "We shall not be moved;
> > throughout all generations we shall not meet adversity." . . .
>
> Why do the wicked renounce God,
> > and say in their hearts, "You will not call us to account"? (Ps. 10:3–4,
> > 6, 13)

In this and other psalms, the psalmists cry out in frustration because their enemies think themselves invulnerable: "We shall not be moved," and "You will not call us to account." Here the prophet senses that attitude of invulnerability among the Edomites but announces that it is a false sense of security. Remembering that the audience for this message is the defeated and exiled communities of Judeans, this is a promise of good news. The prophet then announces that Edom's allies will betray it. Inasmuch as Edom had betrayed Judah, this promise would have sounded like just deserts to the exiles.

Box 33.3

Edom and Esau

Obadiah condemns the Edomites "for the slaughter and violence done to [their] brother Jacob" (v. 10). The language of "brother Jacob" assumes that the Judeans and Edomites are "cousin" peoples. Esau is the ancestor of the Edomites (Gen. 25:30; 32:3; 36:1) and the brother of Jacob. The relationship between these two brothers was contentious from the beginning—literally: as twins in their mother's womb, Jacob and Esau struggled with one another (Gen. 25:22). Their mother, Rebekah, received word from Yahweh that she carried two nations at odds with one another even before they were born. The deep tensions between the Israelites and the Edomites are on full display during the time of the exile, when the latter apparently allied with the Babylonians to ensure the destruction of Judah (see, e.g., Ps. 137; Lam. 4:21–22). Given the deep ties between these two people, Edom's actions against Judah have all the sting of brotherly betrayal.

Edom's guilt and sin (Obad. 10–16). In verses 10–16, the prophet announces the reasons for Edom's judgment. In a series of accusations, he describes Edom's sins against Judah. Central to the prophet's accusation is that Edom violated a covenant of kinship with Judah: "You stood aside, on the day that strangers carried off his wealth, and foreigners entered his gates" (v. 11):

> You should not have gloated over your brother. . . .
> You should not have entered the gate of my people . . . ;
> you should not have looted his goods. . . .
> You should not have stood at the crossings
>   to cut off his fugitives;
> you should not have handed over his survivors. (vv. 12–14)

It may have been that King Zedekiah and Judah expected help from Edom when they rebelled against Babylon; it was not uncommon for several vassal nations to join together and rebel as a group against the empire. But Edom not only gloated over Jerusalem's destruction; apparently some Edomites joined in razing the city, while others hunted down refugees and survivors to turn over to the Babylonians. The prophet sums up the equity of the coming judgment: "As you have done, it shall be done to you" (v. 15). This sense of equity and proportionality in the Lord's judgment was a key feature of prophetic theology; the Lord's judgment never exceeded in scope or severity the crimes of those who were brought to judgment.

God's promised, ideal future (Obad. 17–21). In the last section of Obadiah, the prophet casts a poetic vision of the Lord's promised future, in which he will gather the exiles and the remnants of the scattered Judah. "The house of Jacob shall be a fire" that will burn "the house of Esau" as if it were stubble (v. 18). The Lord will gather the chosen people from the ends of the earth—"those of the Negeb," "those of the Shephelah," "the exiles of the Israelites who are

in Halah," and "the exiles of Jerusalem who are in Sepharad" (vv. 19–20). They will all be returned to the promised land, and all of these "who have been saved shall go up to Mount Zion to rule Mount Esau" (v. 21).

Theological Interpretation

The most intriguing theological feature of the book of Obadiah is what the prophet refers to either as "the day" or "the day of the LORD." It is interesting that the short book has three sections—the pronouncement of judgment against Edom (vv. 1–9), the announcement of Edom's sins (vv. 10–16), and the promise of the ideal future (vv. 17–21)—and in each section, the prophet uses the expression to refer to a different "day."

In the first section, "the day" refers to the day coming in the relatively near future, when Edom would experience punishment for her sins: "On that day, says the LORD, I will destroy the wise out of Edom, and understanding out of Mount Edom" (v. 8). In the second section, the prophet uses the phrase "on the day"

Fig. 33.2. *The Pride and Fall of Esau*, by Nahum HaLevi. The book of Obadiah admonishes Edom for its treachery against Judah. In this image, the central winged figure with a talon-like hand is Esau. The nest, representing the nation of Edom, is being violently shaken by a God-ordained earthquake.

nine times to refer to the day of Jerusalem's fall in 587/586 BCE and the atrocities that were committed immediately after that event—specifically Edom's participation in those atrocities. The staccato repetition of the phrase highlights Judah's vulnerability—"on the day of his misfortune," "on the day of their ruin," "on the day of distress," "on the day of their calamity" (vv. 12–13)—and thus underscores Edom's violation of the covenant of kinship.

Box 33.4

Sepharad

The reference to Sepharad in Obadiah 20 is especially intriguing, a location that is unknowable and disputed. Later in history, Jews who trace their lineage back to the Spanish line of European Judaism took their name from this word; they are known as Sephardic Jews (compared to Ashkenazi Jews, European Jews who trace their line to eastern Europe). In modern Hebrew, Sepharad is the name for Spain.

The third section describes "the day of the LORD" (the phrase occurs in v. 15 but describes the vision in vv. 17–21). Similar to the vision captured in Isaiah 2:1–4 and Micah 4:14, which are introduced by the phrase "in days to come," the vision of the ideal future is cast as occurring on Mount Zion. This represents a development of the theology of Zion, in which God's promises to protect Zion and dwell in Zion are projected into the future. Whereas Micah and Isaiah envision all nations streaming to Zion to learn the ways of peace from the Lord, Obadiah sees the scattered remnants of Israel and Judah being gathered home from the ends of the earth.

Historical Interpretation

As already noted, the primary difficulty in interpreting the book of Obadiah relates to determining its historical context. Assuming that the sixth-century-BCE exilic date is correct, there is no reason to doubt the integrity of the message of the book. The primary contribution the book makes toward understanding the history of Judah is the degree to which Edom participated in the destruction of Jerusalem and the degree to which that participation angered Judah. While neither 2 Kings nor 2 Chronicles relates this betrayal by the Edomites, Obadiah—together with Psalm 137:7, Lamentations 4:21–22, and Ezekiel 35:12–14—helps historians understand Edom's role in the Babylonian coalition that defeated and razed Jerusalem.

FOR FURTHER READING: **Obadiah**

Achtemeier, Elizabeth. *Minor Prophets I.* New International Biblical Commentary. Peabody, MA: Hendrickson, 1996.

Barton, John. *Joel and Obadiah: A Commentary.* Old Testament Library. Louisville: Westminster John Knox, 2001.

Claassens, L. Juliana M. "Obadiah." In *Women's Bible Commentary*, 3rd ed., edited by Carol A. Newsom, Sharon H. Ringe, and Jacqueline E. Lapsley, 319–20. Louisville: Westminster John Knox, 2012.

Collins, John. *Joel, Obadiah, Haggai, Zechariah, Malachi.* New Collegeville Bible Commentary. Collegeville, MN: Liturgical Press, 2013.

Goldingay, John. *Hosea–Micah.* Baker Commentary on the Old Testament Prophetic Books. Grand Rapids: Baker Academic, 2021.

Limburg, James. *Hosea–Micah.* Interpretation: A Bible Commentary for Teaching and Preaching. Atlanta: John Knox, 1988.

Stuart, Douglas. *Hosea–Jonah.* Word Biblical Commentary 31. Waco: Word, 1987.

Jonah

The story of Jonah is one of the most memorable and entertaining Old Testament narratives. A rebellious Israelite prophet flees by boat from the God "who made the sea and the dry land" (1:9); he is swallowed by a fish and vomited on the shore, only to preach one of the Bible's most successful sermons to an audience of oddly openhearted Assyrians.

Jonah can help a reader appreciate the Bible not only as Scripture but also as literature. The book is roll-on-the-floor funny. But through the medium of humor, it also conveys deeply important messages about the compassion of God for all people, animals, and even recalcitrant prophets.

Reading the book of Jonah also provides an opportunity to ponder the book's relationship to history. Questions are often raised about the historicity of Jonah and most especially about his misadventures in the belly of a fish (not a whale!). The fact that Jesus refers to Jonah's undersea journey complicates the matter and raises the stakes (Matt. 12:38–42; Luke 11:29–32). Did the events described in the book actually occur? Did Nineveh truly repent of its ways, and why is there no record of such a significant cultural moment? Was Jonah a historical prophet at all? If Jonah is fiction, can the book be both fictional and true? We will take up these questions directly.

Background

The Prophet Jonah

The prophet Jonah son of Amittai is mentioned both in the book of Jonah and in 2 Kings 14:25 in the regnal formula that introduces Jeroboam II of the Northern Kingdom. There it reports that Jeroboam "reestablished Israel's border from Lebo-hamath to the Dead Sea. This was in agreement with the word that the LORD, the God of Israel, spoke through his servant the prophet Jonah, Amittai's son, who was from Gath-hepher" (CEB). If the two prophets are the same, then this notice locates Jonah as a resident and prophet in the Northern Kingdom of Israel around 786–746 BCE.

Historical Context

As is often the case with biblical books, it is helpful to distinguish between the historical setting of the book and the historical context in which the book was written down. The historical setting of the book of Jonah is the Northern Kingdom around 750 BCE—just a few decades before the nation was conquered by the cruel Assyrians. Israel's leading citizens were deported into exile, where they became known to history as the "lost tribes of Israel." The book of Jonah narrates the repentance of the city of Nineveh, the capital of the Assyrian Empire. The prophet Nahum gives a sense of the rage that Israelites felt toward Nineveh:

> Woe to the city of blood,
> full of lies,
> full of plunder,
> never without victims!
> The crack of whips,
> the clatter of wheels,
> galloping horses
> and jolting chariots!
> Charging cavalry,
> flashing swords
> and glittering spears!
> Many casualties,
> piles of dead,
> bodies without number,
> people stumbling over the corpses . . . (Nah. 3:1–3 NIV)

Most scholars believe, however, that Jonah was written down after the exile, when Ezra and other leaders cast the foreign wives and their children out of the community. After the exile, there was a certain amount of xenophobia among the Second Temple Jews who lived in the land.

Composition and Development

Despite the book's title, the author of Jonah is anonymous. The book gives no indication that "Jonah son of Amittai" (1:1) actually wrote it, though he is the

Fig. 34.1. This fifteenth-century Persian depiction of Jonah demonstrates the cross-cultural appeal of the story and the fact that it also appears in the Qur'an.

main character. Anonymous authorship is common across the biblical corpus, not to mention the ancient Near East. Think, for instance, of the books of Joshua, Samuel, and Ruth. While these books are named after significant characters, nothing in them suggests that these characters actually wrote the books.

The compositional history of Jonah is largely unknown. In terms of a date, most scholars assume that the book was written after the Babylonian exile. This argument is based largely on the presence of Late Hebrew linguistic features. Few details anchor the text in a particular historical period.

Scholars often wonder whether the prayer in chapter 2 was added secondarily. While this scenario is possible, there is insufficient evidence to make the claim with any certainty. Apart from new evidence, the compositional history of Jonah is likely to remain a mystery.

Genre

The book of Jonah is unlike other prophetic books, which are dominated by poetry and largely contain the messages of the prophets whose names they bear. By contrast, Jonah is a narrative about the prophet himself and is more similar

Box 34.1

Outline

1. Jonah's call and flight (1:1–16)
2. Jonah in the belly of a giant fish (1:17–2:10)
3. Jonah's prophecy and Nineveh's repentance (3)
4. Jonah's anger over God's mercy (4)

to Ruth and Esther than to other prophetic books. Presented in the form of a legend, Jonah clearly employs humor, satire, and exaggeration.

But the use of these literary elements does not preclude the book from dealing with very serious topics. Biblical scholar Ehud Ben Zvi refers to "meta-prophetic" features of Jonah:[1] it is not just a text about an individual prophet; it is a text about *prophets* and *prophecy* as concepts. Important questions include, What is the nature of prophetic ministry? Is "true prophecy" always marked by the fulfillment of predictions? How should Israelites think about the future and fate of foreigners, and most especially foreign conquerors? What kind of God do the Israelites worship? How does the God of Israel relate to the nonhuman creation?

We will return to the topic of genre at the end of the chapter when we consider the historicity of the book.

Literary Interpretation

Jonah's call and flight (Jon. 1:1–16). Unlike many prophetic books, Jonah does not begin with a superscription that provides historical context or announces God's message for the prophet to deliver (e.g., Isa. 1:1; Jer. 1:1; Ezek. 1:1; Amos 1:1). Instead, the book jumps immediately into the action. In a series of events that are surely intended to be absurd and surprising, the prophet Jonah becomes a fugitive, trying to flee the presence of God.

Jonah's actions initiate a long process of descent, both literally and figuratively. The Hebrew root *yrd* ("descend," "go down") marks the various steps in this journey, which finally ends with Jonah knocking on the gates of Sheol, the realm of the dead: Jonah "went down to Joppa" (1:3); he "went down" into the ship (1:3); he "had gone down" to sleep (1:5); and finally Jonah "went down" to the place of the dead (2:6). Jonah eventually ascends back to the world of the living but only after his protracted journey into death.

One of the book's deep ironies is the fact that the sailors—foreigners presumably—are far more god fearing and courageous than Jonah. As soon as the storm assaults their ship, they begin praying. Meanwhile, Jonah sleeps (1:5), oblivious to how his disobedience endangers others. The captain (the leader of the foreigners) rouses Jonah, urging him to cry out to the gods (1:6) and appearing far more prophetic than Jonah does. Like the Assyrian king will do later, the ship's captain throws himself on the mercy of God, not knowing what the outcome will be (1:6; cf. 3:6–9). What's more, after learning about Jonah's guilt through the casting of lots (1:7–10), the sailors refuse to throw him overboard and try to spare him by rowing to land (1:13). Alas, circumstances prevail, and they do throw Jonah overboard, but not until after offering a humble and deferential prayer to Yahweh, God of the Hebrews, followed by the offering of a sacrifice and vows (1:14–16).

Jonah in the belly of a giant fish (Jon. 1:17–2:10). Just as God commissioned a giant storm to lash the seas, he now commissions a giant fish to rescue Jonah from drowning. The prophet spends three days and three nights in the belly of the beast, on a journey to the depths of despair and oblivion. Only a poem can express such a journey:

> I cried out to Yahweh out of my distress,
>   and he answered me;
> from Sheol's stomach I cried—
>   you heard my voice.
> You hurled me into the depths,
>   into the heart of the seas.
> A river surrounded me;
>   all your breakers and billows passed over me.
> Then I said, "I was banished from before your eyes.
>   Yet I will again look to your holy temple." (2:2–4 AT)

As Jonah leaves the presence of God, he draws nearer to death, until he finally finds himself at its doorstep. However, the poem changes course suddenly when Jonah proclaims that God rescues "from the Pit" (2:6), and it reaches its zenith when he exclaims, "Salvation belongs to Yahweh!" (2:9 AT).

Jonah's prophecy and Nineveh's repentance (Jon. 3). After the fish spews Jonah onto the shore, Yahweh calls to him a second time. This time, Jonah obeys immediately and sets off toward the city. Like the storm and the fish, Nineveh is "big"—so big, in fact, that a three-day journey would be needed just to traverse it! Jonah travels a day's journey into the city and proclaims what may be the shortest (and lamest?) sermon in all of history: "Forty days more and Nineveh shall be overturned [*nehpaket*]!" (3:4, modified). The same verbal root is used to describe the destruction brought upon Sodom and Gomorrah, when God "overthrew those cities" (Gen. 19:25). The city sits on the edge of destruction.

But in keeping with the book's positive depiction of foreigners, "the king of Nineveh" (the leader of the foreigners!) orders the entire city to repent (3:6). Even the animals are dressed in sackcloth! The entire city believes God, cries out to God for mercy, and repents of its evil and violence. Moved by their dramatic response, God "changed his mind" about the disaster (3:10).

Jonah's anger over God's mercy (Jon. 4). Jonah is thoroughly unimpressed by God's change of heart and launches into a tirade over God's mercy. Citing a common Israelite creed, Jonah spitefully tells God that he fled to Tarshish because he knew that God was a "gracious God and compassionate, slow to anger, and abounding in faithfulness, relenting from disaster" (Jon. 4:2 AT; cf. Exod. 34:6–7). The emphasis in Jonah 4 is on God's choice to show mercy and compassion.

Scholars debate the reasons for Jonah's anger. Perhaps he is concerned about his reputation as a prophet? What good, after all, is a prophet whose predictions don't come true? But if he were really concerned about his reputation, would he have directly disobeyed God's command and run the risk of ruining his image as an obedient prophet?

Jonah is angry because God was gracious. This makes a world of sense. Assyria (Nineveh was one of its capitals) represented one of Israel's most despised historical foes. The Assyrians annihilated the Northern Kingdom, extracted massive amounts of tribute, and laid siege to Jerusalem in 701 BCE—to name but a few things. Other biblical texts describe Assyria as violent, arrogant, and oppressive (see, e.g., Isa. 10:5–34; 36:1–37:38; 2 Kings 18:9–19:37; Nah. 1–3). With few exceptions (Isa. 19:23–25), the Assyrians are almost universally despised. Jonah's anger, then, is not because God is generally merciful but because God chooses to extend that mercy to *Nineveh* in particular.

Despite Jonah's clear displeasure at God's actions, God does not give up on him. The prophet stakes out a seat east of the city, waiting to see what its fate would be. God appoints a bush to protect Jonah from the oppressive heat

---

Box 34.2

Exodus 34:6–7

Jonah cites a creedal formula that first appears in Moses's vision of Yahweh atop Mount Sinai.

> Yahweh passed before him [Moses] and declared:
> Yahweh, Yahweh,
>> a God merciful and compassionate,
>> slow to anger and overflowing with steadfast love and faithfulness,
> maintaining steadfast love for thousands,
>> forgiving iniquity, transgress, and sin.
> But by no means clearing the guilty,
>> rather visiting the sin of the ancestors upon the children,
>> and upon the children's children,
>> upon the third and fourth generations. (AT)

(4:6). At dawn the next day, however, God appoints a worm to destroy the bush, thereby leaving Jonah exposed to the wind and sun (4:8). God uses the opportunity to stir up a sense of compassion for the Ninevites:

The Upside-Down Prophet

One of the delightful literary features of the book of Jonah is the prophet's upside-down behavior. When commanded to journey eastward to preach to the great city of Nineveh, Jonah hops a ship at Joppa and heads west. The plot question is, What will God do with a disobedient prophet?

Jonah's behavior is completely upside down when it comes to prayer. In the midst of a mighty storm, when he should be praying for deliverance with the rest of the sailors, Jonah sleeps. When thrown overboard and swallowed by the great fish, instead of praying for deliverance, he praises God. When Nineveh repents and God shows mercy on the city, Jonah should praise God, but instead he laments and asks to die.

Jonah claims to know the truth about Yahweh and creation—"I worship Yahweh, the God of the heavens, who created the sea and the dry land" (1:9 AT)—but thinks he can flee by sea! He knows Yahweh's character—"I knew that you are a gracious God and merciful, slow to anger, and abounding in steadfast love, and ready to relent from punishing" (4:2)—but he does not like this about God.

So what will God do with a disobedient prophet who praises when he should pray, prays when he should praise, and knows the truth about his God but does not love it?

Maerten van Heemskerck

Fig. 34.2. The book of Jonah closes with the petulant prophet waiting to see if God would destroy the city of Nineveh. The Lord causes a bush to grow over Jonah to provide shade, which gives Jonah joy. But then the Lord causes a worm to attack the bush and cause it to wilt. The Lord then causes a hot wind and sun to beat down on Jonah. Jonah grows so angry that he wishes to die. The Lord answered, "You cared about the bush, for which you did not work or cause to grow, which came and went in a day. Shouldn't I care about Nineveh?" (4:10–11a; author's paraphrase). The book ends with this question, inviting readers to answer it on their own.

You have pity for the plant for which you did not labor and which you did not grow—a thing that came and went in a single night. Should I not have pity for Nineveh, that great city in which there are more than 120,000 people who do not know their right hand from their left hand, including many animals? (4:10–11 AT)

Like the book of Nahum (discussed later), Jonah ends with a question and with no sense of how the prophet responds. One way to think about this question is to consider that the divine question is to be answered not by Jonah but by the book's readers. If we take delight in things like flowers and plants and animals, should we not also learn to take delight in those who are very different from us?

Theological Interpretation

Divine Compassion

Jonah is a deeply theological piece of literature. Chief among its theological concerns is God's deep compassion for Nineveh. The author's choice of Nineveh is intentional. As noted above, Nineveh and Judah have a long and bloody history. Nineveh invaded Judah's territory on multiple occasions, extracted significant resources, and killed countless Judeans. These events deeply shaped the Old Testament, especially books like Kings, Chronicles, Isaiah, and Nahum.

The book of Jonah is a book about God's compassion for gentiles, but this interpretation does not go far enough. The book of Jonah is less about God's compassion for the nations than it is about God's compassion for Israel's *enemies* and his call for Jonah to warn them of impending doom. The book of Jonah says something powerful and disruptive about the God of Israel. This God reaches out with grace, favor, and compassion to the undeserving.

In addition to showing mercy to Nineveh, God also shows tremendous patience and compassion toward Jonah, the recalcitrant and resentful prophet. After Jonah runs, God pursues him to the brink of death itself (chap. 2). After the city is saved from destruction, God continues to pursue Jonah, not in order to secure his obedience but rather to move Jonah's heart to compassion. God wants Jonah to undergo the same change of heart toward Nineveh that God did (3:10). In God's final attempt to sway him, God reminds Jonah that the city of 120,000 people does not know their right hand from their left and that there were also many animals. When God looks upon Nineveh, he sees an entire population that is lost and in need of mercy. God's compassion for Jonah, even in his resentment and anger, offers a very important insight: the God of Israel is full of grace, both for those who repent and for those who haven't yet found their way.

Jonah and Jesus

Jesus refers to the "sign of Jonah" in an exchange with some scribes and Pharisees. He explains that just as Jonah was three days and three nights in the belly of the fish (cf. Jon. 1:17), so the Son of Man would be three days and three nights in the "heart of the earth" (Matt. 12:40). According to the Gospel of Matthew, Jonah's journey from the place of the dead to the land of the living foreshadowed Jesus's own death and resurrection.

But this is only half of Jesus's exposition on Jonah. He also tells his questioners that the people of Nineveh—among the most penitent people in all of the Old Testament!—would rise up in judgment against his generation, since it refused to repent when one even greater than Jonah was present. This text from Matthew represents an important fragment of early Christian Christology, as the early followers of Jesus attempted to understand who he was.

The book ends with a question from God, subtly inviting its readers to consider the state of their own hearts with respect to neighbors and even enemies. This prophetic book stands firmly within the tradition of Jesus's own radical directive in the Sermon on the Mount: "Love your enemies and pray for those who persecute you" (Matt. 5:44).

Divine Agency through Creation

The book of Jonah depicts a God who is deeply and compassionately involved in the world. His involvement happens through the calling and appointing of people, creatures, and natural forces. God calls and employs a wide range of people, creatures, and phenomena: wind (1:4), a fish (1:17; 2:10), the people of Nineveh and their animals (3:5–8), a bush (4:6), a worm (4:7), and an east wind (4:8); the only character who doesn't listen to God's call and obey is Jonah the prophet! In the midst of this irony, the theological point is that the God of Jonah accomplishes things in the world by working through creation, even when the possibility to disobey exists.

In so many ways, creation is a far greater exemplar of obedience than the prophet himself. One cannot imagine the story of Jonah without the dynamic actions of creation: a storm, wind, fish, water, plant life, insects, and cattle. Creation is not only the stage on which the story takes place; creation is a significant actor on that stage.

Historical Interpretation

Historical questions have played an important role in the interpretation of the book of Jonah. Did the events in Jonah really happen? Did Jonah actually spend three days and nights in the belly of the fish? If such a major change of heart happened to the Assyrian king and his subjects, why is there no evidence of it in the expansive archaeological record we have from Assyria? It is true that

Nineveh was a major capital city for the Assyrians, but it did not take three days to traverse. What should we make of this fact?

All of these questions are important and bring us back to the matter of genre, discussed earlier. What kind of literature is Jonah? If the book doesn't provide a historical account of actual events, does that diminish its value as Scripture? In other words, must a biblical book be *factual* in order for it to be *true*?

This question is at the heart of the matter. There is no extrabiblical evidence that the events in the book of Jonah took place. The exaggerated elements of the story (e.g., the size of the city, Jonah's journey to the netherworld in the belly of a fish) suggest that the book is attempting to do something other than recount history. But to deny the historicity of Jonah is not the same thing as denying its truthfulness. Put differently, a thing may be true and not historical.

Consider an example from the New Testament: the parable of the prodigal son (Luke 15:8–32). This famous parable is one of the most well-known of Jesus's didactic stories. The parable speaks powerfully about the compassion of God, the pain of fractured relationships, and the power of reconciliation. Because we know the genre (parable), nobody feels compelled to ask whether the father and sons were historical figures. What were their names? What city did they live in? Were they still alive at the time of the story's telling? The truthfulness of the parable does not depend upon its historicity. The parable is true in the way that all of Jesus's parables are true: they reveal something true about God and God's world. But they communicate truth through the medium of parable. Like the parable of the prodigal son, Jonah can be properly called parable.

FOR FURTHER READING: Jonah

Achtemeier, Elizabeth. *Minor Prophets I.* New International Biblical Commentary. Peabody, MA: Hendrickson, 1996.

Allen, Leslie C. *The Books of Joel, Obadiah, Jonah, and Micah.* New International Commentary on the Old Testament. Grand Rapids: Eerdmans, 1976.

Erickson, Amy. *Jonah: Introduction and Commentary.* Grand Rapids: Eerdmans, 2021.

Goldingay, John. *Hosea–Micah.* Baker Commentary on the Old Testament Prophetic Books. Grand Rapids: Baker Academic, 2021.

Limburg, James. *Hosea–Micah.* Interpretation: A Bible Commentary for Teaching and Preaching. Atlanta: John Knox, 1988.

———. *Jonah: A Commentary.* Old Testament Library. Louisville: Westminster John Knox, 1993.

Murphy, Kelly J. "Jonah." In *Women's Bible Commentary*, 3rd ed., edited by Carol A. Newsom, Sharon H. Ringe, and Jacqueline E. Lapsley, 321–25. Louisville: Westminster John Knox, 2012.

Nowell, Irene. *Jonah, Tobit, Judith*. New Collegeville Bible Commentary: Old Testament 25. Collegeville, MN: Liturgical Press, 2015.

Simon, Uriel. *Jonah*. JPS Bible Commentary. Philadelphia: Jewish Publication Society, 1999.

Stuart, Douglas. *Hosea–Jonah*. Word Biblical Commentary 31. Waco: Word, 1987.

Trible, Phyllis. *Rhetorical Criticism: Context, Method, and the Book of Jonah*. Guides to Biblical Scholarship: Old Testament. Minneapolis: Fortress, 1994.

Shari LeMonnier

Micah

The book of Micah contains one of the most well-known and loved poetic passages in the Old Testament:

> With what shall I come before the Lord,
>   and bow myself before God on high?
> Shall I come before him with burnt offerings,
>   with calves a year old?
> Will the Lord be pleased with thousands of rams,
>   with ten thousands of rivers of oil?
> Shall I give my firstborn for my transgression,
>   the fruit of my body for the sin of my soul?"
> He has told you, O mortal, what is good;
>   and what does the Lord require of you
> but to do justice, and to love kindness,
>   and to walk humbly with your God? (6:6–8)

These powerful lines appear in everything from mission statements to presidential addresses to songs and art. But the book of Micah is about much more than one passage. The entire book of Micah is an extraordinary theological and literary achievement, whose full witness deserves hearing.

Background

The Prophet Micah

The superscription introduces the book as "the word of Micah the Moresheth-ite" (1:1 AT). The precise location of Moresheth is unknown but most likely was a village in the hill country near Jerusalem. Micah was a prophet in the Southern Kingdom. Unlike most prophets, who are introduced according to their parental lineage (e.g., Isaiah son of Amoz; Jeremiah son of Hilkiah; Ezekiel son of Buzi), Micah is identified by his hometown instead. The reason for this may have been that Micah was very critical of Jerusalem in his preaching—he was not from Jerusalem, did not live or worship there on a regular basis, and he had no trouble condemning the city, its rulers, and its temple.

Historical Context

Micah prophesied during the reigns of Judean kings Jotham, Ahaz, and Hezekiah, situating his ministry in the late eighth and early seventh centuries BCE. Given this timing, he was active around the same time as the historical prophets Isaiah, Amos, and Hosea. Accordingly, the ever-present threat of Assyrian military power looms large in the book. Several major historical events shaped Micah's context.

The fall of Samaria and exile of the Northern Kingdom (722/721 BCE). Around 745 BCE, the Northern Kingdom of Israel became an Assyrian vassal state. They rebelled several times, and when Israel's last king, Hoshea, allied with Egypt and rebelled, the Assyrians under Shalmaneser invaded Israel and besieged Samaria for three years. Samaria, the capital city, fell in 722/721 BCE.

The campaigns of Sargon II (720–710 BCE). Several nations along the Mediterranean Sea rebelled against Assyria in the decade spanning 720 to 710 BCE. Assyrian king Sargon responded, putting down these rebellions.

The invasion of Sennacherib (701 BCE). Sargon's son Sennacherib invaded Judah in 701 BCE in order to reconquer the kingdom. This invasion is known both from the biblical sources and also from Sennacherib's annals, where the Assyrian king boasts that he destroyed many of Hezekiah's fortified cities and confined the Judean king in Jerusalem "like a caged bird." Sennacherib was unable to conquer Jerusalem, but the devastation and death he caused were enormous.

Micah, from one of the villages that was overrun by Sennacherib, criticizes Jerusalem's leadership harshly. He recognizes that those in power easily misuse their positions by terrorizing those whom they are called to lead. For Micah, the exercise of cruel and hypocritical leadership invites divine judgment. But the God of Israel is a God of two messages—judgment and restoration. To borrow from Micah's language, Zion may need to be plowed like a field (3:12) before it can become a blessing to the nations (4:1–5).

Composition and Development

There is little reason to doubt that the book of Micah originated in some way from the prophet Micah himself. It seems likely, however, that later editorial activity occurred. For example, scholars argue that Micah 4:10 is strong evidence for a later, sixth-century-BCE addition:

> Writhe and give birth, daughter Zion,
>   like a woman in labor,
> for now you will go forth from the city,
>   and you will dwell in the field,
>   and you will go to Babylon.
> There you will be delivered;
>   there Yahweh will redeem you from the hand of your enemies.
>   (4:10 AT)

The reference to daughter Zion going to Babylon makes almost no sense in the context of the eighth or seventh centuries BCE, but it fits comfortably in a sixth-century context, when Judah was exiled to Babylonia. This verse illustrates the common scribal practice of updating prophetic texts according to changing circumstances. Through such modifications, Judah's scribes ensured the ongoing significance of prophetic texts well beyond the life of the prophet (cf. Jer. 36:32). Further proof of Micah's ongoing influence comes from Jeremiah 26:18, where Micah 3:12 is explicitly cited.

Genre

Like most other prophetic books, Micah is primarily a collection of poetic texts. Within these poems are a range of genres, covering themes such as judgment, restoration, lament, and eschatology. As poetry, Micah should be read with care and appreciation. Hebrew poetry is dense, drawing on images, traditions, and concepts from Israel and its surrounding cultures. Readers will appreciate Hebrew poetry more fully—even in translation—if they read it slowly, with an eye toward the use of poetic and literary devices.

Given the range of genres present in Micah, the book can be somewhat disorienting, leaving the reader wondering whether it has a coherent structure. The book opens with judgment (1:2–7) and ends with forgiveness and restoration

---

Box 35.1

Hebrew Poetry in the Prophets

The Old Testament prophetic books are primarily composed in poetry. Readers can tell the difference between prose and poetry by looking at how the text is laid out on the printed page. Prose will fill the page from margin to margin, like one would see in a newspaper. Look, for instance, at pages from Ruth, Samuel, or Kings—mostly narrative books. When poetry is printed in modern translations, there is significantly more white space. This is because the translators use the page layout to show where poetic lines begin and end. For more detailed information on Hebrew poetry, see chapter 18, "Poetry, Poetic Books, and Wisdom."

(7:18–20), but these two themes are woven throughout the entire composition, with one often following abruptly upon the other. Micah is best interpreted the way one interprets a collage—with attention to the entirety of the image rather than to single constituent elements. The point is not that individual poems don't matter—they certainly do—but that the individual parts should be interpreted in light of the whole.

Literary Interpretation

Superscription (Mic. 1:1). Like many prophetic books, Micah begins with a historical superscription, informing the reader of the historical context in which the prophet operated. In the case of Micah, the book refers to the reigns of Jotham, Ahaz, and Hezekiah. This notice places the prophet in the latter part of the eighth and early part of the seventh centuries BCE.

theophany A revelation of God that often manifests itself in creation.

Poems of judgment, lament, and condemnation (Mic. 1:2–2:11). Micah opens with a fiery theophany: Yahweh emerges from his dwelling place, full of accusation and fury, leaving destruction in his wake. All of this is because of the "transgression of Jacob" and the "sins of the house of Israel" (1:5). Two important questions follow: "What is the transgression of Jacob? Is it not Samaria? And what are the shrines of Judah? Are they not Jerusalem?" (1:5 AT). Samaria is the capital of the Northern Kingdom and—from Micah's perspective—the location of an apostate cult. In what must have been a shock to Micah's audience, Jerusalem (the capital of the Southern Kingdom) is equated with the apostate capital city of Samaria. Micah sees their sins as identical.

In what remains of Micah 1:2–2:11, the prophet inveighs against both the Northern and the Southern Kingdoms. Samaria, for its part, will be turned into ruins for its idolatrous ways, but Samaria's "wound" has also reached the people of Judah, afflicting Jerusalem with incurable sickness (1:9).

Chapter 2 lays out their sins more explicitly: devising evil, coveting and seizing property, and oppressing their neighbors. Yahweh will also devise for them a day of disaster from which escape is hopeless. And all of this is because those who devised evil "[rose] up against my people as an enemy" (2:8).

The God of Micah rages, but that rage is mingled with sorrow:

> On account of this, I will lament and mourn;
>   I will go barefoot and naked;
> I will wail like a jackal,
>   mourn like ostriches;
> Because her wound cannot be healed,
>   it has reached Judah;
>   it has arrived at the gate of my people, to Jerusalem. (1:8–9 AT)

In the verse immediately preceding, God is the first-person actor. One can rightly assume that in these verses God is also the intended subject. His judgment is not the result of fickle anger. God does not delight in exercising judgment. But Samaria's sins now threaten Jerusalem like a spreading infection. This reality weighs heavily upon the heart of God, whose words overflow with both grief and anger.

Promise of restoration for the remnant (Mic. 2:12–13). Doom is abruptly interrupted by the hope of homecoming. God is depicted as a gathering shepherd who breaks the people out of their bondage and leads them into a safer, more secure future.

Oracles against Judah's leaders (Mic. 3:1–12). The third chapter returns to the familiar theme of judgment. In grotesque but memorable images, Micah decries the "rulers of Jacob" because they are "haters of good and lovers of evil" (3:2 AT), ripping skin and flesh from the bones of people and consuming it. Silence is part of God's judgment. These leaders may cry out to God, but God will ignore their prayers. Even the prophets, Israel's "seers," will be denied the word of the Lord. Zion's rulers built the city with blood and bribery and dared to claim divine favor as their own, but their corruption will catch up to them, and Jerusalem will "be plowed as a field" (Mic. 3:10–12; cf. Jer. 26:18).

Oracles about Zion and the nations (Mic. 4:1–5:15). Chapters 4 and 5 contain a series of texts about the future, all with different emphases. The heightened role of foreigners distinguishes this collection of texts. Micah 4:1–5 depicts Zion as the highest of mountains and Yahweh's temple as a sort of school of nations, where people come to seek teaching (*torah*) and arbitration from Yahweh. The increase of divine knowledge results in a time of unprecedented peace when the peoples of the earth will "beat their swords into plowshares, and their spears into pruning hooks" (4:3). Because they are learning torah, they no longer need to learn war.

Box 35.3

Swords into Plowshares

Micah 4:3 contains one of the Old Testament's most well-known promises: one day human beings will "beat their swords into plowshares, and their spears into pruning hooks." This memorable saying looks forward to a time when weapons of war will be transformed into implements that support human life. The verse has inspired hymns, vision statements, and even art. A bronze statue that currently stands in the United Nations gardens in New York City was inspired by Micah 4:3. The statue was created by the Soviet artist Evgeny Vuchetich and presented to the UN by the USSR in 1959.

The subsequent oracles deal with the ingathering of the exiles to Zion (4:6–8), the Judeans' exile to Babylon and subsequent victory over the nations (4:9–5:2), and the rise of a powerful leader who will allow God's people to live in security and peace (5:3–6). Though scattered among the nations, Jacob will be "like a lion among forest animals, like a youthful lion among flocks of sheep" (5:8 AT). The collection ends with a promise from Yahweh to cleanse Israel and the nations for their disobedience (5:10–15).

Yahweh's lawsuit against his people (Mic. 6:1–8). Chapter 6 opens with a lawsuit, brought by Yahweh against the people of God. Creation itself is called as a witness against God's people. Yahweh wonders aloud, "What have I done to you? How have I exasperated you?" (6:3 AT). The poem recounts Yahweh's gracious deeds, and then it suddenly shifts into a dialogue:

> With what shall I come before Yahweh,
>> bow before God on high?
> Shall I come before him with burnt offerings?
>> With one-year-old calves? (6:6 AT)

The answer to these questions is well known:

> He has told you, O mortal, what is good
>> and what Yahweh desires from you,
> do justice, and love faithfulness,
>> and to walk humbly with your God. (6:8, modified)

The point is not that Israel's sacrifices are unimportant—they were commanded by God at Sinai. Rather, the point is that a life of obedience requires faithfulness in all aspects of life. Faithfulness to God is interwoven with faithfulness to the neighbor. Obedience to God necessitates love of and faithfulness to the neighbor.

Condemnation of corruption and exploitation (Mic. 6:9–16). The remaining verses in chapter 6 strongly condemn corrupt economic practices and blame them for the onset of societal ruin. God's people have entered an age of futility: eating will not produce satisfaction, storing up will result in scarcity, and planting will bring forth nothing. In other words, the system that once enriched the unjust will break down entirely.

Poem urging trust in Yahweh (Mic. 7:1–7). Chapter 7 continues the theme of scarcity and famine—only this time, there is a famine of righteous people: "The pious have perished from the land, the upright cannot be found among humanity" (7:2 AT). The scarcity of the righteous makes way for an abundance of evil, especially among the powerful. The rot finds its way into the most intimate of relationships, where trust has also broken down, yet the prophet finds ground to stand on: "I will fix my eyes on Yahweh; I will wait upon the God of my salvation" (7:7 AT).

Fig. 35.1. In this engraving by Gustave Doré, Micah exhorts the people to repent.

Yahweh: Judge and redeemer (Mic. 7:8–20). The book concludes with words of hope, grounded in God's forgiveness. Despair and adversity persist for a season, and during this painful time, enemies say, "Where is Yahweh, your God?" (7:10 AT). Winter turns to spring, however, when Yahweh promises to act "as in the days when you came forth from the land of Egypt" (7:15 AT). An act of forgiveness makes this possible:

> Who is a God like you, forgiving sin
> and overlooking transgression? . . .
> He will again show us compassion;
> he will trample on our iniquities,
> and into the depths of the sea you will cast all of our sins.
> (7:18–19 AT)

The God of Micah is not only forgiving; he is also faithful: "You [Yahweh] show faithfulness to Jacob, loyalty to Abraham, which you swore to our fathers from ancient days" (7:20 AT). Through fire and judgment, sin and wrath, God's promises persist and form the basis for a new future.

Famine, Scarcity, and Natural Disasters

The people of the ancient Near East were vulnerable to natural disasters of many kinds: droughts, locusts, famines, storms, floods, and even earthquakes. The plagues in the book of Exodus and the global flood in Genesis 6–9 are but a few testimonies to these dire realities. Ancient people lacked the technologies that allow many modern societies to mitigate the impact of such disasters and even to live in areas where natural disasters occur regularly.

Natural disasters also provided the prophets with a cache of material for their oracles. These disastrous events were often associated with divine judgment. While this might seem like a strange thing to modern ears, it is important to recognize that in the Old Testament the consequences of human sin are often manifested in the created order itself. For the prophets, creation operates as a conduit both for blessing and for judgment.

Theological Interpretation

The book of Micah deals with some difficult and persistent theological questions. What kind of life does God demand? Why does God judge? What does God say to a society that practices worship but neglects its members? How should one live a pious life in the midst of a corrupt society? What comes after judgment?

Yahweh's Anger and Sorrow over Idolatry

Like so many other prophetic books, the book of Micah is dominated by messages of judgment. Many readers of the Bible hear the word *judgment* and think of a fickle, grumpy despot in the skies, arbitrarily hurling lightning bolts down on unsuspecting sinners. But this caricature does not even begin to describe judgment in the book of Micah.

The torrent of God's rage in Micah intermingles with God's sorrow. In a shocking statement quoted earlier, God says:

> On account of this, I will lament and mourn;
> I will go barefoot and naked;
> I will wail like a jackal,
> mourn like ostriches;
> Because her wound cannot be healed,
> it has reached Judah;
> it has arrived at the gate of my people, to Jerusalem. (1:8–9 AT)

Sorrow bursts the bonds of public decency, and God laments Judah's unhealable wound. This incurable wound is idolatry, which spreads like an infection from the Northern Kingdom to the Southern Kingdom. The God of Micah does not delight in judgment. To the contrary, he is overwhelmed with sorrow.

Divine Suffering

As Micah 1:8–9 indicates, the God of the prophets is a suffering God—meaning one who is moved by the suffering of the world. God is not "the unmoved mover," but rather one who empathizes and sympathizes with creation. Yahweh laments and mourns like a human being in response to the agonizing news that his people cannot be healed. In 1984, Old Testament scholar Terence Fretheim published an important book on this topic: *The Suffering of God: An Old Testament Perspective*.* Fretheim draws attention to texts in which Yahweh is deeply moved by the world, most especially by human beings. The relationship between Yahweh and humanity is real for both parties, and both parties can be impacted by it. This is not to say that the divine-human relationship is equal: God is still God. But human beings can genuinely affect the world, including its Creator.

* Terence E. Fretheim, *The Suffering of God: An Old Testament Perspective*, Overtures to Biblical Theology (Philadelphia: Fortress, 1984).

Yahweh's Anger and Sorrow over Injustice

But idolatry is not God's only concern. Infidelity to God inevitably leads to infidelity to the neighbor. The prophet Micah tears into those who exploit power over others:

> Woe to those who plot wickedness
> and work evil on their beds;
> in the light of the morning they do it
> because they have the power to do so.
> They covet fields and seize them,
> and they carry away houses.
> They oppress a man and his house,
> a man and his inheritance.
> Therefore, thus has Yahweh spoken:
> Look, I am plotting a disaster against this family,
> from which you will not be able to save your necks. (2:1–3 AT)

This text lays bare an important insight about divine judgment: judgment for one is salvation for another. The oracle keenly recognizes that powerful people often have access to tools that allow them to more easily acquire what they covet. In Micah's time, apparently, there weren't strong legal or social checks and balances to ensure that the vulnerable were not taken advantage of. Matching plot for plot, God steps into this gap and chooses to act on behalf of those who cannot defend themselves.

Hope for the Future and Yahweh's Forgiveness

Alongside judgment, Micah also speaks about a hopeful future for God's people. The depictions of this future are diverse throughout the book. They involve the restoration and gathering of God's dispersed people (2:12–13; 4:10), the establishment of Zion as a center of divine teaching and arbitration (4:1–5), and the empowerment of Israel as a mighty nation with a powerful ruler (4:13; 5:2–9). Many of these themes reverberate across the Old Testament and go on to influence the New Testament and Christianity.

Forgiveness also plays an important role in the book of Micah, and the book closes with a poem that makes God's forgiveness the linchpin to Israel's new future:

> Who is a God like you, forgiving sin
>   and overlooking transgression for the remnant of your inheritance?
> He does not cling to his anger forever,
>   because he delights in steadfast love.
> He will again show us compassion;
>   he will trample on our iniquities,
>   and into the depths of the sea you will cast all of our sins.
> You [Yahweh] show faithfulness to Jacob,
>   steadfast love to Abraham,
>   which you swore to our fathers from ancient days. (7:18–20 AT)

Israel's future will be built on God's delight in forgiveness and on his faithfulness to ancient promises.

Historical Interpretation

As noted above, the historical prophet Micah worked in the eighth and seventh centuries BCE, which situates his ministry in the broader context of the Neo-Assyrian period (ca. 1000–609 BCE). The Assyrian Empire began to expand westward in the direction of the Northern and Southern Kingdoms beginning in the mid- to late ninth century BCE under the reigns of Assurnasirpal II (883–859 BCE) and his son Shalmaneser III (859–824 BCE). The earlier part of the eighth century (781–746 BCE) saw a lull in Assyrian expansion, but this changed under the rule of Tiglath-pileser III (745–727 BCE), who set the empire on a trajectory toward its zenith.

The Assyrian Empire would eventually be responsible for a number of destructive and memorable incursions into the territories of the Northern and Southern Kingdoms. The Northern Kingdom in particular met its demise under the Assyrian axe in 722/721 BCE. This back and forth of resistance and submission echoes throughout the prophetic literature of this period, including Micah and his prophetic contemporaries.

Although hard to detect at times, beneath the Prophets' statements of judgment and doom lies a deep sense of geopolitical vulnerability. Many readers of this book—especially those born and raised in the United States—may struggle to imagine what it is like to live in a society with assailable borders and whose fortunes are largely dependent on the strategic priorities of another nation. For the kingdoms of Israel and Judah, security could sometimes be found in alliances (e.g., with Egypt or Levantine coalitions), but even these were highly risky endeavors.

Fig. 35.2. The biblical King Jehu is shown genuflecting before the Assyrian king Shalmaneser, as representatives from various nations bring their tribute to the Assyrian despot.

In the study of the Prophets, we urge readers to keep geopolitics in mind and especially the relatively minimal power held by Israel and Judah. Neither of these kingdoms ever reached the stature of New Kingdom Egypt, the Neo-Assyrian Empire, or the Persian Empire. These political and economic realities profoundly shaped the literature and theology of the Bible.

FOR FURTHER READING: Micah

Achtemeier, Elizabeth. *Minor Prophets I*. New International Biblical Commentary. Peabody, MA: Hendrickson, 1996.

Allen, Leslie C. *The Books of Joel, Obadiah, Jonah, and Micah*. New International Commentary on the Old Testament. Grand Rapids: Eerdmans, 1976.

Fentress-Williams, Judy. "Micah." In *Women's Bible Commentary*, 3rd ed., edited by Carol A. Newsom, Sharon H. Ringe, and Jacqueline E. Lapsley, 326–28. Louisville: Westminster John Knox, 2012.

Gignilliat, Mark S. *Micah*. International Theological Commentary on the Holy Scripture of the Old and New Testaments. London: Bloomsbury T&T Clark, 2019.

Goldingay, John. *Hosea–Micah*. Baker Commentary on the Old Testament Prophetic Books. Grand Rapids: Baker Academic, 2021.

Limburg, James. *Hosea–Micah*. Interpretation: A Bible Commentary for Teaching and Preaching. Atlanta: John Knox, 1988.

Mays, James Luther. *Micah: A Commentary*. Old Testament Library. Philadelphia: Westminster, 1976.

Waltke, Bruce K. *A Commentary on Micah*. Grand Rapids: Eerdmans, 2007.

36

Nahum

Nahum is one of the most fascinating books in the Old Testament. From start to finish, it focuses on a single event: the violent fall of Nineveh (Assyria's capital) to the Medes and Babylonians in 612 BCE. Nahum's interest in this event, however, is not merely of a historical nature. For Nahum, the fall of Nineveh is an act of divine judgment against Israel's imperial oppressors. In Nahum, the divine warrior does to Assyria's capital what Assyria's army had done to so many of its victims. The book of Nahum understands that Yahweh's violent conquest of Nineveh will ultimately be liberation for the nations.

The central theological claim of Nahum is that Yahweh is a warrior who comes to free Israel and the other nations from Assyria's cruel dominion. But Yahweh is not just any warrior. When he marches to battle, his presence stirs up storms, shakes the earth, and terrifies onlookers (1:3–5). The God of Israel is the God of creation, and when that God hits the war path, creation responds.

Background

The Prophet Nahum

We know very little about the prophet himself, Nahum of Elkosh, a Judean village of unknown location. Neither the prophet nor the location is mentioned elsewhere in the Old Testament. Theologically, Nahum stands in the long Israelite tradition of hailing Yahweh as a warrior.

Yahweh as Warrior

Yahweh is frequently depicted as a warrior in the Old Testament. This is espe-cially true for the book of Exodus, where Yahweh goes to war against Pharaoh to free the Israelites from slavery. In the words of the Song of Moses, "Yahweh is a man of war; Yahweh is his name" (Exod. 15:3 AT).

But the image of Yahweh as warrior extends far beyond the book of Exodus. The warrior image is closely tied to Yahweh's identity as a king who protects the Israelites, establishes justice, and defeats chaos. Deuteronomy 33:26–28 captures this idea: "There is no one like the God of Jeshurun, who rides across the heavens to help you and on the clouds in his majesty. The eternal God is your refuge, and underneath are the everlasting arms. He will drive out your enemies before you, saying, 'Destroy them!' So Israel will live in safety; Jacob will dwell secure in a land of grain and new wine, where the heavens drop dew" (AT). The divine warrior is dangerous, but Yahweh's ferocity in the face of threats is precisely what keeps his people safe in a dangerous world. In the case of Nahum, the fury is turned against one of Israel's historic oppressors: As-syria and, in particular, the city of Nineveh.

Historical Context

The book itself provides the strongest clues to its historical context. Nahum 3:8 explicitly references the fall of Thebes (No-amon) at the hand of the Assyr-ian king Assurbanipal (663 BCE). One can safely assume that the book—or at least some form of it—was composed after the fact. In addition, the book of Nahum imagines the fall of Nineveh (612 BCE) to be a future event—something to expect and hope for, rather than something to reflect upon—though how closely the book can be tied to the actual events of Nineveh's fall is uncertain. These two historical frames of reference lead most scholars to conclude that the book of Nahum, in one form or another, was written after 663 and before—or even shortly after—612 BCE. Some date the book to Josiah's reformation in the 620s BCE. For the purposes of understanding the book, it is enough to know that it was written after the fall of Samaria to Assyria and shortly before the sun would set on the Assyrian Empire, which would be replaced by the Baby-lonians and then the Persians.

Composition and Development

There is little reason to doubt that the book in its entirety comes from the hand or mouth of the prophet Nahum. One of the mysteries that puzzles scholars is the incomplete acrostic in Nahum 1:2–8, running from the Hebrew letter *aleph* (א) to *kaph* (כ) (for another famous biblical acrostic, see Ps. 119). Some scholars assume that the incomplete acrostic indicates editorial activity and the need for textual reconstruction, but it is impossible to be conclusive about this.

Genre

Like so many other prophetic books, Nahum is a collection of poems. Topically, the poems focus on Nineveh and Yahweh's wrath toward it. Broadly speaking, Nahum stands among a diverse set of texts in which prophets address the foreign nations of the earth, often with messages of doom and judgment (see, e.g., Isa. 13–23; Jer. 46–51; Amos 1:1–2:3). It is likely that texts like these were actually for domestic consumption. There is no evidence that they were actually presented to foreign powers.

It is not entirely clear how this text functioned socially. Was it used in Israel's ritual life, perhaps as a liturgy? Was it political propaganda, designed to engender solidarity by stoking the flames of vengeance? Was it designed to stir up hope that the oppressor—whether Nineveh or some other imperial power—would one day finally receive its just deserts? None of these questions can be answered with absolute certainty.

Theologically, the assumption behind these texts is that Yahweh, the God of Israel, is king of the nations. As king of the nations, Yahweh takes interest in how the various kingdoms of the earth act, especially when their actions concern the chosen people of Israel.

Literary Interpretation

Superscription (Nah. 1:1). The book of Nahum is singularly focused on announcing judgment on Nineveh, that "city of bloodshed" (3:1). Its superscription identifies the book's contents as an oracle received in a vision by Nahum.

Theophanic hymn about Yahweh's wrath (Nah. 1:2–15). The book begins in familiar territory, with recognizable creedal language that describes God as a great warrior (cf. Exod. 34:6–7; Num. 14:18):

> Yahweh is a jealous and avenging God;
> Yahweh is avenging and supremely wrathful;
> Yahweh takes vengeance against his enemies;
> he fumes against his foes.
> Yahweh is slow to anger and great in power,
> but by no means clearing the guilty. (1:2–3 AT)

Creation responds to the divine warrior, whose way is "in whirlwind and storm" (1:3). He dries the sea with his rebuke (1:4; cf. Exod. 15:8–10) and withers the heights, and before him the earth quakes. The poem asks, "Who can stand before his indignation?" (1:6).

But for those laboring under the yoke of despair, the divine warrior is a welcome sight—a "stronghold in a day of trouble" (1:7). In fact, his arrival is heralded with glad tidings:

> Look upon the hills:
>> the feet of one bringing good news,
>> publishing peace.
> Celebrate your feasts, O Judah;
>> fulfill your vows,
> for never again shall a worthless one pass through you.
>> He is utterly cut down. (1:15 AT)

For the book of Nahum, peace and violence are not contradictions. The violence of the divine warrior represents the possibility of peace. By destroying the "city of bloodshed"—with its deceptive ways and monstrous appetite for victims—and releasing Israel from its heavy yoke (1:13), the divine warrior ends the terrifying reign of the Assyrians and secures a peaceable future for Israel.

Oracle of Nineveh's destruction and Israel's salvation (Nah. 2:1–13). The book continues by announcing Nineveh's destruction. The announcement begins with a double-barreled truth:

> I have afflicted you [Israel];
>> I will afflict you no more.
> Now, I will break his yoke from upon you,
>> and your shackles I will tear off. (1:12–13 AT)

A cursory reading might miss the important claim that Assyria's rule, though violent and brutal, was also understood to be divine judgment (cf. Isa. 10:5–6). The precise reason for God's judgment is not indicated, but such a claim is common in prophetic literature (see also Jer. 27). What is clear is that, for Nahum, the God of Israel judges and saves simultaneously.

Nahum 2:1–13 describes the coming battle in disturbing detail. The first verse directly addresses the city of Nineveh itself:

> A scatterer has come up against you.
>> Man the fortifications;
> watch the way;
>> gird your loins;
> gather much strength. (2:1 AT)

Fig. 36.1. The Assyrian kings often depict themselves as mighty warriors who are able to subdue any enemy.

Dripping with irony, the divine warrior calls for the mighty king of Assyria to protect himself. But nothing will stop the onslaught of battle.

Madness ensues. With clustered staccato lines, the poem portrays blood-soaked soldiers, flashing metal, frenzied war machines, stumbling officers, mournful panic, plundered treasure, buckling knees, and melting hearts (2:3–10). In a stunning reversal of fortune, Yahweh promises to enter the den of the "lion" (a common Assyrian royal image) and "devour your young lions" (2:13). The predator has become the prey.

A taunt of Nineveh (Nah. 3:1–19). Chapter 3 continues the depiction of the carnage, but with a direct address to Nineveh and with greater emphasis placed on Nineveh's wrongdoings. It taunts the bloody city with its ominous fate:

> Woe, city of bloodshed!
> > Fully deceitful,
> full of plunder,
> > prey never ceases. (3:1 AT)

The dramatic shift to addressing the city foreshadows the book's most disturbing imagery. In the ancient Near East, cities were always feminine in linguistic gender and were often portrayed as women. After several more lines describing the battle (3:2–3), the poem returns to the metaphor of city-as-woman, with horrifying results:

> Because of innumerable harlotries,
>   graceful mistress of charms,
> peddling nations in exchange for her whorings
>   and people with her charms.
> Look, I am against you, declares the Lord of hosts.
>   I will lift your skirts over your face;
>   I will cause nations to see your nakedness
>   and kingdoms your shame.
> I will throw filth at you,
>   and I will disgrace you,
>   and I will make you a spectacle. (3:4–6 AT)

Nineveh will be (mis)treated like a woman of harlotry—publicly exposed, shamed, and abused. So deep is the disdain toward Nineveh that no one will be found to comfort her in the hour of distress (3:7).

With victory often comes a sense of exceptionalism and superiority. According to Nahum, the situation was no different in Assyria (cf. Isa. 10:7–11). The poem attacks that sense of exceptionalism directly and mocks Nineveh by stating that it would suffer the same fate as its victims:

> Are you superior to Thebes [No-amon],
>   those who sat by the Nile,
> water surrounding her,
>   sea a rampart,
>   water her wall? (3:8 AT)

As noted earlier, Thebes fell to the Assyrian king Assurbanipal in 663 BCE. Dripping with spite, Nahum announces that Nineveh's fate is to be drunk with defeat and overcome by cowardice. Their fortresses—no doubt symbols of national strength—would fall like ripened fruit shaken from a tree, straight into the mouths of devourers. Drawing further on gendered insults, Nineveh's people will become "women in your midst" (3:13), and their gates open themselves to the world, all but welcoming the pillaging of its treasures.

The remainder of the book continues in a spiteful and disparaging tone, describing in various ways the impending defeat of the once-great city. The poem mocks Nineveh, telling it to "draw water" and "strengthen . . . fortifications" for the coming siege, when it will be devoured like an insect (3:14–15 AT; see also vv. 16–17). Nineveh's shepherds are asleep and incapacitated, its people are scattered, and its wound beyond healing. And lest one think that Nineveh's violent fate will provoke the world's compassion, the poet asserts that "all who

Box 36.3

Nahum and Jonah as Canonical Counterpoints

There are significant literary and theological connections between the books of Nahum and Jonah. Both books concern the fate and destruction of Nineveh. In Jonah, Nineveh's destruction is averted because of the city's thoroughgoing repentance (Jon. 3:10). In Nahum, the city's destruction is predicted and celebrated.

Both books also draw directly from the creedal language of Exodus 34:6–7 to describe God's actions toward the Assyrian city. Nahum 1:2–3 emphasizes the wrathful elements of God's character. Jonah, on the other hand—and with considerable resentment and spite—draws on the same language to describe God's merciful characteristics: "I knew that you are a gracious God and merciful, slow to anger, and abounding in steadfast love" (Jon. 4:2).

Both books also end with a question. Jonah ends with God asking the prophet, "Should I not have pity for Nineveh, that great city in which there are more than 120,000 people who do not know their right hand from their left hand, including many animals?" (4:11 AT). This question begs one to consider God's mercy and care. Nahum, in counterpoint, ends with the prophet asking the Assyrian king a question: "For who has not suffered from your unceasing malice?" (3:19 AT).

The thematic and literary connections between these two prophetic books are even more apparent in the Septuagint, which orders the Book of the Twelve (i.e., the Minor Prophets) so that Nahum follows Jonah rather than Micah. This makes for a striking juxtaposition. In the last verse of Septuagint Jonah, God asks whether he should not spare "Nineveh, that great city" (Jon. 4:11), followed immediately by Septuagint Nahum, which begins with the phrase, "A matter for Nineveh" (Nah. 1:1 AT).

These two prophetic books certainly deserve to be read as independent compositions, but there is also benefit from reading them in conversation with each other. All evidence suggests that they were read that way at one point in their compositional history.

hear your report will clap their hands over you" (3:19 AT). Nineveh's downfall will be a cause for celebration the world round. Like the book of Jonah, the book ends with a question. This question is directed at Nineveh: "For who has not suffered from your unceasing malice?" (3:19 AT).

Theological Interpretation

Nahum can be a deeply uncomfortable book to read. For Christians, Jesus's teachings about loving one's enemy only intensify the problem (see, e.g., Matt. 5:43–48; Luke 6:27–31). What does one do with the fact that Nahum predicts and celebrates the violent downfall of Assyria? One might be inclined to give Nahum a pass if the book showed an ounce of pity for the inhabitants of Nineveh. But it doesn't. The book cheers Nineveh's downfall and taunts it with the claim that the whole earth will celebrate its bad fortune (3:19).

Add to this the fact that God is incontrovertibly at the center of the violence described in Nahum. There is no getting around it. The God of Nahum is a violent warrior, treading furiously upon the earth and wreaking havoc against Israel's oppressor, Nineveh. One could say quite accurately that Nahum describes precisely what Jonah was hoping for. Whereas Jonah wished for the God of wrath, what he got was a God of mercy and compassion. Nahum's violent depictions of Yahweh are important to wrestle with. There are several things to consider while doing so.

God and Violence in Nahum

First, the God of Nahum is the kind of God who is deeply involved in the affairs of humanity—so much so that his hands get dirty, even bloody. As disturbing as that may be, the Hebrew Bible insists on a God who is intertwined with human affairs, small and large. On the one hand, this is bad news for Nineveh, oppressor of nations. On the other hand, it is gospel—good news—for those who live under Nineveh's heel. Human lives matter to God, and this fact is of no small significance. God takes note of people mistreated under Assyrian rule and acts to release them from that yoke of bondage.

Nahum as Post-traumatic Literature

Second, Nahum—like so many other biblical books—is literature of the defeated. Nahum is post-traumatic literature. Both the Northern and the Southern Kingdoms were victims of Assyria's violent, imperial expansion into the west. From this place of relative powerlessness, the book of Nahum places its trust in Yahweh, who alone is capable of meeting and overcoming the brutal forces of Assyria. In Nahum's time, there were no United Nations peacekeepers. One could not simply appeal to the International Criminal Court. The God of Israel alone was capable of bringing about the scale of liberation needed.

To these victims of Assyrian brutality, the arrival of the divine hero offered both comfort and courage:

> Yahweh is good,
>   a stronghold in a day of trouble.
>   He is mindful of those who take refuge in him. (1:7 AT)

The strength of the divine warrior and his ability to defeat the overwhelming power of Assyria signaled an end to a long reign of terror and bloodshed. Imperial brutality did not end with the snap of Yahweh's fingers; it ended when the death-dealing agents of violence were defeated. For Nahum, peace was a result of conflict.

One could easily read the book of Nahum and assume that it is nothing more than a vengeful screed against a bitter foe—a sort of pornography of violence,

Fig. 36.2. An artistic rendering of ancient Assyria's palaces in the capital city of Nineveh.

poetically delighting in the gruesome and brutal downfall of Nineveh. But this would be to miss an important nuance—namely, that Yahweh's violence was a means of securing a future of flourishing in which violence no longer existed (1:15).

Nahum and Compassion

The violence in Nahum serves a third purpose. It acknowledges and mirrors back concrete realities common in Nahum's time: warfare, conquest, and domination. Relative to powerful kingdoms like Assyria and later Babylon, Israel was a fragile nation, vulnerable to a range of geopolitical dynamics, including conquest and defeat. For readers who grew up in prosperous and powerful nations like the United States, it may be difficult to imagine what it might have been like to live in ancient Israel and to experience that level of vulnerability. What does it feel like to live in a country whose military is not the dominant force on the planet? What does it feel like to live between multiple empires, whose vast resources all but ensure military superiority? What does it feel like to know that your kinfolk (the Northern Kingdom) were conquered and exiled by the very kingdom you now serve? To borrow an insight from Ellen Davis, if these experiences are foreign to you, let them instruct your compassion.[1]

Nahum and Sexual Violence

Nahum presents another grave problem. The book graphically depicts Daughter Nineveh's downfall in terms of sexual violence and public humiliation (3:5–7). Throughout the ancient Near East, cities were conceptualized as female (see "daughter Zion" in Ps. 9:14; Isa. 1:8; Lam. 1:6; etc.). This led tragically to defeated cities being portrayed as victimized women. In Nahum, Nineveh has her nakedness exposed publicly, and she is pelted with feces. These truly grotesque and shocking descriptions must be dealt with honestly and carefully. We suggest a number of approaches that attempt to honor the wide range of responses a person might have.

First, one should be fully honest about the horrors of such depictions. For twenty-first-century readers, it is rightfully disturbing to see a male figure engaged in such shocking violence against a female character. One should give careful thought to the consequences of using texts like this in a public setting. We rightfully reject this portrayal of violence against women.

Second, a text like this serves as a potent reminder that the book of Nahum—and the entire Bible, in fact—is a cross-cultural text, whose authors are not only from a different place but also from a different time. What offends in the present may have been acceptable in the past. As modern readers, we are challenged with the difficult, dialectical task of understanding what an ancient text was trying to do in its own time, while also engaging it critically and ethically in our own. In our view, a proper approach will balance both critical, appreciative, and ethical perspectives.

Historical Interpretation

Due to its brevity and sharp focus, Nahum provokes fewer historical controversies than other prophetic books like Isaiah or Jeremiah. Clues within the text provide a date for the book of sometime between 663 BCE (the fall of Thebes, mentioned in 3:8) and the fall of Nineveh in 612 BCE.

The book does, however, leave open a number of historical questions. Who were its primary consumers? The text claims that Nahum is, in fact, a "book" (*sepher*)—or better, a written document. The medium could have been papyrus, stone, leather, or the like. In what social context was such a text taken in? The royal court? The temple? Other public venues?

papyrus An inexpensive but brittle type of writing material made from plant fibers (plural, papyri).

There is also a great deal we don't know about the prophet himself. He is an Elkoshite, but this designation is not known elsewhere, either as a location or as a family name. Did Nahum regularly publish prophecies? Was he a court prophet like Isaiah, or somebody outside of the formal cultic system? How did he relate to Israel's kings? Did he have an amicable or contentious relationship with other prophetic voices of his time? We simply don't have the answers to these kinds of questions.

FOR FURTHER READING: **Nahum**

Galambush, Julie. "Nahum." In *Women's Bible Commentary*, 3rd ed., edited by Carol A. Newsom, Sharon H. Ringe, and Jacqueline E. Lapsley, 329–34. Louisville: Westminster John Knox, 2012.

O'Brien, Julia M. *Nahum, Habakkuk, Zephaniah, Haggai, Zechariah, Malachi*. Abingdon Old Testament Commentaries. Nashville: Abingdon, 2004.

Renz, Thomas. *The Books of Nahum, Habakkuk, and Zephaniah*. New International Commentary on the Old Testament. Grand Rapids: Eerdmans, 2021.

Roberts, J. J. M. *Nahum, Habakkuk, Zephaniah: A Commentary*. Old Testament Library. Louisville: Westminster John Knox, 1991.

Snyman, S. D. *Nahum, Habakkuk and Zephaniah: An Introduction and Commentary*. Tyndale Old Testament Commentaries 27. Downers Grove, IL: IVP Academic, 2020.

Tuell, Steven. *Reading Nahum–Malachi: A Literary and Theological Commentary*. Macon, GA: Smyth & Helwys, 2016.

37

Habakkuk

When people think of a prophet, they often imagine someone communicating heavenly words to an earthly audience. The book of Habakkuk is definitely interested in conveying Yahweh's message, but it unconventionally does so in the form of a dialogue between Habakkuk and Yahweh (chaps. 1–2), followed by a psalm (chap. 3). Habakkuk is similar to the book of Job in that the book's truth claims emerge in the process of a contentious exchange.

Habakkuk deals with weighty questions such as, Why does Yahweh allow violence to go unchecked and justice to be perverted, even among God's own people? How can a God who is pure and holy use the idolatrous and excessively violent Babylonians to accomplish his will? What does it mean to live by faith? In the process of wrestling with these questions, the book of Habakkuk uncovers an understanding of faith that both acknowledges the terror of the present age and also reaches forward toward a more hopeful future.

Background

The Prophet Habakkuk

What we know about the prophet Habakkuk can be derived from his book, which introduces him simply as "the prophet Habakkuk." The title formula does not name his father, his hometown, or the kings during whose reigns he prophesied.

Historical Context

The book of Habakkuk dates to the period just before Jerusalem fell to the Babylonians in 587 BCE, so around 610–590 BCE. During this time, Judah was

Why Does Evil Prevail?

The prophet Habakkuk takes up important and persistent questions about the relationship between good and evil, with special emphasis on why evil seems to prevail. This issue is particularly nettlesome for monotheistic faiths like Judaism and Christianity, both of which claim that God is not only powerful but good. The questions sound something like this: If God is both all-powerful and supremely good, then how could he allow evil to have its way in the world? For Habakkuk, the issue comes in the form of an accusation: "Therefore the law is paralyzed, and justice never prevails. The wicked hem in the righteous, so that justice is perverted" (1:4 AT).

But for Habakkuk, the question is not merely theoretical. When he refers to the perversion of justice, he is referring to the decisive and destructive power of the Babylonian Empire. This issue forms the theological center of the book. As you will see, the book provides a specific and hopeful answer to this question. Whether that answer is both adequate and hopeful today remains an open matter.

governed by a succession of kings whose reigns were cut short. The reformer King Josiah fell in battle with the Egyptian pharaoh Neco in 609 BCE. Jehoahaz reigned just three months before he was dethroned by Neco and exiled to Egypt, where he died (609 BCE). Neco replaced him with Jehoiakim, who reigned for a decade (609–598 BCE), first becoming a vassal of Babylon and then rebelling. His son Jehoiachin (598/597 BCE) was captured by Nebuchadnezzar of Babylon and taken into exile. Nebuchadnezzar replaced him with his uncle Zedekiah (597–586 BCE), who also rebelled against Babylon. When Jerusalem fell and was razed, Zedekiah's sons were slain in front of him, his eyes were put out, and he was taken into exile, where he died.

Composition and Development

The compositional history of Habakkuk is largely unknown. There is little reason to doubt that much of the book is genuinely from the words of the prophet Habakkuk, but several editorial, musical, and liturgical markings suggest some textual development at the hands of Levitical priests (see "a prayer . . . according to Shigionoth," 3:1; "selah," 3:9, 13; and the concluding editorial note in 3:19).

Genre

Like most prophetic books, Habakkuk is largely poetry. Within that framework, it contains several types of literature. Based on its opening lines, the book is prophetic literature: "The oracle that Habakkuk the prophet saw" (1:1 AT). But the bulk of the book is a dialogical exchange between Habakkuk and God: Habakkuk raises a number of serious complaints about Yahweh's governance over the world, and Yahweh responds. Eventually, the book concludes with a prayer that includes a petition and a lengthy description of a theophany (a divine revelation in which creation responds dramatically to God's presence).

Box 37.2

Outline

1. Superscription (1:1)
2. Dialogue between Habakkuk and Yahweh (1:2–2:20)
3. Prayer/psalm of Habakkuk (3)

Literary Interpretation

Superscription (Hab. 1:1). The book begins as many prophetic books do: with a superscription identifying the prophet who received messages from Yahweh. In the case of the book of Habakkuk, the superscription provides only the prophet's name.

Dialogue between Habakkuk and Yahweh (Hab. 1:2–2:20). The dialogue between the prophet and Yahweh begins with the prophet praying a prayer for help (a lament psalm) and asking a question found frequently in the Psalter (not to mention in the hearts of believers!):

> How long shall I plead for help,
>   and you do not hear?
> I cry out "violence" to you,
>   but you do not save. (1:2 AT)

Habakkuk goes on to list other problems emerging from Yahweh's silence:

> As a result, teaching is feeble;
>   justice [*mishpat*] fails to go forth,
> for the wicked surround the righteous;
>   judgment [*mishpat*] goes forth crooked.
>   (1:4 AT)

Habakkuk uses a pun in his complaint. "Justice" and "judgment" are the same Hebrew word with two meanings here—there is no justice because those in charge issue corrupt judgments in court.

Yahweh responds to Habakkuk's accusations in some astonishing ways. He promises to send the Chaldeans (i.e., Babylonians)—a fierce, violent, and bellicose nation set on expanding its reach well beyond its own borders (1:3–6). The Chaldeans are ethically corrupt because they define justice on their own and according to their own interests (*mishpat*, 1:7). They are a terrifying force that is guilty not only of violence but also of idolatry.

Fig. 37.1. This fragment from the Babylonian Chronicles dates from around the time of Habakkuk and uses the ancient cuneiform script.

Habakkuk's response shows that he comprehends Yahweh's words but disagrees with his actions on theological grounds. He contends that the eyes of Yahweh—the holy God—are too pure to look upon evil, and he appeals to Yahweh's divine character:

> Are you not from everlasting,
>   oh Lord my God, my Holy One,
> never dying?
> Yahweh, you have appointed them for judgment;
>   Oh Rock, to rebuke you have established him.
> You who are purer of eyes than to behold evil,
>   who is unable to look upon trouble,
> why do you simply gaze at the faithless,
>   staying silent when a wicked one swallows someone more righteous than
>   he is? (1:12–13 AT)

According to Habakkuk, Yahweh is implicated in the success of the Chaldeans, who slaughter nations "without pity" (1:17 NJPS).

In chapter 2, Habakkuk awaits an answer from Yahweh. He stands watch, vigilantly watching his post "to see what he [Yahweh] will tell me, and what he will reply concerning my protest" (2:1 AT).

Yahweh's response comes in Habakkuk 2:2–20, where he promises, "There will still be a vision for the appointed time," and "If it delays, expect it, for it will surely come and will not linger" (2:3 AT). Yahweh's response sets up the book's key insight: Yahweh is not an indifferent deity who stands idly by as evil gobbles up the world, and neither is justice impotent. His judgment will prevail but only after a season of persistence and waiting. Until the appointed time of the vision arrives, Yahweh commands, "the righteous shall live by faith" (2:4 AT).

The faithful who wait on Yahweh are contrasted with the one who is "puffed up" (2:4 NJPS). The latter will not continue in their destructive behavior without end. Suddenly their "creditors" will arise, because "you plundered many nations" (2:7–8 NJPS). Though the fulfillment of this word would seem to be delayed, according to the oracle, these events will occur "suddenly."

While the world seems to favor those who gain wealth and riches through domination, Yahweh paints a different picture:

> Woe to the one who unjustly gains benefit for his house,
>   placing his nest on high,
>   to preserve it from disaster.
> You have devised shame for your house,
>   cutting off multitudes
>   and violating your own life.

For a stone will cry out from the wall,
    and a beam will reply from the woodwork:
"Woe to the one who constructs a town by means of blood
    and who establishes a city with injustice." (2:9–12 AT)

Like Abel's blood crying out from the ground (Gen. 4:10), the components of the unjustly built house raise a wounded cry that implicates the builder and prophetically signals his demise.

The remainder of the chapter pairs Yahweh's critique of injustice to a critique of idolatry (2:18–20), showing once again that for Israel's prophets, there is a deep and abiding linkage between idolatry and injustice.

Prayer/psalm of Habakkuk (Hab. 3). The third and final chapter contains another psalm in the mouth of Habakkuk, this time a psalm of praise. The first words out of the prophet's mouth are scented with the joy of freshly uncovered truth:

Yahweh, I have heard of your fame;
    I revere you, Lord, your deed.
In the midst of years, renew it;
    in the midst of years announce it;
    in anger, may you remember compassion. (3:2 AT)

The psalm continues with a report of the vision that Yahweh had promised in 2:3. The vision is terrifying: Yahweh arrives on the scene with majesty and splendor. Like a mighty general, he marches with pestilence and plague at his front and rear (3:5). Heaven and earth respond with tectonic fury, quaking, bowing, and scattering before the glory of Yahweh. But this divine display of might is not simply undirected anger; Yahweh marches the earth with furor "for the salvation of [his] people" and to shatter "the head from the evil house" (3:13 AT). This theophany describes the long-awaited moment of fulfillment when God's promises break out of the realm of hope and explode onto the stage of history. Habakkuk is terrified—"I hear, and I tremble within; my lips quiver"—but he has the faith to wait for the day of God's justice: "I wait quietly for the day of calamity to come upon the people who attack us" (3:16).

The last three verses of Habakkuk leave the reader with a poetic, defiant expression of praise that announces Habakkuk's newly realized hope and faith. Here is a picture of what it looks like when "the righteous . . . live by faith":

Though a fig tree does not blossom,
    nor is fruit found on the vines;
though the produce of the olive fails,
    the field makes no food.

Fig. 37.2. This artistic rendering of a fig tree invites the reader to ponder Habakkuk's closing word of praise, "Though the fig tree does not blossom, and no fruit is on the vines; . . . yet I will rejoice in the Lord" (3:17–18). Praise can sometimes be a defiant act of faith in the midst of persecution or an expression of trust in the midst of loss.

> Sheep are cut off from the fold;
>> there are no cattle in the stall.
> Even still, I will rejoice in Yahweh;
>> I will delight in the God of my salvation. (3:17–18 AT)

The book of Habakkuk ends on a note of joy—not because circumstances have changed but because Habakkuk's view of Yahweh's involvement has been transformed. Faith in Yahweh allows Habakkuk to hope in the face of despair.

Theological Interpretation

Habakkuk, Human Injustice, and Divine Justice

The book of Habakkuk engages some of the most persistent and challenging theological questions. Why does evil so often prevail over justice? Why do the strong so often succeed in oppressing the weak? If God is holy and good, how can he tolerate such a world? Why are God's promises so often delayed?

But Habakkuk does not engage these questions in the tranquil vacuum of a theological laboratory. His forceful inquiries erupt from the mouth of a man who is staring Babylonian bellicosity in the face. Their decisive defeat of the Neo-Assyrian Empire indicated that Babylonian actions and capabilities were to be taken with deadly seriousness. For Habakkuk, this is not chiefly a foreign

Habakkuk's Use of Prayer and Praise

It is interesting to compare Habakkuk's prophetic use of prayer and praise with that of the prophet Jonah. Jonah either sleeps or praises God when he should be praying, and he prays a prayer asking to die when he should be praising God. Jonah's actions are understandable from a human point of view: Jonah hates Nineveh and the Assyrians. He hopes they die and is livid when they are spared. Habakkuk, by contrast, praises and rejoices in God when there is absolute famine. Even though the field, vineyard, and flock—the three sources of Israel's food—all fail to produce, he says, "Even still, I will rejoice in Yahweh; I will delight in the God of my salvation" (3:18 AT).

policy problem; it is a life-and-death theological problem, with Yahweh's people and Yahweh's reputation at stake.

As noted above, Habakkuk's complaints have primarily to do with Yahweh's failure to save (1:2) and his tolerance of violence and injustice from evil actors. He interprets Yahweh's inactivity as a violation of divine holiness and purity. From the prophet's perspective, Yahweh's character should not allow him to sit by while the wicked devour the righteous. Habakkuk considers Yahweh's initial response inadequate and unable to properly account for the apparent distance between Habakkuk's understanding of Yahweh and the reality on the ground.

Habakkuk and the Righteous Living by Faith

Yahweh offers another response that ultimately leads Habakkuk to petition Yahweh with newfound confidence in chapter 3. Yahweh's answer includes the following claims:

- Yahweh's prophetic word may be delayed, but its fulfillment is certain (2:3).
- Even though the puffed-up devourer of nations would seem to have victory in the present moment, the righteous are in possession of the true reward (2:4).
- The one who has "harvested nations for himself" (2:5 AT) with an appetite as insatiable as death will have the tables turned on him (2:6–8).
- This plunderer of nations may have designs on world rule, but in the process of engineering its dominion, Babylon unknowingly "devised shame for [its] house" (2:10). In the language of 2:16, "The cup of Yahweh's right hand will come around to you" (AT).
- Yahweh mocks Babylon's worship of handmade idols, thereby directly linking idolatry to imperialistic violence (2:18–19).

Yahweh's response in chapter 2 actually affirms Habakkuk's negative judgment of Babylon's imperialistic activity and idolatrous worship. Yahweh pushes

Fig. 37.3. Twelfth-century Byzantine mosaic of Habakkuk.

back, however, on Habakkuk's accusation that he is indifferent and unwilling to act on behalf of his people. Yahweh's justice is delayed but assured. The prophet is thereby summoned into a posture of faith and hope.

Historical Interpretation

The book of Habakkuk deals with an age in which the Chaldeans (Babylonians) are the preeminent military power, gobbling up land and resources across the ancient Near East. The Neo-Babylonian Empire's rise to imperial dominance began around 612 BCE with the twilight of the Neo-Assyrian Empire. Babylon, in turn, fell to the Persian Empire in 539 BCE.

While the texts that make up Habakkuk fit within this timeline, it is impossible to say with certainty

---

Box 37.4

Promise and Reality

Yahweh's responses to Habakkuk underscore one of the heaviest burdens carried by people of faith: the apparent contradiction between divine promises and earthly realities. For Christians, this contradiction is regularly acknowledged when they utter the Lord's Prayer: "Your kingdom come. Your will be done, on earth as it is in heaven" (Matt. 6:10). The fact that this prayer continues in the church long after Christ's ascension and promise to return (Acts 1:6–11) points directly to the problem of faith identified in Habakkuk: faith requires defiant belief in the face of contradictory realities. To borrow from the language of Hebrews, faith is the "conviction of things not seen" (Heb. 11:1).

Habakkuk expresses this reality in the final verses of chapter 3:

> Though a fig tree does not blossom,
>   nor is fruit found on the vines;
> though the produce of the olive fails,
>   the field makes no food.
> Sheep are cut off from the fold;
>   there are no cattle in the stall.
> Even still, I will rejoice in Yahweh;
>   I will delight in the God of my salvation. (3:17–18 AT)

Habakkuk's hope and praise ring with defiance. Defiance in the face of imperialistic violence. Defiance in the face of contrary evidence. Defiance in the face of despair. In this regard, Paul was certainly right to see in Habakkuk a book about faith, trust, and righteousness (Rom. 1:17; Gal. 3:11).

Box 37.5

Chaldeans

The term *Chaldeans* is an English translation of the Hebrew word *kasdim*. *Chaldean* is an anglicized version derivative of the Greek word *chaldaiōn*. When the Hebrew Bible wants to describe the people of Babylon, this is the term that it typically uses. When it wants to talk about Babylon—both as a geographical region and as an empire—it uses the term *babel*. In some cases, *kasdim* seems to be a technical term for an astrological specialist (Dan. 2:2, 4), but these are the exceptions.

when they were written. Some elements (e.g., the poetic material in chap. 3) may have existed independently and may have been integrated into the larger book at a later time. Whatever the case, the book of Habakkuk represents one of the most theologically creative attempts to deal with the challenges of remaining faithful in a time of national threat.

FOR FURTHER READING: Habakkuk

Merrill Willis, Amy C. "Habakkuk." In *Women's Bible Commentary*, 3rd ed., edited by Carol A. Newsom, Sharon H. Ringe, and Jacqueline E. Lapsley, 335–38. Louisville: Westminster John Knox, 2012.

Renz, Thomas. *The Books of Nahum, Habakkuk, and Zephaniah*. New International Commentary on the Old Testament. Grand Rapids: Eerdmans, 2021.

Roberts, J. J. M. *Nahum, Habakkuk, Zephaniah: A Commentary*. Old Testament Library. Louisville: Westminster John Knox, 1991.

Snyman, S. D. *Nahum, Habakkuk and Zephaniah: An Introduction and Commentary*. Tyndale Old Testament Commentaries 27. Downers Grove, IL: IVP Academic, 2020.

Thomas, Heath A. *Habakkuk*. Two Horizons Old Testament Commentary. Grand Rapids: Eerdmans, 2018.

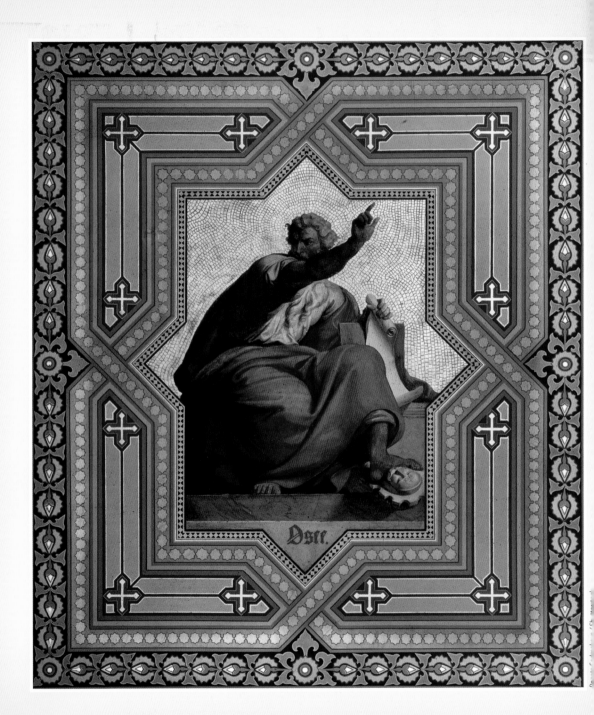

Ofee.

38

Zephaniah

Like many other prophetic books, Zephaniah contains warnings, statements of hope, offers of repentance, and oracles against foreign nations. One of the book's key themes is a familiar topic in the Book of the Twelve: the day of the Lord.

Background

The Prophet Zephaniah

If the information in Zephaniah 1:1 is accurate, Zephaniah came from the royal line but was a prophet rather than a king: "Zephaniah son of Cushi son of Gedaliah son of Amariah son of Hezekiah." According to this pedigree, Zephaniah was a relative of King Josiah, whose reign he may have criticized. Regardless, he is most certainly a southern prophet, focused on matters related to Judah and its rulers.

Historical Context

As noted, the superscription of Zephaniah locates the book in the reign of King Josiah. Zephaniah provides us with a rare glimpse into the reign of one of Judah's most prominent kings, Josiah, whose reforms are described in 2 Kings 22–23 and are often associated with the theology found in the book of Deuteronomy.

With that said, Zephaniah's description of his social environment is starkly different from the image of Josiah's reign in the book of 2 Kings. There the narrator is ebullient in his praise of the king's penitent disposition, faithful reforms, and thorough religious housecleaning. Zephaniah, by contrast, depicts

Box 38.1

The Josianic Reforms

Josiah is one of a small handful of rulers to whom 1–2 Kings gives its approval. Its evaluation is typically noted in the opening verses of a king's narrative. For instance, in 2 Kings 22:2 the text reads, "He [Josiah] did what was right in the eyes of the Lord and followed completely the ways of his father David, not turning aside to the right or to the left" (AT). This glowing review is due in large part to the radical reforms Josiah undertook in response to the discovery of a scroll containing Yahweh's demands and judgments (22:11–13). Yahweh's chief complaint against the people—communicated through Huldah the prophetess—primarily concerned infractions against the first commandment (22:17). Josiah's reforms are described in chapter 23 and involved a renewal of the covenant, the removal of idolatrous implements, the desecration of idolatrous worship sites, actions against personnel who aided in unfaithful worship, and so on.

creation-wide, impending doom because of Judah's sin (see 1:2–18). Josiah is never explicitly mentioned or critiqued, but the circumstances described in Zephaniah are difficult to square with what we read in the pro-Josianic 2 Kings 22–23. These questions will be taken up in greater detail below. Of course, one could assume that the judgment texts in Zephaniah were written prior to Josiah's reforms—and that his allegedly expansive reforms made no meaningful impact on the book of Zephaniah. Josiah came to the throne at age eight, so Zephaniah may have been critiquing the governance of the regent(s) who ruled until he was of age. According to the list of reforms in 2 Kings 23, there were a lot of cobwebs that needed to be swept aside.

Composition and Development

Some biblical scholars find evidence of later expansion and redaction to the prophecies attributed to Zephaniah. This is certainly possible and even likely, but it is difficult to see clearly in the text we have what these changes may have been. We assume, therefore, that the book of Zephaniah is largely a product of the Josianic era, though it probably underwent some minor editing.

Genre

As a whole, Zephaniah is a compendium of multiple genres commonly found in prophetic books: oracles announcing doom, offers of repentance, oracles against foreign nations and their deities, and oracles of salvation. Most of these texts are critical in nature, castigating Judah for its sin—especially idolatry (1:4–6)—and describing the impending consequences. In keeping with a trend we've seen elsewhere, however, Zephaniah concludes with hope. That hope is centered around a remnant in God's holy city of Jerusalem that will emerge after God removes "[their] arrogantly exulting ones" (3:11 AT). Specific leaders are not named, only titles.

Literary Interpretation

Superscription (Zeph. 1:1). The book of Zephaniah begins with a superscription that identifies the prophet as a descendant of King Hezekiah. It limits the prophet's activity to the reign of a single Judean king: Josiah.

Announcement of Judah's doom (Zeph. 1:2–2:2). Verse 2 quickly transitions into a dramatic description of impending doom, brought about because of Judah and Jerusalem's idolatrous devotion to Baal, the heavenly hosts, and Molech. Zephaniah's opening oracle is devastating:

> I will surely sweep away everything from the face of the earth,
>   declares Yahweh.
> I will sweep away man and beast;
>   I will sweep away the birds of the heavens
>   and the fish of the seas. (1:2–3 AT)

Human sin catches all creation up in its destructive consequences. The cosmic scale of these consequences is signaled by the fact that all three realms of creation—the heavens, the land, and the sea—suffer as a result. Zephaniah is not unique in emphasizing the creational consequences of human sin (see, e.g., Hosea 4:3; Joel 1:10–20).

This dire scene takes place on the "day of the LORD" (1:7, 9–10, 14–16, 18). The day of the Lord is a widely used motif in the Book of the Twelve. In Zephaniah's time, it was understood to be a time when Yahweh would defeat his enemies and thereby end the threat to the chosen people. It was a symbol of hope in the power of Judah's deity. But that richly symbolic day could also be rhetorically weaponized and directed against Judah, as we see here in Zephaniah (cf. Amos 5:18–20).

Using ominous imagery, Yahweh promises to "search Jerusalem with lamps" in order to track down those worthy of judgment. The light of divine scrutiny shines brightly on those who "are indifferent, who say to themselves, 'the Lord will do neither good nor bad'" (1:12 AT). The prophet shows himself to be concerned not only with "active" sins but also with sins of inaction, like indifference. For Zephaniah, belief in a God who is morally neutral is repugnant.

Ultimately, both Judah's active sins and its outright indifference open wide the doors to doom. As if to say that language could not contain the terror of

Fig. 38.1. This nineteenth-century painting, *The Great Day of His Wrath*, depicts creation in upheaval. For the Bible, the effect of human sin always ripples out into the world, impacting and corrupting everything it touches—human, beast, bird, and fish.

that day, the poem piles up words, calling the great day of the Lord "bitter," "distress and affliction," "devastation and disaster," "darkness and despair," and "clouds and thick darkness" (1:14–15 AT).

These fierce words, however, are immediately followed by passionate pleas to gather and seek Yahweh:

> Seek Yahweh, all you humble of the land,
> who execute his justice.
> Seek righteousness;
> seek humility.
> Perhaps you will be hidden away
> on the day of Yahweh's wrath. (2:3 AT)

The admonitions in chapter 2 do nothing to negate the fire and fury of chapter 1. The day of the Lord is on the way, and no amount of repentance or reformation will change that. For the righteous and the humble, however, hope exists in finding shelter from the storm. Anticipating the remnant theology of Zephaniah 3:12–13, chapter 2 argues that hope is in the righteous few who will persist beyond the cleansing fires of judgment.

Oracles against the nations (Zeph. 2:3–15). The rest of chapter 2 is a collection of oracles against foreign nations and their gods. The nations include

Fig. 38.2. A fresco of the prophet Zephaniah in the Church of San Giuseppe in Taormina, Italy.

Philistia, Moab, Ammon, Cush/Ethiopia, and Assyria. These texts function theologically as royal decrees, issued from a heavenly king—Yahweh. As head of all divine beings, Yahweh will "emaciate all the gods of the earth, and to him will bow, each from his own place, all of the world's distant lands" (2:11 AT). This verse reflects the ancient belief that the deities of the earth were assigned to specific locations and people (Deut. 32:8).

It is not clear whether readers are meant to associate these acts of judgment with the "day of the Lord," as described in chapter 1. What is clear, however, is that Yahweh's conflicts with the nations are designed to benefit Judah. For example, Zephaniah says that the seacoast will become a possession for the "remnant of the house of Judah" and that Yahweh will "return their fortunes" (2:7 AT). The oracles against foreign nations, both here and elsewhere, make an important theological point—namely, that Yahweh is king of the nations. As king, Yahweh makes pronouncements about the fate of the nations, with special attention to how their futures impact Yahweh's people.

Oracle of Jerusalem's judgment and salvation (Zeph. 3). Chapter 3 turns its attention to the "violent city" (3:1 CEB). Initially, the text is not forthcoming about the identity of the city. From the first few verses, the reader knows that this city is defiled, oppressive, unwilling to obey, unteachable, distrustful toward Yahweh, and led by predatory, deceptive leaders (3:1–4). Typical of prophetic books is the emphasis on the guilt of leaders and public figures, equating their misdeeds with the predatory behavior of lions and wolves. Both the prophets and the priests are also indicted for their corruption.

One might assume the city is Nineveh, one of Assyria's capitals (cf. Nahum and Jonah). But by verse 5, it becomes clear that the city in the crosshairs is none other than Jerusalem itself—Yahweh's chosen domicile (3:5). Like Nathan's parable of the little ewe lamb (2 Sam. 12), the poem secures moral buy-in before springing its trap.

The poem describes a day when God will "rise up as a witness" to gather the nations, unleash his wrath, and consume the earth (3:8 CEB). This fiery display, however, is not the end. The fire not only judges, but it also refines. Yahweh promises to remove arrogant and haughty people from the midst of his people but leave a "humble and powerless" people who seek shelter in Yahweh (3:12 CEB). This remnant will also avoid injustice and rest at ease.

It is unclear to whom the term "remnant" refers. In some ways, the answer depends on how one dates the texts in chapter 3. If verses 12–13 were written in the exilic period, then it may refer to the exiles, to whom the text offers a comforting invitation. If, however, the text is Josianic, then the term may in fact be an invitation to the Northern Kingdom.[1] If the earlier date is accepted, then there is no reason why these verses could not be heard in both ways—initially as an overture to the north and later as a comfort to exiled Judahites.

Finally, Zion is summoned to joy because judgment has come to an end, her enemies have been nullified, and Yahweh arrives as a "mighty one who saves" (3:17 AT). All the threats to Zion's future, human and divine, are ended. The warrior God will delight over Jerusalem and quiet her with his love. The book concludes with the promise that God will gather his people, restore their fortunes, and make them renowned among the people of the earth.

Box 38.3

Judgment and Hope in Zephaniah and Beyond

The judgment of Yahweh is a common theme in the Old Testament. It is also deeply misunderstood by many readers. Christian readers, especially, often raise a skeptical eyebrow at the God of the Old Testament and describe him as capricious, temperamental, and unloving. They consider the God of the Old Testament as wrathful and angry, whereas the God of the New Testament—seen in Jesus—is compassionate and loving.

But for prophets like Zephaniah, Yahweh's judgment is an expression of divine love and faithfulness. In Zephaniah, the haughty and arrogant are removed precisely because they bring destruction on others and suffocate the life out of the lowly. God's love compels him to act on behalf of those whose lives are ground under the boot of the powerful.

Theological Interpretation

Creation, Ecology, and Judgment

More and more interpreters recognize the deep and pervasive creation theology at work in the prophetic texts, and Zephaniah is a good example. Creation is not merely the stage on which God's redemptive work takes place; the redemption of creation itself is the drama. In other words, it is inappropriate to draw a sharp distinction between God's creative acts and God's saving or judging acts.

As an example, Zephaniah begins with a dystopic image of creational destruction:

> I will surely sweep away everything from the face of the earth,
>   declares Yahweh.
> I will sweep away man and beast;
>   I will sweep away the birds of the heavens
>   and the fish of the seas. (1:2–3 AT)

These verses describe a massive depopulation of creatures from their habitats. Once full and fruitful spheres of life are transformed—uncreated—into barren wastelands. The heavens, the earth, and the sea are caught up in the destructive aftermath of human sin. In our own time, there is increasing recognition that human beings contribute significantly to the health of creation. This insight is not an exclusively scientific one; it is an insight recognized already by the Hebrew prophets, who knew deep down that human sin could negatively impact the created world.

Divine Wrath and Salvation

Like many other prophets, Zephaniah is generous in his accusations. He focuses his ire on those who revere foreign gods and embrace foreign influence (1:4–8), who commit violence and fraud (1:9), and those who are indifferent (1:12). He reserves a special dose of wrath for the "oppressing city"—that is, Jerusalem and its leaders, who do not trust or draw near to God and are predatory in their dealings with others (3:1–4). God's wrath in Zephaniah shows that while human beings may be indifferent, God certainly is not. God's judgment shows clearly that he will not let sin run amok, allowing the weak to be victimized and the strong to exercise unjust power unchecked.

Threats of divine judgment, however, are not merely divine rantings on the fractured state of the world. They are appeals to God's people to repent and be spared (2:1–3). Zephaniah urges the people to seek the Lord, seek righteousness, seek humility—not in order to prevent the day of the Lord, but in order that "you may be hidden on the day of Yahweh's wrath" (2:3 AT). Repentance won't

Fig. 38.3. A nineteenth-century depiction of Jerusalem, a city that has captured the imaginations of people over the generations and from many different faiths. Zephaniah is among that great host of people who see the city as sacred.

avert the impending doom, but turning to Yahweh can mitigate its effects on the penitent and, most importantly, allow them to survive.

The City of God

The fate of Zion/Jerusalem is at the center of Zephaniah's theology. In chapter 1, the prophet rails against the holy city's inhabitants and especially its leaders for their idolatry, violence, and fraud. A similar tone marks 3:1–13. The last seven verses of the book, however, turn suddenly from judgment to hope. Shouts of doom are overtaken by songs of joy.

In an initially puzzling move, Zephaniah says, "The King of Israel, Yahweh, is in your midst; you will never fear doom again" (3:15 AT). Prior to this declaration, however, Yahweh's presence was not the problem. Yahweh was there, searching Jerusalem "with lamps" and judging the guilty (1:12). The issue was not that Yahweh was absent. The issue was the manner in which he was present. At the end of the book, Yahweh promises to be present for Jerusalem in a particular kind of way, a way that makes new futures possible through forgiveness and through the gathering of the scattered. Whereas the first part of the book depicts Yahweh primarily in the form of a judge, the very last poem depicts the God of Israel as a savior.

Historical Interpretation

The book of Zephaniah claims that the word of Yahweh came to Zephaniah during King Josiah's reign. Nothing in Zephaniah explicitly calls this claim into question, and it need not be doubted. However, as discussed above, the book's relationship to the reign and reforms of Josiah recorded in 2 Kings 22:1–23:30 raises important historical questions.

Zephaniah has a largely negative depiction of Judah's leaders—though without any specific mention of King Josiah—while 2 Kings 22–23 portrays Josiah in extremely positive terms: "Among those who came before him, he was peerless, someone who turned to Yahweh with all of his heart and with all of his soul and with all of his strength, according to the entire law of Moses. In his wake, no one comparable arose" (2 Kings 23:25 AT). This is rare praise in the book of Kings, which frequently condemns the kings of both Israel and Judah. Zephaniah neither condemns nor praises Josiah. Given the vitriol with which the book scorches its other opponents, these gaps are surprising and noticeable.

A few possibilities exist to explain the disparity between Zephaniah and 2 Kings. The first is that Josiah's reign was far more controversial and contested than 2 Kings suggests, with the book of Zephaniah representing a divergent and even oppositional voice. A second possibility is that the negative oracles against Judah and its rulers describe Judah leading up to Josiah's widespread reforms, perhaps even playing a role in calling Judah to account for their sins. A third is that the narrative in 2 Kings 22–23 of a pious Josiah has little grounding in history. Scholars are divided on the historicity of Josiah's reforms, with some urging readers to be cautious about the historicity of Josiah's legendary status.

FOR FURTHER READING: Zephaniah

Berlin, Adele. *Zephaniah: A New Translation with Introduction and Commentary.* Anchor Bible 25A. New York: Doubleday, 1994.

Heffelfinger, Katie M. "Zephaniah." In *Women's Bible Commentary*, 3rd ed., edited by Carol A. Newsom, Sharon H. Ringe, and Jacqueline E. Lapsley, 339–42. Louisville: Westminster John Knox, 2012.

Renz, Thomas. *The Books of Nahum, Habakkuk, and Zephaniah.* New International Commentary on the Old Testament. Grand Rapids: Eerdmans, 2021.

Roberts, J. J. M. *Nahum, Habakkuk, Zephaniah: A Commentary.* Old Testament Library. Louisville: Westminster John Knox, 1991.

Snyman, S. D. *Nahum, Habakkuk and Zephaniah: An Introduction and Commentary.* Tyndale Old Testament Commentaries 27. Downers Grove, IL: IVP Academic, 2020.

Haggai

The book of Haggai is one of the postexilic prophetic books and the tenth book in the Book of the Twelve. The book is set during the early years after the Babylonian exile, when many Jews had returned to their homeland—now the Persian province of Yehud/Judah—to reestablish their lives there and rebuild their temple. The book is named for a prophet who may have assumed the name Haggai because its meaning—"my festival"—reinforced the basic message he delivered from Yahweh: Rebuild the temple so my people can keep my festivals.

The prophet Zechariah (see chap. 40, "Zechariah") was also active in postexilic Jerusalem during this time. While neither prophet mentions the other, it may be assumed that the two knew of each other, because Jerusalem was a small city.

Background

The Prophet Haggai

We know little about the prophet Haggai other than what we can discern from the messages in the book named for him. There is no reason to doubt that the prophet was a historical figure who lived and prophesied in 520 BCE (Hosea 1:1). Because of his concern for the temple and references to matters of ritual cleanliness and uncleanliness (2:13–14), it is likely that he was a Levitical priest. The prophet was concerned with the welfare of the people, who suffered from hunger because of crop failures and natural calamities.

The name Haggai may not have been the name given to the prophet at birth. As noted, he may have assumed the name because its meaning ("my festival") related to his message that the people needed to rebuild the temple so they could keep the Lord's festivals. Other prophets such as Hosea and Isaiah gave symbolic names to their children in order to communicate their messages, and it is likely that Haggai gave himself the new symbolic name in order to embody his prophetic word. It is not surprising, then, that the prophet's name is given but no information about either his father or his hometown is provided.

Historical Context

The book of Haggai is unique for the specificity of dates it provides. It opens with such a reference: "In the second year of King Darius, in the sixth month, on the first day of the month, the word of the LORD came by the prophet Haggai to Zerubbabel son of Shealtiel, governor of Judah, and to Joshua son of Jehozadak, the high priest" (1:1). This date formula establishes the date of Haggai's first message: August 29, 520 BCE.

Each of the book's four sections includes the exact date of one of the prophet's messages, situating his messages between August and December 520 BCE, two decades after the end of the Babylonian exile, which formally ended in 539 BCE when the Persian emperor Cyrus the Great conquered Babylon and issued a decree that exiles could return home.

The introductory verse mentions three key figures: Darius the Persian emperor, Zerubbabel the Judean governor, and Joshua the high priest. Darius reigned as emperor from 522 to 486 BCE. Zerubbabel and Joshua are also mentioned in the book of Ezra as prominent leaders among those who returned from exile in 539 BCE. Zerubbabel is especially interesting. The governor of Yehud (the name of postexilic Judah, a Persian province), he was from the line of King David and the grandson of King Jehoiachin, Judah's last king, exiled in 597 BCE. The book of 2 Kings ended with a note of hope, recounting that Jehoiachin was released from prison and given a place of honor at the emperor's table. That note of hope continues with his grandson Zerubbabel, a scion of the Davidic line reigning as governor.

Although the exiles who began to return to Judah in 539 BCE came home with great hope, the realities of life in the land quickly tempered and even dimmed that hope. Conditions were difficult. Not only had the land been destroyed during the Babylonian invasion; it also suffered from a combination of drought and plagues, such as locust invasion. In addition, it is clear from the books of Ezra and Nehemiah that those who returned from exile encountered hostility from those who were still living in the land and were less than thrilled to see the exiles return to rebuild Jerusalem and the temple. Meanwhile, those who returned from exile regarded those who remained in the land as less-than-pure-and-faithful Jews. Conflict between these two groups was inevitable.

According to the book of Ezra, in 538 BCE Zerubbabel and Joshua had laid the foundation for the rebuilding of the temple (3:8–10), but apparently work was suspended and had not yet recommenced by 520 BCE. Haggai's messages were delivered to Zerubbabel and others of the cultural elite, whom he blamed for the suffering of the people because they had not rebuilt the temple. Perhaps in response to Haggai's preaching, work on the temple did restart, since it was finished around 516/515 BCE.

Composition and Development

There is little reason to doubt the integrity of the book of Haggai. The four prophetic messages that the book presents were delivered by the prophet between August and December 520 BCE. The book that bears his name does not show evidence of editorial development or rearrangement.

Genre

While most Old Testament scholars distinguish primarily between prophetic messages of judgment and messages of salvation (or hope), that binary approach may not do justice to Haggai's messages. The prophet's messages might best be called messages of admonition, since they upbraid the people for not having rebuilt the temple and also encourage them to do so immediately. Because the book reports the prophet's messages as well as the people's responses, it is likely that the book was written down by one or more of Haggai's followers.

Literary Interpretation

Superscription (Hag. 1:1). The superscription in the book of Haggai identifies the prophet, the historically specific setting of his first message, and his intended audience: August 29, 520 BCE, in Judah/Yehud, to Zerubbabel the governor and Joshua the high priest.

First message (Hag. 1:2–15). Haggai's first message, directed to the leaders of the people who had returned from exile, criticizes them for living in "paneled houses, while this house [the temple] lies in ruins" (1:4). The message continues: "Consider how you have fared. You have sown much, and harvested little; you eat, but you never have enough; you drink, but you never have your fill; you clothe yourselves, but no one is warm" (1:5–6). The prophet proclaims that the land's lack of fertility—due to drought, plague, and the like—is the result of the temple lying unfinished. "Why? says the LORD of hosts. Because my house lies in ruins. . . . Therefore the heavens above you have withheld the dew, and the earth has withheld its produce" (1:9–10). The book then reports

Fig. 39.1. Upon the Jews' return from exile, the temple rebuilding program began but was interrupted. Haggai called for the completion of the rebuilding.

that Zerubbabel and Joshua, "with all the remnant of the people, obeyed the voice of the LORD" and recommenced work on the temple (1:12).

Second message (Hag. 2:1–9). Haggai's second message dates to October 17, 520 BCE. This message is directed to the two leaders and the remnant of the people. The prophet asks those old enough to remember the first temple whether the new building is "not in [their] sight as nothing." The prophet then exhorts the people to "take courage" and offers them God's promises, "I am with you, . . . according to the promise I made you when you came out of Egypt. My spirit abides among you" (2:3–5). The prophet further says that "the treasure of all nations shall come," the "splendor of this house shall be greater than the former," and "I will give prosperity" (2:7, 9).

Third message (Hag. 2:10–19). The third message of Haggai dates to December 18, 520 BCE, and is directed as questions to "the priests." If consecrated food is carried in your robe and the robe touches other food, does that food then become consecrated? No, answer the priests. If a person who is ritually unclean touches food, does the food become unclean? Yes, answer the priests. So it is with this people and every work of their hands and what they offer at the

Signet Rings

Haggai promised Zerubbabel that the Lord would make him "like a signet ring," for the Lord had chosen him (2:23). The Hebrew word *hotam* can refer to any form of a seal—a ring, a stamp, or a cylinder stamp that could be pressed into clay or wax to authorize or validate a document. The promise here implies that just as a king might impress a document with his seal as a sign of royal authority, Zerubbabel was to bear God's authority and validation.

temple, announces the prophet: "I struck you and all the products of your toil with blight and mildew and hail; yet you did not return to me, says the LORD" (2:17). And then the prophet announces, "From this day on I will bless you" (2:19).

Fourth message (Hag. 2:20–23). The fourth and final message from the prophet, delivered the same day as the third message, is given to Zerubbabel. This word is a message of salvation announcing a coming ideal, messianic age. In it, the Lord says through Haggai, "I am about to destroy the strength of the kingdoms of the nations. . . . On that day, says the LORD of hosts, I will take you, O Zerubbabel my servant, son of Shealtiel, says the LORD, and make you like a signet ring; for I have chosen you, says the LORD of hosts" (2:22–23).

Haggai's Use of Biblical Tradition

By the time the exile ended in 539 BCE, significant portions of the Old Testament had been completed. Most scholars believe that the entire Pentateuch and Deuteronomistic History were finished (Genesis–2 Kings, with the exception of Ruth). In addition, many of the pre-exilic prophetic books would have been finished, such as Amos, Hosea, Micah, Habakkuk, Nahum, and Zephaniah, and major portions of Isaiah and Jeremiah would have been as well. It seems that Haggai was familiar with at least parts of these books and that he consciously drew on their rhetoric and theology to give life to his prophetic messages.

In his first message, Haggai asks, "Is it a time for you yourselves to live in your paneled houses, while this house lies in ruins?" (1:4). This seems to play consciously on the important passage in 2 Samuel 7, in which David wants to build a temple (house) for the Lord, but instead the Lord promises to build a dynasty (house) for David. The passage describes David's situation and state of mind: "Now when the king was settled in his house, and the LORD had given him rest from all his enemies around him, the king said to the prophet Nathan, 'See now, I am living in a house of cedar, but the ark of God stays in a tent'" (2 Sam. 7:1–2). Haggai appears to play on this passage and reverse (or advance) the logic. He admonishes Zerubbabel and Joshua for living in "paneled houses" while the house of the Lord lay incomplete. In 1 Kings, the first temple is described as having been "paneled" ("covered," see 6:9; 7:3, 7). The prophet is comparing Zerubbabel—a scion of the Davidic line—to his ancestor David, and it seems that he draws on the scriptural tradition to suggest that Zerubbabel is not living up to his messianic heritage.

In a similar vein, the prophet exhorts Zerubbabel and Joshua in his second message to "take courage . . . ; take courage, all you people of the land, says the LORD; work, for I am with you, says the LORD of hosts, according to the promise that I made you when you came out of Egypt. My spirit abides among you; do not fear" (2:4–5). Especially worth noting is the language "take courage," "I am with you," and "do not fear." Haggai appears to borrow language from the high priest Joshua's namesake and ancestor, Joshua son of Nun. After Moses had died and the people prepared to enter the promised land, the Lord tells Joshua, "I will be with you," and he commands him to be "strong and courageous." He exhorts him, "Do not be frightened" (Josh. 1:5–9). Haggai calls the high priest Joshua to show courage, fearlessness, and obedience to the Lord, drawing on the scriptural tradition to suggest that Joshua was not living up to his spiritual heritage.

Theological Interpretation

The Temple and the Lord's Sovereignty over Creation

The prophet Haggai believes and proclaims that the Lord is sovereign over creation. The Lord can cause the heavens to dry up, blights and droughts to commence, and plagues to ensue. Moreover, the prophet believes that the temple in Jerusalem is the epicenter of God's presence in the world and the place where the heavenly and earthly realms most intimately draw near to each other. Thus, he believes that restoring the temple to its former glory so that worship and offerings might be performed there would please the Lord, and then he would open the heavens to rain water down on the earth, blessing creation so that harvests would be plentiful.

Haggai's Prosperity Theology

Haggai believes that the droughts and plagues suffered by the land in the years following the remnant's return are the result of the temple remaining in shambles. The remedy, therefore, is to rebuild the temple, which would restore prosperity. When the leaders of the people do so, Haggai proclaims that God is pleased and prosperity will ensue. Some leaders in Judah might have questioned spending wealth to rebuild the temple when the land was impoverished. Haggai responds that not rebuilding the temple is why the land is impoverished. When the leaders invest in the temple, Haggai declares the Lord's words: "I will give prosperity" (2:9), and "I will bless you" (2:19).

Haggai's Messianic Theology

The prophet Haggai proclaims a kind of messianic theology. One of the tenets of Judah's royal theology was that the Lord had chosen David as his "son" and the king of his people. In 2 Samuel 7, which Haggai seems to have known, the Lord promises David that one of his descendants will forever be king over his people. When Jerusalem fell, the line of kings ended, but King Jehoiachin

---

Box 39.4

The American Prosperity-Gospel Movement

As the church historian Kate Bowler has chronicled in her book *Blessed: A History of the American Prosperity Gospel*,* a strong strain of prosperity theology reigns in certain sectors of American Christianity (this theology has been most popular in the ministry of Joel Osteen). If American prosperity-gospel theologians were to select one book in the Bible that best supports its theological claims, the book of Haggai might well be their choice.

* Kate Bowler, *Blessed: A History of the American Prosperity Gospel* (Oxford: Oxford University Press, 2018).

remains alive as the book of 2 Kings ends, and therefore hope in God's promise remains alive. God's people kept faith in the Lord's promise to David. In Haggai's version of that faith, he believes that Zerubbabel will be the one to restore Davidic rule of the people. Thus, the book of Haggai ends with a vision of an ideal future in which the nations will be overthrown and the Lord will make Zerubbabel "like a signet ring" (2:23). In the ancient world, the bearer of a ruler's ring carried the ruler's authority, so Haggai is promising that Zerubbabel would reign with the Lord's authority and blessing.

Fig. 39.2. A signet ring.

Historical Interpretation

As noted earlier, there is little reason to doubt the integrity or composition of the book of Haggai. The four messages in the book, along with the precise date formulas and the description of the people's responses to the prophet's preaching, help historians reconstruct the history of Judah in the last twenty years of the sixth century BCE. In particular, the book helps historians understand when and why rebuilding efforts on the temple recommenced. Haggai also sheds light on how the people were governed by Zerubbabel and Joshua, and he provides a perspective on the theology of the temple in the early postexilic period.

FOR FURTHER READING: **Haggai**

Achtemeier, Elizabeth. *Nahum–Malachi*. Interpretation: A Bible Commentary for Teaching and Preaching. Atlanta: John Knox, 1986.

Collins, John. *Joel, Obadiah, Haggai, Zechariah, Malachi*. New Collegeville Bible Commentary. Collegeville, MN: Liturgical Press, 2013.

Jacobs, Mignon R. *The Books of Haggai and Malachi*. New International Commentary on the Old Testament. Grand Rapids: Eerdmans, 2017.

O'Brien, Julia M. "Haggai." In *Women's Bible Commentary*, 3rd ed., edited by Carol A. Newsom, Sharon H. Ringe, and Jacqueline E. Lapsley, 343–45. Louisville: Westminster John Knox, 2012.

Petersen, David L. *Haggai and Zechariah 1–8: A Commentary*. Old Testament Library. Philadelphia: Westminster, 1986.

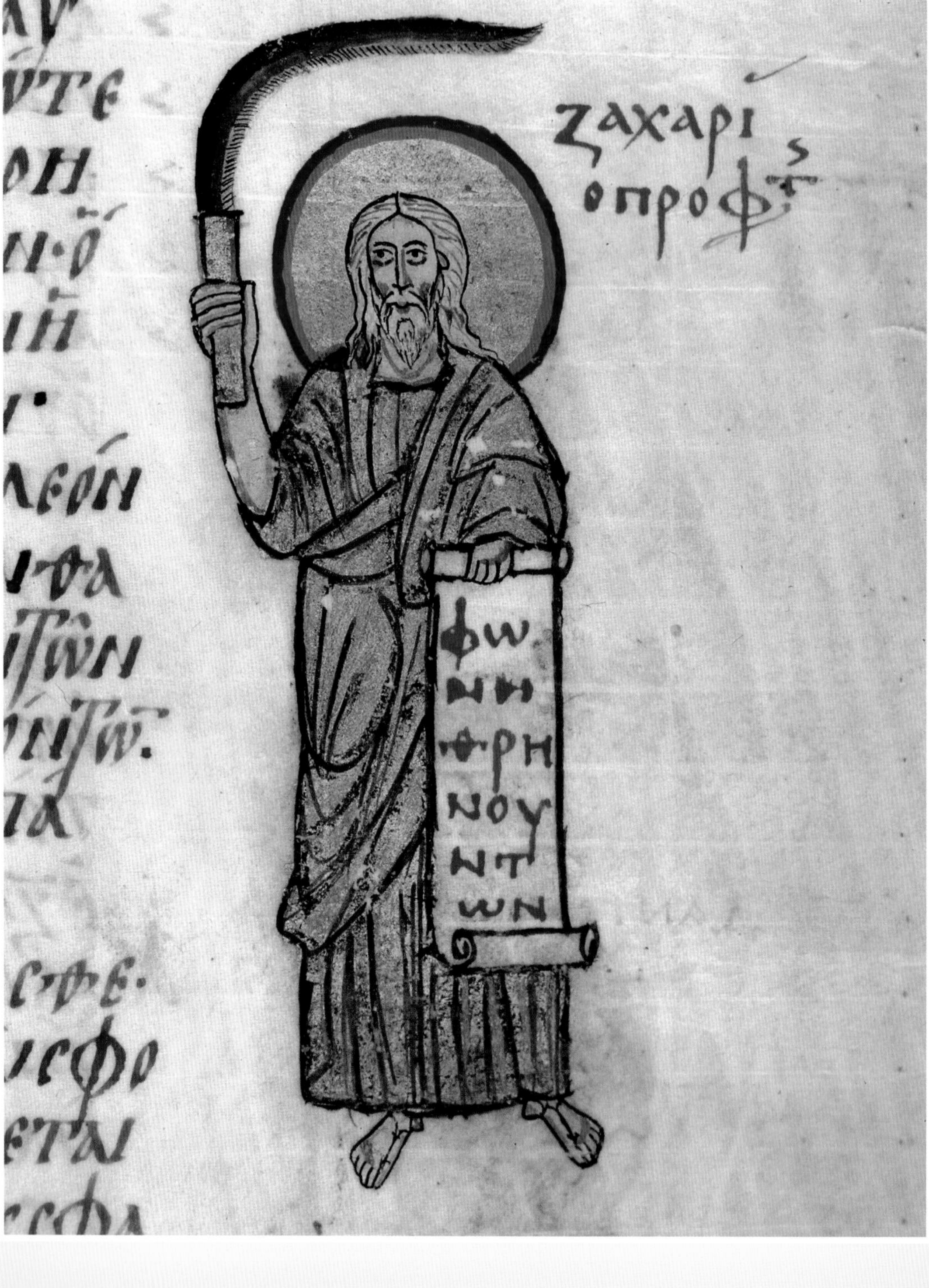
ζαχαρι
οπροφ

Zechariah

The prophets Haggai and Zechariah were contemporaries, living and prophesying in the late sixth century BCE. Like Haggai, the book of Zechariah is set in the Persian province of Yehud/Judah when many Jews had returned to their homeland to reestablish their lives there and rebuild their temple. Zechariah was relatively young when he received the visions in the first eight chapters, and it's possible he continued his ministry long after Haggai had ceased to prophesy.

Background

The Prophet Zechariah

Zechariah, whose name means "Yahweh has remembered," was among the Judeans who were born in exile and returned to the land after the edict of Cyrus gave exiles permission to return home. He came from a priestly family and is identified as "Zechariah son of Berechiah son of Iddo." Iddo is named in Nehemiah 12:4 among the Levites who returned with Zerubbabel in 538 BCE. Nehemiah 12:16 says that Zechariah succeeded his grandfather Iddo as head of the branch of the Levitical tribe, and this suggests that his father, Berechiah, either died young or remained in Babylon. Zechariah is a common name in the Old Testament and, unlike the names of Haggai or Malachi, its meaning most likely does not play a role in the meaning or interpretation of the book. In art, Zechariah is often portrayed as a beardless young man, because he is described as a "young lad" (2:4 AT) when he received his first set of visions (see the image at the beginning of this chapter). He lived and prophesied in Jerusalem.

Historical Context

The opening verse of Zechariah identifies the prophet's first vision as coming in "the eighth month of the second year of Darius" (AT), which was in October or November 520 BCE, two months after Haggai's initial vision. Thus, the historical context of Zechariah is the same as that of Haggai: postexilic Jerusalem and Judah/Yehud, where Zerubbabel served as governor.

Zerubbabel was in the line of King David and, most likely, the next in line to become king. However, under the political conditions of the Persian Empire, Judah/Yehud was not an independent kingdom with its own king but rather a Persian province with an imperially appointed governor. Zerubbabel was the grandson of King Jehoiachin, the last king of Judah who went into exile in 597 BCE. Although the exiles who returned to Judah in 538 BCE initially exhibited high hope, the realities of life in the land quickly tempered that hope. The conditions were difficult. In addition to the destruction caused by the Babylonian invasion, the land suffered from a combination of drought and plagues, such as locust invasion. Those who returned from exile came into conflict with those who were living in the land. The people of the land may have feared that rebuilding Jerusalem and the temple would encourage rebellion against Persia and thus more war and death. Meanwhile, the returnees regarded those who remained in the land as less-than-pure-and-faithful Jews.

According to the book of Ezra, Zerubbabel and Joshua the high priest had laid the foundation for the temple in 538 BCE (Ezra 3:8–10), but apparently the work was suspended and had not yet resumed by 520 BCE. Since Zerubbabel and Joshua apparently responded positively to the first vision of Haggai, which occurred in August of 520 BCE, and resumed construction on the temple, it may be that work on the temple had already begun by the time of Zechariah's first vision.

Composition and Development

Zechariah is fourteen chapters long. Most scholars agree that chapters 1–8 faithfully recount the prophetic visions of the prophet Zechariah. In chapters 9–14, the dominant genres switch from the apocalyptic and traditional prose messages that characterize the first eight chapters to poetic messages and a different kind of prose message. Some critical scholars argue that these differences, along with a change in style and vocabulary, suggest that someone other than Zechariah is responsible for chapters 9–14. Other critical scholars argue that consistency in themes and theology, especially the importance of Zion theology and the purity of the chosen people, supports a single author. Because Zechariah was relatively young when the visions in chapters 1–8 took place (see 2:4), and because he may have continued his ministry beyond that of his contemporary

Haggai (see 7:1), a change in style could reflect the prophet's aging and further development of his perspective.

Genre

There are two dominant genres in the first half of Zechariah: apocalyptic and traditional prophetic messages. In the apocalyptic portions, the prophet sees a vision that he does not understand, and then an angelic interpreter explains its meaning. The second half of the book is characterized by poetic messages and a different style of prose message.

Literary Interpretation

Superscription (Zech. 1:1). The superscription of Zechariah identifies the prophet and his setting. As noted earlier, Zechariah was from a priestly family, and he delivered his messages in the early years of postexilic resettlement back in Yehuh/Judah.

Prophetic introduction (Zech. 1:2–6). Zechariah's message begins with a description of Israel's past sins and failure to respond to the prophetic call to repent, which led to the exile and the ultimate repentance of the exiles. The culminating verse of this introduction states, "So [the exiles] repented and said, 'As the LORD of hosts purposed to deal with us for our ways and deeds, so has he dealt with us'" (1:6 ESV). This introduction provides a theological frame for the entire book, but its meaning is interpreted in different ways. It can be interpreted as a call for ongoing repentance. It also can be interpreted as the basis for the good news that the prophet announces in the first half of the book. Or it can be understood as a broad articulation of the justice of the Lord's ways, including the justice of having sent Israel and Judah into exile.

First set of visions and messages (Zech. 1:7–8:23). In the first eight chapters of the book, apocalyptic visions alternate with traditional prophetic messages. These visions occurred between October 520 and December 518 BCE; the temple was finished in March 516 BCE. In the first vision (1:7–17), the prophet sees a man riding a horse with three other horses behind him. The angel explains that the horses have patrolled the earth and that God has brought peace and will bring grace to Jerusalem and Judah: "I have returned to Jerusalem with compassion. . . . My cities shall again overflow with prosperity" (1:16–17).

The angel explains that the second vision (1:18–21), of four horses and horns, meant that the Lord will strike down the nations that scattered Judah. The third vision (2:1–5), of a man surveying Jerusalem, meant that Jerusalem

Fig. 40.1. In Zechariah's first vision, he sees a man riding a red horse, with a sorrel and a white horse behind him. As is typical in apocalyptic scenes, the prophet cannot understand the meaning without an angel to interpret for him. The angel says that figures have patrolled the earth and that the Lord will be gracious to Jerusalem. The unknown artist who painted this miniature mistakenly portrays Zechariah as an old man.

will again be inhabited and protected. A traditional prophetic message follows that urges the exiles to return to Jerusalem and Judah.

In a fourth vision (3:1–10), Zechariah sees the high priest Joshua dressed in filthy clothes, along with Satan. Satan is rebuked, and Joshua's filthy clothing is replaced with festal apparel. Joshua is then told, "You shall rule my house . . . , and I will give you the right of access" to God's deliberations in the heavenly court (3:7). Prior to the exile, kings had ruled the people, and only prophets had access to the heavenly court (see 1 Kings 22; Isa. 6:1–6). Thus, the vision signals the ascendance of the priests as leaders of the people in the new postexilic era. Yet Joshua is also told, "I am going to bring my servant the Branch" (3:8). "Servant" and "Branch" were names of the Davidic king, here meaning that one day the Lord would send a royal figure—namely, the Messiah.

The fifth vision (4:1–7), in which Zechariah sees a golden lampstand with two olive trees, meant that Zerubbabel would complete the rebuilding of the temple. The sixth vision (5:1–4), of a flying scroll, symbolized judgment that the Lord would send out over the earth for those who violate God's law. The seventh vision (5:5–11), of two women flying a small basket carrying a woman to the land of Shinar (i.e., Babylon), symbolized sin being banished from the land. The eighth vision (6:1–8), of four chariots, symbolized the Spirit of God extending God's reign throughout the earth. This vision forms an inclusio with the first vision, which also featured horses.

A series of traditional prophetic messages follows this cluster of visions. In the first, a crown is placed on the head of the high priest Joshua (signaling priestly

inclusio A literary device in which parallel expressions are used at the beginning and the ending of a literary unit.

leadership of the people), and it is said that a man called "the Branch" (Zerubbabel?) shall rule and rebuild the temple. More traditional messages follow, condemning hypocrisy and disobedience to the law but also announcing the restoration of Zion.

Second set of visions and messages (Zech. 9:1–14:21). The second part of the book begins with a lengthy poetic message (or series of messages) condemning Judah's neighbors (9:1–8) and announcing good news for Judah (9:9–11:3)—the Lord will bring glory and prosperity to Judah and will himself be the shepherd of the people. The message in the rest of chapter 11 is difficult to decipher, but it seems to reflect the prophet's dissatisfaction with human leadership.

The final chapters of the book (12:1–14:21) are held together by the common prophetic phrase "on that day." This phrase is often used to announce a coming redemptive act of the Lord—either in the near future or in the distant, ideal future. The sayings in this section are vivid and

Fig. 40.2. This illumination in a Hebrew Bible portrays Zechariah's vision of a golden menorah flanked by two olive trees (Zech. 4:2–3). The angel explains that the seven lamps of the menorah are the eyes of the Lord that see all the earth and the two olive trees are the anointed ones who stand by the Lord. Zerubbabel would finish building the temple. When modern Israel was reconstituted, it used the images of the menorah and the two olive branches for Israel's coat of arms.

Zechariah's Symbolism

One of the most fascinating aspects of interpreting Zechariah is how to make sense of the vivid prophetic imagery, especially in the second half of the book. In the first half, the angelic interpreter—a standard feature of the apocalyptic genre—explains the meaning of the confusing visions and images. In the second half of the book, there is no interpreting angel to explain the imagery and symbolism. The overall meaning and message of the book seem clear: the Lord will return to Jerusalem as the temple is rebuilt, and Judah/Jerusalem will be restored to its former glory. Yet the book also displays a growing frustration and even disillusionment with human leaders.

Not unlike the developments in Isaiah 55–66, in which the disappointing realities of the return to the land seem to have disillusioned the prophet, the prophet responsible for the last chapters of Zechariah is harshly critical of the people's leaders and yet also staunch in his belief that the Lord would prove faithful to Judah. For example, in 11:1–17 and 13:7–9, confusing language about "my shepherd" occurs. The prophet announces, "Strike the shepherd in order to scatter the flock! I will turn my hand against the little ones" (13:7 CEB). There is then language of two thirds of the people perishing and the remnant being refined as silver. It is difficult to know what to make of such vibrant symbolism, which occurs throughout the book, but it is fertile ground for interpreters.

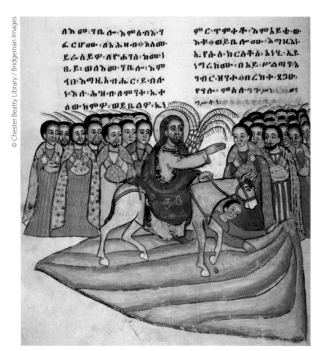

imaginative: "On that day I will make the clans of Judah like a blazing pot on a pile of wood, like a flaming torch among sheaves" (12:6). The messages announce the coming cleansing and victory of Judah and Jerusalem. They also include familiar prophetic themes, such as the condemnation of idol worship, the restoration of the Davidic kingdom, the prosperity of the land, and the ingathering of the people from the diaspora.

Fig. 40.3. In Zechariah 9:9, the prophet promises, "Your king will come to you; he is righteous and delivered, humble and riding on a donkey" (AT). The New Testament sees this promise as fulfilled when Jesus came into Jerusalem on a donkey in the triumphal entry.

Theological Interpretation

The Temple and the Blessings That Flow from True Worship

Like the prophet Haggai, Zechariah's vision of God centered on the temple and the blessings that flow from right worship of God. For Zechariah, right worship of God meant worship and sacrifice in the temple on Mount Zion in Jerusalem—the dwelling place of God on earth, from which his blessings emanate. In Zechariah's vision, the Lord returns to Zion, first purging the city and then moving into the neighborhood. Zechariah proclaims, "I have returned to Jerusalem with compassion; my house shall be built in it, says the LORD of hosts. . . . My cities shall again overflow with prosperity; the LORD will again comfort Zion and again choose Jerusalem" (1:16–17).

The Lord's Fidelity to His Promises

The notion that God had chosen Jerusalem as his dwelling place was a central tenet of Judah's royal theology. The Lord had chosen David and his line as his "sons" to be kings in Jerusalem, and the Lord had chosen Jerusalem as his dwelling place. God would be faithful to both Jerusalem and David's line; but when the people were sinful, the Lord would punish them yet never remove his steadfast love from them (see 2 Sam. 7 and Ps. 89). Zechariah preaches that the exiles deserved the punishment they had received, but the time of punishment was over, and God was returning to Jerusalem. The Lord was also remaining

Box 40.3

Philip, Nathanael, the Fig Tree, and the Messiah

In the Gospel of John, Jesus calls Philip to follow him. Philip then tells Nathanael, "We have found him about whom Moses in the Torah and also the Prophets wrote, Jesus son of Joseph from Nazareth" (John 1:45, modified).

Nathanael scoffs, "Can anything good come out of Nazareth?" (1:46). Why did he scoff? Because Nazareth did not fit expectations of the Messiah according to Nathanael's reading of the Torah and the Prophets.

Jesus then announces, "I saw you under the fig tree before Philip called you." And Nathanael answers, "You are the Son of God! You are the King of Israel!"—that is, the Messiah (1:48–49).

The question is, Why would Nathanael conclude that Jesus was the Messiah because he had seen Nathanael under a fig tree? Jesus is playing a biblical game with Nathanael here. Can Nathanael catch the allusion to Zechariah?

In Zechariah 3:8–10 (ESV), the prophet, speaking for God, had promised, "I will bring my servant the Branch"—Branch being a term for the Messiah, the ideal Davidic descendant and king to come. This is the promise: God would send the messianic Branch. What was the sign that the Branch had arrived? The Branch (Jesus) would call a follower (Philip), who would then in turn "invite his neighbor . . . under his fig tree" (v. 10). Nathanael—who apparently knew his Bible well!—followed Jesus's wordplay and recognized him as the Branch.* Therefore, he addresses Jesus with the messianic titles "Son of God" and "King of Israel."

* See Craig R. Koester, "Messianic Exegesis and the Call of Nathanael (John 1:45–51)," *Journal for the Study of the New Testament* 39 (June 1990): 23–34.

faithful to the Davidic line and would be faithful to "the Branch" (a messianic term for the ideal Davidic king to come), who was later simply called Messiah.

A Holy People, with a Holy Book, Led by a Holy Priesthood

Following the exile, there was a significant change for the people of Judah. Except for a brief period in the second and first centuries BCE, the people of Judah would never again be an independent nation with their own king. Rather than a kingdom, they would be a province in the empire of Persia (and later Greece and Rome). Rather than being the people of a holy nation within geographical boundaries, they would be a holy people, dispersed across the world. Rather than being led by kings and prophets, they would be led by priests. The Lord said to Joshua the high priest, "If you will walk in obedience to me and keep my requirements, then you will govern my house and have charge of my courts, and I will give you a place among these standing here [in the heavenly court]" (3:6–7 NIV). They would still have a governor appointed by Persia, but as a people, they would become Second Temple Jews, primarily led by a religious priesthood. They would also become the people of a holy book—what was later called the Bible.

Fig. 40.4. The book of Zechariah has the distinction of referring to angels more than any other biblical book (twenty times in fourteen chapters). The book presents a series of visions interpreted by "an angel of the Lord." Angels, of course, have been envisioned as taking many different forms. This painting shows an Old Testament angel as imagined by an Iraqi artist.

Historical Interpretation

The theological developments discussed above were not simply of religious importance, but also of political and historical importance. If the people of the province of Judah had continued to rebel against their imperial overlords and try to establish their own kingdom, their survival as a people would have been nearly impossible. So there was both political wisdom and theological rationale behind their becoming a holy people led by holy priests. This decision helped foster the survival of the people. (In fact, when their descendents later rebelled against Rome around 70 CE and again around 132 CE, the Roman legions came down hard and the survival of Jews in the Holy Land was greatly imperiled.) Some Christian interpreters in the nineteenth and twentieth centuries viewed this religious development negatively. Interpreters in an influential strain of European Protestant theology saw historical developments through a lens that feared "works righteousness" and so incorrectly considered the development of Jewish law in this way. But this interpretation misses that these changes were a way to survive in the era of warring empires, to become a holy people rather than a holy nation.

FOR FURTHER READING: **Zechariah**

Achtemeier, Elizabeth. *Nahum–Malachi*. Interpretation: A Bible Commentary for Teaching and Preaching. Atlanta: John Knox, 1986.

Boda, Mark J. *The Book of Zechariah*. New International Commentary on the Old Testament. Grand Rapids: Eerdmans, 2016.

Collins, John. *Joel, Obadiah, Haggai, Zechariah, Malachi*. New Collegeville Bible Commentary. Collegeville, MN: Liturgical Press, 2013.

O'Brien, Julia M. "Zechariah." In *Women's Bible Commentary*, 3rd ed., edited by Carol A. Newsom, Sharon H. Ringe, and Jacqueline E. Lapsley, 346–49. Louisville: Westminster John Knox, 2012.

Petersen, David L. *Haggai and Zechariah 1–8: A Commentary*. Old Testament Library. Philadelphia: Westminster, 1984.

———. *Zechariah 9–14 and Malachi: A Commentary*. Old Testament Library. Louisville: Westminster John Knox, 1995.

Malachi

In the Protestant and Roman Catholic versions of the Bible, Malachi is the last book of the Old Testament. (In the Jewish order, the last book is 2 Chronicles; in the Orthodox versions, the last book is Daniel—see chap. 2, "The Old Testament Writings."[1] This placement is fitting, because of both Malachi's message and also its history. The book was written sometime after the temple was rebuilt and rededicated in 516/515 BCE, and Malachi was concerned with a lack of piety in worship practices in the temple. This similarity of theme with those of Haggai, Zechariah, and Ezra-Nehemiah, along with some late linguistic features in the book, makes it likely that Malachi was written between 450 and 430 BCE.

Background

The Prophet Malachi

The name Malachi means "my messenger," and like the prophet Haggai, who may have taken his name ("my festival") as a part of his prophetic witness, the prophet Malachi may have taken his name to accentuate his identity as a prophetic messenger sent by the Lord. In support of this view, the books of Haggai and Malachi—in contrast with almost all other prophetic books—do not list the parental lineage of either prophet. The prophets are simply called Haggai and Malachi. On the other hand, the name of the book might also come from Malachi 3:1, which says, "See, I am sending my messenger [Hebrew *mal'aki*] to prepare the way before me."

Historical Context

The introductory verses of Malachi do not offer a date or place in which to locate the prophet and his work. However, all the book's messages assume the context of Jerusalem and, as noted above, that the temple had been rebuilt. The prophets Haggai and Zechariah had urged Zerubbabel and Joshua to finish rebuilding the temple, which was completed in 516 BCE. Around 458 BCE, the priest Ezra and a large contingent returned from exile, strengthening the postexilic community but creating some controversy and conflict with the "people of the land." These were people who had been resettled into the promised land by the Assyrians or were Israelites who had intermarried with them. The "people of the land" worshiped the Lord, but the "purist" returnees considered them religiously compromised because "they worshiped the LORD but also served their own gods, after the manner of the nations" (2 Kings 17:33).

This religious conflict included the issues of intermarriage with the people of the land and also whether they could participate in temple worship. Around 444 BCE, Nehemiah had left his post as cupbearer of the Persian king to return to Judah/Yehud, where he served as governor of the province. Nehemiah rebuilt the walls of Jerusalem (Neh. 4:16; 6:15), instituted land reform to grant property to returnees (5:2–13), banned intermarriage with foreign women (10:30), and enforced the Sabbath and temple offerings (10:31–39). The land itself was also a source of hardship, having experienced droughts and famine during these years, along with crop failures, lack of rain, and plagues such as locust invasions (see Haggai and Joel). This was the context in which the prophet Malachi preached.

Composition and Development

Malachi is a short book, only four chapters long with only six verses in the last chapter. Although some scholars question the book's authorship, there is not sufficient reason to doubt that a prophet named Malachi was responsible for the prophetic messages the book contains. The last chapter includes short passages that may have been added sometime after the book had originally been finished. If so, it is not possible to know if these verses represent messages from the prophet Malachi or date to a later time.

Genre

The book of Malachi contains traditional prophetic messages of salvation and judgment. The book opens, for example, with a message of salvation in which the prophet announces to the Israelites on behalf of the Lord, "I have loved you" (1:2). But in the same message, the prophet announces regarding the people of Edom, "Esau I have hated" (1:3 AT). The ensuing messages call the Israelites to faithfulness and justice and offer promises about God's future actions.

Literary Interpretation

The message of Malachi is an answer to the question, Why does the Lord not accept our offerings and bless us? The ultimate answer given is this: God will accept your offerings and bless you when you purify yourselves. The book proceeds through a series of questions and answers, as the prophet addresses a variety of issues plaguing the people.

Superscription (Mal. 1:1). As noted above, the introduction to the book of Malachi includes only the prophet's name. No genealogical or historical information is provided.

First dispute (Mal. 1:2–5). Following the identification of the prophet, the initial message sounds a keynote for the book. The very first words are "I have loved you." God's love for "Jacob" (meaning the nation of Judah) is contrasted with God's hatred of "Esau" (meaning the nation of Edom), and God promises that Judah will see Edom's humiliation. The theme of Judah's anger with Edom, which joined Babylon in destroying Jerusalem, is shared in other exilic and early postexilic books.

Second dispute (Mal. 1:6–2:9). As noted in the previous chapter, the postexilic community was led by priests. The people became a holy people of a holy book led by religious leaders, rather than a political nation led by kings. Malachi, however, condemns the priests for sacrificing impure offerings and for violating "[God's] covenant with Levi" (the original priest, 2:4): "You have turned aside from the way; you have caused many to stumble by your instruction; you have corrupted the covenant of Levi" (2:8). The prophet asks, "Why is the Lord not accepting your offerings?" Then he answers, "Because the offerings are impure and the priests who offer them are impure and fail to teach others faithfully."

Third dispute (Mal. 2:10–16). The prophet asserts, "We all have one Father," and "One God created us all" (2:10 AT). But then he says, "Judah has profaned the sanctuary of the LORD . . . and has married the daughter of a foreign god" (2:11). It may be that this is a condemnation of the practice of marrying foreign women, who may bring with them the worship of foreign gods (similar to how Solomon was criticized for marrying many foreign women; 1 Kings 11:1–8). Why does the Lord not accept our offerings? Because of the worship of foreign gods.

Govert Flinck

Fig. 41.1. Malachi's announcement "I have loved Jacob, but Esau I have hated" (1:2–3 AT) is controversial. To a people who doubted God's love ("How have you loved us?"), Malachi contrasts God's regard for them (Jacob) and Esau (Edom). But people wonder, "Does God hate anyone?" Furthermore, some interpreters have wondered if the passage supports the controversial concept of double predestination—that God chooses some to be saved and others to be damned. Paul draws on this passage to assert, "Before [Jacob and Esau] were born or had done anything good or bad—in order that God's purpose in election might stand: not by works but by him who calls—[Rebecca] was told, 'The older will serve the younger'" (Rom. 9:11–12 NIV).

The next section is controversial. Again the prophet asks, "Why does God not accept our offerings?" Because of divorce. What follows is the strongest condemnation of divorce in the Bible:

> Because the LORD was a witness between you and the wife of your youth, to whom you have been faithless, though she is your companion and your wife by covenant. Did not one God make her? Both flesh and spirit are his. And what does the one God desire? Godly offspring. So look to yourselves, and do not let anyone be faithless to the wife of his youth. For I hate divorce, says the LORD, the God of Israel, and covering one's garment with violence, says the LORD of hosts. So take heed to yourselves and do not be faithless. (2:14–16)

Because this passage on divorce follows the passage about Judah as a whole marrying "the daughter of a foreign god" (2:11), it is often interpreted as a condemnation of the act of divorcing a Jewish wife in order to marry a foreign wife. But the passage does not actually say this. Rather, it is simply a general condemnation of any man who is unfaithful to and divorces the "wife of his youth." It is more straightforward to interpret the passage as a general condemnation of divorce, as an act of faithlessness to a covenant sworn in the Lord's presence, before his altar. As such, Malachi may actually be against Ezra and Nehemiah's decision to ban foreign intermarriage and especially their decision to drive foreign wives out of the community. While Malachi is critical of worshiping foreign gods, he is equally critical of all divorce—including, it would seem, the casting out of foreign wives. As such, it may be that Malachi may have been joining the anonymous prophet known as Third Isaiah (Isa. 56:1–8) in welcoming foreigners who have joined themselves to the Lord.

Fourth dispute (Mal. 2:17–3:5). The next brief passage again asks, "How have we wearied him?" By doing evil and injustice in the sight of God (2:17). Altogether, chapters 1–2 offer several answers to the question, Why is God not accepting our offerings?—because the offerings are impure, because the priests are impure, because the people worship foreign gods alongside the Lord, because men unjustly divorce the wives of their youth. In sum, because of idolatry, impurity, and injustice.

So what will God do about such an impure people? Answer: God will first send "my messenger" to purify the people:

> I am sending my messenger to prepare the way before me, and the Lord whom you seek will suddenly come to his temple. The messenger of the covenant . . . is like a refiner's fire and like fullers' soap; he will sit as a refiner and purifier of silver, and he will purify the descendants of Levi and refine them like gold and silver, until they present offerings to the Lord in righteousness. Then the offering of Judah and Jerusalem will be pleasing to the Lord as in the days of old and as in former years. (3:1–4)

When the Lord comes, the prophet continues, he will "bear witness against the sorcerers, against the adulterers, against those who swear falsely, against those who oppress the hired workers in their wages, the widow and the orphan, against those who thrust aside the alien, and do not fear me" (3:5). It is striking to note, again, that there is no condemnation of foreigners or those who marry foreign wives, only of those who commit the above sins—notice especially the concern for the poor and the oppressed: "those who oppress the hired workers in their wages, the widow and the orphan, against those who thrust aside the alien."

Fifth dispute (Mal. 3:6–12). In the next passage, the prophet exhorts the people to "bring the full tithe" to the storehouse and promises that then God will "open the windows of heaven for you and pour down for you an overflowing

God, God's People, and Divorce

The translation of Malachi 2:16 is controversial. The traditional translation is "I hate divorce, says the LORD" (so NRSV). Other versions translate the verse, "The man who hates and divorces his wife . . . does violence to the one he should protect" (so NIV). But both agree that the next phrase warns something like, "Take care in your spirit! Do not be unfaithful!" Either way, the verse is difficult for people who have experienced divorce—whether one's own, one's parents, or that of other loved ones. It is clear from other passages in Scripture (see Matt. 5:27–32) that divorce was allowed in certain cases, but it was seen as a sign of the brokenness of the world.

Research has shown that divorce is devasting for children. The theologian Andrew Root, himself a child of divorce, writes, "Divorce does the impossible to young people; it divides a child's *Dasein* [the act of wrestling with one's being]." He describes this as the "*Back To the Future* effect, feeling like, in the chasm that now separates your parents, your being is slipping from you."* The problem with divorce is that it creates injustice—especially for children, but also for women and men. In some occasions, it is necessary, and as with all experiences of sin, there is forgiveness and reconciliation.

* Andrew Root, "Young People, Divorce, and Youth Ministry: Leveraging Ecclesial Community to Create Ontological Security," *Immerse*, accessed April 14, 2022, http://andrewroot.org/wp-content/uploads/2012/04/Young-People-Divorce-And-Youth-Ministry.pdf. See also his *The Children of Divorce: The Loss of Family as the Loss of Being*, Youth, Family, and Culture (Grand Rapids: Baker Academic, 2010).

blessing. I will rebuke the locust for you, so that it will not destroy the produce of your soil; and your vine in the field shall not be barren" (3:10–11). (See the sidebar "The American Prosperity-Gospel Movement" in chap. 39, "Haggai.") The chapter ends by reasserting the value of serving the Lord and the reward promised for the faithful.

Sixth dispute (Mal. 3:13–4:3). In the sixth dispute, God takes notice of the faithful, those who fear the Lord. The arrogant and evildoers will be caught in a judgment that burns like an oven.

Conclusion (Mal. 4:4–6). The previous section ends by promising that "the day is coming" when the wicked shall be judged, but "for you who revere my name the sun of righteousness will rise, with healing in its wings" (4:1–2). The book then concludes with references to Moses and Elijah: "Remember the teaching of my servant Moses, the statutes and ordinances that I commanded him at Horeb for all Israel. Lo, I will send you the prophet Elijah before the great and terrible day of the LORD comes. He will turn the hearts of parents to their children and the hearts of children to their parents, so that I will not come and strike the land with a curse" (4:4–6).

Theological Interpretation

Why, O Lord?

Like so many people through history, the people of Jerusalem during Malachi's ministry wondered, Why does the Lord not bless us with rain and bountiful crops? Why does the Lord allow blight and invasions of locust? Some people gave up on the Lord, simply abandoning piety: "You have said, 'It is vain to serve God'" (3:14). Others acted wickedly, believing that God would not punish them (2:17; 3:13–15).

The prophet answers such questions with the traditional answer of Old Testament theology: Wait. Trust in the Lord. He will prove faithful. But Malachi also offers an answer that may seem theologically simplistic to some: The Lord is refusing to receive our offerings and bless us because the priests offer impure offerings (1:6–14), the priests are impure (2:1–9), the people worship foreign gods and cheat on their tithes (2:10–12; 3:8–12), and the men divorce the wives of their youth (2:13–16). Stop doing those things, Malachi says, and the Lord will grant prosperity.

Fig. 41.2. In Jewish tradition, at the Passover Seder meal, a place is set and a chair is left for Elijah, who ascended into heaven in a fiery chariot and who will come again "before the great and terrible day of the Lᴏʀᴅ" (Mal. 4:5). Later a prayer is said, such as the following: "May the merciful One send us Elijah the prophet, of blessed memory, and may he bring us good tidings of salvation and consolation."

The Coming Messenger

The most interesting question of Malachi revolves around the promised messenger. This messenger can be understood in three different ways. First, the messenger may be Malachi himself, whose name means "my messenger." He brings the prophetic messages contained in the book that bears his name—messages from God to the people. If we extend this understanding, the prophet Malachi may have understood himself to be the messenger promised—the messenger who would refine and purge the people so that God can again come to them (3:1).

A second way of understanding the promised messenger is that the prophet may have been promising a different person than himself—either someone that he knew or some future figure that he did not know—who would come to refine and purge the people.

Fig. 41.3. According to New Testament tradition, John the Baptist played the role of Elijah to come "before the great and terrible day of the LORD" (Mal. 4:5; see Mark 9:9–13). In this portrayal of the transfiguration (see Mark 9:1–8), Elijah and Moses flank Jesus as he is transfigured, while Peter, James, and John react in terror.

A third understanding involves the figure of Elijah. The book ends by promising, "I will send you the prophet Elijah before the great and terrible day of the LORD comes. He will turn the hearts of parents to their children and the hearts of children to their parents, so that I will not come and strike the land with a curse" (3:5–6). Because Elijah will fulfill essentially the same task as "my messenger"—the purging of the people so that God's coming will result in blessing and not curse—the prophet (or perhaps an editor who added this verse) may have understood that Elijah was to be the messenger. Recall that, according to 2 Kings 2, Elijah did not die but was taken to heaven directly in a fiery chariot. Malachi thus ends with the theological promise that Elijah would return before the day of the Lord.

The New Testament takes up the promise of Elijah's return. The Gospel of Mark, the earliest Gospel to be written, begins by casting John the Baptist in the role of Elijah. John dresses like Elijah, wearing "a leather belt around his waist" (cf. Mark 1:6 with 2 Kings 1:8), and eats locust and honey, the food of prophets. Jesus later says, "Elijah has come, and they did to him whatever they pleased" (Mark 9:13)—seemingly a reference to Herod's murder of John the Baptist. Thus, in the Protestant and Catholic order of the biblical books, the Old Testament ends with Malachi's promise of the coming of Elijah, which is fulfilled in the messenger who prepared the way for the Lord's coming, as the New Testament opens—John the Baptist.

In rabbinic Judaism, the waiting for Elijah is symbolized at the Passover meal by pouring a cup of wine for him and opening the door for him. The cup is poured in the hope that Elijah will come and precede the coming of the Messiah.

Historical Interpretation

As noted above, Malachi shares many historical themes with Haggai, Zechariah, Third Isaiah (Isa. 56–66), and Ezra-Nehemiah (and perhaps Joel). Historians include Malachi among those books that help them reconstruct the deflating and difficult early postexilic years. One particularly interesting element in Malachi is the issue of divorce and how it relates to the decision made by the postexilic community to put foreign wives out of the community. Ezra 10 describes how Ezra coerced the men to cast foreign wives and children out of the community, but the book of Ezra notes, "Jonathan the son of Asahel and Jahzeiah the son of Tikvah opposed this, and Meshullam and Shabbethai the Levite supported them" (10:15 ESV). It may be, if the above interpretation of Malachi 2:13–16 is correct, that the prophet Malachi also opposed this action, joining Third Isaiah in welcoming those foreigners who were joined to the Lord and kept his Sabbaths.

FOR FURTHER READING: **Malachi**

Achtemeier, Elizabeth. *Nahum–Malachi*. Interpretation: A Bible Commentary for Teaching and Preaching. Atlanta: John Knox, 1986.

Collins, John. *Joel, Obadiah, Haggai, Zechariah, Malachi*. New Collegeville Bible Commentary. Collegeville, MN: Liturgical Press, 2013.

Jacobs, Mignon R. *The Books of Haggai and Malachi*. New International Commentary on the Old Testament. Grand Rapids: Eerdmans, 2017.

Myers, Carol. "Malachi." In *Women's Bible Commentary*, 3rd ed., edited by Carol A. Newsom, Sharon H. Ringe, and Jacqueline E. Lapsley, 354–61. Louisville: Westminster John Knox, 2012.

Petersen, David L. *Zechariah 9–14 and Malachi: A Commentary*. Old Testament Library. Louisville: Westminster John Knox, 1995.

Glossary

allegory A type of figurative speech in which the elements or characters that make up a story signify concepts or other entities in the real world.

anachronism Something that appears in a text from a different time (e.g., an automobile appearing in a medieval text).

ancestors Sometimes referred to as the patriarchs or matriarchs; generally includes Abraham/Sarah, Isaac/Rebekah, Jacob/Rachel/Leah.

ancient Near East Geographical area that runs east-west from Egypt to Mesopotamia and north-south from Turkey to the Arabian Peninsula.

angel A heavenly messenger.

anoint To use oil to symbolize the selection of a royal figure.

Antiochus IV Epiphanes A second-century-BCE king of the Seleucid Empire (based in Syria) who was responsible for religiously persecuting Jews living in Judea. These events influenced the latter chapters of the book of Daniel.

apocalypticism A religious worldview that combines a radical dualistic outlook (clear distinction between good and evil) with a deterministic view of history (the idea that everything is proceeding according to a divine plan).

apocalyptic literature A genre of heavily symbolic, eschatologically oriented literature that displays distinctive literary characteristics and claims to unveil the truth about the world as viewed from a dualistic and deterministic perspective.

Apocrypha Books of the Old Testament with varying degrees of scriptural status and authority among Protestant, Roman Catholic, and Orthodox Christians; many of these books were included in the Septuagint but not the Hebrew Bible. *See also* deuterocanonical writings.

Aram The ancestor of the Arameans, according to the Bible (Gen. 10:22). In some cases the term also describes a geographical location, referring to the Aramaic city-state of Damascus or locations where Arameans live.

Aramaic A Semitic language similar to Hebrew and used primarily in the Old Testament books of Daniel and Ezra-Nehemiah. It was also the native tongue for Jesus and many other Jews living in Palestine during the New Testament period.

archaeology The study of human history and prehistory through the excavation of sites and analysis of artifacts, material culture, and other physical remains.

Assyria A northern Mesopotamian empire that had a significant impact on the Northern and Southern Kingdoms of Israel and Judah, especially during the eighth and seventh centuries BCE. *See also* Neo-Assyrian Empire.

atonement In the context of Levitical law, atonement is most prominently associated with the Day of Atonement, a day of purification and confession when the people are cleansed before Yahweh.

baal/Baal A Hebrew word meaning "master" or "lord" and also used for a Canaanite deity encountered in the Old Testament.

Babylon A southern Mesopotamian power responsible for the destruction of Jerusalem and the deportation of Jews to Mesopotamia. *See also* Neo-Babylonian Empire.

BCE An abbreviation for "before the common era"; in academic studies, BCE is typically used for dates in place of BC ("before Christ").

Canaanite A term used to describe the inhabitants of the Holy Land prior to Israel's emergence there.

canon Literally, "rule" or "standard"; refers to an authoritative list of books officially accepted as Scripture.

casting lots A divination practice akin to "drawing straws" and used to select a person for a given task; lots were marked stones similar to dice (see Jon. 1:7; Acts 1:26).

CE An abbreviation for "common era"; in academic studies, CE is typically used for dates in place of AD (*anno Domini*, "in the year of the Lord").

Chaldean An alternative term for "Babylonian."

circumcision A surgical procedure to remove the foreskin of a penis; in the Jewish tradition, the rite is a sign of the covenant God made with Israel.

compositional history A description of how a text came to be in its present form.

covenant In the Bible, an agreement or pact between God and human beings that establishes the terms of their ongoing relationship.

creed A confessional statement summarizing key articles of faith.

cult Every aspect of a given group's worship life, including its practices, sacred spaces, personnel, implements, etc.

Cyrus the Great Persian emperor who conquered the ancient Near East and permitted exiled Jews to return to their land and rebuild their temple.

Dead Sea Scrolls A collection of Jewish documents copied and preserved between 250 BCE and 70 CE. *See also* Essenes; Qumran.

Decalogue A synonym for the Ten Commandments.

demon An evil (or "unclean") spirit capable of possessing people and incapacitating them with some form of illness or disability.

deuterocanonical writings A term used primarily by Roman Catholics for eleven of the fifteen books that Protestants call the Apocrypha; the books are regarded as a "secondary canon," part of Scripture but distinct from both Old and New Testament writings. *See also* Apocrypha.

Deuteronomistic History / Deuteronomic History An academic term for the narrative unit from Deuteronomy through Kings.

diaspora Jews living in exile outside the Holy Land; also called the dispersion.

divided kingdom A reference to the Northern and Southern Kingdoms, which split shortly after Solomon's death. *See also* united kingdom.

divination Any practice used to discern the will of divine beings and/or to predict the future.

doctrine A belief or set of recognized beliefs held and taught by a religious group.

Documentary Hypothesis A theory that explains the composition of the Pentateuch by proposing that its final form is compiled from at least four different sources, commonly referred to as the J, E, D, and P sources.

doublet In literature, a pair or duplication of references.

doxology A hymn or group of words that expresses praise to God.

Egypt An ancient imperial power in northeast Africa, organized around the Nile River.

election In theology, the notion or doctrine that people may be chosen by God for salvation or some predetermined destiny.

eschatology The study or focus on "last things," such as the restoration of Jerusalem, the return of Christ, final judgment, or other phenomena associated with the end times.

Essenes Ascetic, separatist Jews who lived in private communities; they probably are to be identified with the group that lived at Qumran and preserved a library of manuscripts now known as the Dead Sea Scrolls. *See also* Dead Sea Scrolls; Qumran.

eunuch A castrated male who typically served in royal courts.

exegesis The scholarly study of the Bible with an emphasis on the explication of texts using various academic approaches (called exegetical methods).

exile Shorthand for the sixth-century-BCE period in which many Jews were forcibly deported from the Holy Land and relocated to Mesopotamia, most notably Babylon.

exiles In Israelite history, the Jews who were deported to Mesopotamia after Jerusalem was conquered by the Babylonians.

Exodus The second book of the Pentateuch. It describes the liberation of the Israelites from the oppressive rule of Pharaoh and the subsequent giving of the law at Sinai.

expiation A ritual that cleanses or removes defilement.

faith A strong belief in God or religious doctrines; often an orientation of complete trust and confidence in God that transforms one's life and being.

feminist criticism An academic approach that analyzes texts from a feminist perspective.

fertility A condition that results in abundance in agriculture, sustenance, and descendants.

firstfruits An agricultural term for crops collected at the beginning of the harvest season; Jesus is called the "firstfruits of the resurrection" because his resurrection is thought to precede and anticipate the general resurrection of all.

form criticism An academic approach that classifies literary materials by type or genre and identifies the purposes for which such materials were intended.

genre A type or form of literature (e.g., poetry, letter, narrative).

Hanukkah An eight-day Jewish festival commemorating the rededication of the temple in 164 BCE after it had been defiled by Antiochus IV Epiphanes; also called the Feast of Dedication and the Feast of Lights.

Hasmonean The family name of the Jewish rebels who led a successful revolt against the Syrians in 167 BCE. *See also* Maccabees; Seleucids.

Hellenistic Affected by Hellenism, that is, the influence of Greek and Roman culture, customs, philosophy, and modes of thought. For example, Jewish people were said to be "hellenized" when they adopted Greco-Roman customs or came to believe propositions derived from Greek philosophy.

henotheism A belief in multiple gods but with the added belief that one god rules over the others. *See also* monolatry; monotheism; polytheism.

hermeneutical Relating to hermeneutics, the philosophical reflection on the process of biblical interpretation, including consideration of what the goal of interpretation should be, different ways in which passages might be regarded as meaningful, and ways in which authority is ascribed to biblical texts.

historical criticism An academic approach that deals with matters pertinent to the historical composition of a writing (author, date, and place of writing, intended audience, etc.); increasingly the term is used more precisely to refer to investigations concerning what can be verified as authentic historical data in accord with accepted criteria of such analysis.

historiography "The writing of history"; a written work that offers a particular representation of historical events.

Holy Land A term used to describe the land promised to Abraham, Sarah, and their descendants.

honor The positive status that one has in the eyes of those whom one considers to be significant. *See also* shame.

Horeb, Mount An alternative name for Mount Sinai where Moses received the law of God on behalf of the Israelites.

idolatry The forbidden practice of worshiping images of deities fashioned by human hands.

Immanuel A Hebrew name meaning "God with us," first used in Isaiah 7:14 and later applied to Jesus in Matthew 1:23; sometimes spelled *Emmanuel* in the New Testament.

inclusio A literary device in which parallel expressions are used at the beginning and the ending of a literary unit.

Iron Age The period of human culture from 1200 BCE to 586 BCE; the period in which Israel developed from a loose confederation of tribes into a kingdom.

Israel (1) The entire people descended from Abraham and Sarah; (2) the Northern Kingdom centered in Samaria; (3) a symbolic name given to Jacob, the patriarch.

Jordan River A major river system in Israel running north-south and connecting the Sea of Galilee and the Dead Sea.

Judah The Southern Kingdom centered in Jerusalem.

Judaism A general term for the religious systems and beliefs of the Jewish people. In Jesus's day, there were varieties of Judaism, though all shared certain fundamental ideas and practices.

judges The translation of a Hebrew term more properly translated "deliverers" or "saviors."

kingdom of God / kingdom of heaven Phrases that describe the phenomenon of God ruling, wherever and whenever that might be; sometimes the phrases refer to a more precise manifestation of God's reign (e.g., in heaven or at the end of time).

law, the The law of Moses or any regulations the Jewish people understood as delineating faithfulness to God in terms of the covenant he had made with Israel; often used synonymously with Torah.

Lord of Hosts A title given to Yahweh, describing his command over heavenly armies.

lots *See* casting lots.

Maccabees Literally, "hammers"; the nickname given to Jewish rebels who led a successful revolt against the Syrians in 167 BCE. *See also* Hasmonean.

manuscript In biblical studies, an ancient handwritten document containing a book or portion of the Bible.

messiah A word meaning "anointed one"; it designated a promised and expected deliverer of the Jewish people; when capitalized, it refers to Jesus.

Mishnah A collection of rabbinic discussions about the interpretation of the law of Moses; the Mishnah forms one major part of the Jewish Talmud. *See also* Talmud.

monolatry The worship of a single god without denying the existence of others. *See also* henotheism; monotheism; polytheism.

monotheism The belief that there is only one God. *See also* henotheism; monolatry; polytheism.

mystery In the biblical world, something hidden that can be known only if and when it is revealed by God. *See also* revelation.

Neo-Assyrian Empire An empire based in northern Mesopotamia that ruled much of the ancient Near East from the middle of the eighth century BCE until approximately 609 BCE. *See also* Assyria.

Neo-Babylonian Empire An empire based in southern Mesopotamia that ruled much of the ancient Near East from 612 to 539 BCE. *See also* Babylon.

Northern Kingdom The ten tribes that broke away from Judah after Solomon's reign. It had alternative cultic sites at Dan and Bethel. *See also* Israel.

oral tradition Material passed on by word of mouth; early Christians relied on oral tradition as well as written sources when writing the Gospels.

ostraca Shards of pottery, sometimes used as small tablets for writing.

papyrus An inexpensive but brittle type of writing material made from plant fibers (plural, papyri).

parable A figurative story or saying that conveys spiritual truth through reference to mundane and earthly phenomena.

Pentateuch The first five books of the Bible, sometimes called the Torah: Genesis, Exodus, Leviticus, Numbers, Deuteronomy.

Pentecost The Greek term for the Jewish harvest festival called the Feast of Weeks, situated chronologically between Passover and the Feast of Tabernacles.

persecution A program or campaign to exterminate, drive away, or subjugate people based on their membership in a religious, ethnic, or social group.

Persia A large area east of Mesopotamia and north of the Persian Gulf; the center of the Persian Empire, which ruled large portions of the ancient Near East from 539 to 332 BCE.

Pharaoh The traditional title for the king of Egypt.

Pharisees One of the major Jewish groups active during the Second Temple period. The Pharisees were largely associated with synagogues and placed high value on faithfulness to Torah; most rabbis and many scribes were Pharisees.

phylactery A small case containing Scripture texts and worn on the forehead or left arm by pious Jews in obedience to the law (see Exod. 13:9, 16; Deut. 6:8; 11:18).

polytheism The belief that there are multiple gods. *See also* henotheism; monolatry; monotheism.

predestination The concept or doctrine that some or all events are predetermined by God or that individual and national destinies may likewise be predetermined.

priests In Second Temple Judaism, people authorized to oversee the sacrificial system in the Jerusalem temple; closely associated with the Sadducees. *See also* Sadducees.

principalities Powerful spiritual beings that exercise their influence in a dimension not perceptible to human senses.

prophet Someone claiming to bear a message from a divine source.

prophetic actions Unconventional public displays intended to reveal something that God wishes to communicate.

Protestant Reformation A religious movement of the sixteenth century that sought to reform the Roman Catholic Church and that led to the establishment of Protestant churches.

pseudonymity The practice of ancient authors attributing their own writings to other people, such as a revered teacher or prominent church leader who had influenced their thinking, using a pseudonym ("false name").

pseudonymous author An author who uses a pseudonym (fictitious name); the author of a pseudepigraphic text.

Ptolemies The Egyptian dynastic family that ruled Palestine during the years 320–198 BCE. *See also* Seleucids.

purity codes Regulations derived from the Torah that specified what was clean or unclean or holy or profane for the Jewish people, enabling them to live in the presence of a holy God and in a way that was distinct from their neighbors.

Qumran A site in Palestine near the Dead Sea where it is believed the Essenes had their monastic community; many of the Dead Sea Scrolls were found in close proximity to this settlement. *See also* Dead Sea Scrolls; Essenes.

rabbis Jewish teachers, many of whom had disciples or followers; closely associated with the Pharisees.

redemption A theological term derived from commerce (where it means "purchase" or "buy back"); associated with the concept that human salvation was costly to God, requiring the death of Jesus.

Reformation *See* Protestant Reformation.

resurrection The reanimation of dead human bodies; this teaching is generally understood to be a later theological development in Judaism and Christianity that is based on core understandings of the Old Testament God as a deity who saves from death.

revelation In theology, the disclosure (usually by God) of things that could not be known otherwise. *See also* mystery.

rhetorical criticism An academic approach that focuses on strategies employed by biblical authors to achieve particular purposes.

Sabbath A day of the week set aside for worship and for rest from normal endeavors; for Jews, the Sabbath is the last day of the week (Saturday); for most Christians, it is the first (Sunday).

sacrifice The offering of something valuable (e.g., crops from a field or an animal from one's flock) as an expression of worship.

Sadducees One of the major Jewish groups during the Second Temple period; the Sadducees were closely associated with the temple in Jerusalem and were concerned with maintaining the sacrificial system; most priests appear to have been Sadducees. *See also* priests.

Samaritans Semitic people who lived in Samaria at the time of Jesus and claimed to be the true Israel; descendants of the tribes taken into captivity by the Assyrians.

scribes Professionals skilled in teaching, copying, and interpreting texts; in Second Temple Judaism, closely associated with the Pharisees.

Scripture The sacred writings of the Bible, believed to be inspired by God and viewed as authoritative for faith and practice.

Second Temple Judaism A general term for the diverse culture, practices, and beliefs of Jewish people during the Second Temple period (515 BCE–70 CE).

Second Temple period The era in Jewish history between the dedication of the second Jerusalem temple in 515 BCE and its destruction in 70 CE.

Seleucids The Syrian dynastic family that ruled Palestine during the years 198–167 BCE. *See also* Antiochus IV Epiphanes.

Septuagint A Greek translation of the Old Testament produced during the last three centuries BCE. The Septuagint (abbreviated LXX) includes fifteen extra books that Protestants call the Apocrypha (eleven of these are classed as deuterocanonical writings by Roman Catholics). *See also* Apocrypha; deuterocanonical writings.

shame A negative status, implying disgrace and unworthiness. *See also* honor.

Shema The central affirmation of Jewish faith. Based on Deuteronomy 6:4–9; 11:13–21; Numbers 15:37–41, it was recited daily. *Shema* is the Hebrew word for "Hear!"

Sheol The underworld, or place where all the dead dwell; called Hades in the New Testament, where it sometimes appears to be synonymous with hell.

signs and wonders Spectacular acts (miracles) performed by people who access either divine or demonic supernatural power.

sin Any act, thought, word, or state of being contrary to the will of God.

social location A person's social identity in terms of factors such as age, gender, race, nationality, social class, and marital status.

source criticism An academic approach that tries to identify and sometimes reconstruct materials that the biblical authors used in composing their documents.

synagogue A congregation of Jews who gather for worship, prayer, and Bible study, or the place where they gather for these purposes.

tabernacle The portable tent-shrine that housed the ark of the covenant and was used as the central place of worship for the Israelites prior to the construction of the temple in Jerusalem.

Talmud A collection of sixty-three books that contain Jewish civil and canonical law based on interpretations of Scripture. *See also* Mishnah.

Tanak (TNK) An acronym for the Jewish Bible: Torah (Pentateuch), Nevi'im (Prophets), Ketuvim (Writings).

testament A written account of a covenant. It is in this sense that parts of the Bible are called the Old Testament and the New Testament.

theophany A revelation of God that often manifests itself in creation.

Torah The law of Moses, as contained in the Pentateuch; or, frequently, a synonym for the Pentateuch (referring, then, to the first five books of the Hebrew Bible).

Transjordan The geographic region of Israel east of the Jordan River.

united kingdom The kingdom of Israel ruled by Saul, David, and Solomon. It divided into Northern and Southern Kingdoms after Solomon's death. *See also* divided kingdom.

vision A revelatory, visual medium typically experienced by prophets and apocalyptic visionaries.

Vulgate A Latin translation of the Bible produced by Jerome in the fourth century CE; it was virtually the only Bible used in Western Christianity for over a thousand years.

wisdom literature / wisdom tradition Biblical and other ancient materials that focus on commonsense observations about life; examples include the books of Proverbs, Job, and Ecclesiastes.

womanist criticism An academic approach that focuses on the lived experiences of African American women, with a focus on experiences of oppression and the longing for liberation.

Yehud A term for the province of Judah during the Persian period.

Notes

Preface

1. Mark Allan Powell, *Introducing the New Testament: A Historical, Literary, and Theological Survey*, 2nd ed. (Grand Rapids: Baker Academic, 2018), 11.

2. Powell, *Introducing the New Testament*, 13.

Chapter 2 The Old Testament Writings

1. See Patrick D. Miller, *Deuteronomy*, Interpretation: A Bible Commentary for Teaching and Preaching (Louisville: John Knox, 1990), 5–8.

Chapter 3 The Pentateuch

1. Wellhausen had argued that the D document was written in Jerusalem around the time of King Josiah's reformation (622 BCE). But for reasons that will be explored in chapter 8, there is a strong basis for regarding D as having been written in the northern country of Israel, perhaps 100–140 years earlier.

Chapter 5 Exodus

1. Terence E. Fretheim, *Exodus*, Interpretation: A Bible Commentary for Teaching and Preaching (Louisville: John Knox, 1991), 18.

2. Our translation, following the NJPS and other versions. Others, such as the NRSV, translate: "Come, make gods for us." But in the story, Aaron only makes one calf. The passage is complicated, but it seems the singular "a god" is to be preferred. See Rolf Jacobson, "Moses, the Golden Calf, and False Images of the True God," *Word & World* 33 (Spring 2013): 130–39.

3. Fretheim, *Exodus*, 12, 13. See also his *God and World in the Old Testament: A Relational Theology of Creation* (Nashville: Abingdon, 2010).

4. Fretheim, *Exodus*, 13.

5. Fretheim, *Exodus*, 14.

6. Reinhard Feldmeier and Hermann Spieckermann, *God of the Living: A Biblical Theology*, trans. Mark E. Biddle (Waco: Baylor University Press, 2011), 18.

7. Feldmeier and Spieckermann, *God of the Living*, 25.

8. As translated by John A. Wilson in *Ancient Near Eastern Texts Relating to the Old Testament*, ed. James B. Prichard, 3rd ed. (Princeton: Princeton University Press, 1969), 378, quoted in Mark S. Smith, "Ugarit and the Ugaritians," in *The World around the Old Testament: The*

People and Places of the Ancient Near East, ed. Bill T. Arnold and Brent A. Strawn (Grand Rapids: Baker Academic, 2016), 142.

Chapter 6 Leviticus

1. Andy Crouch, "The Emergent Mystique," *Christianity Today*, November 1, 2004, https://www.christianitytoday.com/ct/2004/november/12.36.html.

2. Moshe Weinfeld, *Social Justice in Ancient Israel and in the Ancient Near East* (Minneapolis: Fortress, 1995).

Chapter 7 Numbers

1. Dennis T. Olson, *Numbers*, Interpretation: A Bible Commentary for Teaching and Preaching (Louisville: John Knox, 1996), 156.

2. Katharine Doob Sakenfeld, "In the Wilderness, Awaiting the Land: The Daughters of Zelophehad and Feminist Interpretation," *Princeton Seminary Bulletin* (1988): 180 (179–96).

3. Karl Jacobson, "Numbers," in *Fortress Commentary on the Bible: The Old Testament and Apocrypha*, ed. Gale A. Yee, Hugh R. Page Jr., and Matthew J. M. Coomber (Minneapolis: Fortress, 2014), 215–16.

Chapter 8 Deuteronomy

1. Patrick D. Miller, *Deuteronomy*, Interpretation: A Bible Commentary for Teaching and Preaching (Louisville: John Knox, 1990), 6–8.

2. Miller, *Deuteronomy*, 11–12.

3. Dennis T. Olson, *Deuteronomy and the Death of Moses: A Theological Reading*, Overtures to Biblical Theology (Minneapolis: Fortress, 1994), 126.

4. Olson, *Deuteronomy and the Death of Moses*, 126–27.

5. Ronald Clements, "The Book of Deuteronomy," in *The New Interpreter's Bible*, vol. 1 (Nashville: Abingdon, 1998), 537.

6. Miller, *Deuteronomy*, 15.

7. Terence E. Fretheim, "Law in the Service of Life: A Dynamic Understanding of Law in Deuteronomy," in *A God So Near: Essays in Old Testament Theology in Honor of Patrick D. Miller*, ed. Brent A. Strawn and Nancy R. Bowen (Winona Lake, IN: Eisenbrauns, 2003), 190.

8. See also Foster R. McCurley Jr., "The Home of Deuteronomy Revisited: A Methodological Analysis of the Northern Theory," in *A Light unto My Path: Old Testament Studies in Honor of Jacob M. Myers*, ed. Howard N. Bream, Ralph D. Heim, and Carey A. Moore, Gettysburg Theological Studies 4 (Philadelphia: Temple University Press, 1974), 295–317.

Chapter 9 The Historical Books

1. See Martin Noth, *The Deuteronomistic History*, ed. J. Barton, trans. J. Doull, 2nd ed. (Sheffield: Sheffield University Press, 1991), 1–110; trans. of *Überlieferungsgeschichtliche Studien*, 2nd ed. (Tübingen: Max Niemeyer, 1943).

2. Noth, *Deuteronomistic History*, 89.

3. Noth, *Deuteronomistic History*, 97.

4. Richard D. Nelson, *The Double Redaction of the Deuteronomistic History*, Journal for the Study of the Old Testament Supplement Series 18 (Sheffield: JSOT Press, 1981), 42.

5. Gerhard von Rad, "The Deuteronomistic Theology of History," in *Studies in Deuteronomy*, trans. David Stalker, Studies in Biblical Theology 9 (London: SCM, 1953), 74–90.

6. Robert Alter, *The Art of Biblical Narrative*, 2nd ed. (New York: Basic Books, 2011). See also Phyllis Trible, *Rhetorical Criticism: Context, Method, and the Book of Jonah* (Minneapolis: Fortress, 1994).

7. Von Rad, "Deuteronomistic Theology of History," 91.

8. Terence E. Fretheim, *First and Second Kings*, Westminster Bible Companion (Louisville: Westminster John Knox, 1999), 225.

Chapter 10 Joshua

1. Richard D. Nelson, *Joshua: A Commentary*, Old Testament Library (Louisville: Westminster John Knox, 1997), 18.
2. Nelson, *Joshua*, 18.
3. Richard D. Nelson, *The Historical Books*, Interpreting Biblical Texts (Nashville: Abingdon, 1998), 87.
4. Miriam Lichtheim and Hans-W Fischer-Elfert, *Ancient Egyptian Literature*, vol. 2, *The New Kingdom*, 2nd ed. (Berkeley: University of California Press, 2006), 77.

Chapter 13 1–2 Samuel

1. See P. Kyle McCarter, *2 Samuel: A New Translation with Introduction, Notes, and Commentary*, Anchor Bible 9 (New York: Doubleday, 1984).
2. For a survey of the various arguments in this debate, see Hallvard Hagelia, *The Dan Debate: The Tel Dan Inscription in Recent Research*, Recent Research in Biblical Studies 4 (Sheffield: Sheffield Phoenix, 2009).

Chapter 17 Esther

1. Martin Luther, "Sermon on John 21:19–24 (1522)," WA 10 I:308, translation by Mark Tranvik, *Martin Luther and the Called Life* (Minneapolis: Fortress, 2016), 33.

Chapter 18 Poetry, the Poetic Books, and Wisdom

1. John Donne, "Holy Sonnet 6," in *The Major Works*, ed. John Carey, Oxford World's Classics (Oxford: Oxford University Press, 1990), 175.
2. James L. Kugel, *The Idea of Biblical Poetry* (New Haven: Yale University Press, 1981), 15.
3. See Fred W. Dobbs-Allsopp, "Poetry, Hebrew," in *The New Interpreter's Dictionary of the Bible*, ed. Katharine Doob Sakenfeld (Nashville: Abingdon, 2009), 4:550–58.

Chapter 19 Job

1. C. L. Seow, *Job 1–21: Interpretation and Commentary*, Illuminations (Grand Rapids: Eerdmans, 2013), 45.
2. Seow, *Job 1–21*, 61.
3. Matitiahu Tsevat, "The Meaning of the Book of Job," *Hebrew Union College Annual* 37 (1966): 78.
4. Tsevat, "The Meaning of the Book of Job," 78.
5. The Hebrew text reads "You know," but a note in the Hebrew margin agrees with the ancient Greek translation, "I know."
6. William P. Brown, "Job and the 'Comforting' Chaos," in *Seeking Wisdom's Depths and Torah's Heights: Essays in Honor of Samuel E. Balentine*, ed. Barry R. Huff and Patricia Vesely (Macon, GA: Smyth & Helwys, 2020), 252.
7. Tsevat, "The Meaning of the Book of Job," 74.
8. Tsevat, "The Meaning of the Book of Job," 91.
9. Tsevat, "The Meaning of the Book of Job," 97.
10. Tsevat, "The Meaning of the Book of Job," 104.
11. See the introduction in Seow, *Job 1–21*.

Chapter 20 Psalms

1. Recent research shows, however, that the division of the Psalter into 150 psalms only reached stability with the invention of the movable-type printing press and the printing of the Second

Rabbinic Bible in 1525. Prior to that, the text of the Hebrew and Greek copies of the Psalter was stable, but the division of the text into different poems varied somewhat. William Larchin, "Is There an Authoritative Shape for the Hebrew Book of Psalms? Profiling the Manuscripts of the Hebrew Psalter," *Revue biblique* 3 (2015): 355–70.

2. Hebrews 4:7 quotes Psalm 95, which bears no superscription, but the Greek version of the psalm does.

3. *Bava Batra* 14b.

4. Psalms 94 and 100 lack the phrase "the LORD reigns," which marks the other psalms; however, some Psalms scholars include them in this collection.

Chapter 21 Proverbs

1. Ellen F. Davis, *Proverbs, Ecclesiastes, and the Song of Songs*, Westminster Bible Companion (Louisville: Westminster John Knox, 2000), 11.

2. Carol A. Newsom, "Woman and the Discourse of Patriarchal Wisdom," in *Reading Bibles, Writing Bodies: Identity and the Book*, ed. Timothy K. Beal and David M. Gunn, Biblical Limits (London: Routledge, 1997), 116–31.

3. Christine Roy Yoder, "Proverbs," in *Women's Bible Commentary*, 3rd ed., ed. Carol A. Newsom, Sharon H. Ringe, and Jacqueline E. Lapsley (Louisville: Westminster John Knox, 2012), 235.

4. For this translation, see the important works of Christine Roy Yoder: *Wisdom as a Woman of Substance: A Socioeconomic Reading of Proverbs 1–9 and 31:10–31*, Beihefte zur Zeitschrift für die alttestamentliche Wissenshaft 304 (Berlin: de Gruyter, 2001); *Proverbs*, Abingdon Old Testament Commentaries (Nashville: Abingdon, 2009).

5. Karel van der Toorn, *Scribal Culture and the Making of the Hebrew Bible* (Cambridge, MA: Harvard University Press, 2007).

Chapter 22 Ecclesiastes

1. Eunny P. Lee, *The Vitality of Enjoyment in Qohelet's Theological Rhetoric*, Beihefte zur Zeitschrift für die alttestamentliche Wissenshaft 353 (Berlin: de Gruyter, 2005), 34.

2. William P. Brown, *Ecclesiastes*, Interpretation: A Bible Commentary for Teaching and Preaching (Louisville: John Knox, 2000), 127.

3. Brown, *Ecclesiastes*, 128.

Chapter 24 Prophecy and the Prophetic Books

1. Gene M. Tucker, "The Role of the Prophets and the Role of the Church," in *Prophecy in Israel*, ed. David L. Petersen, Issues in Religion and Theology 10 (Philadelphia: Fortress, 1987), 159–74.

2. Bryan D. Bibb, *God's Servants, the Prophets* (Macon, GA: Smyth & Helwys, 2014), 1.

3. Gerhard von Rad, *Old Testament Theology*, trans. D. M. G. Stalker (New York: Harper & Row, 1965), 2:38; translation altered.

4. Abraham J. Heschel, *The Prophets*, Perennial Classics (New York: HarperCollins, 2001), 3, 4.

5. Heschel, *The Prophets*, 5.

6. Heschel, *The Prophets*, 16.

7. Heschel, *The Prophets*, 26.

8. Gerhard von Rad, *Old Testament Theology*, trans. D. M. G. Stalker (New York: Harper & Row, 1962), 1:106.

9. See Claus Westermann, *Basic Forms of Prophetic Speech*, trans. Hugh Clayton White (Louisville: Westminster John Knox, 1991); and Westermann, *Prophetic Oracles of Salvation in the Old Testament*, trans. Keith Crim (Louisville: Westminster John Knox, 1991).

Chapter 25 Isaiah

1. "Index of Quotations" and "Index of Allusions and Verbal Parallels," in *The Greek New Testament*, ed. B. Aland et al., 5th rev. ed. (Stuttgart: Deutsche Bibelgesellschaft, 2014), 859, 874–77. See Craig A. Evans, "From Gospel to Gospel: The Function of Isaiah in the New Testament," in *Writing and Reading the Scroll of Isaiah: Studies of an Interpretive Tradition*, ed. Craig C. Broyles and Craig A. Evans (Leiden: Brill, 1997), 2:651.

2. For this language, see H. G. M. Williamson, *The Book Called Isaiah: Deutero-Isaiah's Role in Composition and Redaction* (Oxford: Clarendon, 1994).

3. See Karel van der Toorn, *Scribal Culture and the Making of the Hebrew Bible* (Cambridge, MA: Harvard University Press, 2007), 173–204.

4. David L. Petersen, *The Prophetic Literature: An Introduction* (Louisville: Westminster John Knox, 2002), 63–64.

5. Here we partially follow the divisions suggested by Benjamin Sommer, especially with respect to Isaiah 1–39. See "Isaiah," in *The Jewish Study Bible* (Oxford: Oxford University Press, 2004), 780–84.

6. Michael J. Chan, "Rhetorical Reversal and Usurpation: Isaiah 10:5–34 and the Use of Neo-Assyrian Royal Idiom in the Construction of an Anti-Assyrian Theology," *Journal of Biblical Literature* 128 (2009): 717–33.

7. Martin Luther, *Lectures on Isaiah Chapters 40–66*, Luther's Works 17 (St. Louis: Concordia, 1955), 3.

8. John F. A. Sawyer, *The Fifth Gospel: Isaiah in the History of Christianity* (Cambridge: Cambridge University Press, 1996).

Chapter 27 Lamentations

1. In Orthodox Bibles, the deuterocanonical book of Baruch, attributed to Jeremiah's scribe, Baruch, is inserted between Jeremiah and Lamentations.

2. F. W. Dobbs-Allsopp, *Lamentations*, Interpretation: A Bible Commentary for Teaching and Preaching (Louisville: John Knox, 2002), 4.

3. Dobbs-Allsopp, *Lamentations*, 7. See also F. W. Dobbs-Allsopp, *Weep, O Daughter Zion: A Study of the City-Lament Genre in the Hebrew Bible* (Rome: Editrice Pontificio Istituto Biblico, 1993).

4. Dobbs-Allsopp, *Lamentations*, 9.

Chapter 28 Ezekiel

1. See, e.g., David Garber, "Trauma Theory and Biblical Studies," *Currents in Biblical Research* 14 (2015): 24–44.

Chapter 30 Hosea

1. See also James B. Pritchard, ed., *Ancient Near Eastern Texts Relating to the Old Testament*, 3rd ed. (Princeton: Princeton University Press, 1969), 283.

2. Terence E. Fretheim, *The Pentateuch*, Interpreting Biblical Texts (Nashville: Abingdon, 1996), 24.

Chapter 34 Jonah

1. Ehud Ben Zvi, *Signs of Jonah: Reading and Rereading in Ancient Yehud*, Journal for the Study of the Old Testament Supplement Series 367 (Sheffield: Sheffield Academic, 2003), 80–98.

Chapter 36 Nahum

1. Ellen F. Davis, *Getting Involved with God: Rediscovering the Old Testament* (Lanham, MD: Cowley, 2001), 20.

Chapter 38 Zephaniah

1. See Marvin A. Sweeney, *Zephaniah*, Hermeneia (Minneapolis: Fortress, 2003), 191–92; Christopher B. Hays, *The Origins of Isaiah 24–27: Josiah's Festival Scroll for the Fall of Assyria* (Cambridge: Cambridge University Press, 2019), 139.

Chapter 41 Malachi

1. Orthodox Christians base the order of the Old Testament on a list written by the Greek church father Athanasius, in his 39th Festal Letter, section 4.

Art Credits

Weisgerber. Bridgeman Images. **CHAPTER 10: Frontispiece** *Joshua* (13th c.) by the French School, from the Morgan Picture Bible. Bridgeman Images. **10.1** *The Ark of the Covenant* by Frans Francken II the Younger. National Trust Photographic Library. John Hammond. Bridgeman Images. **10.2** *Sarah, Rahab and Bathsheba* by Sieger Koder, from St. Stephen's Church in Wasseralfingen, Germany. Photo by Zvonimir Atletic. Shutterstock.com. **CHAPTER 11: Frontispiece** *The Lament of Jephthah's Daughter* (1871) George Elgar Hicks. Photo © Christie's Images. Bridgeman Images. **11.1** *Deborah—Words Women and War* (2013) by Nahum HaLevi. **11.2** *Battle of Gideon against the Midianites* (1625–26) by Nicolas Poussin. **11.3** *Samson and the Lion* (1932) by Edward Cyril Power. Photo © Osborne Samuel Ltd, London. Bridgeman Images. **11.4** *The Death of Abimelech* (1885) by Gustave Doré. Photo by Nicku. Shutterstock.com. **CHAPTER 12: Frontispiece** *Ruth* (1999) by Laura James. Bridgeman Images. **12.1** *Ruth and Naomi* by Phili Hermogenes Calderon. Yale Center for British Art, Gift of David Doret, Yale BA 1968, and Linda Mitchell. **12.2** *Summer,* or *Ruth and Boaz* (1660–64) by Nicolas Poussin. Bridgeman Images. **CHAPTER 13: Frontispiece** *David* by Michelangelo. Photo by ndphoto. Shutterstock.com. **13.1** *Eli and Samuel* by William Brassey Hole. Photo © Look and Learn. Bridgeman Images. **13.2** *David and Jonathan* by He Qi. Heqigallery.com. **13.3** *Bethsabée* (1885–90) by Paul Cézanne. **13.4** *Rizpah* by Rev. Lauren Wright Pittman. © A Sanctified Art LLC. Sanctifiedart.org. **CHAPTER 14: Frontispiece** *Elijah and Elisha* (1986) by Hans Feibusch. © The Estate of Hans Feibusch. Bridgeman Images. **14.1** *Solomon's Judgement* (1832–83) by Gustave Doré, later coloring. Photo Stefano Bianchetti. Bridgeman Images. **14.4** *Banquet Given by King Solomon in Honour of the Queen of Sheba* (20th c.) by the Ethiopian School. Bridgeman Images. **14.7** *Elijah Runs before the Chariot of Ahab* by James Jaques Joseph Tissot. Lebrecht History. Bridgeman Images. **14.8** *Elisha* (1192) from the Church of Panagia Tou Arakos, Lagoudera, Cyprus. Sonia Halliday Photographs. Bridgeman Images. **CHAPTER 15: Frontispiece** *David Dancing Alone* (2001) by Richard Mcbee. Bridgeman Images. **15.1** *2 Samuel 6 1–5 David Brings the Ark to Jerusaelm* (15th c.) by the German School, from the *Nuremberg Bible (Biblia Sacra Germanica)*. The Stapleton Collection. Bridgeman Images. **15.2** *Construction du Temple de Jérusalem* (1470–75) by Jean Fouquet, from *Les Antiquities judaïques* by Flavius Josèphe. **CHAPTER 16: 16.1** *Ezra Reads the Law* (3rd c.) from the Dura Europos Synagogue. Photo © Zev Radovan. Bridgeman Images. **16.2** *Nehemiah Makes His Petition to Artaxerxes* by William Brassey Hole. Photo © Look and Learn. Bridgeman Images. **16.3** *Synagogue, Reading the Torah*, engraving. Photo by Tarker. Bridgeman Images. **CHAPTER 17: Frontispiece** *Queen Esther* (2014) by Jodi Simmons. Bridgeman Images. **17.1** *Esther before Ahasuerus* (1548) by Jacopo Tintoretto. **17.2** Overdoor of *La Toiletter D'Esther* (1738) by Jean-Francios de Troy. This copy of the original oil painting is from 1825 by an unknown artist. **CHAPTER 18: Frontispiece** *David and the Temple Singers* (1490–97) from the *Isabella Breviary*. **18.1** *Psalm 85* (2003) by John August Swanson. **CHAPTER 19: Frontispiece** *Behemoth and Leviathan* by William Blake (Linnell set), from *Illustrations of the Book of Job*. **19.1** *Job* (2003) Xavier Cortada. Bridgeman Images. **19.2** *Job and his Friends* by Gustave Doré. Lebrecht History. Bridgeman Images. **19.3** *Then the Lord Answered Job out of the Whirlwind* (1916) by Mary Tongue, from *The Book of Job*, with an introduction by G. K. Chesterton. Photo © Hilary Morgan. Bridgeman Images. **19.4** *Job Restored to Prosperity* (1648) by Laurent de La Hyre. **CHAPTER 20: Frontispiece** *Psalm 23* (2010) by John August Swanson. **20.1** *I Will Lift Up Mine Eyes unto the Hills* (1922) by William Ladd Taylor, from Charles Scribner, *The Children's Bible*. © Look and Learn. Bridgeman Images. **20.3** *Stained Glass* (1929–34) by Frantisek Kysela, from the Thunov Chapel of St. Vitus Cathedral in Prague, Czech Republic. Photo by Shmuel Magal. Alamay Stock Photo. **20.4** *Psalm 100* (2004) by Laura James. Bridgeman Images. **CHAPTER 21: Frontispiece** *The Ancient of Days* (1794) by William Blake. **21.1** *Parabole* or *Proverbs* (1455) from *The Gutenberg Bible*. Photo © British Library Board. Bridgeman Images. **21.2** *Wisdom* (1560) by Titian. **21.3** *The Virtuous Woman* (1890) by Matthew Maris, from Holy Trinity Church, Leamington Spa, UK. Photo © Alastair Carew-Cox. Bridgeman Images. **21.4** *Solomon Dictating Proverbs* (15th c.) by Pierre Gilbert, from Guyart Des Moulins, *La Bible historiale*. **CHAPTER 22: Frontispiece** *King Solomon* (1940) Leon Schulman Gaspard. Photo © Fred Jones Jr. Museum of Art. Given in memory of Roxanne P. Thams by William Thams, 2003. Bridgeman Images. **22.1** *Grace* (1918) by Eric Enstrom. **CHAPTER 23: Frontispiece** *The Song of Songs (B)* by He Qi. Heqigallery.com. **23.1** *Osculatur me (Let me kiss you),* initial letter "O" (12th c.) by the English School, from the Winchester Bible. Bridgeman Images. **23.2** *The Song of Songs* (15th c.) by the Italian School, from the *Borso d'Este Bible*. Bridgeman Images. **23.3** *Song of Songs Triptych* (1993) by Laura James. Bridgeman Images. **23.5** *Minstrel Playing before King Solomon* (1492) from the *Rothschild Mahzor*. **CHAPTER 24: Frontispiece** *The Prophet Jeremiah* by Michelangelo, from the Sistine Chapel. Bridgeman Images. **24.1** *Christ with the Twelve Minor Prophets* (12th c.) by the French School, from St. Jerome, *Explanatio in Prophetas et Ecclesiasten*. © British

Library Board. Bridgeman Images. **24.2** *Jeremiah, Isaiah and Ezekiel* from *The Books of Prophets* (1995) by Alek Rapoport. Bridgeman Images. **24.3** *Four Minor Prophets* by Joseph Manning, from the Bristol Cathedral. Photo © Bristol Museums, Galleries & Archives. Bequest of William Jerdone Braikenridge, 1908. Bridgeman Images. **CHAPTER 25: Frontispiece** *The Prophet Isaiah* by Sieger Koder, from St. Joseph's Church, Bad Urach, Germany. Photo by Zvonimir Atletic. Shutterstock.com. **25.2** *Seraphim Purifying the Lips of Isaiah, Catalan School* (12th c.) by Spanish School. Bridgeman Images. **25.3** *Lion and the Lambs* (1984) by Duncan Hannah. Bridgeman Images. **CHAPTER 26: Frontispiece** *The Prophet Jeremiah* from the Cathedral of Saint Rumbold, Mechelen, Belgium. Photo by jorisvo. Shutterstock.com. **26.1** *The Prophet Jeremiah* (1306–11) from Rashid Al-Din, *History of the World*. Photo by Pictures from History. Bridgeman Images. **26.2** *The Prophet Baruch* (1451) by Giusto d'Allamagna. Photo © Dario Grimaldi. Bridgeman Images. **26.3** *New Roots* by Lauren Wright Pittman. © A Sanctified Art LLC. Sanctifiedart.org. **26.4** *Jeremiah Lamenting the Destruction of Jerusalem* (1628) by Rembrandt. Everett Collection. Shutterstock.com. **CHAPTER 27: Frontispiece** *Lamentation* (1963) by Craigie Aitchison. Photo © Peter Nahum at The Leicester Galleries, London. Bridgeman Images. **27.1** *The Wailing Wall* (1880) by Jean Leon Gerome. **27.2** *The Destruction of Jerusalem by Nebuzar-Adan* by William Brassey Hole. Lebrecht History. Bridgeman Images. **CHAPTER 28: Frontispiece** *The Vision of Ezekiel*, illuminated manuscript from the Armenian church. Armenianmanuscripts. org. **28.1** *Cherubim and Chariot Vision of the Prophet Ezekiel* from the Cathedral of Brussels, Belgium. Photo by jorisvo. Shutterstock.com. **28.2** *Ezekiel's Vision* (3rd c.) from the Dura Europos Synagogue. **28.3** *Ezekiel Kneeling by the Death-Bed of His Wife* by William Blake. Lebrecht Authors. Bridgeman Images. **CHAPTER 29: Frontispiece** *Daniel in the Lion's Den* (1613–16) by Peter Paul Rubens. **29.1** *Nebuchadnezzar* (1795) by William Blake. **29.2** *Belshazzar's Feast* (1635-38) by Rembrandt. **29.3** *The Three Hebrews, Shadrach, Meshach, and Abed-nego Cast into the Furnace by Nebuchadnezzar* (960) by the Spanish School, from the Visigothic-Mozarabic Bible of St. Isidore. Bridgeman Images. **CHAPTER 30: Frontispiece** *The Prophet Hosea* by the Byzantine School, from Saint Mark's Basilica, Venice Italy. Photo by Cameraphoto Arte Venezia. Bridgeman Images. **30.1** *Marriage of Hosea and the Prostitute* (12th c.) by the German School, from the *Bible of St. Andre aux-Bois*. Bridgeman Images. **CHAPTER 31:Frontispiece** *The Descent of the Holy Spirit on the Apostles and Mary at Pentecost* (2001) by Elizabeth Wang. Photo © Radiant Light. Bridgeman Images. **31.1** *Locusts* from

Hartmann Schedel, *The Nuremberg Chronicle*. **31.2** *The Prophet Joel* from the Biblical Garden, Yad HaShmona, Israel. Photo by Wagner Santos de Almeida. Shutterstock.com. **CHAPTER 32: Frontispiece** *Judah* from the series *Twelve Tribes of Israel* (2017) by Joy Lions. Bridgeman Images. **32.1** *God of Justice* by Lisle Gwynn Garrity. © A Sanctified Art LLC. Sanctifiedart. org. **32.2** *Mean Collection* (1891) by A. Mrevlishvili. Bridgeman Images. **CHAPTER 33: Frontispiece** *Obadiah* by Eugen Spiro. SuperStock. Bridgeman Images. **33.1** *Obadiah* (19th c.) by the French School, educational card. Photo © Look and Learn. Bridgeman Images. **33.2** *Obadiah—The Pride and Fall of Esau* by Nahum HaLevi. **CHAPTER 34: Frontispiece** *Jonah Vomited by the Great Fish on the Shore*, engraving. Tarker. Bridgeman Images. **34.1** *Jonah and the Whale* (ca. 1400) from a Jami al-Tavarikh (Compendium of Chronicles). Purchase, Joseph Pulitzer Bequest, 1933. The MET. **34.2** *Jonah under His Gourd* (1561) by Maerten van Heemskerck. **CHAPTER 35: Frontispiece** *Swords into Plowshares* by Shari LeMonnier. **35.1** *Micah the Moreshite Prophet Preaching to the Israelites* (1860) by Gustave Doré. Photo by Stefano Bianchetti. Bridgeman Images. **CHAPTER 36: Frontispiece** *Nahum* by James Jacques Joseph Tissot. Bridgeman Images. **36.2** *Majestic Palaces of Ancient Assyria's Great Capital Nineveh as It Was More Than Twenty-Five Centuries Ago* (19th c.) European School, from J. A. Hammerton, *Wonders of the Past*. © Look and Learn. Bridgeman Images. **CHAPTER 37: Frontispiece** *Habakkuk Prophet* by Mikhail Vrubel, from St. Cyril's Church, Kiev, Ukraine. Photo by Ivan Vdovin. Alamy Stock Photo. **37.2** *Fig Tree* (1930) by Christopher Patrick Hussey Murphy. Morris Museum of Art, Augusta, Georgia. Bridgeman Images. **37.3** *Mosaic of the Prophet Habakkuk* (12th c.) from St. Mark's Basilica, Venice, Italy. **CHAPTER 38: Frontispiece** *Fresco of Zephaniah* (19th c.) by Carl Mayer, from Alterchenfelder Church, Vienna, Italy. Photo by Renata Sedmakova. Shutterstock.com. **38.1** *The Great Day of His Wrath* (1853) by John Martin. **38.2** *Fresco of Prophet Zephaniah* from Chiesa di San Giuseppe, Taormina, Italy. Photo by Renata Sedmakova. Shutterstock.com. **38.3** *Jerusalem from the Mount of Olives* (1858–59) by Edward Lear. Presented by the executors of the estate of Flora Koch, through British Friends of the Art Museums of Israel. **CHAPTER 39: Frontispiece** *Haggai* by James Jacques Joseph Tissot. Lebrecht History. Bridgeman Images. **39.1** *Joash Repairs the Temple* (1602) by Anton Möller. **CHAPTER 40: Frontispiece** *Representation de Zacharie, pretre et prophete juif* (9th c.) from *Codex de San Gregorio di Nazianza*. Photo © Giancarlo Costa. Bridgeman Images. **40.1** *The Vision of Zechariah* (1300) by unknown artist. **40.2** *Menorah de Zacarias* (1299–1300) by Josef Asarfati, from *Biblia de Cervera*. National

Index

acrostics, 323–24, 461–63, 568
Acts, book of, 16, 441–42
Addition to Esther, 306
agency, 66. *See also* God: agency; prophets
    (people): agents of God; Cyrus the Great:
    agent of God
Aleppo Codex, 42–43
Alexander the Great, 8
allegory, 391, 397–98
Alter, Robert, 177–79
Amos, book of
    composition, 520, 526
    genre, 520–21
    historical context, 520, 532
    outline, 520
    summary, 521–26
    theological themes, 526–32
Amos, the prophet, 519–20
anachronism, 52
ancestors, 4, 84, 247
ancient Near East, 8, 12, 15–17
angels, 186, 611, 614
anoint, 20
Antiochus IV Epiphanes, 8–9, 480–82, 487–90
apocalyptic literature, 435, 482, 488, 609
Apocrypha, 33. *See also* canon(s)
Aram, 10
Aramaic, 25, 32, 292–93, 481–82, 486
archaeology, 89, 197–98. *See also* cylinder seals;
    high places; ostraca
ark of the covenant, 240, 242–43
Artaxerxes, 301
Asherah, 505

Assyria
    emergence, 6, 11, 265, 276
    and Israel, 11, 264–65, 429, 497, 556, 564
Astruc, Jean, 52
atonement, 119, 121–23
Augustine, 450

baal/Baal, 136, 502
"Baal-peor," 502
Babylon, 6, 11–12, 264, 267, 586–87
Balaam, 408
Baruch, book of, 639n1 (chap. 27)
Baruch, the scribe, 449
BCE, 4
Bel and the Dragon, 492. *See also* canon(s)
bet, 246
Bible, 32, 613. *See also* canon(s); canonization
Black Obelisk of Shalmaneser, 276
blasphemy, 419–20. *See also* idolatry; sin
blessing, 84–85, 142–43, 155–56, 228–29
Boaz, 228
book of the law, 38–40, 149–50, 161–62, 216–17

calling. *See* vocation
call stories. *See under* literary forms
call to worship. *See under* literary forms
Canaan(ites), 4–5, 13–15, 203, 217. *See also* con-
    quest of Canaan
canon(s)
    Christian, 28–34, 640n1 (chap. 41)
    definition, 26
    Jewish, 27–31
canonical criticism, 58–59